C000261676

ROAD ATLAS
of
Great Britain

CONTENTS

Edition 10 2003 © Copyright of Geographers' A-Z Map Company Ltd. **2002**
No reproduction by any method whatsoever of any part of this publication is permitted without the prior consent of the copyright owners.

This product includes mapping data licenced from Ordnance Survey® with the permission of the Controller of Her Majesty's Stationery Office.
© Crown copyright 2002. Licence Number (100017302).

The Shopmobility logo is a registered symbol of The National Federation of Shopmobility.

An AtoZ Publication

Geographers' A-Z Map Company Ltd.

Head Office : (General Enquiries & Trade Sales) Fairfield Road, Borough Green, Sevenoaks, Kent TN15 8PP Telephone : 01732- 781000
Showrooms : (Retail Sales) 44 Gray's Inn Road, London, WC1X 8HX Telephone 020- 7440 9500
www.a-zmaps.co.uk

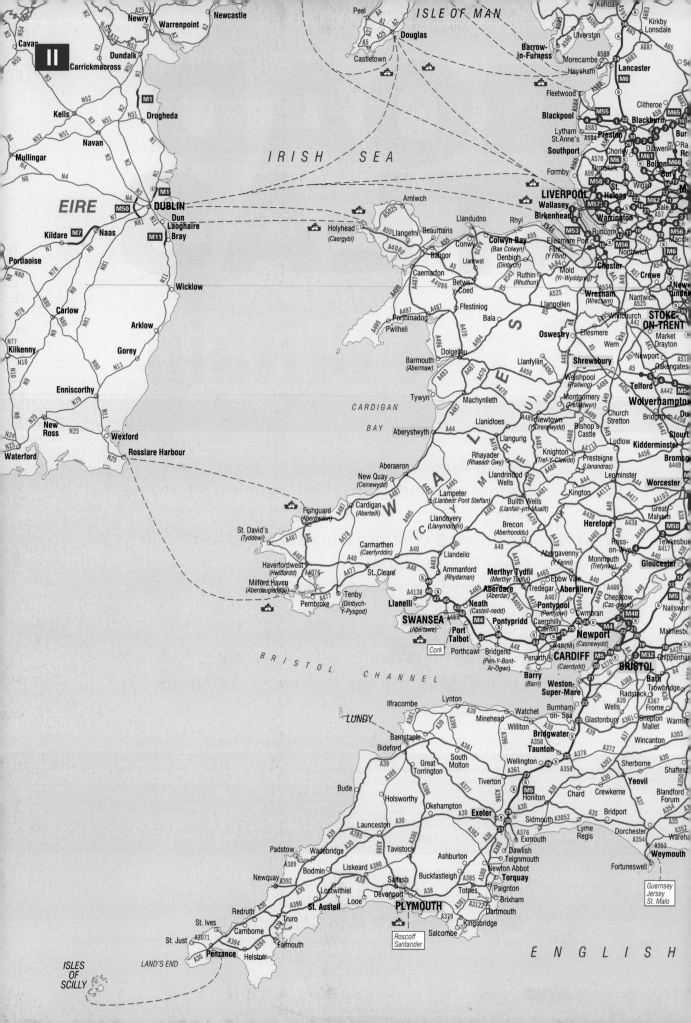

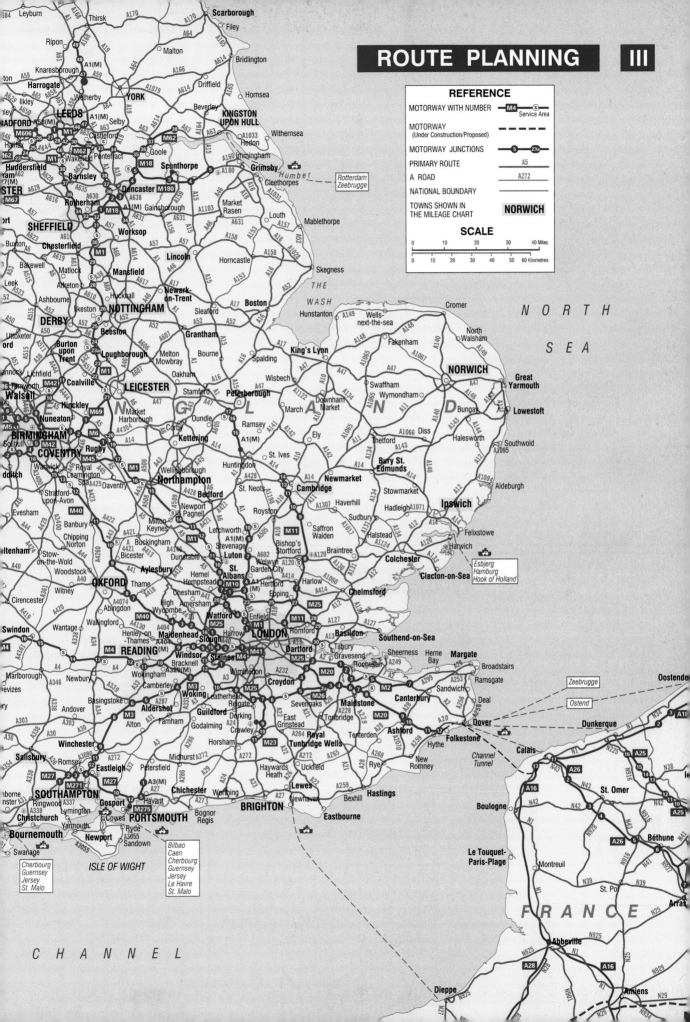

REFERENCE

MOTORWAY WITH NUMBER	M4 (S) Service Area
MOTORWAY (Under Construction/Proposed)	– – – –
MOTORWAY JUNCTIONS	5 23a
PRIMARY ROUTE	A5
A ROAD	A272
NATIONAL BOUNDARY	
TOWNS SHOWN IN THE MILEAGE CHART	NORWICH

SCALE

0   10   20   30   40 Miles
0   10   20   30   40   50   60 Kilometres

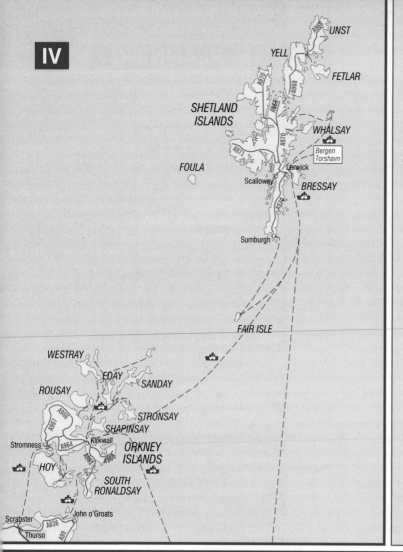

MILEAGE CHART

Places featured in this mileage chart are highlighted in YELLOW on the routeplanning maps.

PRIMARY ROUTES, Shown in green throughout this atlas, are a national network of recommended through routes which compliment the motorway system. Selected places of major traffic importance are known as Primary Route Destinations and on road signs have a green background.

The distances for the mileage chart have been compiled by using a combination of Primary Routes and Motorways between any two towns shown.

To find the distance between any two towns shown, follow the horizontal line of one town and the vertical line of the other; at the intersection read off the mileage.

ie : Horizontal - LONDON

Intersection 216 miles

Vertical - Liverpool

```
ABERDEEN
449 ABERYSTWYTH
181 324 AYR
400 114 272 BIRMINGHAM
330 159 196 124 BRADFORD
562 258 441 169 263 BRIGHTON
503 122 375 88 215 129 BRISTOL
447 198 366 102 156 117 167 CAMBRIDGE
505 106 377 106 233 168 42 201 CARDIFF
217 232 89 183 107 345 286 256 288 CARLISLE
437 134 297 18 124 157 102 84 129 200 COVENTRY
397 137 269 41 88 188 134 99 159 180 43 DERBY
340 192 239 95 40 232 184 117 210 150 94 57 DONCASTER
558 315 477 195 284 81 194 118 233 393 180 208 244 DOVER
125 340 75 284 198 466 377 326 379 91 303 266 212 444 EDINBURGH
553 199 425 161 282 170 75 232 107 336 166 213 257 244 439 EXETER
148 430 136 391 305 568 478 456 486 198 415 387 345 591 131 549 FORT WILLIAM
148 322 36 291 203 468 378 355 384 96 313 282 245 491 46 449 100 GLASGOW
445 109 317 53 171 152 35 53 228 59 93 149 189 331 107 435 324 GLOUCESTER
520 258 411 170 224 130 64 234 323 152 167 185 129 397 262 524 419 171 HARWICH
443 96 315 151 158 330 204 252 209 226 167 156 168 316 279 423 323 189 315 HOLYHEAD
357 235 255 139 68 243 228 134 239 165 123 94 37 254 290 367 255 195 204 218 HULL
107 192 198 449 353 620 536 490 558 260 458 421 369 601 157 607 63 162 496 554 481 387 INVERNESS
505 268 420 156 210 126 54 240 311 138 155 171 127 381 264 510 409 177 21 307 189 538 IPSWICH
269 182 139 151 62 324 235 215 232 50 170 136 99 344 141 307 248 146 200 279 180 127 310 268 KENDAL
316 171 198 119 9 256 209 144 226 111 117 74 32 275 190 279 309 218 162 60 345 197 72 LEEDS
407 155 294 43 99 163 118 70 140 214 24 30 73 183 282 189 412 312 83 146 182 98 431 125 166 97 LEICESTER
376 208 249 87 80 207 170 88 192 178 76 53 41 206 247 241 376 274 135 152 204 46 402 124 140 72 52 LINCOLN
327 120 199 99 67 267 180 179 169 110 163 110 90 294 201 240 308 213 142 265 95 370 236 75 73 110 118 LIVERPOOL
321 128 204 87 37 252 167 159 188 117 99 58 51 273 208 239 315 215 132 230 120 96 363 211 72 42 95 87 34 MANCHESTER
273 233 181 174 69 316 265 196 287 193 130 84 316 147 337 254 127 134 106 MIDDLESBROUGH
236 266 146 209 98 345 300 232 312 58 209 165 115 350 104 369 237 152 263 297 130 263 287 88 96 188 153 167 136 40 NEWCASTLE
476 270 348 163 185 174 234 62 256 280 142 146 142 169 351 284 478 378 193 72 289 145 505 44 249 178 112 103 222 177 221 252 NORWICH
381 155 267 54 78 191 140 84 165 188 52 15 48 210 256 218 386 108 165 177 92 410 141 72 37 107 68 128 159 118 NOTTINGHAM
485 151 335 68 167 106 73 92 106 267 57 101 138 142 358 151 465 365 47 134 208 175 515 128 223 162 76 123 168 178 253 159 104 OXFORD
680 301 552 269 394 279 184 343 218 463 278 316 369 355 551 109 663 561 217 374 388 412 715 375 419 391 310 359 353 344 449 481 393 323 261 PENZANCE
87 366 85 336 245 509 412 370 412 94 346 309 254 481 63 362 439 290 244 254 191 148 394 299 404 598 PERTH
589 332 461 203 325 206 111 274 159 329 209 254 300 286 485 43 592 490 150 305 322 648 305 348 323 231 284 299 281 379 412 327 255 193 75 529 PLYMOUTH
575 231 440 147 274 90 95 138 308 357 132 184 231 147 555 455 114 161 363 268 603 358 200 191 83 235 486 170 PORTSMOUTH
526 180 399 103 213 79 77 90 112 309 90 138 184 115 402 141 506 406 75 129 264 209 554 126 263 207 113 168 193 197 264 295 152 129 25 221 445 184 60 READING
529 178 383 121 245 82 53 140 101 312 113 159 207 158 400 91 510 408 73 177 262 251 569 177 265 230 132 187 213 208 287 318 200 162 65 201 443 132 43 57 SALISBURY
355 173 239 71 85 211 155 84 200 225 63 31 21 268 250 218 386 108 164 66 387 176 102 3 360 200 61 160 203 SHEFFIELD
388 73 260 47 100 216 116 140 107 171 64 67 114 249 262 175 369 267 25 154 163 424 195 122 73 43 159 56 97 166 203 196 86 105 286 309 218 195 147 150 85 SHREWSBURY
547 213 401 128 251 85 91 75 64 272 84 124 171 85 482 41 557 455 120 258 296 629 306 345 348 253 308 320 190 162 66 217 476 149 20 47 23 206 175 SOUTHAMPTON
520 258 431 152 220 85 177 64 211 342 129 168 185 89 395 226 548 438 152 97 303 200 549 57 283 213 139 156 225 262 299 96 160 337 173 126 SOUTHEND
374 108 243 47 75 217 137 137 140 50 64 36 74 236 241 202 348 248 95 201 112 17 410 179 121 71 55 87 56 36 142 273 91 105 331 287 201 147 148 50 35 133 199 STOKE
496 76 368 103 235 168 144 127 150 184 244 264 370 154 477 375 9 271 172 262 578 279 226 148 196 256 164 78 159 268 457 169 268 604 657 589 492 108 604 452 403 544 510 463 417 410 367 613 519 621 823 220 758 709 662 664 506 523 682 659 502 631 THURSO
437 96 309 29 135 162 62 119 73 220 46 68 117 197 306 116 418 311 28 168 151 166 480 174 169 146 72 118 108 101 203 225 85 57 244 350 177 146 95 101 103 49 124 156 65 97 572 WORCESTER
312 193 201 129 34 269 227 151 237 116 129 28 143 185 38 344 200 81 34 170 130 324 231 217 244 54 12 168 234 166 78 43 161 160 78 43 160 187 636 193 YORK
501 206 390 118 203 53 118 58 150 305 97 128 165 76 373 171 503 403 101 79 264 188 527 76 283 416 214 77 38 41 134 208 234 74 161 160 187 636 318 160 203 LONDON
```

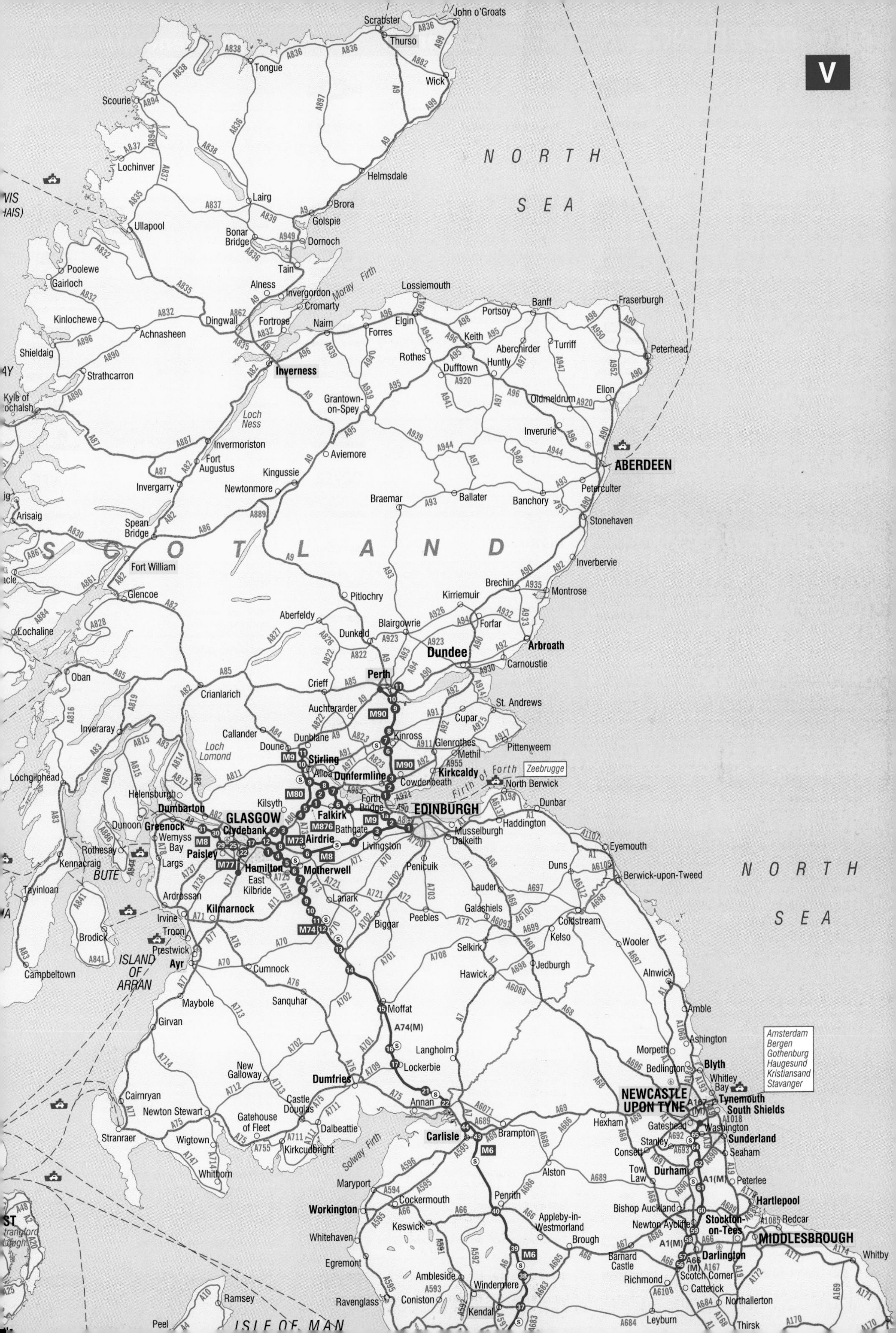

V

NORTH SEA

NORTH SEA

SCOTLAND

Scrabster John o'Groats
Thurso Wick
Tongue
Scourie
Lochinver
Lairg Helmsdale
Ullapool Bonar Bridge Brora
Poolewe Golspie
Gairloch Dornoch
Kinlochewe Dingwall Tain
Achnasheen Alness Invergordon Cromarty Lossiemouth
Shieldaig Strathcarron Fortrose Nairn Elgin Portsoy Banff Fraserburgh
Kyle of Lochalsh INVERNESS Forres Keith Aberchirder Turriff
Invermoriston Rothes Dufftown Huntly Peterhead
Fort Augustus Grantown-on-Spey Oldmeldrum Ellon
Invergarry Aviemore Inverurie
Arisaig Kingussie ABERDEEN
Spean Bridge Newtonmore Peterculter
Fort William Braemar Ballater Banchory Stonehaven
Glencoe Pitlochry Kirriemuir Inverbervie
Lochaline Aberfeldy Brechin Montrose
Oban Dunkeld Blairgowrie Forfar
Crianlarich Crieff DUNDEE Arbroath
Inveraray Callander PERTH Carnoustie
Doune Auchterarder St. Andrews
Dunblane Kinross Cupar Pittenweem
STIRLING Glenrothes Methil
Lochgilphead Alloa DUNFERMLINE KIRKCALDY Zeebrugge
Helensburgh Kilsyth Cowdenbeath Forth Bridge North Berwick
DUMBARTON FALKIRK EDINBURGH Dunbar
Rothesay GLASGOW Bathgate Musselburgh Haddington
GREENOCK CLYDEBANK AIRDRIE Livingston Dalkeith Eyemouth
Wemyss Bay PAISLEY Penicuik Duns
BUTE HAMILTON MOTHERWELL Lauder Berwick-upon-Tweed
Largs East Kilbride Lanark Galashiels
Ardrossan KILMARNOCK Biggar Peebles Coldstream
Tayinloan Irvine Troon Selkirk Kelso
ISLAND OF ARRAN Prestwick AYR Hawick Jedburgh Wooler
Brodick Cumnock Moffat Alnwick
Campbeltown Maybole Langholm Amble
Girvan Lockerbie Ashington
New Galloway Morpeth Blyth
Sanquhar Bedlington Whitley Bay
Cairnryan DUMFRIES Annan NEWCASTLE UPON TYNE Tynemouth
Newton Stewart Castle Douglas Brampton South Shields
Stranraer Wigtown Dalbeattie CARLISLE Hexham Gateshead SUNDERLAND
Whithorn Kirkcudbright Stanley Washington Seaham
Maryport Penrith Consett DURHAM Peterlee
Workington Cockermouth Alston Tow Law Bishop Auckland HARTLEPOOL
Whitehaven Keswick Appleby-in-Westmorland Newton Aycliffe STOCKTON-on-Tees Redcar
Egremont Brough Barnard Castle DARLINGTON MIDDLESBROUGH Whitby
Ravenglass Ambleside Richmond Scotch Corner
Coniston Windermere Catterick Northallerton
Peel Ramsey Kendal Leyburn Thirsk
ISLE OF MAN

Amsterdam
Bergen
Gothenburg
Haugesund
Kristiansand
Stavanger

Loch Ness
Loch Lomond
Moray Firth
Firth of Forth
Solway Firth

M90 M9 M80 M8 M77 M74 M73 M876 M6
A9 A90 A82 A74(M) A1(M)

REFERENCE	Légende	Zeichenerklärung
MOTORWAY — M1	Autoroute — M1	Autobahn — M1
MOTORWAY UNDER CONSTRUCTION	Autoroute en construction	Autobahn im Bau
MOTORWAY PROPOSED	Autoroute prévue	Geplante Autobahn
MOTORWAY JUNCTIONS WITH NUMBERS — 4 Unlimited interchange 4 Limited interchange 5	Echangeur numéroté — 4 Echangeur non limité 4 Echangeur limité 5	Autobahnanschlußstelle mit Nummer — 4 Unbeschränkter Fahrtrichtungswechsel 4 Beschränkter Fahrtrichtungswechsel 5
MOTORWAY SERVICE AREA — HESTON (S) with access from one carriageway only (S)	Aire de services d'autoroute — HESTON (S) à sens unique (S)	Rastplatz oder Raststätte — HESTON (S) Einbahn (S)
MAJOR ROAD SERVICE AREAS with 24 hour Facilities Primary Route — LEEMING (S) Class A Road — GRASBY (S)	Aire de services de route prioriataire Ouverte 24h sur 24 Route à grande circulation — LEEMING (S) Route de type A — GRASBY (S)	Raststätte Durchgehend geöffnet Hauptverkehrsstraße — LEEMING (S) A-Straße — GRASBY (S)
PRIMARY ROUTE — A41	Route à grande circulation — A41	Hauptverkehrsstraße — A41
PRIMARY ROUTE JUNCTION WITH NUMBER — 5	Echangeur numéroté — 5	Hauptverkehrsstraßenkreuzung mit Nummer — 5
PRIMARY ROUTE DESTINATION — DOVER	Route prioritaire, direction — DOVER	Hauptverkehrsstraße Richtung — DOVER
DUAL CARRIAGEWAYS (A & B Roads)	Route à deux chaussées séparées (route A & B)	Zweispurige Schnellstraße (A- und B-Straßen)
CLASS A ROAD — A129	Route de type A — A129	A-Straße — A129
CLASS B ROAD — B177	Route de type B — B177	B-Straße — B177
NARROW MAJOR ROAD (Passing Places)	Route prioritaire étroite (possibilité de dépassement)	Schmale Hauptverkehrsstaße (mit Überholmöglichkeit)
MAJOR ROADS UNDER CONSTRUCTION	Route prioritaire en construction	Hauptverkehrsstraße im Bau
MAJOR ROADS PROPOSED	Route prioritaire prévue	Geplante Hauptverkehrsstraße
GRADIENT 1:5(20%) & STEEPER (Ascent in direction of arrow)	Pente égale et supérieure à 20% (dans le sens de la montée)	20% Steigung und steiler (in Pfeilrichtung)
TOLL — TOLL	Péage — TOLL	Gebührenpflichtig — TOLL
MILEAGE BETWEEN MARKERS — 8	Distance en milles entre les flèches — 8	Strecke zwischen Markierungen in Meilen — 8
RAILWAY AND STATION	Voie ferrée et gare	Eisenbahnlinie und Bahnhof
LEVEL CROSSING AND TUNNEL	Passage à niveau et tunnel	Bahnübergang und Tunnel
RIVER OR CANAL	Rivière ou canal	Fluß oder Kanal
COUNTY OR UNITARY AUTHORITY BOUNDARY	Limite des comté ou de division administrative	Grafschafts- oder Verwaltungsbezirksgrenze
NATIONAL BOUNDARY — + — +	Frontière nationale — + — +	Landesgrenze — + — +
BUILT-UP AREA	Agglomération	Geschlossene Ortschaft
VILLAGE OR HAMLET	Village ou hameau	Dorf oder Weiler
WOODED AREA	Zone boisée	Waldgebiet
SPOT HEIGHT IN FEET — • 813	Altitude (en pieds) — • 813	Höhe in Fuß — • 813
HEIGHT ABOVE SEA LEVEL 400' - 1,000' 122m - 305m 1,000' - 1,400' 305m - 427m 1,400' - 2,000' 427m - 610m 2,000'+ 610m +	Altitude par rapport au niveau de la mer 400' - 1,000' 122m - 305m 1,000' - 1,400' 305m - 427m 1,400' - 2,000' 427m - 610m 2,000'+ 610m +	Höhe über Meeresspiegel 400' - 1,000' 122m - 305m 1,000' - 1,400' 305m - 427m 1,400' - 2,000' 427m - 610m 2,000'+ 610m +
NATIONAL GRID REFERENCE (Kilometres) — 100	Coordonnées géographiques nationales (Kilometres) — 100	Nationale geographische Koordinaten (Kilometer) — 100
PAGE CONTINUATION — ▲ 48	Suite à la page indiquée — ▲ 48	Seitenfortsetzung — ▲ 48
AREA COVERED BY MAIN ROUTE MAP	Répartition des cartes des principaux axes routiers	Von Karten mit Hauptverkehrsstrecken
AREA COVERED BY TOWN PLAN — SEE PAGE 188	Répartition des cartes des plans des villes — SEE PAGE 188	Von Karten mit Stadtplänen erfaßter Bereich — SEE PAGE 188

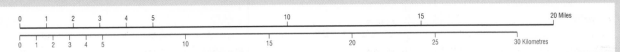

Tourist Information	Information	Touristeninformationen
AIRPORT	Aéroport	Flughafen
AIRFIELD	Terrain d' aviation	Flugplatz
HELIPORT	Héliport	Hubschrauberlandeplatz
BATTLE SITE AND DATE *1066*	Champ de bataille avec date *1066*	Schlachtfeld mit Datum *1066*
CASTLE (Open to Public)	Château (ouvert au public)	Schloss / Burg (für die Öffentlichkeit zugänglich)
CASTLE WITH GARDEN (Open to Public)	Château et parc (ouvert au public)	Schloß mit Garten (für die Öffentlichkeit zugänglich)
CATHEDRAL, ABBEY, CHURCH, FRIARY, PRIORY	Cathédrale, abbaye, église, monastère, prieuré	Kathedrale, Abtei, Kirche, Mönchskloster, Kloster
COUNTRY PARK	Parc régional	Landschaftspark
FERRY (Vehicular, sea) (Vehicular, river) (Foot only)	Bac (véhicules, mer) (véhicules, rivière) (Piétons)	Fähre (Autos, meer) (Autos, fluß) (nur für Personen)
GARDEN (Open to Public)	Jardin ouvert au public	Garten (für die Öffentlichkeit zugänglich)
GOLF COURSE (9 Hole) (18 Hole)	Terrain de golf (9 trous) (18 trous)	Golfplatz (9 Löcher) (18 Löcher)
HISTORIC BUILDING (Open to Public)	Monument historique (ouvert au public)	Historisches Gebäude (für die Öffentlichkeit zugänglich)
HISTORIC BUILDING WITH GARDEN (Open to Public)	Monument historique avec jardin (ouvert au public)	Historisches Gebäude mit Garten (für die Öffentlichkeit zugänglich)
HORSE RACECOURSE	Hippodrome	Pferderennbahn
INFORMATION CENTRE	Syndicat d'initiative	Information
LIGHTHOUSE	Phare	Leuchtturm
MOTOR RACING CIRCUIT	Circuit automobile	Automobilrennbahn
MUSEUM, ART GALLERY	Musée	Museum, Galerie
NATIONAL PARK OR FOREST PARK	Parc national ou forêt domaniale	National- oder Waldpark
NATIONAL TRUST PROPERTY (Open) *NT* (Restricted Opening) *NT* (National Trust of Scotland) *NTS NTS*	National Trust Property (ouvert) *NT* (heures d'ouverture) *NT* (National Trust of Scotland) *NTS NTS*	National Trust-Eigentum (geöffnet) *NT* (beschränkte Öffnungszeit) *NT* (National Trust of Scotland) *NTS NTS*
NATURE RESERVE OR BIRD SANCTUARY	Réserve naturelle botanique ou ornithologique	Natur- oder Vogelschutzgebiet
NATURE TRAIL OR FOREST WALK	Chemin forestier, piste verte	Naturpfad oder Waldweg
PLACE OF INTEREST *Monument* •	Site, curiosité *Monument* •	Sehenswürdigkeit *Monument* •
PICNIC SITE	Lieu pour pique-nique	Picknickplatz
RAILWAY, STEAM OR NARROW GAUGE	Chemin de fer, à vapeur ou à voie étroite	Eisenbahn, Dampf- oder Schmalspurbahn
THEME PARK	Centre de loisir	Vergnügungspark
VIEWPOINT (360 degrees) (180 degrees)	Vue panoramique (360 degré) (180 degré)	Aussichtspunkt (360 grade) (180 grade)
WILDLIFE PARK	Réserve de faune	Wildpark
WINDMILL	Moulin à vent	Windmühle
ZOO OR SAFARI PARK	Parc ou réserve zoologique	Zoo oder Safari-Park

10   20   30   40

Ⓐ   Ⓑ   68   Ⓒ   Ⓓ

❶

90

❷

80

C A R D I G A N   B A Y

(B A E   C E R E D I G I O N)

70

❸

❹

Sea
Aquarium

Aberaeron
Honey
Bee

60

New Quay
(Ceinewydd)   Ffos-y-ffin

Llwyncelyn

Maen-y-
groes   Gilfachreda

Bird & Wildlife
Hospital   **Llanarth**

Cwmtudu   *NT*   Cross Inn   Oakfo
(Derwen)

Nanternis   Geneva

Caerwedros   Pen-cae

Ynys-Lochtyn   Honey
Farm

Llwyndafydd

❺   *NT*   Blaen Celyn   **Mydr**

Llangranog   Pontgarreg   Synod Inn or
Post-mawr

Morfa   **A487**

Penbryn   Plwmp

**Cardigan
Island**   Pentregat

Bird Sanctuary   Parcllyn   **Aberporth**

NT   Sarnau   **Talgarreg**

Cemaes Head   Farm
Park   Rainforest &
Butterfly Centre   Tresaith   Brynhoffnant   Ⓒ

250   Gwbert   Aberporth
Castell   15

Ⓐ   44   ynt   Ⓑ   Gwythian   Tan-y-groes   Countryside
Collection   Bwlch-y-fadfa   Ⓓ

Allt-y-coed   Blannerch   Capel
Cynon   *Castell
Howell*

Y Ferwig   Tremain   **Blaenporth**   Glynarthen   Ffostrasol   40

Pwllvgranant   Cippyn   **A487**   Penparc   Brithdir   Pont-sian

Cardigan   Noyadd   Felin   **Rhydlewis**
(Aberteifi)   Trefawr   Beulah   Hwnda   Penrhiw-pal   11

**Bettws
Ifan**

St. Dogmaels   Pantgwyn   **Troedyraur**

400

10   20   30   40

A   **B**   **C**   **D**

1

Middle Mouse
(Ynys Badrig)

The Skerries
(Ynysoedd y Moelrhoniaid)

West Mouse
(Maen y Bugael)

Wylfa Nuclear
Power Station

NT   NT   Porth
Wen   East Mo
(Ynys Amlv

Cemaes
Bay   Cemlyn
Bay   Penrhyn   Llanbadrig
(Porthllechog)   Bull Bay   Po

NT   Cemaes   Bull Bay

Carmel Head
(Trwyn y Gader)   Tregele   A5025   Burwen   Amlwch

90

Llanfairynghornwy   *Thomas Mon*   Bodewryd

Llanfechell

Llanrhyddlad   Llanfflewyn   Carreglefn   Rhosgoch

Church Bay
(Porth Swtan)   Rhydwyn   Llyn   Parys   Rhosybol   Llaneudd
Llygeirian   Mountain   City

Llanfaethlu   Anglesey   Llanbabo   Gwredog   Llandyfry
Birds
of Prey

A5025   Llynnon   Llanddeusant   B5111

Llanfwrog   Melin Howell   Llanerchymedd   Maenaddwyn   Bachau

2   HOLYHEAD   Tregwhelydd   B5112   B5111

BAY   Standing
Stone   Carmel   Tryfil   Driel Llynfaes

Holyhead to:
Dublin 3hrs. 15mins.
Dublin 1hr. 50mins.
(Fast Ferry)
Dun Laoghaire 1hr. 40mins.
(Fast Ferry)   ANGLES
Llanfachraeth   Pen-llyn   Trefor   Llangwyllog

(YNYS

Breakwater   Porth-y-felin   Salt Island

Gogarth   Caer y Twr   March

South Stack   Hut Fort   HOLYHEAD   Bodedern   B5109   Llynfaes
Cliffs   Mountain   (Caergybi)   Presaddfed
Hut   Penrhos   Llanynghenedl   Burial Chamber   Llanfaes   Cefni
Group   Stryd   Valley   Rest
Ellin's Tower   Kingsland   Penrhos   (Dyffryn)   Bryngwran   Bodffordd   Llangefni
Penrhos Feilw   Ty-Mawr   Burial   A55   A5   Rhostrenw
Standing   Hut   Chamber   Caergeiliog   Mona

80   Stones   Circle   Treaddur   2   Gwalchmai

Valley Lakes   Llyn Traffwll   Heneglwys   6   Rhostrer

(YNYS   Four Mile   Llanfihangel   A5

Bridge   Llyn Dinam   yn Nhowyn   A4080

Rhoscolyn   Llanfairyn   Capel   Cerrigceinwen   Langristiolus

GYBI)   neubwll   Penrhyn   Gwyn   Mona   5   ANGLE

Ty-newydd   Pentre B
St. Gwenfaen's   Valley   Burial
Well   Chamber   Llanrhistiolus
Farm Park
Cymyran   Llantaelog   Pencarnisiog   Henblas
Bay   Rhosneigr   Bryn Du   B4422   Capel Mawr
Bodorgan   Llyn   Capel Mawr   A5
Coron   Bethel   Trefdraeth   Malltraeth Marsh   B4419
Cors Ddyga
70   Llyn   Trefdraeth   Malltraeth   B4421
Maelog   Barclodiad y Gawres   Llangwyfan   Langadwaladr   Llangaffo
Burial Chamber   -isaf   Afon Cefni   Gast
Anglesey   Aberffraw   A4080   Hermon   Malltraeth   Gwy
Llys Llywelyn   Bodowr
Aberffraw   Bodorgan   Llyn   B4421
Bay   Parc   Langaff
Mawr   Bird
World   Dwyran
Newborough
(Niwbwrch)   Model
Village
Malltraeth   Newborough   Newborough
Bay   Forest   Warren   Aberr
mena
4   Llanddwyn Island   Llanddwyn   Point
(Ynys Llanddwyn)   Bay   Welsh Highl
Railway   Caer
Llanfag
Foryd
Bay   Llanwrog
Caernarfon

60   CAERNARFON   Air
World
Dinas
Dinlle
Llandwrog
A499   Glynllifo
Slate Wo

5   A487   Penygro

B A Y   Pontllyfni

Aberdesach   Old
Welsh
Life   Tai'n Lon

St. Beuno
Church   Clynnog
350   Fawr   Capel Uchaf   D

10   20   30   40

St. Beuno's
Well
Trefor   Bwlch Mawr   Bwlchderwi
1712
Trwyn y   Gyrn Ddu
Gorlech   Yr Eifl

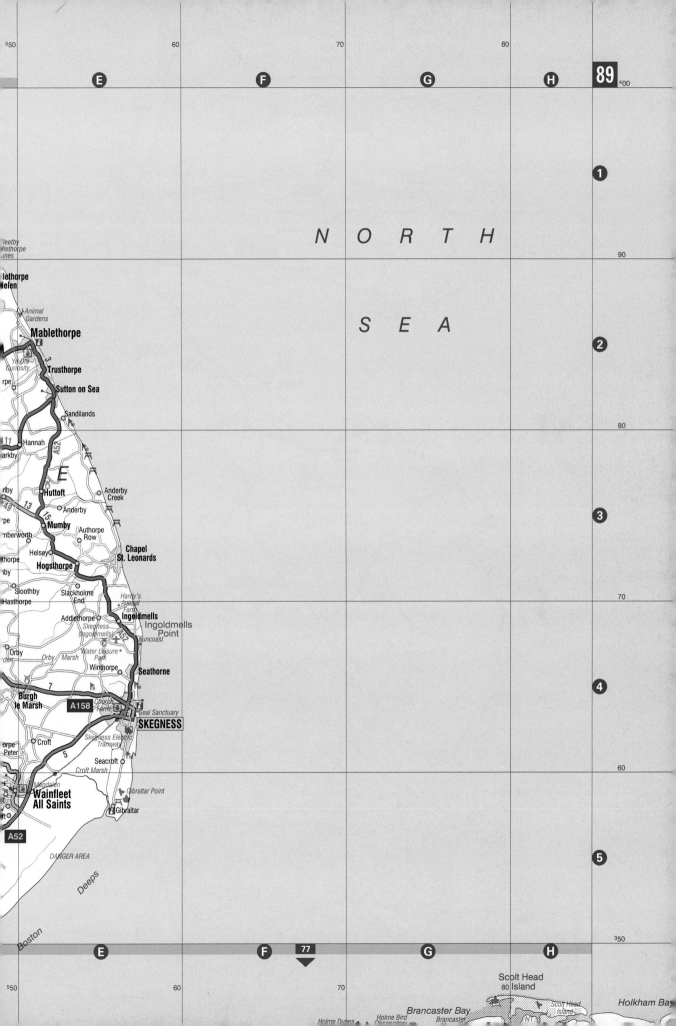

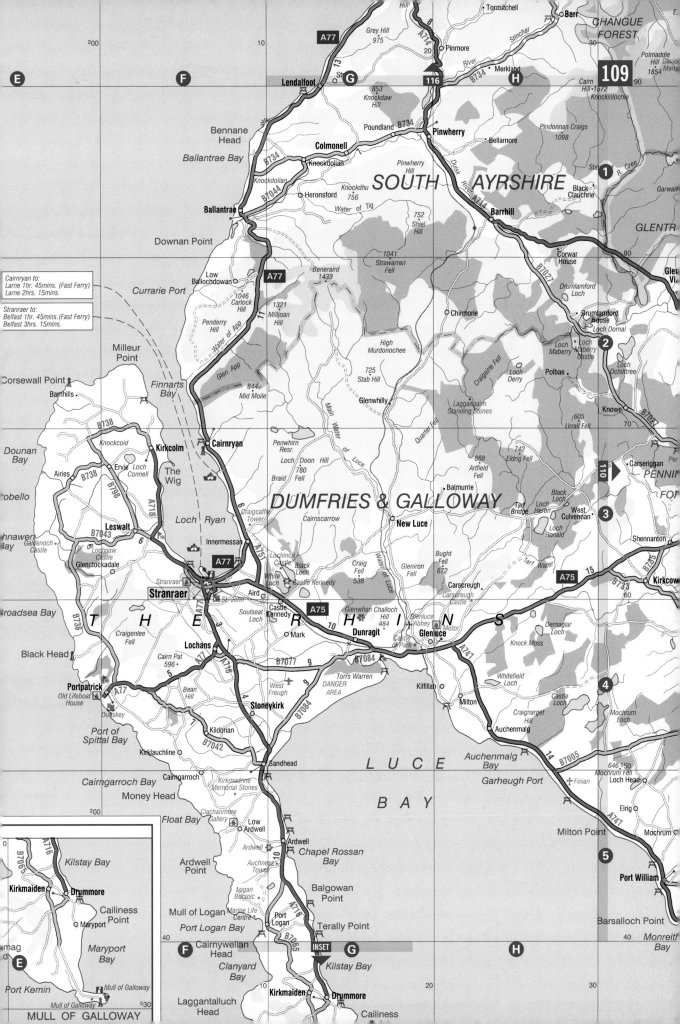

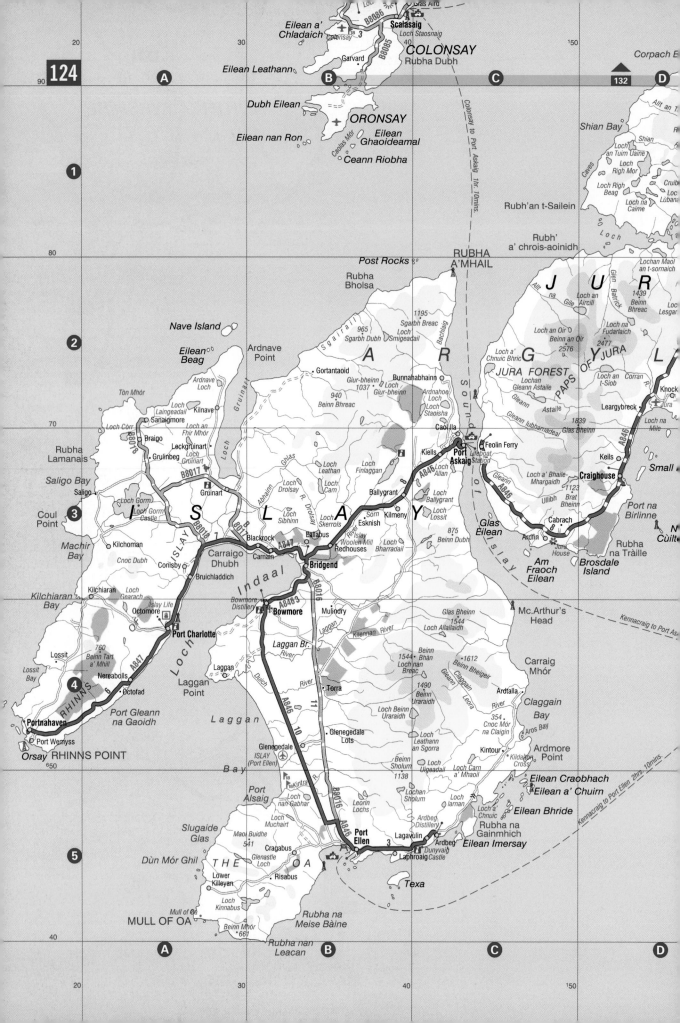

NORTH SEA

Fast Castle
Head

Fast Castle
Telegraph
Hill

ST. ABB'S HEAD
NTS

Lumsdaine
Cross Law •744
Coldingham Moor
11
Press

St. Abbs
Lifeboat
Station
Coldingham
Bay
Coldingham
Priory
Lifeboat Station
Buss Craig
Eyemouth
Gunsgreenhill

Houndwood

Reston
Ayton
18
Burnmouth
Ross

Auchencrow

B6437
12

B6355

B6435
8

Chirnside
15

Lamberton
Clappers
Chirnside-
bridge
Whiteadder
Water
Foulden
Hutton
Tithe Barn
Halidon
Hill
1333
Old Toll House
Marshall
Meadows
A1
Highfields
Scottish Borderers
BERWICK-
UPON-TWEED

Allanton
B6437
Hutton
B6460
Paxton
B6461
A6105
Tweed
Walk

Whitsome
B6460

Fishwick
Church
B6461
Horncliffe
Union
Bridge
Tweed
Loanend
East
Ord
2
Tweedmouth
Spittal
Redshin
Cove

Horndean
Church
Norham
Murton
Thornton
Scremerston

Ladykirk
Norham
B6470
Shoreswood
Shoresdean
West
Allerdean
Cheswick

B6470
12
Railway
Upsettlington
Simprim
Grindon
Felkington
West
Ancroft
Berrington Law
Berrington
Goswick
Haggerston

Twizel
Bridge
Chapel
Duddo
Duddo Tower
Bowsden
Beal
Fenham

LINDISFARNE
HOLY ISLAND
Keel
Head
Holy
Island
NT Lindisfarne
Priory
Castle Point
Burrows
Hole

NORTHUMBERLAND

Castle
Heaton
Melkington
A698
Lennel
Cornhill-
on-Tweed
Bareless
Pallinsburn
House
Etal
Etal
Manor
Waterford
Hall
Barmoor
Lowick
West
Kyloe
East
Kyloe
A1
121
Fenwick

Crookham
Mill
B6353
Ford
Kyloe
Hills
Buckton

West
mouth
A697
East
Learmouth
Branxton
1513
Flodden
Field
B6525
Holburn
St. Cuthbert's
Cave
Detchant
Elwick
Ross
Budle
Bay

FARNE
ISLANDS
NT
Staple
Sound

Bamburgh
Inner

Pressen
Flodden

80

100   A   B   C   D

Oban to
Lochboisdale 5hrs. 15mins.

70

1

Oban to
Castlebay 5hrs. 10mins.

2

Cairns of C

Eag na
Maoile

Eilean Mór

Rubha Mór

Bousd

Cornaigmore

Rubh'a' Bhinnein

Sorisdale

60

COLL

Loch
Fada

Cliad Bay

Grishipoll

Rubha Hogh

7

Clabbach

Loch Cliad

Bagh Feisdlum

Hogh Bay

340

B8071

H

Ben
Nogh

Loch nan
Cinneachan

Arinagour

E

3

Totronald

Loch
Anlaimh

B8070

Loch Eatharna

B

Feall
Bay

Coll
Uig

Acha

5

Eilean
Ornsay

R

Calgary Point

Coll

Breachacha
Castle

Port na
h-Eathar

I

Caolas
Ban

Breachacha

Port
Friesland
Bay

750

Gunna

Crossapol
Bay

Soa

Miodar

Vaul
Bay

Carnan

Hough
Skerries

Balephetrish
Bay

Vaul
Salum

Gunna Sound

Rubha Dubh

Tresh

Cornaigmore

Loch
Riaghain

B8069

Ruaig

Caolas

Coll to Tiree 1hr. 10mins.

Sraid Ruadh

Balephetrish

Gott

Rubha Hogh

Balevullin

Cornaigbeg

Kirkapol

Gott Bay

Cairn
Burgh

Hough

Kilmoluaig

Kenovay
Tiree

4

Kilkenneth

B8068

5

Scarinish

Moss

Loch an
Eilein

B8065

Baugh

Flao

Sandaig

Heylipol

3

Crossapol

Rubha Tràigh
an Duin

Lunga

Middleton

Barrapol

Hanish

Port Mor
Thatched House
Port
Bharrapool

2

TIREE

Loch a
Phuill

Hynish
Bay

Balephuil

B8067

Balemartine

Mannal

40

Balephuil
Bay

West
Hynish

Bac Mor or
Dutchman's Cap

Hynish

Signal
Tower

Bac Beag

Port Snoig

5

I N N E R

30

A   B   C   D

100   10   20

30

Réidh
Eilean

Eilean
Annraidh

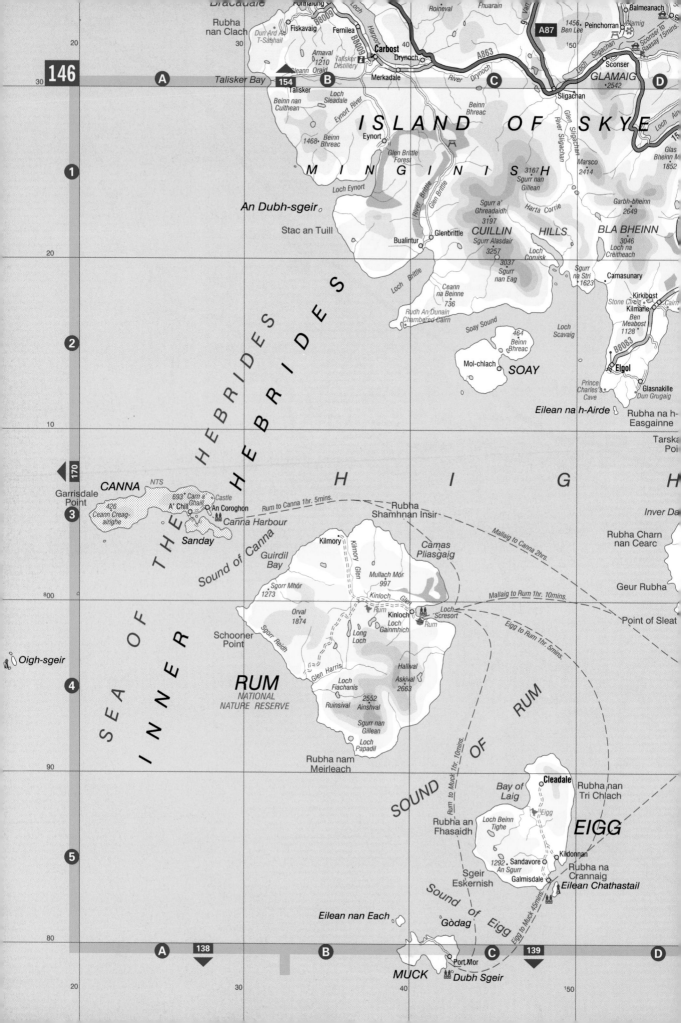

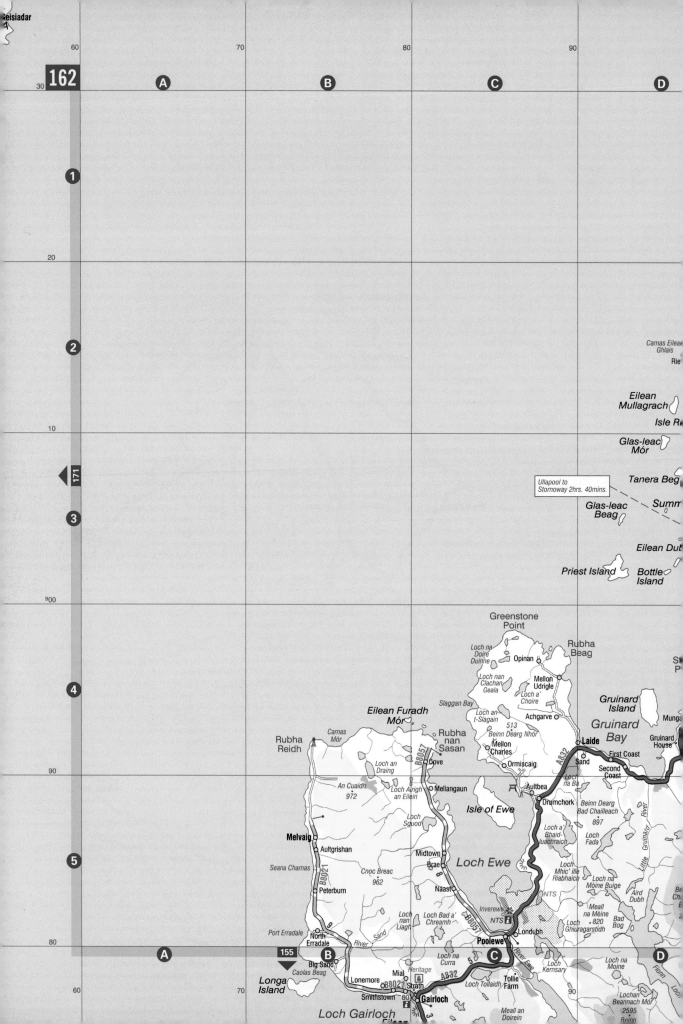

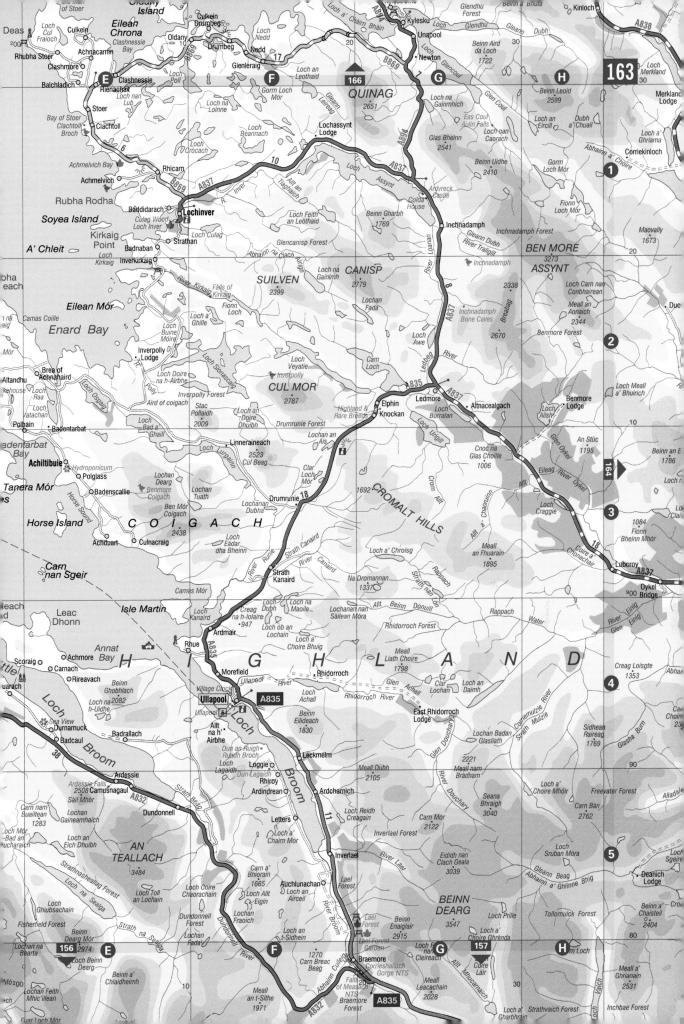

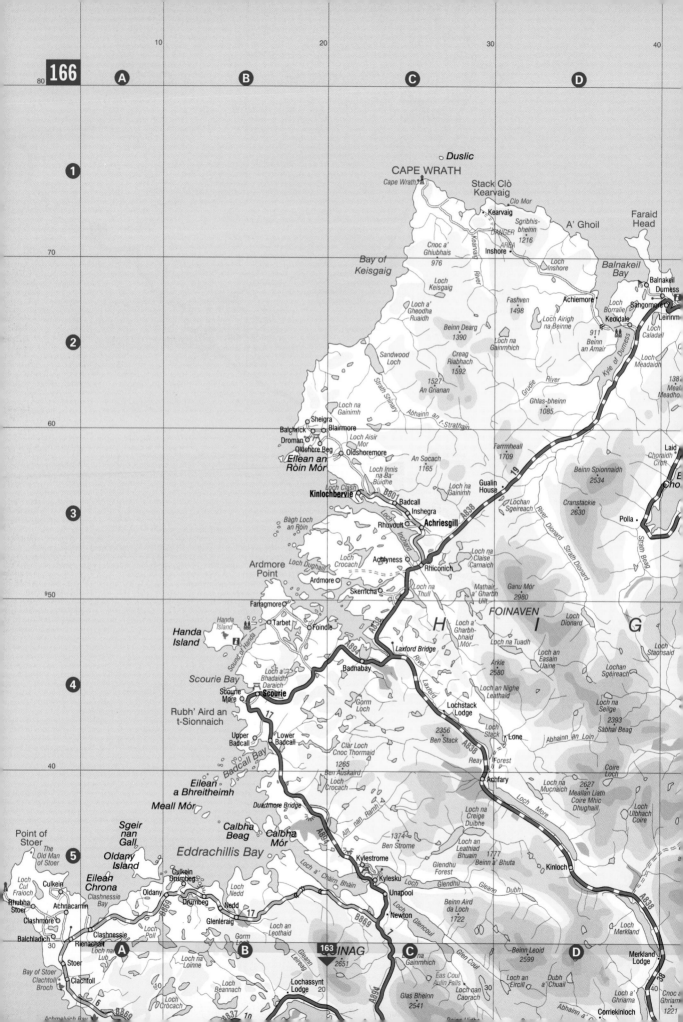

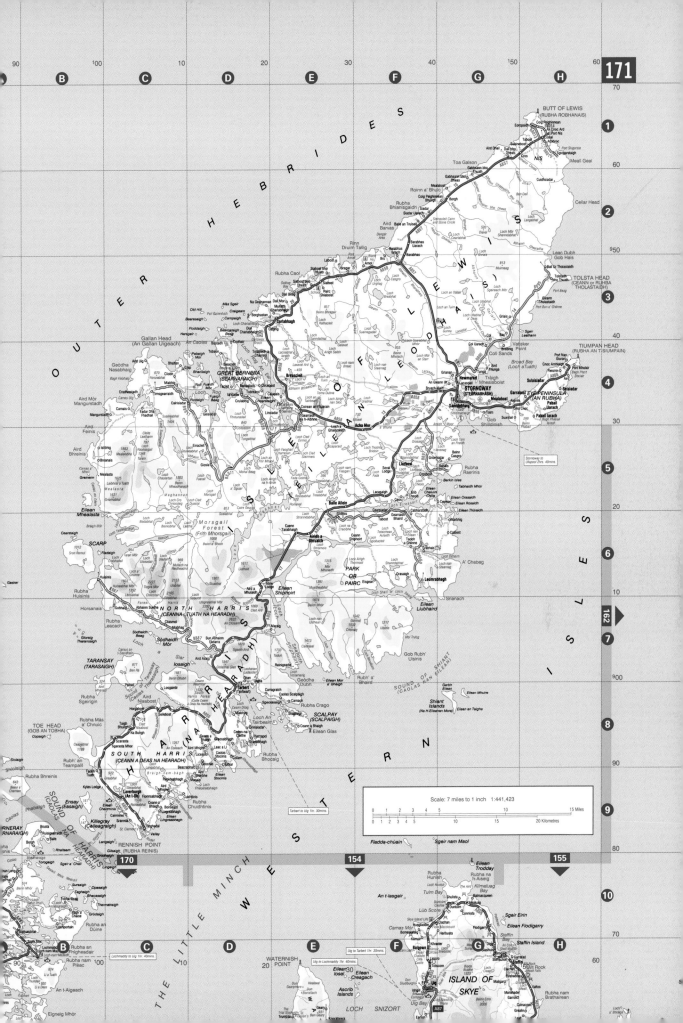

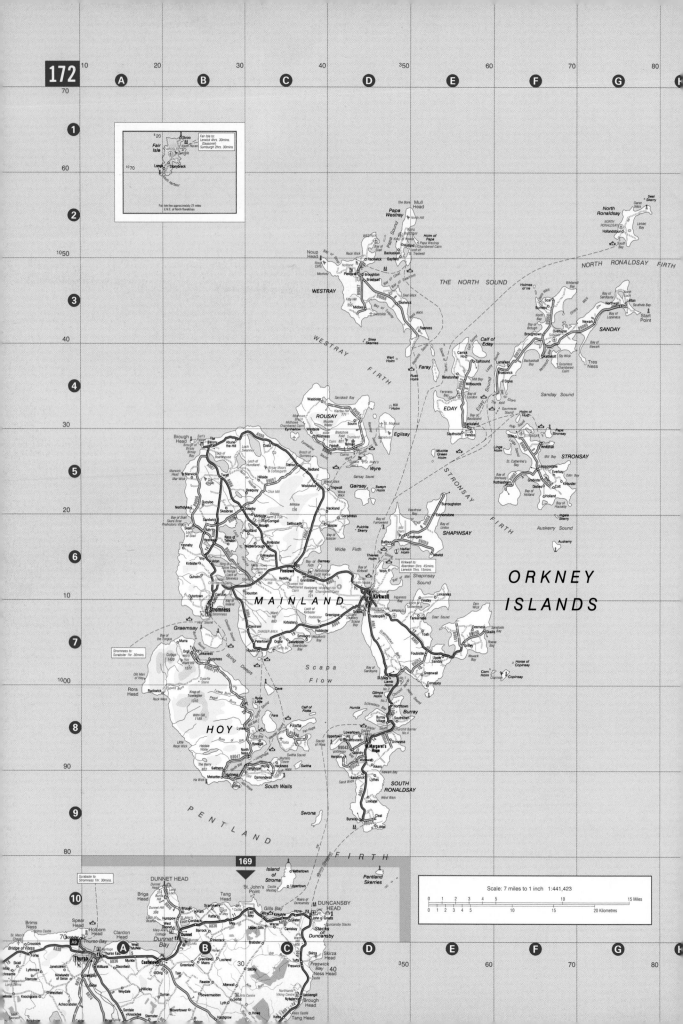

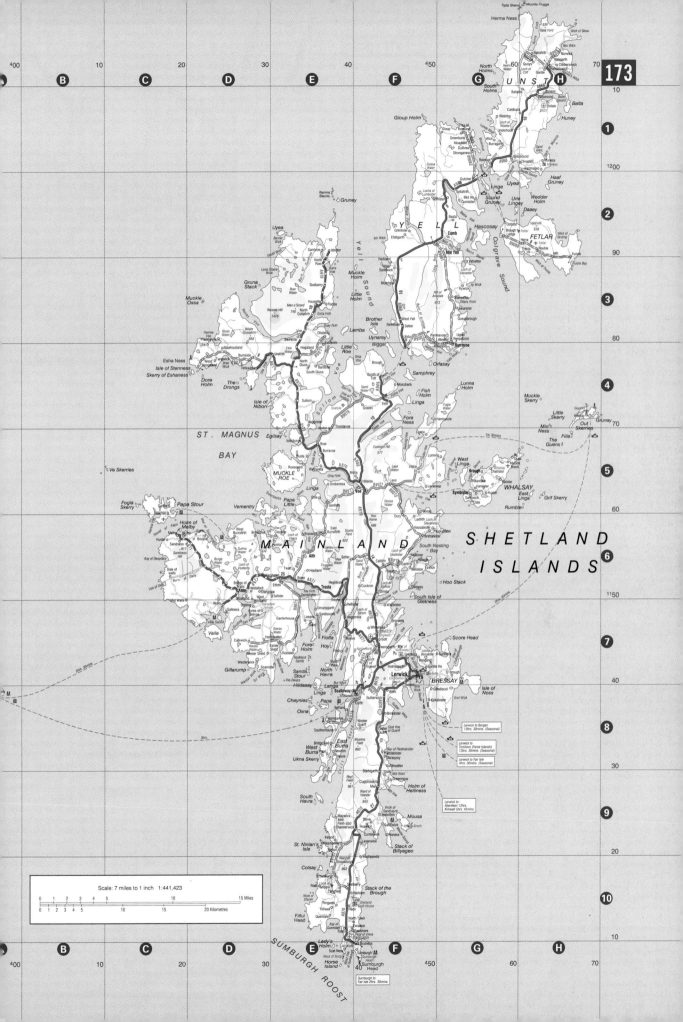

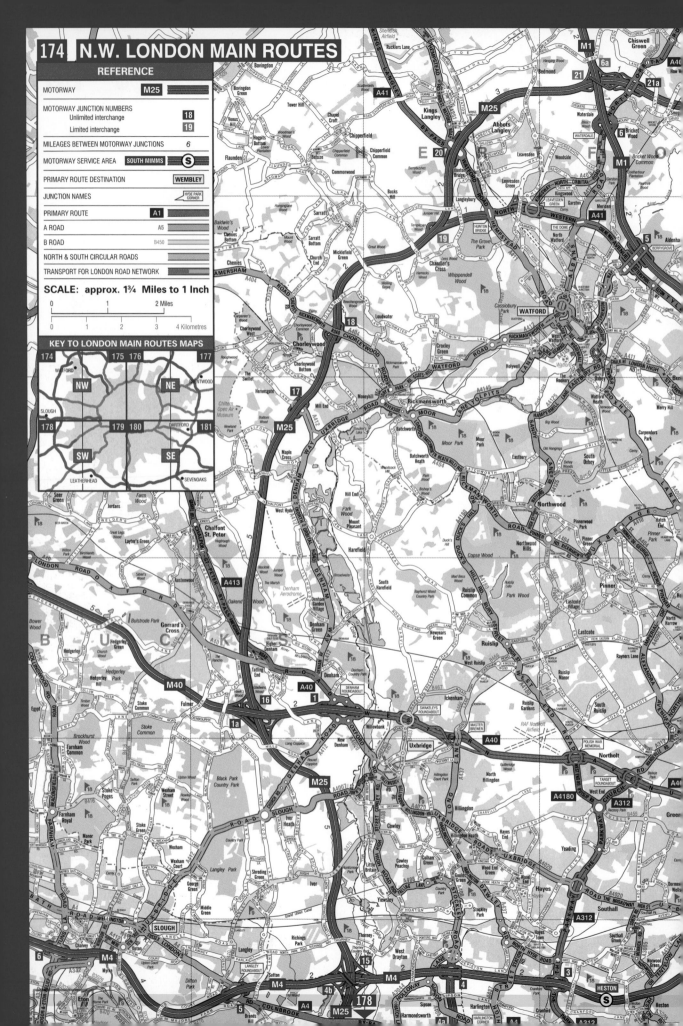

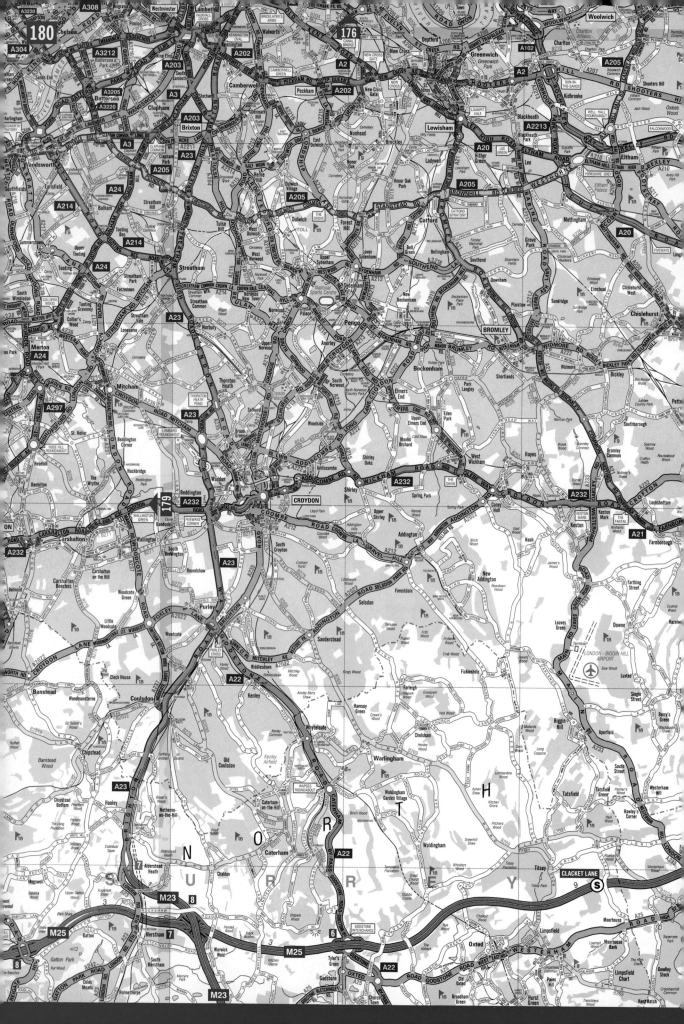

SCALE: approx. 1¾ Miles to 1 Inch

0   1   2 Miles

0   1   2   3   4 Kilometres

Town Plans

The Shetland Islands lie approximately 135 miles N.N.E. of John o' Groats

Reference to Town Plans	Légende	Zeichenerklärung
MOTORWAY — M1	Autoroute	Autobahn
MOTORWAY UNDER CONSTRUCTION	Autoroute en construction	Autobahn im Bau
MOTORWAY PROPOSED	Autoroute prévue	Geplante Autobahn
MOTORWAY JUNCTIONS WITH NUMBERS	Autoroute echangeur numéroté	Autobahnanschluß mit Nummer
Unlimited Interchange 4	Echangeur non limité 4	4 Unbeschränkter Fahrtrichtungswechsel
Limited Interchange 5	Echangeur limité 5	5 Beschränkter Fahrtrichtungswechsel
PRIMARY ROUTE — A41	Route prioritaire, direction	Hauptverbindungsstraße
DUAL CARRIAGEWAY — A129	Route à deux chaussées séparées	Zweispurige Schnellstraße (A- und B-Straßen)
CLASS A ROAD — B177	Route de type A	A-Straße
CLASS B ROAD	Route de type B	B-Straße
MAJOR ROAD UNDER CONSTRUCTION	Route prioritaire en construction	Hauptverkehrsstraße im Bau
MAJOR ROAD PROPOSED	Route prioritaire prévue	Geplante Hauptverkehrsstraße
MINOR ROAD	Route secondaire	Nebenstraße
RESTRICTED ACCESS	Accès réglementé	Beschränkte Zufahrt
PEDESTRIAN ROAD & MAIN FOOTWAY	Route piétonnière et chemin réservé aux piétons	Fußgängerstraße und Fußweg
ONE WAY STREET	Sens unique	Einbahnstraße
TOLL	Péage	Gebührenpflichtig
RAILWAY AND B.R. STATION	Voie ferrée et gare B.R.	Eisenbahnlinie und Bahnhof
UNDERGROUND, D.L.R. & METRO STATION	Station de metro et D.L.R.	U-Bahnstation und D.L.R.-Station
LEVEL CROSSING AND TUNNEL	Passage à niveau et tunnel	Bahnübergang und Tunnel
TRAM STOP AND ONE WAY TRAM STOP	Arrêt de Tramway	Straßenbahnhaltestelle
BUILT UP AREA	Agglomération	Geschlossene Ortschaft
ABBEY, CATHEDRAL, PRIORY ETC. †	Abbaye, Cathédrale, Prieuré etc. †	Abtei, Kathedrale, Kloster usw.
AIRPORT	Aéroport	Flughafen
BUS STATION	Gare routière	Bushaltestelle
CAR PARK (Selection of) P	Choix de Parking P	Auswahl von Parkplatz
CHURCH †	Eglise †	Kirche
CITY WALL	Murs d'enceinte	Stadtmauer
FERRY (Vehicular)	Bac (Véhicules)	Fähre (Autos)
(Foot only)	(Piétons)	(nur für Personen)
GOLF COURSE	Terrain de golf	Golfplatz
HELIPORT	Héliport	Hubschrauberlandeplatz
HOSPITAL H	Hôpital H	Krankenhaus
INFORMATION CENTRE	Syndicat d'initiative	Information
LIGHTHOUSE	Phare	Leuchtturm
MARKET	Marché	Markt
NATIONAL TRUST PROPERTY (Open) NT	National Trust Property (Ouvert) NT	National Trust-Eigentum (geöffnet)
(Restricted opening) NT	(Heures d'ouverture) NT	(Beschränkte Öffnungszeit)
(National Trust of Scotland) NTS	(National Trust of Scotland) NTS	(National Trust of Scotland)
PARK & RIDE	Choix de Parking	Auswahl von Parkplatz
PLACE OF INTEREST	Endroits Intéressants	Sehenswürdigkeiten
POLICE STATION ▲	Commissariat de police ▲	Polizeirevier
POST OFFICE ★	Bureau de poste ★	Postamt
SHOPPING AREA (Main street and precinct)	Quartier commerçant (Rue et zone principales)	Einkaufsviertel (Hauptgeschäftsstraße, Fußgängerzone)
SHOPMOBILITY	Shopmobility	Shopmobility
TOILET ▽	Toilettes ▽	Toilette
VIEWPOINT	Vue Panoramique	Aussichtspunkt

ABERDEEN

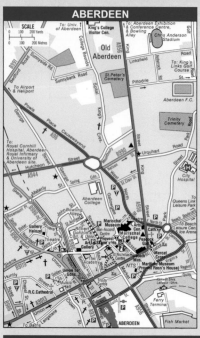

BATH

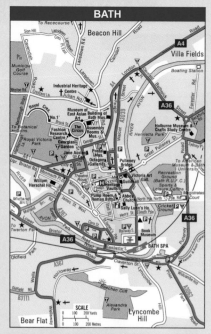

BLACKPOOL

BIRMINGHAM (CITY CENTRE)

BOURNEMOUTH

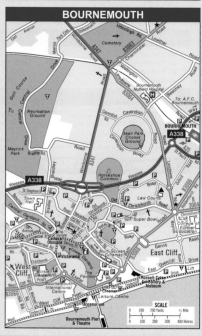

BRADFORD

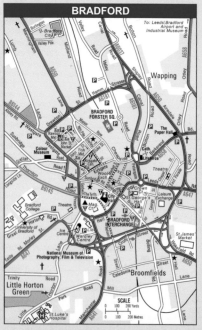

BRIGHTON and HOVE

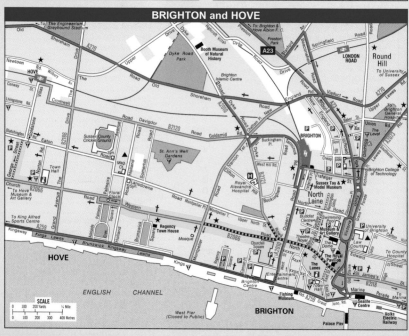

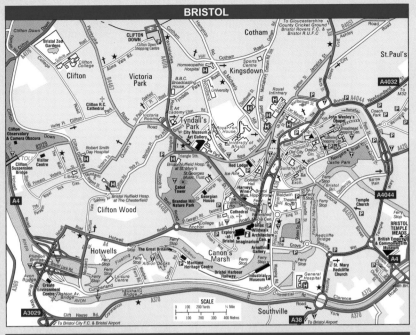

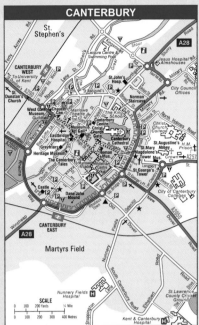

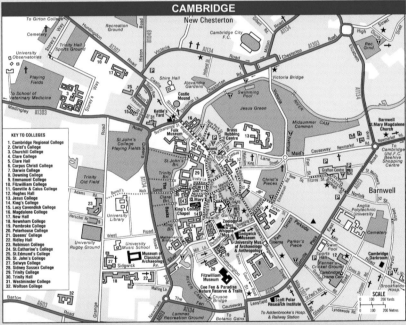

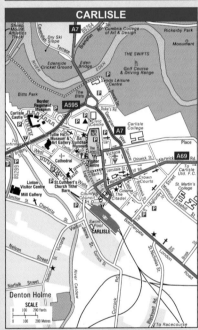

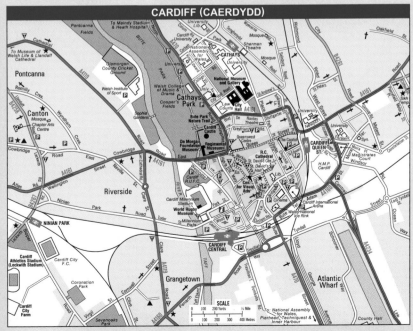

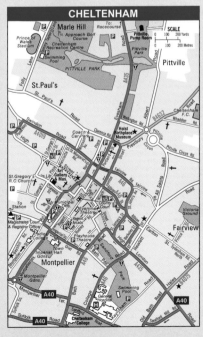

CHESTER
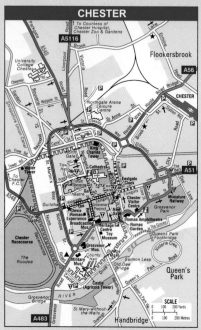

COVENTRY
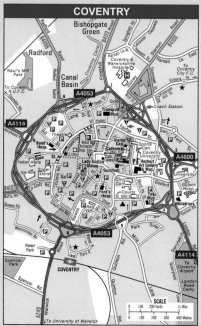

DERBY
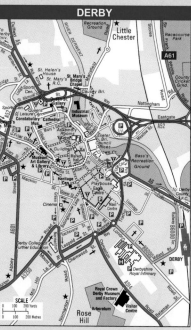

DOVER
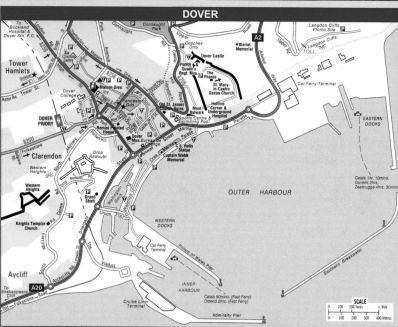

DUMFRIES
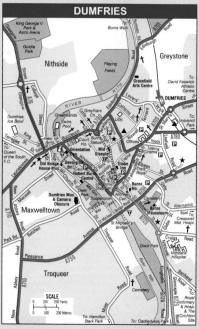

DUNDEE
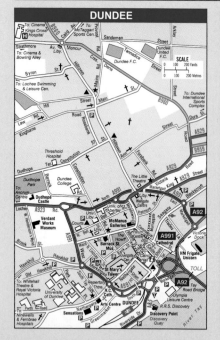

DURHAM
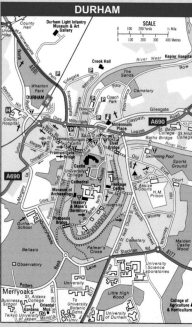

EASTBOURNE
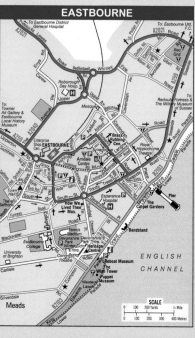

EDINBURGH

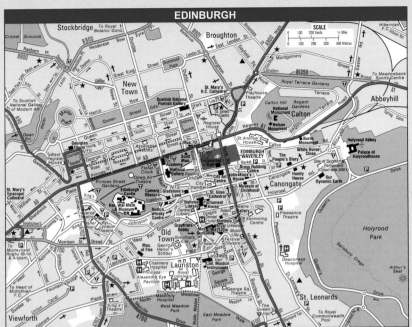

FOLKESTONE

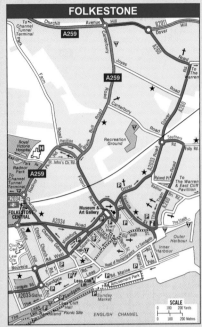

EXETER

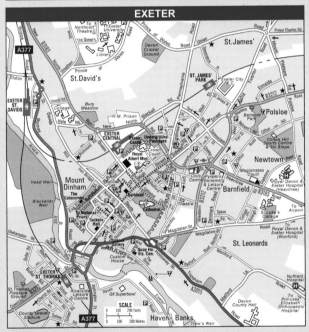

GUILDFORD

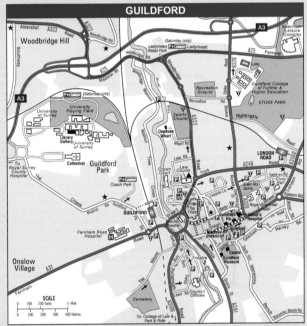

GLASGOW

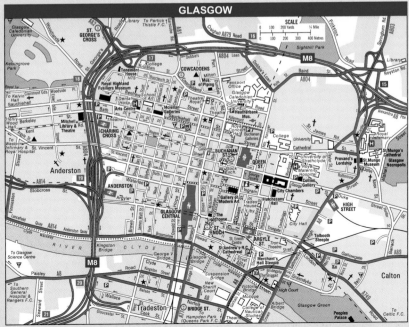

GLOUCESTER

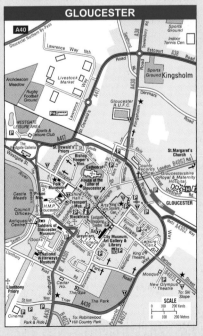

HARROGATE

INVERNESS
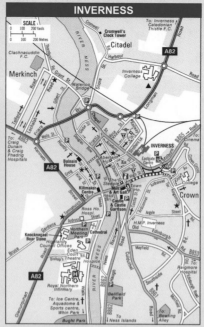

IPSWICH
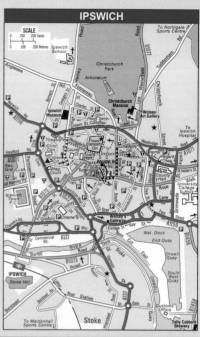

KILMARNOCK

LEEDS
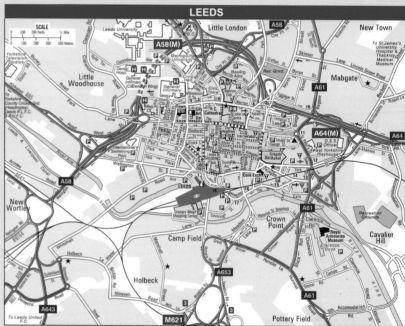

KINGSTON UPON HULL
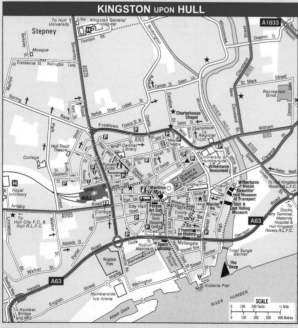

LEICESTER
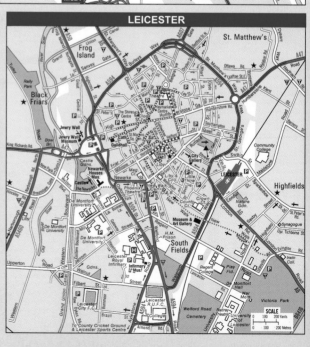

LINCOLN

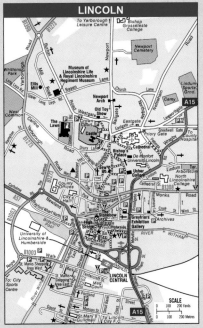

LIVERPOOL

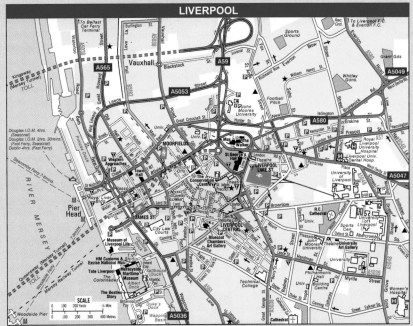

MANCHESTER (CITY CENTRE)

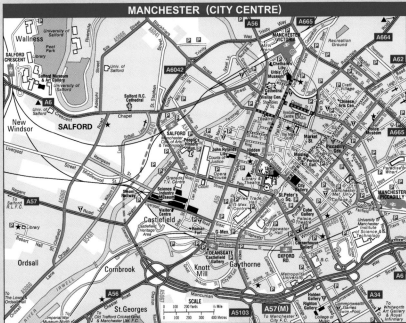

MIDDLESBROUGH

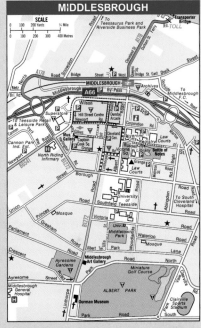

MEDWAY TOWNS

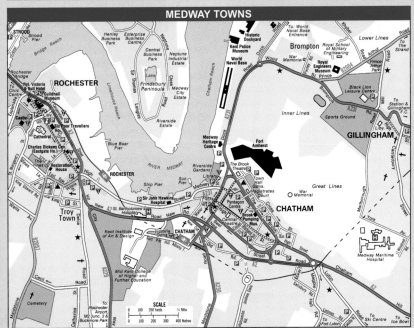

NEWCASTLE UPON TYNE

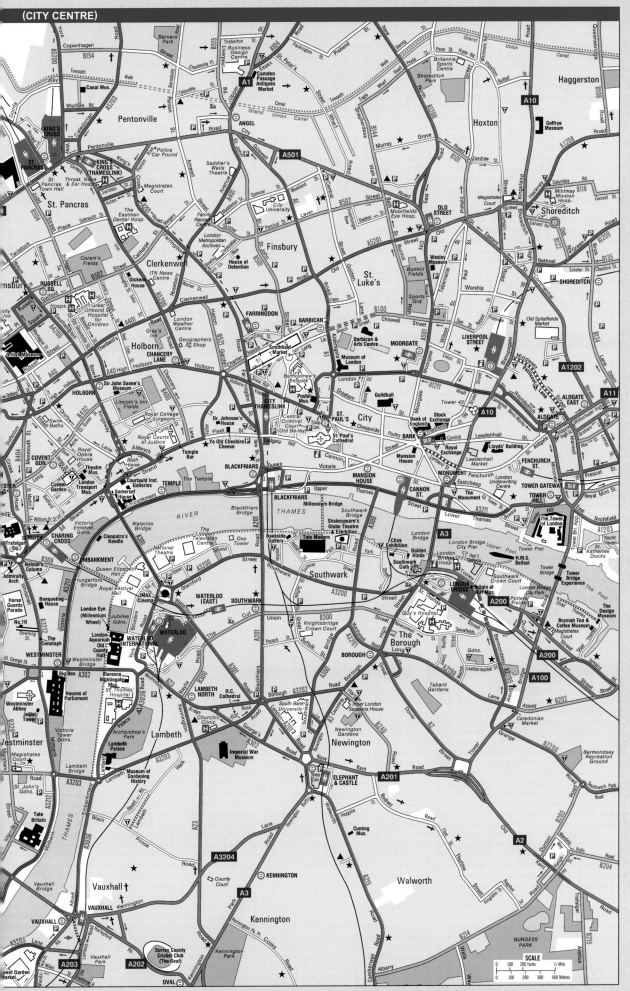

MILTON KEYNES

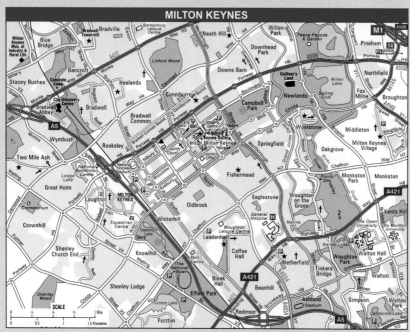

NEWPORT (CASNEWYDD)

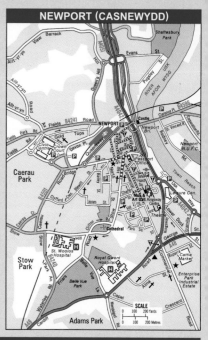

NORWICH

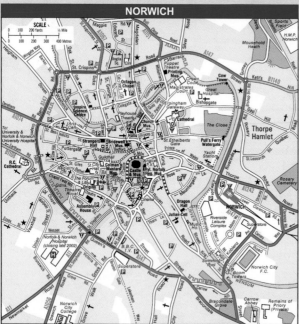

NOTTINGHAM

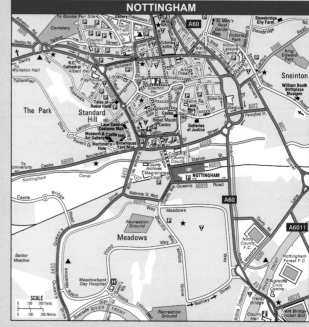

NORTHAMPTON

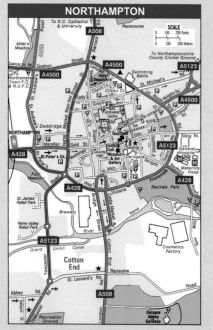

OXFORD

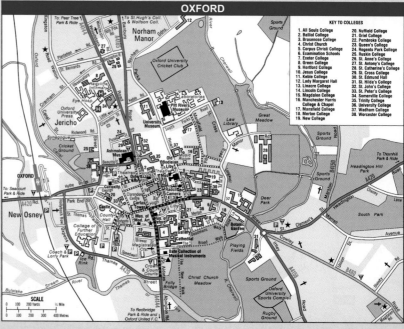

KEY TO COLLEGES

1. All Souls College
2. Balliol College
3. Brasenose College
4. Christ Church
5. Corpus Christi College
6. Examination Schools
7. Exeter College
8. Green College
9. Hertford College
10. Jesus College
11. Keble College
12. Lady Margaret Hall
13. Linacre College
14. Lincoln College
15. Magdalen College
16. Manchester Harris College & Chapel
17. Mansfield College
18. Merton College
19. New College
20. Nuffield College
21. Oriel College
22. Pembroke College
23. Queen's College
24. Regents Park College
25. Ruskin College
26. St. Anne's College
27. St. Antony's College
28. St. Catherine's College
29. St. Cross College
30. St. Edmund Hall
31. St. Hilda's College
32. St. John's College
33. St. Peter's College
34. Somerville College
35. Trinity College
36. University College
37. Wadham College
38. Worcester College

OBAN
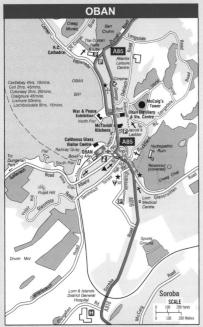

PERTH
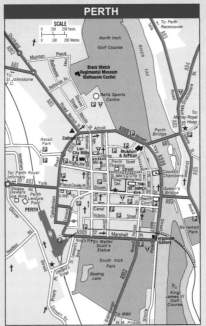

PETERBOROUGH

PLYMOUTH
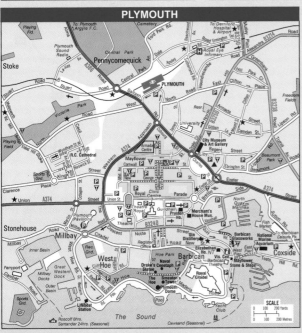

PORTSMOUTH
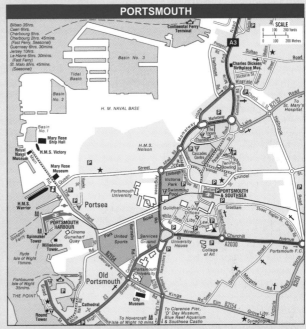

PRESTON
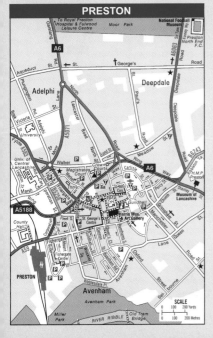

READING
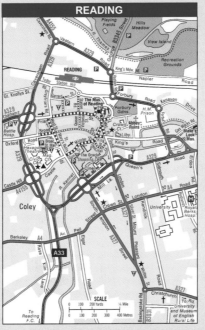

SALISBURY
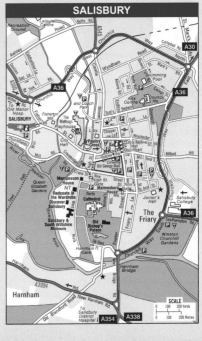

SHEFFIELD

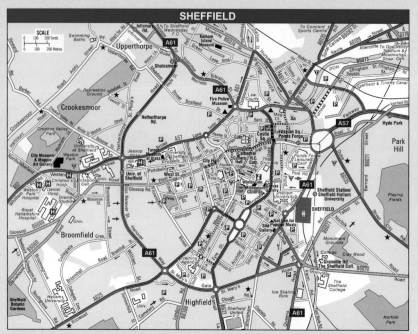

SHREWSBURY

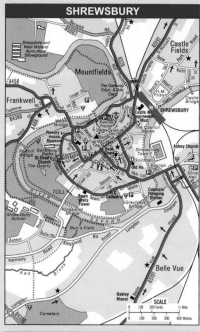

SOUTHAMPTON

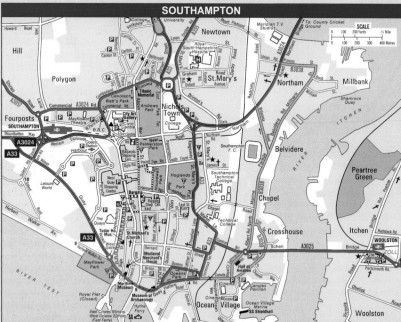

STIRLING

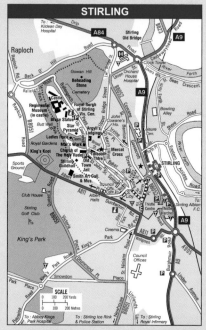

STOKE-ON-TRENT

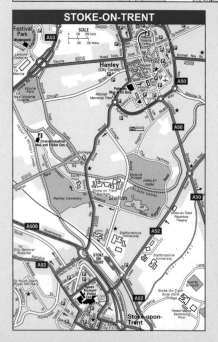

STRATFORD UPON AVON

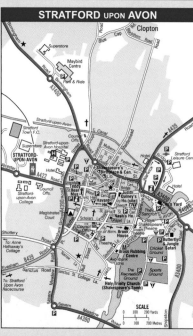

SUNDERLAND

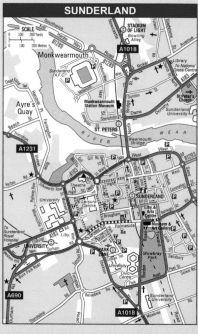

SWANSEA

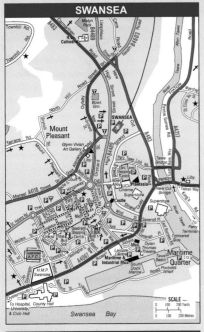

SWINDON

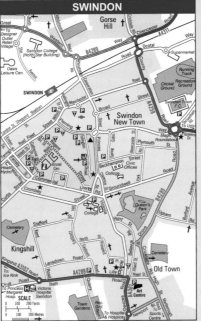

TAUNTON

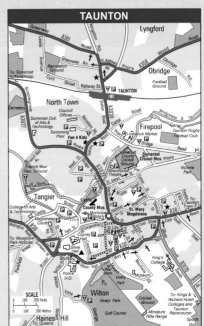

WINCHESTER

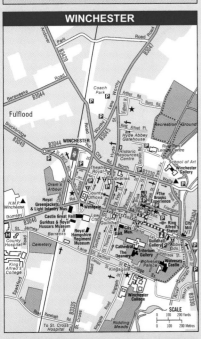

WINDSOR

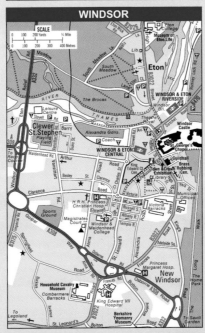

WOLVERHAMPTON

WORCESTER

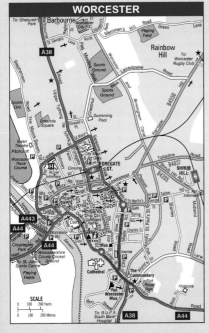

YORK

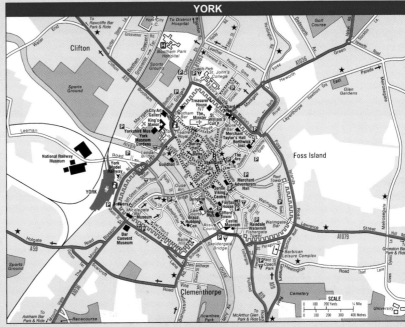

HARWICH

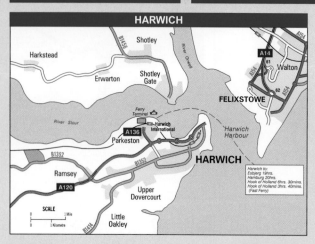

Harwich to:
Esbjerg 19hrs.
Hamburg 20hrs.
Hook of Holland 6hrs. 30mins.
Hook of Holland 3hrs. 40mins.
(Fast Ferry)

KINGSTON UPON HULL

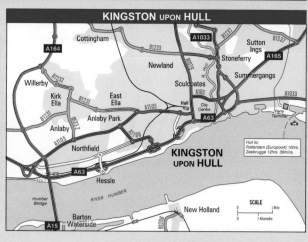

Hull to:
Rotterdam (Europoort) 10hrs.
Zeebrugge 12hrs. 30mins.

NEWCASTLE UPON TYNE

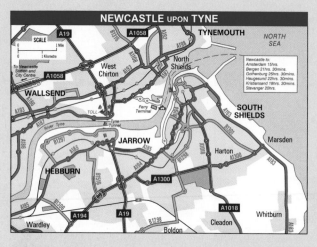

Newcastle to:
Amsterdam 15hrs.
Bergen 21hrs. 30mins.
Gothenburg 25hrs. 30mins.
Haugesund 22hrs. 30mins.
Kristiansand 18hrs. 30mins.
Stavanger 20hrs.

NEWHAVEN

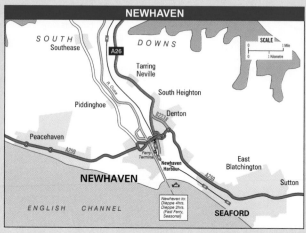

Newhaven to:
Dieppe 4hrs.
Dieppe 2hrs.
(Fast Ferry,
Seasonal)

POOLE

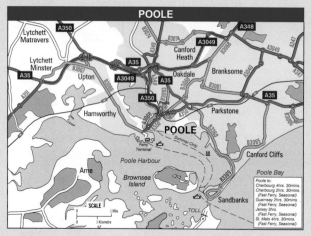

Poole to:
Cherbourg 4hrs. 30mins.
Cherbourg 2hrs. 30mins.
(Fast Ferry, Seasonal)
Guernsey 3hrs. 30mins.
(Fast Ferry,
Seasonal)
Jersey 3hrs.
(Fast Ferry,
Seasonal)
St. Malo 3hrs. 30mins.
(Fast Ferry, Seasonal)

PORTSMOUTH

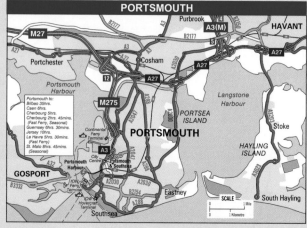

Portsmouth to:
Bilbao 35hrs.
Caen 6hrs.
Cherbourg 5hrs.
Cherbourg 2hrs. 45mins.
(Fast Ferry, Seasonal)
Guernsey 6hrs. 30mins.
Jersey 10hrs.
Le Havre 5hrs. 30mins.
(Fast Ferry)
St. Malo 8hrs. 45mins.
(Seasonal)

SWANSEA

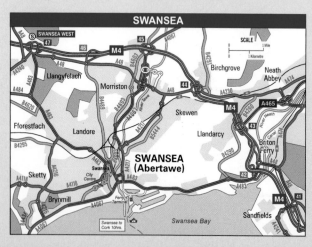

Swansea to:
Cork 10hrs.

WEYMOUTH

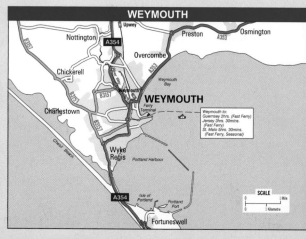

Weymouth to:
Guernsey 2hrs. (Fast Ferry)
Jersey 3hrs. 30mins.
(Fast Ferry)
St. Malo 5hrs. 30mins.
(Fast Ferry, Seasonal)

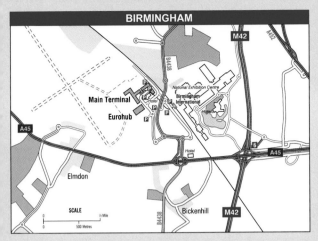

BIRMINGHAM

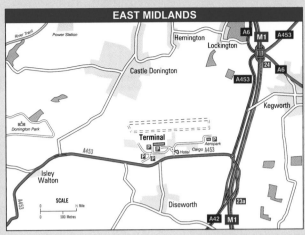

EAST MIDLANDS

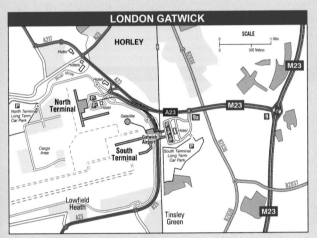

LONDON GATWICK

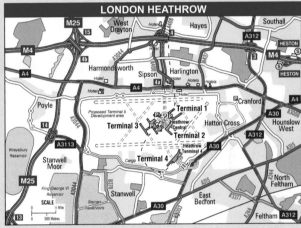

LONDON HEATHROW

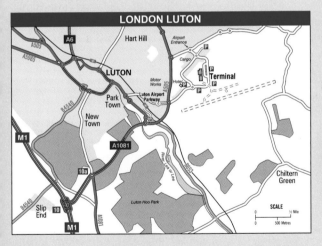

LONDON LUTON

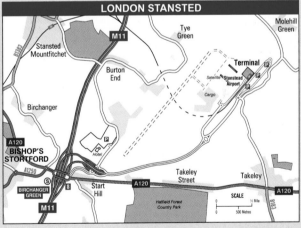

LONDON STANSTED

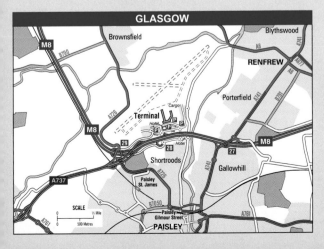

GLASGOW

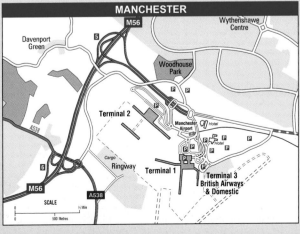

MANCHESTER

INDEX TO CITIES, TOWNS, VILLAGES, HAMLETS & LOCATIONS

(1) A strict alphabetical order is used e.g Abbotstone follows Abbot's Salford but precedes Abbots Worthy.

(2) The map reference given refers to the actual map square in which the town spot or built-up area is located and not to the place name.

(3) Where two or more places of the same name occur in the same County or Unitary Authority, the nearest large town is also given; e.g. Achiemore. *High* —2D **166** (nr. Durness) indicates that Achiemore is located in square 2D on page **166** and is situated near Durness in the Unitary Authority of Highland.

(4) Only one reference is given although due to page overlaps the place may appear on more than one page.

COUNTIES and UNITARY AUTHORITIES with the abbreviations used in this index

Aberdeen (City) : *Aber C*
Aberdeenshire : *Aber*
Angus : *Ang*
Argyll & Bute : *Arg*
Bath & N E Somerset : *Bath*
Bedfordshire : *Beds*
Blackburn with Darwen : *Bkbn*
Blackpool : *Bkpl*
Blaenau Gwent : *Blae*
Bournemouth : *Bour*
Bracknell Forest : *Brac*
Bridgend : *B'end*
Brighton & Hove (City) : *Brig*
Bristol (City) : *Bris*
Buckinghamshire : *Buck*
Caerphilly : *Cphy*
Cambridgeshire : *Cambs*
Cardiff : *Card*
Carmarthenshire : *Carm*
Ceredigion : *Cdgn*
Cheshire : *Ches*
Clackmannanshire : *Clac*
Conwy : *Cnwy*
Cornwall : *Corn*
Cumbria : *Cumb*
Darlington : *Darl*
Denbighshire : *Den*
Derby (City) : *Dby C*
Derbyshire : *Derbs*
Devon : *Devn*
Dorset : *Dors*
Dumfries & Galloway : *Dum*
Dundee : *D'dee*
Durham : *Dur*
East Ayrshire : *E Ayr*
East Dunbartonshire : *E Dun*
East Lothian : *E Lot*
East Renfrewshire : *E Ren*
East Riding of Yorkshire : *E Yor*
East Sussex : *E Sus*
Edinburgh : *Edin*
Essex : *Essx*
Falkirk : *Falk*
Fife : *Fife*
Flintshire : *Flin*
Glasgow : *Glas*
Gloucestershire : *Glos*
Greater London : *G Lon*
Greater Manchester : *G Man*
Gwynedd : *Gwyn*
Halton : *Hal*
Hampshire : *Hants*
Hartlepool : *Hart*
Herefordshire : *Here*
Hertfordshire : *Herts*
Highland : *High*
Inverclyde : *Inv*
Isle of Anglesey : *IOA*
Isle of Man : *IOM*
Isle of Wight : *IOW*
Isles of Scilly : *IOS*
Kent : *Kent*
Kingston upon Hull : *Hull*
Lancashire : *Lanc*
Leicester (City) : *Leic C*
Leicestershire : *Leics*
Lincolnshire : *Linc*
Luton : *Lutn*
Medway : *Medw*
Merseyside : *Mers*
Merthyr Tydfil : *Mer T*
Middlesbrough : *Midd*
Midlothian : *Midl*
Milton Keynes : *Mil*
Monmouthshire : *Mon*
Moray : *Mor*
Neath Port Talbot : *Neat*
Newport : *Newp*
Norfolk : *Norf*
Northamptonshire : *Nptn*
North Ayrshire : *N Ayr*
North East Lincolnshire : *NE Lin*
North Lanarkshire : *N Lan*
North Lincolnshire : *N Lin*
North Somerset : *N Som*
Northumberland : *Nmbd*
North Yorkshire : *N Yor*
Nottingham (City) : *Not C*
Nottinghamshire : *Notts*
Orkney : *Orkn*
Oxfordshire : *Oxon*
Pembrokeshire : *Pemb*
Perth & Kinross : *Per*
Peterborough : *Pet*
Plymouth : *Plym*
Poole : *Pool*
Portsmouth : *Port*
Powys : *Powy*
Reading : *Read*
Redcar & Cleveland : *Red C*
Renfrewshire : *Ren*
Rhondda Cynon Taff : *Rhon*
Rutland : *Rut*
Scottish Borders : *Scot*
Shetland : *Shet*
Shropshire : *Shrp*
Slough : *Slo*
Somerset : *Som*
Southampton : *Sotn*
South Ayrshire : *S Ayr*
Southend-on-Sea : *S'end*
South Gloucestershire : *S Glo*
South Lanarkshire : *S Lan*
South Yorkshire : *S Yor*
Staffordshire : *Staf*
Stirling : *Stir*
Stockton-on-Tees : *Stoc T*
Stoke-on-Trent : *Stoke*
Suffolk : *Suff*
Surrey : *Surr*
Swansea : *Swan*
Swindon : *Swin*
Telford & Wrekin : *Telf*
Thurrock : *Thur*
Torbay : *Torb*
Torfaen : *Torf*
Tyne & Wear : *Tyne*
Vale of Glamorgan, The : *V Glam*
Warrington : *Warr*
Warwickshire : *Warw*
West Berkshire : *W Ber*
West Dunbartonshire : *W Dun*
Western Isles : *W Isl*
West Lothian : *W Lot*
West Midlands : *W Mid*
West Sussex : *W Sus*
West Yorkshire : *W Yor*
Wiltshire : *Wilts*
Windsor & Maidenhead : *Wind*
Wokingham : *Wok*
Worcestershire : *Worc*
Wrexham : *Wrex*
York (City) : *York*

INDEX

Abbas Combe. *Som* —4C **22**
Abberley. *Worc* —4B **60**
Abberley Common. *Worc* —4B **60**
Abberton. *Essx* —4D **54**
Abberton. *Worc* —5D **61**
Abberwick. *Nmbd* —3F **121**
Abbess Roding. *Essx* —4F **53**
Abbey. *Devn* —1E **13**
Abbey-cwm-hir. *Powy* —3C **58**
Abbeydale. *S Yor* —2H **85**
Abbeydale Park. *S Yor* —2H **85**
Abbey Dore. *Here* —2G **47**
Abbey Hulton. *Stoke* —1D **72**
Abbey St Bathans. *Scot* —3D **130**
Abbeystead. *Lanc* —4E **97**
Abbeytown. *Cumb* —4C **112**
Abbey Village. *Lanc* —2E **91**
Abbey Wood. *G Lon* —3F **39**
Abbots Ann. *Hants* —2B **24**
Abbots Bickington. *Devn* —1D **11**
Abbots Bromley. *Staf* —3E **73**
Abbotsbury. *Dors* —4A **14**
Abbotsham. *Devn* —4E **19**
Abbotskerswell. *Devn* —2E **9**
Abbots Langley. *Herts* —5A **52**
Abbots Leigh. *N Som* —4A **34**
Abbotsley. *Cambs* —5B **64**
Abbots Morton. *Worc* —5E **61**
Abbots Ripton. *Cambs* —3B **64**
Abbot's Salford. *Warw* —5E **61**
Abbotstone. *Hants* —3D **24**
Abbots Worthy. *Hants* —3C **24**
Abcott. *Shrp* —3F **59**
Abdon. *Shrp* —2H **59**
Abenhall. *Glos* —4B **48**
Aber. *Cdgn* —1E **45**
Aberaeron. *Cdgn* —4D **56**
Aberafan. *Neat* —3A **32**
Aberaman. *Rhon* —5D **46**
Aberangell. *Powy* —4H **69**
Aberarad. *Carm* —1H **43**
Aberarder. *High* —1A **150**
Aberargie. *Per* —2D **136**
Aberarth. *Cdgn* —4D **57**
Aberavon. *Neat* —3A **32**
Aber-banc. *Cdgn* —1D **44**
Aberbargoed. *Cphy* —2E **33**
Aberbechan. *Powy* —1D **58**
Aberbeeg. *Blae* —5F **47**
Aberbowlan. *Carm* —2G **45**
Aberbran. *Powy* —3C **46**
Abercanaid. *Mer T* —5D **46**
Abercarn. *Cphy* —2F **33**
Abercastle. *Pemb* —1C **42**
Abercegir. *Powy* —5H **69**
Aberchalder. *High* —3F **149**
Aberchirder. *Aber* —3D **160**
Abercorn. *W Lot* —2D **129**
Abercraf. *Powy* —4B **46**
Abercregan. *Neat* —2B **32**
Abercrombie. *Fife* —3H **137**
Abercwmboi. *Rhon* —2D **32**
Abercych. *Pemb* —1C **44**
Abercynon. *Rhon* —2D **32**
Aber-Cywarch. *Gwyn* —4A **70**
Aberdalgie. *Per* —1C **136**
Aberdar. *Rhon* —5C **46**
Aberdare. *Rhon* —5C **46**
Aberdaron. *Gwyn* —3A **68**
Aberdaugleddau. *Pemb* —4D **42**
Aberdeen. *Aber C* —3G **153**
Aberdeen Airport. *Aber C* —2F **153**
Aberdesach. *Gwyn* —5D **80**
Aberdour. *Fife* —1E **129**
Aberdovey. *Gwyn* —1F **57**
Aberdulais. *Neat* —5A **46**
Aberdyfi. *Gwyn* —1F **57**
Aberedw. *Powy* —1D **46**
Abereiddy. *Pemb* —1B **42**
Abererch. *Gwyn* —2C **68**
Aberfan. *Mer T* —5D **46**
Aberfeldy. *Per* —4F **143**
Aberffraw. *IOA* —4C **80**
Aberffrwd. *Cdgn* —3F **57**
Aberford. *W Yor* —1E **93**
Aberfoyle. *Stir* —3E **135**
Abergarw. *B'End* —3C **32**
Abergarwed. *Neat* —5B **46**
Abergavenny. *Mon* —4G **47**
Abergele. *Cnwy* —3B **82**
Aber-Giar. *Carm* —1F **45**
Abergorlech. *Carm* —2F **45**
Abergwaun. *Pemb* —1D **42**
Abergwesyn. *Powy* —5A **58**
Abergwili. *Carm* —3E **45**
Abergwynfi. *Neat* —2B **32**
Abergwyngregyn. *Gwyn* —3F **81**
Abergynolwyn. *Gwyn* —5F **69**
Aberhafesp. *Powy* —1C **58**
Aberhonddu. *Powy* —3D **46**
Aberhosan. *Powy* —1H **57**
Aberkenfig. *B'End* —3B **32**
Aberlady. *E Lot* —2A **130**
Aberlemno. *Ang* —3E **145**
Aberllefenni. *Cdgn* —5G **69**
Abermaw. *Gwyn* —4F **69**
Abermeurig. *Cdgn* —5E **57**
Aber-miwl. *Powy* —1D **58**
Abermule. *Powy* —1D **58**
Abernant. *Carm* —2H **43**
Abernant. *Rhon* —5D **46**
Abernethy. *Per* —2D **136**
Abernyte. *Per* —5B **144**
Aber-oer. *Wrex* —1E **71**
Aberpennar. *Rhon* —2D **32**
Aberporth. *Cdgn* —5B **56**
Aberriw. *Powy* —5D **70**
Abersoch. *Gwyn* —3C **68**
Abersychan. *Torf* —5F **47**
Abertawe. *Swan* —3F **31**
Aberteifi. *Cdgn* —1B **44**
Aberthin. *V Glam* —4D **32**
Abertillery. *Blae* —5F **47**
Abertridwr. *Cphy* —3E **32**
Abertridwr. *Powy* —4C **70**
Abertyleri. *Blae* —5F **47**
Abertysswg. *Cphy* —5E **47**
Aberuthven. *Per* —2B **136**
Aber Village. *Powy* —3E **46**
Aberyscir. *Powy* —3D **46**
Aberystwyth. *Cdgn* —2E **57**
Abhainn Suidhe. *W Isl* —7C **171**
Abingdon. *Oxon* —2C **36**
Abinger Common. *Surr* —1C **26**
Abinger Hammer. *Surr* —1B **26**
Abington. *S Lan* —2B **118**
Abington Pigotts. *Cambs* —1D **52**
Ab Kettleby. *Leics* —3E **74**
Ab Lench. *Worc* —5E **61**
Ablington. *Glos* —5G **49**
Ablington. *Wilts* —2G **23**
Abney. *Derbs* —3F **85**
Aboyne. *Aber* —4C **152**
Abram. *G Man* —4E **90**
Abriachan. *High* —5H **157**
Abridge. *Essx* —1F **39**
Abronhill. *N Lan* —2A **128**
Abson. *S Glo* —4C **34**
Abthorpe. *Nptn* —1E **51**
Abune-the-Hill. *Orkn* —5B **172**
Aby. *Linc* —3D **88**
Acarsaid Mhor. *W Isl* —8C **170**
Acaster Malbis. *York* —5H **99**
Acaster Selby. *N Yor* —5H **99**
Accott. *Devn* —3G **19**
Accrington. *Lanc* —2F **91**
Acha. *Arg* —3C **138**
Achachork. *High* —4D **155**
Achahoish. *Arg* —2F **125**
Achaleven. *Arg* —5D **140**
Achallader. *Arg* —4H **141**
Acha Mor. *W Isl* —5F **171**
Achanalt. *High* —2E **157**
Achandunie. *High* —1A **158**
Ach'an Todhair. *High* —1E **141**
Achany. *High* —3C **164**
Achaphubuil. *High* —1E **141**
Acharacle. *High* —2A **140**
Acharn. *Ang* —1B **144**
Acharn. *Per* —4E **143**
Acharole. *High* —3E **169**
Achateny. *High* —2G **139**
Achavanich. *High* —4D **169**
Achdalieu. *High* —1E **141**
Achduart. *High* —3E **163**
Achentoul. *High* —5A **168**
Achfary. *High* —5C **166**
Achfrish. *High* —2C **164**
Achgarve. *High* —4C **162**
Achiemore. *High* —2D **166** (nr. Durness)
Achiemore. *High* —3A **168** (nr. Thurso)
A'Chill. *High* —3A **146**
Achiltibuie. *High* —3E **163**
Achina. *High* —2H **167**
Achinahuagh. *High* —2F **167**
Achindarroch. *High* —3E **141**
Achinduich. *High* —3C **164**
Achinduin. *Arg* —5C **140**
Achininver. *High* —2F **167**
Achintee. *High* —4B **156**
Achintraid. *High* —5H **155**
Achleck. *Arg* —4F **139**
Achlorachan. *High* —3F **157**
Achluachrach. *High* —5E **149**
Achlyness. *High* —3C **166**
Achmelvich. *High* —1E **163**
Achmony. *High* —5H **157**
Achmore. *High* —5A **156** (nr. Stromeferry)
Achmore. *High* —4E **163** (nr. Ullapool)
Achnacarnin. *High* —1E **163**
Achnacarry. *High* —5D **148**
Achnaclerach. *High* —2G **157**
Achnacloich. *High* —3D **147**
Achnaconeran. *High* —2G **149**
Achnacroish. *Arg* —4C **140**
Achnafalnich. *Arg* —1B **134**
Achnagarron. *High* —2A **158**
Achnaha. *High* —2F **139**
Achnahanat. *High* —4C **164**
Achnahannet. *High* —1D **151**
Achnairn. *High* —2C **164**
Achnaluachrach. *High* —3D **164**
Achnamara. *Arg* —1F **125**
Achnanellan. *High* —5C **148**
Achnangoul. *Arg* —3H **133**
Achnasheen. *High* —3D **156**
Achnashellach. *High* —4C **156**
Achosnich. *High* —2F **139**
Achow. *High* —5E **169**
Achranich. *High* —4B **140**
Achreamie. *High* —2C **168**
Achriabhach. *High* —2F **141**
Achriesgill. *High* —3C **166**
Achrimsdale. *High* —3G **165**
Achscrabster. *High* —2C **168**
Achtoty. *High* —2G **167**
Achurch. *Nptn* —2H **63**
Achuvoldrach. *High* —3F **167**
Achvaich. *High* —4E **164**
Achvoan. *High* —3E **165**
Ackergill. *High* —3F **169**
Ackergillshore. *High* —3F **169**
Acklam. *Midd* —3B **106**
Acklam. *N Yor* —3B **100**
Ackleton. *Shrp* —1B **60**
Acklington. *Nmbd* —4G **121**
Ackton. *W Yor* —2E **93**
Ackworth Moor Top. *W Yor* —3E **93**
Acle. *Norf* —4G **79**
Acock's Green. *W Mid* —2F **61**
Acol. *Kent* —4H **41**
Acomb. *Nmbd* —3C **114**
Acomb. *York* —4H **99**
Aconbury. *Here* —2A **48**
Acre. *G Man* —4H **91**
Acre. *Lanc* —2F **91**
Acrefair. *Wrex* —1E **71**
Acrise. *Kent* —1F **29**
Acton. *Ches* —5A **84**
Acton. *Dors* —5E **15**
Acton. *G Lon* —2C **38**
Acton. *Shrp* —2F **59**
Acton. *Staf* —1C **72**
Acton. *Suff* —1B **54**
Acton. *Worc* —4C **60**
Acton. *Wrex* —5F **83**
Acton Beauchamp. *Here* —5A **60**
Acton Bridge. *Ches* —3H **83**
Acton Burnell. *Shrp* —5H **71**
Acton Green. *Here* —5A **60**
Acton Pigott. *Shrp* —5H **71**
Acton Round. *Shrp* —1A **60**
Acton Scott. *Shrp* —2G **59**
Acton Trussell. *Staf* —4D **72**
Acton Turville. *S Glo* —3D **34**
Adabroc. *W Isl* —1H **171**
Adam's Hill. *Worc* —3D **60**
Adbaston. *Staf* —3B **72**
Adber. *Dors* —4B **22**
Adderbury. *Oxon* —2C **50**
Adderley. *Shrp* —2A **72**
Adderstone. *Nmbd* —1F **121**
Addiewell. *W Lot* —3C **128**
Addingham. *W Yor* —5C **98**
Addington. *Buck* —3F **51**
Addington. *G Lon* —4E **39**
Addington. *Kent* —5A **40**
Addinston. *Scot* —4B **130**
Addiscombe. *G Lon* —4E **39**
Addlestone. *Surr* —4B **38**
Addlethorpe. *Linc* —4E **89**
Adeney. *Telf* —4B **72**
Adfa. *Powy* —5C **70**
Adforton. *Here* —3G **59**
Adgestone. *IOW* —4D **16**
Adisham. *Kent* —5G **41**
Adlestrop. *Glos* —3H **49**
Adlingfleet. *E Yor* —2B **94**
Adlington. *Ches* —2D **84**
Adlington. *Lanc* —3E **90**
Admaston. *Staf* —3E **73**
Admaston. *Telf* —4A **72**
Admington. *Warw* —1G **49**
Adpar. *Cdgn* —1D **44**
Adsborough. *Som* —4F **21**
Adstock. *Buck* —2F **51**
Adstone. *Nptn* —5C **62**
Adversane. *W Sus* —3B **26**
Advie. *High* —5F **159**
Adwalton. *W Yor* —2C **92**
Adwell. *Oxon* —2E **37**
Adwick le Street. *S Yor* —4F **93**
Adwick upon Dearne. *S Yor* —4E **93**
Adziel. *Aber* —3G **161**
Ae. *Dum* —1A **112**
Affleck. *Aber* —1F **153**
Affpuddle. *Dors* —3D **14**
Affric Lodge. *High* —1D **148**
Afon-wen. *Flin* —3D **82**
Afton Bridgend. *E Ayr* —3F **117**
Agglethorpe. *N Yor* —1C **98**
Aglionby. *Cumb* —4F **113**
Aigburth. *Mers* —2F **83**
Aiginis. *W Isl* —4G **171**
Aike. *E Yor* —5E **101**
Aikers. *Orkn* —8D **172**
Aiketgate. *Cumb* —5F **113**
Aikhead. *Cumb* —5D **112**
Aikton. *Cumb* —4D **112**
Ailey. *Here* —1G **47**
Ailsworth. *Pet* —1A **64**
Ainderby Quernhow. *N Yor* —1F **99**
Ainderby Steeple. *N Yor* —5A **106**
Aingers Green. *Essx* —3E **54**
Ainsdale. *Mers* —3B **90**
Ainsdale-on-Sea. *Mers* —3A **90**
Ainstable. *Cumb* —5G **113**
Ainsworth. *G Man* —3F **91**
Ainthorpe. *N Yor* —4E **107**
Aintree. *Mers* —1F **83**
Aird. *Arg* —3E **133**
Aird. *Dum* —3F **109**
Aird. *High* —1G **155**
Aird. *W Isl* —3C **170** (on Benbecula)
Aird. *W Isl* —4H **171** (on Lewis)
Aird a Mhachair. *W Isl* —4C **170**
Aird a Mhulaidh. *W Isl* —6D **171**
Aird Asaig. *W Isl* —7D **171**
Aird Dhail. *W Isl* —1G **171**
Airdens. *High* —4D **164**
Airdeny. *Arg* —1G **133**
Aird Mhidhinis. *W Isl* —8C **170**
Aird Mhighe. *W Isl* —8D **171** (nr. Ceann a Bhaigh)
Aird Mhighe. *W Isl* —9C **171** (nr. Fionnsbhagh)
Aird Mhor. *W Isl* —8C **170** (on Barra)
Aird Mhor. *W Isl* —4D **170** (on South Uist)
Aird of Sleat. *High* —3D **147**
Airdrie. *N Lan* —3A **128**
Aird Shleibhe. *W Isl* —9D **171**
Aird, The. *High* —3D **154**
Aird Thunga. *W Isl* —4G **171**
Aird Uig. *W Isl* —4C **171**
Airedale. *W Yor* —2E **93**
Airidh a Bhruaich. *W Isl* —6E **171**
Airies. *Dum* —3E **109**
Airmyn. *E Yor* —2H **93**
Airntully. *Per* —5H **143**
Airor. *High* —3F **147**
Airth. *Falk* —1C **128**
Airton. *N Yor* —4B **98**
Aisby. *Linc* —1F **87** (nr. Gainsborough)
Aisby. *Linc* —2H **75** (nr. Grantham)
Aisgernis. *W Isl* —6C **170**
Aish. *Devn* —2C **8** (nr. Buckfastleigh)
Aish. *Devn* —3E **9** (nr. Totnes)
Aisholt. *Som* —3E **21**
Aiskew. *N Yor* —1E **99**
Aislaby. *N Yor* —1B **100** (nr. Pickering)
Aislaby. *N Yor* —4F **107** (nr. Whitby)
Aislaby. *Stoc T* —3B **106**
Aisthorpe. *Linc* —3G **87**
Aith. *Shet* —2H **173** (on Fetlar)
Aith. *Shet* —6E **173** (on Mainland)
Aithsetter. *Shet* —8F **173**
Akeld. *Nmbd* —2D **120**
Akeley. *Buck* —2F **51**
Akenham. *Suff* —1E **55**
Albaston. *Corn* —5E **11**
Alberbury. *Shrp* —4F **71**
Albert Town. *Pemb* —3D **42**
Albert Village. *Leics* —4H **73**
Albourne. *W Sus* —4D **26**
Albrighton. *Shrp* —4G **71** (nr. Shrewsbury)
Albrighton. *Shrp* —5C **72** (nr. Telford)
Alburgh. *Norf* —2E **67**
Albury. *Herts* —3E **53**
Albury. *Surr* —1B **26**
Albyfield. *Cumb* —4G **113**
Alby Hill. *Norf* —2D **78**
Alcaig. *High* —3H **157**
Alcaston. *Shrp* —2G **59**
Alcester. *Warw* —5E **61**
Alciston. *E Sus* —5G **27**
Alcombe. *Som* —2C **20**
Alconbury. *Cambs* —3A **64**
Alconbury Weston. *Cambs* —3A **64**
Aldborough. *Norf* —2D **78**
Aldborough. *N Yor* —3G **99**
Aldbourne. *Wilts* —4A **36**
Aldbrough. *E Yor* —1F **95**
Aldbrough St John. *N Yor* —3F **105**
Aldbury. *Herts* —4H **51**
Aldcliffe. *Lanc* —3D **96**
Aldclune. *Per* —2G **143**

Aldeburgh—Ashton

Aldeburgh. *Suff* —5G **67**
Aldeby. *Norf* —1G **67**
Aldenham. *Herts* —1C **38**
Alderbury. *Wilts* —4G **23**
Aldercar. *Derbs* —1B **74**
Alderford. *Norf* —4D **78**
Alderholt. *Dors* —1G **15**
Alderley. *Glos* —2C **34**
Alderley Edge. *Ches* —3C **84**
Aldermaston. *W Ber* —5D **36**
Aldermaston Stoke. *W Ber* —5E **36**
Aldermaston Wharf. *W Ber* —5E **36**
Alderminster. *Warw* —1H **49**
Alder Moor. *Staf* —3G **73**
Aldersey Green. *Ches* —5G **83**
Aldershot. *Hants* —1G **25**
Alderton. *Glos* —2E **49**
Alderton. *Nptn* —1F **51**
Alderton. *Shrp* —3G **71**
Alderton. *Suff* —1G **55**
Alderton. *Wilts* —3D **34**
Alderton Fields. *Glos* —2F **49**
Alderwasley. *Derbs* —5H **85**
Aldfield. *N Yor* —3E **99**
Aldford. *Ches* —5G **83**
Aldgate. *Rut* —5G **75**
Aldham. *Essx* —3C **54**
Aldham. *Suff* —1D **54**
Aldingbourne. *W Sus* —5A **26**
Aldingham. *Cumb* —2B **96**
Aldington. *Kent* —2E **29**
Aldington. *Worc* —1F **49**
Aldochlay. *Arg* —4C **134**
Aldon. *Shrp* —3G **59**
Aldoth. *Cumb* —5C **112**
Aldreth. *Cambs* —3D **64**
Aldridge. *W Mid* —5E **73**
Aldringham. *Suff* —4G **67**
Aldsworth. *Glos* —4G **49**
Aldsworth. *W Sus* —2F **17**
Aldwark. *Derbs* —5G **85**
Aldwark. *N Yor* —3G **99**
Aldwick. *W Sus* —3H **17**
Aldwincle. *Nptn* —2H **63**
Aldworth. *W Ber* —4D **36**
Alexandria. *W Dun* —1E **127**
Aley. *Som* —3E **21**
Aley Green. *Beds* —4A **52**
Alfardisworthy. *Devn* —1C **10**
Alfington. *Devn* —3E **12**
Alfold. *Surr* —2B **26**
Alfold Bars. *W Sus* —2B **26**
Alfold Crossways. *Surr* —2B **26**
Alford. *Aber* —2C **152**
Alford. *Linc* —3D **88**
Alford. *Som* —3B **22**
Alfreton. *Derbs* —5B **86**
Alfrick. *Worc* —5B **60**
Alfrick Pound. *Worc* —5B **60**
Alfriston. *E Sus* —5G **27**
Algarkirk. *Linc* —2B **76**
Alhampton. *Som* —3B **22**
Aline Lodge. *W Isl* —6D **171**
Alkborough. *N Lin* —2B **94**
Alkerton. *Oxon* —1B **50**
Alkham. *Kent* —1G **29**
Alkington. *Shrp* —2H **71**
Alkmonton. *Derbs* —2F **73**
Alladale Lodge. *High* —5B **164**
Allaleigh. *Devn* —3E **9**
Allanton. *N Lan* —4B **128**
Allanton. *Scot* —4E **131**
Allaston. *Glos* —5B **48**
Allbrook. *Hants* —4C **24**
All Cannings. *Wilts* —5F **35**
Allendale Town. *Nmbd* —4B **114**
Allen End. *Warw* —1F **61**
Allenheads. *Nmbd* —5B **114**
Allensford. *Dur* —5D **115**
Allen's Green. *Herts* —4E **53**
Allensmore. *Here* —2H **47**
Allenton. *Dby C* —2A **74**
Aller. *Som* —4H **21**
Allerby. *Cumb* —1B **102**
Allercombe. *Devn* —3D **12**
Allerford. *Som* —2C **20**
Allerston. *N Yor* —1C **100**
Allerthorpe. *E Yor* —5B **100**
Allerton. *Mers* —2G **83**
Allerton. *W Yor* —1B **92**
Allerton Bywater. *W Yor* —2E **93**
Allerton Mauleverer. *N Yor* —4G **99**
Allesley. *W Mid* —2G **61**
Allestree. *Dby C* —2H **73**
Allet. *Corn* —4B **6**
Allexton. *Leics* —5F **75**
Allgreave. *Ches* —4D **84**
Allhallows. *Medw* —3C **40**
Allhallows-on-Sea. *Medw* —3C **40**
Alligin Shuas. *High* —3H **155**
Allimore Green. *Staf* —4C **72**
Allington. *Kent* —5B **40**
Allington. *Linc* —1F **75**
Allington. *Wilts* —3H **23**
(nr. Amesbury)
Allington. *Wilts* —5F **35**
(nr. Devizes)
Allithwaite. *Cumb* —2C **96**
Alloa. *Clac* —4A **136**
Allonby. *Cumb* —5B **112**
Alloway. *S Ayr* —3C **116**
Allowenshay. *Som* —1G **13**
All Saints South Elmham. *Suff* —2F **67**
Allscott. *Shrp* —1B **60**
Allscott. *Telf* —4A **72**
All Stretton. *Shrp* —1G **59**
Allt. *Carm* —5F **45**
Alltami. *Flin* —4E **83**
Alltgobhlach. *N Ayr* —5G **125**
Alltmawr. *Powy* —1D **46**
Alltnacaillich. *High* —4E **167**
Allt na h-Airbhe. *High* —4F **163**
Alltour. *High* —5E **148**
Alltsigh. *High* —2G **149**
Alltwalis. *Carm* —2E **45**
Alltwen. *Neat* —5H **45**
Alltyblacca. *Cdgn* —1F **45**
Allt-y-goed. *Pemb* —1B **44**
Allweston. *Dors* —1B **14**
Almeley. *Here* —5F **59**
Almeley Wooton. *Here* —5F **59**
Almer. *Dors* —3E **15**
Almholme. *S Yor* —4F **93**
Almington. *Staf* —2B **72**
Alminstone Cross. *Devn* —4D **18**
Almodington. *W Sus* —3G **17**
Almondbank. *Per* —1C **136**
Almondbury. *W Yor* —3B **92**
Almondsbury. *S Glo* —3B **34**
Alne. *N Yor* —3G **99**
Alness. *High* —2A **158**
Alnessferry. *High* —2A **158**
Alnham. *Nmbd* —3D **121**
Alnmouth. *Nmbd* —3G **121**
Alnwick. *Nmbd* —3F **121**
Alphamstone. *Essx* —2B **54**
Alpheton. *Suff* —5A **66**
Alphington. *Devn* —3C **12**
Alpington. *Norf* —5E **79**
Alport. *Derbs* —4G **85**
Alport. *Powy* —1E **59**
Alpraham. *Ches* —5H **83**
Alresford. *Essx* —3D **54**
Alrewas. *Staf* —4F **73**
Alsager. *Ches* —5B **84**
Alsagers Bank. *Staf* —1C **72**
Alsop en le Dale. *Derbs* —5F **85**
Alston. *Cumb* —5A **114**
Alstone. *Glos* —2E **49**
Alstone. *Som* —2G **21**
Alstonefield. *Staf* —5F **85**
Alston Sutton. *Som* —1H **21**
Alswear. *Devn* —4H **19**
Altandhu. *High* —2D **163**
Altanduin. *High* —1F **165**
Altarnun. *Corn* —4C **10**
Altass. *High* —3B **164**
Alterwall. *High* —2E **169**
Altgaltraig. *Arg* —2B **126**
Altham. *Lanc* —1F **91**
Althorne. *Essx* —1D **40**
Althorpe. *N Lin* —4B **94**
Altnabreac. *High* —4C **168**
Altnacealgach. *High* —2G **163**
Altnafeadh. *High* —3G **141**
Altnaharra. *High* —5F **167**
Altofts. *W Yor* —2D **92**
Alton. *Derbs* —4A **86**
Alton. *Hants* —3F **25**
Alton. *Staf* —1E **73**
Alton Barnes. *Wilts* —5G **35**
Altonhill. *E Ayr* —1D **116**
Alton Pancras. *Dors* —2C **14**
Alton Priors. *Wilts* —5G **35**
Altrincham. *G Man* —2B **84**
Altrua. *High* —4E **149**
Alva. *Clac* —4A **136**
Alvanley. *Ches* —3G **83**
Alvaston. *Dby C* —2A **74**
Alvechurch. *Worc* —3E **61**
Alvecote. *Warw* —5G **73**
Alvediston. *Wilts* —4E **23**
Alveley. *Shrp* —2B **60**
Alverdiscott. *Devn* —4F **19**
Alverstoke. *Hants* —3E **16**
Alverstone. *IOW* —4D **16**
Alverthorpe. *W Yor* —2D **92**
Alverton. *Notts* —1E **75**
Alves. *Mor* —2F **159**
Alvescot. *Oxon* —5A **50**
Alveston. *S Glo* —3B **34**
Alveston. *Warw* —5G **61**
Alvie. *High* —3C **150**
Alvingham. *Linc* —1C **88**
Alvington. *Glos* —5B **48**
Alwalton. *Pet* —1A **64**
Alwinton. *Nmbd* —4D **120**
Alwoodley. *W Yor* —5E **99**
Alyth. *Per* —4B **144**
Amatnatua. *High* —4B **164**
Am Baile. *W Isl* —7C **170**
Ambaston. *Derbs* —2B **74**
Ambergate. *Derbs* —5H **85**
Amber Hill. *Linc* —1B **76**
Amberley. *Glos* —5D **48**
Amberley. *W Sus* —4B **26**
Amble. *Nmbd* —4G **121**
Amblecote. *W Mid* —2C **60**
Ambler Thorn. *W Yor* —2A **92**
Ambleside. *Cumb* —4E **103**
Ambleston. *Pemb* —2D **43**
Ambrosden. *Oxon* —4E **50**
Amcotts. *N Lin* —3B **94**
Amersham. *Buck* —1A **38**
Amerton. *Staf* —3D **73**
Amesbury. *Wilts* —2G **23**
Amisfield Town. *Dum* —1B **112**
Amlwch. *IOA* —1D **80**
Amlwch Port. *IOA* —1D **80**
Ammanford. *Carm* —4G **45**
Amotherby. *N Yor* —2B **100**
Ampfield. *Hants* —4B **24**
Ampleforth. *N Yor* —2H **99**
Ampleforth College. *N Yor* —2H **99**
Ampney Crucis. *Glos* —5F **49**
Ampney St Mary. *Glos* —5F **49**
Ampney St Peter. *Glos* —5F **49**
Amport. *Hants* —2A **24**
Ampthill. *Beds* —2A **52**
Ampton. *Suff* —3A **66**
Amroth. *Pemb* —4F **43**
Amulree. *Per* —5G **143**
Amwell. *Herts* —4B **52**
Anaheilt. *High* —2C **140**
Ancaster. *Linc* —1G **75**
Anchor. *Shrp* —2D **58**
Anchorsholme. *Lanc* —5C **96**
An Cnoc. *W Isl* —4G **171**
An Cnoc Ard. *W Isl* —1H **171**
An Coroghon. *High* —3A **146**
Ancroft. *Nmbd* —5G **131**
Ancrum. *Scot* —2A **120**
Ancton. *W Sus* —5A **26**
Anderby. *Linc* —3E **89**
Anderby Creek. *Linc* —3E **89**
Anderson. *Dors* —3D **15**
Anderton. *Ches* —3A **84**
Andertons Mill. *Lanc* —3D **90**
Andover. *Hants* —2B **24**
Andover Down. *Hants* —2B **24**
Andoversford. *Glos* —4F **49**
Andreas. *IOM* —2D **108**
Andwell. *Hants* —1E **25**
Anelog. *Gwyn* —3A **68**
Anfield. *Mers* —1F **83**
Angarrack. *Corn* —3C **4**
Angelbank. *Shrp* —3H **59**
Angerton. *Cumb* —4D **112**
Angle. *Pemb* —4C **42**
An Gleann Ur. *W Isl* —4G **171**
Angmering. *W Sus* —5B **26**
Angmering-on-Sea. *W Sus* —5B **26**
Angram. *N Yor* —5B **104**
(nr. Keld)
Angram. *N Yor* —5H **99**
(nr. York)
Anick. *Nmbd* —3C **114**
Ankerbold. *Derbs* —4A **86**
Ankerville. *High* —1C **158**
Anlaby. *E Yor* —2D **94**
Anlaby Park. *Hull* —2D **94**
An Leth Meadhanach. *W Isl* —7C **170**
Anmer. *Norf* —3G **77**
Anmore. *Hants* —1E **17**
Annan. *Dum* —3C **112**
Annaside. *Cumb* —1A **96**
Annat. *Arg* —1H **133**
Annat. *High* —3A **156**
Annathill. *N Lan* —2A **128**
Anna Valley. *Hants* —2B **24**
Annbank. *S Ayr* —2D **116**
Annesley. *Notts* —5C **86**
Annesley Woodhouse. *Notts* —5C **86**
Annfield Plain. *Dur* —4E **115**
Annscroft. *Shrp* —5G **71**
Ansdell. *Lanc* —2B **90**
Ansford. *Som* —3B **22**
Ansley. *Warw* —1H **61**
Anslow. *Staf* —3G **73**
Anslow Gate. *Staf* —3F **73**
Ansteadbrook. *Surr* —2A **26**
Anstey. *Herts* —2E **53**
Anstey. *Leics* —5C **74**
Anston. *S Lan* —5D **128**
Anstruther Easter. *Fife* —3H **137**
Anstruther Wester. *Fife* —3H **137**
Ansty. *Warw* —2A **62**
Ansty. *W Sus* —3D **27**
Ansty. *Wilts* —4E **23**
Anthill Common. *Hants* —1E **17**
Anthorn. *Cumb* —4C **112**
Antingham. *Norf* —2E **79**
An-t-Ob. *W Isl* —9C **171**
Anton's Gowt. *Linc* —1B **76**
Antony. *Corn* —3A **8**
Antrobus. *Ches* —3A **84**
Anvil Corner. *Devn* —2D **11**
Anwick. *Linc* —5A **88**
Anwoth. *Dum* —4C **110**
Apethorpe. *Nptn* —1H **63**
Apeton. *Staf* —4C **72**
Apley. *Linc* —3A **88**
Apperknowle. *Derbs* —3A **86**
Apperley. *Glos* —3D **48**
Apperley Dene. *Nmbd* —4D **114**
Appersett. *N Yor* —5B **104**
Appin. *Arg* —4D **140**
Appleby. *N Lin* —3C **94**
Appleby-in-Westmorland. *Cumb* —2H **103**
Appleby Magna. *Leics* —5H **73**
Appleby Parva. *Leics* —5H **73**
Applecross. *High* —4G **155**
Appledore. *Devn* —3E **19**
(nr. Bideford)
Appledore. *Devn* —1D **12**
(nr. Tiverton)
Appledore. *Kent* —3D **28**
Appledore Heath. *Kent* —2D **28**
Appleford. *Oxon* —2D **36**
Applegarthtown. *Dum* —1C **112**
Applemore. *Hants* —2B **16**
Appleshaw. *Hants* —2B **24**
Applethwaite. *Cumb* —2D **102**
Appleton. *Hal* —2H **83**
Appleton. *Oxon* —5C **50**
Appleton-le-Moors. *N Yor* —1B **100**
Appleton-le-Street. *N Yor* —2B **100**
Appleton Roebuck. *N Yor* —5H **99**
Appleton Thorn. *Warr* —2A **84**
Appleton Wiske. *N Yor* —4A **106**
Appletree. *Nptn* —1C **50**
Appletreehall. *Scot* —3H **119**
Appletreewick. *N Yor* —3C **98**
Appley. *Som* —4D **20**
Appley Bridge. *Lanc* —4D **90**
Apse Heath. *IOW* —4D **16**
Apsley End. *Beds* —2B **52**
Apuldram. *W Sus* —2G **17**
Arabella. *High* —1C **158**
Arbeadie. *Aber* —4D **152**
Arberth. *Pemb* —3F **43**
Arbirlot. *Ang* —4F **145**
Arborfield. *Wok* —5F **37**
Arborfield Cross. *Wok* —5F **37**
Arborfield Garrison. *Wok* —5F **37**
Arbourthorne. *S Yor* —2A **86**
Arbroath. *Ang* —4F **145**
Arbuthnott. *Aber* —1H **145**
Arcan. *High* —3H **157**
Archargary. *High* —3H **167**
Archdeacon Newton. *Darl* —3F **105**
Archiestown. *Mor* —4G **159**
Arclid. *Ches* —4B **84**
Arclid Green. *Ches* —4B **84**
Ardachu. *High* —3D **164**
Ardalanish. *Arg* —1A **132**
Ardaneaskan. *High* —5H **155**
Ardarroch. *High* —5H **155**
Ardbeg. *Arg* —3B **126**
(nr. Bute)
Ardbeg. *Arg* —1C **126**
(nr. Dunoon)
Ardbeg. *Arg* —5C **124**
(nr. Islay)
Ardcharnich. *High* —5F **163**
Ardchiavaig. *Arg* —1A **132**
Ardchonnell. *Arg* —2G **133**
Ardchrishnish. *Arg* —1B **132**
Ardchronie. *High* —5D **164**
Ardchullarie. *Stir* —2E **135**
Ardchyle. *Stir* —1E **135**
Ard-dhubh. *High* —4G **155**
Arddleen. *Powy* —4E **71**
Arddlin. *Powy* —4E **71**
Ardechive. *High* —4D **148**
Ardeley. *Herts* —3D **52**
Ardelve. *High* —1A **148**
Arden. *Arg* —1E **127**
Ardendrain. *High* —5H **157**
Arden Hall. *N Yor* —5C **106**
Ardens Grafton. *Warw* —5F **61**
Ardentinny. *Arg* —1C **126**
Ardeonaig. *Stir* —5D **142**
Ardersier. *High* —3B **158**
Ardery. *High* —2B **140**
Ardessie. *High* —5E **163**
Ardfern. *Arg* —3F **133**
Ardfernal. *High* —2D **124**
Ardfin. *Arg* —3C **124**
Ardgartan. *Arg* —3B **134**
Ardgay. *High* —5C **164**
Ardgour. *High* —2E **141**
Ardheslaig. *High* —3G **155**
Ardindrean. *High* —5F **163**
Ardingly. *W Sus* —3E **27**
Ardington. *Oxon* —3C **36**
Ardlamont House. *Arg* —3A **126**
Ardleigh. *Essx* —3D **54**
Ardler. *Per* —4B **144**
Ardley. *Oxon* —3D **50**
Ardlui. *Arg* —2C **134**
Ardlussa. *Arg* —1E **125**
Ardlussa. *High* —1E **125**
Ardmair. *High* —4F **163**
Ardmay. *Arg* —3B **134**
Ardminish. *Arg* —5E **125**
Ardmolich. *High* —1B **140**
Ardmore. *High* —3C **166**
(nr. Kinlochbervie)
Ardmore. *High* —5E **164**
(nr. Tain)
Ardnacross. *Arg* —4G **139**
Ardnadam. *Arg* —1C **126**
Ardnagrask. *High* —4H **157**
Ardnamurach. *High* —4G **147**
Ardnarff. *High* —5A **156**
Ardnastang. *High* —2C **140**
Ardoch. *Per* —5H **143**
Ardochy House. *High* —3E **148**
Ardpatrick. *Arg* —3F **125**
Ardrishaig. *Arg* —1G **125**
Ardroag. *High* —4B **154**
Ardross. *High* —1A **158**
Ardrossan. *N Ayr* —5D **126**
Ardshealach. *High* —2A **140**
Ardsley. *S Yor* —4D **93**
Ardslignish. *High* —2G **139**
Ardtalla. *Arg* —4C **124**
Ardtalnaig. *Per* —5E **142**
Ardtoe. *High* —1A **140**
Arduaine. *Arg* —2E **133**
Ardullie. *High* —2H **157**
Ardvasar. *High* —3E **147**
Ardvorlich. *Per* —1F **135**
Ardwell. *Dum* —5G **109**
Ardwell. *Mor* —5A **160**
Arean. *High* —1A **140**
Areley Common. *Worc* —3C **60**
Areley Kings. *Worc* —3B **60**
Arford. *Hants* —3G **25**
Argoed. *Cphy* —2E **33**
Argoed Mill. *Powy* —4B **58**
Aridhglas. *Arg* —2B **132**
Arinacrinachd. *High* —3G **155**
Arinagour. *Arg* —3D **138**
Arisaig. *High* —5E **147**
Ariundle. *High* —2C **140**
Arivegaig. *High* —2A **140**
Arkendale. *N Yor* —3F **99**
Arkesden. *Essx* —2E **53**
Arkholme. *Lanc* —2E **97**
Arkle Town. *N Yor* —4D **104**
Arkley. *G Lon* —1D **38**
Arksey. *S Yor* —4F **93**
Arkwright Town. *Derbs* —3B **86**
Arlecdon. *Cumb* —3B **102**
Arlescote. *Warw* —1B **50**
Arlesey. *Beds* —2B **52**
Arleston. *Telf* —4A **72**
Arley. *Ches* —2A **84**
Arlingham. *Glos* —4C **48**
Arlington. *Devn* —2G **19**
Arlington. *E Sus* —5G **27**
Arlington. *Glos* —5G **49**
Arlington Beccott. *Devn* —2G **19**
Armadale. *High* —2H **167**
Armadale. *W Lot* —3C **128**
Armathwaite. *Cumb* —5G **113**
Arminghall. *Norf* —5E **79**
Armitage. *Staf* —4E **73**
Armitage Bridge. *W Yor* —3B **92**
Armley. *W Yor* —1C **92**
Armscote. *Warw* —1H **49**
Arms, The. *Norf* —1A **66**
Armston. *Nptn* —2H **63**
Armthorpe. *S Yor* —4G **93**
Arncliffe. *N Yor* —2B **98**
Arncliffe Cote. *N Yor* —2B **98**
Arncroach. *Fife* —3H **137**
Arne. *Dors* —4E **15**
Arnesby. *Leics* —1D **62**
Arnicle. *Arg* —2B **122**
Arnisdale. *High* —2G **147**
Arnish. *High* —4E **155**
Arniston. *Midl* —3G **129**
Arnol. *W Isl* —3F **171**
Arnold. *E Yor* —5F **101**
Arnold. *Notts* —1C **74**
Arnprior. *Stir* —4F **135**
Arnside. *Cumb* —2D **96**
Aros Mains. *Arg* —4G **139**
Arpafeelie. *High* —3A **158**
Arrad Foot. *Cumb* —1C **96**
Arram. *E Yor* —5E **101**
Arras. *E Yor* —5D **100**
Arrathorne. *N Yor* —5F **105**
Arreton. *IOW* —4D **16**
Arrington. *Cambs* —5C **64**
Arrochar. *Arg* —3B **134**
Arrow. *Warw* —5E **61**
Arscaig. *High* —2C **164**
Artafallie. *High* —4A **158**
Arthington. *W Yor* —5E **99**
Arthingworth. *Nptn* —2E **63**
Arthog. *Gwyn* —4F **69**
Arthrath. *Aber* —5G **161**
Arthurstone. *Per* —4B **144**
Arundel. *W Sus* —5B **26**
Asby. *Cumb* —2B **102**
Ascog. *Arg* —3C **126**
Ascot. *Wind* —4A **38**
Ascott-under-Wychwood. *Oxon* —4B **50**
Asenby. *N Yor* —2F **99**
Asfordby. *Leics* —4E **74**
Asfordby Hill. *Leics* —4E **74**
Asgarby. *Linc* —4C **88**
(nr. Horncastle)
Asgarby. *Linc* —1A **76**
(nr. Sleaford)
Ash. *Devn* —4E **9**
Ash. *Dors* —1D **14**
Ash. *Kent* —5G **41**
(nr. Sandwich)
Ash. *Kent* —4H **39**
(nr. Swanley)
Ash. *Som* —4H **21**
Ash. *Surr* —1G **25**
Ashampstead. *W Ber* —4D **36**
Ashbocking. *Suff* —5D **66**
Ashbourne. *Derbs* —1F **73**
Ashbrittle. *Som* —4D **20**
Ashbrook. *Shrp* —1G **59**
Ashburton. *Devn* —2D **8**
Ashbury. *Devn* —3F **11**
Ashbury. *Oxon* —3A **36**
Ashby. *N Lin* —4B **94**
Ashby by Partney. *Linc* —4D **88**
Ashby cum Fenby. *NE Lin* —4F **95**
Ashby de la Launde. *Linc* —5H **87**
Ashby-de-la-Zouch. *Leics* —4A **74**
Ashby Folville. *Leics* —4E **74**
Ashby Magna. *Leics* —1C **62**
Ashby Parva. *Leics* —2C **62**
Ashby Puerorum. *Linc* —3C **88**
Ashby St Ledgars. *Nptn* —4C **62**
Ashby St Mary. *Norf* —5F **79**
Ashcombe. *Devn* —5C **12**
Ashcott. *Som* —3H **21**
Ashcurch. *Glos* —2E **49**
Ashdon. *Essx* —1F **53**
Ashe. *Hants* —1D **24**
Asheldham. *Essx* —5C **54**
Ashen. *Essx* —1H **53**
Ashendon. *Buck* —4F **51**
Ashey. *IOW* —4D **16**
Ashfield. *Hants* —1B **16**
Ashfield. *Here* —3A **48**
Ashfield. *Shrp* —2H **59**
Ashfield. *Stir* —3G **135**
Ashfield. *Suff* —4E **66**
Ashfield Green. *Suff* —3E **67**
Ashfold Crossways. *W Sus* —3D **26**
Ashford. *Devn* —3F **19**
(nr. Barnstaple)
Ashford. *Devn* —4C **8**
(nr. Kingsbridge)
Ashford. *Hants* —1G **15**
Ashford. *Kent* —1E **28**
Ashford. *Surr* —3B **38**
Ashford Bowdler. *Shrp* —3H **59**
Ashford Carbonel. *Shrp* —3H **59**
Ashford Hill. *Hants* —5D **36**
Ashford in the Water. *Derbs* —4F **85**
Ashgill. *S Lan* —5A **128**
Ash Green. *W Mid* —3H **61**
Ashgrove. *Mor* —2G **159**
Ashill. *Devn* —1D **12**
Ashill. *Norf* —5A **78**
Ashill. *Som* —1G **13**
Ashingdon. *Essx* —1C **40**
Ashington. *Nmbd* —1F **115**
Ashington. *W Sus* —4C **26**
Ashkirk. *Scot* —2G **119**
Ashlett. *Hants* —2C **16**
Ashleworth. *Glos* —3D **48**
Ashley. *Cambs* —4F **65**
Ashley. *Ches* —2B **84**
Ashley. *Dors* —2G **15**
Ashley. *Glos* —2E **35**
Ashley. *Hants* —3A **16**
(nr. New Milton)
Ashley. *Hants* —3B **24**
(nr. Winchester)
Ashley. *Kent* —1H **29**
Ashley. *Nptn* —1E **63**
Ashley. *Staf* —2B **72**
Ashley. *Wilts* —5D **34**
Ashley Green. *Buck* —5H **51**
Ashley Heath. *Dors* —2G **15**
Ashley Heath. *Staf* —2B **72**
Ashley Moor. *Here* —4G **59**
Ash Magna. *Shrp* —2H **71**
Ashmanhaugh. *Norf* —3F **79**
Ashmansworth. *Hants* —1C **24**
Ashmansworthy. *Devn* —1D **10**
Ashmead Green. *Glos* —2C **34**
Ashmill. *Devn* —3D **11**
(nr. Holsworthy)
Ash Mill. *Devn* —4A **20**
(nr. South Molton)
Ashmore. *Dors* —1E **15**
Ashmore Green. *W Ber* —5D **36**
Ashorne. *Warw* —5H **61**
Ashover. *Derbs* —4A **86**
Ashow. *Warw* —3H **61**
Ash Parva. *Shrp* —2H **71**
Ashperton. *Here* —1B **48**
Ashprington. *Devn* —3E **9**
Ash Priors. *Som* —4E **21**
Ashreigney. *Devn* —1G **11**
Ash Street. *Suff* —1D **54**
Ashtead. *Surr* —5C **38**
Ash Thomas. *Devn* —1D **12**
Ashton. *Ches* —4H **83**
Ashton. *Corn* —4D **4**
Ashton. *Here* —4H **59**
Ashton. *Inv* —2D **126**

Ashton—Barcombe

Ashton. Nptn —2H 63 (nr. Oundle)
Ashton. Nptn —1F 51 (nr. Roade)
Ashton. Pet —5A 76
Ashton Common. Wilts —1D 23
Ashton-in-Makerfield. G Man —4D 90
Ashton Keynes. Wilts —2F 35
Ashton under Hill. Worc —2E 49
Ashton-under-Lyne. G Man —1D 84
Ashton upon Mersey. G Man —1B 84
Ashurst. Hants —1B 16
Ashurst. Kent —2G 27
Ashurst. Lanc —4C 90
Ashurst. W Sus —4C 26
Ashurstwood. W Sus —2F 27
Ash Vale. Surr —1G 25
Ashwater. Devn —3D 11
Ashwell. Herts —2C 52
Ashwell. Rut —4F 75
Ashwellthorpe. Norf —1D 66
Ashwick. Som —2B 22
Ashwicken. Norf —4G 77
Ashwood. Staf —2C 60
Askam in Furness. Cumb —2B 96
Askern. S Yor —3F 93
Askerswell. Dors —3A 14
Askett. Buck —5G 51
Askham. Cumb —2G 103
Askham. Notts —3E 87
Askham Bryan. York —5H 99
Askham Richard. York —5H 99
Askrigg. N Yor —5C 104
Askwith. N Yor —5D 98
Aslackby. Linc —2H 75
Aslacton. Norf —1D 66
Aslockton. Notts —1E 75
Aspatria. Cumb —5C 112
Aspenden. Herts —3D 52
Asperton. Linc —2B 76
Aspley Guise. Beds —2H 51
Aspley Heath. Beds —2H 51
Aspull. G Man —4E 90
Asselby. E Yor —2H 93
Assington. Suff —2C 54
Assington Green. Suff —5G 65
Astbury. Ches —4C 84
Astcote. Nptn —5D 62
Asterby. Linc —3B 88
Asterley. Shrp —5F 71
Asterton. Shrp —1F 59
Asthall. Oxon —4A 50
Asthall Leigh. Oxon —4B 50
Astle. High —4E 165
Astley. G Man —4F 91
Astley. Shrp —4H 71
Astley. Warw —2H 61
Astley. Worc —4B 60
Astley Abbotts. Shrp —1B 60
Astley Bridge. G Man —3F 91
Astley Cross. Worc —4C 60
Aston. Ches —3H 83 (nr. Frodsham)
Aston. Ches —1A 72 (nr. Nantwich)
Aston. Derbs —2F 85
Aston. Flin —4F 83
Aston. Here —4G 59
Aston. Herts —3C 52
Aston. Oxon —5B 50
Aston. Shrp —1C 60 (nr. Bridgnorth)
Aston. Shrp —3H 71 (nr. Wem)
Aston. S Yor —2B 86
Aston. Staf —1B 72
Aston. Telf —5A 72
Aston. W Mid —2E 61
Aston. Wok —3F 37
Aston Abbotts. Buck —3G 51
Aston Botterell. Shrp —2A 60
Aston-by-Stone. Staf —2D 72
Aston Cantlow. Warw —5F 61
Aston Clinton. Buck —4G 51
Aston Crews. Here —3B 48
Aston Cross. Glos —2E 49
Aston End. Herts —3C 52
Aston Eyre. Shrp —1A 60
Aston Fields. Worc —4D 60
Aston Flamville. Leics —1B 62
Aston Ingham. Here —3B 48
Aston juxta Mondrum. Ches —5A 84
Astonlane. Shrp —1A 60
Aston le Walls. Nptn —5B 62
Aston Magna. Glos —2G 49
Aston Munslow. Shrp —2H 59
Aston on Carrant. Glos —2E 49
Aston on Clun. Shrp —2F 59
Aston-on-Trent. Derbs —3B 74
Aston Pigott. Shrp —5F 71
Aston Rogers. Shrp —5F 71
Aston Rowant. Oxon —2F 37
Aston Sandford. Buck —5F 51
Aston Somerville. Worc —2F 49
Aston Subedge. Glos —1G 49
Aston Tirrold. Oxon —3D 36
Aston Upthorne. Oxon —3D 36
Astrop. Nptn —2D 50
Astwick. Beds —2C 52
Astwood. Mil —1H 51
Astwood Bank. Worc —4E 61
Aswarby. Linc —2H 75
Aswardby. Linc —3C 88
Atcham. Shrp —5H 71
Atch Lench. Worc —5E 61
Athelhampton. Dors —3C 14
Athelington. Suff —3E 66
Athelney. Som —4G 21
Athelstaneford. E Lot —2B 130
Atherfield. IOW —4C 16
Atherington. Devn —4F 19
Atherington. W Sus —5B 26
Athersley. S Yor —4D 92
Atherstone. Warw —1H 61
Atherstone on Stour. Warw —5G 61
Atherton. G Man —4E 91
Atlow. Derbs —1G 73
Attadale. High —5B 156
Attenborough. Notts —2C 74
Atterby. Linc —1G 87
Atterley. Shrp —1A 60
Attleborough. Norf —1C 66
Attleborough. Warw —1A 62
Attlebridge. Norf —4D 78
Atwick. E Yor —4F 101
Atworth. Wilts —5D 34
Auberrow. Here —1H 47
Aubourn. Linc —4G 87
Aucharnie. Aber —4D 160
Auchattie. Aber —4D 152
Auchavan. Ang —2A 144
Auchbreck. Mor —1G 151
Auchenback. E Ren —4G 127
Auchenblae. Aber —1G 145
Auchenbrack. Dum —5G 117
Auchenbreck. Arg —1B 126
Auchencairn. Dum —4E 111 (nr. Dalbeattie)
Auchencairn. Dum —1A 112 (nr. Dumfries)
Auchencarroch. W Dun —1F 127
Auchencrow. Scot —3E 131
Auchendennan. Arg —1E 127
Auchendinny. Midl —3F 129
Auchengray. S Lan —4C 128
Auchenhalrig. Mor —2A 160
Auchenheath. S Lan —5B 128
Auchenlochan. Arg —2A 126
Auchenmade. N Ayr —5E 127
Auchenmaig. Dum —4H 109
Auchentiber. E Ayr —5E 127
Auchenvennel. Arg —1D 126
Auchindrain. Arg —3H 133
Auchininna. Aber —4D 160
Auchinleck. Dum —2B 110
Auchinleck. E Ayr —2E 117
Auchinloch. N Lan —2H 127
Auchinstarry. N Lan —2A 128
Auchleven. Aber —1D 152
Auchlochan. S Lan —1H 117
Auchlunachan. High —5F 163
Auchmillan. E Ayr —2E 117
Auchmithie. Ang —4F 145
Auchmuirbridge. Per —3E 136
Auchmull. Ang —1E 145
Auchnacree. Ang —2D 144
Auchnafree. Per —5F 143
Auchnagallin. High —5E 159
Auchnagatt. Aber —4G 161
Aucholzie. Aber —4H 151
Auchreddie. Aber —4F 161
Auchterarder. Per —2B 136
Auchteraw. High —3F 149
Auchterderran. Fife —4E 136
Auchterhouse. Ang —5C 144
Auchtermuchty. Fife —2E 137
Auchterneed. High —3G 157
Auchtertool. Fife —4E 136
Auchtertyre. High —1G 147
Auchtubh. Stir —1E 135
Auckengill. High —2F 169
Auckley. S Yor —4G 93
Audenshaw. G Man —1D 84
Audlem. Ches —1A 72
Audley. Staf —5B 84
Audley End. Essx —2F 53
Audmore. Staf —3C 72
Auds. Aber —2D 160
Aughton. E Yor —1H 93
Aughton. Lanc —3E 97 (nr. Lancaster)
Aughton. Lanc —4B 90 (nr. Ormskirk)
Aughton. S Yor —2B 86
Aughton. Wilts —1H 23
Aughton Park. Lanc —4C 90
Auldearn. High —3D 158
Aulden. Here —5G 59
Auldgirth. Dum —1G 111
Auldhouse. S Lan —4H 127
Ault a' chruinn. High —1B 148
Aultbea. High —5C 162
Aultdearg. High —2E 157
Aultgrishan. High —5B 162
Aultguish Inn. High —1F 157
Ault Hucknall. Derbs —4B 86
Aultibea. High —1H 165
Aultiphurst. High —2A 168
Aultivullin. High —2A 168
Aultmore. Mor —3B 160
Aultnamain Inn. High —5D 164
Aunby. Linc —4H 75
Aunsby. Linc —2H 75
Aust. S Glo —3A 34
Austerfield. S Yor —1D 86
Austin Fen. Linc —1C 88
Austrey. Warw —5G 73
Austwick. N Yor —3G 97
Authorpe. Linc —2D 88
Authorpe Row. Linc —3E 89
Avebury. Wilts —5G 35
Avebury Trusloe. Wilts —5F 35
Aveley. Thur —2G 39
Avening. Glos —2D 35
Averham. Notts —5E 87
Aveton Gifford. Devn —4C 8
Avielochan. High —2D 150
Aviemore. High —2C 150
Avington. Hants —3D 24
Avoch. High —3B 158
Avon. Hants —3G 15
Avonbridge. Falk —2C 128
Avon Dassett. Warw —5B 62
Avonmouth. Bris —4A 34
Avonwick. Devn —3D 8
Awbridge. Hants —4B 24
Awliscombe. Devn —2E 13
Awre. Glos —5C 48
Awsworth. Notts —1B 74
Axbridge. Som —1H 21
Axford. Hants —2E 24
Axford. Wilts —5H 35
Axminster. Devn —3F 13
Axmouth. Devn —3F 13
Aycliffe. Dur —2F 105
Aydon. Nmbd —3D 114
Aykley Heads. Dur —5F 115
Aylburton. Glos —5B 48
Aylburton Common. Glos —5B 48
Ayle. Nmbd —5A 114
Aylesbeare. Devn —3D 12
Aylesbury. Buck —4G 51
Aylesby. NE Lin —4F 95
Aylescott. Devn —1G 11
Aylesford. Kent —5B 40
Aylesham. Kent —5G 41
Aylestone. Leic C —5C 74
Aylmerton. Norf —2D 78
Aylsham. Norf —3D 78
Aylton. Here —2B 48
Aylworth. Glos —3G 49
Aymestrey. Here —4G 59
Aynho. Nptn —2D 50
Ayot Green. Herts —4C 52
Ayot St Lawrence. Herts —4B 52
Ayot St Peter. Herts —4C 52
Ayr. S Ayr —2C 116
Ayreville. Torb —2E 9
Aysgarth. N Yor —1C 98
Ayshford. Devn —1D 12
Ayside. Cumb —1C 96
Ayston. Rut —5F 75
Ayton. Scot —3F 131
Aywick. Shet —3G 173
Azerley. N Yor —2E 99

Babbacombe. Torb —2F 9
Babbinswood. Shrp —3F 71
Babb's Green. Herts —4D 53
Babcary. Som —4A 22
Babel. Carm —2B 46
Babell. Flin —3D 82
Babingley. Norf —3F 77
Babraham. Cambs —5E 65
Babworth. Notts —2D 86
Bac. W Isl —3G 171
Bachau. IOA —2D 80
Bacheldre. Powy —1E 59
Bachymbyd Fawr. Den —4C 82
Backaland. Orkn —4E 172
Backaskaill. Orkn —2D 172
Backbarrow. Cumb —1C 96
Backe. Carm —3G 43
Backfolds. Aber —3H 161
Backford. Ches —3G 83
Backhill. Aber —5E 161
Backhill of Clackriach. Aber —4G 161
Backies. High —3F 165
Backmuir of New Gilston. Fife —3G 137
Back of Keppoch. High —5E 147
Back Street. Suff —5G 65
Backwell. N Som —5H 33
Backworth. Tyne —2G 115
Bacon End. Essx —4G 53
Baconsthorpe. Norf —2D 78
Bacton. Here —2G 47
Bacton. Norf —2F 79
Bacton. Suff —4C 66
Bacton Green. Norf —2F 79
Bacup. Lanc —2G 91
Badachonacher. High —1A 158
Badachro. High —1G 155
Badanloch Lodge. High —5H 167
Badavanich. High —3D 156
Badbury. Swin —3G 35
Badby. Nptn —5C 62
Badcall. High —3C 166
Badcaul. High —4E 163
Baddeley Green. Stoke —5D 84
Baddesley Clinton. W Mid —3G 61
Baddesley Ensor. Warw —1G 61
Baddidarach. High —1E 163
Baddoch. Aber —5F 151
Badenscallie. High —3E 163
Badenscoth. Aber —5D 160
Badentarbat. High —2E 163
Badgall. Corn —4C 10
Badgers Mount. Kent —4F 39
Badgeworth. Glos —4E 49
Badgworth. Som —1G 21
Badicaul. High —1F 147
Badingham. Suff —4F 67
Badlesmere. Kent —5E 40
Badlipster. High —4E 169
Badluarach. High —4D 163
Badminton. S Glo —3D 34
Badnaban. High —1E 163
Badnabay. High —4C 166
Badnagie. High —5D 168
Badnellan. High —3F 165
Badninish. High —4E 165
Badrallach. High —4E 163
Badsey. Worc —1F 49
Badshot Lea. Surr —2G 25
Badsworth. W Yor —3E 93
Badwell Ash. Suff —4B 66
Bae Cinmel. Cnwy —2B 82
Bae Colwyn. Cnwy —3A 82
Bae Penrhyn. Cnwy —2H 81
Bagby. N Yor —1G 99
Bag Enderby. Linc —3C 88
Bagendon. Glos —5F 49
Bagginswood. Shrp —2A 60
Baggrave. Leics —5D 74
Bagh a Chaise. W Isl —1E 170
Bagh a'Chaisteil. W Isl —9B 170
Bagham. Kent —5E 41
Baghasdal. W Isl —7C 170
Bagh Mor. W Isl —3D 170
Bagh Shiarabhagh. W Isl —8C 170
Bagillt. Flin —3E 83
Baginton. Warw —3H 61
Baglan. Neat —2A 32
Bagley. Shrp —3G 71
Bagley. Som —2H 21
Bagnall. Staf —5D 84
Bagnor. W Ber —5C 36
Bagshot. Surr —4A 38
Bagshot. Wilts —5B 36
Bagstone. S Glo —3B 34
Bagthorpe. Norf —2G 77
Bagthorpe. Notts —5B 86
Bagworth. Leics —5B 74
Bagwy Llydiart. Here —3H 47
Baildon. W Yor —1B 92
Baildon Green. W Yor —1B 92
Baile. W Isl —1E 170
Baile Ailein. W Isl —5E 171
Baile an Truiseil. W Isl —2F 171
Baile Boidheach. Arg —2F 125
Baile Glas. W Isl —3D 170
Bailemeonach. Arg —4A 140
Baile Mhanaich. W Isl —3C 170
Baile Mhartainn. W Isl —1C 170
Baile MhicPhail. W Isl —1D 170
Baile Mor. Arg —2A 132
Baile Mor. W Isl —2C 170
Baile nan Cailleach. W Isl —3C 170
Baile Raghaill. W Isl —2C 170
Bailey Green. Hants —4E 25
Baileyhead. Cumb —1G 113
Bailiesward. Aber —5B 160
Bail Iochdrach. W Isl —3D 170
Baillieston. Glas —3H 127
Bailrigg. Lanc —4D 97
Bail Uachdraich. W Isl —2D 170
Bail Ur Tholastaidh. W Isl —3H 171
Bainbridge. N Yor —5C 104
Bainsford. Falk —1B 128
Bainshole. Aber —5D 160
Bainton. E Yor —4D 100
Bainton. Oxon —3D 50
Bainton. Pet —5H 75
Baintown. Fife —3F 137
Baker Street. Thur —2H 39
Bakewell. Derbs —4G 85
Bala. Gwyn —2B 70
Balbeg. High —5G 157 (nr. Glen Urquhart)
Balbeg. High —1G 149 (nr. Loch Ness)
Balbeggie. Per —1D 136
Balblair. High —4C 164 (nr. Bonar Bridge)
Balblair. High —2B 158 (nr. Invergordon)
Balblair. High —4H 157 (nr. Inverness)
Balby. S Yor —4F 93
Balcathie. Ang —5F 145
Balcherry. High —5F 165
Balchladich. High —1E 163
Balchraggan. High —4H 157
Balchrick. High —3B 166
Balcombe. W Sus —2E 27
Balcombe Lane. W Sus —2E 27
Balcurvie. Fife —3F 137
Baldersby. N Yor —2F 99
Baldersby St James. N Yor —2F 99
Balderstone. Lanc —1E 91
Balderton. Ches —4F 83
Balderton. Notts —5F 87
Baldinnie. Fife —2G 137
Baldock. Herts —2C 52
Baldrine. IOM —3D 108
Baldslow. E Sus —4C 28
Baldwin. IOM —3C 108
Baldwinholme. Cumb —4E 113
Baldwins Gate. Staf —1B 72
Bale. Norf —2C 78
Balearn. Aber —3H 161
Balemartine. Arg —4A 138
Balephretrish. Arg —4B 138
Balephuil. Arg —4A 138
Balerno. Edin —3E 129
Balevullin. Arg —4A 138
Balfield. Ang —2E 145
Balfour. Orkn —6D 172
Balfron. Stir —1G 127
Balgaveny. Aber —4D 160
Balgonar. Fife —4C 136
Balgowan. High —4A 150
Balgown. High —2C 154
Balgrochan. E Dun —2H 127
Balgy. High —3H 155
Balhalgardy. Aber —1E 153
Baliasta. Shet —1G 173
Baligill. High —2A 168
Balintore. Ang —3B 144
Balintore. High —1C 158
Balintraid. High —1B 158
Balk. N Yor —1G 99
Balkeerie. Ang —4C 144
Balkholme. E Yor —2A 94
Ball. Shrp —3F 71
Ballabeg. IOM —4B 108
Ballacannell. IOM —3D 108
Ballacarnane Beg. IOM —3C 108
Ballachulish. High —3E 141
Ballagyr. IOM —3B 108
Ballajora. IOM —2D 108
Ballaleigh. IOM —3C 108
Ballamodha. IOM —4B 108
Ballantrae. S Ayr —1F 109
Ballards Gore. Essx —1D 40
Ballasalla. IOM —4B 108 (nr. Castletown)
Ballasalla. IOM —2C 108 (nr. Kirk Michael)
Ballater. Aber —4A 152
Ballaugh. IOM —2C 108
Ballencrieff. E Lot —2A 130
Ballencrieff Toll. W Lot —2C 128
Ballentoul. Per —2F 143
Ball Hill. Hants —5C 36
Ballidon. Derbs —5G 85
Balliemore. Arg —1B 126 (nr. Dunoon)
Balliemore. Arg —1F 133 (nr. Oban)
Ballieward. High —5E 159
Ballig. IOM —3B 108
Ballimore. Stir —2E 135
Ballingdon. Suff —1B 54
Ballingdon Bulmer. Essx —1B 54
Ballinger Common. Buck —5H 51
Ballingham. Here —2A 48
Ballingry. Fife —4D 136
Ballinluig. Per —3G 143
Ballintuim. Per —3A 144
Balliveolan. Arg —4C 140
Balloan. High —3C 164
Balloch. High —4B 158
Balloch. N Lan —2A 128
Balloch. Per —2H 135
Balloch. W Dun —1E 127
Ballochan. Aber —4C 152
Ballochgoy. Arg —3B 126
Ballochmyle. E Ayr —2E 117
Ballochroy. Arg —4F 125
Balls Cross. W Sus —3A 26
Ball's Green. E Sus —2F 27
Ballygown. Arg —4F 139
Ballygrant. Arg —3B 124
Ballymichael. N Ayr —2D 122
Balmacara. High —1G 147
Balmaclellan. Dum —2D 110
Balmacqueen. High —1D 154
Balmaha. Stir —4D 134
Balmalcolm. Fife —3F 137
Balmalloch. N Lan —2A 128
Balmeanach. High —5E 155
Balmedie. Aber —2G 153
Balmerino. Fife —1F 137
Balmerlawn. Hants —2B 16
Balmore. E Dun —2H 127
Balmore. High —4B 154
Balmuir. Ang —5D 144
Balmullo. Fife —1G 137
Balmurrie. Dum —3H 109
Balnaboth. Ang —2C 144
Balnabruaich. High —1B 158
Balnabruich. High —5D 168
Balnacoil. High —2F 165
Balnacra. High —4B 156
Balnacroft. Aber —4G 151
Balnageith. Mor —3E 159
Balnaglaic. High —5G 157
Balnagrantach. High —5G 157
Balnaguard. Per —3G 143
Balnahard. Arg —3B 132
Balnain. High —5G 157
Balnakeil. High —2D 166
Balnamoon. Aber —3G 161
Balnamoon. Ang —2E 145
Balnapaling. High —2B 158
Balornock. Glas —3H 127
Balquhidder. Stir —1E 135
Balsall. W Mid —3G 61
Balsall Common. W Mid —3G 61
Balscote. Oxon —1B 50
Balsham. Cambs —5E 65
Balstonia. Thur —2A 40
Baltasound. Shet —1H 173
Balterley. Staf —5B 84
Baltersan. Dum —3B 110
Balthangie. Aber —3F 161
Baltonsborough. Som —3A 22
Balvaird. High —3H 157
Balvaird. Per —2D 136
Balvenie. Mor —4H 159
Balvicar. Arg —2E 133
Balvraid. High —2G 147
Balvraid Lodge. High —5C 158
Bamber Bridge. Lanc —2D 90
Bamber's Green. Essx —3F 53
Bamburgh. Nmbd —1F 121
Bamford. Derbs —2G 85
Bampton. Cumb —3G 103
Bampton. Devn —4C 20
Bampton. Oxon —5B 50
Bampton Grange. Cumb —3G 103
Banavie. High —1F 141
Banbury. Oxon —1C 50
Bancffosfelen. Carm —4E 45
Banchory. Aber —4D 152
Banchory-Devenick. Aber —3G 153
Bancycapel. Carm —4E 45
Bancyfelin. Carm —3H 43
Banc-y-ffordd. Carm —2E 45
Banff. Aber —2D 160
Bangor. Gwyn —3E 81
Bangor-is-y-coed. Wrex —1F 71
Bangors. Corn —3C 10
Bangor's Green. Lanc —4B 90
Bangrove. Suff —3B 66
Banham. Norf —2C 66
Bank. Hants —2A 16
Bankend. Dum —3B 112
Bankfoot. Per —5H 143
Bankglen. E Ayr —3E 117
Bankhead. Aber C —2F 153
Bankhead. Aber —3D 152
Bankhead. S Lan —5B 128
Bankland. Som —4G 21
Bank Newton. N Yor —4B 98
Banknock. Falk —2A 128
Banks. Cumb —3G 113
Banks. Lanc —2B 90
Bankshill. Dum —1C 112
Bank Street. Worc —4A 60
Bank, The. Ches —5C 84
Bank, The. Shrp —1A 60
Bank Top. Lanc —4D 90
Banners Gate. W Mid —1E 61
Banningham. Norf —3E 78
Banniskirk. High —3D 168
Bannister Green. Essx —3G 53
Bannockburn. Stir —4H 135
Banstead. Surr —5D 38
Bantham. Devn —4C 8
Banton. N Lan —2A 128
Banwell. N Som —1G 21
Banyard's Green. Suff —3F 67
Bapchild. Kent —4D 40
Bapton. Wilts —3E 23
Barabhas. W Isl —2F 171
Barabhas Iarach. W Isl —2F 171
Barabhas Uarach. W Isl —2F 171
Baramore. High —1A 140
Barassie. S Ayr —1C 116
Baravullin. Arg —4D 140
Barbaraville. High —1B 158
Barber Booth. Derbs —2F 85
Barber Green. Cumb —1C 96
Barbieston. E Ayr —3C 116
Barbieston. S Ayr —3D 116
Barbon. Cumb —1F 97
Barbourne. Worc —5C 60
Barbridge. Ches —5A 84
Barbrook. Devn —2H 19
Barby. Nptn —3C 62
Barby Nortoft. Nptn —3C 62
Barcaldine. Arg —4D 140
Barcheston. Warw —1A 50
Barclose. Cumb —3F 113
Barcombe. E Sus —4F 27

Berwick-upon-Tweed—Bodiam

Berwick-upon-Tweed. Nmbd —4G 131
Berwyn. Den —1D 70
Bescaby. Leics —3F 75
Bescar. Lanc —3B 90
Besford. Worc —1E 49
Bessacarr. S Yor —4G 93
Bessels Leigh. Oxon —5C 50
Bessingby. E Yor —3F 101
Bessingham. Norf —2D 78
Best Beech Hill. E Sus —2H 27
Besthorpe. Norf —1C 66
Besthorpe. Notts —4F 87
Bestwood Village. Notts —1C 74
Beswick. E Yor —5E 101
Betchworth. Surr —5D 38
Bethania. Cdgn —4E 57
Bethania. Gwyn —1G 69 (nr. Blaenau Ffestiniog)
Bethania. Gwyn —5F 81 (nr. Caernarfon)
Bethel. Gwyn —2B 70 (nr. Bala)
Bethel. Gwyn —4E 81 (nr. Caernarfon)
Bethel. IOA —3C 80
Bethersden. Kent —1D 28
Bethesda. Gwyn —4F 81
Bethesda. Pemb —3E 43
Bethlehem. Carm —3G 45
Bethnal Green. G Lon —2E 39
Betishill. N Lan —3A 128
Betley. Staf —1B 72
Betsham. Kent —3H 39
Betteshanger. Kent —5H 41
Bettiscombe. Dors —3H 13
Bettisfield. Wrex —2G 71
Betton. Shrp —2A 72
Betton Strange. Shrp —5H 71
Bettws. B'End —3B 32
Bettws. Newp —2F 33
Bettws Bledrws. Cdgn —5E 57
Bettws Cedewain. Powy —1D 58
Bettws Gwerfil Goch. Den —1C 70
Bettws Ifan. Cdgn —1D 44
Bettws Newydd. Mon —5G 47
Bettyhill. High —2H 167
Betws. Carm —4G 45
Betws Garmon. Gwyn —5E 81
Betws-y-Coed. Cnwy —5G 81
Betws-yn-Rhos. Cnwy —3B 82
Beulah. Cdgn —1C 44
Beulah. Powy —5B 58
Bevendean. Brig —5E 27
Bevercotes. Notts —3D 86
Beverley. E Yor —1D 94
Beverston. Glos —2D 34
Bevington. Glos —2B 34
Bewaldeth. Cumb —1D 102
Bewcastle. Cumb —2G 113
Bewdley. Worc —3B 60
Bewerley. N Yor —3D 98
Bewholme. E Yor —5F 101
Bexfield. Norf —3C 78
Bexhill. E Sus —5B 28
Bexley. G Lon —3F 39
Bexleyheath. G Lon —3F 39
Bexleyhill. W Sus —3A 26
Bexwell. Norf —5F 77
Beyton. Suff —4B 66
Beyton Green. Suff —4B 66
Bhalton. W Isl —4C 171
Bhatarsaigh. W Isl —9B 170
Bibbington. Derbs —3E 85
Bibury. Glos —5G 49
Bicester. Oxon —3D 50
Bickenhall. Som —1F 13
Bickenhill. W Mid —2F 61
Bicker. Linc —2B 76
Bicker Bar. Linc —2B 76
Bicker Gauntlet. Linc —2B 76
Bickershaw. G Man —4E 91
Bickerstaffe. Lanc —4C 90
Bickerton. Ches —5H 83
Bickerton. Nmbd —4D 121
Bickerton. N Yor —4G 99
Bickford. Staf —4C 72
Bickington. Devn —3F 19 (nr. Barnstaple)
Bickington. Devn —5A 12 (nr. Newton Abbot)
Bickleigh. Devn —2B 8 (nr. Plymouth)
Bickleigh. Devn —2C 12 (nr. Tiverton)
Bickleton. Devn —3F 19
Bickley. N Yor —5G 107
Bickley Moss. Ches —1H 71
Bickmarsh. Warw —5F 61
Bicknacre. Essx —5A 54
Bicknoller. Som —3E 20
Bicknor. Kent —5C 40
Bickton. Hants —1G 15
Bicton. Here —4G 59
Bicton. Shrp —2E 59 (nr. Bishop's Castle)
Bicton. Shrp —4G 71 (nr. Shrewsbury)
Bicton Heath. Shrp —4G 71
Bidborough. Kent —1G 27
Biddenden. Kent —2C 28
Biddenden Green. Kent —1C 28
Biddenham. Beds —1A 52
Biddestone. Wilts —4D 34
Biddisham. Som —1G 21
Biddlesden. Buck —1E 51
Biddlestone. Nmbd —4D 120
Biddulph. Staf —5C 84
Biddulph Moor. Staf —5D 84
Bideford. Devn —4E 19
Bidford-on-Avon. Warw —5E 61
Bidlake. Devn —4F 11
Bidston. Mers —2E 83
Bielby. E Yor —5B 100
Bieldside. Aber C —3F 153
Bierley. IOW —5D 16
Bierley. W Yor —1B 92
Bierton. Buck —4G 51
Bigbury. Devn —4C 8
Bigbury-on-Sea. Devn —4C 8
Bigby. Linc —4D 94
Big Corlae. Dum —5F 117
Biggar. Cumb —3A 96
Biggar. S Lan —1C 118
Biggin. Derbs —5F 85 (nr. Hartington)
Biggin. Derbs —1G 73 (nr. Hulland)
Biggin. N Yor —1F 93
Biggings. Shet —5C 173
Biggin Hill. G Lon —5F 39
Biggin Hill (London) Airport. Kent —4F 39
Biggleswade. Beds —1B 52
Bighouse. High —2A 168
Bighton. Hants —3E 24
Biglands. Cumb —4D 112
Bignor. W Sus —4A 26
Big Sand. High —1G 155
Bigton. Shet —9E 173
Bilberry. Corn —2E 6
Bilborough. Not C —1C 74
Bilbrook. Som —2D 20
Bilbrook. Staf —5C 72
Bilbrough. N Yor —5H 99
Bilbster. High —3E 169
Bilby. Notts —2D 86
Bildershaw. Dur —2F 105
Bildeston. Suff —1C 54
Billericay. Essx —1A 40
Billesdon. Leics —5E 74
Billesley. Warw —5F 61
Billingborough. Linc —2A 76
Billinge. Mers —4D 90
Billingford. Norf —3D 66 (nr. Diss)
Billingford. Norf —3C 78 (nr. East Dereham)
Billingham. Stoc T —2B 106
Billinghay. Linc —5A 88
Billingley. S Yor —4E 93
Billingshurst. W Sus —3B 26
Billingsley. Shrp —2B 60
Billington. Beds —3H 51
Billington. Lanc —1F 91
Billington. Staf —3C 72
Billockby. Norf —4G 79
Billy Row. Dur —1E 105
Bilsborrow. Lanc —5E 97
Bilsby. Linc —3D 88
Bilsham. W Sus —5A 26
Bilsington. Kent —2E 29
Bilson Green. Glos —4B 48
Bilsthorpe. Notts —4D 86
Bilsthorpe Moor. Notts —5D 86
Bilston. Midl —3F 129
Bilston. W Mid —1D 60
Bilstone. Leics —5A 74
Bilting. Kent —1E 29
Bilton. E Yor —1E 95
Bilton. Nmbd —3G 121
Bilton. N Yor —4E 99 (nr. Harrogate)
Bilton. N Yor —5G 99 (nr. York)
Bilton. Warw —3B 62
Bilton Banks. Nmbd —3G 121
Bimbister. Orkn —6C 172
Binbrook. Linc —1B 88
Binchester Blocks. Dur —1F 105
Bincombe. Dors —4B 14
Bindal. High —5G 165
Binegar. Som —2B 22
Bines Green. W Sus —4C 26
Binfield. Brac —4G 37
Binfield Heath. Oxon —4F 37
Bingfield. Nmbd —2C 114
Bingham. Notts —1E 74
Bingham's Melcombe. Dors —2C 14
Bingley. W Yor —1B 92
Bings Heath. Shrp —4H 71
Binham. Norf —2B 78
Binley. Hants —1C 24
Binley. W Mid —3A 62
Binnegar. Dors —4D 15
Binniehill. Falk —2B 128
Binsoe. N Yor —2E 99
Binstead. IOW —3D 16
Binstead. W Sus —5A 26
Binsted. Hants —2F 25
Binton. Warw —5F 61
Bintree. Norf —3C 78
Binweston. Shrp —5F 71
Birch. Essx —4C 54
Birchall. Staf —5D 85
Bircham Newton. Norf —2G 77
Bircham Tofts. Norf —2G 77
Birchanger. Essx —3F 53
Birchburn. N Ayr —3D 122
Birch Cross. Staf —2F 73
Bircher. Here —4G 59
Birch Green. Essx —4C 54
Birchgrove. Card —4E 33
Birchgrove. Swan —3G 31
Birch Heath. Ches —4H 83
Birch Hill. Ches —3H 83
Birchington. Kent —4G 41
Birch Langley. G Man —4G 91
Birchley Heath. Warw —1G 61
Birchmoor. Warw —5G 73
Birchmoor Green. Beds —2H 51
Birchover. Derbs —4G 85
Birch Vale. Derbs —2E 85
Birchview. Mor —5F 159
Birchwood. Linc —4G 87
Birchwood. Som —1F 13
Birchwood. Warr —1A 84
Bircotes. Notts —1D 86
Birdbrook. Essx —1H 53
Birdham. W Sus —2G 17
Birdingbury. Warw —4B 62
Birdlip. Glos —4E 49
Birdsall. N Yor —3C 100
Birds Edge. W Yor —4C 92
Birds Green. Essx —5F 53
Birdsgreen. Shrp —2B 60
Birdsmoor Gate. Dors —2G 13
Birdston. E Dun —2H 127
Birdwell. S Yor —4D 92
Birdwood. Glos —4C 48
Birgham. Scot —1B 120
Birichen. High —4E 165
Birkby. Cumb —1B 102
Birkby. N Yor —4A 106
Birkdale. Mers —3B 90
Birkenhead. Mers —2F 83
Birkenhills. Aber —4E 161
Birkenshaw. N Lan —3H 127
Birkenshaw. W Yor —2C 92
Birkhall. Aber —4H 151
Birkhill. Ang —5C 144
Birkholme. Linc —3G 75
Birkin. N Yor —2F 93
Birley. Here —5G 59
Birling. Kent —4A 40
Birling. Nmbd —4G 121
Birling Gap. E Sus —5G 27
Birlingham. Worc —1E 49
Birmingham. W Mid —2E 61
Birmingham Airport. W Mid —2F 61
Birnam. Per —4H 143
Birsay. Orkn —5B 172
Birse. Aber —4C 152
Birsemore. Aber —4C 152
Birstall. Leics —5C 74
Birstall Smithies. W Yor —2C 92
Birstwith. N Yor —4E 99
Birthorpe. Linc —2A 76
Birtle. Lanc —3G 91
Birtley. Here —4F 59
Birtley. Nmbd —2B 114
Birtley. Tyne —4F 115
Birtsmorton. Worc —2D 48
Birts Street. Worc —2C 48
Bisbrooke. Rut —1F 63
Bisham. Wind —3G 37
Bishampton. Worc —5D 61
Bish Mill. Devn —4H 19
Bishop Auckland. Dur —2F 105
Bishopbridge. Linc —1H 87
Bishopbriggs. E Dun —2H 127
Bishop Burton. E Yor —5D 101
Bishopdown. Wilts —3G 23
Bishop Middleham. Dur —1A 106
Bishopmill. Mor —2G 159
Bishop Monkton. N Yor —3F 99
Bishop Norton. Linc —1G 87
Bishopsbourne. Kent —5F 41
Bishops Cannings. Wilts —5F 35
Bishop's Castle. Shrp —2F 59
Bishop's Caundle. Dors —1B 14
Bishop's Cleeve. Glos —3E 49
Bishop's Down. Dors —1B 14
Bishop's Frome. Here —1B 48
Bishop's Green. Essx —4G 53
Bishop's Green. Hants —5D 36
Bishop's Hull. Som —4F 21
Bishop's Itchington. Warw —5A 62
Bishop's Lydeard. Som —4E 21
Bishop's Norton. Glos —3D 48
Bishop's Nympton. Devn —4A 20
Bishop's Offley. Staf —3B 72
Bishop's Stortford. Herts —3E 53
Bishops Sutton. Hants —3E 24
Bishop's Tachbrook. Warw —4H 61
Bishop's Tawton. Devn —3F 19
Bishopsteignton. Devn —5C 12
Bishopstoke. Hants —1C 16
Bishopston. Swan —4E 31
Bishopstone. Buck —4G 51
Bishopstone. E Sus —5F 27
Bishopstone. Here —1H 47
Bishopstone. Swin —3H 35
Bishopstone. Wilts —4F 23
Bishopstrow. Wilts —2D 23
Bishop Sutton. Bath —1A 22
Bishop's Waltham. Hants —1D 16
Bishopswood. Som —1F 13
Bishop's Wood. Staf —5C 72
Bishopsworth. Bris —5A 34
Bishop Thornton. N Yor —3E 99
Bishopthorpe. York —5H 99
Bishopton. Darl —2A 106
Bishopton. Dum —5B 110
Bishopton. N Yor —2F 99
Bishopton. Ren —2F 127
Bishopton. Warw —5F 61
Bishop Wilton. E Yor —4B 100
Bishton. Newp —3G 33
Bishton. Staf —3E 73
Bisley. Glos —5E 49
Bisley. Surr —5A 38
Bispham. Bkpl —5C 96
Bispham Green. Lanc —3C 90
Bissoe. Corn —4B 6
Bisterne. Hants —2G 15
Bisterne Close. Hants —2H 15
Bitchfield. Linc —3G 75
Bittadon. Devn —2F 19
Bittaford. Devn —3C 8
Bittering. Norf —4B 78
Bitterley. Shrp —3H 59
Bitterne. Sotn —1C 16
Bitteswell. Leics —2C 62
Bitton. S Glo —5B 34
Bix. Oxon —3F 37
Bixter. Shet —6E 173
Blaby. Leics —1C 62
Blackawton. Devn —3E 9
Black Bank. Cambs —2E 65
Black Barn. Linc —3D 76
Blackborough. Devn —2D 12
Blackborough. Norf —4F 77
Blackborough End. Norf —4F 77
Black Bourton. Oxon —5A 50
Blackboys. E Sus —3G 27
Blackbrook. Derbs —1H 73
Blackbrook. Mers —1H 83
Blackbrook. Staf —2B 72
Blackbrook. Surr —1C 26
Blackburn. Aber —2F 153
Blackburn. Bkbn —2E 91
Blackburn. W Lot —3C 128
Black Callerton. Tyne —3E 115
Black Car. Norf —1C 66
Black Clauchrie. S Ayr —1H 109
Black Corries. High —3G 141
Black Crofts. Arg —5D 140
Black Cross. Corn —2D 6
Blackden Heath. Ches —3B 84
Blackditch. Oxon —5C 50
Blackdog. Aber —2G 153
Black Dog. Devn —2B 12
Blackdown. Dors —2G 13
Blackdyke. Cumb —4C 112
Blacker Hill. S Yor —4D 92
Blackfen. G Lon —3F 39
Blackfield. Hants —2C 16
Blackford. Cumb —3E 113
Blackford. Per —3A 136
Blackford. Shrp —2H 59
Blackford. Som —2H 21 (nr. Burnham-on-Sea)
Blackford. Som —4B 22 (nr. Wincanton)
Blackfordby. Leics —4H 73
Blackgang. IOW —5C 16
Blackhall. Edin —2F 129
Blackhall. Ren —3F 127
Blackhall Colliery. Dur —1B 106
Blackhall Mill. Tyne —4E 115
Blackhall Rocks. Dur —1B 106
Blackham. E Sus —2F 27
Blackheath. Essx —3D 54
Blackheath. G Lon —3E 39
Blackheath. Suff —3G 67
Blackheath. Surr —1B 26
Blackheath. W Mid —2D 61
Black Heddon. Nmbd —2D 115
Blackhill. Aber —4H 161
Blackhill. High —3C 154
Black Hill. Warw —5G 61
Blackhills. Aber —2G 161
Blackhills. High —3D 158
Blackjack. Linc —2B 76
Blackland. Wilts —5F 35
Black Lane. G Man —4F 91
Blackleach. Lanc —1C 90
Blackley. G Man —4G 91
Blackley. W Yor —3B 92
Blacklunans. Per —2A 144
Blackmill. B'End —3C 32
Blackmoor. G Man —4E 91
Blackmoor. Hants —3F 25
Blackmoor Gate. Devn —2G 19
Blackmore. Essx —5G 53
Blackmore End. Essx —2H 53
Blackmore End. Herts —4B 52
Black Mount. Arg —4G 141
Blackness. Falk —2D 128
Blacknest. Hants —2F 25
Blackney. Dors —3H 13
Blacknoll. Dors —4D 14
Black Notley. Essx —3A 54
Blacko. Lanc —5A 98
Black Pill. Swan —3F 31
Blackpool. Bkpl —1B 90
Blackpool. Devn —4E 9
Blackpool Airport. Lanc —1B 90
Blackpool Gate. Cumb —2G 113
Blackridge. W Lot —3B 128
Blackrock. Arg —3B 124
Blackrock. Mon —4F 47
Blackrod. G Man —3E 90
Blackshaw. Dum —3B 112
Blackshaw Head. W Yor —2H 91
Blacksmith's Green. Suff —4D 66
Blacksnape. Bkbn —2F 91
Blackstone. W Sus —4D 26
Black Street. Suff —2H 67
Black Tar. Pemb —4D 43
Blackthorn. Oxon —4E 50
Blackthorpe. Suff —4B 66
Blacktoft. E Yor —2B 94
Blacktop. Aber C —3F 153
Black Torrington. Devn —2E 11
Blacktown. Newp —3F 33
Blackwater. Corn —4B 6
Blackwater. Hants —1G 25
Blackwater. IOW —4D 16
Blackwater. Som —1F 13
Blackwaterfoot. N Ayr —3C 122
Blackwell. Darl —3F 105
Blackwell. Derbs —5B 86 (nr. Alfreton)
Blackwell. Derbs —3F 85 (nr. Buxton)
Blackwell. Som —4D 20
Blackwell. Warw —1H 49
Blackwell. Worc —3D 61
Blackwood. Cphy —2E 33
Blackwood. Dum —1G 111
Blackwood. S Lan —5A 128
Blackwood Hill. Staf —5D 84
Blacon. Ches —4F 83
Bladnoch. Dum —4B 110
Bladon. Oxon —4C 50
Blaenannerch. Cdgn —1C 44
Blaenau Dolwyddelan. Cnwy —5F 81
Blaenau Ffestiniog. Gwyn —1G 69
Blaenavon. Torf —5F 47
Blaenawey. Mon —4F 47
Blaen Celyn. Cdgn —5C 56
Blaen Clydach. Rhon —2C 32
Blaendulais. Neat —5B 46
Blaenffos. Pemb —1F 43
Blaengarw. B'End —2C 32
Blaen-geuffordd. Cdgn —2F 57
Blaengwrach. Neat —5B 46
Blaengwynfi. Neat —2B 32
Blaenllechau. Rhon —2D 32
Blaenpennal. Cdgn —4F 57
Blaenplwyf. Cdgn —3E 57
Blaenporth. Cdgn —1C 44
Blaenrhondda. Rhon —2C 32
Blaenwaun. Carm —2G 43
Blaen-y-coed. Carm —2H 43
Blaen-y-cwm. Blae —4E 47
Blaenycwm. Rhon —2C 32
Blagdon. N Som —1A 22
Blagdon. Torb —2E 9
Blagdon Hill. Som —1F 13
Blaguegate. Lanc —4C 90
Blaich. High —1E 141
Blain. High —2A 140
Blaina. Blae —5F 47
Blair Atholl. Per —2F 143
Blair Drummond. Stir —4G 135
Blairgowrie. Per —4A 144
Blairhall. Fife —1D 128
Blairingone. Per —4B 136
Blairlogie. Stir —4H 135
Blairmore. Aber —5B 160
Blairmore. Arg —1C 126
Blairmore. High —3B 166
Blairquhanan. W Dun —1F 127
Blaisdon. Glos —4C 48
Blakebrook. Worc —3C 60
Blakedown. Worc —3C 60
Blake End. Essx —3H 53
Blakemere. Here —1G 47
Blakeney. Glos —5B 48
Blakeney. Norf —1C 78
Blakenhall. Ches —1B 72
Blakenhall. W Mid —1C 60
Blakeshall. Worc —2C 60
Blakesley. Nptn —5D 62
Blanchland. Nmbd —4C 114
Blandford Camp. Dors —2E 15
Blandford Forum. Dors —2D 15
Blandford St Mary. Dors —2D 15
Bland Hill. N Yor —4E 98
Blandy. High —3G 167
Blanefield. Stir —2G 127
Blankney. Linc —4H 87
Blantyre. S Lan —4H 127
Blarmachfoldach. High —2E 141
Blashford. Hants —2G 15
Blaston. Leics —1F 63
Blatchbridge. Som —2C 22
Blathaisbhal. W Isl —1D 170
Blatherwycke. Nptn —1G 63
Blawith. Cumb —1B 96
Blaxhall. Suff —5F 67
Blaxton. S Yor —4G 93
Blaydon. Tyne —3E 115
Bleadney. Som —2H 21
Bleadon. N Som —1G 21
Blean. Kent —4F 41
Bleasby. Linc —2A 88
Bleasby. Notts —1E 74
Bleasby Moor. Linc —2A 88
Blebocraigs. Fife —2G 137
Bleddfa. Powy —4E 58
Bledington. Glos —3H 49
Bledlow. Buck —5F 51
Bledlow Ridge. Buck —2F 37
Blencarn. Cumb —1H 103
Blencogo. Cumb —5C 112
Blendworth. Hants —1F 17
Blenheim. Oxon —5D 50
Blennerhasset. Cumb —5C 112
Bletchingdon. Oxon —4D 50
Bletchingley. Surr —5E 39
Bletchley. Mil —2G 51
Bletchley. Shrp —2A 72
Bletherston. Pemb —2E 43
Bletsoe. Beds —5H 63
Blewbury. Oxon —3D 36
Blickling. Norf —3D 78
Blidworth. Notts —5C 86
Blindburn. Nmbd —3C 120
Blindcrake. Cumb —1C 102
Blindley Heath. Surr —1E 27
Blisland. Corn —5A 10
Blissford. Hants —1G 15
Bliss Gate. Worc —3B 60
Blists Hill. Telf —5A 72
Blisworth. Nptn —5E 63
Blithbury. Staf —3E 73
Blitterlees. Cumb —4C 112
Blockley. Glos —2G 49
Blofield. Norf —5F 79
Blofield Heath. Norf —4F 79
Blo' Norton. Norf —3C 66
Bloomfield. Scot —2H 119
Blore. Staf —1F 73
Blount's Green. Staf —2E 73
Bloxham. Oxon —2C 50
Bloxholm. Linc —5H 87
Bloxwich. W Mid —5E 73
Bloxworth. Dors —3D 15
Blubberhouses. N Yor —4D 98
Blue Anchor. Som —2D 20
Blue Anchor. Swan —3E 31
Blue Bell Hill. Kent —4B 40
Blue Row. Essx —4D 54
Bluetown. Kent —5D 40
Blundeston. Suff —1H 67
Blunham. Beds —5A 64
Blunsdon St Andrew. Swin —3G 35
Bluntington. Worc —3C 60
Bluntisham. Cambs —3C 64
Blunts. Corn —2H 7
Blurton. Stoke —1C 72
Blyborough. Linc —1G 87
Blyford. Suff —3G 67
Blymhill. Staf —4C 72
Blymhill Lawns. Staf —4C 72
Blyth. Nmbd —1G 115
Blyth. Notts —2D 86
Blyth. Scot —5E 129
Blyth Bank. Scot —5E 129
Blyth Bridge. Scot —5E 129
Blythburgh. Suff —3G 67
Blythe Bridge. Staf —1D 72
Blythe Marsh. Staf —1D 72
Blythe, The. Staf —3E 73
Blyton. Linc —1F 87
Boarhills. Fife —2H 137
Boarhunt. Hants —2E 16
Boarshead. E Sus —2G 27
Boar's Head. G Man —4D 90
Boars Hill. Oxon —5C 50
Boarstall. Buck —4E 51
Boasley Cross. Devn —3F 11
Boath. High —1H 157
Boat of Garten. High —2D 150
Bobbing. Kent —4C 40
Bobbington. Staf —1C 60
Bobbingworth. Essx —5F 53
Bocaddon. Corn —3F 7
Bocking. Essx —3A 54
Bocking Churchstreet. Essx —3A 54
Boddam. Aber —4H 161
Boddam. Shet —10E 173
Boddington. Glos —3D 49
Bodedern. IOA —2C 80
Bodelwyddan. Den —3C 82
Bodenham. Here —5H 59
Bodenham. Wilts —4G 23
Bodewryd. IOA —1C 80
Bodfari. Den —3C 82
Bodffordd. IOA —3D 80
Bodham. Norf —1D 78
Bodiam. E Sus —3B 28

Bodicote—Breanais

Bodicote. Oxon —2C 50
Bodieve. Corn —1D 6
Bodinnick. Corn —3F 7
Bodle Street Green. E Sus —4A 28
Bodmin. Corn —2E 7
Bodnant. Cnwy —3H 81
Bodney. Norf —1H 65
Bodorgan. IOA —4C 80
Bodrane. Corn —2G 7
Bodsham Green. Kent —1F 29
Boduan. Gwyn —2C 68
Bodymoor Heath. Warw —1F 61
Bogallan. High —3A 158
Bogbrae. Aber —5H 161
Bogend. S Ayr —1C 116
Boghall. Midl —3F 129
Boghall. W Lot —3C 128
Boghead. S Lan —5A 128
Bogindollo. Ang —3D 144
Bogmoor. Mor —2A 160
Bognor Regis. W Sus —3H 17
Bograxie. Aber —2E 152
Bogside. N Lan —4B 128
Bog, The. Shrp —1F 59
Bogton. Aber —3D 160
Bogue. Dum —1D 110
Bohenie. High —5E 149
Bohortha. Corn —5C 6
Boirseam. W Isl —9C 171
Bojewyan. Corn —3A 4
Bokiddick. Corn —2E 7
Bolam. Dur —2E 105
Bolam. Nmbd —1D 115
Bolberry. Devn —5C 8
Bold Heath. Mers —2H 83
Boldon. Tyne —3G 115
Boldon Colliery. Tyne —3G 115
Boldre. Hants —3B 16
Boldron. Dur —3D 104
Bole. Notts —2E 87
Bolehall. Staf —5G 73
Bolehill. Derbs —5G 85
Bolenowe. Corn —5A 6
Boleside. Scot —1G 119
Bolham. Devn —1C 12
Bolham Water. Devn —1E 13
Bolingey. Corn —3B 6
Bollington. Ches —3D 84
Bolney. W Sus —3D 26
Bolnhurst. Beds —5H 63
Bolshan. Ang —3F 145
Bolsover. Derbs —3B 86
Bolsterstone. S Yor —1G 85
Bolstone. Here —2A 48
Boltachan. Per —3F 143
Boltby. N Yor —1G 99
Bolton. Cumb —2H 103
Bolton. E Lot —2B 130
Bolton. E Yor —4B 100
Bolton. G Man —4F 91
Bolton. Nmbd —3F 121
Bolton Abbey. N Yor —4C 98
Bolton by Bowland. Lanc —5G 97
Boltonfellend. Cumb —3F 113
Boltongate. Cumb —5D 112
Bolton Green. Lanc —3D 90
Bolton-le-Sands. Lanc —3D 97
Bolton Low Houses. Cumb —5D 112
Bolton New Houses. Cumb —5D 112
Bolton-on-Swale. N Yor —5F 105
Bolton Percy. N Yor —5H 99
Bolton Town End. Lanc —3D 97
Bolton upon Dearne. S Yor —4E 93
Bolton Wood Lane. Cumb —5D 112
Bolventor. Corn —5B 10
Bomarsund. Nmbd —1F 115
Bomere Heath. Shrp —4G 71
Bonar Bridge. High —4D 164
Bonawe. Arg —5E 141
Bonawe Quarries. Arg —5E 141
Bonby. N Lin —3D 94
Boncath. Pemb —1G 43
Bonchester Bridge. Scot —3H 119
Bonchurch. IOW —5D 16
Bond End. Staf —4F 73
Bondleigh. Devn —2G 11
Bonds. Lanc —5D 97
Bonehill. Devn —5H 11
Bonehill. Staf —5F 73
Bo'ness. Falk —1C 128
Boney Hay. Staf —4E 73
Bonham. Wilts —3C 22
Bonhill. W Dun —2E 127
Boningale. Shrp —5C 72
Bonjedward. Scot —2A 120
Bonkle. N Lan —4B 128
Bonnington. Ang —5E 145
Bonnington. Edin —3E 129
Bonnington. Kent —2E 29
Bonnybank. Fife —3F 137
Bonnybridge. Falk —1B 128
Bonnykelly. Aber —3F 161
Bonnyrigg & Lasswade. Midl —3G 129
Bonnyton. Ang —5C 144
Bonnytown. Fife —2H 137
Bonsall. Derbs —5G 85
Bont. Mon —4G 47
Bontddu. Gwyn —4F 69
Bont Dolgadfan. Powy —5A 70
Bontgoch. Cdgn —2F 57
Bonthorpe. Linc —3D 89
Bontnewydd. Cdgn —4F 57
Bont-newydd. Cnwy —3C 82
Bontnewydd. Gwyn —4D 81
(nr. Caernarfon)
Bont Newydd. Gwyn —1G 69
(nr. Ffestiniog)
Bontuchel. Den —5C 82
Bonvilston. V Glam —4D 32
Bon-y-maen. Swan —3F 31
Booker. Buck —2G 37
Booley. Shrp —3H 71
Boorley Green. Hants —1D 16
Boosbeck. Red C —3D 106
Boot. Cumb —4C 102
Booth. W Yor —2A 92
Boothby Graffoe. Linc —5G 87
Boothby Pagnell. Linc —2G 75
Booth Green. Ches —2D 84
Booth of Toft. Shet —4F 173
Boothstown. G Man —4F 91
Boothville. Nptn —4E 63
Booth Wood. W Yor —3A 92
Bootle. Cumb —1A 96
Bootle. Mers —1F 83
Booton. Norf —3D 78
Booze. N Yor —4D 104
Boquhan. Stir —1G 127
Boraston. Shrp —3A 60
Borden. Kent —4C 40
Borden. W Sus —4G 25
Bordlands. Scot —5E 129
Bordley. N Yor —3B 98
Bordon. Hants —3G 25
Boreham. Essx —5A 54
Boreham. Wilts —2D 23
Boreham Street. E Sus —4A 28
Borehamwood. Herts —1C 38
Boreland. Dum —5D 118
Boreston. Devn —3D 8
Borestone Brae. Stir —4H 135
Boreton. Shrp —5H 71
Borgh. W Isl —8B 170
(on Barra)
Borgh. W Isl —3C 170
(on Benbecula)
Borgh. W Isl —1E 170
(on Berneray)
Borgh. W Isl —2G 171
(on Lewis)
Borghastan. W Isl —3D 171
Borgie. High —3G 167
Borgue. Dum —5D 110
Borgue. High —1H 165
Borley. Essx —1B 54
Borley Green. Essx —1B 54
Borley Green. Suff —4B 66
Borlum. High —1H 149
Bornais. W Isl —6C 170
Bornesketaig. High —1C 154
Boroughbridge. N Yor —3F 99
Borough Green. Kent —5H 39
Borras Head. Wrex —5F 83
Borreraig. High —3A 154
Borrobol Lodge. High —1F 165
Borrodale. High —4A 154
Borrowash. Derbs —2A 74
Borrowby. N Yor —1G 99
(nr. Northallerton)
Borrowby. N Yor —3E 107
(nr. Whitby)
Borrowdale. Cumb —3D 102
Borrowston. High —4F 169
Borrowstoun. Falk —1C 128
Borstal. Medw —4B 40
Borth. Cdgn —2F 57
Borthwick. Midl —4G 129
Borth-y-Gest. Gwyn —2E 69
Borve. High —4D 154
Borwick. Lanc —2E 97
Bosbury. Here —1B 48
Boscastle. Corn —3B 10
Boscombe. Bour —3G 15
Boscombe. Wilts —3H 23
Boscoppa. Corn —3E 7
Bosham. W Sus —2G 17
Bosherston. Pemb —5D 42
Bosley. Ches —4D 84
Bossall. N Yor —3B 100
Bossiney. Corn —4A 10
Bossingham. Kent —1F 29
Bossington. Som —2B 20
Bostadh. W Isl —3D 171
Bostock Green. Ches —4A 84
Boston. Linc —1C 76
Boston Spa. W Yor —5G 99
Boswarthen. Corn —3B 4
Boswinger. Corn —4D 6
Botallack. Corn —3A 4
Botany Bay. G Lon —1D 39
Botcheston. Leics —5B 74
Botesdale. Suff —3C 66
Bothal. Nmbd —1F 115
Bothampstead. W Ber —4D 36
Bothamsall. Notts —3D 86
Bothel. Cumb —1C 102
Bothenhampton. Dors —3H 13
Bothwell. S Lan —4H 127
Botley. Buck —5H 51
Botley. Hants —1D 16
Botley. Oxon —5C 50
Botloe's Green. Glos —3C 48
Botolph Claydon. Buck —3F 51
Botolphs. W Sus —5C 26
Bottacks. High —2G 157
Bottesford. Leics —2F 75
Bottesford. N Lin —4B 94
Bottisham. Cambs —4E 65
Bottlesford. Wilts —1G 23
Bottomcraig. Fife —1F 137
Bottom o' th' Moor. G Man —3E 91
Botton Head. Lanc —3F 97
Botusfleming. Corn —2A 8
Botwnnog. Gwyn —2B 68
Bough Beech. Kent —1F 27
Boughrood. Powy —2E 47
Boughspring. Glos —2A 34
Boughton. Norf —5F 77
Boughton. Nptn —4E 63
Boughton. Notts —4D 86
Boughton Aluph. Kent —1E 29
Boughton Green. Kent —5B 40
Boughton Lees. Kent —1E 28
Boughton Malherbe. Kent —1C 28
Boughton Monchelsea. Kent —5B 40
Boughton under Blean. Kent —5E 41
Boulby. Red C —3E 107
Bouldnor. IOW —4B 16
Bouldon. Shrp —2H 59
Boulmer. Nmbd —3G 121
Boulston. Pemb —3D 42
Boultham. Linc —4G 87
Boulton. Dby C —2A 74
Boundary. Staf —1D 73
Bounds. Here —2B 48
Bourn. Cambs —5C 64
Bournbrook. W Mid —2E 61
Bourne. Linc —3H 75
Bourne End. Beds —1H 51
(nr. Cranfield)
Bourne End. Beds —4H 63
(nr. Sharnbrook)
Bourne End. Buck —3G 37
Bourne End. Herts —5A 52
Bournemouth. Bour —3F 15
Bournemouth Airport. Dors —3G 15
Bournes Green. Glos —5E 49
Bournes Green. S'end —2D 40
Bourne, The. Surr —2G 25
Bournheath. Worc —3D 60
Bournmoor. Dur —4G 115
Bournville. W Mid —2E 61
Bourton. Dors —3C 22
Bourton. N Som —5G 33
Bourton. Oxon —3H 35
Bourton. Shrp —1H 59
Bourton. Wilts —5F 35
Bourton on Dunsmore. Warw —3B 62
Bourton-on-the-Hill. Glos —2G 49
Bourton-on-the-Water. Glos —3G 49
Bousd. Arg —2D 138
Boustead Hill. Cumb —4D 112
Bouth. Cumb —1C 96
Bouthwaite. N Yor —2D 98
Boveney. Buck —3A 38
Boveridge. Dors —1F 15
Boverton. V Glam —5C 32
Bovey Tracey. Devn —5B 12
Bovingdon. Herts —5A 52
Bovingdon Green. Buck —3G 37
Bovinger. Essx —5F 53
Bovington Camp. Dors —4D 14
Bow. Devn —2H 11
Bowbank. Dur —2C 104
Bow Brickhill. Mil —2H 51
Bowbridge. Glos —5D 48
Bowburn. Dur —1A 106
Bowcombe. IOW —4C 16
Bowd. Devn —4E 12
Bowden. Devn —4E 9
Bowden. Scot —1H 119
Bowden Hill. Wilts —5E 35
Bowdon. G Man —2B 84
Bower. Nmbd —1A 114
Bowerchalke. Wilts —4F 23
Bowerhill. Wilts —5E 35
Bower Hinton. Som —1H 13
Bowermadden. High —2E 169
Bowers. Staf —2C 72
Bowers Gifford. Essx —2B 40
Bowershall. Fife —4C 136
Bowertower. High —2E 169
Bowes. Dur —3C 104
Bowgreave. Lanc —5D 97
Bowhousebog. N Lan —4B 128
Bowithick. Corn —4B 10
Bowland Bridge. Cumb —1D 96
Bowlees. Dur —2C 104
Bowley. Here —5H 59
Bowlhead Green. Surr —2A 26
Bowling. W Dun —2F 127
Bowling. W Yor —1B 92
Bowling Bank. Wrex —1G 71
Bowling Green. Worc —5C 60
Bowlish. Som —2B 22
Bowmanstead. Cumb —5E 102
Bowmore. Arg —4B 124
Bowness-on-Solway. Cumb —3D 112
Bowness-on-Windermere. Cumb —5F 103
Bow of Fife. Fife —2F 137
Bowood. Dors —3H 13
Bowriefauld. Ang —4E 145
Bowscale. Cumb —1E 103
Bowsden. Nmbd —5F 131
Bowside Lodge. High —2A 168
Bowston. Cumb —5F 103
Bow Street. Cdgn —2F 57
Bowthorpe. Norf —5D 78
Box. Glos —5D 48
Box. Wilts —5D 34
Boxbush. Glos —3B 48
Box End. Beds —1A 52
Boxford. Suff —1C 54
Boxford. W Ber —4C 36
Boxgrove. W Sus —5A 26
Boxley. Kent —5B 40
Box's Shop. Corn —2C 10
Boxted. Essx —2C 54
Boxted. Suff —5H 65
Boxted Cross. Essx —2C 54
Boxworth. Cambs —4C 64
Boxworth End. Cambs —4C 64
Boyden End. Suff —5G 65
Boyden Gate. Kent —4G 41
Boylestone. Derbs —2F 73
Boylestonfield. Derbs —2F 73
Boyndie. Aber —2D 160
Boyndlie. Aber —2G 161
Boynton. E Yor —3F 101
Boys Hill. Dors —1B 14
Boythorpe. Derbs —4A 86
Boyton. Corn —3D 10
Boyton. Suff —1G 55
Boyton. Wilts —3E 23
Boyton Cross. Essx —5G 53
Boyton End. Essx —2G 53
Boyton End. Suff —1H 53
Bozeat. Nptn —5G 63
Braaid. IOM —4C 108
Braal Castle. High —3D 168
Brabling Green. Suff —4E 67
Brabourne. Kent —1F 29
Brabourne Lees. Kent —1E 29
Brabster. High —2F 169
Bracadale. High —5C 154
Braceborough. Linc —4H 75
Bracebridge. Linc —4G 87
Bracebridge Heath. Linc —4G 87
Bracebridge Low Fields. Linc —4G 87
Braceby. Linc —2H 75
Bracewell. Lanc —5A 98
Brackenfield. Derbs —5A 86
Brackenlands. Cumb —5D 112
Brackenthwaite. Cumb —5D 112
Brackenthwaite. N Yor —4E 99
Brackla. B'End —4C 32
Brackla. High —3C 158
Bracklesham. W Sus —3G 17
Brackletter. High —5D 148
Brackley. Nptn —2D 50
Brackley Hatch. Nptn —1E 51
Bracknell. Brac —5G 37
Braco. Per —3H 135
Bracobrae. Mor —3C 160
Bracon. N Lin —4A 94
Bracon Ash. Norf —1D 66
Bracora. High —4F 147
Bradbourne. Derbs —5G 85
Bradbury. Dur —2A 106
Bradda. IOM —4A 108
Bradden. Nptn —1E 51
Bradenham. Buck —2G 37
Bradenham. Norf —5B 78
Bradenstoke. Wilts —4F 35
Bradfield. Essx —2E 55
Bradfield. Norf —2E 79
Bradfield. W Ber —4E 36
Bradfield Combust. Suff —5A 66
Bradfield Green. Ches —5A 84
Bradfield Heath. Essx —3E 55
Bradfield St Clare. Suff —5B 66
Bradfield St George. Suff —4B 66
Bradford. Derbs —4G 85
Bradford. Devn —2E 11
Bradford. Nmbd —1F 121
Bradford. W Yor —1B 92
Bradford Abbas. Dors —1A 14
Bradford Barton. Devn —1B 12
Bradford Leigh. Wilts —5D 34
Bradford-on-Avon. Wilts —5D 34
Bradford-on-Tone. Som —4E 21
Bradford Peverell. Dors —3B 14
Bradiford. Devn —3F 19
Brading. IOW —4E 16
Bradley. Ches —3H 83
Bradley. Cumb —1H 103
Bradley. Derbs —1G 73
Bradley. Glos —2C 34
Bradley. Hants —2E 25
Bradley. NE Lin —4F 95
Bradley. N Yor —1C 98
Bradley. Staf —4C 72
Bradley. W Mid —1D 60
Bradley. W Yor —2B 92
Bradley. Wrex —5F 83
Bradley Cross. Som —1H 21
Bradley Green. Ches —1H 71
Bradley Green. Som —3F 21
Bradley Green. Warw —5G 73
Bradley Green. Worc —4D 61
Bradley in the Moors. Staf —1E 73
Bradley Mount. Ches —3D 84
Bradley Stoke. S Glo —3B 34
Bradlow. Here —2C 48
Bradmore. Notts —2C 74
Bradmore. W Mid —1C 60
Bradninch. Devn —2D 12
Bradnop. Staf —5E 85
Bradpole. Dors —3H 13
Bradshaw. G Man —3F 91
Bradstone. Devn —4D 11
Bradwall Green. Ches —4B 84
Bradway. S Yor —3H 85
Bradwell. Derbs —2F 85
Bradwell. Essx —3B 54
Bradwell. Mil —2G 51
Bradwell. Norf —5H 79
Bradwell-on-Sea. Essx —5D 54
Bradwell Waterside. Essx —5C 54
Bradworthy. Devn —1D 10
Brae. High —5C 162
Brae. Shet —5E 173
Braeantra. High —1H 157
Braefield. High —5G 157
Braefindon. High —3A 158
Braegrum. Per —1C 136
Braehead. Ang —3F 145
Braehead. Dum —4B 110
Braehead. S Lan —1H 117
(nr. Coalburn)
Braehead. S Lan —4C 128
(nr. Forth)
Braehoulland. Shet —4D 173
Braemar. Aber —4F 151
Braemore. High —5C 168
(nr. Dunbeath)
Braemore. High —1D 156
(nr. Ullapool)
Brae of Achnahaird. High —2E 163
Brae Roy Lodge. High —4F 149
Braeside. Aber —5G 161
Braeside. Inv —2D 126
Braes of Coul. Ang —3B 144
Braeswick. Orkn —4F 172
Braetongue. High —3F 167
Braeval. Stir —3E 135
Braevallich. Arg —3G 133
Braewick. Shet —6E 173
Brafferton. Darl —2F 105
Brafferton. N Yor —2G 99
Brafield-on-the-Green. Nptn —5F 63
Bragar. W Isl —3E 171
Bragbury End. Herts —3C 52
Bragleenbeg. Arg —1G 133
Braichmelyn. Gwyn —4F 81
Braides. Lanc —4D 96
Braidwood. S Lan —5B 128
Braigo. Arg —3A 124
Brailsford. Derbs —1G 73
Braintree. Essx —3A 54
Braiseworth. Suff —3D 66
Braishfield. Hants —4B 24
Braithwaite. Cumb —2D 102
Braithwaite. S Yor —3G 93
Braithwaite. W Yor —5C 98
Braithwell. S Yor —1C 86
Brakefield Green. Norf —5C 78
Bramber. W Sus —4C 26
Brambledown. Kent —3D 40
Brambridge. Hants —4C 24
Bramcote. Notts —2C 74
Bramcote. Warw —2B 62
Bramdean. Hants —4E 24
Bramerton. Norf —5E 79
Bramfield. Herts —4C 52
Bramfield. Suff —3F 67
Bramford. Suff —1E 54
Bramhall. G Man —2C 84
Bramham. W Yor —5G 99
Bramhope. W Yor —5E 99
Bramley. Hants —1E 25
Bramley. S Yor —1B 86
Bramley. Surr —1B 26
Bramley. W Yor —1C 92
Bramley Green. Hants —1E 25
Bramley Head. N Yor —4D 98
Bramley Vale. Derbs —4B 86
Bramling. Kent —5G 41
Brampford Speke. Devn —3C 12
Brampton. Cambs —3B 64
Brampton. Cumb —2H 103
(nr. Appleby)
Brampton. Cumb —3G 113
(nr. Carlisle)
Brampton. Linc —3F 87
Brampton. Norf —3E 78
Brampton. S Yor —4E 93
Brampton. Suff —2G 67
Brampton Abbotts. Here —3B 48
Brampton Ash. Nptn —2E 63
Brampton Bryan. Here —3F 59
Brampton en le Morthen. S Yor —2B 86
Bramshall. Staf —2E 73
Bramshaw. Hants —1A 16
Bramshill. Hants —5F 37
Bramshott. Hants —3G 25
Branault. High —2G 139
Brancaster. Norf —1G 77
Brancaster Staithe. Norf —1G 77
Brancepeth. Dur —1F 105
Branch End. Nmbd —3D 114
Branchill. Mor —3E 159
Brand End. Linc —1C 76
Branderburgh. Mor —1G 159
Brandesburton. E Yor —5F 101
Brandeston. Suff —4E 67
Brand Green. Glos —3C 48
Brandhill. Shrp —3G 59
Brandis Corner. Devn —2E 11
Brandish Street. Som —2C 20
Brandiston. Norf —3D 78
Brandon. Dur —1F 105
Brandon. Linc —1G 75
Brandon. Nmbd —3E 121
Brandon. Suff —2G 65
Brandon. Warw —3B 62
Brandon Bank. Cambs —2F 65
Brandon Creek. Norf —1F 65
Brandon Parva. Norf —5C 78
Brandsby. N Yor —2H 99
Brandy Wharf. Linc —1H 87
Brane. Corn —4B 4
Bran End. Essx —3G 53
Branksome. Pool —3F 15
Bransbury. Hants —2C 24
Bransby. Linc —3G 87
Branscombe. Devn —4E 13
Bransford. Worc —5B 60
Bransgore. Hants —3G 15
Bransholme. Hull —1D 94
Bransley. Shrp —3A 60
Branston. Leics —3F 75
Branston. Linc —4H 87
Branston. Staf —3G 73
Branston Booths. Linc —4H 87
Branstone. IOW —4D 16
Bransty. Cumb —3A 102
Brant Broughton. Linc —5G 87
Brantham. Suff —2E 54
Branthwaite. Cumb —1D 102
(nr. Caldbeck)
Branthwaite. Cumb —2B 102
(nr. Workington)
Brantingham. E Yor —1C 94
Branton. Nmbd —3E 121
Branton. S Yor —4G 93
Branton Green. N Yor —3G 99
Branxholme. Scot —3G 119
Branxton. Nmbd —1C 120
Brassington. Derbs —5G 85
Brasted. Kent —5F 39
Brasted Chart. Kent —5F 39
Bratch, The. Staf —1C 60
Brathens. Aber —4D 152
Bratoft. Linc —4D 88
Brattleby. Linc —2G 87
Bratton. Telf —4A 72
Bratton. Wilts —1E 23
Bratton Clovelly. Devn —3E 11
Bratton Fleming. Devn —3G 19
Bratton Seymour. Som —4B 22
Braughing. Herts —3D 53
Braulen Lodge. High —5E 157
Braunston. Nptn —4C 62
Braunston. Rut —5F 75
Braunstone. Leics —5C 74
Braunton. Devn —3E 19
Brawby. N Yor —2B 100
Brawl. High —2A 168
Brawlbin. High —3C 168
Bray. Wind —3A 38
Braybrooke. Nptn —2E 63
Brayford. Devn —3G 19
Bray Shop. Corn —5D 10
Braystones. Cumb —4B 102
Brayton. N Yor —1G 93
Bray Wick. Wind —4G 37
Brazacott. Corn —3C 10
Brea. Corn —5A 6
Breach. W Sus —2F 17
Breachwood Green. Herts —3B 52
Breacleit. W Isl —4D 171
Breaden Heath. Shrp —2G 71
Breadsall. Derbs —1A 74
Breadstone. Glos —5C 48
Breage. Corn —4D 4
Breakachy. High —4G 157
Bream. Glos —5B 48
Breamore. Hants —1G 15
Bream's Meend. Glos —5B 48
Brean. Som —1F 21
Breanais. W Isl —5B 171

Brynteg—Calverhall

Brynteg. IOA —2D 81
Brynteg. Wrex —5F 83
Brynygwenyn. Mon —4G 47
Bryn-y-maen. Cnwy —3H 81
Buaile nam Bodach. W Isl —8C 170
Bualintur. High —1C 146
Bubbenhall. Warw —3A 62
Bubwith. E Yor —1H 93
Buccleuch. Scot —3F 119
Buchanan Smithy. Stir —1F 127
Buchanhaven. Aber —4H 161
Buchanty. Per —1B 136
Buchany. Stir —3G 135
Buchley. E Dun —2G 127
Buchlyvie. Stir —4E 135
Buckabank. Cumb —5E 113
Buckden. Cambs —4A 64
Buckden. N Yor —2B 98
Buckenham. Norf —5F 79
Buckerell. Devn —2E 13
Buckfast. Devn —2D 8
Buckfastleigh. Devn —2D 8
Buckhaven. Fife —4F 137
Buckholm. Scot —1G 119
Buckholt. Here —4A 48
Buckhorn Weston. Dors —4C 22
Buckhurst Hill. Essx —1F 39
Buckie. Mor —2B 160
Buckingham. Buck —2E 51
Buckland. Buck —4G 51
Buckland. Devn —4C 8
Buckland. Glos —2F 49
Buckland. Here —5H 59
Buckland. Herts —2D 52
Buckland. Kent —1H 29
Buckland. Oxon —2B 36
Buckland. Surr —5D 38
Buckland Brewer. Devn —4E 19
Buckland Common. Buck —5H 51
Buckland Dinham. Som —1C 22
Buckland Filleigh. Devn —2E 11
Buckland in the Moor. Devn —5H 11
Buckland Monachorum. Corn —2A 8
Buckland Newton. Dors —2B 14
Buckland Ripers. Dors —4B 14
Buckland St Mary. Som —1F 13
Buckland-tout-Saints. Devn —4D 8
Bucklebury. W Ber —4D 36
Bucklegate. Linc —2C 76
Buckleigh. Devn —4E 19
Bucklers Hard. Hants —3C 16
Bucklesham. Suff —1F 55
Buckley. Flin —4E 83
Buckley Green. Warw —4F 61
Buckley Hill. Mers —1F 83
Bucklow Hill. Ches —2B 84
Buckminster. Leics —3F 75
Bucknall. Linc —4A 88
Bucknall. Stoke —1D 72
Bucknell. Oxon —3D 50
Bucknell. Shrp —3F 59
Buckpool. Mor —2B 160
Bucksburn. Aber C —3F 153
Buck's Cross. Devn —4D 18
Bucks Green. W Sus —2B 26
Bucks Hill. Herts —5A 52
Bucks Horn Oak. Hants —2G 25
Buck's Mills. Devn —4D 18
Buckton. E Yor —2F 101
Buckton. Here —3F 59
Buckton. Nmbd —1E 121
Buckton Vale. G Man —4H 91
Buckworth. Cambs —3A 64
Budby. Notts —4D 86
Bude. Corn —2C 10
Budge's Shop. Corn —3H 7
Budlake. Devn —2C 12
Budle. Nmbd —1F 121
Budleigh Salterton. Devn —4D 12
Budock Water. Corn —5B 6
Buerton. Ches —1A 72
Buffler's Holt. Buck —2E 51
Bugbrooke. Nptn —5D 62
Buglawton. Ches —4C 84
Bugle. Corn —3E 6
Bugthorpe. E Yor —4B 100
Buildwas. Shrp —5A 72
Builth Road. Powy —5C 58
Builth Wells. Powy —5C 58
Bulbourne. Herts —4H 51
Bulby. Linc —3H 75
Bulcote. Notts —1D 74
Buldoo. High —2C 168
Bulford. Wilts —2G 23
Bulford Camp. Wilts —2G 23
Bulkeley. Ches —5H 83
Bulkington. Warw —2A 62
Bulkington. Wilts —1E 23
Bulkworthy. Devn —1D 11
Bullamoor. N Yor —5A 106
Bull Bay. IOA —1D 80
Bullbridge. Derbs —5A 86
Bullgill. Cumb —1B 102
Bull Hill. Hants —3B 16
Bullinghope. Here —2A 48
Bull's Green. Herts —4C 52
Bullwood. Arg —2C 126
Bulmer. Essx —1B 54
Bulmer. N Yor —3A 100
Bulmer Tye. Essx —2B 54
Bulphan. Thur —2H 39
Bulverhythe. E Sus —5B 28
Bulwark. Aber —4G 161
Bulwell. Not C —1C 74
Bulwick. Nptn —1G 63
Bumble's Green. Essx —5E 53
Bun Abhainn Eadarra. W Isl —7D 171
Bunacaimb. High —5E 147
Bun a Mhuillinn. W Isl —7C 170
Bunarkaig. High —5D 148
Bunbury. Ches —5H 83
Bunchrew. High —4A 158
Bundalloch. High —1A 148
Buness. Shet —1H 173
Bunessan. Arg —1A 132
Bungay. Suff —2F 67
Bunkegivie. High —2H 149
Bunker's Hill. Cambs —5D 76
Bunkers Hill. Linc —5B 88
Bunker's Hill. Suff —5H 79
Bunloit. High —1H 149
Bunnahabhain. Arg —2C 124
Bunny. Notts —3C 74
Bunoich. High —3F 149
Bunree. High —2E 141
Bunroy. High —5E 149
Buntait. High —5F 157
Buntingford. Herts —3D 52
Buntings Green. Essx —2B 54
Bunwell. Norf —1D 66
Burbage. Derbs —3E 85
Burbage. Leics —1B 62
Burbage. Wilts —5H 35
Burcher. Here —4F 59
Burchett's Green. Wind —3G 37
Burcombe. Wilts —3F 23
Burcot. Oxon —2D 36
Burcote. Shrp —1B 60
Burcott. Buck —3G 51
Burcott. Som —2A 22
Burdale. N Yor —3C 100
Burdrop. Oxon —2B 50
Bures. Suff —2C 54
Burford. Oxon —4A 50
Burford. Shrp —4H 59
Burf, The. Worc —4C 60
Burg. Arg —4E 139
Burgate Great Green. Suff —3C 66
Burgate Little Green. Suff —3C 66
Burgess Hill. W Sus —4E 27
Burgh. Suff —5E 67
Burgh by Sands. Cumb —4E 113
Burgh Castle. Norf —5G 79
Burghclere. Hants —5C 36
Burghead. Mor —2F 159
Burghfield. W Ber —5E 37
Burghfield Common. W Ber —5E 37
Burghfield Hill. W Ber —5E 37
Burgh Heath. Surr —5D 38
Burghill. Here —1H 47
Burgh le Marsh. Linc —4E 89
Burgh Muir. Aber —2E 153
Burgh next Aylsham. Norf —3E 78
Burgh on Bain. Linc —2B 88
Burgh St Margaret. Norf —4G 79
Burgh St Peter. Norf —1G 67
Burghwallis. S Yor —3F 93
Burgie. Mor —3E 159
Burham. Kent —4B 40
Buriton. Hants —4F 25
Burland. Ches —5A 84
Burland. Shet —8E 173
Burlawn. Corn —2D 6
Burleigh. Brac —3A 38
Burleigh. Glos —5D 48
Burlescombe. Devn —1D 12
Burleston. Dors —3C 14
Burlestone. Devn —4E 9
Burley. Hants —2H 15
Burley. Rut —4F 75
Burley. W Yor —1C 92
Burley Gate. Here —1A 48
Burley in Wharfedale. W Yor —5D 98
Burley Street. Hants —2H 15
Burley Woodhead. W Yor —5D 98
Burlingjobb. Powy —5E 59
Burlton. Shrp —3G 71
Burmantofts. W Yor —1D 92
Burmarsh. Kent —2F 29
Burmington. Warw —2A 50
Burn. N Yor —2F 93
Burnage. G Man —1C 84
Burnaston. Derbs —2G 73
Burnbanks. Cumb —3G 103
Burnby. E Yor —5C 100
Burncross. S Yor —1H 85
Burneside. Cumb —5G 103
Burness. Orkn —3F 172
Burneston. N Yor —1F 99
Burnett. Bath —5B 34
Burnfoot. Per —3B 136
Burnfoot. Scot —3H 119 (nr. Hawick)
Burnfoot. Scot —3G 119 (nr. Roberton)
Burngreave. S Yor —2A 86
Burnham. Buck —2A 38
Burnham. N Lin —3D 94
Burnham Deepdale. Norf —1H 77
Burnham Green. Herts —4C 52
Burnham Market. Norf —1H 77
Burnham Norton. Norf —1H 77
Burnham-on-Crouch. Essx —1D 40
Burnham-on-Sea. Som —2G 21
Burnham Overy Staithe. Norf —1H 77
Burnham Overy Town. Norf —1H 77
Burnham Thorpe. Norf —1A 78
Burnhaven. Aber —4H 161
Burnhead. Dum —5A 118
Burnhervie. Aber —2E 153
Burnhill Green. Staf —5B 72
Burnhope. Dur —5E 115
Burnhouse. N Ayr —4E 127
Burniston. N Yor —5H 107
Burnlee. W Yor —4B 92
Burnley. Lanc —1G 91
Burnleydam. Wrex —1A 72
Burnmouth. Scot —3F 131
Burn Naze. Lanc —5C 96
Burn of Cambus. Stir —3G 135
Burnopfield. Dur —4E 115
Burnsall. N Yor —3C 98
Burnside. Ang —3E 145
Burnside. E Ayr —3E 117
Burnside. Per —3D 136
Burnside. Shet —4D 173
Burnside. S Lan —4H 127
Burnside. W Lot —2D 129 (nr. Broxburn)
Burnside. W Lot —2D 128 (nr. Winchburgh)
Burntcommon. Surr —5B 38
Burntheath. Derbs —2G 73
Burnt Heath. Essx —3D 54
Burnt Hill. W Ber —4D 36
Burnt Houses. Dur —2E 105
Burntisland. Fife —1F 129
Burnt Oak. G Lon —1D 38
Burnton. E Ayr —4D 117
Burntstalk. Norf —2G 77
Burntwood. Staf —5E 73
Burntwood Green. Staf —5E 73
Burnt Yates. N Yor —3E 99
Burnwynd. Edin —3E 129
Burpham. Surr —5B 38
Burpham. W Sus —5B 26
Burradon. Nmbd —4D 121
Burradon. Tyne —2F 115
Burrafirth. Shet —1H 173
Burragarth. Shet —1G 173
Burras. Corn —5A 6
Burraton. Corn —3A 8
Burravoe. Shet —5E 173 (on Mainland)
Burravoe. Shet —4G 173 (on Yell)
Burray Village. Orkn —8D 172
Burrells. Cumb —3H 103
Burrelton. Per —5A 144
Burridge. Devn —2G 13
Burridge. Hants —1D 16
Burrigill. High —5E 169
Burrill. N Yor —1E 99
Burringham. N Lin —4B 94
Burrington. Devn —1G 11
Burrington. Here —3G 59
Burrington. N Som —1H 21
Burrough End. Cambs —5F 65
Burrough Green. Cambs —5F 65
Burrough on the Hill. Leics —4E 75
Burroughston. Orkn —5E 172
Burrow. Devn —4D 12
Burrow. Som —2C 20
Burrowbridge. Som —4G 21
Burrowhill. Surr —4A 38
Burry. Swan —3D 30
Burry Green. Swan —3D 30
Burry Port. Carm —5E 45
Burscough. Lanc —3C 90
Burscough Bridge. Lanc —3C 90
Bursea. E Yor —1B 94
Burshill. E Yor —5E 101
Bursledon. Hants —2C 16
Burslem. Stoke —1C 72
Burstall. Suff —1D 54
Burstock. Dors —2H 13
Burston. Devn —2H 11
Burston. Norf —2D 66
Burston. Staf —2D 72
Burstow. Surr —1E 27
Burstwick. E Yor —2F 95
Burtersett. N Yor —1A 98
Burtholme. Cumb —3G 113
Burthorpe. Suff —4G 65
Burthwaite. Cumb —5F 113
Burtle. Som —2H 21
Burtoft. Linc —2B 76
Burton. Ches —4H 83 (nr. Kelsall)
Burton. Ches —3F 83 (nr. Neston)
Burton. Dors —3G 15 (nr. Christchurch)
Burton. Dors —3B 14 (nr. Dorchester)
Burton. Linc —3G 87
Burton. Nmbd —1F 121
Burton. Pemb —4D 43
Burton. Som —2E 21
Burton. Wilts —4D 34 (nr. Chippenham)
Burton. Wilts —3D 22 (nr. Warminster)
Burton. Wrex —5F 83
Burton Agnes. E Yor —3F 101
Burton Bradstock. Dors —4H 13
Burton Coggles. Linc —3G 75
Burton Constable. E Yor —1E 95
Burton Corner. Linc —1C 76
Burton End. Cambs —1G 53
Burton End. Essx —3F 53
Burton Fleming. E Yor —2E 101
Burton Green. W Mid —3G 61
Burton Green. Wrex —5F 83
Burton Hastings. Warw —2B 62
Burton-in-Kendal. Cumb —2E 97
Burton in Lonsdale. N Yor —2F 97
Burton Joyce. Notts —1D 74
Burton Latimer. Nptn —3G 63
Burton Lazars. Leics —4E 75
Burton Leonard. N Yor —3F 99
Burton on the Wolds. Leics —3C 74
Burton Overy. Leics —1D 62
Burton Pedwardine. Linc —1A 76
Burton Pidsea. E Yor —1F 95
Burton Salmon. N Yor —2E 93
Burton's Green. Essx —3B 54
Burton Stather. N Lin —3B 94
Burton upon Stather. N Lin —3B 94
Burton upon Trent. Staf —3G 73
Burton Wolds. Leics —3D 74
Burtonwood. Warr —1H 83
Burwardsley. Ches —5H 83
Burwarton. Shrp —2A 60
Burwash. E Sus —3A 28
Burwash Common. E Sus —3H 27
Burwash Weald. E Sus —3A 28
Burwell. Cambs —4E 65
Burwell. Linc —3C 88
Burwen. IOA —1D 80
Burwick. Orkn —9D 172
Bury. Cambs —2B 64
Bury. G Man —3G 91
Bury. Som —4C 20
Bury. W Sus —4B 26
Bury End. Worc —2F 49
Bury Green. Herts —3E 53
Bury Hill. S Glo —3C 34
Bury St Edmunds. Suff —4A 66
Burythorpe. N Yor —3B 100
Busbridge. Surr —1A 26
Busby. E Ren —4G 127
Busby. Per —1C 136
Buscot. Oxon —2H 35
Bush. Corn —2C 10
Bush Bank. Here —5G 59
Bushbury. W Mid —5D 72
Bushby. Leics —5D 74
Bushey. Dors —4E 15
Bushey. Herts —1C 38
Bushey Heath. Herts —1C 38
Bush Green. Norf —1C 66 (nr. Attleborough)
Bush Green. Norf —2E 66 (nr. Harleston)
Bush Green. Suff —5B 66
Bushley. Worc —2D 49
Bushley Green. Worc —2D 48
Bushmead. Beds —4A 64
Bushmoor. Shrp —2G 59
Bushton. Wilts —4F 35
Bushy Common. Norf —4B 78
Busk. Cumb —5H 113
Buslingthorpe. Linc —2H 87
Bussage. Glos —5D 49
Bussex. Som —3G 21
Busta. Shet —5E 173
Bustard Green. Essx —3G 53
Butcher's Cross. E Sus —3G 27
Butcombe. N Som —5A 34
Bute Town. Cphy —5E 46
Butleigh. Som —3A 22
Butleigh Wootton. Som —3A 22
Butlers Marston. Warw —5H 61
Butley. Suff —5F 67
Butley High Corner. Suff —1G 55
Butterburn. Cumb —2H 113
Buttercrambe. N Yor —4B 100
Butterknowle. Dur —2E 105
Butterleigh. Devn —2C 12
Buttermere. Cumb —3C 102
Buttermere. Wilts —5B 36
Buttershaw. W Yor —2B 92
Butterstone. Per —4H 143
Butterton. Staf —5E 85 (nr. Leek)
Butterton. Staf —1C 72 (nr. Stoke-on-Trent)
Butterwick. Dur —2A 106
Butterwick. Linc —1C 76
Butterwick. N Yor —2B 100 (nr. Malton)
Butterwick. N Yor —2D 101 (nr. Weaverthorpe)
Butteryhaugh. Nmbd —5A 120
Butt Green. Ches —5A 84
Buttington. Powy —5E 71
Buttonbridge. Shrp —3B 60
Buttonoak. Shrp —3B 60
Buttsash. Hants —2C 16
Butt's Green. Essx —5A 54
Butt Yeats. Lanc —3E 97
Buxhall. Suff —5C 66
Buxted. E Sus —3F 27
Buxton. Derbs —3E 85
Buxton. Norf —3E 79
Buxworth. Derbs —2E 85
Bwcle. Flin —4E 83
Bwlch. Powy —3E 47
Bwlchderwin. Gwyn —1D 68
Bwlchgwyn. Wrex —5E 83
Bwlch-Llan. Cdgn —5E 57
Bwlchnewydd. Carm —3D 44
Bwlchtocyn. Gwyn —3C 68
Bwlch-y-cibau. Powy —4D 70
Bwlchyddar. Powy —3D 70
Bwlch-y-fadfa. Cdgn —1E 45
Bwlch-y-ffridd. Powy —1C 58
Bwlch y Garreg. Powy —1C 58
Bwlch-y-groes. Pemb —1G 43
Bwlch-yr-haiarn. Cnwy —5G 81
Bwlch-y-sarnau. Powy —3C 58
Bybrook. Kent —1E 28
Byermoor. Tyne —4E 115
Byers Garth. Dur —5G 115
Byers Green. Dur —1F 105
Byfield. Nptn —5C 62
Byfleet. Surr —4B 38
Byford. Here —1G 47
Bygrave. Herts —2C 52
Byker. Tyne —3F 115
Byland Abbey. N Yor —2H 99
Bylchau. Cnwy —4B 82
Byley. Ches —4B 84
Bynea. Carm —3E 31
Byram. N Yor —2E 93
Byrness. Nmbd —4B 120
Bythorn. Cambs —3H 63
Byton. Here —4F 59
Bywell. Nmbd —3D 114
Byworth. W Sus —3A 26

Cabharstadh. W Isl —6F 171
Cabourne. Linc —4E 95
Cabrach. Arg —3C 124
Cabrach. Mor —1A 152
Cabus. Lanc —5D 97
Cadbury. Devn —2C 12
Cadder. E Dun —2H 127
Caddington. Beds —4A 52
Caddonfoot. Scot —1G 119
Cadeby. Leics —5B 74
Cadeby. S Yor —4F 93
Cadeleigh. Devn —2C 12
Cade Street. E Sus —3H 27
Cadgwith. Corn —5E 5
Cadham. Fife —3E 137
Cadishead. G Man —1B 84
Cadley. Lanc —1D 90
Cadley. Wilts —1H 23 (nr. Ludgershall)
Cadley. Wilts —5H 35 (nr. Marlborough)
Cadmore End. Buck —2F 37
Cadnam. Hants —1B 16
Cadney. N Lin —4D 94
Cadole. Flin —4E 82
Cadoxton-Juxta-Neath. Neat —2A 32
Cadwell. Herts —2B 52
Cadwst. Den —2C 70
Cadzow. S Lan —4A 128
Caeathro. Gwyn —4E 81
Caehopkin. Powy —4B 46
Caenby. Linc —2H 87
Caenn-na-Cleithe. W Isl —8D 171
Caerau. B'End —2B 32
Caerau. Card —4E 33
Cae'r-bont. Powy —4B 46
Cae'r-bryn. Carm —4F 45
Caerdeon. Gwyn —4F 69
Caerdydd. Card —4E 33
Caerfarchell. Pemb —2B 42
Caerffili. Cphy —3E 33
Caerfyrddin. Carm —4E 45
Caergeiliog. IOA —3C 80
Caergwrle. Flin —5F 83
Caergybi. IOA —2B 80
Caerlaverock. Per —2A 136
Caerleon. Newp —2G 33
Caerlleon. Carm —2G 43
Caerllion. Newp —2G 33
Caernarfon. Gwyn —4D 81
Caerphilly. Cphy —3E 33
Caersws. Powy —1C 58
Caerwedros. Cdgn —5C 56
Caerwent. Mon —2H 33
Caerwys. Flin —3D 82
Caigenhouses. Arg —3D 124
Caim. IOA —2F 81
Caio. Carm —2G 45
Cairinis. W Isl —2D 170
Cairisiadar. W Isl —4C 171
Cairminis. W Isl —9C 171
Cairnbaan. Arg —4F 133
Cairnbulg. Aber —2H 161
Cairncross. Ang —1D 145
Cairndow. Arg —2A 134
Cairness. Aber —2H 161
Cairneyhill. Fife —1D 128
Cairngarroch. Dum —4F 109
Cairnhill. Aber —5D 160
Cairnie. Aber —4B 160
Cairnorrie. Aber —4F 161
Cairnryan. Dum —3F 109
Cairntable. E Ayr —3D 116
Cairnston. Orkn —6B 172
Caister-on-Sea. Norf —4H 79
Caister St Edmund. Norf —5E 79
Caistor. Linc —4E 95
Caistron. Nmbd —4D 121
Cakebole. Worc —3C 60
Cake Street. Suff —3F 65
Calais Street. Suff —1C 54
Calanais. W Isl —4E 171
Calbost. W Isl —6G 171
Calbourne. IOW —4C 16
Calceby. Linc —3C 88
Calcot. Glos —4F 49
Calcot Row. W Ber —4E 37
Calcott. Kent —4F 41
Calcott. Shrp —4G 71
Caldback. Shet —1H 173
Caldbeck. Cumb —1E 102
Caldbergh. N Yor —1C 98
Caldecote. Cambs —5C 64 (nr. Cambridge)
Caldecote. Cambs —2A 64 (nr. Peterborough)
Caldecote. Herts —2C 52
Caldecote. Warw —1A 62
Caldecott. Nptn —4G 63
Caldecott. Oxon —2C 36
Caldecott. Rut —1F 63
Calderbank. N Lan —3A 128
Calder Bridge. Cumb —4B 102
Calderbrook. G Man —3H 91
Caldercruix. N Lan —3B 128
Calder Grove. W Yor —3D 92
Calder Mains. High —3C 168
Caldermill. S Lan —5H 127
Calder Vale. Lanc —5E 97
Calderwood. S Lan —4H 127
Caldescote. Nptn —5D 62
Caldicot. Mon —3H 33
Caldwell. N Yor —3E 105
Caldy. Mers —2E 83
Calebrack. Cumb —1E 103
Caledfwlch. Carm —3G 45
Calford Green. Suff —1G 53
Calfsound. Orkn —4E 172
Calgary. Arg —3E 139
Califer. Mor —3E 159
California. Falk —2C 128
California. Norf —4H 79
California. Suff —1E 55
Calke. Derbs —3A 74
Callakille. High —3F 155
Callaly. Nmbd —4E 121
Callander. Stir —3F 135
Callaughton. Shrp —1A 60
Callendoun. Arg —1E 127
Callestick. Corn —3B 6
Calligarry. High —3E 147
Callington. Corn —2H 7
Callingwood. Staf —3F 73
Callow. Here —2H 47
Callowell. Glos —5D 48
Callow End. Worc —1D 48
Callow Hill. Wilts —3F 35
Callow Hill. Worc —3B 60 (nr. Bewdley)
Callow Hill. Worc —4E 61 (nr. Redditch)
Calmore. Hants —1B 16
Calmsden. Glos —5F 49
Calne. Wilts —4E 35
Calow. Derbs —3B 86
Calshot. Hants —2C 16
Calstock. Corn —2A 8
Calstone Wellington. Wilts —5F 35
Calthorpe. Norf —2D 78
Calthorpe Street. Norf —3G 79
Calthwaite. Cumb —5F 113
Calton. N Yor —4B 98
Calveley. Ches —5H 83
Calver. Derbs —3G 85
Calverhall. Shrp —2A 72

Calverleigh—Chapel Brampton

Calverleigh. Devn —1C 12
Calverley. W Yor —1C 92
Calvert. Buck —3E 51
Calverton. Mil —2F 51
Calverton. Notts —1D 74
Calvine. Per —2F 143
Calvo. Cumb —4C 112
Cam. Glos —2C 34
Camaghael. High —1F 141
Camas-luinie. High —1B 148
Camasnacroise. High —3C 140
Camastianavaig. High —5E 155
Camasunary. High —2D 146
Camault Muir. High —4H 157
Camb. Shet —2G 173
Camber. E Sus —4D 28
Camberley. Surr —5G 37
Camberwell. G Lon —3E 39
Camblesforth. N Yor —2G 93
Cambo. Nmbd —1D 114
Cambois. Nmbd —1G 115
Camborne. Corn —5A 6
Cambourne. Cambs —5C 64
Cambridge. Cambs —5D 64
Cambridge. Glos —5C 48
Cambridge Airport. Cambs —5D 65
Cambrose. Corn —4A 6
Cambus. Clac —4A 136
Cambusbarron. Stir —4G 135
Cambuskenneth. Stir —4H 135
Cambuslang. S Lan —3H 127
Cambusnethan. N Lan —4B 128
Cambus o'May. Aber —4B 152
Camden Town. G Lon —2D 39
Cameley. Bath —1B 22
Camelford. Corn —4B 10
Camelon. Falk —1B 128
Camelsdale. Surr —2A 26
Camer's Green. Worc —2C 48
Camerton. Bath —1B 22
Camerton. Cumb —1B 102
Camerton. E Yor —2F 95
Camghouran. Per —3C 142
Cammachmore. Aber —4G 153
Cammeringham. Linc —2G 87
Camore. High —4E 165
Campbelton. N Ayr —4C 126
Campbeltown. Arg —3B 122
Campbeltown Airport. Arg —3A 122
Cample. Dum —5B 118
Campmuir. Per —5B 144
Campsall. S Yor —3F 93
Campsea Ashe. Suff —5F 67
Camps End. Cambs —1G 53
Camp, The. Glos —5E 49
Campton. Beds —2B 52
Camptoun. E Lot —2B 130
Camptown. Scot —3A 120
Camrose. Pemb —3D 42
Camserney. Per —4F 143
Camster. High —4E 169
Camus Croise. High —2E 147
Camusdarach. High —4E 147
Camusnagaul. High —1E 141 (nr. Fort William)
Camusnagaul. High —5E 163 (nr. Loch Broom)
Camusteel. High —4G 155
Camusterrach. High —4G 155
Camusvrachan. Per —4D 142
Canada. Hants —1A 16
Canadia. E Sus —4B 28
Canaston Bridge. Pemb —3E 43
Candlesby. Linc —4D 88
Candle Street. Suff —3C 66
Candy Mill. S Lan —5D 128
Cane End. Oxon —4E 37
Canewdon. Essx —1C 40
Canford Cliffs. Pool —4F 15
Canford Magna. Pool —3F 15
Cangate. Norf —3F 79
Canham's Green. Suff —4C 66
Canholes. Derbs —3E 85
Canisbay. High —1F 169
Canley. W Mid —3H 61
Cann. Dors —4D 22
Cann Common. Dors —4D 23
Cannich. High —5F 157
Cannington. Som —3F 21
Cannock. Staf —4D 73
Cannock Wood. Staf —4E 73
Canonbie. Dum —2E 113
Canon Bridge. Here —1H 47
Canon Frome. Here —1B 48
Canon Pyon. Here —1H 47
Canons Ashby. Nptn —5C 62
Canonstown. Corn —3C 4
Canterbury. Kent —5F 41
Cantley. Norf —5F 79
Cantley. S Yor —4G 93
Cantlop. Shrp —5H 71
Canton. Card —4E 33
Cantray. High —4B 158
Cantraybruich. High —4B 158
Cantraywood. High —4B 158
Cantsdam. Fife —4D 136
Cantsfield. Lanc —2F 97
Canvey Island. Essx —2B 40
Canwick. Linc —4G 87
Canworthy Water. Corn —3C 10
Caol. High —1F 141
Caolas. W Isl —9B 170
Caolas Liubharsaigh. W Isl —4D 170
Caolas Scalpaigh. W Isl —8E 171
Caolas Stocinis. W Isl —8D 171
Caoles. Arg —4B 138
Caol Ila. Arg —3C 124
Capel. Kent —1H 27
Capel. Surr —1C 26
Capel Bangor. Cdgn —2F 57
Capel Betws Lleucu. Cdgn —5F 57
Capel Coch. IOA —2D 80
Capel Curig. Cnwy —5G 81
Capel Cynon. Cdgn —1D 45
Capel Dewi. Carm —3E 45
Capel Dewi. Cdgn —2F 57 (nr. Aberystwyth)
Capel Dewi. Cdgn —1E 45 (nr. Llandyssul)
Capel Garmon. Cnwy —5H 81
Capel Green. Suff —1G 55
Capel Gwyn. IOA —3C 80
Capel Gwynfe. Carm —3H 45
Capel Hendre. Carm —4F 45
Capel Isaac. Carm —3F 45
Capel Iwan. Carm —1G 43
Capel-le-Ferne. Kent —2G 29
Capel Llanilterne. Card —4D 32
Capel Mawr. IOA —3D 80
Capel Newydd. Pemb —1G 43
Capel St Andrew. Suff —1G 55
Capel St Mary. Suff —2D 54
Capel Seion. Carm —4F 45
Capel Seion. Cdgn —3F 57
Capel Uchaf. Gwyn —1D 68
Capel-y-ffin. Powy —2F 47
Capenhurst. Ches —3F 83
Capernwray. Lanc —2E 97
Capheaton. Nmbd —1D 114
Cappercleuch. Scot —2E 119
Capplegill. Dum —3D 118
Capton. Devn —3E 9
Capton. Som —3D 20
Caputh. Per —5H 143
Caradon Town. Corn —5C 10
Carbis Bay. Corn —3C 4
Carbost. High —5C 154 (nr. Loch Harport)
Carbost. High —4D 154 (nr. Portree)
Carbrook. S Yor —2A 86
Carbrooke. Norf —5B 78
Carburton. Notts —3D 86
Carcluie. S Ayr —3C 116
Car Colston. Notts —1E 74
Carcroft. S Yor —4F 93
Cardenden. Fife —4E 136
Cardeston. Shrp —4F 71
Cardewless. Cumb —4E 113
Cardiff. Card —4E 33
Cardiff Airport. V Glam —5D 32
Cardigan. Cdgn —1B 44
Cardinal's Green. Cambs —1G 53
Cardington. Beds —1A 52
Cardington. Shrp —1H 59
Cardinham. Corn —2F 7
Cardno. Aber —2G 161
Cardow. Mor —4F 159
Cardross. Arg —2E 127
Cardurnock. Cumb —4C 112
Careby. Linc —4H 75
Careston. Ang —2E 145
Carew. Pemb —4E 43
Carew Cheriton. Pemb —4E 43
Carew Newton. Pemb —4E 43
Carey. Here —2A 48
Carfin. N Lan —4A 128
Carfrae. Scot —4B 130
Cargate Green. Norf —4F 79
Cargenbridge. Dum —2G 111
Cargill. Per —5A 144
Cargo. Cumb —4E 113
Cargreen. Corn —2A 8
Carham. Nmbd —1B 120
Carhampton. Som —2D 20
Carharrack. Corn —4B 6
Carie. Per —3D 142 (nr. Loch Rannah)
Carie. Per —5D 142 (nr. Loch Tay)
Carisbrooke. IOW —4C 16
Cark. Cumb —2C 96
Carkeel. Corn —2A 8
Carlabhagh. W Isl —3E 171
Carland Cross. Corn —3C 6
Carlbury. Darl —3F 105
Carlby. Linc —4H 75
Carlecotes. S Yor —4B 92
Carleen. Corn —4D 4
Carlesmoor. N Yor —2D 98
Carleton. Cumb —4F 113 (nr. Carlisle)
Carleton. Cumb —4B 102 (nr. Egremont)
Carleton. Cumb —2G 103 (nr. Penrith)
Carleton. Lanc —1B 90
Carleton. N Yor —5B 98
Carleton. W Yor —2E 93
Carleton Forehoe. Norf —5C 78
Carleton Rode. Norf —1D 66
Carleton St Peter. Norf —5F 79
Carlidnack. Corn —4E 5
Carlingcott. Bath —1B 22
Carlin How. Red C —3E 107
Carlisle. Cumb —4E 113
Carloonan. Arg —2H 133
Carlops. Scot —4E 129
Carlton. Beds —5G 63
Carlton. Cambs —5F 65
Carlton. Leics —5A 74
Carlton. N Yor —1A 100 (nr. Helmsley)
Carlton. N Yor —1C 98 (nr. Middleham)
Carlton. N Yor —2G 93 (nr. Selby)
Carlton. Notts —1C 74
Carlton. S Yor —3D 92
Carlton. Stoc T —2A 106
Carlton. Suff —4F 67
Carlton. W Yor —2D 92
Carlton Colville. Suff —1H 67
Carlton Curlieu. Leics —1D 62
Carlton Husthwaite. N Yor —2G 99
Carlton in Cleveland. N Yor —4C 106
Carlton in Lindrick. Notts —2C 86
Carlton-le-Moorland. Linc —5G 87
Carlton Miniott. N Yor —1F 99
Carlton-on-Trent. Notts —4E 87
Carlton Scroop. Linc —1G 75
Carluke. S Lan —4B 128
Carlyon Bay. Corn —3E 7
Carmarthen. Carm —4E 45
Carmel. Carm —4F 45
Carmel. Flin —3D 82
Carmel. Gwyn —5D 81
Carmel. IOA —2C 80
Carmichael. S Lan —1B 118
Carmunnock. Glas —4H 127
Carmyle. S Lan —3H 127
Carmyllie. Ang —4E 145
Carnaby. E Yor —3F 101
Carnach. High —1C 148 (nr. Lochcarron)
Carnach. High —4E 163 (nr. Ullapool)
Carnach. Mor —4E 159
Carnach. W Isl —8E 171
Carnachy. High —3H 167
Carnain. Arg —3B 124
Carnais. W Isl —4C 171
Carnan. Arg —4B 138
Carnan. W Isl —4C 170
Carnbee. Fife —3H 137
Carnbo. Per —3C 136
Carn Brea. Corn —4A 6
Carndu. High —1A 148
Carne. Corn —5D 6
Carnell. S Ayr —1D 116
Carnforth. Lanc —2E 97
Carn-gorm. High —1B 148
Carnhedryn. Pemb —2B 42
Carnhell Green. Corn —3D 4
Carnie. Aber —3F 153
Carnkie. Corn —5B 6 (nr. Falmouth)
Carnkie. Corn —5A 6 (nr. Redruth)
Carnkief. Corn —3B 6
Carno. Powy —1B 58
Carnock. Fife —1D 128
Carnon Downs. Corn —4C 6
Carnoustie. Ang —5E 145
Carntyne. Glas —3H 127
Carn Vale. Derbs —4B 86
Carnwath. S Lan —5C 128
Carnyorth. Corn —3A 4
Carol Green. W Mid —3G 61
Carpalla. Corn —3D 6
Carperby. N Yor —1C 98
Carradale. Arg —2C 122
Carragraich. W Isl —8D 171
Carrbridge. High —1D 150
Carr Cross. Lanc —3B 90
Carreglefn. IOA —2C 80
Carrhouse. N Lin —4A 94
Carrick. Arg —4A 134
Carrick Castle. Arg —4A 134
Carrick Ho. Orkn —4E 172
Carriden. Falk —1D 128
Carrington. G Man —1B 84
Carrington. Linc —5C 88
Carrington. Midl —3G 129
Carrog. Cnwy —1G 69
Carrog. Den —1D 70
Carron. Falk —1B 128
Carron. Mor —4G 159
Carronbridge. Dum —5A 118
Carronshore. Falk —1B 128
Carrow Hill. Mon —2H 33
Carr Shield. Nmbd —5B 114
Carrutherstown. Dum —2C 112
Carrville. Dur —5G 115
Carrycoats Hall. Nmbd —2C 114
Carsaig. Arg —1C 132
Carscreugh. Dum —3H 109
Carsegowan. Dum —4B 110
Carse House. Arg —3F 125
Carseriggan. Dum —3A 110
Carsethorn. Dum —4A 112
Carshalton. G Lon —4D 38
Carsington. Derbs —5G 85
Carskiey. Arg —5A 122
Carsluith. Dum —4B 110
Carsphairn. Dum —5E 117
Carstairs. S Lan —5C 128
Carstairs Junction. S Lan —5C 128
Cartbridge. Surr —5B 38
Carterhaugh. Ang —4D 144
Carter's Clay. Hants —4B 24
Carterton. Oxon —5A 50
Carterway Heads. Nmbd —4D 114
Carthew. Corn —3E 6
Carthorpe. N Yor —1F 99
Cartington. Nmbd —4E 121
Cartland. S Lan —5B 128
Cartmel. Cumb —2C 96
Cartmel Fell. Cumb —1D 96
Cartworth. W Yor —4B 92
Carwath. Cumb —5E 112
Carway. Carm —5E 45
Carwinley. Cumb —2F 113
Cascob. Powy —4E 59
Cas-gwent. Mon —2A 34
Cash Feus. Fife —3E 136
Cashlie. Per —4B 142
Cashmoor. Dors —1E 15
Cas-Mael. Pemb —2E 43
Casnewydd. Newp —3G 33
Cassington. Oxon —4C 50
Cassop. Dur —1A 106
Castell. Cnwy —4G 81
Castell. Den —4D 82
Castell Hendre. Pemb —2E 43
Castell-nedd. Neat —2A 32
Castell Newydd Emlyn. Carm —1D 44
Castell-y-bwch. Torf —2F 33
Casterton. Cumb —1F 97
Castle. Som —2A 22
Castle Acre. Norf —4H 77
Castle Ashby. Nptn —5F 63
Castlebay. W Isl —9B 170
Castle Bolton. N Yor —5D 104
Castle Bromwich. W Mid —2F 61
Castle Bytham. Linc —4G 75
Castlebythe. Pemb —2E 43
Castle Caereinion. Powy —5D 70
Castle Camps. Cambs —1G 53
Castle Carrock. Cumb —4G 113
Castlecary. N Lan —2A 128
Castle Cary. Som —3B 22
Castle Combe. Wilts —4D 34
Castlecraig. High —2C 158
Castle Donington. Leics —3B 74
Castle Douglas. Dum —3E 111
Castle Eaton. Swin —2G 35
Castle Eden. Dur —1B 106
Castleford. W Yor —2E 93
Castle Frome. Here —1B 48
Castle Green. Surr —4A 38
Castle Green. Warw —3G 61
Castle Gresley. Derbs —4G 73
Castle Heaton. Nmbd —5F 131
Castle Hedingham. Essx —2A 54
Castle Hill. Kent —1A 28
Castlehill. Per —5B 144
Castlehill. S Lan —4B 128
Castle Hill. Suff —1E 55
Castlehill. W Dun —2E 127
Castle Kennedy. Dum —4G 109
Castle Lachlan. Arg —4H 133
Castlemartin. Pemb —5D 42
Castlemilk. Glas —4H 127
Castlemorris. Pemb —1D 42
Castlemorton. Worc —2C 48
Castle O'er. Dum —5E 119
Castle Park. N Yor —3F 107
Castlerigg. Cumb —2D 102
Castle Rising. Norf —3F 77
Castleside. Dur —5D 115
Castlethorpe. Mil —1F 51
Castleton. Aber —4F 151
Castleton. Arg —1G 125
Castleton. Derbs —2F 85
Castleton. G Man —3G 91
Castleton. Mor —1F 151
Castleton. Newp —3F 33
Castleton. N Yor —4D 107
Castleton. Per —2B 136
Castletown. Cumb —1G 103
Castletown. Dors —5B 14
Castletown. High —2D 169
Castletown. IOM —5B 108
Castletown. Tyne —4G 115
Castley. N Yor —5E 99
Caston. Norf —1B 66
Castor. Pet —1A 64
Caswell. Swan —4E 31
Catacol. N Ayr —5H 125
Catbrook. Mon —5A 48
Catchems End. Worc —3B 60
Catchgate. Dur —4E 115
Catcleugh. Nmbd —4B 120
Catcliffe. S Yor —2B 86
Catcott. Som —3G 21
Caterham. Surr —5E 39
Catfield. Norf —3F 79
Catfield Common. Norf —3F 79
Catfirth. Shet —6F 173
Catford. G Lon —3E 39
Catforth. Lanc —1C 90
Cathcart. Glas —3G 127
Cathedine. Powy —3E 47
Catherine-de-Barnes. W Mid —2F 61
Catherington. Hants —1E 17
Catherston Leweston. Dors —3G 13
Catherton. Shrp —3A 60
Catisfield. Hants —2D 16
Catlodge. High —4A 150
Catlowdy. Cumb —2F 113
Catmore. W Ber —3C 36
Caton. Devn —5A 12
Caton. Lanc —3E 97
Catrine. E Ayr —2E 117
Cat's Ash. Newp —2G 33
Catsfield. E Sus —4B 28
Catsgore. Som —4A 22
Catshill. Worc —3D 60
Cattal. N Yor —4G 99
Cattawade. Suff —2E 54
Catterall. Lanc —5E 97
Catterick. N Yor —5F 105
Catterick Bridge. N Yor —5F 105
Catterick Garrison. N Yor —5E 105
Catterlen. Cumb —1F 103
Catterline. Aber —1H 145
Catterton. N Yor —5H 99
Catteshall. Surr —1A 26
Catthorpe. Leics —3C 62
Cattistock. Dors —3A 14
Catton. Norf —4E 78
Catton. Nmbd —4B 114
Catton. N Yor —2F 99
Catton Hall. Derbs —4G 73
Catwick. E Yor —5F 101
Catworth. Cambs —3H 63
Caudle Green. Glos —4E 49
Caulcott. Oxon —3D 50
Cauldhame. Stir —4F 135
Cauldmill. Scot —3H 119
Cauldon. Staf —1E 73
Cauldon Lowe. Staf —1E 73
Cauldwell. Derbs —4G 73
Caulkerbush. Dum —4G 111
Caulside. Dum —1F 113
Caunsall. Worc —2C 60
Caunton. Notts —4E 87
Causewayend. S Lan —1C 118
Causewayhead. Stir —4H 135
Causey Park. Nmbd —5F 121
Caute. Devn —1E 11
Cautley. Cumb —5H 103
Cavendish. Suff —1B 54
Cavendish Bridge. Leics —3B 74
Cavenham. Suff —4G 65
Caversfield. Oxon —3D 50
Caversham. Read —4F 37
Caversham Heights. Read —4E 37
Caverswall. Staf —1D 72
Cawdor. High —4C 158
Cawkwell. Linc —3B 88
Cawood. N Yor —1F 93
Cawsand. Corn —4A 8
Cawston. Norf —3D 78
Cawston. Warw —3B 62
Cawthorne. N Yor —1B 100
Cawthorne. S Yor —4C 92
Cawthorpe. Linc —3H 75
Cawton. N Yor —2A 100
Caxton. Cambs —5C 64
Caynham. Shrp —3H 59
Caythorpe. Linc —1G 75
Caythorpe. Notts —1D 74
Cayton. N Yor —1E 101
Ceallan. W Isl —3D 170
Ceann a Bhaigh. W Isl —8D 171 (on Harris)
Ceann a Bhaigh. W Isl —2C 170 (on North Uist)
Ceann a Bhaigh. W Isl —8E 171 (on Scalpay)
Ceann a Bhaigh. W Isl —9C 171 (on South Harris)
Ceannacroc Lodge. High —2E 149
Ceann a Tuath Loch Baghasdail. W Isl —6C 170
Ceann Loch Shiphoirt. W Isl —6E 171
Ceann Tarabhaigh. W Isl —6E 171
Cearsiadar. W Isl —5F 171
Ceathramh Meadhanach. W Isl —1D 170
Cefn Berain. Cnwy —4B 82
Cefn-brith. Cnwy —5B 82
Cefn-bryn-brain. Carm —4H 45
Cefn Bychan. Cphy —2F 33
Cefn-bychan. Flin —4D 82
Cefncaeau. Carm —3E 31
Cefn Canol. Powy —2E 71
Cefn-coch. Powy —3D 70
Cefn-coed-y-cymmer. Mer T —5D 46
Cefn Cribwr. B'End —3B 32
Cefn-ddwysarn. Gwyn —2B 70
Cefn Einion. Shrp —2E 59
Cefneithin. Carm —4F 45
Cefn Glas. B'End —3B 32
Cefngorwydd. Powy —1C 46
Cefn Llwyd. Cdgn —2F 57
Cefn-mawr. Wrex —1E 71
Cefn-y-bedd. Wrex —5F 83
Cefn-y-coed. Powy —1D 58
Cefn-y-pant. Carm —2F 43
Cegidfa. Powy —4E 70
Ceinewydd. Cdgn —5C 56
Cellan. Cdgn —1G 45
Cellardyke. Fife —3H 137
Cellarhead. Staf —1D 72
Celleron. Cumb —2F 103
Cemaes. IOA —1C 80
Cemmaes. Powy —5H 69
Cemmaes Road. Powy —5H 69
Cenarth. Carm —1C 44
Cenin. Gwyn —1D 68
Ceos. W Isl —5F 171
Ceres. Fife —2G 137
Ceri. Powy —2D 58
Cerist. Powy —2B 58
Cerne Abbas. Dors —2B 14
Cerney Wick. Glos —2F 35
Cerrigceinwen. IOA —3D 80
Cerrigydrudion. Cnwy —1B 70
Cess. Norf —4G 79
Cessford. Scot —2B 120
Ceunant. Gwyn —4E 81
Chaceley. Glos —2D 48
Chacewater. Corn —4B 6
Chackmore. Buck —2E 51
Chacombe. Nptn —1C 50
Chadderton. G Man —4H 91
Chaddesden. Derbs —2A 74
Chaddesden Common. Dby C —2A 74
Chaddesley Corbett. Worc —3C 60
Chaddlehanger. Devn —5E 11
Chaddleworth. W Ber —4C 36
Chadlington. Oxon —3B 50
Chadshunt. Warw —5H 61
Chadstone. Nptn —5F 63
Chad Valley. W Mid —2E 61
Chadwell. Leics —3E 75
Chadwell. Shrp —4B 72
Chadwell Heath. G Lon —2F 39
Chadwell St Mary. Thur —3H 39
Chadwick End. W Mid —3G 61
Chadwick Green. Mers —1H 83
Chaffcombe. Som —1G 13
Chafford Hundred. Thur —3H 39
Chagford. Devn —4H 11
Chailey. E Sus —4E 27
Chainbridge. Cambs —5D 76
Chain Bridge. Linc —1C 76
Chainhurst. Kent —1B 28
Chalbury. Dors —2F 15
Chalbury Common. Dors —2F 15
Chaldon. Surr —5E 39
Chaldon Herring. Dors —4C 14
Chale. IOW —5C 16
Chale Green. IOW —5C 16
Chalfont Common. Buck —1B 38
Chalfont St Giles. Buck —1A 38
Chalfont St Peter. Buck —2B 38
Chalford. Glos —5D 49
Chalgrove. Oxon —2E 37
Chalk. Kent —3A 40
Chalk End. Essx —4G 53
Chalk Hill. Glos —3G 49
Challaborough. Devn —4C 8
Challacombe. Devn —2G 19
Challister. Shet —5G 173
Challoch. Dum —3A 110
Challock. Kent —5E 40
Chalton. Beds —5A 64 (nr. Bedford)
Chalton. Beds —3A 52 (nr. Luton)
Chalton. Hants —1F 17
Chalvington. E Sus —5G 27
Champany. Falk —2D 128
Chance Inn. Fife —2F 137
Chancery. Cdgn —3E 57
Chandler's Cross. Herts —1B 38
Chandler's Cross. Worc —2C 48
Chandler's Ford. Hants —4C 24
Chanlockfoot. Dum —4G 117
Channel End. Beds —5A 64
Channel Tunnel. Kent —2F 29
Channerwick. Shet —9F 173
Chantry. Som —2C 22
Chantry. Suff —1E 55
Chapel. Cumb —1D 102
Chapel. Fife —4E 137
Chapel Allerton. Som —1H 21
Chapel Allerton. W Yor —1D 92
Chapel Amble. Corn —1D 6
Chapel Brampton. Nptn —4E 63

Clapham—Conisholme

Clapham. G Lon —3D 39
Clapham. N Yor —3G 97
Clapham. W Sus —5B 26
Clap Hill. Kent —2E 29
Clappers. Scot —4F 131
Clappersgate. Cumb —4E 103
Clapphoulk. Shet —9F 173
Clapton. Som —2H 13
(nr. Crewkerne)
Clapton. Som —1B 22
(nr. Radstock)
Clapton-in-Gordano.
N Som —4H 33
Clapton-on-the-Hill. Glos
—4G 49
Clapworthy. Devn —4G 19
Clara Vale. Tyne —3E 115
Clarbeston. Pemb —2E 43
Clarbeston Road. Pemb —2E 43
Clarborough. Notts —2E 87
Clare. Suff —1A 54
Clarebrand. Dum —3E 111
Clarencefield. Dum —3B 112
Clarilaw. Scot —3H 119
Clark's Green. Surr —2C 26
Clark's Hill. Linc —3C 76
Clarkston. E Ren —4G 127
Clasheddy. High —2G 167
Clashindarroch. Aber —5B 160
Clashmore. High —5E 165
(nr. Dornoch)
Clashmore. High —1E 163
(nr. Stoer)
Clashnessie. High —5A 166
Clashnoir. Mor —1G 151
Clate. Shet —5G 173
Clathick. Per —1H 135
Clathy. Per —2B 136
Clatt. Aber —1C 152
Clatter. Powy —1B 58
Clatterford. IOW —4C 16
Clatworthy. Som —3D 20
Claughton. Lanc —3E 97
(nr. Caton)
Claughton. Lanc —5E 97
(nr. Garstang)
Claughton. Mers —2F 83
Claverdon. Warw —4F 61
Claverham. N Som —5H 33
Clavering. Essx —2E 53
Claverley. Shrp —1B 60
Claverton. Bath —5C 34
Clawdd-coch. V Glam —4D 32
Clawdd-newydd. Den —5C 82
Clawson Hill. Leics —3E 75
Clawton. Devn —3D 10
Claxby. Linc —3D 88
(nr. Alford)
Claxby. Linc —1A 88
(nr. Market Rasen)
Claxton. Norf —5F 79
Claxton. N Yor —4A 100
Claybrooke Magna. Leics
—2B 62
Claybrooke Parva. Leics
—2B 62
Clay Common. Suff —2G 67
Clay Coton. Nptn —3C 62
Clay Cross. Derbs —4A 86
Claydon. Oxon —5B 62
Claydon. Suff —5D 66
Clay End. Herts —3D 52
Claygate. Kent —1B 28
Claygate. Surr —4C 38
Claygate Cross. Kent —5H 39
Clayhall. Hants —3E 16
Clayhanger. Devn —4D 20
Clayhanger. W Mid —5E 73
Clayhidon. Devn —1E 13
Clay Hill. Bris —4B 34
Clayhill. E Sus —3C 28
Clayhill. Hants —2B 16
Clayholes. Ang —5E 145
Clayhythe. Cambs —4E 65
Claylake. Dors —2F 15
Clay Lake. Linc —3B 76
Clayock. High —3D 168
Claypits. Glos —5C 48
Claypole. Linc —1F 75
Claythorpe. Linc —3D 88
Clayton. G Man —1C 84
Clayton. S Yor —4E 93
Clayton. Staf —1C 72
Clayton. W Sus —4E 27
Clayton. W Yor —1B 92
Clayton Green. Lanc —2D 90
Clayton-le-Moors. Lanc —1F 91
Clayton-le-Woods. Lanc
—2D 90
Clayton West. W Yor —3C 92
Clayworth. Notts —2E 87
Cleadale. High —5C 146
Cleadon. Tyne —3G 115
Clearbrook. Devn —2B 8
Clearwell. Glos —5A 48
Cleasby. N Yor —3F 105
Cleat. Orkn —9D 172
Cleatlam. Dur —3E 105
Cleator. Cumb —3B 102
Cleator Moor. Cumb —3B 102
Cleckheaton. W Yor —2B 92
Cleedownton. Shrp —2H 59
Cleehill. Shrp —3H 59
Cleekhimin. N Lan —4A 128
Clee St Margaret. Shrp —2H 59
Cleestanton. Shrp —3H 59
Cleethorpes. NE Lin —4G 95
Cleeton St Mary. Shrp —3A 60
Cleeve. N Som —5H 33
Cleeve. Oxon —3E 36
Cleeve Hill. Glos —3E 49
Cleeve Prior. Worc —1F 49
Clehonger. Here —2H 47
Cleigh. Arg —1F 133
Cleish. Per —4C 136
Cleland. N Lan —4B 128
Clench Common. Wilts —5G 35
Clenchwarton. Norf —3E 77
Clennell. Nmbd —4D 120
Clent. Worc —3D 60
Cleobury Mortimer. Shrp
—3A 60
Cleobury North. Shrp —2A 60
Clephanton. High —3C 158
Clerkhill. High —2H 167
Clestrain. Orkn —7C 172
Clevancy. Wilts —4F 35
Clevedon. N Som —4H 33
Cleveley. Oxon —3B 50
Cleveleys. Lanc —5C 96
Clevelode. Worc —1D 48
Cleverton. Wilts —3E 35
Clewer. Som —1H 21
Cley next the Sea. Norf —1C 78
Cliaid. W Isl —8B 170
Cliasmol. W Isl —7C 171
Clibberswick. Shet —1H 173
Cliburn. Cumb —2G 103
Cliddesden. Hants —2E 25
Clieves Hills. Lanc —4B 90
Cliff. Warw —1G 61
Cliffburn. Ang —4F 145
Cliffe. Medw —3B 40
Cliffe. N Yor —3F 105
(nr. Darlington)
Cliffe. N Yor —1G 93
(nr. Selby)
Cliff End. E Sus —4C 28
Cliffe Woods. Medw —3B 40
Clifford. W Yor —5G 99
Clifford Chambers. Warw
—5F 61
Clifford's Mesne. Glos —3B 48
Cliffs End. Kent —4H 41
Clifton. Beds —2B 52
Clifton. Bris —4A 34
Clifton. Cumb —2G 103
Clifton. Derbs —1F 73
Clifton. Devn —2G 19
Clifton. G Man —4F 91
Clifton. Lanc —1C 90
Clifton. Nmbd —1F 115
Clifton. N Yor —5D 98
Clifton. Not C —2C 74
Clifton. Oxon —2C 50
Clifton. S Yor —1C 86
Clifton. Stir —5H 141
Clifton. W Yor —2B 92
Clifton. Worc —1D 48
Clifton. York —4H 99
Clifton Campville. Staf —4G 73
Clifton Hampden. Oxon —2D 36
Clifton Hill. Worc —4B 60
Clifton Reynes. Mil —5G 63
Clifton upon Dunsmore.
Warw —3C 62
Clifton-upon-Teme. Worc
—4B 60
Cliftonville. Kent —3H 41
Cliftonville. Norf —2F 79
Climping. W Sus —5A 26
Climpy. S Lan —4C 128
Clint. N Yor —4E 99
Clint Green. Norf —4C 78
Clintmains. Scot —1A 120
Cliobh. W Isl —4C 171
Clipiau. Gwyn —4H 69
Clippesby. Norf —4G 79
Clippings Green. Norf —4C 78
Clipsham. Rut —4G 75
Clipston. Nptn —2E 62
Clipston. Notts —2D 74
Clipstone. Notts —4C 86
Clitheroe. Lanc —5G 97
Cliuthar. W Isl —8D 171
Clive. Shrp —3H 71
Clivocast. Shet —1H 173
Clixby. Linc —4E 94
Clocaenog. Den —5C 82
Clochan. Mor —2B 160
Clochforbie. Aber —3F 161
Clock Face. Mers —1H 83
Cloddiau. Powy —5E 70
Cloddymoss. Mor —3D 159
Clodock. Here —3G 47
Cloford. Som —2C 22
Clola. Aber —4H 161
Clophill. Beds —2A 52
Clopton. Nptn —2H 63
Clopton Corner. Suff —5E 66
Clopton Green. Suff —5G 65
Closeburn. Dum —5A 118
Close Clark. IOM —4B 108
Closworth. Som —1A 14
Clothall. Herts —2C 52
Clotton. Ches —4H 83
Clough. G Man —3H 91
Clough. W Yor —3A 92
Clough Foot. W Yor —2H 91
Cloughton. N Yor —5H 107
Cloughton Newlands.
N Yor —5H 107
Clousta. Shet —6E 173
Clouston. Orkn —6B 172
Clova. Aber —1B 152
Clova. Ang —1C 144
Clovelly. Devn —4D 18
Clovenfords. Scot —1G 119
Clovenstone. Aber —2E 153
Clovullin. High —2E 141
Clowne. Derbs —3B 86
Clows Top. Worc —3B 60
Cloy. Wrex —1F 71
Cluanie Inn. High —2C 148
Cluanie Lodge. High —2C 148
Cluddley. Telf —5A 72
Clun. Shrp —2F 59
Clunas. High —4C 158
Clunbury. Shrp —2F 59
Clunderwen. Carm —3F 43
Clune. High —1B 150
Clunes. High —5E 148
Clungunford. Shrp —3F 59
Clunie. Per —4A 144
Clunton. Shrp —2F 59
Cluny. Fife —4E 137
Clutton. Bath —1B 22
Clutton. Ches —5G 83
Clwt-y-bont. Gwyn —4E 81
Clwydfagwyr. Mer T —5D 46
Clydach. Mon —4F 47
Clydach. Swan —5G 45
Clydach Vale. Rhon —2C 32
Clydebank. W Dun —3G 127
Clydey. Pemb —1G 43
Clyffe Pypard. Wilts —4F 35
Clynder. Arg —1D 126
Clyne. Neat —5B 46
Clynelish. High —3F 165
Clynnog-fawr. Gwyn —1D 68
Clyro. Powy —1F 47
Clyst Honiton. Devn —3C 12
Clyst Hydon. Devn —2D 12
Clyst St George. Devn —4C 12
Clyst St Lawrence. Devn
—2D 12
Clyst St Mary. Devn —3C 12
Clyth. High —5E 169
Cnip. W Isl —4C 171
Cnoc Amhlaigh. W Isl —4H 171
Cnwcau. Pemb —1C 44
Cnwch Coch. Cdgn —3F 57
Coad's Green. Corn —5C 10
Coal Aston. Derbs —3A 86
Coalbrookdale. Telf —5A 72
Coalbrookvale. Blae —5F 47
Coalburn. S Lan —1H 117
Coalburns. Tyne —3E 115
Coalcleugh. Nmbd —5B 114
Coaley. Glos —5C 48
Coalford. Aber —4F 153
Coalhall. E Ayr —3D 116
Coalhill. Essx —1B 40
Coalpit Heath. S Glo —3B 34
Coal Pool. W Mid —5E 73
Coalport. Telf —5A 72
Coalsnaughton. Clac —4B 136
Coaltown of Balgonie.
Fife —4F 137
Coaltown of Wemyss.
Fife —4F 137
Coalville. Leics —4B 74
Coalway. Glos —4A 48
Coanwood. Nmbd —4H 113
Coat. Som —4H 21
Coatbridge. N Lan —3A 128
Coatdyke. N Lan —3A 128
Coate. Swin —3G 35
Coate. Wilts —5F 35
Coates. Cambs —1C 64
Coates. Glos —5E 49
Coates. Linc —2G 87
Coates. W Sus —4A 26
Coatham. Red C —2C 106
Coatham Mundeville.
Darl —2F 105
Cobbaton. Devn —4G 19
Coberley. Glos —4E 49
Cobhall Common. Here
—2H 47
Cobham. Kent —4A 40
Cobham. Surr —4C 38
Cobnash. Here —4G 59
Coburg. Devn —5B 12
Cockayne. N Yor —5D 106
Cockayne Hatley. Beds —1C 52
Cock Bank. Wrex —1F 71
Cock Bridge. Aber —3G 151
Cockburnspath. Scot —2D 130
Cock Clarks. Essx —5B 54
Cockenzie & Port Seton.
E Lot —2H 129
Cockerham. Lanc —4D 96
Cockermouth. Cumb —1C 102
Cockernhoe. Herts —3B 52
Cockfield. Dur —2E 105
Cockfield. Suff —5B 66
Cockfosters. G Lon —1D 39
Cock Gate. Here —4G 59
Cock Green. Essx —4G 53
Cocking. W Sus —1G 17
Cocking Causeway.
W Sus —1G 17
Cockington. Torb —2F 9
Cocklake. Som —2H 21
Cocklaw. Aber —4H 161
Cocklaw. Nmbd —2C 114
Cockley Beck. Cumb —4D 102
Cockley Cley. Norf —5G 77
Cockmuir. Aber —3G 161
Cockpole Green. Wind —3G 37
Cockshutford. Shrp —2H 59
Cockshutt. Shrp —3G 71
Cockthorpe. Norf —1B 78
Cockwood. Devn —4C 12
Cockyard. Derbs —3E 85
Cockyard. Here —2H 47
Codda. Corn —5B 10
Coddenham. Suff —5D 66
Coddenham Green. Suff
—5D 66
Coddington. Ches —5G 83
Coddington. Here —1C 48
Coddington. Notts —5F 87
Codford St Mary. Wilts —3E 23
Codford St Peter. Wilts —3E 23
Codicote. Herts —4C 52
Codmore Hill. W Sus —3B 26
Codnor. Derbs —1B 74
Codrington. S Glo —4C 34
Codsall. Staf —5C 72
Codsall Wood. Staf —5C 72
Coed Duon. Cphy —2E 33
Coedely. Rhon —3D 32
Coedglasson. Powy —4C 58
Coedkernew. Newp —3F 33
Coed Morgan. Mon —4G 47
Coedpoeth. Wrex —5E 83
Coedway. Powy —4F 71
Coed-y-bryn. Cdgn —1D 44
Coed-y-paen. Mon —2G 33
Coed-yr-ynys. Powy —3E 47
Coed Ystumgwern. Gwyn
—3E 69
Coelbren. Powy —4B 46
Coffinswell. Devn —2E 9
Cofton Hackett. Worc —3E 61
Cogan. V Glam —4E 33
Cogenhoe. Nptn —4F 63
Cogges. Oxon —5B 50
Coggeshall. Essx —3B 54
Coggeshall Hamlet. Essx
—3B 54
Coggins Mill. E Sus —3G 27
Coignafearn Lodge.
High —2A 150
Coig Peighinnean. W Isl
—1H 171
Coig Peighinnean
Bhuirgh. W Isl —2G 171
Coille Mhorgil. High —3D 148
Coilliemore. High —1A 158
Coillore. High —5C 154
Coire an Fhuarain. W Isl
—4E 171
Coity. B'End —3C 32
Cokhay Green. Derbs —3G 73
Col. W Isl —3G 171
Colaboll. High —2C 164
Colan. Corn —2C 6
Colaton Raleigh. Devn —4D 12
Colbost. High —4B 154
Colburn. N Yor —5E 105
Colby. Cumb —2H 103
Colby. IOM —4B 108
Colby. Norf —2E 78
Colchester. Essx —3D 54
Cold Ash. W Ber —5D 36
Cold Ashby. Nptn —3D 62
Cold Ashton. S Glo —4C 34
Cold Aston. Glos —4G 49
Coldbackie. High —3G 167
Cold Blow. Pemb —3F 43
Cold Brayfield. Mil —5G 63
Cold Cotes. N Yor —2G 97
Coldean. Brig —5E 27
Coldeast. Devn —5B 12
Colden. W Yor —2H 91
Colden Common. Hants
—4C 24
Coldfair Green. Suff —4G 67
Coldham. Cambs —5D 76
Coldham. Staf —5C 72
Cold Hanworth. Linc —2H 87
Coldharbour. Corn —4B 6
Cold Harbour. Dors —3E 15
Coldharbour. Glos —5A 48
Coldharbour. Kent —5G 39
Coldharbour. Surr —1C 26
Cold Hatton. Telf —3A 72
Cold Hatton Heath. Telf —3A 72
Cold Hesledon. Dur —5H 115
Cold Hiendley. W Yor —3D 92
Cold Higham. Nptn —5D 62
Coldingham. Scot —3F 131
Cold Kirby. N Yor —1H 99
Coldmeece. Staf —2C 72
Cold Northcott. Corn —4C 10
Cold Norton. Essx —5B 54
Cold Overton. Leics —5F 75
Coldrain. Per —3C 136
Coldred. Kent —1G 29
Coldridge. Devn —2H 11
Cold Row. Lanc —5C 96
Coldstream. Scot —5E 131
Coldwaltham. W Sus —4B 26
Coldwell. Here —2H 47
Coldwells. Aber —5H 161
Coldwells Croft. Aber —1C 152
Cole. Shet —5E 173
Cole. Som —3B 22
Colebatch. Shrp —2F 59
Colebrook. Devn —2D 12
Colebrooke. Devn —2A 12
Coleburn. Mor —3G 159
Coleby. Linc —4G 87
Coleby. N Lin —3B 94
Cole End. Warw —2F 61
Coleford. Devn —2A 12
Coleford. Glos —4A 48
Coleford. Som —2B 22
Colegate End. Norf —2D 66
Cole Green. Herts —4C 52
Cole Henley. Hants —1C 24
Colehill. Dors —2F 15
Coleman Green. Herts —4B 52
Coleman's Hatch. E Sus —2F 27
Colemere. Shrp —2G 71
Colemore. Hants —3F 25
Colemore Green. Shrp —1B 60
Colenden. Per —1D 136
Coleorton. Leics —4B 74
Colerne. Wilts —4D 34
Colesbourne. Glos —4E 49
Colesden. Beds —5A 64
Coles Green. Worc —5B 60
Coleshill. Buck —1A 38
Coleshill. Oxon —2H 35
Coleshill. Warw —2G 61
Colestocks. Devn —2D 12
Colethrop. Glos —4D 48
Coley. Bath —1A 22
Colgate. W Sus —2D 26
Colinsburgh. Fife —3G 137
Colinton. Edin —3F 129
Colintraive. Arg —2B 126
Colkirk. Norf —3B 78
Collace. Per —5B 144
Collam. W Isl —8D 171
Collaton. Devn —5D 8
Collaton St Mary. Torb —3E 9
College of Roseisle. Mor
—2F 159
Collessie. Fife —2E 137
Collier Row. G Lon —1F 39
Colliers End. Herts —3D 52
Collier Street. Kent —1B 28
Colliery Row. Tyne —5G 115
Collieston. Aber —1H 153
Collin. Dum —2B 112
Collingbourne Ducis.
Wilts —1H 23
Collingbourne Kingston.
Wilts —1H 23
Collingham. Notts —4F 87
Collingham. W Yor —5F 99
Collingtree. Nptn —5E 63
Collins Green. Warr —1H 83
Collins Green. Worc —5B 60
Colliston. Ang —4F 145
Colliton. Devn —2D 12
Collydean. Fife —3E 137
Collyweston. Nptn —5G 75
Colmonell. S Ayr —1G 109
Colmworth. Beds —5A 64
Colnbrook. Buck —3B 38
Colne. Cambs —3C 64
Colne. Lanc —5A 98
Colne Engaine. Essx —2B 54
Colney. Norf —5D 78
Colney Heath. Herts —5C 52
Colney Street. Herts —5B 52
Coln Rogers. Glos —5F 49
Coln St Aldwyns. Glos —5G 49
Coln St Dennis. Glos —4F 49
Colpitts Grange. Nmbd
—4C 114
Colpy. Aber —5D 160
Colscott. Devn —1D 10
Colsterdale. N Yor —1D 98
Colsterworth. Linc —3G 75
Colston Bassett. Notts —2D 74
Colstoun House. E Lot
—2B 130
Coltfield. Mor —2F 159
Colthouse. Cumb —5E 103
Coltishall. Norf —4E 79
Coltness. N Lan —4A 128
Colton. Cumb —1C 96
Colton. Norf —5D 78
Colton. N Yor —5H 99
Colton. Staf —3E 73
Colton. W Yor —1D 92
Colt's Hill. Kent —1H 27
Col Uarach. W Isl —4G 171
Colvend. Dum —4F 111
Colvister. Shet —2G 173
Colwall Green. Here —1C 48
Colwall Stone. Here —1C 48
Colwell. Nmbd —2C 114
Colwich. Staf —3E 73
Colwick. Notts —1D 74
Colwinston. V Glam —4C 32
Colworth. W Sus —5A 26
Colwyn Bay. Cnwy —3A 82
Colyford. Devn —3F 13
Colyton. Devn —3F 13
Combe. Devn —2D 8
Combe. Here —4F 59
Combe. Oxon —4C 50
Combe. W Ber —5B 36
Combe Almer. Dors —3E 15
Combebow. Devn —4E 11
Combe Common. Surr —2A 26
Combe Down. Bath —5C 34
Combe Fishacre. Devn —2E 9
Combe Florey. Som —3E 21
Combe Hay. Bath —1C 22
Combeinteignhead. Devn
—5C 12
Combe Martin. Devn —2F 19
Combe Moor. Here —4F 59
Combe Raleigh. Devn —2E 13
Comberbach. Ches —3A 84
Comberford. Staf —5F 73
Comberton. Cambs —5C 64
Comberton. Here —4G 59
Combe St Nicholas. Som
—1G 13
Combpyne. Devn —3F 13
Combridge. Staf —2E 73
Combrook. Warw —5H 61
Combs. Derbs —3E 85
Combs. Suff —5C 66
Combs Ford. Suff —5C 66
Combwich. Som —2F 21
Comers. Aber —3D 152
Comhampton. Worc —4C 60
Comins Coch. Cdgn —2F 57
Comley. Shrp —1G 59
Commercial End. Cambs
—4E 65
Commins. Powy —3D 70
Commins Coch. Powy —5H 69
Commondale. N Yor —3D 106
Common End. Cumb —2B 102
Common Hill. Here —2A 48
Common Moor. Corn —2G 7
Common Platt. Wilts —3G 35
Commonside. Ches —3H 83
Common Side. Derbs —3H 85
(nr. Chesterfield)
Commonside. Derbs —1G 73
(nr. Derby)
Common, The. Wilts —3H 23
(nr. Salisbury)
Common, The. Wilts —3F 35
(nr. Swindon)
Compstall. G Man —1D 84
Compton. Devn —2E 9
Compton. Hants —4C 24
Compton. Plym —3A 8
Compton. Staf —2C 60
Compton. Surr —1A 26
Compton. W Ber —4D 36
Compton. W Sus —1F 17
Compton. Wilts —1G 23
Compton Abbas. Dors —1D 15
Compton Abdale. Glos —4F 49
Compton Bassett. Wilts —4F 35
Compton Beauchamp.
Oxon —3A 36
Compton Bishop. Som —1G 21
Compton Chamberlayne.
Wilts —4F 23
Compton Dando. Bath —5B 34
Compton Dundon. Som
—3H 21
Compton Greenfield.
S Glo —3A 34
Compton Martin. Bath —1A 22
Compton Pauncefoot.
Som —4B 22
Compton Valence. Dors
—3A 14
Comrie. Fife —1D 128
Comrie. Per —1G 135
Conaglen. High —2E 141
Conchra. Arg —1B 126
Conchra. High —1A 148
Conder Green. Lanc —4D 96
Conderton. Worc —2E 49
Condicote. Glos —3G 49
Condorrat. N Lan —2A 128
Condover. Shrp —5G 71
Coneyhurst Common.
W Sus —3C 26
Coneysthorpe. N Yor —2B 100
Coneythorpe. N Yor —4F 99
Coney Weston. Suff —3B 66
Conford. Hants —3G 25
Congdon's Shop. Corn —5C 10
Congerstone. Leics —5A 74
Congham. Norf —3G 77
Congleton. Ches —4C 84
Congl-y-wal. Gwyn —1G 69
Congresbury. N Som —5H 33
Congreve. Staf —4D 72
Conham. S Glo —4B 34
Conicaval. Mor —3D 159
Coningsby. Linc —5B 88
Conington. Cambs —4C 64
(nr. Fenstanton)
Conington. Cambs —2A 64
(nr. Sawtry)
Conisbrough. S Yor —1C 86
Conisby. Arg —3A 124
Conisholme. Linc —1D 88

Coniston—Croeserw

Coniston. Cumb —5E 102
Coniston. E Yor —1E 95
Coniston Cold. N Yor —4B 98
Conistone. N Yor —3B 98
Connah's Quay. Flin —4E 83
Connel. Arg —5D 140
Connel Park. E Ayr —3F 117
Connista. High —1D 154
Connor Downs. Corn —3C 4
Conock. Wilts —1F 23
Conon Bridge. High —3H 157
Cononley. N Yor —5B 98
Cononsyth. Ang —4E 145
Conordan. High —5E 155
Consall. Staf —1D 73
Consett. Dur —4E 115
Constable Burton. N Yor —5E 105
Constantine. Corn —4E 5
Constantine Bay. Corn —1C 6
Contin. High —3G 157
Contullich. High —1A 158
Conwy. Cnwy —3G 81
Conyer. Kent —4D 40
Conyers Green. Suff —4A 66
Cooden. E Sus —5B 28
Cooil. IOM —4C 108
Cookbury. Devn —2E 11
Cookbury Wick. Devn —2D 11
Cookham. Wind —3G 37
Cookham Dean. Wind —3G 37
Cookham Rise. Wind —3G 37
Cookhill. Worc —5E 61
Cookley. Suff —3F 67
Cookley. Worc —2C 60
Cookley Green. Oxon —2E 37
Cookney. Aber —4F 153
Cooksbridge. E Sus —4F 27
Cooksey Corner. Worc —4D 60
Cooksey Green. Worc —4D 60
Cookshill. Staf —1D 72
Cooksmill Green. Essx —5G 53
Coolham. W Sus —3C 26
Cooling. Medw —3B 40
Cooling Street. Medw —3B 40
Coombe. Corn —1C 10
(nr. Bude)
Coombe. Corn —3D 6
(nr. St Austell)
Coombe. Corn —4C 6
(nr. Truro)
Coombe. Devn —3E 12
(nr. Sidmouth)
Coombe. Devn —5C 12
(nr. Teignmouth)
Coombe. Glos —2C 34
Coombe. Hants —4E 25
Coombe. Wilts —1G 23
Coombe Bissett. Wilts —4G 23
Coombe Hill. Glos —3D 49
Coombe Keynes. Dors —4D 14
Coombes. W Sus —5C 26
Coombe Street. Som —3C 22
Coopersale Common. Essx —5E 53
Coopersale Street. Essx —5E 53
Cooper's Corner. Kent —1F 27
Cooper Street. Kent —5H 41
Cootham. W Sus —4B 26
Copalder Corner. Cambs —1C 64
Copdock. Suff —1E 54
Copford. Essx —3C 54
Copford Green. Essx —3C 54
Copgrove. N Yor —3F 99
Cople. Beds —1B 52
Copley. Dur —2D 105
Coplow Dale. Derbs —3F 85
Copmanthorpe. York —5H 99
Copp. Lanc —1C 90
Coppathorne. Corn —2C 10
Coppenhall. Ches —5B 84
Coppenhall. Staf —4D 72
Coppenhall Moss. Ches —5B 84
Copperhouse. Corn —3C 4
Coppicegate. Shrp —2B 60
Coppingford. Cambs —2A 64
Copplestone. Devn —2A 12
Coppull. Lanc —3D 90
Coppull Moor. Lanc —3D 90
Copsale. W Sus —3C 26
Copster Green. Lanc —1E 91
Copston Magna. Warw —2B 62
Copt Green. Warw —4F 61
Copthall Green. Essx —5E 53
Copt Heath. W Mid —3F 61
Copt Hewick. N Yor —2F 99
Copthill. Dur —5B 114
Copthorne. W Sus —2E 27
Coptiviney. Shrp —2G 71
Copy's Green. Norf —2B 78
Copythorne. Hants —1B 16
Corbridge. Nmbd —3C 114
Corby. Nptn —2G 63
Corby Glen. Linc —3H 75
Cordon. N Ayr —2E 123
Coreley. Shrp —3A 60
Corfe. Som —1F 13
Corfe Castle. Dors —4E 15
Corfe Mullen. Dors —3E 15
Corfton. Shrp —2G 59
Corgarff. Aber —3G 151
Corhampton. Hants —4E 24
Corlannau. Neat —2A 32
Corley. Warw —2H 61
Corley Ash. Warw —2G 61
Corley Moor. Warw —2G 61
Cormiston. S Lan —1C 118
Cornaa. IOM —3D 108
Cornaigbeg. Arg —4A 138
Cornaigmore. Arg —2D 138
(on Coll)
Cornaigmore. Arg —4A 138
(on Tiree)
Corner Row. Lanc —1C 90
Corney. Cumb —5C 102
Cornforth. Dur —1A 106
Cornhill. Aber —3C 160
Cornhill. High —4C 164
Cornhill-on-Tweed. Nmbd —1C 120
Cornholme. W Yor —2H 91
Cornish Hall End. Essx —2G 53
Cornquoy. Orkn —7E 172
Cornriggs. Dur —5B 114
Cornsay. Dur —5E 115
Cornsay Colliery. Dur —5E 115
Corntown. High —3H 157
Corntown. V Glam —4C 32
Cornwell. Oxon —3A 50
Cornwood. Devn —3C 8
Cornworthy. Devn —3E 9
Corpach. High —1E 141
Corpusty. Norf —3D 78
Corra. Dum —3F 111
Corran. High —2E 141
(nr. Arnisdale)
Corran. High —3A 148
(nr. Fort William)
Corrany. IOM —3D 108
Corribeg. High —1D 141
Corrie. N Ayr —5B 126
Corrie Common. Dum —1D 112
Corriecravie. N Ayr —3D 122
Corriekinloch. High —1A 164
Corriemoillie. High —2F 157
Corrievarkie Lodge. Per —1C 142
Corrievorrie. High —1B 150
Corrigall. Orkn —6C 172
Corrimony. High —5F 157
Corringham. Linc —1F 87
Corringham. Thur —2B 40
Corris. Gwyn —5G 69
Corris Uchaf. Gwyn —5G 69
Corrour Shooting Lodge. High —2B 142
Corry. High —1E 147
Corrybrough. High —1C 150
Corrygills. N Ayr —2E 123
Corry of Ardnagrask. High —4H 157
Corsback. High —1E 169
(nr. Dunnet)
Corsback. High —3E 169
(nr. Halkirk)
Corscombe. Dors —2A 14
Corse. Aber —4D 160
Corsehill. Aber —3G 161
Corse Lawn. Worc —2D 48
Corse of Kinnoir. Aber —4C 160
Corsham. Wilts —4D 34
Corsley. Wilts —2D 22
Corsley Heath. Wilts —2D 22
Corsock. Dum —2E 111
Corston. Bath —5B 34
Corston. Wilts —3E 35
Corstorphine. Edin —2F 129
Cortachy. Ang —3C 144
Corton. Suff —1H 67
Corton. Wilts —2E 23
Corton Denham. Som —4B 22
Corwar House. S Ayr —1H 109
Corwen. Den —1C 70
Coryates. Dors —4B 14
Coryton. Devn —4E 11
Coryton. Thur —2B 40
Cosby. Leics —1C 62
Coscote. Oxon —3D 36
Coseley. W Mid —1D 60
Cosgrove. Nptn —1F 51
Cosham. Port —2E 17
Cosheston. Pemb —4E 43
Coskills. N Lin —3D 94
Cosmeston. V Glam —5E 33
Cossall. Notts —1B 74
Cossington. Leics —4D 74
Cossington. Som —2G 21
Costa. Orkn —5C 172
Costessey. Norf —4D 78
Costock. Notts —3C 74
Coston. Leics —3F 75
Coston. Norf —5C 78
Cote. Oxon —5B 50
Cotebrook. Ches —4H 83
Cotehill. Cumb —5F 113
Cotes. Cumb —1D 97
Cotes. Leics —3C 74
Cotes. Staf —2C 72
Cotesbach. Leics —2C 62
Cotes Heath. Staf —2C 72
Cotgrave. Notts —2D 74
Cothall. Aber —2F 153
Cotham. Notts —1E 75
Cothelstone. Som —3E 21
Cotheridge. Worc —5B 60
Cotherstone. Dur —3D 104
Cothill. Oxon —2C 36
Cotland. Mon —5A 48
Cotleigh. Devn —2F 13
Cotmanhay. Derbs —1B 74
Coton. Cambs —5D 64
Coton. Nptn —3D 62
Coton. Staf —4C 72
(nr. Gnosall)
Coton. Staf —2D 73
(nr. Stone)
Coton. Staf —5F 73
(nr. Tamworth)
Coton Clanford. Staf —3C 72
Coton Hayes. Staf —2D 73
Coton Hill. Shrp —4G 71
Coton in the Clay. Staf —3F 73
Coton in the Elms. Derbs —4G 73
Cotonwood. Shrp —2H 71
Cotonwood. Staf —3C 72
Cott. Devn —2D 9
Cott. Orkn —5F 172
Cottam. E Yor —3D 101
Cottam. Lanc —1D 90
Cottam. Notts —3F 87
Cottartown. High —5E 159
Cottarville. Nptn —4E 63
Cottenham. Cambs —4D 64
Cotterdale. N Yor —5B 104
Cottered. Herts —3D 52
Cotterstock. Nptn —1H 63
Cottesbrooke. Nptn —3E 62
Cottesmore. Rut —4G 75
Cotteylands. Devn —1C 12
Cottingham. E Yor —1D 94
Cottingham. Nptn —1F 63
Cottingley. W Yor —1B 92
Cottisford. Oxon —2D 50
Cotton. Staf —1E 73
Cotton. Suff —4C 66
Cotton End. Beds —1A 52
Cot-town. Aber —4F 161
Cotts. Devn —2A 8
Cotwalton. Staf —2D 72
Couch's Mill. Corn —3F 7
Coughton. Here —3A 48
Coughton. Warw —4E 61
Coulags. High —4B 156
Coulderton. Cumb —4A 102
Coulin Lodge. High —3C 156
Coull. Aber —3C 152
Coulport. Arg —1D 126
Coulsdon. Surr —5D 39
Coulter. S Lan —1C 118
Coultershaw Bridge. W Sus —4A 26
Coultings. Som —2F 21
Coulton. N Yor —2A 100
Cound. Shrp —5H 71
Coundon. Dur —2F 105
Coundon Grange. Dur —2F 105
Countersett. N Yor —1B 98
Countess. Wilts —2G 23
Countess Cross. Essx —2B 54
Countesthorpe. Leics —1C 62
Countisbury. Devn —2A 20
Coupar Angus. Per —4B 144
Coupe Green. Lanc —2D 90
Coupland. Cumb —3A 104
Coupland. Nmbd —1D 120
Cour. Arg —5G 125
Courance. Dum —5C 118
Court-at-Street. Kent —2E 29
Courteachan. High —4E 147
Courteenhall. Nptn —5E 63
Court Henry. Carm —3F 45
Courtsend. Essx —1E 41
Courtway. Som —3F 21
Cousland. Midl —3G 129
Cousley Wood. E Sus —2A 28
Coustonn. Arg —2B 126
Cove. Arg —1D 126
Cove. Devn —1C 12
Cove. Hants —1G 25
Cove. High —4C 162
Cove. Scot —2D 130
Cove Bay. Aber C —3G 153
Covehithe. Suff —2H 67
Coven. Staf —5D 72
Coveney. Cambs —2D 65
Covenham St Bartholomew. Linc —1C 88
Covenham St Mary. Linc —1C 88
Coven Heath. Staf —5D 72
Coventry. W Mid —3H 61
Coverack. Corn —5E 5
Coverham. N Yor —1D 98
Covesea. Mor —1F 159
Covingham. Swin —3G 35
Covington. Cambs —3H 63
Covington. S Lan —1B 118
Cowan Bridge. Lanc —2F 97
Cowbar. Red C —3E 107
Cowbeech. E Sus —4H 27
Cowbit. Linc —4B 76
Cowbridge. V Glam —4C 32
Cowden. Kent —1F 27
Cowdenbeath. Fife —4D 136
Cowdenburn. Scot —4F 129
Cowdenend. Fife —1E 129
Cowen Head. Cumb —5F 103
Cowers Lane. Derbs —1H 73
Cowes. IOW —3C 16
Cowesby. N Yor —1G 99
Cowfold. W Sus —3D 26
Cowfords. Mor —2H 159
Cowgate. Cumb —5B 112
Cowgill. Cumb —1G 97
Cowie. Aber —5F 153
Cowie. Stir —1B 128
Cowlam. N Yor —3D 100
Cowley. Devn —3C 12
Cowley. Glos —4E 49
Cowley. G Lon —2B 38
Cowley. Oxon —5D 50
Cowley. Staf —4C 72
Cowleymoor. Devn —1C 12
Cowling. Lanc —3D 90
Cowling. N Yor —1E 99
(nr. Bedale)
Cowling. N Yor —5B 98
(nr. Glusburn)
Cowlinge. Suff —5G 65
Cowmes. W Yor —3B 92
Cowpe. Lanc —2G 91
Cowpen. Nmbd —1F 115
Cowpen Bewley. Stoc T —2B 106
Cowplain. Hants —1E 17
Cowshill. Dur —5B 114
Cowslip Green. N Som —5H 33
Cowstrandburn. Fife —4C 136
Cowthorpe. N Yor —4G 99
Coxall. Here —3F 59
Coxbank. Ches —1A 72
Coxbench. Derbs —1A 74
Cox Common. Suff —2G 67
Coxford. Norf —3H 77
Coxgreen. Staf —2C 60
Cox Green. Surr —2B 26
Cox Green. Tyne —4G 115
Coxheath. Kent —5B 40
Coxhoe. Dur —1A 106
Coxley. Som —2A 22
Coxwold. N Yor —2H 99
Coychurch. V Glam —4C 32
Coylton. S Ayr —3D 116
Coylumbridge. High —2D 150
Coynach. Aber —3B 152
Coynachie. Aber —5B 160
Coytrahen. B'End —3B 32
Crabbs Cross. Worc —4E 61
Crabgate. Norf —3C 78
Crab Orchard. Dors —2F 15
Crabtree. W Sus —3D 26
Crabtree Green. Wrex —1F 71
Crackaig. High —2G 165
Crackenthorpe. Cumb —2H 103
Crackington Haven. Corn —3B 10
Crackley. Staf —5C 84
Crackley. Warw —3G 61
Crackleybank. Shrp —4B 72
Crackpot. N Yor —5C 104
Cracoe. N Yor —4B 98
Craddock. Devn —1D 12
Cradhlastadh. W Isl —4C 171
Cradley. Here —1C 48
Cradley. W Mid —2D 60
Cradoc. Powy —2D 46
Crafthole. Corn —3H 7
Crafton. Buck —4G 51
Cragabus. Arg —5B 124
Crag Foot. Lanc —2D 97
Craggan. Arg —4B 134
Craggan. High —1E 151
Cragganmore. Mor —5F 159
Cragganvallie. High —5H 157
Craggie. High —2F 165
Craggiemore. High —5B 158
Cragg Vale. W Yor —2A 92
Craghead. Dur —4F 115
Crai. Powy —3B 46
Craibstone. Aber C —2F 153
Craichie. Ang —4E 145
Craig. Arg —5E 141
Craig. Dum —2D 111
Craig. High —4C 156
(nr. Achnashellach)
Craig. High —2G 155
(nr. Lower Diabaig)
Craig. High —5H 155
(nr. Stromeferry)
Craiganour Lodge. Per —3D 142
Craigbrack. Arg —4A 134
Craig-cefn-parc. Swan —5G 45
Craigdallie. Per —1E 137
Craigdam. Aber —5F 161
Craigdarroch. E Ayr —4F 117
Craigdarroch. High —3G 157
Craigdhu. High —4G 157
Craigearn. Aber —2E 152
Craigellachie. Mor —4G 159
Craigend. Per —2D 136
Craigends. Ren —3F 127
Craigenputtock. Dum —1E 111
Craigens. E Ayr —3E 117
Craiggiecat. Aber —4F 153
Craighall. Edin —2E 129
Craighead. Fife —2H 137
Craighouse. Arg —3D 124
Craigie. Aber —2G 153
Craigie. D'dee —5D 144
Craigie. Per —4A 144
(nr. Blairgowrie)
Craigie. Per —1D 136
(nr. Perth)
Craigie. S Ayr —1D 116
Craigielaw. E Lot —2A 130
Craiglemine. Dum —5B 110
Craig-llwyn. Shrp —3E 71
Craiglockhart. Edin —2F 129
Craig Lodge. Arg —2B 126
Craigmalloch. E Ayr —5D 117
Craigmaud. Aber —3F 161
Craigmill. Stir —4H 135
Craigmillar. Edin —2F 129
Craigmore. Arg —3C 126
Craigmuie. Dum —1E 111
Craignair. Dum —3F 111
Craignant. Shrp —2E 71
Craigneuk. N Lan —3A 128
(nr. Airdrie)
Craigneuk. N Lan —4A 128
(nr. Motherwell)
Craignure. Arg —5B 140
Craigo. Ang —2F 145
Craigrory. High —4A 158
Craigrothie. Fife —2F 137
Craigs. Dum —2D 112
Craigsglen. Aber —3E 161
Craigshill. W Lot —3D 128
Craigside. Dur —1E 105
Craigs, The. High —4B 164
Craigton. Aber C —3F 153
Craigton. Aber —3E 152
Craigton. Ang —5E 145
(nr. Carnoustie)
Craigton. Ang —3C 144
(nr. Kirriemuir)
Craigton. High —4A 158
Craigtown. High —3A 168
Craig-y-Duke. Neat —5H 45
Craigyloch. Ang —3B 144
Craig-y-nos. Powy —4B 46
Craik. Scot —4F 119
Crail. Fife —3H 137
Crailing. Scot —2A 120
Crailinghall. Scot —2B 120
Craiselound. N Lin —1E 87
Crakehill. N Yor —2G 99
Crakemarsh. Staf —2E 73
Crambe. N Yor —3B 100
Crambeck. N Yor —3B 100
Cramlington. Nmbd —2F 115
Cramond. Edin —2E 129
Cramond Bridge. Edin —2E 129
Cranage. Ches —4B 84
Cranberry. Staf —2C 72
Cranborne. Dors —1F 15
Cranbourne. Brac —3A 38
Cranbrook. Kent —2B 28
Cranbrook Common. Kent —2B 28
Crane Moor. S Yor —4D 92
Crane's Corner. Norf —4B 78
Cranfield. Beds —1H 51
Cranford. G Lon —3B 38
Cranford St Andrew. Nptn —3G 63
Cranford St John. Nptn —3G 63
Cranham. Glos —4D 49
Cranham. G Lon —2G 39
Crank. Mers —1H 83
Cranleigh. Surr —2B 26
Cranley. Suff —3D 66
Cranloch. Mor —3G 159
Cranmer Green. Suff —3C 66
Cranmore. IOW —3B 16
Cranmore. Linc —5A 76
Crannich. Arg —4G 139
Crannoch. Mor —3B 160
Cranoe. Leics —1E 63
Cransford. Suff —4F 67
Cranshaws. Scot —3C 130
Cranstal. IOM —1D 108
Crantock. Corn —2B 6
Cranwell. Linc —5H 87
Cranwich. Norf —1G 65
Cranworth. Norf —5B 78
Craobh Haven. Arg —3E 133
Craobhnaclag. High —4G 157
Crapstone. Devn —2B 8
Crarae. Arg —4G 133
Crask. High —2H 167
Crask Inn. High —1C 164
Crask of Aigas. High —4G 157
Craster. Nmbd —3G 121
Cratfield. Suff —3F 67
Crathes. Aber —4E 153
Crathie. Aber —4G 151
Crathie. High —4H 149
Crathorne. N Yor —4B 106
Craven Arms. Shrp —2G 59
Crawcrook. Tyne —3E 115
Crawford. Lanc —4C 90
Crawford. S Lan —2B 118
Crawforddyke. S Lan —4B 128
Crawfordjohn. S Lan —2A 118
Crawick. Dum —3G 117
Crawley. Devn —2F 13
Crawley. Hants —3C 24
Crawley. Oxon —4B 50
Crawley. W Sus —2D 26
Crawley Down. W Sus —2E 27
Crawley Side. Dur —5C 114
Crawshawbooth. Lanc —2G 91
Crawton. Aber —5F 153
Cray. N Yor —2B 98
Cray. Per —2A 144
Crayford. G Lon —3G 39
Crayke. N Yor —2H 99
Craymere Beck. Norf —2C 78
Crays Hill. Essx —1B 40
Cray's Pond. Oxon —3E 37
Crazies Hill. Wok —3F 37
Creacombe. Devn —1B 12
Creagan. Arg —4D 141
Creag Aoil. High —1F 141
Creag Ghoraidh. W Isl —4C 170
Creaguaineach Lodge. High —2H 141
Creamore Bank. Shrp —2H 71
Creaton. Nptn —3E 62
Creca. Dum —2D 112
Credenhill. Here —1H 47
Crediton. Devn —2B 12
Creebridge. Dum —3B 110
Creech. Dors —4E 15
Creech Heathfield. Som —4F 21
Creech St Michael. Som —4F 21
Creed. Corn —4D 6
Creekmoor. Pool —3E 15
Creekmouth. G Lon —2F 39
Creeting St Mary. Suff —5C 66
Creeting St Peter. Suff —5C 66
Creeton. Linc —3H 75
Creetown. Dum —4B 110
Creggans. Arg —3H 133
Cregneash. IOM —5A 108
Cregrina. Powy —5D 58
Creighton. Staf —2E 73
Creigiau. Card —3D 32
Cremyll. Corn —3A 8
Crendell. Dors —1F 15
Crepkill. High —4D 154
Cressage. Shrp —5H 71
Cressbrook. Derbs —3F 85
Cresselly. Pemb —4E 43
Cressing. Essx —3A 54
Cresswell. Nmbd —5G 121
Cresswell. Staf —2D 73
Cresswell Quay. Pemb —4E 43
Creswell. Derbs —3C 86
Creswell Green. Staf —4E 73
Cretingham. Suff —4E 67
Crewe. Ches —5G 83
(nr. Farndon)
Crewe. Ches —5B 84
(nr. Nantwich)
Crewgreen. Powy —4F 71
Crewkerne. Som —2H 13
Crews Hill. G Lon —5D 52
Crewton. Dby C —2A 74
Crianlarich. Stir —1C 134
Cribbs Causeway. S Glo —4A 34
Cribyn. Cdgn —5E 57
Criccieth. Gwyn —2D 69
Crich. Derbs —5A 86
Crichton. Midl —3G 129
Crick. Mon —2H 33
Crick. Nptn —3C 62
Crickadarn. Powy —1D 46
Cricket Hill. Hants —5G 37
Cricket Malherbie. Som —1G 13
Cricket St Thomas. Som —2G 13
Crickham. Som —2H 21
Crickheath. Shrp —3E 71
Crickhowell. Powy —4F 47
Cricklade. Wilts —2G 35
Cricklewood. G Lon —2D 38
Cridling Stubbs. N Yor —2F 93
Criech. Fife —1F 137
Crieff. Per —1A 136
Criftins. Shrp —2F 71
Criggion. Powy —4E 71
Crigglestone. W Yor —3D 92
Crimchard. Som —2G 13
Crimdon Park. Dur —1B 106
Crimond. Aber —3H 161
Crimonmogate. Aber —3H 161
Crimplesham. Norf —5F 77
Crimscote. Warw —1H 49
Crinan. Arg —4E 133
Cringleford. Norf —5D 78
Crinow. Pemb —3F 43
Cripplesease. Corn —3C 4
Cripplestyle. Dors —1F 15
Cripp's Corner. E Sus —3B 28
Croanford. Corn —5A 10
Crockenhill. Kent —4G 39
Crocker End. Oxon —3F 37
Crockerhill. Hants —2D 16
Crockernwell. Devn —3A 12
Crocker's Ash. Here —4A 48
Crockerton. Wilts —2D 22
Crocketford. Dum —2F 111
Crockey Hill. York —5A 100
Crockham Hill. Kent —5F 39
Crockhurst Street. Kent —1H 27
Crockleford Heath. Essx —3D 54
Croeserw. Neat —2B 32

Croes-Goch—David's Well

Croes-Goch. Pemb —1C 42
Croes Hywel. Mon —4G 47
Croes-lan. Cdgn —1D 45
Croesor. Gwyn —1F 69
Croesowallt. Shrp —3E 71
Croesyceiliog. Carm —4E 45
Croesyceiliog. Torf —2G 33
Croes-y-mwyalch. Newp —2G 33
Croesywaun. Gwyn —5E 81
Croford. Som —4E 20
Croft. Leics —1C 62
Croft. Linc —4E 89
Croft. Warr —1A 84
Croftamie. Stir —1F 127
Croftfoot. Glas —3H 127
Croftmill. Per —5F 143
Crofton. Cumb —4E 112
Crofton. W Yor —3D 93
Crofton. Wilts —5A 36
Croft-on-Tees. N Yor —4F 105
Crofts. Dum —2E 111
Crofts of Benachielt. High —5D 169
Crofts of Dipple. Mor —3H 159
Crofty. Swan —3E 31
Croggan. Arg —1E 132
Croglin. Cumb —5G 113
Croich. High —4B 164
Croick. High —3A 168
Croig. Arg —3E 139
Croir. W Isl —4D 171
Cromarty. High —2B 158
Crombie. Fife —1D 128
Cromdale. High —1E 151
Cromer. Herts —3C 52
Cromer. Norf —1E 78
Cromford. Derbs —5G 85
Cromhall. S Glo —2B 34
Cromhall Common. S Glo —3B 34
Cromor. W Isl —5G 171
Cromra. High —5H 149
Cromwell. Notts —4E 87
Cronberry. E Ayr —2F 117
Crondall. Hants —2F 25
Cronk, The. IOM —2C 108
Cronk-y-Voddy. IOM —3C 108
Cronton. Mers —2G 83
Crook. Cumb —5F 103
Crook. Dur —1E 105
Crookdake. Cumb —5C 112
Crooke. G Man —4D 90
Crookedholm. E Ayr —1D 116
Crooked Soley. Wilts —4B 36
Crookes. S Yor —2H 85
Crookgate Bank. Dur —4E 115
Crookhall. Dur —4E 115
Crookham. Nmbd —1D 120
Crookham. W Ber —5D 36
Crookham Village. Hants —1F 25
Crooklands. Cumb —1E 97
Crook of Devon. Per —3C 136
Crookston. Ren —3G 127
Cropredy. Oxon —1C 50
Cropston. Leics —4C 74
Cropthorne. Worc —1E 49
Cropton. N Yor —1B 100
Cropwell Bishop. Notts —2D 74
Cropwell Butler. Notts —2D 74
Cros. W Isl —1H 171
Crosbie. N Ayr —4D 126
Crosbost. W Isl —5F 171
Crosby. Cumb —1B 102
Crosby. IOM —4C 108
Crosby. Mers —1F 83
Crosby. N Lin —3B 94
Crosby Court. N Yor —5A 106
Crosby Garrett. Cumb —4A 104
Crosby Ravensworth. Cumb —3H 103
Crosby Villa. Cumb —1B 102
Croscombe. Som —2A 22
Crosland Moor. W Yor —3B 92
Cross. Som —1H 21
Crossaig. Arg —4G 125
Crossapol. Arg —4A 138
Cross Ash. Mon —4H 47
Cross-at-Hand. Kent —1B 28
Crossbush. W Sus —5B 26
Crosscanonby. Cumb —1B 102
Crossdale Street. Norf —2E 79
Cross End. Essx —2B 54
Crossens. Mers —3B 90
Crossford. Fife —1D 128
Crossford. S Lan —5B 128
Cross Foxes. Gwyn —4G 69
Crossgate. Orkn —6D 172
Crossgate. Staf —2D 72
Crossgatehall. E Lot —3G 129
Crossgates. Fife —1E 129
Crossgates. N Yor —1E 101
Crossgates. Powy —4C 58
Cross Gates. W Yor —1D 92
Crossgill. Lanc —3E 97
Cross Green. Devn —4D 11
Cross Green. Staf —5D 72
Cross Green. Suff —5A 66 (nr. Cockfield)
Cross Green. Suff —5B 66 (nr. Hitcham)
Cross Hands. Carm —4F 45 (nr. Ammanford)
Crosshands. Carm —2F 43 (nr. Whitland)
Crosshands. E Ayr —1D 117
Crosshill. E Ayr —2D 117
Crosshill. Fife —4D 136
Cross Hill. Glos —2A 34
Crosshill. S Ayr —4C 116
Crosshills. High —2A 158
Cross Hills. N Yor —5C 98
Cross Holme. N Yor —5C 106
Crosshouse. E Ayr —1C 116
Cross Houses. Shrp —5H 71
Crossings. Cumb —2G 113
Cross in Hand. E Sus —3G 27
Cross Inn. Cdgn —4E 57 (nr. Aberaeron)
Cross Inn. Cdgn —5C 56 (nr. New Quay)
Cross Inn. Rhon —3D 32
Crosskeys. Cphy —2F 33
Crosskirk. High —2C 168
Crosslands. Cumb —1C 96
Cross Lane Head. Shrp —1B 60
Cross Lanes. Corn —4D 5
Cross Lanes. Dur —3D 104
Cross Lanes. N Yor —3H 99
Crosslanes. Shrp —4F 71
Cross Lanes. Wrex —1F 71
Crosslee. Ren —3F 127
Crossmichael. Dum —3E 111
Crossmoor. Lanc —1C 90
Cross Oak. Powy —3E 46
Cross of Jackston. Aber —5E 161
Cross o' th' Hands. Derbs —1G 73
Crossroads. Aber —3G 153 (nr. Aberdeen)
Crossroads. Aber —4E 153 (nr. Banchory)
Crossroads. E Ayr —1D 116
Cross Side. Devn —4B 20
Cross Street. Suff —3D 66
Crosston. Ang —3E 145
Cross Town. Ches —3B 84
Crossway. Mon —4H 47
Crossway. Powy —5C 58
Crossway Green. Mon —2A 34
Crossway Green. Worc —4C 60
Crossways. Dors —4C 14
Crosswell. Pemb —1F 43
Crosswood. Cdgn —3F 57
Crosthwaite. Cumb —5F 103
Croston. Lanc —3C 90
Crostwick. Norf —4E 79
Crostwight. Norf —3F 79
Crothair. W Isl —4D 171
Crouch. Kent —5H 39
Croucheston. Wilts —4F 23
Crouch Hill. Dors —1C 14
Croughton. Nptn —2D 50
Crovie. Aber —2F 161
Crow. Hants —2G 15
Crowan. Corn —3D 4
Crowborough. E Sus —2G 27
Crowcombe. Som —3E 21
Crowcroft. Worc —5B 60
Crowdecote. Derbs —4F 85
Crowden. Derbs —1E 85
Crowden. Devn —3E 11
Crowdhill. Hants —1C 16
Crowdon. N Yor —5G 107
Crow Edge. S Yor —4B 92
Crow End. Cambs —5C 64
Crowfield. Nptn —1E 50
Crowfield. Suff —5D 66
Crow Green. Essx —1G 39
Crow Hill. Here —3B 48
Crowhurst. E Sus —4B 28
Crowhurst. Surr —1E 27
Crowhurst Lane End. Surr —1E 27
Crowland. Linc —4B 76
Crowland. Suff —3C 66
Crowlas. Corn —3C 4
Crowle. N Lin —3A 94
Crowle. Worc —5D 60
Crowle Green. Worc —5D 60
Crowmarsh Gifford. Oxon —3E 36
Crown Corner. Suff —3E 67
Crownthorpe. Norf —5C 78
Crowntown. Corn —3D 4
Crows-an-wra. Corn —4A 4
Crowshill. Norf —5B 78
Crowthorne. Brac —5G 37
Crowton. Ches —3H 83
Croxall. Staf —4F 73
Croxby. Linc —1A 88
Croxdale. Dur —1F 105
Croxden. Staf —2E 73
Croxley Green. Herts —1B 38
Croxton. Cambs —4B 64
Croxton. Norf —2B 78 (nr. Fakenham)
Croxton. Norf —2A 66 (nr. Thetford)
Croxton. N Lin —3D 94
Croxton. Staf —2B 72
Croxtonbank. Staf —2B 72
Croxton Green. Ches —5H 83
Croxton Kerrial. Leics —3F 75
Croy. High —4B 158
Croy. N Lan —2A 128
Croyde. Devn —3E 19
Croydon. Cambs —1D 52
Croydon. G Lon —4E 39
Crubenbeg. High —4A 150
Crubenmore Lodge. High —4A 150
Cruckmeore. Shrp —5G 71
Cruckton. Shrp —4G 71
Cruden Bay. Aber —5H 161
Crudgington. Telf —4A 72
Crudie. Aber —3E 161
Crudwell. Wilts —2E 35
Cruft. Devn —3F 11
Crug. Powy —3D 58
Crughywel. Powy —4F 47
Crugmeer. Corn —1D 6
Crugybar. Carm —2G 45
Crug-y-byddar. Powy —2D 58
Crulabhig. W Isl —4D 171
Crumlin. Cphy —2F 33
Crumpsall. G Man —4G 91
Crumpsbrook. Shrp —3A 60
Crundale. Kent —1E 29
Crundale. Pemb —3D 42
Cruwys Morchard. Devn —1B 12
Crux Easton. Hants —1C 24
Crwbin. Carm —4E 45
Cryers Hill. Buck —2G 37
Crymych. Pemb —1F 43
Crynant. Neat —5A 46
Crystal Palace. G Lon —3E 39
Cuaich. High —5A 150
Cuaig. High —3G 155
Cuan. Arg —2E 133
Cubbington. Warw —4H 61
Cubert. Corn —3B 6
Cubley. S Yor —4C 92
Cubley Common. Derbs —2F 73
Cublington. Buck —3G 51
Cublington. Here —2G 47
Cuckfield. W Sus —3E 27
Cucklington. Som —4C 22
Cuckney. Notts —3C 86
Cuckoo Bridge. Linc —3B 76
Cuckron. Shet —6F 173
Cuddesdon. Oxon —5E 50
Cuddington. Buck —4F 51
Cuddington. Ches —3A 84
Cuddington Heath. Ches —1G 71
Cuddy Hill. Lanc —1C 90
Cudham. G Lon —5F 39
Cudlipptown. Devn —5F 11
Cudworth. Som —1G 13
Cudworth. S Yor —4D 93
Cudworth. Surr —1D 26
Cuerdley Cross. Warr —2H 83
Cuffley. Herts —5D 52
Cuidhir. W Isl —8B 170
Cuidhsiadar. W Isl —2H 171
Cuidhtinis. W Isl —9C 171
Culbo. High —2A 158
Culbokie. High —3A 158
Culburnie. High —4G 157
Culcabock. High —4A 158
Culcharry. High —3C 158
Culcheth. Warr —1A 84
Culduie. High —4G 155
Culeave. High —4C 164
Culford. Suff —4H 65
Culgaith. Cumb —2H 103
Culham. Oxon —2D 36
Culkein. High —1E 163
Culkein Drumbeg. High —5B 166
Culkerton. Glos —2E 35
Cullen. Mor —2C 160
Cullercoats. Tyne —2G 115
Cullicudden. High —2A 158
Cullingworth. W Yor —1A 92
Cullipool. Arg —2E 133
Cullivoe. Shet —1G 173
Culloch. Per —2G 135
Cullompton. Devn —2D 12
Culm Davy. Devn —1E 13
Culmington. Shrp —2G 59
Culmstock. Devn —1E 12
Culnacnoc. High —2E 155
Culnacraig. High —3E 163
Culrain. High —4C 164
Culross. Fife —1C 128
Culroy. S Ayr —3C 116
Culswick. Shet —7D 173
Cults. Aber C —3F 153
Cults. Aber —5C 160
Cults. Fife —3F 137
Cultybraggan Camp. Per —1G 135
Culver. Devn —3B 12
Culverlane. Devn —2D 8
Culverstone Green. Kent —4H 39
Culverthorpe. Linc —1H 75
Culworth. Nptn —1D 50
Culzie Lodge. High —1H 157
Cumberlow Green. Herts —2D 52
Cumbernauld. N Lan —2A 128
Cumbernauld Village. N Lan —2A 128
Cumberworth. Linc —3E 89
Cumdivock. Cumb —5E 113
Cuminestown. Aber —3F 161
Cumledge Mill. Scot —4D 130
Cumlewick. Shet —9F 173
Cummersdale. Cumb —4E 113
Cummertrees. Dum —3C 112
Cummingstown. Mor —2F 159
Cumnock. E Ayr —3E 117
Cumnor. Oxon —5C 50
Cumrew. Cumb —4G 113
Cumwhinton. Cumb —4F 113
Cumwhitton. Cumb —4G 113
Cundall. N Yor —2G 99
Cunninghamhead. N Ayr —5E 127
Cunning Park. S Ayr —3C 116
Cunnister. Shet —2G 173
Cupar. Fife —2F 137
Cupar Muir. Fife —2F 137
Cupernham. Hants —4B 24
Curbar. Derbs —3G 85
Curborough. Staf —4F 73
Curbridge. Hants —1D 16
Curbridge. Oxon —5B 50
Curdridge. Hants —1D 16
Curdworth. Warw —1F 61
Curland. Som —1F 13
Curridge. W Ber —4C 36
Currie. Edin —3E 129
Curry Mallet. Som —4G 21
Curry Rivel. Som —4G 21
Curtisden Green. Kent —1B 28
Curtisknowle. Devn —3D 8
Cury. Corn —4D 5
Cusgarne. Corn —4B 6
Cusop. Here —1F 47
Cusworth. S Yor —4F 93
Cutcombe. Som —3C 20
Cuthill. E Lot —2G 129
Cutiau. Gwyn —4F 69
Cutlers Green. Essx —2F 53
Cutmadoc. Corn —2E 7
Cutnall Green. Worc —4C 60
Cutsdean. Glos —2F 49
Cutthorpe. Derbs —3H 85
Cuttivett. Corn —2H 7
Cutts. Shet —8F 173
Cuttybridge. Pemb —3D 42
Cuttyhill. Aber —3H 161
Cuxham. Oxon —2E 37
Cuxton. Medw —4B 40
Cuxwold. Linc —4E 95
Cwm. Blae —5E 47
Cwm. Den —3C 82
Cwm. Powy —1E 59
Cwmafan. Neat —2A 32
Cwmaman. Rhon —2C 32
Cwmann. Carm —1F 45
Cwmbach. Carm —2G 43
Cwmbach. Powy —2E 47
Cwmbach. Rhon —5D 46
Cwmbach Llechryd. Powy —5C 58
Cwmbelan. Powy —2B 58
Cwmbran. Torf —2F 33
Cwmbrwyno. Cdgn —2G 57
Cwm Capel. Carm —5E 45
Cwmcarn. Cphy —2F 33
Cwmcarvan. Mon —5H 47
Cwm-celyn. Blae —5F 47
Cwmcerdinen. Swan —5G 45
Cwm-Cewydd. Gwyn —4A 70
Cwmcoy. Cdgn —1C 44
Cwmcrawnon. Powy —4E 47
Cwmcych. Pemb —1G 43
Cwmdare. Rhon —5C 46
Cwmdu. Carm —2G 45
Cwmdu. Powy —3E 47
Cwmduad. Carm —2D 45
Cwm Dulais. Swan —5G 45
Cwmerfyn. Cdgn —2F 57
Cwmfelin. B'End —3B 32
Cwmfelin Boeth. Carm —3F 43
Cwmfelinfach. Cphy —2E 33
Cwmfelin Mynach. Carm —2G 43
Cwmffrwd. Carm —4E 45
Cwmgiedd. Powy —4A 46
Cwmgors. Neat —4H 45
Cwmgwili. Carm —4F 45
Cwmgwrach. Neat —5B 46
Cwmhiraeth. Carm —1H 43
Cwmifor. Carm —3G 45
Cwmisfael. Carm —4E 45
Cwm-Llinau. Powy —5H 69
Cwmllynfell. Neat —4H 45
Cwm-mawr. Carm —4F 45
Cwm-miles. Carm —2F 43
Cwmorgan. Carm —1G 43
Cwmparc. Rhon —2C 32
Cwm Penmachno. Cnwy —1G 69
Cwmpennar. Rhon —5D 46
Cwm Plysgog. Pemb —1B 44
Cwmrhos. Powy —3E 47
Cwmsychpant. Cdgn —1E 45
Cwmsyfiog. Cphy —5E 47
Cwmsymlog. Cdgn —2F 57
Cwmtillery. Blae —5F 47
Cwm-twrch Isaf. Powy —5A 46
Cwm-twrch Uchaf. Powy —4A 46
Cwmwysg. Powy —3B 46
Cwm-y-glo. Gwyn —4E 81
Cwmyoy. Mon —3G 47
Cwmystwyth. Cdgn —3G 57
Cwrt. Gwyn —1F 57
Cwrtnewydd. Cdgn —1E 45
Cwrt-y-Cadno. Carm —1G 45
Cydweli. Carm —5E 45
Cyffylliog. Den —5C 82
Cymau. Flin —5E 83
Cymer. Rhon —2B 32
Cymmer. Neat —2B 32
Cymmer. Rhon —2D 32
Cyncoed. Card —3E 33
Cynghordy. Carm —2B 46
Cynghordy. Swan —5G 45
Cynheidre. Carm —5E 45
Cynonville. Neat —2B 32
Cynwyd. Den —1C 70
Cynwyl Elfed. Carm —3D 44
Cywarch. Gwyn —4A 70

Dacre. Cumb —2F 103
Dacre. N Yor —3D 98
Dacre Banks. N Yor —3D 98
Daddry Shield. Dur —1B 104
Dadford. Buck —2E 51
Dadlington. Leics —1B 62
Dafen. Carm —5F 45
Daffy Green. Norf —5B 78
Dagdale. Staf —2E 73
Dagenham. G Lon —2F 39
Daggons. Dors —1G 15
Daglingworth. Glos —5E 49
Dagnall. Buck —4H 51
Dagtail End. Worc —4E 61
Dail. Arg —5E 141
Dail Beag. W Isl —3E 171
Dail bho Dheas. W Isl —1G 171
Dailly. S Ayr —4B 116
Dail Mor. W Isl —3E 171
Dairsie. Fife —2G 137
Daisy Bank. W Mid —1E 61
Daisy Hill. G Man —4E 91
Daisy Hill. W Yor —1B 92
Dalabrog. W Isl —6C 170
Dalavich. Arg —2G 133
Dalbeattie. Dum —3F 111
Dalblair. E Ayr —3F 117
Dalbury. Derbs —2G 73
Dalby. IOM —4B 108
Dalby Wolds. Leics —3D 74
Dalchalm. High —3G 165
Dalcharn. High —3G 167
Dalchork. High —2C 164
Dalchreichart. High —2E 149
Dalchruin. Per —2G 135
Dalcross. High —4B 158
Dalderby. Linc —4B 88
Dale. Cumb —5G 113
Dale. Derbs —2B 74
Dale. Pemb —4C 42
Dalebank. Derbs —4A 86
Dale Bottom. Cumb —2D 102
Dalebrook. Derbs —2F 73
Dale Head. Cumb —3F 103
Dalehouse. N Yor —3E 107
Dalelia. High —2B 140
Dale of Walls. Shet —6C 173
Dalgarven. N Ayr —5D 126
Dalgety Bay. Fife —1E 129
Dalginross. Per —1G 135
Dalguise. Per —4G 143
Dalhalvaig. High —3A 168
Dalham. Suff —4G 65
Dalintart. Arg —1F 133
Dalkeith. Midl —3G 129
Dallas. Mor —3F 159
Dalleagles. E Ayr —3E 117
Dallinghoo. Suff —5E 67
Dallington. E Sus —4A 28
Dallow. N Yor —2D 98
Dalmally. Arg —1A 134
Dalmarnock. Glas —3H 127
Dalmellington. E Ayr —4D 117
Dalmeny. Edin —2E 129
Dalmigavie. High —2B 150
Dalmilling. S Ayr —2C 116
Dalmore. High —2A 158 (nr. Alness)
Dalmore. High —3E 164 (nr. Rogart)
Dalmuir. W Dun —2F 127
Dalmunach. Mor —4G 159
Dalnabreck. High —2B 140
Dalnacardoch Lodge. Per —1E 142
Dalnamein Lodge. Per —2E 143
Dalnaspidal Lodge. Per —1D 142
Dalnatrat. High —3D 140
Dalnavie. High —1A 158
Dalnawillan Lodge. High —4C 168
Dalness. High —3F 141
Dalnessie. High —2D 164
Dalqueich. Per —3C 136
Dalquhairn. S Ayr —5C 116
Dalreavoch. High —3E 165
Dalreoch. Per —2C 136
Dalry. Edin —2F 129
Dalry. N Ayr —5D 126
Dalrymple. S Ayr —3C 116
Dalscote. Nptn —5D 62
Dalserf. S Lan —4A 128
Dalsmirren. Arg —4A 122
Dalston. Cumb —5E 113
Dalswinton. Dum —1G 111
Dalton. Dum —2C 112
Dalton. Lanc —4C 90
Dalton. Nmbd —4C 114 (nr. Hexham)
Dalton. Nmbd —2E 115 (nr. Ponteland)
Dalton. N Yor —4E 105 (nr. Richmond)
Dalton. N Yor —2G 99 (nr. Thirsk)
Dalton. S Lan —4H 127
Dalton. S Yor —1B 86
Dalton-in-Furness. Cumb —2B 96
Dalton-le-Dale. Dur —5H 115
Dalton Magna. S Yor —1B 86
Dalton-on-Tees. N Yor —4F 105
Dalton Piercy. Hart —1B 106
Daltot. Arg —1F 125
Dalvey. High —5F 159
Dalwhinnie. High —5A 150
Dalwood. Devn —2F 13
Damerham. Hants —1G 15
Damgate. Norf —5G 79 (nr. Acle)
Damgate. Norf —4G 79 (nr. Martham)
Dam Green. Norf —2C 66
Danaway. Kent —4C 40
Danbury. Essx —5A 54
Danby. N Yor —4E 107
Danby Botton. N Yor —4D 107
Danby Wiske. N Yor —5A 106
Danderhall. Midl —3G 129
Danebank. Ches —2D 85
Danebridge. Ches —4D 84
Dane End. Herts —3D 52
Danehill. E Sus —3F 27
Danesford. Shrp —1B 60
Daneshill. Hants —1E 25
Danesmoor. Derbs —4A 86
Danestone. Aber C —3G 153
Dangerous Corner. Lanc —3D 90
Daniel's Water. Kent —1D 28
Dan's Castle. Dur —1E 105
Danshillock. Aber —3E 160
Danzey Green. Warw —4F 61
Dapple Heath. Staf —3E 73
Daren. Powy —4F 47
Darenth. Kent —3G 39
Daresbury. Hal —2H 83
Darfield. S Yor —4E 93
Dargate. Kent —4E 41
Dargill. Per —2A 136
Darite. Corn —2G 7
Darlaston. Staf —2C 72
Darlaston. W Mid —1D 60
Darley. N Yor —4E 98
Darley Abbey. Dby C —2A 74
Darley Bridge. Derbs —4G 85
Darley Dale. Derbs —4G 85
Darley Head. N Yor —4D 98
Darlingscott. Warw —1H 49
Darlington. Darl —3F 105
Darliston. Shrp —2H 71
Darlton. Notts —3E 87
Darmsden. Suff —5C 66
Darnall. S Yor —2A 86
Darnford. Aber —4E 153
Darnick. Scot —1H 119
Darowen. Powy —5H 69
Darra. Aber —4E 161
Darracott. Devn —3E 19
Darras Hall. Nmbd —2E 115
Darrington. W Yor —2E 93
Darrow Green. Norf —2E 67
Darsham. Suff —4G 67
Dartfield. Aber —3H 161
Dartford. Kent —3G 39
Dartford Crossing. Kent —3G 39
Dartington. Devn —2D 9
Dartmeet. Devn —5G 11
Dartmouth. Devn —3E 9
Darton. S Yor —3D 92
Darvel. E Ayr —1E 117
Darwen. Bkbn —2E 91
Dassels. Herts —3D 53
Datchet. Wind —3A 38
Datchworth. Herts —4C 52
Datchworth Green. Herts —4C 52
Daubhill. G Man —4F 91
Dauntsey. Wilts —3E 35
Dauntsey Green. Wilts —3E 35
Dauntsey Lock. Wilts —3E 35
Dava. Mor —5E 159
Davenham. Ches —3A 84
Daventry. Nptn —4C 62
Davidson's Mains. Edin —2F 129
Davidston. High —2B 158
Davidstow. Corn —4B 10
David's Well. Powy —3C 58

Davington—Duddon

Davington. Dum —4E 119
Daviot. Aber —1E 153
Daviot. High —5B 158
Davyhulme. G Man —1B 84
Daw Cross. N Yor —4F 99
Dawdon. Dur —5H 115
Dawesgreen. Surr —1D 26
Dawley. Telf —5A 72
Dawlish. Devn —5C 12
Dawlish Warren. Devn —5C 12
Dawn. Cnwy —3A 82
Daws Heath. Essx —2C 40
Dawshill. Worc —5C 60
Daw's House. Corn —4D 10
Dawsmere. Linc —2D 76
Dayhills. Staf —2D 72
Dayhouse Bank. Worc —3D 60
Daylesford. Glos —3H 49
Daywall. Shrp —2E 71
Ddol. Flin —3D 82
Ddol Cownwy. Powy —4C 70
Deadwater. Nmbd —5A 120
Deaf Hill. Dur —1A 106
Deal. Kent —5H 41
Dean. Cumb —2B 102
Dean. Devn —2G 19
(nr. Combe Martin)
Dean. Devn —2F 19
(nr. Ilfracombe)
Dean. Devn —2H 19
(nr. Lynton)
Dean. Dors —1E 15
Dean. Hants —1D 16
(nr. Bishop's Waltham)
Dean. Hants —3C 24
(nr. Winchester)
Dean. Som —2B 22
Dean Bank. Dur —1F 105
Deanburnhaugh. Scot —3F 119
Deane. Hants —1D 24
Deanich Lodge. High —5A 164
Deanland. Dors —1E 15
Deanlane End. W Sus —1F 17
Dean Park. Shrp —4H 59
Dean Prior. Devn —2D 8
Dean Row. Ches —2C 84
Deans. W Lot —3D 128
Deanscales. Cumb —2B 102
Deanshanger. Nptn —2F 51
Deanston. Stir —3G 135
Dearham. Cumb —1B 102
Dearne. S Yor —4E 93
Dearne Valley. S Yor —4E 93
Debach. Suff —5E 67
Debden. Essx —2F 53
Debden Green. Essx —1F 39
(nr. Loughton)
Debden Green. Essx —2F 53
(nr. Saffron Walden)
Debenham. Suff —4D 66
Dechmont. W Lot —2D 128
Deddington. Oxon —2C 50
Dedham. Essx —2D 54
Dedham Heath. Essx —2D 54
Deebank. Aber —4D 152
Deene. Nptn —1G 63
Deenethorpe. Nptn —1G 63
Deepcar. S Yor —1G 85
Deepcut. Surr —5A 38
Deepdale. Cumb —1G 97
Deepdale. N Lin —3D 94
Deepdale. N Yor —2A 98
Deeping Gate. Pet —5A 76
Deeping St James. Linc —5A 76
Deeping St Nicholas. Linc —4B 76
Deerhill. Mor —3B 160
Deerhurst. Glos —3D 48
Deerhurst Walton. Glos —3D 49
Deerness. Orkn —7E 172
Defford. Worc —1E 49
Defynnog. Powy —3C 46
Deganwy. Cnwy —3G 81
Deighton. N Yor —4A 106
Deighton. W Yor —3B 92
Deighton. York —5A 100
Deiniolen. Gwyn —4E 81
Delabole. Corn —4A 10
Delamere. Ches —4H 83
Delfour. High —3C 150
Dellieture. High —5E 159
Dell, The. Suff —1G 67
Delly End. Oxon —4B 50
Delny. High —1B 158
Delph. G Man —4H 91
Delves. Dur —5E 115
Delves, The. W Mid —1E 61
Delvin End. Essx —2A 54
Dembleby. Linc —2H 75
Demelza. Corn —2D 6
Denaby Main. S Yor —1B 86
Denbeath. Fife —4F 137
Denbigh. Den —4C 82
Denbury. Devn —2E 9
Denby. Derbs —1A 74
Denby Common. Derbs —1B 74
Denby Dale. W Yor —4C 92
Denchworth. Oxon —2B 36
Dendron. Cumb —2B 96
Deneside. Dur —5H 115
Denford. Nptn —3G 63
Dengie. Essx —5C 54
Denham. Buck —2B 38
Denham. Suff —4G 65
(nr. Bury St Edmunds)
Denham. Suff —3D 66
(nr. Eye)
Denham Green. Buck —2B 38
Denham Street. Suff —3D 66
Denhead. Aber —5G 161
(nr. Ellon)
Denhead. Aber —3G 161
(nr. Strichen)
Denhead. Fife —2G 137
Denholm. Scot —3H 119
Denholme. W Yor —1A 92
Denholme Clough. W Yor —1A 92
Denholme Gate. W Yor —1A 92
Denio. Gwyn —2C 68
Denmead. Hants —1E 17
Dennington. Suff —4E 67
Denny. Falk —1B 128
Denny End. Cambs —4D 65
Dennyloanhead. Falk —1B 128
Den of Lindores. Fife —2E 137
Denshaw. G Man —3H 91
Denside. Aber —4F 153
Densole. Kent —1G 29
Denston. Suff —5G 65
Denstone. Staf —1F 73
Denstroude. Kent —4F 41
Dent. Cumb —1G 97
Den, The. N Ayr —4E 127
Denton. Cambs —2A 64
Denton. Darl —3F 105
Denton. E Sus —5F 27
Denton. G Man —1D 84
Denton. Kent —1G 29
Denton. Linc —2F 75
Denton. Norf —2E 67
Denton. Nptn —5F 63
Denton. N Yor —5D 98
Denton. Oxon —5D 50
Denver. Norf —5F 77
Denwick. Nmbd —3G 121
Deopham. Norf —5C 78
Deopham Green. Norf —1C 66
Depden. Suff —5G 65
Depden Green. Suff —5G 65
Deptford. G Lon —3E 39
Deptford. Wilts —3F 23
Derby. Dby C —2A 74
Derbyhaven. IOM —5B 108
Derculich. Per —3F 143
Dereham. Norf —4B 78
Deri. Cphy —5E 47
Derril. Devn —2D 10
Derringstone. Kent —1G 29
Derrington. Shrp —1A 60
Derrington. Staf —3C 72
Derriton. Devn —2D 10
Derryguaig. Arg —5F 139
Derry Hill. Wilts —4E 35
Derrythorpe. N Lin —4B 94
Dersingham. Norf —2F 77
Dervaig. Arg —3F 139
Derwen. Den —5C 82
Derwen Gam. Cdgn —5D 56
Derwenlas. Powy —1G 57
Desborough. Nptn —2F 63
Desford. Leics —5B 74
Detchant. Nmbd —1E 121
Dethick. Derbs —5H 85
Detling. Kent —5B 40
Deuchar. Ang —2D 144
Deuddwr. Powy —4E 71
Devauden. Mon —2H 33
Devil's Bridge. Cdgn —3G 57
Devitts Green. Warw —1G 61
Devizes. Wilts —5F 35
Devonport. Plym —3A 8
Devonside. Clac —4B 136
Devoran. Corn —5B 6
Dewartown. Midl —3G 129
Dewlish. Dors —3C 14
Dewsbury. W Yor —2C 92
Dewshall Court. Here —2H 47
Dexbeer. Devn —2C 10
Dhoon. IOM —3D 108
Dhoor. IOM —2D 108
Dhowin. IOM —1D 108
Dial Green. W Sus —3A 26
Dial Post. W Sus —4C 26
Dibberford. Dors —2H 13
Dibden. Hants —2C 16
Dibden Purlieu. Hants —2C 16
Dickleburgh. Norf —2D 66
Didbrook. Glos —2F 49
Didcot. Oxon —2D 36
Diddington. Cambs —4A 64
Diddlebury. Shrp —2H 59
Didley. Here —2H 47
Didling. W Sus —1G 17
Didmarton. Glos —3D 34
Didsbury. G Man —1C 84
Didworthy. Devn —2C 8
Digby. Linc —5H 87
Digg. High —2D 154
Diggle. G Man —4A 92
Digmoor. Lanc —4C 90
Digswell. Herts —4C 52
Dihewyd. Cdgn —5D 57
Dilham. Norf —3F 79
Dilhorne. Staf —1D 73
Dillarburn. S Lan —5B 128
Dillington. Cambs —4A 64
Dilston. Nmbd —3C 114
Dilton Marsh. Wilts —2D 22
Dilwyn. Here —5G 59
Dimmer. Som —3B 22
Dimple. G Man —3F 91
Dinas. Carm —1G 43
Dinas. Gwyn —5D 81
Dinas. Gwyn —2B 68
Dinas. Pemb —1E 43
Dinas Dinlle. Gwyn —5D 80
Dinas Mawddwy. Gwyn —4A 70
Dinas Powys. V Glam —4E 33
Dinbych. Den —4C 82
Dinbych-y-Pysgod. Pemb —4F 43
Dinckley. Lanc —1E 91
Dinder. Som —2A 22
Dinedor. Here —2A 48
Dinedor Cross. Here —2A 48
Dingestow. Mon —4H 47
Dingle. Mers —2F 83
Dingleden. Kent —2C 28
Dingleton. Scot —1H 119
Dingley. Nptn —2E 63
Dingwall. High —3H 157
Dinmael. Cnwy —1C 70
Dinnet. Aber —4B 152
Dinnington. Som —1H 13
Dinnington. S Yor —2C 86
Dinnington. Tyne —2F 115
Dinorwic. Gwyn —4E 81
Dinton. Buck —4F 51
Dinton. Wilts —3F 23
Dinworthy. Devn —1D 10
Dipley. Hants —1F 25
Dippen. Arg —2B 122
Dippenhall. Surr —2G 25
Dippertown. Devn —4E 11
Dippin. N Ayr —3E 123
Dipple. S Ayr —4B 116
Diptford. Devn —3D 8
Dipton. Dur —4E 115
Dirleton. E Lot —1B 130
Dirt Pot. Nmbd —5B 114
Discoed. Powy —4E 59
Diseworth. Leics —3B 74
Dishes. Orkn —5F 172
Dishforth. N Yor —2F 99
Disley. Ches —2D 85
Diss. Norf —3D 66
Disserth. Powy —5C 58
Distington. Cumb —2B 102
Ditchampton. Wilts —3F 23
Ditcheat. Som —3B 22
Ditchingham. Norf —1F 67
Ditchling. E Sus —4E 27
Ditteridge. Wilts —5D 34
Dittisham. Devn —3E 9
Ditton. Hal —2G 83
Ditton. Kent —5B 40
Ditton Green. Cambs —5F 65
Ditton Priors. Shrp —2A 60
Divach. High —1G 149
Dixonfield. High —2D 168
Dixton. Glos —2E 49
Dixton. Mon —4A 48
Dizzard. Corn —3B 10
Dobcross. G Man —4H 91
Dobs Hill. Flin —4F 83
Dobson's Bridge. Shrp —2G 71
Dobwalls. Corn —2G 7
Doccombe. Devn —4A 12
Dochgarroch. High —4A 158
Docking. Norf —2G 77
Docklow. Here —5H 59
Dockray. Cumb —2E 103
Doc Penfro. Pemb —4D 42
Dodbrooke. Devn —4D 8
Doddenham. Worc —5B 60
Doddinghurst. Essx —1G 39
Doddington. Cambs —1C 64
Doddington. Kent —5D 40
Doddington. Linc —4F 87
Doddington. Nmbd —1D 121
Doddington. Shrp —3A 60
Doddiscombsleigh. Devn —4B 12
Doddshill. Norf —2G 77
Dodford. Nptn —4D 62
Dodford. Worc —3D 60
Dodington. Som —2E 21
Dodington. S Glo —4C 34
Dodleston. Ches —4F 83
Dods Leigh. Staf —2E 73
Dodworth. S Yor —4D 92
Doe Lea. Derbs —4B 86
Dogdyke. Linc —5B 88
Dogmersfield. Hants —1F 25
Dogsthorpe. Pet —5B 76
Dog Village. Devn —3C 12
Dolanog. Powy —4C 70
Dolau. Powy —4D 58
Dolau. Rhon —3D 32
Dolbenmaen. Gwyn —1E 69
Doley. Shrp —3B 72
Dol-fach. Powy —5B 70
(nr. Llanbrynmair)
Dolfach. Powy —3B 58
(nr. Llanidloes)
Dolfor. Powy —2D 58
Dolgarrog. Cnwy —4G 81
Dolgellau. Gwyn —4G 69
Dolgoch. Gwyn —5F 69
Dol-gran. Carm —2E 45
Dolhelfa. Powy —3B 58
Doll. High —3F 165
Dollar. Clac —4B 136
Dolley Green. Powy —4E 59
Dollwen. Cdgn —2F 57
Dolphin. Flin —3D 82
Dolphingstone. E Lot —2G 129
Dolphinholme. Lanc —4E 97
Dolphinton. S Lan —5E 129
Dolton. Devn —1F 11
Dolwen. Cnwy —3A 82
Dolwyddelan. Cnwy —5G 81
Dol-y-Bont. Cdgn —2F 57
Dolyhir. Powy —5E 59
Domgay. Powy —4E 71
Doncaster. S Yor —4F 93
Donhead St Andrew. Wilts —4E 23
Donhead St Mary. Wilts —4E 23
Doniford. Som —2D 20
Donington. Linc —2B 76
Donington. Shrp —5C 72
Donington Eaudike. Linc —2B 76
Donington on Bain. Linc —2B 88
Donington South Ing. Linc —2B 76
Donisthorpe. Leics —4H 73
Donkey Town. Surr —4A 38
Donna Nook. Linc —1D 88
Donnington. Glos —3G 49
Donnington. Here —2C 48
Donnington. Shrp —5H 71
Donnington. Telf —4B 72
Donnington. W Ber —5C 36
Donnington. W Sus —2G 17
Donnington le Heath. Leics —4B 74
Donyatt. Som —1G 13
Doomsday Green. W Sus —2C 26
Doonbank. E Ayr —4D 116
Doonfoot. S Ayr —3C 116
Doonholm. S Ayr —3C 116
Dorback Lodge. High —2E 151
Dorchester. Dors —3B 14
Dorchester. Oxon —2D 36
Dordon. Warw —5G 73
Dore. S Yor —2H 85
Dores. High —5H 157
Dorking. Surr —1C 26
Dorking Tye. Suff —2C 54
Dormansland. Surr —1F 27
Dormans Park. Surr —1E 27
Dormanstown. Red C —2C 106
Dormington. Here —1A 48
Dormston. Worc —5D 61
Dorn. Glos —2H 49
Dorney. Buck —3A 38
Dornie. High —1A 148
Dornoch. High —5E 165
Dornock. Dum —3D 112
Dorridge. W Mid —3F 61
Dorrington. Linc —5H 87
Dorrington. Shrp —5G 71
Dorsington. Warw —1G 49
Dorstone. Here —1G 47
Dorton. Buck —4E 51
Dottery. Dors —3H 13
Doublebois. Corn —2F 7
Dougarie. N Ayr —2C 122
Doughton. Glos —2D 35
Douglas. IOM —4C 108
Douglas. S Lan —1H 117
Douglastown. Ang —4D 144
Douglas Water. S Lan —1A 118
Doulting. Som —2B 22
Dounby. Orkn —5B 172
Doune. High —3C 150
(nr. Kingussie)
Doune. High —3B 164
(nr. Lairg)
Doune. Stir —3G 135
Dounie. High —4C 164
(nr. Bonar Bridge)
Dounie. High —5D 164
(nr. Tain)
Dounreay. High —2B 168
Doura. N Ayr —5E 127
Dousland. Devn —2B 8
Dovaston. Shrp —3F 71
Dove Holes. Derbs —3E 85
Dovenby. Cumb —1B 102
Dover. Kent —1H 29
Dovercourt. Essx —2F 55
Doverdale. Worc —4C 60
Doveridge. Derbs —2F 73
Doversgreen. Surr —1D 26
Dowally. Per —4H 143
Dowbridge. Lanc —1C 90
Dowdeswell. Glos —4F 49
Dowlais. Mer T —5D 46
Dowland. Devn —1F 11
Dowlands. Devn —3F 13
Dowles. Worc —3B 60
Dowlesgreen. Wok —5G 37
Dowlish Wake. Som —1G 13
Downall Green. G Man —4D 90
Down Ampney. Glos —2F 35
Downderry. Corn —3H 7
(nr. Looe)
Downderry. Corn —3D 6
(nr. St Austell)
Downe. G Lon —4F 39
Downend. IOW —4D 16
Downend. S Glo —4B 34
Downend. W Ber —4C 36
Downfield. Cambs —3F 65
Downfield. D'dee —5C 144
Downgate. Corn —5D 10
(nr. Kelly Brae)
Downgate. Corn —5C 10
(nr. Upton Cross)
Downham. Essx —1B 40
Downham. Lanc —5G 97
Downham. Nmbd —1C 120
Downham Market. Norf —5F 77
Down Hatherley. Glos —3D 48
Downhead. Som —2B 22
(nr. Frome)
Downhead. Som —4A 22
(nr. Yeovil)
Downhill. Per —5H 143
Downholland Cross. Lanc —4B 90
Downholme. N Yor —5E 105
Downies. Aber —4G 153
Downley. Buck —2G 37
Down St Mary. Devn —2H 11
Downside. Som —1B 22
(nr. Chilcompton)
Downside. Som —2B 22
(nr. Shepton Mallet)
Downside. Surr —5C 38
Down, The. Shrp —1A 60
Down Thomas. Devn —4B 8
Downton. Hants —3A 16
Downton. Wilts —4G 23
Downton on the Rock. Here —3G 59
Dowsby. Linc —3A 76
Dowsdale. Linc —4B 76
Dowthwaitehead. Cumb —2E 103
Doxey. Staf —3D 72
Doxford. Nmbd —2F 121
Doynton. S Glo —4C 34
Drabblegate. Norf —3E 78
Draethen. Cphy —3F 33
Draffan. S Lan —5A 128
Dragonby. N Lin —3B 94
Dragons Green. W Sus —3C 26
Drakelow. Worc —2C 60
Drakemyre. N Ayr —4D 126
Drakes Broughton. Worc —1E 49
Drakes Cross. Worc —3E 61
Drakewalls. Corn —5E 11
Draughton. Nptn —3E 63
Draughton. N Yor —4C 98
Drax. N Yor —2G 93
Draycot. Oxon —5E 51
Draycote. Warw —4B 62
Draycot Foliat. Swin —4G 35
Draycott. Derbs —2B 74
Draycott. Glos —2G 49
Draycott. Shrp —1C 60
Draycott. Som —1H 21
(nr. Cheddar)
Draycott. Som —4A 22
(nr. Yeovil)
Draycott. Worc —1D 48
Draycott in the Clay. Staf —3F 73
Draycott in the Moors. Staf —1D 73
Drayford. Devn —1A 12
Drayton. Leics —1F 63
Drayton. Linc —2B 76
Drayton. Norf —4D 78
Drayton. Nptn —4C 62
Drayton. Oxon —2C 36
(nr. Abingdon)
Drayton. Oxon —1C 50
(nr. Banbury)
Drayton. Port —2E 17
Drayton. Som —4H 21
Drayton. Warw —5F 61
Drayton. Worc —3D 60
Drayton Bassett. Staf —5F 73
Drayton Beauchamp. Buck —4H 51
Drayton Parslow. Buck —3G 51
Drayton St Leonard. Oxon —2D 36
Drebley. N Yor —4C 98
Dreenhill. Pemb —3D 42
Drefach. Carm —4F 45
(nr. Meidrim)
Drefach. Carm —2D 44
(nr. Newcastle Emlyn)
Drefach. Carm —2G 43
(nr. Tumble)
Drefach. Cdgn —1F 45
Dreghorn. N Ayr —1C 116
Drellingore. Kent —1G 29
Drem. E Lot —2B 130
Dreumasdal. W Isl —5C 170
Drewsteignton. Devn —3H 11
Drewston. Devn —4H 11
Driby. Linc —3C 88
Driffield. E Yor —4E 101
Driffield. Glos —2F 35
Drift. Corn —4B 4
Drigg. Cumb —5B 102
Drighlington. W Yor —2C 92
Drimnin. High —3G 139
Drimpton. Dors —2H 13
Dringhoe. E Yor —4F 101
Drinisiadar. W Isl —8D 171
Drinkstone. Suff —4B 66
Drinkstone Green. Suff —4B 66
Drointon. Staf —3E 73
Droitwich. Worc —4C 60
Droman. High —3B 166
Dron. Per —2D 136
Dronfield. Derbs —3A 86
Dronfield Woodhouse. Derbs —3H 85
Drongan. E Ayr —3D 116
Dronley. Ang —5C 144
Droop. Dors —2C 14
Drope. V Glam —4E 32
Droxford. Hants —1E 16
Droylsden. G Man —1C 84
Druggers End. Worc —2C 48
Druid. Den —1C 70
Druid's Heath. W Mid —5E 73
Druidston. Pemb —3C 42
Druim. High —3D 158
Druimarbin. High —1E 141
Druimindarroch. High —5E 147
Drum. Per —3C 136
Drumbeg. High —5B 166
Drumblade. Aber —4C 160
Drumbuie. Dum —1C 110
Drumbuie. High —5G 155
Drumburgh. Cumb —4D 112
Drumburn. Dum —3A 112
Drumchapel. Glas —2G 127
Drumchardine. High —4H 157
Drumchork. High —5C 162
Drumclog. S Lan —1F 117
Drumeldrie. Fife —3G 137
Drumelzier. Scot —1D 118
Drumfearn. High —2E 147
Drumgask. High —4A 150
Drumgelloch. N Lan —3A 128
Drumgley. Ang —3D 144
Drumguish. High —4B 150
Drumin. Mor —5F 159
Drumindorsair. High —4G 157
Drumlamford House. S Ayr —2H 109
Drumlasie. Aber —3D 152
Drumlemble. Arg —4A 122
Drumlithie. Aber —5E 153
Drummoddie. Dum —5A 110
Drummond. High —2A 158
Drummore. Dum —5E 109
Drummuir. Mor —4A 160
Drumnadrochit. High —5H 157
Drumnagorrach. Mor —3C 160
Drumoak. Aber —4E 153
Drumrunie. High —3F 163
Drumry. W Dun —2G 127
Drums. Aber —1G 153
Drumsleet. Dum —2G 111
Drumsmittal. High —4A 158
Drums of Park. Aber —3C 160
Drumsturdy. Ang —5D 145
Drumtochty Castle. Aber —5D 152
Drumuie. High —4D 154
Drumuillie. High —1D 150
Drumvaich. Stir —3F 135
Drumwhindle. Aber —5G 161
Drunkendub. Ang —4F 145
Drury. Flin —4E 83
Drury Square. Norf —4B 78
Drybeck. Cumb —3H 103
Drybridge. Mor —2B 160
Drybridge. N Ayr —1C 116
Drybrook. Glos —4B 48
Drybrook. Here —4A 48
Dryburgh. Scot —1H 119
Dry Doddington. Linc —1F 75
Dry Drayton. Cambs —4C 64
Drym. Corn —3D 4
Drymen. Stir —1F 127
Drymuir. Aber —4G 161
Drynachan Lodge. High —5C 158
Drynie Park. High —3H 157
Drynoch. High —5D 154
Dry Sandford. Oxon —5C 50
Dryslwyn. Carm —3F 45
Dry Street. Essx —2A 40
Dryton. Shrp —5H 71
Dubford. Aber —2E 161
Dubiton. Aber —3D 160
Dubton. Ang —3E 145
Duchally. High —2A 164
Duck End. Essx —3G 53
Duckington. Ches —5G 83
Ducklington. Oxon —5B 50
Duckmanton. Derbs —3B 86
Duck Street. Hants —2B 24
Dudbridge. Glos —5D 48
Duddenhoe End. Essx —2E 53
Duddingston. Edin —2F 129
Duddington. Nptn —5G 75
Duddo. Nmbd —5F 131
Duddon. Ches —4H 83

Duddon Bridge—East Village

Duddon Bridge. Cumb —1A 96
Dudleston. Shrp —2F 71
Dudleston Heath. Shrp —2F 71
Dudley. Tyne —2F 115
Dudley. W Mid —2D 60
Dudsbury. Dors —3F 15
Dudston. Shrp —1E 59
Dudwells. Pemb —2D 42
Duffield. Derbs —1H 73
Duffryn. Neat —2B 32
Dufftown. Mor —4H 159
Duffus. Mor —2F 159
Dufton. Cumb —2H 103
Duggleby. N Yor —3C 100
Duirinish. High —5G 155
Duisdalemore. High —2E 147
Duisky. High —1E 141
Dukesfield. Nmbd —4C 114
Dukestown. Blae —4E 47
Dukinfield. G Man —1D 84
Dulas. IOA —2D 81
Dulcote. Som —2A 22
Dulford. Devn —2D 12
Dull. Per —4F 143
Dullatur. N Lan —2A 128
Dullingham. Cambs —5F 65
Dullingham Ley. Cambs —5F 65
Dulnain Bridge. High —1D 151
Duloe. Beds —4A 64
Duloe. Corn —3G 7
Dulverton. Som —4C 20
Dulwich. G Lon —3E 39
Dumbarton. W Dun —2F 127
Dumbleton. Glos —2F 49
Dumfries. Dum —2A 112
Dumfrin. Arg —1E 127
Dumgoyne. Stir —1G 127
Dummer. Hants —2D 24
Dumpford. W Sus —4G 25
Dun. Ang —3F 145
Dunagoil. Arg —4B 126
Dunalastair. Per —3E 142
Dunan. High —1D 147
Dunball. Som —2G 21
Dunbar. E Lot —2C 130
Dunbeath. High —5D 168
Dunbeg. Arg —5C 140
Dunblane. Stir —3G 135
Dunbog. Fife —2E 137
Dunbridge. Hants —4B 24
Duncanston. Aber —1C 152
Duncanston. High —3H 157
Dun Charlabhaigh. W Isl —3D 171
Dunchurch. Warw —3B 62
Duncote. Nptn —5D 62
Duncow. Dum —1A 112
Duncrievie. Per —3D 136
Duncton. W Sus —4A 26
Dundee. D'dee —5D 144
Dundee Airport. D'dee —1F 137
Dundon. Som —3H 21
Dundonald. S Ayr —1C 116
Dundonnell. High —5E 163
Dundraw. Cumb —5D 112
Dundreggan. High —2F 149
Dundrennan. Dum —5E 111
Dundridge. Hants —1D 16
Dundry. N Som —5A 34
Dunecht. Aber —3E 153
Dunfermline. Fife —1D 129
Dunford Bridge. S Yor —4B 92
Dungate. Kent —5D 40
Dunge. Wilts —1D 23
Dungeness. Kent —4E 29
Dungworth. S Yor —2G 85
Dunham-on-the-Hill. Ches —3G 83
Dunham on Trent. Notts —3F 87
Dunhampton. Worc —4C 60
Dunham Town. G Man —2B 84
Dunham Woodhouses. G Man —2B 84
Dunholme. Linc —3H 87
Dunino. Fife —2H 137
Dunipace. Falk —1B 128
Dunira. Per —1G 135
Dunkeld. Per —4H 143
Dunkerton. Bath —1C 22
Dunkeswell. Devn —2E 13
Dunkeswick. N Yor —5E 99
Dunkirk. Kent —5E 41
Dunkirk. S Glo —3C 34
Dunkirk. Staf —5C 84
Dunkirk. Wilts —5E 35
Dunk's Green. Kent —5H 39
Dunlappie. Ang —2E 145
Dunley. Hants —1C 24
Dunley. Worc —4B 60
Dunlichity Lodge. High —5A 158
Dunlop. E Ayr —5F 127
Dunmaglass Lodge. High —1H 149
Dunmail Raise. Cumb —3E 103
Dunmore. Arg —3F 125
Dunmore. Falk —1B 128
Dunmore. High —4H 157
Dunnet. High —1E 169
Dunnichen. Ang —4E 145
Dunning. Per —2C 136
Dunnington. E Yor —4F 101
Dunnington. Warw —5E 61
Dunnington. York —4A 100
Dunnockshaw. Lanc —2G 91
Dunoon. Arg —2C 126
Dunphail. Mor —4E 159
Dunragit. Dum —4G 109
Dunrostan. Arg —1F 125
Duns. Scot —4D 130
Dunsby. Linc —3A 76
Dunscar. G Man —3F 91
Dunscore. Dum —1F 111
Dunscroft. S Yor —4G 93
Dunsdale. Red C —3D 106
Dunsden Green. Oxon —4F 37
Dunsfold. Surr —2B 26
Dunsford. Devn —4B 12
Dunshalt. Fife —2E 137
Dunshillock. Aber —4G 161
Dunsley. N Yor —3F 107
Dunsley. Staf —2C 60
Dunsmore. Buck —5G 51
Dunsop Bridge. Lanc —4F 97
Dunstable. Beds —3A 52
Dunstal. Staf —3E 73
Dunstall. Staf —3F 73
Dunstall Green. Suff —4G 65
Dunstall Hill. W Mid —1D 60
Dunstan. Nmbd —3G 121
Dunster. Som —2C 20
Duns Tew. Oxon —3C 50
Dunston. Linc —4H 87
Dunston. Norf —5E 79
Dunston. Staf —4D 72
Dunston. Tyne —3F 115
Dunstone. Devn —5H 11
(nr. Ashburton)
Dunstone. Devn —3B 8
(nr. Plymouth)
Dunston Heath. Staf —4D 72
Dunsville. S Yor —4G 93
Dunswell. E Yor —1D 94
Dunsyre. S Lan —5D 128
Dunterton. Devn —5D 11
Duntisbourne Abbots. Glos —5E 49
Duntisbourne Leer. Glos —5E 49
Duntisbourne Rouse. Glos —5E 49
Duntish. Dors —2B 14
Duntocher. W Dun —2F 127
Dunton. Beds —1C 52
Dunton. Buck —3G 51
Dunton. Norf —2A 78
Dunton Bassett. Leics —1C 62
Dunton Green. Kent —5G 39
Dunton Patch. Norf —2A 78
Duntulm. High —1D 154
Dunure. S Ayr —3B 116
Dunvant. Swan —3E 31
Dunvegan. High —4B 154
Dunwich. Suff —3G 67
Dunwood. Staf —5D 84
Durdar. Cumb —4F 113
Durgates. E Sus —2H 27
Durham. Dur —5F 115
Durisdeer. Dum —4A 118
Durisdeermill. Dum —4A 118
Durkar. W Yor —3D 92
Durleigh. Som —3F 21
Durley. Hants —1D 16
Durley. Wilts —5H 35
Durley Street. Hants —1D 16
Durlow Common. Here —2B 48
Durnamuck. High —4E 163
Durness. High —2E 166
Durno. Aber —1E 152
Durns Town. Hants —3A 16
Duror. High —3D 141
Durran. Arg —3G 133
Durran. High —2D 169
Durrant Green. Kent —2C 28
Durrants. Hants —1F 17
Durrington. W Sus —5C 26
Durrington. Wilts —2G 23
Dursley. Glos —2C 34
Dursley Cross. Glos —4B 48
Durston. Som —4F 21
Durweston. Dors —2D 14
Dury. Shet —6F 173
Duston. Nptn —4E 62
Duthil. High —1D 150
Dutlas. Powy —3E 58
Duton Hill. Essx —3G 53
Dutson. Corn —4D 10
Dutton. Ches —3H 83
Duxford. Cambs —1E 53
Duxford. Oxon —2B 36
Dwygyfylchi. Cnwy —3G 81
Dwyran. IOA —4D 80
Dyce. Aber C —2F 153
Dye House. Nmbd —4C 114
Dyffryn. B'End —2B 32
Dyffryn. Carm —2H 43
Dyffryn. IOA —3B 80
Dyffryn. Pemb —1D 42
Dyffryn. V Glam —4D 32
Dyffryn Ardudwy. Gwyn —3E 69
Dyffryn Castell. Cdgn —2G 57
Dyffryn Ceidrych. Carm —3H 45
Dyffryn Cellwen. Neat —5B 46
Dyke. Linc —3A 76
Dyke. Mor —3D 159
Dykehead. Ang —2C 144
Dykehead. N Lan —3B 128
Dykehead. Stir —4E 135
Dykends. Ang —3B 144
Dykesfield. Cumb —4E 112
Dylife. Powy —1A 58
Dymchurch. Kent —3F 29
Dymock. Glos —2C 48
Dyrham. S Glo —4C 34
Dysart. Fife —4F 137
Dyserth. Den —3C 82

Eachwick. Nmbd —2E 115
Eadar Dha Fhadhail. W Isl —4C 171
Eagland Hill. Lanc —5D 96
Eagle. Linc —4F 87
Eagle Barnsdale. Linc —4F 87
Eagle Moor. Linc —4F 87
Eaglescliffe. Stoc T —3B 106
Eaglesfield. Cumb —2B 102
Eaglesfield. Dum —2D 112
Eaglesham. E Ren —4G 127
Eaglethorpe. Nptn —1H 63
Eagley. G Man —3F 91
Eairy. IOM —4C 108
Eakley Lanes. Mil —5F 63
Eakring. Notts —4D 86
Ealand. N Lin —3A 94
Ealing. G Lon —2C 38
Eallabus. Arg —3B 124
Eals. Nmbd —4H 113
Eamont Bridge. Cumb —2G 103
Earby. Lanc —5B 98
Earcroft. Bkbn —2E 91
Eardington. Shrp —1B 60
Eardisland. Here —5G 59
Eardisley. Here —1G 47
Eardiston. Shrp —3F 71
Eardiston. Worc —4A 60
Earith. Cambs —3C 64
Earle. Nmbd —2D 121
Earlesfield. Linc —2G 75
Earlestown. Mers —1H 83
Earley. Wok —4F 37
Earlham. Norf —5D 78
Earlish. High —2C 154
Earls Barton. Nptn —4F 63
Earls Colne. Essx —3B 54
Earls Common. Worc —5D 60
Earl's Croome. Worc —1D 48
Earlsdon. W Mid —3H 61
Earlsferry. Fife —3G 137
Earlsford. Aber —5F 161
Earl's Green. Suff —4C 66
Earlsheaton. W Yor —2C 92
Earl Shilton. Leics —1B 62
Earl Soham. Suff —4E 67
Earl Sterndale. Derbs —4E 85
Earlston. E Ayr —1D 116
Earlston. Scot —1H 119
Earl Stonham. Suff —5D 66
Earlstoun. Dum —1D 110
Earlswood. Mon —2H 33
Earlswood. Warw —3F 61
Earlyvale. Scot —4F 129
Earnley. W Sus —3G 17
Earsairidh. W Isl —9C 170
Earsdon. Tyne —2G 115
Earsham. Norf —2F 67
Earsham Street. Suff —3E 67
Earswick. York —4A 100
Eartham. W Sus —5A 26
Earthcott Green. S Glo —3B 34
Easby. N Yor —4C 106
(nr. Great Ayton)
Easby. N Yor —4E 105
(nr. Richmond)
Easdale. Arg —2E 133
Easebourne. W Sus —4G 25
Easenhall. Warw —3B 62
Eashing. Surr —1A 26
Easington. Buck —4E 51
Easington. Dur —5H 115
Easington. E Yor —3G 95
Easington. Nmbd —1F 121
Easington. Oxon —2C 50
(nr. Banbury)
Easington. Oxon —2E 37
(nr. Watlington)
Easington. Red C —3E 107
Easington Colliery. Dur —5H 115
Easington Lane. Tyne —5G 115
Easingwold. N Yor —3H 99
Easole Street. Kent —5G 41
Eassie. Ang —4C 144
Eassie & Nevay. Ang —4C 144
East Aberthaw. V Glam —5D 32
Eastacombe. Devn —4F 19
Eastacott. Devn —4G 19
East Allington. Devn —4D 8
East Anstey. Devn —4B 20
East Anton. Hants —2B 24
East Appleton. N Yor —5F 105
East Ardsley. W Yor —2D 92
East Ashley. Devn —1G 11
East Ashling. W Sus —2G 17
East Aston. Hants —2C 24
East Ayton. N Yor —1D 101
East Bagborough. Som —3E 21
East Barkwith. Linc —2A 88
East Barming. Kent —5B 40
East Barnby. N Yor —3F 107
East Barnet. G Lon —1D 39
East Barns. E Lot —2D 130
East Barsham. Norf —2B 78
East Beach. W Sus —3G 17
East Beckham. Norf —1D 78
East Bedfont. G Lon —3B 38
East Bennan. N Ayr —3D 123
East Bergholt. Suff —2D 54
East Bierley. W Yor —2B 92
East Blatchington. E Sus —5F 27
East Bliney. Norf —4B 78
East Bloxworth. Dors —3D 15
East Boldre. Hants —2B 16
East Bolton. Nmbd —3F 121
Eastbourne. Darl —3F 105
Eastbourne. E Sus —5H 27
East Brent. Som —1G 21
Eastbridge. Devn —1E 11
East Bridge. Suff —4G 67
East Bridgford. Notts —1D 74
East Briscoe. Dur —3C 104
East Brunton. Tyne —2F 115
East Buckland. Devn —3G 19
East Budleigh. Devn —4D 12
Eastburn. W Yor —5C 98
East Burnham. Buck —2A 38
East Burrafirth. Shet —6E 173
East Burton. Dors —4D 14
Eastbury. Herts —1B 38
Eastbury. W Ber —4B 36
East Butsfield. Dur —5E 115
East Butterleigh. Devn —2C 12
East Butterwick. N Lin —4B 94
Eastby. N Yor —4C 98
East Calder. W Lot —3D 129
East Carleton. Norf —5D 78
East Carlton. Nptn —2F 63
East Carlton. W Yor —5E 98
East Chaldon. Dors —4C 14
East Challow. Oxon —3B 36
East Charlton. Devn —4D 8
East Chelborough. Dors —2A 14
East Chiltington. E Sus —4E 27
East Chinnock. Som —1H 13
East Chisenbury. Wilts —1G 23
Eastchurch. Kent —3D 40
East Clandon. Surr —5B 38
East Claydon. Buck —3F 51
East Clevedon. N Som —4H 33
East Clyne. High —3F 165
East Clyth. High —5E 169
East Coker. Som —1A 14
Eastcombe. Glos —5D 49
East Combe. Som —3E 21
East Common. N Yor —1G 93
East Compton. Som —2B 22
East Cornworthy. Devn —3E 9
Eastcote. G Lon —2C 38
Eastcote. Nptn —5D 62
Eastcote. W Mid —3F 61
Eastcott. Corn —1C 10
Eastcott. Wilts —1F 23
East Cottingwith. E Yor —5B 100
East Coulston. Wilts —1E 23
Eastcourt. Wilts —5H 35
(nr. Pewsey)
Eastcourt. Wilts —2E 35
(nr. Tetbury)
East Cowes. IOW —3D 16
East Cowick. E Yor —2G 93
East Cowton. N Yor —4A 106
East Cramlington. Nmbd —2F 115
East Cranmore. Som —2B 22
East Creech. Dors —4E 15
East Croachy. High —1A 150
East Dean. E Sus —5G 27
East Dean. Glos —3B 48
East Dean. Hants —4A 24
East Dean. W Sus —4A 26
East Down. Devn —2G 19
East Drayton. Notts —3E 87
East Dundry. N Som —5A 34
East Ella. Hull —2D 94
East End. Cambs —3C 64
East End. Dors —3E 15
East End. E Yor —4F 101
(nr. Ulrome)
East End. E Yor —2F 95
(nr. Withernsea)
East End. Hants —3B 16
(nr. Lymington)
East End. Hants —5C 36
(nr. Newbury)
East End. Herts —3E 53
East End. Kent —3D 40
(nr. Minster)
East End. Kent —2C 28
(nr. Tenterden)
East End. N Som —5H 33
East End. Oxon —4B 50
East End. Som —1A 22
East End. Suff —2E 54
Easter Ardross. High —1A 158
Easter Balgedie. Per —3D 136
Easter Balmoral. Aber —4G 151
Easter Brae. High —2A 158
Easter Buckieburn. Stir —1A 128
Easter Bush. Midl —3F 129
Easter Compton. S Glo —3A 34
Easter Fearn. High —5D 164
Easter Galcantray. High —4C 158
Eastergate. W Sus —5A 26
Easterhouse. Glas —3H 127
Easter Howgate. Midl —3F 129
Easter Kinkell. High —3H 157
Easter Lednathie. Ang —2C 144
Easter Ogil. Ang —2D 144
Easter Ord. Aber —3F 153
Easter Quarff. Shet —8F 173
Easter Skeld. Shet —7E 173
Easter Suddie. High —3A 158
Easterton. Wilts —1F 23
Eastertown. Som —1G 21
Eastertown of Auchleuchries. Aber —5H 161
Easter Tulloch. Aber —1G 145
East Everleigh. Wilts —1H 23
East Farleigh. Kent —5B 40
East Farndon. Nptn —2E 62
East Ferry. Linc —1F 87
Eastfield. N Lan —3B 128
(nr. Caldercruix)
Eastfield. N Lan —3B 128
(nr. Harthill)
Eastfield. N Yor —1E 101
Eastfield. S Lan —3H 127
Eastfield Hall. Nmbd —4G 121
East Fortune. E Lot —2B 130
East Garforth. W Yor —1E 93
East Garston. W Ber —4B 36
Eastgate. Dur —1C 104
Eastgate. Norf —3D 78
East Ginge. Oxon —3C 36
East Gores. Essx —3B 54
East Goscote. Leics —4D 74
East Grafton. Wilts —5A 36
East Grimstead. Wilts —4H 23
East Grinstead. W Sus —2E 27
East Guldeford. E Sus —3D 28
East Haddon. Nptn —4D 62
East Hagbourne. Oxon —3D 36
East Halton. N Lin —2E 95
East Ham. G Lon —2F 39
Eastham. Mers —2F 83
Eastham. Worc —4A 60
Eastham Ferry. Mers —2F 83
Easthampstead. Brac —5G 37
Easthampton. Here —4G 59
East Hanney. Oxon —2C 36
East Hanningfield. Essx —5A 54
East Hardwick. W Yor —3E 93
East Harling. Norf —2B 66
East Harlsey. N Yor —5B 106
East Harnham. Wilts —4G 23
East Harptree. Bath —1A 22
East Hartford. Nmbd —2F 115
East Harting. W Sus —1G 17
East Hatch. Wilts —4E 23
East Hatley. Cambs —5B 64
Easthaugh. Norf —4C 78
East Hauxwell. N Yor —5E 105
East Haven. Ang —5E 145
Eastheath. Wok —5G 37
East Heckington. Linc —1A 76
East Hedleyhope. Dur —5E 115
East Hendred. Oxon —3C 36
East Heslerton. N Yor —2D 100
East Hoathly. E Sus —4G 27
Easthope. Shrp —1H 59
Easthorpe. Essx —3C 54
Easthorpe. Leics —2F 75
East Horrington. Som —2A 22
East Horsley. Surr —5B 38
East Horton. Nmbd —1E 121
Easthouses. Midl —3G 129
East Howe. Bour —3F 15
East Huntspill. Som —2G 21
East Hyde. Beds —4B 52
East Ilsley. W Ber —3C 36
Eastington. Devn —2H 11
Eastington. Glos —4G 49
(nr. Northleach)
Eastington. Glos —5C 48
(nr. Stonehouse)
East Keal. Linc —4C 88
East Kennett. Wilts —5G 35
East Keswick. W Yor —5F 99
East Kilbride. S Lan —4H 127
East Kirkby. Linc —4C 88
East Knapton. N Yor —2C 100
East Knighton. Dors —4D 14
East Knowstone. Devn —4B 20
East Knoyle. Wilts —3D 23
East Kyloe. Nmbd —1E 121
East Lambrook. Som —1H 13
East Langdon. Kent —1H 29
East Langton. Leics —1E 63
East Langwell. High —3E 164
East Lavant. W Sus —2G 17
East Lavington. W Sus —4A 26
East Layton. N Yor —4E 105
Eastleach Martin. Glos —5H 49
Eastleach Turville. Glos —5G 49
East Leake. Notts —3C 74
East Learmouth. Nmbd —1C 120
Eastleigh. Devn —4E 19
(nr. Bideford)
East Leigh. Devn —2H 11
(nr. Crediton)
East Leigh. Devn —3C 8
(nr. Modbury)
Eastleigh. Hants —1C 16
East Lexham. Norf —4A 78
East Lilburn. Nmbd —2E 121
Eastling. Kent —5D 40
East Linton. E Lot —2B 130
East Liss. Hants —4F 25
East Lockinge. Oxon —3C 36
East Looe. Corn —3G 7
East Lound. N Lin —1E 87
East Lulworth. Dors —4D 14
East Lutton. N Yor —3D 100
East Lydford. Som —3A 22
East Mains. Aber —4D 152
East Malling. Kent —5B 40
East Marden. W Sus —1G 17
East Markham. Notts —3E 87
East Marton. N Yor —4B 98
East Meon. Hants —4E 25
East Mersea. Essx —4D 54
East Mey. High —1F 169
East Midlands Airport. Leics —3B 74
East Molesey. Surr —4C 38
Eastmoor. Norf —5G 77
East Morton. W Yor —5C 98
East Ness. N Yor —2A 100
East Newton. E Yor —1F 95
East Newton. N Yor —2A 100
Eastney. Port —3E 17
Eastnor. Here —2C 48
East Norton. Leics —5E 75
East Oakley. Hants —1D 24
Eastoft. N Lin —3B 94
East Ogwell. Devn —5B 12
Easton. Cambs —3A 64
Easton. Cumb —4D 112
(nr. Burgh by Sands)
Easton. Cumb —2F 113
(nr. Longtown)
Easton. Devn —4H 11
Easton. Dors —5B 14
Easton. Hants —3D 24
Easton. Linc —3G 75
Easton. Norf —4D 78
Easton. Som —2A 22
Easton. Suff —5E 67
Easton. Wilts —4D 35
Easton Grey. Wilts —3D 35
Easton-in-Gordano. N Som —4A 34
Easton Maudit. Nptn —5F 63
Easton on the Hill. Nptn —5H 75
Easton Royal. Wilts —5H 35
East Orchard. Dors —1D 14
East Ord. Nmbd —4F 131
East Panson. Devn —3D 10
East Peckham. Kent —1A 28
East Pennard. Som —3A 22
East Perry. Cambs —4A 64
East Pitcorthie. Fife —3H 137
East Portlemouth. Devn —5D 8
East Prawle. Devn —5D 9
East Preston. W Sus —5B 26
East Putford. Devn —1D 10
East Quantoxhead. Som —2E 21
East Rainton. Tyne —5G 115
East Ravendale. NE Lin —1B 88
East Raynham. Norf —3A 78
Eastrea. Cambs —1B 64
East Rhidorroch Lodge. High —4G 163
Eastriggs. Dum —3D 112
East Rigton. W Yor —5F 99
Eastrington. E Yor —1A 94
East Rounton. N Yor —4B 106
East Row. N Yor —3F 107
East Rudham. Norf —3H 77
East Runton. Norf —1D 78
East Ruston. Norf —3F 79
Eastry. Kent —5H 41
East Saltoun. E Lot —3A 130
East Shaws. Dur —3D 105
East Shefford. W Ber —4B 36
Eastshore. Shet —10F 173
East Sleekburn. Nmbd —1F 115
East Somerton. Norf —4G 79
East Stockwith. Linc —1E 87
East Stoke. Dors —4D 14
East Stoke. Notts —1E 75
East Stoke. Som —1H 13
East Stour. Dors —4D 22
East Stourmouth. Kent —4G 41
East Stowford. Devn —4G 19
East Stratton. Hants —2D 24
East Studdal. Kent —1H 29
East Taphouse. Corn —2F 7
East-the-Water. Devn —4E 19
East Thirston. Nmbd —5F 121
East Tilbury. Thur —3A 40
East Tisted. Hants —3F 25
East Torrington. Linc —2A 88
East Tuddenham. Norf —4C 78
East Tytherley. Hants —4A 24
East Tytherton. Wilts —4E 35
East Village. Devn —2B 12

Eastville—Fanagmore

Eastville. *Linc* —5D **88**
East Wall. *Shrp* —1H **59**
East Walton. *Norf* —4G **77**
East Week. *Devn* —3G **11**
Eastwell. *Leics* —3E **75**
East Wellow. *Hants* —4B **24**
East Wemyss. *Fife* —4F **137**
East Whitburn. *W Lot* —3C **128**
Eastwick. *Herts* —4E **53**
Eastwick. *Shet* —4E **173**
East Williamston. *Pemb* —4E **43**
East Winch. *Norf* —4F **77**
East Winterslow. *Wilts* —3H **23**
East Wittering. *W Sus* —3F **17**
East Witton. *N Yor* —1D **98**
Eastwood. *Notts* —1B **74**
Eastwood. *S'end* —2C **40**
East Woodburn. *Nmbd* —1C **114**
Eastwood End. *Cambs* —1D **64**
East Woodhay. *Hants* —5C **36**
East Woodlands. *Som* —2C **22**
East Worldham. *Hants* —3F **25**
East Worlington. *Devn* —1A **12**
East Youlstone. *Devn* —1C **10**
Eathorpe. *Warw* —4A **62**
Eaton. *Ches* —4C **84**
(nr. Congleton)
Eaton. *Ches* —4H **83**
(nr. Kelsall)
Eaton. *Leics* —3E **75**
Eaton. *Norf* —2F **77**
(nr. Heacham)
Eaton. *Norf* —5E **78**
(nr. Norwich)
Eaton. *Notts* —3E **86**
Eaton. *Oxon* —5C **50**
Eaton. *Shrp* —2F **59**
(nr. Bishop's Castle)
Eaton. *Shrp* —1H **59**
(nr. Church Stretton)
Eaton Bishop. *Here* —2H **47**
Eaton Bray. *Beds* —3H **51**
Eaton Constantine. *Shrp* —5H **71**
Eaton Green. *Beds* —3H **51**
Eaton Hastings. *Oxon* —2A **36**
Eaton Socon. *Cambs* —5A **64**
Eaton upon Tern. *Shrp* —3A **72**
Eau Brink. *Norf* —4E **77**
Eaves Green. *W Mid* —2G **61**
Ebberston. *N Yor* —1C **100**
Ebbesbourne Wake. *Wilts* —4E **23**
Ebblake. *Dors* —2G **15**
Ebbw Vale. *Blae* —5E **47**
Ebchester. *Dur* —4E **115**
Ebford. *Devn* —4C **12**
Ebley. *Glos* —5D **48**
Ebnal. *Ches* —1G **71**
Ebrington. *Glos* —1G **49**
Ebsworthy Town. *Devn* —3F **11**
Ecchinswell. *Hants* —1D **24**
Ecclefechan. *Dum* —2C **112**
Eccles. *G Man* —1B **84**
Eccles. *Kent* —4B **40**
Eccles. *Scot* —5D **130**
Ecclesall. *S Yor* —2H **85**
Ecclesfield. *S Yor* —1A **86**
Eccles Green. *Here* —1G **47**
Eccleshall. *Staf* —3C **72**
Eccleshill. *W Yor* —1B **92**
Ecclesmachan. *W Lot* —2D **128**
Eccles on Sea. *Norf* —3G **79**
Eccles Road. *Norf* —1C **66**
Eccleston. *Ches* —4G **83**
Eccleston. *Lanc* —3D **90**
Eccleston. *Mers* —1G **83**
Eccup. *W Yor* —5E **99**
Echt. *Aber* —3E **153**
Eckford. *Scot* —2B **120**
Eckington. *Derbs* —3B **86**
Eckington. *Worc* —1E **49**
Ecton. *Nptn* —4F **63**
Edale. *Derbs* —2F **85**
Eday Airport. *Orkn* —4E **172**
Edburton. *W Sus* —4D **26**
Edderside. *Cumb* —5C **112**
Edderton. *High* —5E **164**
Eddington. *W Ber* —5B **36**
Eddleston. *Scot* —5F **129**
Eddlewood. *S Lan* —4A **128**
Edenbridge. *Kent* —1F **27**
Edendonich. *Arg* —1A **134**
Edenfield. *Lanc* —3G **91**
Edenhall. *Cumb* —1G **103**
Edenham. *Linc* —3H **75**
Edensor. *Derbs* —4G **85**
Edentaggart. *Arg* —4C **134**
Edenthorpe. *S Yor* —4G **93**
Eden Vale. *Dur* —1B **106**
Edern. *Gwyn* —2B **68**
Edgarley. *Som* —3A **22**
Edgbaston. *W Mid* —2E **61**
Edgcott. *Buck* —3E **51**
Edgcott. *Som* —3B **20**
Edge. *Glos* —5D **48**
Edge. *Shrp* —5F **71**
Edgebolton. *Shrp* —3H **71**
Edge End. *Glos* —4A **48**
Edgefield. *Norf* —2C **78**
Edgefield Street. *Norf* —2C **78**
Edge Green. *Ches* —5G **83**
Edgehead. *Midl* —3G **129**
Edgeley. *Shrp* —1H **71**
Edgeside. *Lanc* —2G **91**
Edgeworth. *Glos* —5E **49**
Edgiock. *Worc* —4E **61**
Edgmond. *Telf* —4B **72**
Edgmond Marsh. *Telf* —3B **72**
Edgton. *Shrp* —2F **59**
Edgware. *G Lon* —1C **38**
Edgworth. *Bkbn* —3F **91**
Edinbane. *High* —3C **154**
Edinburgh. *Edin* —2F **129**
Edinburgh Airport. *Edin* —2E **129**
Edingale. *Staf* —4G **73**
Edingley. *Notts* —5D **86**
Edingthorpe. *Norf* —2F **79**
Edington. *Som* —3G **21**
Edington. *Wilts* —1E **23**
Edingworth. *Som* —1G **21**
Edistone. *Devn* —4C **18**
Edithmead. *Som* —2G **21**
Edith Weston. *Rut* —5G **75**
Edlaston. *Derbs* —1F **73**
Edlesborough. *Buck* —4H **51**
Edlingham. *Nmbd* —4F **121**
Edlington. *Linc* —3B **88**
Edmondsham. *Dors* —1F **15**
Edmondsley. *Dur* —5F **115**
Edmondthorpe. *Leics* —4F **75**
Edmonstone. *Orkn* —5E **172**
Edmonton. *Corn* —1D **6**
Edmonton. *G Lon* —1E **39**
Edmundbyers. *Dur* —4D **114**
Ednam. *Scot* —1B **120**
Ednaston. *Derbs* —1G **73**
Edney Common. *Essx* —5G **53**
Edrom. *Scot* —4E **131**
Edstaston. *Shrp* —2H **71**
Edstone. *Warw* —4F **61**
Edwalton. *Notts* —2D **74**
Edwardstone. *Suff* —1C **54**
Edwardsville. *Mer T* —2D **32**
Edwinsford. *Carm* —2G **45**
Edwinstowe. *Notts* —4D **86**
Edworth. *Beds* —1C **52**
Edwyn Ralph. *Here* —5A **60**
Edzell. *Ang* —2F **145**
Efail-fach. *Neat* —2A **32**
Efail Isaf. *Rhon* —3D **32**
Efailnewydd. *Gwyn* —2C **68**
Efail-rhyd. *Powy* —3D **70**
Efailwen. *Carm* —2F **43**
Efenechtyd. *Den* —5D **82**
Effingham. *Surr* —5C **38**
Effingham Common. *Surr* —5C **38**
Effirth. *Shet* —6E **173**
Efflinch. *Staf* —4F **73**
Efford. *Devn* —2B **12**
Efstigarth. *Shet* —2F **173**
Egbury. *Hants* —1C **24**
Egdon. *Worc* —5D **60**
Egerton. *G Man* —3F **91**
Egerton. *Kent* —1D **28**
Egerton Forstal. *Kent* —1C **28**
Eggborough. *N Yor* —2F **93**
Eggbuckland. *Plym* —3A **8**
Eggesford. *Devn* —1G **11**
Eggington. *Beds* —3H **51**
Egginton. *Derbs* —3G **73**
Egglescliffe. *Stoc T* —3B **106**
Eggleston. *Dur* —2C **104**
Egham. *Surr* —3B **38**
Egham Hythe. *Surr* —3B **38**
Egleton. *Rut* —5F **75**
Eglingham. *Nmbd* —3F **121**
Egloshayle. *Corn* —5A **10**
Egloskerry. *Corn* —4C **10**
Eglwysbach. *Cnwy* —3H **81**
Eglwys Brewis. *V Glam* —5D **32**
Eglwys Fach. *Cdgn* —1F **57**
Eglwyswrw. *Pemb* —1F **43**
Egmanton. *Notts* —4E **87**
Egremont. *Cumb* —3B **102**
Egremont. *Mers* —1F **83**
Egton. *N Yor* —4F **107**
Egton Bridge. *N Yor* —4F **107**
Egypt. *Buck* —2A **38**
Egypt. *Hants* —2C **24**
Eight Ash Green. *Essx* —3C **54**
Eight Mile Burn. *Midl* —4E **129**
Eignaig. *High* —4B **140**
Eilanreach. *High* —2G **147**
Eildon. *Scot* —1H **119**
Eileanach Lodge. *High* —2H **157**
Eilean Fhlodaigh. *W Isl* —3D **170**
Eilean Iarmain. *High* —2F **147**
Einacleit. *W Isl* —5D **171**
Eisgean. *W Isl* —6F **171**
Eishken. *W Isl* —6F **171**
Eisingrug. *Gwyn* —2F **69**
Elan Village. *Powy* —4B **58**
Elberton. *S Glo* —3B **34**
Elbridge. *W Sus* —5A **26**
Elburton. *Plym* —3B **8**
Elcho. *Per* —1D **136**
Elcombe. *Swin* —3G **35**
Elcot. *W Ber* —5B **36**
Eldernell. *Cambs* —1C **64**
Eldersfield. *Worc* —2D **48**
Elderslie. *Ren* —3F **127**
Elder Street. *Essx* —2F **53**
Eldon. *Dur* —2F **105**
Eldroth. *N Yor* —3G **97**
Eldwick. *W Yor* —5D **98**
Elfhowe. *Cumb* —5F **103**
Elford. *Nmbd* —1F **121**
Elford. *Staf* —4F **73**
Elford Closes. *Cambs* —3D **65**
Elgin. *Mor* —2G **159**
Elgol. *High* —2D **146**
Elham. *Kent* —1F **29**
Elie. *Fife* —3G **137**
Eling. *Hants* —1B **16**
Eling. *W Ber* —4D **36**
Elishaw. *Nmbd* —5C **120**
Elizafield. *Dum* —2B **112**
Elkesley. *Notts* —3D **86**
Elkington. *Nptn* —3D **62**
Elkins Green. *Essx* —5G **53**
Elkstone. *Glos* —4E **49**
Ellan. *High* —1C **150**
Ellanbeich. *Arg* —2E **133**
Elland. *W Yor* —2B **92**
Ellary. *Arg* —2F **125**
Ellastone. *Staf* —1F **73**
Ellbridge. *Corn* —2A **8**
Ellel. *Lanc* —4D **97**
Ellemford. *Scot* —3D **130**
Ellenborough. *Cumb* —1B **102**
Ellenbrook. *Herts* —5C **52**
Ellenhall. *Staf* —3C **72**
Ellen's Green. *Surr* —2B **26**
Ellerbec. *N Yor* —5B **106**
Ellerburn. *N Yor* —1C **100**
Ellerby. *N Yor* —3E **107**
Ellerdine. *Telf* —3A **72**
Ellerdine Heath. *Telf* —3A **72**
Ellerhayes. *Devn* —2C **12**
Elleric. *Arg* —4E **141**
Ellerker. *E Yor* —2C **94**
Ellerton. *E Yor* —1H **93**
Ellerton. *N Yor* —5F **105**
Ellerton. *Shrp* —3B **72**
Ellesborough. *Buck* —5G **51**
Ellesmere. *Shrp* —2G **71**
Ellesmere Port. *Ches* —3G **83**
Ellingham. *Hants* —2G **15**
Ellingham. *Norf* —1F **67**
Ellingham. *Nmbd* —2F **121**
Ellingstring. *N Yor* —1D **98**
Ellington. *Cambs* —3A **64**
Ellington. *Nmbd* —5G **121**
Ellington Thorpe. *Cambs* —3A **64**
Ellisfield. *Hants* —2E **25**
Ellishadder. *High* —2E **155**
Ellistown. *Leics* —4B **74**
Ellon. *Aber* —5G **161**
Ellonby. *Cumb* —1F **103**
Ellough. *Suff* —2G **67**
Elloughton. *E Yor* —2C **94**
Ellwood. *Glos* —5A **48**
Elm. *Cambs* —5D **76**
Elmbridge. *Glos* —4D **48**
Elmbridge. *Worc* —4D **60**
Elmdon. *Essx* —2E **53**
Elmdon. *W Mid* —2F **61**
Elmdon Heath. *W Mid* —2F **61**
Elmesthorpe. *Leics* —1B **62**
Elmfield. *IOW* —3D **16**
Elm Hill. *Dors* —4D **22**
Elmhurst. *Staf* —4F **73**
Elmley Castle. *Worc* —1E **49**
Elmley Lovett. *Worc* —4C **60**
Elmore. *Glos* —4C **48**
Elmore Back. *Glos* —4C **48**
Elm Park. *G Lon* —2G **39**
Elmscott. *Devn* —4C **18**
Elmsett. *Suff* —1D **54**
Elmstead. *Essx* —3D **54**
Elmstead Heath. *Essx* —3D **54**
Elmstead Market. *Essx* —3D **54**
Elmsted. *Kent* —1F **29**
Elmstone. *Kent* —4G **41**
Elmstone Hardwicke. *Glos* —3E **49**
Elmswell. *E Yor* —4D **101**
Elmswell. *Suff* —4B **66**
Elmton. *Derbs* —3C **86**
Elphin. *High* —2G **163**
Elphinstone. *E Lot* —2G **129**
Elrick. *Aber* —3F **153**
Elrick. *Mor* —1B **152**
Elrig. *Dum* —5A **110**
Elsdon. *Nmbd* —5D **120**
Elsecar. *S Yor* —1A **86**
Elsenham. *Essx* —3F **53**
Elsfield. *Oxon* —4D **50**
Elsham. *N Lin* —3D **94**
Elsing. *Norf* —4C **78**
Elslack. *N Yor* —5B **98**
Elsrickle. *S Lan* —5D **128**
Elstead. *Surr* —1A **26**
Elsted. *W Sus* —1G **17**
Elsted Marsh. *W Sus* —4G **25**
Elsthorpe. *Linc* —3H **75**
Elstob. *Dur* —2A **106**
Elston. *Devn* —2A **12**
Elston. *Lanc* —1E **90**
Elston. *Notts* —1E **75**
Elston. *Wilts* —2F **23**
Elstone. *Devn* —1G **11**
Elstow. *Beds* —1A **52**
Elstree. *Herts* —5D **40**
Elstronwick. *E Yor* —1F **95**
Elswick. *Lanc* —1C **90**
Elswick. *Tyne* —3F **115**
Elsworth. *Cambs* —4C **64**
Elterwater. *Cumb* —4E **103**
Eltham. *G Lon* —3F **39**
Eltisley. *Cambs* —5B **64**
Elton. *Cambs* —1H **63**
Elton. *Ches* —3G **83**
Elton. *Derbs* —4G **85**
Elton. *Glos* —4C **48**
Elton. *G Man* —3F **91**
Elton. *Here* —3G **59**
Elton. *Notts* —2E **75**
Elton. *Stoc T* —3B **106**
Elton Green. *Ches* —3G **83**
Eltringham. *Nmbd* —3D **114**
Elvanfoot. *S Lan* —3B **118**
Elvaston. *Derbs* —2B **74**
Elveden. *Suff* —3H **65**
Elvingston. *E Lot* —2A **130**
Elvington. *Kent* —5G **41**
Elvington. *York* —5B **100**
Elwick. *Hart* —1B **106**
Elwick. *Nmbd* —1F **121**
Elworth. *Ches* —4B **84**
Elworth. *Dors* —4A **14**
Elworthy. *Som* —3D **20**
Ely. *Cambs* —2E **65**
Ely. *Card* —4E **33**
Emberton. *Mil* —1G **51**
Embleton. *Cumb* —1C **102**
Embleton. *Dur* —2B **106**
Embleton. *Nmbd* —2G **121**
Embo. *High* —4F **165**
Emborough. *Som* —1B **22**
Embo Street. *High* —4F **165**
Embsay. *N Yor* —4C **98**
Emery Down. *Hants* —2A **16**
Emley. *W Yor* —3C **92**
Emmbrook. *Wok* —5F **37**
Emmer Green. *Read* —4F **37**
Emmington. *Oxon* —5F **51**
Emneth. *Norf* —5D **77**
Emneth Hungate. *Norf* —5E **77**
Empingham. *Rut* —5G **75**
Empshott. *Hants* —3F **25**
Emsworth. *Hants* —2F **17**
Enborne. *W Ber* —5C **36**
Enborne Row. *W Ber* —5C **36**
Enchmarsh. *Shrp* —1H **59**
Enderby. *Leics* —1C **62**
Endmoor. *Cumb* —1E **97**
Endon. *Staf* —5D **84**
Endon Bank. *Staf* —5D **84**
Enfield. *G Lon* —1E **39**
Enfield Wash. *G Lon* —1E **39**
Enford. *Wilts* —1G **23**
Engine Common. *S Glo* —3B **34**
Englefield. *W Ber* —4E **36**
Englefield Green. *Surr* —3A **38**
Engleseabrook. *Ches* —5B **84**
English Bicknor. *Glos* —4A **48**
Englishcombe. *Bath* —5C **34**
English Frankton. *Shrp* —3G **71**
Enham Alamein. *Hants* —2B **24**
Enmore. *Som* —3F **21**
Ennerdale Bridge. *Cumb* —3B **102**
Enniscaven. *Corn* —3D **6**
Enoch. *Dum* —4A **118**
Enochdhu. *Per* —2H **143**
Ensay. *Arg* —4E **139**
Ensbury. *Bour* —3F **15**
Ensdon. *Shrp* —4G **71**
Ensis. *Devn* —4F **19**
Enson. *Staf* —3D **72**
Enstone. *Oxon* —3B **50**
Enterkinfoot. *Dum* —4A **118**
Enville. *Staf* —2C **60**
Eolaigearraidh. *W Isl* —8C **170**
Eorabus. *Arg* —1A **132**
Eoropaidh. *W Isl* —1H **171**
Epney. *Glos* —4C **48**
Epperstone. *Notts* —1D **74**
Epping. *Essx* —5E **53**
Epping Green. *Essx* —5E **53**
Epping Green. *Herts* —5C **52**
Epping Upland. *Essx* —5E **53**
Eppleby. *N Yor* —3E **105**
Eppleworth. *E Yor* —1D **94**
Epsom. *Surr* —4D **38**
Epwell. *Oxon* —1B **50**
Epworth. *N Lin* —4A **94**
Epworth Turbary. *N Lin* —4A **94**
Erbistock. *Wrex* —1F **71**
Erbusaig. *High* —1F **147**
Erchless Castle. *High* —4G **157**
Erdington. *W Mid* —1F **61**
Eredine. *Arg* —3G **133**
Eriboll. *High* —3E **167**
Ericstane. *Dum* —3C **118**
Eridge Green. *E Sus* —2G **27**
Erines. *Arg* —2G **125**
Eriswell. *Suff* —3G **65**
Erith. *G Lon* —3G **39**
Erlestoke. *Wilts* —1E **23**
Ermine East. *Linc* —3G **87**
Ermine West. *Linc* —3G **87**
Ermington. *Devn* —3C **8**
Ernesettle. *Plym* —3A **8**
Erpingham. *Norf* —2D **78**
Erriottwood. *Kent* —5D **40**
Errogie. *High* —1H **149**
Errol. *Per* —1E **137**
Erskine. *Ren* —2F **127**
Ervie. *Dum* —3F **109**
Erwarton. *Suff* —2F **55**
Erwood. *Powy* —1D **46**
Eryholme. *N Yor* —4A **106**
Eryrys. *Den* —5E **82**
Escalls. *Corn* —4A **4**
Escomb. *Dur* —2E **105**
Escrick. *N Yor* —5A **100**
Esgair. *Carm* —3D **45**
(nr. Carmarthen)
Esgair. *Carm* —3G **43**
(nr. St Clears)
Esgairgeiliog. *Powy* —5G **69**
Esh. *Dur* —5E **115**
Esher. *Surr* —4C **38**
Esholt. *W Yor* —5D **98**
Eshott. *Nmbd* —5G **121**
Eshton. *N Yor* —4B **98**
Esh Winning. *Dur* —5E **115**
Eskadale. *High* —5G **157**
Eskbank. *Midl* —3G **129**
Eskdale Green. *Cumb* —4C **102**
Eskdalemuir. *Dum* —5E **119**
Eskham. *Linc* —1C **88**
Esknish. *Arg* —3B **124**
Esk Valley. *N Yor* —4F **107**
Eslington Hall. *Nmbd* —3E **121**
Espley Hall. *Nmbd* —5F **121**
Esprick. *Lanc* —1C **90**
Essendine. *Rut* —4H **75**
Essendon. *Herts* —5C **52**
Essich. *High* —5A **158**
Essington. *Staf* —5D **72**
Eston. *Red C* —3C **106**
Estover. *Plym* —3B **8**
Eswick. *Shet* —6F **173**
Etal. *Nmbd* —1D **120**
Etchilhampton. *Wilts* —5F **35**
Etchingham. *E Sus* —3B **28**
Etchinghill. *Kent* —2F **29**
Etchinghill. *Staf* —4E **73**
Ethie Haven. *Ang* —4F **145**
Etling Green. *Norf* —4C **78**
Etloe. *Glos* —5B **48**
Eton. *Wind* —3A **38**
Eton Wick. *Wind* —3A **38**
Etteridge. *High* —4A **150**
Ettersgill. *Dur* —2B **104**
Ettiley Heath. *Ches* —4B **84**
Ettington. *Warw* —1A **50**
Etton. *E Yor* —5D **101**
Etton. *Pet* —5A **76**
Ettrick. *Scot* —3E **119**
Ettrickbridge. *Scot* —2F **119**
Etwall. *Derbs* —2G **73**
Eudon Burnell. *Shrp* —2B **60**
Eudon George. *Shrp* —2A **60**
Euston. *Suff* —3A **66**
Euxton. *Lanc* —3D **90**
Evanstown. *B'End* —3C **32**
Evanton. *High* —2A **158**
Evedon. *Linc* —1H **75**
Evelix. *High* —4E **165**
Evendine. *Here* —1C **48**
Evenjobb. *Powy* —4E **59**
Evenley. *Nptn* —2D **50**
Evenlode. *Glos* —3H **49**
Even Swindon. *Swin* —3G **35**
Evenwood. *Dur* —2E **105**
Evenwood Gate. *Dur* —2E **105**
Everbay. *Orkn* —5F **172**
Evercreech. *Som* —3B **22**
Everdon. *Nptn* —5C **62**
Everingham. *E Yor* —5C **100**
Everleigh. *Wilts* —1H **23**
Everley. *N Yor* —1D **100**
Eversholt. *Beds* —2H **51**
Evershot. *Dors* —2A **14**
Eversley. *Hants* —5F **37**
Eversley Cross. *Hants* —5F **37**
Everthorpe. *E Yor* —1C **94**
Everton. *Beds* —5B **64**
Everton. *Hants* —3A **16**
Everton. *Mers* —1F **83**
Everton. *Notts* —1D **86**
Evertown. *Dum* —2E **113**
Evesbatch. *Here* —1B **48**
Evesham. *Worc* —1F **49**
Evington. *Leic C* —5D **74**
Ewden Village. *S Yor* —1G **85**
Ewdness. *Shrp* —1B **60**
Ewell. *Surr* —4D **38**
Ewell Minnis. *Kent* —1G **29**
Ewelme. *Oxon* —2E **37**
Ewen. *Glos* —2F **35**
Ewenny. *V Glam* —4C **32**
Ewerby. *Linc* —1A **76**
Ewes. *Dum* —5F **119**
Ewesley. *Nmbd* —5E **121**
Ewhurst. *Surr* —1B **26**
Ewhurst Green. *E Sus* —3B **28**
Ewhurst Green. *Surr* —2B **26**
Ewlo. *Flin* —4F **83**
Ewloe. *Flin* —4F **83**
Ewood Bridge. *Lanc* —2F **91**
Eworthy. *Devn* —3E **11**
Ewshot. *Hants* —2G **25**
Ewyas Harold. *Here* —3G **47**
Exbourne. *Devn* —2G **11**
Exbury. *Hants* —2C **16**
Exceat. *E Sus* —5G **27**
Exebridge. *Som* —4C **20**
Exelby. *N Yor* —1E **99**
Exeter. *Devn* —3C **12**
Exeter Airport. *Devn* —3D **12**
Exford. *Som* —3B **20**
Exfords Green. *Shrp* —5G **71**
Exhall. *Warw* —5F **61**
Exlade Street. *Oxon* —3E **37**
Exminster. *Devn* —4C **12**
Exmouth. *Devn* —4D **12**
Exnaboe. *Shet* —10E **173**
Exning. *Suff* —4F **65**
Exton. *Devn* —4C **12**
Exton. *Hants* —4E **24**
Exton. *Rut* —4G **75**
Exton. *Som* —3C **20**
Exwick. *Devn* —3C **12**
Eyam. *Derbs* —3G **85**
Eydon. *Nptn* —5C **62**
Eye. *Here* —4G **59**
Eye. *Pet* —5B **76**
Eye. *Suff* —3D **66**
Eye Green. *Pet* —5B **76**
Eyemouth. *Scot* —3F **131**
Eyeworth. *Beds* —1C **52**
Eyhorne Street. *Kent* —5C **40**
Eyke. *Suff* —5F **67**
Eynesbury. *Cambs* —5A **64**
Eynort. *High* —1B **146**
Eynsford. *Kent* —4G **39**
Eynsham. *Oxon* —5C **50**
Eype. *Dors* —3H **13**
Eyre. *High* —5E **155**
(on Raasay)
Eyre. *High* —3D **154**
(on Skye)
Eythorne. *Kent* —1G **29**
Eyton. *Here* —4G **59**
Eyton. *Shrp* —2F **59**
(nr. Bishop's Castle)
Eyton. *Shrp* —4F **71**
(nr. Shrewsbury)
Eyton. *Wrex* —1F **71**
Eyton on Severn. *Shrp* —5H **71**
Eyton upon the Weald Moors. *Telf* —4A **72**

Faccombe. *Hants* —1B **24**
Faceby. *N Yor* —4B **106**
Faddiley. *Ches* —5H **83**
Fadmoor. *N Yor* —1A **100**
Fagwyr. *Swan* —5G **45**
Faichem. *High* —3E **149**
Faifley. *W Dun* —2G **127**
Fail. *S Ayr* —2D **116**
Failand. *N Som* —4A **34**
Failford. *S Ayr* —2D **116**
Failsworth. *G Man* —4H **91**
Fairbourne. *Gwyn* —4F **69**
Fairbourne Heath. *Kent* —5C **40**
Fairburn. *N Yor* —2E **93**
Fairfield. *Derbs* —3E **85**
Fairfield. *Kent* —3D **28**
Fairfield. *Worc* —3D **60**
(nr. Bromsgrove)
Fairfield. *Worc* —1F **49**
(nr. Evesham)
Fairford. *Glos* —5G **49**
Fair Green. *Norf* —4F **77**
Fair Hill. *Cumb* —1G **103**
Fairhill. *S Lan* —4A **128**
Fair Isle Airport. *Shet* —1B **172**
Fairlands. *Surr* —5A **38**
Fairlie. *N Ayr* —4D **126**
Fairlight. *E Sus* —4C **28**
Fairlight Cove. *E Sus* —4C **28**
Fairmile. *Devn* —3D **12**
Fairmile. *Surr* —4C **38**
Fairmilehead. *Edin* —3F **129**
Fair Oak. *Devn* —1D **12**
Fair Oak. *Hants* —1C **16**
(nr. Eastleigh)
Fair Oak. *Hants* —5D **36**
(nr. Kingsclere)
Fairoak. *Staf* —2B **72**
Fair Oak Green. *Hants* —5E **37**
Fairseat. *Kent* —4H **39**
Fairstead. *Essx* —4A **54**
Fairstead. *Norf* —4F **77**
Fairwarp. *E Sus* —3F **27**
Fairwater. *Card* —4E **33**
Fairy Cross. *Devn* —4E **19**
Fakenham. *Norf* —3B **78**
Fakenham Magna. *Suff* —3B **66**
Fala. *Midl* —3H **129**
Fala Dam. *Midl* —3H **129**
Falcon. *Here* —2B **48**
Faldingworth. *Linc* —2H **87**
Falfield. *S Glo* —2B **34**
Falkenham. *Suff* —2F **55**
Falkirk. *Falk* —2B **128**
Falkland. *Fife* —3E **137**
Fallin. *Stir* —4H **135**
Fallowfield. *G Man* —1C **84**
Falmer. *E Sus* —5E **27**
Falmouth. *Corn* —5C **6**
Falsgrave. *N Yor* —1E **101**
Falstone. *Nmbd* —1A **114**
Fanagmore. *High* —4B **166**

Fancott—Four Ashes

Fancott. Beds —3A 52
Fanellan. High —4G 157
Fangdale Beck. N Yor —5C 106
Fangfoss. E Yor —4B 100
Fankerton. Falk —1A 128
Fanmore. Arg —4F 139
Fanner's Green. Essx —4G 53
Fannich Lodge. High —2E 156
Fans. Scot —5C 130
Far Cotton. Nptn —5E 63
Fareham. Hants —2D 16
Farewell. Staf —4E 73
Far Forest. Worc —3B 60
Farforth. Linc —3C 88
Far Green. Glos —5C 48
Far Hoarcross. Staf —3F 73
Faringdon. Oxon —2A 36
Farington. Lanc —2D 90
Farlam. Cumb —4G 113
Farleigh. N Som —5H 33
Farleigh. Surr —4E 39
Farleigh Hungerford. Som —1D 22
Farleigh Wallop. Hants —2E 24
Farleigh Wick. Wilts —5D 34
Farlesthorpe. Linc —3D 88
Farleton. Cumb —1E 97
Farleton. Lanc —3E 97
Farley. High —4G 157
Farley. N Som —4H 33
Farley. Shrp —5F 71
(nr. Shrewsbury)
Farley. Shrp —5A 72
(nr. Telford)
Farley. Staf —1E 73
Farley. Wilts —4H 23
Farley Green. Suff —5G 65
Farley Green. Surr —1B 26
Farley Hill. Wok —5F 37
Farley's End. Glos —4C 48
Farlington. N Yor —3A 100
Farlington. Port —2E 17
Farlow. Shrp —2A 60
Farmborough. Bath —5B 34
Farmcote. Glos —3F 49
Farmcote. Shrp —1B 60
Farmington. Glos —4G 49
Far Moor. G Man —4D 90
Farmoor. Oxon —5C 50
Farmtown. Mor —3C 160
Farnah Green. Derbs —1H 73
Farnborough. G Lon —4F 39
Farnborough. Hants —1G 25
Farnborough. Warw —1C 50
Farnborough. W Ber —3C 36
Farncombe. Surr —1A 26
Farndish. Beds —4G 63
Farndon. Ches —5G 83
Farndon. Notts —5E 87
Farnell. Ang —3F 145
Farnham. Dors —1E 15
Farnham. Essx —3E 53
Farnham. N Yor —3F 99
Farnham. Suff —4F 67
Farnham. Surr —2G 25
Farnham Common. Buck —2A 38
Farnham Green. Essx —3E 53
Farnham Royal. Buck —2A 38
Farnhill. N Yor —5C 98
Farningham. Kent —4G 39
Farnley. N Yor —5E 98
Farnley Tyas. W Yor —3B 92
Farnsfield. Notts —5D 86
Farnworth. G Man —4F 91
Farnworth. Hal —2H 83
Far Oakridge. Glos —5E 49
Far Orrest. Cumb —4F 103
Farr. High —2H 167
(nr. Bettyhill)
Farr. High —5A 158
(nr. Inverness)
Farr. High —3C 150
(nr. Kingussie)
Farraline. High —1H 149
Farringdon. Devn —3D 12
Farrington. Dors —1D 14
Farrington Gurney. Bath —1B 22
Far Sawrey. Cumb —5E 103
Farsley. W Yor —1C 92
Farthinghoe. Nptn —2D 50
Farthingstone. Nptn —5D 62
Farthorpe. Linc —3B 88
Fartown. W Yor —3B 92
Farway. Devn —3E 13
Fasag. High —3A 156
Fascadale. High —1G 139
Fasnacloich. Arg —4E 141
Fassfern. High —1E 141
Fatfield. Tyne —4G 115
Faugh. Cumb —4G 113
Fauld. Staf —3F 73
Fauldhouse. W Lot —3C 128
Faulkbourne. Essx —4A 54
Faulkland. Som —1C 22
Fauls. Shrp —2H 71
Faverdale. Darl —3F 105
Faversham. Kent —4E 40
Fawdington. N Yor —2G 99
Fawfieldhead. Staf —4E 85
Fawkham Green. Kent —4G 39
Fawler. Oxon —4B 50
Fawley. Buck —3F 37
Fawley. Hants —2C 16
Fawley. W Ber —3B 36
Fawley Chapel. Here —3A 48
Fawton. Corn —2F 7
Faxfleet. E Yor —2B 94
Faygate. W Sus —2D 26
Fazakerley. Mers —1F 83
Fazeley. Staf —5F 73
Feabuie. High —4B 158
Feagour. High —4H 149
Fearby. N Yor —1D 98
Fearn. High —1C 158
Fearnan. Per —4E 142
Fearnbeg. High —3G 155
Fearnhead. Warr —1A 84
Fearnmore. High —2G 155
Featherstone. Staf —5D 72
Featherstone. W Yor —2E 93
Featherstone Castle. Nmbd —3H 113
Feckenham. Worc —4E 61
Feering. Essx —3B 54
Feetham. N Yor —5C 104
Feizor. N Yor —3G 97
Felbridge. Surr —2E 27
Felbrigg. Norf —2E 78
Felcourt. Surr —1E 27
Felden. Herts —5A 52
Felhampton. Shrp —2G 59
Felindre. Carm —3F 45
(nr. Llandeilo)
Felindre. Carm —2G 45
(nr. Llandovery)
Felindre. Carm —2D 44
(nr. Newcastle Emlyn)
Felindre. Powy —2D 58
Felindre. Swan —5G 45
Felindre Farchog. Pemb —1F 43
Felinfach. Cdgn —5E 57
Felinfach. Powy —2D 46
Felinfoel. Carm —5F 45
Felingwmisaf. Carm —3F 45
Felingwmuchaf. Carm —3F 45
Felin Newydd. Powy —5C 70
(nr. Newtown)
Felin Newydd. Powy —3E 70
(nr. Oswestry)
Felin Wnda. Cdgn —1D 44
Felinwynt. Cdgn —5B 56
Felixkirk. N Yor —1G 99
Felixstowe. Suff —2F 55
Felixstowe Ferry. Suff —2G 55
Felkington. Nmbd —5F 131
Fell End. Cumb —5A 104
Felling. Tyne —3F 115
Fell Side. Cumb —1E 102
Felmersham. Beds —5G 63
Felmingham. Norf —3E 79
Felpham. W Sus —3H 17
Felsham. Suff —5B 66
Felsted. Essx —3G 53
Feltham. G Lon —3C 38
Felthamhill. G Lon —3B 38
Felthorpe. Norf —4D 78
Felton. Here —1A 48
Felton. N Som —5A 34
Felton. Nmbd —4F 121
Felton Butler. Shrp —4F 71
Feltwell. Norf —1G 65
Fenay Bridge. W Yor —3B 92
Fence. Lanc —1G 91
Fence Houses. Tyne —4G 115
Fencott. Oxon —4D 50
Fen Ditton. Cambs —4D 65
Fen Drayton. Cambs —4C 64
Fen End. Linc —3B 76
Fen End. W Mid —3G 61
Fenham. Nmbd —5G 131
Fenham. Tyne —3F 115
Fenhouses. Linc —1B 76
Feniscowles. Bkbn —2E 91
Feniton. Devn —3E 12
Fenn Green. Shrp —2B 60
Fenn's Bank. Wrex —2H 71
Fenn Street. Medw —3B 40
Fenny Bentley. Derbs —5F 85
Fenny Bridges. Devn —3E 12
Fenny Compton. Warw —5B 62
Fenny Drayton. Leics —1A 62
Fenny Stratford. Mil —2G 51
Fenrother. Nmbd —5F 121
Fenstanton. Cambs —4C 64
Fen Street. Norf —1C 66
Fenton. Cambs —3C 64
Fenton. Cumb —4G 113
Fenton. Linc —5F 87
(nr. Caythorpe)
Fenton. Linc —3F 87
(nr. Saxilby)
Fenton. Nmbd —1D 120
Fenton. Notts —2E 87
Fenton. Stoke —1C 72
Fentonadle. Corn —5A 10
Fenton Barns. E Lot —1B 130
Fenwick. E Ayr —5F 127
Fenwick. Nmbd —5G 131
(nr. Berwick)
Fenwick. Nmbd —2D 114
(nr. Hexham)
Fenwick. S Yor —3F 93
Feochaig. Arg —4B 122
Feock. Corn —5C 6
Feolin Ferry. Arg —3C 124
Feorlan. Arg —5A 122
Feriniquarrie. High —3A 154
Fern. Ang —2D 145
Ferndale. Rhon —2C 32
Ferndown. Dors —2F 15
Ferness. High —4D 158
Fernham. Oxon —2A 36
Fernhill. W Sus —1D 27
Fernhill Heath. Worc —5C 60
Fernhurst. W Sus —4G 25
Fernieflatt. Aber —1H 145
Ferniegair. S Lan —4A 128
Fernilea. High —5C 154
Fernilee. Derbs —3E 85
Ferrensby. N Yor —3F 99
Ferriby Sluice. N Lin —2C 94
Ferrindonald. High —3E 147
Ferring. W Sus —5C 26
Ferrybridge. W Yor —2E 93
Ferryden. Ang —3G 145
Ferryhill. Aber C —3G 153
Ferry Hill. Cambs —2C 64
Ferryhill. Dur —1F 105
Ferryhill Station. Dur —1F 105
Ferryside. Carm —4D 44
Ferryton. High —2A 158
Fersfield. Norf —2C 66
Fersit. High —1A 142
Feshiebridge. High —3C 150
Fetcham. Surr —5C 38
Fetterangus. Aber —3G 161
Fettercairn. Aber —1F 145
Fewcott. Oxon —3D 50
Fewston. N Yor —4D 98
Ffairfach. Carm —3G 45
Ffair Rhos. Cdgn —4G 57
Ffaldybrenin. Carm —1G 45
Ffarmers. Carm —1G 45
Ffawyddog. Powy —4F 47
Ffestiniog. Gwyn —1G 69
Ffodun. Powy —5E 71
Ffont-y-gari. V Glam —5D 32
Fforest. Carm —5F 45
Fforest-fach. Swan —3F 31
Fforest Goch. Neat —5H 45
Ffostrasol. Cdgn —1D 45
Ffos-y-ffin. Cdgn —4D 56
Ffrith. Flin —5E 83
Ffrwdgrech. Powy —3D 46
Ffynnon-ddrain. Carm —3E 45
Ffynnongroyw. Flin —2D 82
Ffynnon Gynydd. Powy —1E 47
Ffynnonoer. Cdgn —5E 57
Fiag Lodge. High —1B 164
Fidden. Arg —2B 132
Fiddington. Glos —2E 49
Fiddington. Som —2F 21
Fiddleford. Dors —1D 14
Fiddlers Hamlet. Essx —5E 53
Field. Staf —2E 73
Field Assarts. Oxon —4B 50
Field Broughton. Cumb —1C 96
Field Dalling. Norf —2C 78
Fieldhead. Cumb —1F 103
Field Head. Leics —5B 74
Fifehead Magdalen. Dors —4C 22
Fifehead Neville. Dors —1C 14
Fifehead St Quintin. Dors —1C 14
Fife Keith. Mor —3B 160
Fifield. Oxon —4H 49
Fifield. Wilts —1G 23
Fifield. Wind —3A 38
Fifield Bavant. Wilts —4F 23
Figheldean. Wilts —2G 23
Filby. Norf —4G 79
Filey. N Yor —1F 101
Filford. Dors —3H 13
Filgrave. Mil —1G 51
Filkins. Oxon —5H 49
Filleigh. Devn —1H 11
(nr. Crediton)
Filleigh. Devn —4G 19
(nr. South Molton)
Fillingham. Linc —2G 87
Fillongley. Warw —2G 61
Filton. Bris —4B 34
Fimber. E Yor —3C 100
Finavon. Ang —3D 145
Fincham. Norf —5F 77
Finchampstead. Wok —5F 37
Fincharn. Arg —3G 133
Finchdean. Hants —1F 17
Finchingfield. Essx —2G 53
Finchley. G Lon —1D 38
Findern. Derbs —2H 73
Findhorn. Mor —2E 159
Findhorn Bridge. High —1C 150
Findochty. Mor —2B 160
Findo Gask. Per —1C 136
Findon. Aber —4G 153
Findon. W Sus —5C 26
Findon Mains. High —2A 158
Findon Valley. W Sus —5C 26
Finedon. Nptn —3G 63
Fingal Street. Suff —3E 66
Fingest. Buck —2F 37
Finghall. N Yor —1D 98
Fingland. Cumb —4D 112
Fingland. Dum —3G 117
Finglesham. Kent —5H 41
Fingringhoe. Essx —3D 54
Finiskaig. High —4A 148
Finmere. Oxon —2E 51
Finnart. Per —3C 142
Finningham. Suff —4C 66
Finningley. S Yor —1D 86
Finnyguad. Aber —3D 160
Finsbury. G Lon —2E 39
Finstall. Worc —3D 61
Finsthwaite. Cumb —1C 96
Finstock. Oxon —4B 50
Finstown. Orkn —6C 172
Fintry. Aber —3E 161
Fintry. D'dee —5D 144
Fintry. Stir —1H 127
Finwood. Warw —4F 61
Finzean. Aber —4D 152
Fionnphort. Arg —2B 132
Fionnsabhagh. W Isl —9C 171
Firbeck. S Yor —2C 86
Firby. N Yor —1E 99
(nr. Bedale)
Firby. N Yor —3B 100
(nr. Malton)
Firgrove. G Man —3H 91
Firsby. Linc —4D 88
Firsdown. Wilts —3H 23
First Coast. High —4D 162
Firth. Shet —4F 173
Fir Tree. Dur —1E 105
Fishbourne. IOW —3D 16
Fishbourne. W Sus —2G 17
Fishburn. Dur —1A 106
Fishcross. Clac —4B 136
Fisherford. Aber —5D 160
Fisherrow. E Lot —2G 129
Fisher's Pond. Hants —4C 24
Fisher's Row. Lanc —5D 96
Fisherstreet. W Sus —2A 26
Fisherton. High —3B 158
Fisherton. S Ayr —3B 116
Fisherton de la Mere. Wilts —3E 23
Fishguard. Pemb —1D 42
Fishlake. S Yor —3G 93
Fishley. Norf —4G 79
Fishnish. Arg —4A 140
Fishpond Bottom. Dors —3G 13
Fishponds. Bris —4B 34
Fishpool. Glos —3B 48
Fishpool. G Man —4G 91
Fishpools. Powy —4D 58
Fishtoft. Linc —1C 76
Fishtoft Drove. Linc —1C 76
Fishwick. Scot —4F 131
Fiskavaig. High —5C 154
Fiskerton. Linc —3H 87
Fiskerton. Notts —5E 87
Fitch. Shet —7E 173
Fitling. E Yor —1F 95
Fittleton. Wilts —2G 23
Fittleworth. W Sus —4B 26
Fitton End. Cambs —4D 76
Fitz. Shrp —4G 71
Fitzhead. Som —4E 20
Fitzwilliam. W Yor —3E 93
Fiunary. High —4A 140
Five Ash Down. E Sus —3F 27
Five Ashes. E Sus —3G 27
Five Bells. Som —2D 20
Five Bridges. Here —1B 48
Fivehead. Som —4G 21
Five Lane Ends. Lanc —4E 97
Fivelanes. Corn —4C 10
Five Oak Green. Kent —1H 27
Five Oaks. W Sus —3B 26
Five Roads. Carm —5E 45
Five Ways. Warw —3G 61
Flack's Green. Essx —4A 54
Flackwell Heath. Buck —3G 37
Fladbury. Worc —1E 49
Fladda. Shet —3E 173
Fladdabister. Shet —8F 173
Flagg. Derbs —4F 85
Flamborough. E Yor —2G 101
Flamstead. Herts —4A 52
Flansham. W Sus —5A 26
Flasby. N Yor —4B 98
Flash. Staf —4E 85
Flashader. High —3C 154
Flatt, The. Cumb —2G 113
Flaunden. Herts —5A 52
Flawborough. Notts —1E 75
Flawith. N Yor —3G 99
Flax Bourton. N Som —5A 34
Flaxby. N Yor —4F 99
Flaxholme. Derbs —1H 73
Flaxley. Glos —4B 48
Flaxley Green. Staf —4E 73
Flaxpool. Som —3E 21
Flaxton. N Yor —3A 100
Fleck. Shet —10E 173
Fleckney. Leics —1D 62
Flecknoe. Warw —4C 62
Fledborough. Notts —3F 87
Fleet. Dors —4B 14
Fleet. Hants —1G 25
(nr. Farnborough)
Fleet. Hants —2F 17
(nr. South Hayling)
Fleet. Linc —3C 76
Fleet Hargate. Linc —3C 76
Fleetville. Herts —5B 52
Fleetwood. Lanc —5C 96
Fleggburgh. Norf —4G 79
Fleisirin. W Isl —4H 171
Flemingston. V Glam —4D 32
Flemington. S Lan —3H 127
(nr. Glasgow)
Flemington. S Lan —5A 128
(nr. Strathaven)
Flempton. Suff —4H 65
Fleoideabhagh. W Isl —9C 171
Fletcher's Green. Kent —1G 27
Fletchertown. Cumb —5D 112
Fletching. E Sus —3F 27
Fleuchary. High —4E 165
Flexbury. Corn —2C 10
Flexford. Surr —5A 38
Flimby. Cumb —1B 102
Flimwell. E Sus —2B 28
Flint. Flin —3E 83
Flintham. Notts —1E 75
Flint Mountain. Flin —3E 83
Flinton. E Yor —1F 95
Flintsham. Here —5F 59
Flishinghurst. Kent —2B 28
Flitcham. Norf —3G 77
Flitton. Beds —2A 52
Flitwick. Beds —2A 52
Flixborough. N Lin —3B 94
Flixton. G Man —1B 84
Flixton. N Yor —2E 101
Flixton. Suff —2F 67
Flockton. W Yor —3C 92
Flodden. Nmbd —1D 120
Flodigarry. High —1D 154
Flood's Ferry. Cambs —1C 64
Flookburgh. Cumb —2C 96
Flordon. Norf —1D 66
Flore. Nptn —4D 62
Flotterton. Nmbd —4E 121
Flowton. Suff —1D 54
Flushing. Aber —4H 161
Flushing. Corn —5C 6
Fluxton. Devn —3D 12
Flyde, The. Lanc —1C 90
Flyford Flavell. Worc —5D 61
Fobbing. Thur —2B 40
Fochabers. Mor —3H 159
Fochriw. Cphy —5E 46
Fockerby. N Lin —3B 94
Fodderty. High —3H 157
Foddington. Som —4A 22
Foel. Powy —4B 70
Foffarty. Ang —4D 144
Foggathorpe. E Yor —1A 94
Fogo. Scot —5D 130
Fogorig. Scot —5D 130
Foindle. High —4B 166
Folda. Ang —2A 144
Fole. Staf —2E 73
Foleshill. W Mid —2A 62
Foley Park. Worc —3C 60
Folke. Dors —1B 14
Folkestone. Kent —2G 29
Folkingham. Linc —2H 75
Folkington. E Sus —5G 27
Folksworth. Cambs —1A 64
Folkton. N Yor —2E 101
Folla Rule. Aber —5E 161
Follifoot. N Yor —4F 99
Folly Cross. Devn —2E 11
Folly Gate. Devn —3F 11
Folly, The. Herts —4B 52
Folly, The. W Ber —5C 36
Fonthill Bishop. Wilts —3E 23
Fonthill Gifford. Wilts —3E 23
Fontmell Magna. Dors —1D 14
Fontwell. W Sus —5A 26
Font-y-gary. V Glam —5D 32
Foodieash. Fife —2F 137
Foolow. Derbs —3F 85
Footdee. Aber C —3G 153
Footherley. Staf —5F 73
Foots Cray. G Lon —3F 39
Forbestown. Aber —2A 152
Force Forge. Cumb —5E 103
Force Mills. Cumb —5E 103
Forcett. N Yor —3E 105
Ford. Arg —3F 133
Ford. Buck —5F 51
Ford. Derbs —3B 86
Ford. Devn —4E 19
(nr. Bideford)
Ford. Devn —3C 8
(nr. Holbeton)
Ford. Devn —4D 9
(nr. Salcombe)
Ford. Glos —3F 49
Ford. Nmbd —1D 120
Ford. Plym —3A 8
Ford. Shrp —4G 71
Ford. Som —1A 22
(nr. Wells)
Ford. Som —4D 20
(nr. Wiveliscombe)
Ford. Staf —5E 85
Ford. W Sus —5B 26
Ford. Wilts —4D 34
(nr. Chippenham)
Ford. Wilts —3G 23
(nr. Salisbury)
Ford Barton. Devn —1C 12
Fordcombe. Kent —1G 27
Fordell. Fife —1E 129
Forden. Powy —5E 71
Ford End. Essx —4G 53
Forder Green. Devn —2D 9
Ford Green. Lanc —5D 97
Fordham. Cambs —3F 65
Fordham. Essx —3C 54
Fordham. Norf —1F 65
Fordham Heath. Essx —3C 54
Ford Heath. Shrp —4G 71
Fordhouses. W Mid —5D 72
Fordie. Per —1G 135
Fordingbridge. Hants —1G 15
Fordington. Linc —3D 88
Fordon. E Yor —2E 101
Fordoun. Aber —1G 145
Ford Street. Essx —3C 54
Ford Street. Som —1E 13
Fordton. Devn —3B 12
Fordwells. Oxon —4B 50
Fordwich. Kent —5F 41
Fordyce. Aber —2C 160
Forebridge. Staf —3D 72
Foremark. Derbs —3H 73
Forest. N Yor —4F 105
Forestburn Gate. Nmbd —5E 121
Foresterseat. Mor —3F 159
Forest Green. Glos —2D 34
Forest Green. Surr —1C 26
Forest Hall. Cumb —4G 103
Forest Head. Cumb —4G 113
Forest Hill. Oxon —5D 50
Forest-in-Teesdale. Dur —2B 104
Forest Lodge. Per —1G 143
Forest Mill. Clac —4B 136
Forest Row. E Sus —2F 27
Forestside. W Sus —1F 17
Forest Town. Notts —4C 86
Forfar. Ang —3D 144
Forgandenny. Per —2C 136
Forge. Powy —1G 57
Forge Side. Torf —5F 47
Forge, The. Here —5F 59
Forgewood. N Lan —4A 128
Forgie. Mor —3A 160
Forgue. Aber —4D 160
Formby. Mers —4A 90
Forncett End. Norf —1D 66
Forncett St Mary. Norf —1D 66
Forncett St Peter. Norf —1D 66
Forneth. Per —4H 143
Fornham All Saints. Suff —4H 65
Fornham St Martin. Suff —4A 66
Forres. Mor —3E 159
Forrestfield. N Lan —3B 128
Forrest Lodge. Dum —1C 110
Forsbrook. Staf —1D 72
Forse. High —5E 169
Forsinard. High —4A 168
Forss. High —2C 168
Forstal, The. Kent —2E 29
Forston. Dors —3B 14
Fort Augustus. High —3F 149
Forteviot. Per —2C 136
Fort George. High —3B 158
Forth. S Lan —4C 128
Forthampton. Glos —2D 48
Forthay. Glos —2C 34
Fortingall. Per —4E 143
Fort Matilda. Inv —2D 126
Forton. Hants —2C 24
Forton. Lanc —4D 97
Forton. Shrp —4G 71
Forton. Som —2G 13
Forton. Staf —3B 72
Forton Heath. Shrp —4G 71
Fortrie. Aber —4D 160
Fortrose. High —3B 158
Fortuneswell. Dors —5B 14
Fort William. High —1F 141
Forty Green. Buck —1A 38
Forty Hill. G Lon —1E 39
Forward Green. Suff —5C 66
Fosbury. Wilts —1B 24
Foscot. Oxon —3H 49
Fosdyke. Linc —2C 76
Foss. Per —3E 143
Fossebridge. Glos —4F 49
Foster Street. Essx —5E 53
Foston. Derbs —2F 73
Foston. Leics —1D 62
Foston. Linc —1F 75
Foston. N Yor —3A 100
Foston on the Wolds. E Yor —4F 101
Fotherby. Linc —1C 88
Fothergill. Cumb —1B 102
Fotheringhay. Nptn —1H 63
Foubister. Orkn —7E 172
Foul Anchor. Cambs —4D 76
Foulbridge. Cumb —5F 113
Foulden. Norf —1G 65
Foulden. Scot —4F 131
Foul Mile. E Sus —4H 27
Foulridge. Lanc —5A 98
Foulsham. Norf —3C 78
Fountainhall. Scot —5H 129
Four Alls, The. Shrp —2A 72
Four Ashes. Staf —5D 72
(nr. Cannock)

Four Ashes—Glan-yr-afon

Four Ashes. Staf —2C 60 (nr. Kinver)
Four Ashes. Suff —3C 66
Four Crosses. Powy —5C 70 (nr. Llanerfyl)
Four Crosses. Powy —4E 71 (nr. Llanymynech)
Four Crosses. Staf —5D 72
Four Elms. Kent —1F 27
Four Forks. Som —3F 21
Four Gotes. Cambs —4D 76
Four Lane End. S Yor —4C 92
Four Lane Ends. Lanc —5C 96 (nr. Blackpool)
Four Lane Ends. Lanc —4E 97 (nr. Lancaster)
Four Lanes. Corn —5A 6
Fourlanes End. Ches —5C 84
Four Marks. Hants —3E 25
Four Mile Bridge. IOA —3B 80
Four Oaks. E Sus —3C 28
Four Oaks. Glos —3B 48
Four Oaks. W Mid —2G 61
Four Roads. Carm —5E 45
Four Roads. IOM —5B 108
Fourstones. Nmbd —3B 114
Four Throws. Kent —3B 28
Fovant. Wilts —4F 23
Foveran. Aber —1G 153
Fowey. Corn —3F 7
Fowlershill. Aber —2G 153
Fowley Common. Warr —1A 84
Fowlis. Ang —5C 144
Fowlis Wester. Per —1B 136
Fowlmere. Cambs —1E 53
Fownhope. Here —2A 48
Foxcombe Hill. Oxon —5C 50
Fox Corner. Surr —5A 38
Foxcote. Glos —4F 49
Foxcote. Som —1C 22
Foxdale. IOM —4B 108
Foxearth. Essx —1B 54
Foxfield. Cumb —1B 96
Foxham. Wilts —4E 35
Fox Hatch. Essx —1G 39
Foxhole. Corn —3D 6
Foxholes. N Yor —2E 101
Foxhunt Green. E Sus —4G 27
Fox Lane. Hants —1G 25
Foxlediate. Worc —4E 61
Foxley. Norf —3C 78
Foxley. Nptn —5D 62
Foxley. Wilts —3D 35
Fox Street. Essx —3D 54
Foxt. Staf —1E 73
Foxton. Cambs —1E 53
Foxton. Dur —2A 106
Foxton. Leics —1D 62
Foxton. N Yor —5B 106
Foxup. N Yor —2A 98
Foxwist Green. Ches —4A 84
Foxwood. Shrp —3A 60
Foy. Here —3A 48
Foyers. High —1G 149
Foynesfield. High —3C 158
Fraddam. Corn —3C 4
Fraddon. Corn —3D 6
Fradley. Staf —4F 73
Fradswell. Staf —2D 73
Fraisthorpe. E Yor —3F 101
Framfield. E Sus —3F 27
Framingham Earl. Norf —5E 79
Framingham Pigot. Norf —5E 79
Framlingham. Suff —4E 67
Frampton. Dors —3B 14
Frampton. Linc —2C 76
Frampton Cotterell. S Glo —3B 34
Frampton Mansell. Glos —5E 49
Frampton on Severn. Glos —5C 48
Frampton West End. Linc —1B 76
Framsden. Suff —5D 66
Framwellgate Moor. Dur —5F 115
Franche. Worc —3C 60
Frandley. Ches —3A 84
Frankby. Mers —2E 83
Frankfort. Norf —3F 79
Frankley. Worc —2D 61
Frank's Bridge. Powy —5D 58
Frankton. Warw —3B 62
Frankwell. Shrp —4G 71
Frant. E Sus —2G 27
Fraserburgh. Aber —2G 161
Frating Green. Essx —3D 54
Fratton. Port —2E 17
Freathy. Corn —3A 8
Freckenham. Suff —3F 65
Freckleton. Lanc —2C 90
Freeby. Leics —3F 75
Freefolk Priors. Hants —2C 24
Freeland. Oxon —4C 50
Freester. Shet —6F 173
Freethorpe. Norf —5G 79
Freiston. Linc —1C 76
Freiston Shore. Linc —1C 76
Fremington. Devn —3F 19
Fremington. N Yor —5D 104
Frenchbeer. Devn —4G 11
French Street. Kent —5F 39
Frenich. Stir —3D 134
Frensham. Surr —2G 25
Frenze. Norf —2D 66
Fresgoe. High —2B 168
Freshfield. Mers —4A 90
Freshford. Bath —5C 34
Freshwater. IOW —4B 16
Freshwater Bay. IOW —4B 16
Freshwater East. Pemb —5E 43
Fressingfield. Suff —3E 67
Freston. Suff —2E 55
Freswick. High —2F 169
Fretherne. Glos —5C 48
Frettenham. Norf —4E 79
Freuchie. Fife —3E 137
Freystrop. Pemb —3D 42
Friar's Gate. E Sus —2F 27
Friar Waddon. Dors —4B 14
Friday Bridge. Cambs —5D 76
Friday Street. E Sus —5H 27
Friday Street. Surr —1C 26
Fridaythorpe. E Yor —4C 100
Friden. Derbs —4F 85
Friern Barnet. G Lon —1D 39
Friesthorpe. Linc —2H 87
Frieston. Linc —1G 75
Frieth. Buck —2F 37
Friezeland. Notts —5B 86
Frilford. Oxon —2C 36
Frilsham. W Ber —4D 36
Frimley. Surr —1G 25
Frimley Green. Surr —1G 25
Frindsbury. Medw —4B 40
Fring. Norf —2G 77
Fringford. Oxon —3E 50
Frinsted. Kent —5C 40
Frinton-on-Sea. Essx —4F 55
Friockheim. Ang —4E 145
Friog. Gwyn —4F 69
Frisby on the Wreak. Leics —4D 74
Friskney. Linc —5D 88
Friskney Eaudyke. Linc —5D 88
Friston. E Sus —5G 27
Friston. Suff —4G 67
Fritchley. Derbs —5A 86
Fritham. Hants —1H 15
Frith Bank. Linc —1C 76
Frith Common. Worc —4A 60
Frithelstock. Devn —1E 11
Frithelstock Stone. Devn —1E 11
Frithsden. Herts —5A 52
Frithville. Linc —5C 88
Frittenden. Kent —1C 28
Frittiscombe. Devn —4E 9
Fritton. Norf —5G 79 (nr. Great Yarmouth)
Fritton. Norf —1E 67 (nr. Long Stratton)
Fritwell. Oxon —3D 50
Frizinghall. W Yor —1B 92
Frizington. Cumb —3B 102
Frobost. W Isl —6C 170
Frocester. Glos —5C 48
Frochas. Powy —5D 70
Frodesley. Shrp —5H 71
Frodingham. N Lin —3C 94
Frodsham. Ches —3H 83
Froggat. Derbs —3G 85
Froghall. Staf —1E 73
Frogham. Hants —1G 15
Frogham. Kent —5G 41
Frogmore. Devn —4D 9
Frogmore. Hants —5G 37
Frogmore. Herts —5B 52
Frognall. Linc —4A 76
Frogshall. Norf —2E 79
Frogwell. Corn —2H 7
Frolesworth. Leics —1C 62
Frome. Som —2C 22
Fromefield. Som —2C 22
Frome St Quintin. Dors —2A 14
Fromes Hill. Here —1B 48
Fron. Carm —2A 46
Fron. Gwyn —5E 81 (nr. Caernarfon)
Fron. Gwyn —2C 68 (nr. Pwllheli)
Fron. Powy —4C 58 (nr. Llandrindod Wells)
Fron. Powy —1D 58 (nr. Newtown)
Fron. Powy —5E 71 (nr. Welshpool)
Froncysyllte. Den —1E 71
Frongoch. Gwyn —2B 70
Fron Isaf. Wrex —1E 71
Fronoleu. Gwyn —2G 69
Frosterley. Dur —1D 104
Frotoft. Orkn —5D 172
Froxfield. Beds —2H 51
Froxfield. Wilts —5A 36
Froxfield Green. Hants —4F 25
Fryern Hill. Hants —4C 24
Fryerning. Essx —5G 53
Fryton. N Yor —2A 100
Fugglestone St Peter. Wilts —3G 23
Fulbeck. Linc —5G 87
Fulbourn. Cambs —5E 65
Fulbrook. Oxon —4A 50
Fulflood. Hants —4C 24
Fulford. Som —4F 21
Fulford. Staf —2D 72
Fulford. York —5A 100
Fulham. G Lon —3D 38
Fulking. W Sus —4D 26
Fuller's Moor. Ches —5G 83
Fuller Street. Essx —4H 53
Fullerton. Hants —3B 24
Fulletby. Linc —3B 88
Full Sutton. E Yor —4B 100
Fullwood. E Ayr —4F 127
Fulmer. Buck —2A 38
Fulmodestone. Norf —2B 78
Fulnetby. Linc —3A 88
Fulney. Linc —3B 76
Fulstow. Linc —1C 88
Fulthorpe. Stoc T —2B 106
Fulwell. Tyne —4G 115
Fulwood. Lanc —1D 90
Fulwood. Notts —5B 86
Fulwood. Som —4F 21
Fulwood. S Yor —2G 85
Fundenhall. Norf —1D 66
Funtington. W Sus —2G 17
Funtley. Hants —2D 16
Funzie. Shet —2H 173
Furley. Devn —2F 13
Furnace. Arg —3H 133
Furnace. Carm —5F 45
Furnace. Cdgn —1F 57
Furner's Green. E Sus —3F 27
Furness Vale. Derbs —2E 85
Furneux Pelham. Herts —3E 53
Furzebrook. Dors —4E 15
Furzehill. Devn —2H 19
Furzeley Corner. Hants —1E 17
Furzey Lodge. Hants —2B 16
Furzley. Hants —1A 16
Fyfield. Essx —5F 53
Fyfield. Glos —5H 49
Fyfield. Hants —2A 24
Fyfield. Oxon —2C 36
Fyfield. Wilts —5G 35
Fylingthorpe. N Yor —4G 107
Fyning. W Sus —4G 25
Fyvie. Aber —5E 161

Gabhsann bho Dheas. W Isl —2G 171
Gabhsann bho Thuath. W Isl —2G 171
Gabroc Hill. E Ayr —4F 127
Gadbrook. Surr —1D 26
Gaddesby. Leics —4D 74
Gadgirth. S Ayr —2D 116
Gaer. Powy —3E 47
Gaerwen. IOA —3D 81
Gagingwell. Oxon —3C 50
Gaick Lodge. High —5B 150
Gailey. Staf —4D 72
Gainford. Dur —3E 105
Gainsborough. Linc —1F 87
Gainsborough. Suff —1E 55
Gainsford End. Essx —2H 53
Gairletter. Arg —1C 126
Gairloch. Aber —3E 153
Gairloch. High —1H 155
Gairlochy. High —5D 148
Gairney Bank. Per —4D 136
Gairnshiel Lodge. Aber —3G 151
Gaisgill. Cumb —4H 103
Gaitsgill. Cumb —5E 113
Galashiels. Scot —1G 119
Galgate. Lanc —4D 97
Galhampton. Som —4B 22
Gallatown. Fife —4E 137
Galley Common. Warw —1H 61
Galleyend. Essx —5H 53
Galleywood. Essx —5H 53
Gallin. Per —4C 142
Gallowfauld. Ang —4D 144
Gallowhill. E Dun —2H 127
Gallowhill. Per —5A 144
Gallowhill. Ren —3F 127
Gallowhills. Aber —3H 161
Gallows Green. Staf —1E 73
Gallows Green. Worc —4D 60
Gallowstree Common. Oxon —3E 37
Galltair. High —1G 147
Gallt Melyd. Den —2C 82
Galmington. Som —4F 21
Galmisdale. High —5C 146
Galmpton. Devn —4C 8
Galmpton. Torb —3E 9
Galmpton Warborough. Torb —3E 9
Galphay. N Yor —2E 99
Galston. E Ayr —1D 117
Galton. Dors —4C 14
Galtrigill. High —3A 154
Gamblesby. Cumb —1H 103
Gamelsby. Cumb —4D 112
Gamesley. Derbs —1E 85
Gamlingay. Cambs —5B 64
Gamlingay Cinques. Cambs —5B 64
Gamlingay Great Heath. Cambs —5B 64
Gammersgill. N Yor —1C 98
Gamrie. Aber —2E 161
Gamston. Notts —3E 86 (nr. East Retford)
Gamston. Notts —2D 74 (nr. Nottingham)
Ganarew. Here —4A 48
Ganavan. Arg —5C 140
Ganborough. Glos —3G 49
Gang. Corn —2H 7
Ganllwyd. Gwyn —3G 69
Gannochy. Ang —1E 145
Gannochy. Per —1D 136
Gansclet. High —4F 169
Ganstead. E Yor —1E 95
Ganthorpe. N Yor —2A 100
Ganton. N Yor —2D 101
Gappah. Devn —5B 12
Garboldisham. Norf —2C 66
Garden City. Flin —4F 83
Gardeners Green. Wok —5G 37
Gardenstown. Aber —2F 161
Garden Village. S Yor —1G 85
Garden Village. Swan —3E 31
Garden Village. W Yor —1E 93
Garderhouse. Shet —7E 173
Gardham. E Yor —5D 100
Gardie. Shet —5C 173 (on Papa Stour)
Gardie. Shet —1H 173 (on Unst)
Gardie Ho. Shet —7F 173
Gare Hill. Som —2C 22
Garelochhead. Arg —4B 134
Garford. Oxon —2C 36
Garforth. W Yor —1E 93
Gargrave. N Yor —4B 98
Gargunnock. Stir —4G 135
Garlieston. Dum —5B 110
Garlinge Green. Kent —5F 41
Garlogie. Aber —3E 153
Garmelow. Staf —3B 72
Garmond. Aber —3F 161
Garmondsway. Dur —1A 106
Garmony. Arg —4A 140
Garmouth. Mor —2H 159
Garmston. Shrp —5A 72
Garnant. Carm —4G 45
Garndiffaith. Torf —5F 47
Garndolbenmaen. Gwyn —1D 69
Garnett Bridge. Cumb —5G 103
Garnfadryn. Gwyn —2B 68
Garnkirk. N Lan —3H 127
Garnlydan. Blae —4E 47
Garnsgate. Linc —3D 76
Garnswllt. Swan —5G 45
Garn-yr-erw. Torf —4F 47
Garrabost. W Isl —4H 171
Garrafad. High —2D 155
Garrallan. E Ayr —3E 117
Garras. Corn —4E 5
Garreg. Gwyn —1F 69
Garrigill. Cumb —5A 114
Garriston. N Yor —5E 105
Garrogie Lodge. High —2H 149
Garros. High —2D 155
Garrow. Per —5F 143
Garsdale. Cumb —1G 97
Garsdale Head. Cumb —5A 104
Garsdon. Wilts —3E 35
Garshall Green. Staf —2D 72
Garsington. Oxon —5D 50
Garstang. Lanc —5D 97
Garston. Mers —2G 83
Garswood. Mers —1H 83
Gartcosh. N Lan —3H 127
Garth. B'End —2B 32
Garth. Cdgn —2F 57
Garth. Den —1E 71
Garth. Gwyn —2E 69
Garth. IOM —4C 108
Garth. Powy —1C 46 (nr. Builth Wells)
Garth. Powy —3E 59 (nr. Knighton)
Garth. Shet —6F 173
Garthamlock. Glas —3H 127
Garthbrengy. Powy —2D 46
Gartheli. Cdgn —5E 57
Garthmyl. Powy —1D 58
Garthorpe. Leics —3F 75
Garthorpe. N Lin —3B 94
Garth Owen. Powy —1D 58
Garth Row. Cumb —5G 103
Gartly. Aber —5C 160
Gartmore. Stir —4E 135
Gartness. N Lan —3A 128
Gartness. Stir —1G 127
Gartocharn. W Dun —1F 127
Garton. E Yor —1F 95
Garton-on-the-Wolds. E Yor —4D 101
Gartsherrie. N Lan —3A 128
Gartymore. High —2H 165
Garvald. E Lot —2B 130
Garvamore. High —4H 149
Garvard. Arg —4A 132
Garvault. High —5H 167
Garve. High —2F 157
Garvestone. Norf —5C 78
Garvie. Arg —4H 133
Garvock. Aber —1G 145
Garvock. Inv —2D 126
Garway. Here —3H 47
Garway Common. Here —3H 47
Garway Hill. Here —3H 47
Garwick. Linc —1A 76
Gaskan. High —1B 140
Gasper. Wilts —3C 22
Gastard. Wilts —5D 35
Gasthorpe. Norf —2B 66
Gatcombe. IOW —4C 16
Gateacre. Mers —2G 83
Gatebeck. Cumb —1E 97
Gate Burton. Linc —2F 87
Gateforth. N Yor —2F 93
Gatehead. E Ayr —1C 116
Gate Helmsley. N Yor —4A 100
Gatehouse. Nmbd —1A 114
Gatehouse of Fleet. Dum —4C 110
Gatelawbridge. Dum —5B 118
Gateley. Norf —3B 78
Gatenby. N Yor —1F 99
Gatesgarth. Cumb —3C 102
Gateshead. Tyne —3F 115
Gatesheath. Ches —4G 83
Gateside. Ang —4D 144 (nr. Forfar)
Gateside. Ang —4C 144 (nr. Kirriemuir)
Gateside. Fife —3D 136
Gateside. N Ayr —4E 127
Gathurst. G Man —4D 90
Gatley. G Man —2C 84
Gatton. Surr —5D 39
Gattonside. Scot —1H 119
Gatwick (London) Airport. G Lon —1D 27
Gaufron. Powy —4B 58
Gaulby. Leics —5D 74
Gauldry. Fife —1F 137
Gaultree. Norf —5D 77
Gaunt's Common. Dors —2F 15
Gaunt's Earthcott. S Glo —3B 34
Gautby. Linc —3A 88
Gavinton. Scot —4D 130
Gawber. S Yor —4D 92
Gawcott. Buck —2E 51
Gawsworth. Ches —4C 84
Gawthorpe. W Yor —2C 92
Gawthrop. Cumb —1F 97
Gawthwaite. Cumb —1B 96
Gay Bowers. Essx —5A 54
Gaydon. Warw —5A 62
Gayfield. Orkn —2D 172
Gayhurst. Mil —1G 51
Gayle. N Yor —1A 98
Gayles. N Yor —4E 105
Gay Street. W Sus —3B 26
Gayton. Mers —2E 83
Gayton. Norf —4G 77
Gayton. Nptn —5E 62
Gayton. Staf —3D 73
Gayton le Marsh. Linc —2D 88
Gayton le Wold. Linc —2B 88
Gayton Thorpe. Norf —4G 77
Gaywood. Norf —3F 77
Gazeley. Suff —4G 65
Geanies. High —1C 158
Gearraidh Bhailteas. W Isl —6C 170
Gearraidh Bhaird. W Isl —6F 171
Gearraidh ma Monadh. W Isl —7C 170
Gearraidh na h-Aibhne. W Isl —4E 171
Geary. High —2B 154
Geddes. High —3C 158
Gedding. Suff —5B 66
Geddington. Nptn —2F 63
Gedintailor. High —5E 155
Gedling. Notts —1D 74
Gedney. Linc —3D 76
Gedney Broadgate. Linc —3D 76
Gedney Drove End. Linc —3D 76
Gedney Dyke. Linc —3D 76
Gedney Hill. Linc —4C 76
Gee Cross. G Man —1D 84
Geeston. Rut —5G 75
Geilston. Arg —2E 127
Geirinis. W Isl —4C 170
Geise. High —2D 168
Geisiadar. W Isl —4D 171
Gelder Shiel. Aber —5G 151
Geldeston. Norf —1F 67
Gell. Cnwy —4A 82
Gelli. Pemb —3E 43
Gelli. Rhon —2C 32
Gellifor. Den —4D 82
Gelligaer. Cphy —2E 32
Gellilydan. Gwyn —2F 69
Gellinudd. Neat —5H 45
Gellyburn. Per —5H 143
Gellywen. Carm —2G 43
Gelston. Dum —4E 111
Gelston. Linc —1G 75
Gembling. E Yor —4F 101
Geneva. Cdgn —5D 56
Gentleshaw. Staf —4E 73
Geocrab. W Isl —8D 171
George Green. Buck —2A 38
Georgeham. Devn —3E 19
George Nympton. Devn —4H 19
Georgetown. Blae —5E 47
Georgetown. Ren —3F 127
Georth. Orkn —5C 172
Gerlan. Gwyn —4F 81
Germansweek. Devn —3E 11
Germoe. Corn —4C 4
Gerrard's Bromley. Staf —2B 72
Gerrards Cross. Buck —2A 38
Gerston. High —3D 168
Gervans. Corn —5C 6
Gestingthorpe. Essx —2B 54
Gethsemane. Pemb —1A 44
Geuffordd. Powy —4E 70
Gibraltar. Linc —5E 89
Gibraltar. Suff —5D 66
Gibralter. Buck —4F 51
Gibsmere. Notts —1E 74
Giddeahall. Wilts —4D 34
Gidea Park. G Lon —2G 39
Gidleigh. Devn —4G 11
Giffnock. E Ren —4G 127
Gifford. E Lot —3B 130
Giffordtown. Fife —2E 137
Giggetty. Staf —1C 60
Giggleswick. N Yor —3H 97
Gignog. Pemb —2C 42
Gilberdyke. E Yor —2B 94
Gilbert's End. Worc —1D 48
Gilbert's Green. Warw —3F 61
Gilchriston. E Lot —3A 130
Gilcrux. Cumb —1C 102
Gildersome. W Yor —2C 92
Gildingwells. S Yor —2C 86
Gilesgate Moor. Dur —5F 115
Gileston. V Glam —5D 32
Gilfach. Cphy —2E 33
Gilfach Goch. Rhon —2C 32
Gilfachreda. Cdgn —5D 56
Gill. Cumb —2F 103
Gillamoor. N Yor —1A 100
Gillar's Green. Mers —1G 83
Gillen. High —3B 154
Gilling East. N Yor —2A 100
Gillingham. Dors —4D 22
Gillingham. Medw —4B 40
Gillingham. Norf —1G 67
Gilling West. N Yor —4E 105
Gillock. High —3E 169
Gillow Heath. Staf —5C 84
Gills. High —1F 169
Gill's Green. Kent —2B 28
Gilmanscleuch. Scot —2F 119
Gilmerton. Edin —3F 129
Gilmerton. Per —1A 136
Gilmonby. Dur —3C 104
Gilmorton. Leics —2C 62
Gilsland. Nmbd —3H 113
Gilsland Spa. Cumb —3H 113
Gilston. Midl —4H 129
Giltbrook. Notts —1B 74
Gilwern. Mon —4F 47
Gimingham. Norf —2E 79
Giosla. W Isl —5D 171
Gipping. Suff —4C 66
Gipsey Bridge. Linc —1B 76
Gipton. W Yor —1D 92
Girdle Toll. N Ayr —5E 127
Girlsta. Shet —6F 173
Girsby. N Yor —4A 106
Girthon. Dum —4D 110
Girton. Cambs —4D 64
Girton. Notts —4F 87
Girvan. S Ayr —5A 116
Gisburn. Lanc —5H 97
Gisleham. Suff —2H 67
Gislingham. Suff —3C 66
Gissing. Norf —2D 66
Gittisham. Devn —3E 13
Gladestry. Powy —5E 59
Gladsmuir. E Lot —2A 130
Glaichbea. High —5H 157
Glais. Swan —5H 45
Glaisdale. N Yor —4E 107
Glame. High —4E 155
Glamis. Ang —4C 144
Glamisdale. High —5C 146
Glanaman. Carm —4G 45
Glan-Conwy. Cnwy —5H 81
Glandford. Norf —1C 78
Glan Duar. Carm —1F 45
Glandwr. Blae —5F 47
Glandwr. Pemb —2F 43
Glan-Dwyfach. Gwyn —1D 69
Glandy Cross. Carm —2F 43
Glandyfi. Cdgn —1F 57
Glangrwyney. Powy —4F 47
Glanmule. Powy —1D 58
Glanrhyd. Gwyn —2B 68
Glan-rhyd. Neat —5A 46
Glanrhyd. Pemb —1B 44 (nr. Cardigan)
Glan-rhyd. Pemb —1F 43 (nr. Crymmych)
Glanton. Nmbd —3E 121
Glanton Pike. Nmbd —3E 121
Glanvilles Wootton. Dors —2B 14
Glan-y-don. Flin —3D 82
Glan-y-nant. Powy —2B 58
Glan-yr-afon. Gwyn —1C 70
Glan-yr-afon. IOA —2F 81

Glan-yr-afon—Great Preston

Glan-yr-afon. Powy —5C 70
Glan-y-wern. Gwyn —2F 69
Glapthorn. Nptn —1H 63
Glapwell. Derbs —4B 86
Glas Aird. Arg —4A 132
Glas-allt Shiel. Aber —5G 151
Glasbury. Powy —2E 47
Glascoed. Den —3B 82
Glascoed. Mon —5G 47
Glascote. Staf —5G 73
Glascwm. Powy —5D 58
Glasfryn. Cnwy —5B 82
Glasgow. Glas —3G 127
Glasgow Airport. Ren —3F 127
Glashvin. High —2D 154
Glasinfryn. Gwyn —4E 81
Glasnakille. High —2D 146
Glasnarcardoch. High —4E 147
Glaspwll. Powy —1G 57
Glassburn. High —5F 157
Glassenbury. Kent —2B 28
Glasserton. Dum —5B 110
Glassford. S Lan —5A 128
Glasshouse. Glos —3C 48
Glasshouses. N Yor —3D 98
Glasson. Cumb —3D 112
Glasson. Lanc —4D 96
Glassonby. Cumb —1G 103
Glasterlaw. Ang —3E 145
Glaston. Rut —5F 75
Glastonbury. Som —3H 21
Glatton. Cambs —2A 64
Glazebrook. Warr —1A 84
Glazebury. Warr —1A 84
Glazeley. Shrp —2B 60
Gleadless. S Yor —2A 86
Gleadsmoss. Ches —4C 84
Gleann Dail bho Dheas. W Isl —7C 170
Gleann Tholastaidh. W Isl —3H 171
Gleaston. Cumb —2B 96
Glecknabae. Arg —3B 126
Gledrid. Shrp —2E 71
Gleiniant. Powy —1B 58
Glemsford. Suff —1B 54
Glen. Dum —4C 110
Glenancross. High —4E 147
Glen Audlyn. IOM —2D 108
Glenbarr. Arg —2A 122
Glenbeg. High —2G 139
Glen Bernisdale. High —4D 154
Glenbervie. Aber —5E 153
Glenboig. N Lan —3A 128
Glenborrodale. High —2A 140
Glenbranter. Arg —4A 134
Glenbreck. Scot —2C 118
Glenbrein Lodge. High —2G 149
Glenbrittle. High —1C 146
Glenbuchat Lodge. Aber —2H 151
Glenbuck. E Ayr —2G 117
Glenburn. Ren —3F 127
Glencalvie Lodge. High —5B 164
Glencaple. Dum —3A 112
Glencarron Lodge. High —3C 156
Glencarse. Per —1D 136
Glencassley Castle. High —3B 164
Glencat. Aber —4C 152
Glencoe. High —3F 141
Glen Cottage. High —5E 147
Glencraig. Fife —4D 136
Glendale. High —4A 154
Glendevon. Per —3B 136
Glendoebeg. High —3G 149
Glendoick. Per —1E 136
Glendoune. S Ayr —5A 116
Glenduckie. Fife —2E 137
Gleneagles. Per —3B 136
Glenegedale. Arg —4B 124
Glenegedale Lots. Arg —4B 124
Glenelg. High —2G 147
Glenernie. Mor —4E 159
Glenesslin. Dum —1F 111
Glenfarg. Per —2D 136
Glenfarquhar Lodge. Aber —5E 152
Glenferness Mains. High —4D 158
Glenfeshie Lodge. High —4C 150
Glenfiddich Lodge. Mor —5H 159
Glenfield. Leics —5C 74
Glenfinnan. High —5B 148
Glenfintaig Lodge. High —5E 149
Glenfoot. Per —2D 136
Glenfyne Lodge. Arg —2B 134
Glengap. Dum —4D 110
Glengarnock. N Ayr —4E 126
Glengolly. High —2C 168
Glengorm Castle. Arg —3F 139
Glengrasco. High —4D 154
Glenhead Farm. Ang —2B 144
Glenholm. Scot —1D 118
Glen House. Scot —1E 119
Glenhurich. High —2C 140
Glenkerry. Scot —3E 119
Glenkiln. Dum —2F 111
Glenkindle. Aber —2B 152
Glenkinglass Lodge. Arg —5F 141
Glenkirk. Scot —1C 118
Glenlean. Arg —1B 126
Glenlee. Dum —1D 110
Glenleraig. High —5B 166
Glenlichorn. Per —2G 135
Glenlivet. Mor —1F 151
Glenlochar. Dum —3E 111
Glenlochsie Lodge. Per —1H 143
Glenluce. Dum —4G 109
Glenmarskie. High —3F 157
Glenmassan. Arg —1C 126
Glenmavis. N Lan —3A 128
Glenmaye. IOM —3B 108
Glenmazeran Lodge. High —1B 150
Glenmidge. Dum —1F 111
Glen Mona. IOM —3D 108
Glenmore. High —2G 139
(nr. Glenborrodale)
Glenmore. High —3D 151
(nr. Kingussie)
Glenmore. High —5D 154
(on Skye)
Glenmoy. Ang —2D 144
Glennoe. Arg —5E 141
Glen of Coachford. Aber —4B 160
Glenogil. Ang —2D 144
Glen Parva. Leics —1C 62
Glenprosen Village. Ang —2C 144
Glenree. N Ayr —3D 122
Glenridding. Cumb —3E 103
Glenrisdell. Arg —4G 125
Glenrosa. N Ayr —2E 123
Glenrothes. Fife —3E 137
Glensanda. High —4C 140
Glensaugh. Aber —1F 145
Glenshero Lodge. High —4H 149
Glensluain. Arg —4H 133
Glenstockadale. Dum —3F 109
Glenstriven. Arg —2B 126
Glen Tanar House. Aber —4B 152
Glentham. Linc —1H 87
Glenton. Aber —1D 152
Glentress. Scot —1E 119
Glentromie Lodge. High —4B 150
Glentrool Lodge. Dum —1B 110
Glentrool Village. Dum —2A 110
Glentruim House. High —4A 150
Glentworth. Linc —2G 87
Glenuig. High —1A 140
Glen Village. Falk —2B 128
Glen Vine. IOM —4C 108
Glenwhilly. Dum —2G 109
Glenzierfoot. Dum —2E 113
Glespin. S Lan —2H 117
Gletness. Shet —6F 173
Glewstone. Here —3A 48
Glib Cheois. W Isl —5F 171
Glinton. Pet —5A 76
Glooston. Leics —1E 63
Glossop. Derbs —1E 85
Gloster Hill. Nmbd —4G 121
Gloucester. Glos —4D 48
Gloup. Shet —1G 173
Glusburn. N Yor —5C 98
Glutt Lodge. High —5B 168
Glutton Bridge. Derbs —4E 85
Gluvian. Corn —2D 6
Glympton. Oxon —3C 50
Glyn. Cnwy —3A 82
Glynarthen. Cdgn —1D 44
Glynbrochan. Powy —2B 58
Glyn Ceiriog. Wrex —2E 70
Glyncoch. Rhon —2D 32
Glyncorrwg. Neat —2B 32
Glynde. E Sus —5F 27
Glyndebourne. E Sus —4F 27
Glyndyfrdwy. Den —1D 70
Glyn Ebwy. Blae —5E 47
Glynllan. B'End —3C 32
Glyn-neath. Neat —5B 46
Glynogwr. B'End —3C 32
Glyntaff. Rhon —3D 32
Glyntawe. Powy —4B 46
Glynteg. Carm —2D 44
Gnosall. Staf —3C 72
Gnosall Heath. Staf —3C 72
Goadby. Leics —1E 63
Goadby Marwood. Leics —3E 75
Goatacre. Wilts —4F 35
Goathill. Dors —1B 14
Goathland. N Yor —4F 107
Goathurst. Som —3F 21
Goathurst Common. Kent —5F 39
Goat Lees. Kent —1E 28
Gobernuisgach Lodge. High —4E 167
Gobernuisgeach. High —5B 168
Gobhaig. W Isl —7C 171
Gobowen. Shrp —2F 71
Godalming. Surr —1A 26
Goddard's Corner. Suff —4E 67
Goddard's Green. Kent —2C 28
(nr. Benenden)
Goddard's Green. Kent —2B 28
(nr. Cranbrook)
Goddards Green. W Sus —3D 27
Godford Cross. Devn —2E 13
Godleybrook. Staf —1D 73
Godmanchester. Cambs —3B 64
Godmanstone. Dors —3B 14
Godmersham. Kent —5E 41
Godolphin Cross. Corn —3D 4
Godre'r-graig. Neat —5A 46
Godshill. Hants —1G 15
Godshill. IOW —4D 16
Godstone. Staf —2E 73
Godstone. Surr —5E 39
Godwell. Devn —3C 8
Goetre. Mon —5G 47
Goff's Oak. Herts —5D 52
Gogar. Edin —2E 129
Goginan. Cdgn —2F 57
Golan. Gwyn —1E 69
Golant. Corn —3F 7
Golberdon. Corn —5D 10
Golborne. G Man —1A 84
Golcar. W Yor —3A 92
Goldcliff. Newp —3G 33
Golden Cross. E Sus —4G 27
Golden Green. Kent —1H 27
Golden Grove. Carm —4F 45
Golden Grove. N Yor —4F 107
Golden Hill. Pemb —2D 43
Goldenhill. Stoke —5C 84
Golden Pot. Hants —2F 25
Golden Valley. Glos —3E 49
Golders Green. G Lon —2D 38
Goldhanger. Essx —5C 54
Gold Hill. Norf —1E 65
Golding. Shrp —5H 71
Goldington. Beds —5H 63
Goldsborough. N Yor —4F 99
(nr. Harrogate)
Goldsborough. N Yor —3F 107
(nr. Whitby)
Goldsithney. Corn —3C 4
Goldstone. Kent —4G 41
Goldstone. Shrp —3B 72
Goldthorpe. S Yor —4E 93
Goldworthy. Devn —4D 19
Golfa. Powy —3D 70
Gollanfield. High —3C 158
Gollinglith Foot. N Yor —1D 98
Golsoncott. Som —3D 20
Golspie. High —4F 165
Gomeldon. Wilts —3G 23
Gomersal. W Yor —2C 92
Gometra House. Arg —4E 139
Gomshall. Surr —1B 26
Gonalston. Notts —1D 74
Gonerby Hill Foot. Linc —2G 75
Gonfirth. Shet —5E 173
Gonnabarn. Corn —3D 6
Good Easter. Essx —4G 53
Gooderstone. Norf —5G 77
Goodleigh. Devn —3G 19
Goodmanham. E Yor —5C 100
Goodmayes. G Lon —2F 39
Goodnestone. Kent —5G 41
(nr. Aylesham)
Goodnestone. Kent —4E 41
(nr. Faversham)
Goodrich. Here —4A 48
Goodrington. Torb —3E 9
Goodshaw. Lanc —2G 91
Goodshaw Fold. Lanc —2G 91
Goodstone. Devn —5A 12
Goodwick. Pemb —1D 42
Goodworth Clatford. Hants —2B 24
Goole. E Yor —2H 93
Goom's Hill. Worc —5E 61
Goonbell. Corn —4B 6
Goonhavern. Corn —3B 6
Goonvrea. Corn —4B 6
Goose Green. Cumb —1E 97
Goose Green. S Glo —3C 34
Gooseham. Corn —1C 10
Goosewell. Plym —3B 8
Goosey. Oxon —2B 36
Goosnargh. Lanc —1D 90
Goostrey. Ches —4B 84
Gorcott Hill. Warw —4E 61
Gord. Shet —9F 173
Gordon. Scot —5C 130
Gordonbush. High —3F 165
Gordonstown. Aber —3C 160
(nr. Cornhill)
Gordonstown. Aber —5E 160
(nr. Fyvie)
Gorebridge. Midl —3G 129
Gorefield. Cambs —4D 76
Gores. Wilts —1G 23
Gorgie. Edin —2F 129
Goring. Oxon —3E 36
Goring-by-Sea. W Sus —5C 26
Goring Heath. Oxon —4E 37
Gorleston-on-Sea. Norf —5H 79
Gornalwood. W Mid —1D 60
Gorran Churchtown. Corn —4D 6
Gorran Haven. Corn —4E 6
Gorran High Lanes. Corn —4D 6
Gors. Cdgn —3F 57
Gorsedd. Flin —3D 82
Gorseinon. Swan —3E 31
Gorseness. Orkn —6D 172
Gorseybank. Derbs —5G 85
Gorsgoch. Cdgn —5D 57
Gorslas. Carm —4F 45
Gorsley. Glos —3B 48
Gorsley Common. Here —3B 48
Gorstan. High —2F 157
Gorstella. Ches —4F 83
Gorsty Common. Here —2H 47
Gorsty Hill. Staf —3E 73
Gortantaoid. Arg —2B 124
Gorteneorn. High —2A 140
Gortenfern. High —2A 140
Gorton. G Man —1C 84
Gosbeck. Suff —5D 66
Gosberton. Linc —2B 76
Gosberton Clough. Linc —3A 76
Goseley Dale. Derbs —3H 73
Gosfield. Essx —3A 54
Gosford. Oxon —4D 50
Gosforth. Cumb —4B 102
Gosforth. Tyne —3F 115
Gosmore. Herts —3B 52
Gospel End Village. Staf —1C 60
Gosport. Hants —2D 16
Gossabrough. Shet —3G 173
Gossington. Glos —5C 48
Gossops Green. W Sus —2D 26
Goswick. Nmbd —5G 131
Gotham. Notts —2C 74
Gotherington. Glos —3E 49
Gott. Arg —4B 138
Gott. Shet —7F 173
Goudhurst. Kent —2B 28
Goulceby. Linc —3B 88
Gourdon. Aber —1H 145
Gourock. Inv —2D 126
Govan. Glas —3G 127
Govanhill. Glas —3G 127
Goverton. Notts —5E 86
Goveton. Devn —4D 8
Govilon. Mon —4F 47
Gowanhill. Aber —2H 161
Gowdall. E Yor —2G 93
Gowerton. Swan —3E 31
Gowkhall. Fife —1D 128
Gowthorpe. E Yor —4B 100
Goxhill. E Yor —5F 101
Goxhill. N Lin —2E 94
Goxhill Haven. N Lin —2E 94
Goytre. Neat —3A 32
Grabhair. W Isl —6F 171
Graby. Linc —3H 75
Graffham. W Sus —4A 26
Grafham. Cambs —4A 64
Grafham. Surr —1B 26
Grafton. Here —2H 47
Grafton. N Yor —3G 99
Grafton. Oxon —5A 50
Grafton. Shrp —4G 71
Grafton. Worc —2E 49
(nr. Evesham)
Grafton. Worc —4H 59
(nr. Leominster)
Grafton Flyford. Worc —5D 60
Grafton Regis. Nptn —1F 51
Grafton Underwood. Nptn —2G 63
Grafty Green. Kent —1C 28
Graianrhyd. Den —5E 82
Graig. Carm —5E 45
Graig. Cnwy —3H 81
Graig. Den —3C 82
Graig-fechan. Den —5D 82
Graig Penllyn. V Glam —4C 32
Grain. Medw —3C 40
Grainsby. Linc —1B 88
Grainthorpe. Linc —1C 88
Grainthorpe Fen. Linc —1C 88
Gramasdail. W Isl —3D 170
Grampound. Corn —4D 6
Grampound Road. Corn —3D 6
Granborough. Buck —3F 51
Granby. Notts —2E 75
Grandborough. Warw —4B 62
Grandpont. Oxon —5D 50
Grandtully. Per —3G 143
Grange. Cumb —3D 102
Grange. E Ayr —1D 116
Grange. Here —3G 59
Grange. Mers —2E 83
Grange. Per —1E 137
Grange Crossroads. Mor —3B 160
Grange Hill. G Lon —1F 39
Grangemill. Derbs —5G 85
Grange Moor. W Yor —3C 92
Grangemouth. Falk —1C 128
Grange of Lindores. Fife —2E 137
Grange-over-Sands. Cumb —2D 96
Grangepans. Falk —1D 128
Grange, The. N Yor —5C 106
Grangetown. Card —4E 33
Grangetown. Red C —2C 106
Grange Villa. Dur —4F 115
Granish. High —2C 150
Gransmoor. E Yor —4F 101
Granston. Pemb —1C 42
Grantchester. Cambs —5D 64
Grantham. Linc —2G 75
Grantley. N Yor —3E 99
Grantlodge. Aber —2E 152
Granton. Edin —2F 129
Grantown-on-Spey. High —1E 151
Grantshouse. Scot —3E 130
Grappenhall. Warr —2A 84
Grasby. Linc —4D 94
Grasmere. Cumb —4E 103
Grasscroft. G Man —4H 91
Grassendale. Mers —2F 83
Grassgarth. Cumb —5E 113
Grassholme. Dur —2C 104
Grassington. N Yor —3C 98
Grassmoor. Derbs —4B 86
Grassthorpe. Notts —4E 87
Grateley. Hants —2A 24
Gratton. Devn —1D 11
Gratton. Staf —5D 84
Gratwich. Staf —2E 73
Graveley. Cambs —4B 64
Graveley. Herts —3C 52
Gravelhill. Shrp —4G 71
Gravel Hole. G Man —4H 91
Gravelly Hill. W Mid —1F 61
Graven. Shet —4F 173
Graveney. Kent —4E 41
Gravesend. Kent —3H 39
Grayingham. Linc —1G 87
Grayrigg. Cumb —5G 103
Grays. Thur —3H 39
Grayshott. Hants —3G 25
Grayson Green. Cumb —2A 102
Grayswood. Surr —2A 26
Graythorp. Hart —2C 106
Grazeley. Wok —5E 37
Grealin. High —2E 155
Greasby. Mers —2E 83
Greaseborough. S Yor —1B 86
Great Abington. Cambs —1F 53
Great Addington. Nptn —3G 63
Great Alne. Warw —5F 61
Great Altcar. Lanc —4B 90
Great Amwell. Herts —4D 52
Great Asby. Cumb —3H 103
Great Ashfield. Suff —4B 66
Great Ayton. N Yor —3C 106
Great Baddow. Essx —5H 53
Great Bardfield. Essx —2G 53
Great Barford. Beds —5A 64
Great Barr. W Mid —1E 61
Great Barrington. Glos —4H 49
Great Barrow. Ches —4G 83
Great Barton. Suff —4A 66
Great Barugh. N Yor —2B 100
Great Bavington. Nmbd —1C 114
Great Bealings. Suff —1F 55
Great Bedwyn. Wilts —5A 36
Great Bentley. Essx —3E 54
Great Billing. Nptn —4F 63
Great Bircham. Norf —2G 77
Great Blakenham. Suff —5D 66
Great Blencow. Cumb —1F 103
Great Bolas. Telf —3A 72
Great Bookham. Surr —5C 38
Great Bosullow. Corn —3B 4
Great Bourton. Oxon —1C 50
Great Bowden. Leics —2E 63
Great Bradley. Suff —5F 65
Great Braxted. Essx —4B 54
Great Bricett. Suff —5C 66
Great Brickhill. Buck —2H 51
Great Bridgeford. Staf —3C 72
Great Brington. Nptn —4D 62
Great Bromley. Essx —3D 54
Great Broughton. Cumb —1B 102
Great Broughton. N Yor —4C 106
Great Budworth. Ches —3A 84
Great Burdon. Darl —3A 106
Great Burstead. Essx —1A 40
Great Busby. N Yor —4C 106
Great Canfield. Essx —4F 53
Great Carlton. Linc —2D 88
Great Casterton. Rut —5H 75
Great Chalfield. Wilts —5D 34
Great Chart. Kent —1D 28
Great Chatwell. Staf —4B 72
Great Chesterford. Essx —1F 53
Great Cheverell. Wilts —1E 23
Great Chilton. Dur —1F 105
Great Chishill. Cambs —2E 53
Great Clacton. Essx —4E 55
Great Cliff. W Yor —3D 92
Great Clifton. Cumb —2B 102
Great Coates. NE Lin —3F 95
Great Comberton. Worc —1E 49
Great Corby. Cumb —4F 113
Great Cornard. Suff —1B 54
Great Cowden. E Yor —5G 101
Great Coxwell. Oxon —2A 36
Great Crakehall. N Yor —1E 99
Great Cransley. Nptn —3F 63
Great Cressingham. Norf —5H 77
Great Crosby. Mers —1F 83
Great Cubley. Derbs —2F 73
Great Dalby. Leics —4E 75
Great Doddington. Nptn —4F 63
Great Doward. Here —4A 48
Great Dunham. Norf —4A 78
Great Dunmow. Essx —3G 53
Great Durnford. Wilts —3G 23
Great Easton. Essx —3G 53
Great Easton. Leics —1F 63
Great Eccleston. Lanc —5D 96
Great Edstone. N Yor —1B 100
Great Ellingham. Norf —1C 66
Great Elm. Som —2C 22
Great Eppleton. Tyne —5G 115
Great Eversden. Cambs —5C 64
Great Fencote. N Yor —5F 105
Great Finborough. Suff —5C 66
Greatford. Linc —4H 75
Great Fransham. Norf —4A 78
Great Gaddesden. Herts —4A 52
Greatgate. Staf —1E 73
Great Gidding. Cambs —2A 64
Great Givendale. E Yor —4C 100
Great Glemham. Suff —4F 67
Great Glen. Leics —1D 62
Great Gonerby. Linc —2G 75
Great Gransden. Cambs —5B 64
Great Green. Norf —2E 67
Great Green. Suff —5B 66
(nr. Lavenham)
Great Green. Suff —3D 66
(nr. Palgrave)
Great Habton. N Yor —2B 100
Great Hale. Linc —1A 76
Great Hallingbury. Essx —4F 53
Greatham. Hants —3F 25
Greatham. Hart —2B 106
Greatham. W Sus —4B 26
Great Hampden. Buck —5G 51
Great Harrowden. Nptn —3F 63
Great Harwood. Lanc —1F 91
Great Haseley. Oxon —5E 51
Great Hatfield. E Yor —5F 101
Great Haywood. Staf —3D 73
Great Heath. W Mid —2H 61
Great Heck. N Yor —2F 93
Great Henny. Essx —2B 54
Great Hinton. Wilts —1E 23
Great Hockham. Norf —1B 66
Great Holland. Essx —4F 55
Great Horkesley. Essx —2C 54
Great Hormead. Herts —2E 53
Great Horton. W Yor —1B 92
Great Horwood. Buck —2F 51
Great Houghton. Nptn —5E 63
Great Houghton. S Yor —4E 93
Great Hucklow. Derbs —3F 85
Great Kelk. E Yor —4F 101
Great Kendale. E Yor —4E 101
Great Kimble. Buck —5G 51
Great Kingshill. Buck —2G 37
Great Langdale. Cumb —4D 102
Great Langton. N Yor —5F 105
Great Leighs. Essx —4H 53
Great Limber. Linc —4E 95
Great Linford. Mil —1G 51
Great Livermere. Suff —3A 66
Great Longstone. Derbs —3G 85
Great Lumley. Dur —5F 115
Great Lyth. Shrp —5G 71
Great Malvern. Worc —1C 48
Great Maplestead. Essx —2B 54
Great Marton. Bkpl —1B 90
Great Massingham. Norf —3G 77
Great Melton. Norf —5D 78
Great Milton. Oxon —5E 51
Great Missenden. Buck —5G 51
Great Mitton. Lanc —1F 91
Great Mongeham. Kent —5H 41
Great Moulton. Norf —1D 66
Great Munden. Herts —3D 52
Great Musgrave. Cumb —3A 104
Great Ness. Shrp —4G 71
Great Notley. Essx —3H 53
Great Oak. Mon —5G 47
Great Oakley. Essx —3E 55
Great Oakley. Nptn —2F 63
Great Offley. Herts —3B 52
Great Ormside. Cumb —3A 104
Great Orton. Cumb —4E 113
Great Ouseburn. N Yor —3G 99
Great Oxendon. Nptn —2E 63
Great Oxney Green. Essx —5G 53
Great Parndon. Essx —5E 53
Great Paxton. Cambs —4B 64
Great Plumpton. Lanc —1B 90
Great Plumstead. Norf —4F 79
Great Ponton. Linc —2G 75
Great Potheridge. Devn —1F 11
Great Preston. W Yor —2E 93

Great Raveley—Hamstall Ridware

Great Raveley. Cambs —2B 64
Great Rissington. Glos —4G 49
Great Rollright. Oxon —2B 50
Great Ryburgh. Norf —3B 78
Great Ryle. Nmbd —3E 121
Great Ryton. Shrp —5G 71
Great Saling. Essx —3G 53
Great Salkeld. Cumb —1G 103
Great Sampford. Essx —2G 53
Great Sankey. Warr —2H 83
Great Saredon. Staf —5D 72
Great Saxham. Suff —4G 65
Great Shefford. W Ber —4B 36
Great Shelford. Cambs —5D 64
Great Shoddesden. Hants —2A 24
Great Smeaton. N Yor —4A 106
Great Snoring. Norf —2B 78
Great Somerford. Wilts —3E 35
Great Stainton. Darl —2A 106
Great Stambridge. Essx —1C 40
Great Staughton. Cambs —4A 64
Great Steeping. Linc —4D 88
Great Stonar. Kent —5H 41
Greatstone-on-Sea. Kent —3E 29
Great Strickland. Cumb —2G 103
Great Stukeley. Cambs —3B 64
Great Sturton. Linc —3B 88
Great Sutton. Ches —3F 83
Great Sutton. Shrp —2H 59
Great Swinburne. Nmbd —2C 114
Great Tew. Oxon —3B 50
Great Tey. Essx —3B 54
Great Thirkleby. N Yor —2G 99
Great Thorness. IOW —3C 16
Great Thurlow. Suff —5F 65
Great Torr. Devn —4C 8
Great Torrington. Devn —1E 11
Great Tosson. Nmbd —4E 121
Great Totham North. Essx —4B 54
Great Totham South. Essx —4B 54
Great Tows. Linc —1B 88
Great Urswick. Cumb —2B 96
Great Wakering. Essx —2D 40
Great Waldingfield. Suff —1C 54
Great Walsingham. Norf —2B 78
Great Waltham. Essx —4G 53
Great Warley. Essx —1G 39
Great Washbourne. Glos —2E 49
Great Welnetham. Suff —5A 66
Great Wenham. Suff —2D 54
Great Whittington. Nmbd —2D 114
Great Wigborough. Essx —4C 54
Great Wilbraham. Cambs —5E 65
Great Wilne. Derbs —2B 74
Great Wishford. Wilts —3F 23
Great Witchingham. Norf —4D 78
Great Witcombe. Glos —4E 49
Great Witley. Worc —4B 60
Great Wolford. Warw —2H 49
Greatworth. Nptn —1D 50
Great Wratting. Suff —1G 53
Great Wymondley. Herts —3C 52
Great Wyrley. Staf —5D 73
Great Wytheford. Shrp —4H 71
Great Yarmouth. Norf —5H 79
Great Yeldham. Essx —2A 54
Grebby. Linc —4D 88
Greeba Castle. IOM —3C 108
Greenbank. Shet —1G 173
Green Bottom. Corn —4B 6
Greenburn. W Lot —3C 128
Greencroft. Dur —4E 115
Greencroft Hall. Dur —5E 115
Greendikes. Nmbd —2E 121
Greendown. Som —1A 22
Green End. Beds —1A 52
Green End. Herts —2D 52
(nr. Buntingford)
Green End. Herts —3D 52
(nr. Stevenage)
Green End. N Yor —4F 107
Green End. Warw —2G 61
Greenfield. Arg —4B 134
Greenfield. Beds —2A 52
Greenfield. Flin —3D 82
Greenfield. G Man —4H 91
Greenfield. Oxon —2F 37
Greenfoot. N Lan —3A 128
Greenford. G Lon —2C 38
Greengairs. N Lan —2A 128
Greengate. Norf —4C 78
Greengill. Cumb —1C 102
Greenhalgh. Lanc —1C 90
Greenham. Dors —2H 13
Greenham. Som —4D 20
Greenham. W Ber —5C 36
Green Hammerton. N Yor —4G 99
Greenhaugh. Nmbd —1A 114
Greenhead. Nmbd —3H 113
Green Heath. Staf —4D 73
Greenhill. Dum —2C 112
Greenhill. Falk —2B 128
Greenhill. Kent —4F 41
Greenhill. S Yor —2H 85
Greenhill. Worc —3C 60
Greenhills. N Ayr —4E 127
Greenhithe. Kent —3G 39
Greenholm. E Ayr —1E 117
Greenhow Hill. N Yor —3D 98
Greenigo. Orkn —7D 172
Greenland. High —2E 169
Greenland Mains. High —2E 169
Greenlands. Worc —4E 61
Green Lane. Shrp —3A 72
Green Lane. Warw —4E 61
Greenlaw. Scot —5D 130
Greenlea. Dum —2B 112
Greenloaning. Per —3H 135
Greenmount. G Man —3F 91
Greenmow. Shet —9F 173
Greenock. Inv —2D 126
Greenodd. Cumb —1C 96
Green Ore. Som —1A 22
Greenrow. Cumb —4C 112
Greens. Aber —4F 161
Greensgate. Norf —4C 78
Greenside. Tyne —3E 115
Greensidehill. Nmbd —3D 121
Greens Norton. Nptn —1E 51
Greenstead Green. Essx —3B 54
Greensted Green. Essx —5F 53
Green Street. Herts —1C 38
Green Street. Suff —3D 66
Green Street Green. G Lon —4F 39
Green Street Green. Kent —3G 39
Greenstreet Green. Suff —1D 54
Green, The. Cumb —1A 96
Green, The. Wilts —3D 22
Green Tye. Herts —4E 53
Greenwall. Orkn —7E 172
Greenway. Pemb —2E 43
Greenway. V Glam —4D 32
Greenwell. Cumb —4G 113
Greenwich. G Lon —3E 39
Greet. Glos —2F 49
Greete. Shrp —3H 59
Greetham. Linc —3C 88
Greetham. Rut —4G 75
Greetland. W Yor —2A 92
Gregson Lane. Lanc —2D 90
Grein. W Isl —8B 170
Greinetobht. W Isl —1D 170
Greinton. Som —3H 21
Gremista. Shet —7F 173
Grenaby. IOM —4B 108
Grendon. Nptn —4F 63
Grendon. Warw —1G 61
Grendon Common. Warw —1G 61
Grendon Green. Here —5H 59
Grendon Underwood. Buck —3E 51
Grenofen. Devn —5E 11
Grenoside. S Yor —1H 85
Greosabhagh. W Isl —8D 171
Gresford. Wrex —5F 83
Gresham. Norf —2D 78
Greshornish. High —3C 154
Gressenhall. Norf —4B 78
Gressingham. Lanc —2E 97
Greta Bridge. Dur —3D 105
Gretna. Dum —3E 112
Gretna Green. Dum —3E 112
Gretton. Glos —2F 49
Gretton. Nptn —1G 63
Gretton. Shrp —1H 59
Grewelthorpe. N Yor —2E 99
Greygarth. N Yor —2D 98
Grey Green. N Lin —4A 94
Greylake. Som —3G 21
Greysouthern. Cumb —2B 102
Greystoke. Cumb —1F 103
Greystone. Ang —4E 145
Greystones. S Yor —2H 85
Greywell. Hants —1F 25
Griais. W Isl —3G 171
Grianan. W Isl —4G 171
Gribthorpe. E Yor —1A 94
Gribun. Arg —5F 139
Griff. Warw —2A 62
Griffithstown. Torf —2F 33
Griffydam. Leics —4B 74
Grigghall. Cumb —5F 103
Griggs Green. Hants —3G 25
Grimbister. Orkn —6C 172
Grimeford Village. Lanc —3E 90
Grimeston. Orkn —6C 172
Grimethorpe. S Yor —4E 93
Griminis. W Isl —3C 170
(on Benbecula)
Griminis. W Isl —1C 170
(on North Uist)
Grimister. Shet —2F 173
Grimley. Worc —4C 60
Grimness. Orkn —8D 172
Grimoldby. Linc —2C 88
Grimpo. Shrp —3F 71
Grimsargh. Lanc —1D 90
Grimsby. NE Lin —3F 95
Grimscote. Nptn —5D 62
Grimscott. Corn —2C 10
Grimshaw. Bkbn —2F 91
Grimshaw Green. Lanc —3C 90
Grimsthorpe. Linc —3H 75
Grimston. E Yor —1F 95
Grimston. Leics —3D 74
Grimston. Norf —3G 77
Grimston. York —4A 100
Grimstone. Dors —3B 14
Grimstone End. Suff —4B 66
Grinacombe Moor. Devn —3E 11
Grindale. E Yor —2F 101
Grindhill. Devn —3E 11
Grindiscol. Shet —8F 173
Grindle. Shrp —5B 72
Grindleford. Derbs —3G 85
Grindleton. Lanc —5G 97
Grindley. Staf —3E 73
Grindley Brook. Shrp —1H 71
Grindlow. Derbs —3F 85
Grindon. Nmbd —5F 131
Grindon. Staf —5E 85
Gringley on the Hill. Notts —1E 87
Grinsdale. Cumb —4E 113
Grinshill. Shrp —3H 71
Grinton. N Yor —5D 104
Griomsidar. W Isl —5G 171
Grishipoll. Arg —3C 138
Grisling Common. E Sus —3F 27
Gristhorpe. N Yor —1E 101
Griston. Norf —1B 66
Gritley. Orkn —7E 172
Grittenham. Wilts —3F 35
Grittleton. Wilts —4D 34
Grizebeck. Cumb —1B 96
Grizedale. Cumb —5E 103
Grobister. Orkn —5F 172
Grobsness. Shet —5E 173
Groby. Leics —5C 74
Groes. Cnwy —4C 82
Groes. Neat —3A 32
Groes-faen. Rhon —3D 32
Groesffordd. Gwyn —2B 68
Groesffordd. Powy —3D 46
Groeslon. Gwyn —5D 81
Groes-lwyd. Powy —4E 70
Groes-wen. Cphy —3E 33
Grogport. Arg —5G 125
Groigearraidh. W Isl —4C 170
Gromford. Suff —5F 67
Gronant. Flin —2C 82
Groombridge. E Sus —2G 27
Grosmont. Mon —3H 47
Grosmont. N Yor —4F 107
Groton. Suff —1C 54
Grove. Dors —5B 14
Grove. Kent —4G 41
Grove. Notts —3E 87
Grove. Oxon —2B 36
Grovehill. E Yor —5E 101
Grove Park. G Lon —3E 39
Grovesend. Swan —5F 45
Grove, The. Dum —2A 112
Grove, The. Worc —1D 48
Grub Street. Staf —3B 72
Grudie. High —2F 157
Gruids. High —3C 164
Gruinard House. High —4D 162
Grulinart. Arg —3A 124
Grulinbeg. Arg —3A 124
Gruline. Arg —4G 139
Grummore. High —5G 167
Grundisburgh. Suff —5E 66
Gruting. Shet —7D 173
Gualachulain. High —4F 141
Guardbridge. Fife —2G 137
Guarlford. Worc —1D 48
Guay. Per —4H 143
Gubblecote. Herts —4H 51
Guestling Green. E Sus —4C 28
Guestling Thorn. E Sus —4C 28
Guestwick. Norf —3C 78
Guestwick Green. Norf —3C 78
Guide. Bkbn —2F 91
Guide Post. Nmbd —1F 115
Guilden Down. Shrp —2F 59
Guilden Morden. Cambs —1C 52
Guilden Sutton. Ches —4G 83
Guildford. Surr —1A 26
Guildtown. Per —5A 144
Guilsborough. Nptn —3D 62
Guilsfield. Powy —4E 70
Guineaford. Devn —3F 19
Guisborough. Red C —3D 106
Guiseley. W Yor —5D 98
Guist. Norf —3B 78
Guiting Power. Glos —3F 49
Gulberwick. Shet —8F 173
Gullane. E Lot —1A 130
Gulling Green. Suff —5H 65
Gulval. Corn —3B 4
Gumfreston. Pemb —4F 43
Gumley. Leics —1D 62
Gunby. E Yor —1H 93
Gunby. Linc —3G 75
Gundleton. Hants —3E 24
Gun Green. Kent —2B 28
Gun Hill. E Sus —4G 27
Gunn. Devn —3G 19
Gunnerside. N Yor —5C 104
Gunnerton. Nmbd —2C 114
Gunness. N Lin —3B 94
Gunnislake. Corn —5E 11
Gunnista. Shet —7G 173
Gunsgreenhill. Scot —3F 131
Gunstone. Staf —5C 72
Gunthorpe. Norf —2C 78
Gunthorpe. N Lin —1F 87
Gunthorpe. Notts —1D 74
Gunthorpe. Pet —5A 76
Gunville. IOW —4C 16
Gupworthy. Som —3C 20
Gurnard. IOW —3C 16
Gurney Slade. Som —2B 22
Gurnos. Powy —5A 46
Gussage All Saints. Dors —1F 15
Gussage St Andrew. Dors —1E 15
Gussage St Michael. Dors —1E 15
Guston. Kent —1H 29
Gutcher. Shet —2G 173
Guthram Gowt. Linc —3A 76
Guthrie. Ang —3E 145
Guyhirn. Cambs —5D 76
Guyhirn Gull. Cambs —5C 76
Guy's Head. Linc —3D 77
Guy's Marsh. Dors —4D 22
Guyzance. Nmbd —4G 121
Gwaelod-y-garth. Card —3E 32
Gwaenynog Bach. Den —4C 82
Gwaenysgor. Flin —2C 82
Gwalchmai. IOA —3C 80
Gwastad. Pemb —2E 43
Gwaun-Cae-Gurwen. Neat —4H 45
Gwaun-y-bara. Cphy —3E 33
Gwbert. Cdgn —5A 56
Gweek. Corn —4E 5
Gwehelog. Mon —5G 47
Gwenddwr. Powy —1D 46
Gwennap. Corn —4B 6
Gwenter. Corn —5E 5
Gwernaffield. Flin —4E 82
Gwernesney. Mon —5H 47
Gwernogle. Carm —2F 45
Gwern-y-go. Powy —1E 58
Gwernymynydd. Flin —4E 82
Gwersyllt. Wrex —5F 83
Gwespyr. Flin —2D 82
Gwinear. Corn —3D 4
Gwithian. Corn —2C 4
Gwredog. IOA —2D 80
Gwyddelwern. Den —1C 70
Gwyddgrug. Carm —2E 45
Gwynfryn. Wrex —5E 83
Gwystre. Powy —4C 58
Gwytherin. Cnwy —4A 82
Gyfelia. Wrex —1F 71
Gyffin. Cnwy —3G 81

Haa of Houlland. Shet —1G 173
Habberley. Shrp —5F 71
Habergham. Lanc —1G 91
Habin. W Sus —4G 25
Habrough. NE Lin —3E 95
Hacconby. Linc —3A 76
Haceby. Linc —2H 75
Hacheston. Suff —5F 67
Hackenthorpe. S Yor —2B 86
Hackford. Norf —5C 78
Hackforth. N Yor —5F 105
Hackland. Orkn —5C 172
Hackleton. Nptn —5F 63
Hackness. N Yor —5G 107
Hackness. Orkn —8C 172
Hackney. G Lon —2E 39
Hackthorn. Linc —2G 87
Hackthorpe. Cumb —2G 103
Haclait. W Isl —4D 170
Hadden. Scot —1B 120
Haddenham. Buck —5F 51
Haddenham. Cambs —3D 64
Haddenham End. Cambs —3D 64
Haddington. E Lot —2B 130
Haddington. Linc —4G 87
Haddiscoe. Norf —1G 67
Haddo. Aber —5F 161
Haddon. Cambs —1A 64
Hademore. Staf —5F 73
Hadfield. Derbs —1E 85
Hadham Cross. Herts —4E 53
Hadham Ford. Herts —3E 53
Hadleigh. Essx —2C 40
Hadleigh. Suff —1D 54
Hadleigh Heath. Suff —1C 54
Hadley. Telf —4A 72
Hadley. Worc —4C 60
Hadley End. Staf —3F 73
Hadley Wood. G Lon —1D 38
Hadlow. Kent —1H 27
Hadlow Down. E Sus —3G 27
Hadnall. Shrp —3H 71
Hadstock. Essx —1F 53
Hady. Derbs —3B 86
Hadzor. Worc —4D 60
Haffenden Quarter. Kent —1C 28
Haggate. Lanc —1G 91
Haggbeck. Cumb —2F 113
Haggersta. Shet —7E 173
Haggerston. Nmbd —5G 131
Hagget End. Cumb —3B 102
Haggrister. Shet —4E 173
Hagley. Here —1A 48
Hagley. Worc —2D 60
Hagnaby. Linc —4C 88
Hagworthingham. Linc —4C 88
Haigh. G Man —4E 90
Haigh Moor. W Yor —2C 92
Haighton Green. Lanc —1D 90
Haile. Cumb —4B 102
Hailes. Glos —2F 49
Hailey. Oxon —4D 52
Hailsham. E Sus —5G 27
Hail Weston. Cambs —4A 64
Hainault. G Lon —1F 39
Hainford. Norf —4E 78
Hainton. Linc —2A 88
Hainworth. W Yor —1A 92
Haisthorpe. E Yor —3F 101
Hakin. Pemb —4C 42
Halam. Notts —5D 86
Halbeath. Fife —1E 129
Halberton. Devn —1D 12
Halcro. High —2E 169
Hale. Cumb —2E 97
Hale. G Man —2B 84
Hale. Hal —2G 83
Hale. Hants —1G 15
Hale. Surr —2G 25
Hale Bank. Hal —2G 83
Halebarns. G Man —2B 84
Hales. Norf —1F 67
Hales. Staf —2B 72
Halesgate. Linc —3C 76
Hales Green. Derbs —1F 73
Halesowen. W Mid —2D 60
Hale Street. Kent —1A 28
Halesworth. Suff —3F 67
Halewood. Mers —2G 83
Halford. Devn —5B 12
Halford. Shrp —2G 59
Halford. Warw —1A 50
Halfpenny. Cumb —1E 97
Halfpenny Furze. Carm —3G 43
Halfpenny Green. Staf —1C 60
Halfway. Carm —2G 45
Halfway. Powy —2B 46
Halfway. S Yor —2B 86
Halfway. W Ber —5C 36
Halfway House. Shrp —4F 71
Halfway Houses. Kent —3D 40
Halgabron. Corn —4A 10
Halifax. W Yor —2A 92
Halistra. High —3B 154
Halket. E Ayr —4F 127
Halkirk. High —3D 168
Halkyn. Flin —3E 82
Hall. E Ren —4F 127
Hallam Fields. Derbs —1B 74
Halland. E Sus —4G 27
Hallands, The. N Lin —2D 94
Hallaton. Leics —1E 63
Hallatrow. Bath —1B 22
Hallbank. Cumb —5H 103
Hallbankgate. Cumb —4G 113
Hall Dunnerdale. Cumb —5D 102
Hallen. S Glo —3A 34
Hall End. Beds —1A 52
Halley. Herts —4D 52
Hallgarth. Dur —5G 115
Hall Green. Ches —5C 84
Hall Green. Norf —2D 66
Hall Green. W Mid —2F 61
Hall Green. W Yor —3D 92
Hall Green. Wrex —1G 71
Halliburton. Scot —5C 130
Hallin. High —3B 154
Halling. Medw —4B 40
Hallington. Linc —2C 88
Hallington. Nmbd —2C 114
Halloughton. Notts —5D 86
Hallow. Worc —5C 60
Hallow Heath. Worc —5C 60
Hallowsgate. Ches —4H 83
Hallsands. Devn —5E 9
Hall's Green. Herts —3C 52
Hallspill. Devn —4E 19
Hallthwaites. Cumb —1A 96
Hall Waberthwaite. Cumb —5C 102
Hallwood Green. Glos —2B 48
Hallworthy. Corn —4B 10
Hallyne. Scot —5E 129
Halmer End. Staf —1C 72
Halmond's Frome. Here —1B 48
Halmore. Glos —5B 48
Halnaker. W Sus —5A 26
Halsall. Lanc —3B 90
Halse. Nptn —1D 50
Halse. Som —4E 21
Halsetown. Corn —3C 4
Halsham. E Yor —2F 95
Halsinger. Devn —3F 19
Halstead. Essx —2B 54
Halstead. Kent —4F 39
Halstead. Leics —5E 75
Halstock. Dors —2A 14
Halstow. Devn —3B 12
Halsway. Som —3E 21
Haltcliff Bridge. Cumb —1E 103
Haltham. Linc —4B 88
Haltoft End. Linc —1C 76
Halton. Buck —5G 51
Halton. Hal —2H 83
Halton. Lanc —3E 97
Halton. Nmbd —3C 114
Halton. W Yor —1D 92
Halton. Wrex —2F 71
Halton East. N Yor —4C 98
Halton Fenside. Linc —4D 88
Halton Gill. N Yor —2A 98
Halton Holegate. Linc —4D 88
Halton Lea Gate. Nmbd —4H 113
Halton Moor. W Yor —1D 92
Halton Shields. Nmbd —3D 114
Halton West. N Yor —4H 97
Haltwhistle. Nmbd —3A 114
Halvergate. Norf —5G 79
Halwell. Devn —3D 9
Halwill. Devn —3E 11
Halwill Junction. Devn —3E 11
Ham. Devn —2F 13
Ham. Glos —2B 34
Ham. G Lon —3C 38
Ham. High —1E 169
Ham. Kent —5H 41
Ham. Plym —3A 8
Ham. Shet —8A 173
Ham. Som —1F 13
(nr. Ilminster)
Ham. Som —4F 21
(nr. Taunton)
Ham. Wilts —5B 36
Hambleden. Buck —3F 37
Hambledon. Hants —1E 17
Hambledon. Surr —2A 26
Hamble-le-Rice. Hants —2C 16
Hambleton. Lanc —5C 96
Hambleton. N Yor —1F 93
Hambridge. Som —4G 21
Hambrook. S Glo —4B 34
Hambrook. W Sus —2F 17
Ham Common. Dors —4D 22
Hameringham. Linc —4C 88
Hamerton. Cambs —3A 64
Ham Green. Here —1C 48
Ham Green. Kent —4C 40
Ham Green. N Som —4A 34
Ham Green. Worc —4E 61
Ham Hill. Kent —4A 40
Hamilton. Leics —5D 74
Hamilton. S Lan —4A 128
Hamister. Shet —5G 173
Hammer. W Sus —3G 25
Hammersmith. G Lon —3D 38
Hammerwich. Staf —5E 73
Hammerwood. E Sus —2F 27
Hammill. Kent —5G 41
Hammond Street. Herts —5D 52
Hammoon. Dors —1D 14
Hamnavoe. Shet —3D 173
(nr. Braehoulland)
Hamnavoe. Shet —8E 173
(nr. Burland)
Hamnavoe. Shet —4F 173
(nr. Lunna)
Hamnavoe. Shet —3F 173
(on Yell)
Hamp. Som —3G 21
Hampden Park. E Sus —5H 27
Hampen. Glos —3F 49
Hamperden End. Essx —2F 53
Hamperley. Shrp —2G 59
Hampnett. Glos —4F 49
Hampole. S Yor —3F 93
Hampreston. Dors —3F 15
Hampstead. G Lon —2D 38
Hampstead Norreys. W Ber —4D 36
Hampsthwaite. N Yor —4E 99
Hampton. Devn —3F 13
Hampton. G Lon —3C 38
Hampton. Kent —4F 41
Hampton. Shrp —2B 60
Hampton. Swin —2G 35
Hampton. Worc —1F 49
Hampton Bishop. Here —2A 48
Hampton Fields. Glos —2D 35
Hampton Heath. Ches —1H 71
Hampton in Arden. W Mid —2G 61
Hampton Loade. Shrp —2B 60
Hampton Lovett. Worc —4C 60
Hampton Lucy. Warw —5G 61
Hampton Magna. Warw —4G 61
Hampton on the Hill. Warw —4G 61
Hampton Poyle. Oxon —4D 50
Hampton Wick. G Lon —4C 38
Hamptworth. Wilts —1H 15
Hamrow. Norf —3B 78
Hamsey. E Sus —4F 27
Hamsey Green. Surr —5E 39
Hamstall Ridware. Staf —4F 73

Hamstead—Helpringham

Hamstead. IOW —3B 16
Hamstead. W Mid —1E 61
Hamstead Marshall. W Ber —5C 36
Hamsterley. Dur —4E 115
(nr. Consett)
Hamsterley. Dur —1E 105
(nr. Wolsingham)
Hamsterley Mill. Dur —4E 115
Hamstreet. Kent —2E 28
Ham Street. Som —3A 22
Hamworthy. Pool —3E 15
Hanbury. Staf —3F 73
Hanbury. Worc —4D 60
Hanbury Woodend. Staf —3F 73
Hanby. Linc —2H 75
Hanchurch. Staf —1C 72
Hand and Pen. Devn —3D 12
Handbridge. Ches —4G 83
Handcross. W Sus —3D 26
Handforth. Ches —2C 84
Handley. Ches —5G 83
Handley. Derbs —4A 86
Handsacre. Staf —4E 73
Handsworth. S Yor —2B 86
Handsworth. W Mid —1E 61
Handy Cross. Buck —2G 37
Hanford. Stoke —1C 72
Hangersley Hill. Hants —2G 15
Hanging Haughton. Nptn —3E 63
Hanging Langford. Wilts —3F 23
Hangleton. Brig —5D 26
Hangleton. W Sus —5B 26
Hanham. S Glo —4B 34
Hanham Green. S Glo —4B 34
Hankelow. Ches —1A 72
Hankerton. Wilts —2E 35
Hankham. E Sus —5H 27
Hanley. Stoke —1C 72
Hanley Castle. Worc —1D 48
Hanley Childe. Worc —4A 60
Hanley Swan. Worc —1D 48
Hanley William. Worc —4A 60
Hanlith. N Yor —3B 98
Hanmer. Wrex —2G 71
Hannaborough. Devn —2F 11
Hannaford. Devn —4G 19
Hannah. Linc —3E 89
Hannington. Hants —1D 24
Hannington. Nptn —3F 63
Hannington. Swin —2G 35
Hannington Wick. Swin —2G 35
Hanscombe End. Beds —2B 52
Hanslope. Mil —1G 51
Hanthorpe. Linc —3H 75
Hanwell. G Lon —2C 38
Hanwell. Oxon —1C 50
Hanwood. Shrp —5G 71
Hanworth. G Lon —3C 38
Hanworth. Norf —2D 78
Happas. Ang —4D 144
Happendon. S Lan —1A 118
Happisburgh. Norf —2F 79
Happisburgh Common. Norf —3F 79
Hapsford. Ches —3G 83
Hapton. Lanc —1F 91
Hapton. Norf —1D 66
Harberton. Devn —3D 9
Harbertonford. Devn —3D 9
Harbledown. Kent —5F 41
Harborne. W Mid —2E 61
Harborough Magna. Warw —3B 62
Harbottle. Nmbd —4D 120
Harbourneford. Devn —2D 8
Harbours Hill. Worc —4D 60
Harbridge. Hants —1G 15
Harbury. Warw —5A 62
Harby. Leics —2E 75
Harby. Notts —3F 87
Harcombe. Devn —3E 13
Harcombe Bottom. Devn —3G 13
Harcourt. Corn —5C 6
Harden. W Yor —1A 92
Hardenhuish. Wilts —4E 35
Hardgate. Aber —3E 153
Hardgate. Dum —3F 111
Hardham. W Sus —4B 26
Hardingham. Norf —5C 78
Hardingstone. Nptn —5E 63
Hardings Wood. Ches —5C 84
Hardington. Som —1C 22
Hardington Mandeville. Som —1A 14
Hardington Marsh. Som —2A 14
Hardington Moor. Som —1A 14
Hardley. Hants —2C 16
Hardley Street. Norf —5F 79
Hardmead. Mil —1H 51
Hardraw. N Yor —5B 104
Hardstoft. Derbs —4B 86
Hardway. Hants —2E 16
Hardway. Som —3C 22
Hardwick. Buck —4G 51
Hardwick. Cambs —5C 64
Hardwick. Norf —2E 66
Hardwick. Nptn —4F 63
Hardwick. Oxon —3D 50
(nr. Bicester)
Hardwick. Oxon —5B 50
(nr. Witney)
Hardwick. Shrp —1F 59
Hardwick. S Yor —2B 86
Hardwick. Stoc T —2B 106
Hardwick. W Mid —1E 61
Hardwicke. Glos —3E 49
(nr. Cheltenham)
Hardwicke. Glos —4C 48
(nr. Gloucester)
Hardwicke. Here —1F 47
Hardwick Village. Notts —3D 86
Hardy's Green. Essx —3C 54
Hareby. Linc —4C 88
Hareden. Lanc —4F 97
Harefield. G Lon —1B 38
Hare Green. Essx —3D 54
Hare Hatch. Wok —4G 37
Harehill. Derbs —2F 73
Harehills. W Yor —1D 92
Harehope. Nmbd —2E 121
Harelaw. Dum —2F 113
Harelaw. Dur —4E 115
Hareplain. Kent —2C 28
Haresceugh. Cumb —5H 113
Harescombe. Glos —4D 48
Haresfield. Glos —4D 48
Haresfinch. Mers —1H 83
Hareshaw. N Lan —3B 128
Hare Street. Essx —5E 53
Hare Street. Herts —3D 53
Harewood. W Yor —5F 99
Harewood End. Here —3A 48
Harford. Devn —3C 8
Hargate. Norf —1D 66
Hargatewall. Derbs —3F 85
Hargrave. Ches —4G 83
Hargrave. Nptn —3H 63
Hargrave. Suff —5G 65
Harker. Cumb —3E 113
Harkland. Shet —3F 173
Harkstead. Suff —2E 55
Harlaston. Staf —4G 73
Harlaxton. Linc —2F 75
Harlech. Gwyn —2E 69
Harlequin. Notts —2D 74
Harlescott. Shrp —4H 71
Harleston. Devn —4D 9
Harleston. Norf —2E 67
Harleston. Suff —4C 66
Harlestone. Nptn —4E 62
Harley. Shrp —5H 71
Harley. S Yor —1A 86
Harling Road. Norf —2B 66
Harlington. Beds —2A 52
Harlington. G Lon —3B 38
Harlington. S Yor —4E 93
Harlosh. High —4B 154
Harlow. Essx —5E 53
Harlow Hill. Nmbd —3D 115
Harlsey Castle. N Yor —5B 106
Harlthorpe. E Yor —1H 93
Harlton. Cambs —5C 64
Harlyn. Corn —1C 6
Harman's Cross. Dors —4E 15
Harmby. N Yor —1D 98
Harmer Green. Herts —4C 52
Harmer Hill. Shrp —3G 71
Harmondsworth. G Lon —3B 38
Harmston. Linc —4G 87
Harnage. Shrp —5H 71
Harnham. Nmbd —1D 115
Harnhill. Glos —5F 49
Harold Hill. G Lon —1G 39
Haroldston West. Pemb —3C 42
Haroldswick. Shet —1H 173
Harold Wood. G Lon —1G 39
Harome. N Yor —1A 100
Harpenden. Herts —4B 52
Harpford. Devn —3D 12
Harpham. E Yor —3E 101
Harpley. Norf —3G 77
Harpley. Worc —4A 60
Harpole. Nptn —4D 62
Harpsdale. High —3D 168
Harpsden. Oxon —3F 37
Harpswell. Linc —2G 87
Harpurhey. G Man —4G 91
Harpur Hill. Derbs —3E 85
Harraby. Cumb —4F 113
Harracott. Devn —4F 19
Harrapool. High —1E 147
Harrietfield. Per —1B 136
Harrietsham. Kent —5C 40
Harrington. Cumb —2A 102
Harrington. Linc —3C 88
Harrington. Nptn —2E 63
Harringworth. Nptn —1G 63
Harriseahead. Staf —5C 84
Harriston. Cumb —5C 112
Harrogate. N Yor —4F 99
Harrold. Beds —5G 63
Harrop Dale. G Man —4A 92
Harrow. G Lon —2C 38
Harrowbarrow. Corn —2H 7
Harrowden. Beds —1A 52
Harrowgate Hill. Darl —3F 105
Harrow on the Hill. G Lon —2C 38
Harrow Weald. G Lon —1C 38
Harry Stoke. S Glo —4B 34
Harston. Cambs —5D 64
Harston. Leics —2F 75
Harswell. E Yor —5C 100
Hart. Hart —1B 106
Hartburn. Nmbd —1D 115
Hartburn. Stoc T —3B 106
Hartest. Suff —5H 65
Hartfield. E Sus —2F 27
Hartford. Cambs —3B 64
Hartford. Ches —3A 84
Hartfordbridge. Hants —1F 25
Hartford End. Essx —4G 53
Harthill. Ches —5H 83
Harthill. N Lan —3C 128
Harthill. S Yor —2B 86
Hartington. Derbs —4F 85
Hartland. Devn —4C 18
Hartland Quay. Devn —4C 18
Hartle. Worc —3D 60
Hartlebury. Worc —3C 60
Hartlepool. Hart —1C 106
Hartley. Cumb —4A 104
Hartley. Kent —2B 28
(nr. Cranbrook)
Hartley. Kent —4H 39
(nr. Dartford)
Hartley. Nmbd —2G 115
Hartley Green. Staf —2D 73
Hartley Mauditt. Hants —3F 25
Hartley Wespall. Hants —1E 25
Hartley Wintney. Hants —1F 25
Hartlip. Kent —4C 40
Hartmount. High —1B 158
Hartoft End. N Yor —5E 107
Harton. N Yor —3B 100
Harton. Shrp —2G 59
Harton. Tyne —3G 115
Hartpury. Glos —3C 48
Hartshead. W Yor —2B 92
Hartshill. Warw —1H 61
Hartshorne. Derbs —3H 73
Hartsop. Cumb —3F 103
Hart Station. Hart —1B 106
Hartswell. Som —4D 20
Hartwell. Nptn —5E 63
Hartwood. Lanc —3D 90
Hartwood. N Lan —4B 128
Harvel. Kent —4A 40
Harvington. Worc —1F 49
(nr. Evesham)
Harvington. Worc —3C 60
(nr. Kidderminster)
Harwell. Oxon —3C 36
Harwich. Essx —2F 55
Harwood. Dur —1B 104
Harwood. G Man —3F 91
Harwood Dale. N Yor —5G 107
Harworth. Notts —1D 86
Hascombe. Surr —1A 26
Haselbech. Nptn —3E 62
Haselbury Plucknett. Som —1H 13
Haseley. Warw —4G 61
Haselor. Warw —5F 61
Hasfield. Glos —3D 48
Hasguard. Pemb —4C 42
Haskayne. Lanc —4B 90
Hasketon. Suff —5E 67
Hasland. Derbs —4A 86
Haslemere. Surr —2A 26
Haslingden. Lanc —2F 91
Haslingden Grane. Lanc —2F 91
Haslingfield. Cambs —5D 64
Haslington. Ches —5B 84
Hassall. Ches —5B 84
Hassall Green. Ches —5B 84
Hassell Street. Kent —1E 29
Hassendean. Scot —2H 119
Hassingham. Norf —5F 79
Hassness. Cumb —3C 102
Hassocks. W Sus —4E 27
Hassop. Derbs —3G 85
Haste Hill. Surr —2A 26
Haster. High —3F 169
Hasthorpe. Linc —4D 89
Hastigrow. High —2E 169
Hastingleigh. Kent —1E 29
Hastings. E Sus —5C 28
Hastingwood. Essx —5E 53
Hastoe. Herts —5H 51
Haston. Shrp —3H 71
Haswell. Dur —5G 115
Haswell Plough. Dur —5G 115
Hatch. Beds —1B 52
Hatch Beauchamp. Som —4G 21
Hatch End. G Lon —1C 38
Hatch Green. Som —1G 13
Hatching Green. Herts —4B 52
Hatchmere. Ches —3H 83
Hatch Warren. Hants —2E 24
Hatcliffe. NE Lin —4F 95
Hatfield. Here —5H 59
Hatfield. Herts —5C 52
Hatfield. S Yor —4G 93
Hatfield. Worc —5C 60
Hatfield Broad Oak. Essx —4F 53
Hatfield Heath. Essx —4F 53
Hatfield Hyde. Herts —4C 52
Hatfield Peverel. Essx —4A 54
Hatfield Woodhouse. S Yor —4G 93
Hatford. Oxon —2B 36
Hatherden. Hants —1B 24
Hatherleigh. Devn —2F 11
Hathern. Leics —3C 74
Hatherop. Glos —5G 49
Hathersage. Derbs —2G 85
Hathersage Booths. Derbs —2G 85
Hatherton. Ches —1A 72
Hatherton. Staf —4D 72
Hatley St George. Cambs —5B 64
Hatt. Corn —2H 7
Hattersley. G Man —1D 85
Hattingley. Hants —3E 25
Hatton. Aber —5H 161
Hatton. Derbs —2G 73
Hatton. G Lon —3B 38
Hatton. Linc —3A 88
Hatton. Shrp —1G 59
Hatton. Warr —2H 83
Hatton. Warw —4G 61
Hattoncrook. Aber —1F 153
Hatton Heath. Ches —4G 83
Hatton of Fintray. Aber —2F 153
Haugh. E Ayr —2D 117
Haugh. Linc —3D 88
Haugham. Linc —2C 88
Haugh Head. Nmbd —2E 121
Haughley. Suff —4C 66
Haughley Green. Suff —4C 66
Haugh of Ballechin. Per —3G 143
Haugh of Glass. Mor —5B 160
Haugh of Urr. Dum —3F 111
Haughton. Notts —3D 86
Haughton. Shrp —1A 60
(nr. Bridgnorth)
Haughton. Shrp —3F 71
(nr. Oswestry)
Haughton. Shrp —5B 72
(nr. Shifnal)
Haughton. Shrp —4H 71
(nr. Shrewsbury)
Haughton. Staf —3C 72
Haughton Green. G Man —1D 84
Haughton le Skerne. Darl —3A 106
Haughton Moss. Ches —5H 83
Haultwick. Herts —3D 52
Haunn. Arg —4E 139
Haunn. W Isl —7C 170
Haunton. Staf —4G 73
Hauxley. Nmbd —4G 121
Hauxton. Cambs —5D 64
Havannah. Ches —4C 84
Havant. Hants —2F 17
Haven. Here —5G 59
Haven Bank. Linc —5B 88
Havenside. E Yor —2E 95
Havenstreet. IOW —3D 16
Haven, The. W Sus —2B 26
Havercroft. W Yor —3D 93
Haverfordwest. Pemb —3D 42
Haverhill. Suff —1G 53
Haverigg. Cumb —2A 96
Havering-atte-Bower. G Lon —1G 39
Havering's Grove. Essx —1A 40
Haversham. Mil —1G 51
Haverthwaite. Cumb —1C 96
Haverton Hill. Stoc T —2B 106
Havyatt. Som —3A 22
Hawarden. Flin —4F 83
Hawcoat. Cumb —2B 96
Hawcross. Glos —2C 48
Hawen. Cdgn —1D 44
Hawes. N Yor —1A 98
Hawes Green. Norf —1E 67
Hawick. Scot —3H 119
Hawkchurch. Devn —2G 13
Hawkedon. Suff —5G 65
Hawkenbury. Kent —1C 28
Hawkeridge. Wilts —1D 22
Hawkerland. Devn —4D 12
Hawkesbury. S Glo —3C 34
Hawkesbury Upton. S Glo —3C 34
Hawkes End. W Mid —2G 61
Hawk Green. G Man —2D 84
Hawkhill. Nmbd —3G 121
Hawkhurst. Kent —2B 28
Hawkhurst Common. E Sus —4G 27
Hawkinge. Kent —1G 29
Hawkley. Hants —4F 25
Hawkridge. Som —3B 20
Hawksdale. Cumb —5E 113
Hawkshaw. G Man —3F 91
Hawkshead. Cumb —5E 103
Hawkshead Hill. Cumb —5E 103
Hawkswick. N Yor —2B 98
Hawksworth. Notts —1E 75
Hawksworth. W Yor —5D 98
Hawkwell. Essx —1C 40
Hawley. Hants —1G 25
Hawley. Kent —3G 39
Hawling. Glos —3F 49
Hawnby. N Yor —1H 99
Haworth. W Yor —1A 92
Hawstead. Suff —5A 66
Hawthorn. Dur —5H 115
Hawthorn Hill. Brac —4G 37
Hawthorn Hill. Linc —5B 88
Hawthorpe. Linc —3H 75
Hawton. Notts —5E 87
Haxby. York —4A 100
Haxey. N Lin —1E 87
Haybridge. Shrp —3A 60
Haybridge. Som —2A 22
Haydock. Mers —1H 83
Haydon. Bath —1B 22
Haydon. Dors —1B 14
Haydon. Som —4F 21
Haydon Bridge. Nmbd —3B 114
Haydon Wick. Swin —3G 35
Haye. Corn —2H 7
Hayes. G Lon —4F 39
(nr. Bromley)
Hayes. G Lon —2B 38
(nr. Uxbridge)
Hayfield. Derbs —2E 85
Hay Green. Norf —4E 77
Hayhill. E Ayr —3D 116
Haylands. IOW —3D 16
Hayle. Corn —3C 4
Hayley Green. W Mid —2D 60
Hayne. Devn —2B 12
Haynes. Beds —1A 52
Haynes West End. Beds —1A 52
Hay-on-Wye. Powy —1F 47
Hayscastle. Pemb —2C 42
Hayscastle Cross. Pemb —2D 42
Haysden. Kent —1G 27
Hayshead. Ang —4F 145
Hay Street. Herts —3D 53
Hayton. Aber C —3G 153
Hayton. Cumb —5C 112
(nr. Aspatria)
Hayton. Cumb —4G 113
(nr. Brampton)
Hayton. E Yor —5C 100
Hayton. Notts —2E 87
Hayton's Bent. Shrp —2H 59
Haytor Vale. Devn —5A 12
Haytown. Devn —1D 11
Haywards Heath. W Sus —3E 27
Haywood. S Lan —4C 128
Hazelbank. S Lan —5B 128
Hazelbury Bryan. Dors —2C 14
Hazeleigh. Essx —5B 54
Hazeley. Hants —1F 25
Hazel Grove. G Man —2D 84
Hazelhead. S Yor —4B 92
Hazelslade. Staf —4E 73
Hazel Street. Kent —2A 28
Hazelton Walls. Fife —1F 137
Hazelwood. Derbs —1H 73
Hazlemere. Buck —2G 37
Hazler. Shrp —1G 59
Hazlerigg. Tyne —2F 115
Hazles. Staf —1E 73
Hazleton. Glos —4F 49
Hazon. Nmbd —4F 121
Heacham. Norf —2F 77
Headbourne Worthy. Hants —3C 24
Headcorn. Kent —1C 28
Headingley. W Yor —1C 92
Headington. Oxon —5D 50
Headlam. Dur —3E 105
Headless Cross. Worc —4E 61
Headley. Hants —3G 25
(nr. Haslemere)
Headley. Hants —5D 36
(nr. Kingsclere)
Headley. Surr —5D 38
Headley Down. Hants —3G 25
Headley Heath. Worc —3E 61
Headley Park. Bris —5A 34
Head of Muir. Falk —1B 128
Headon. Notts —3E 87
Heads Nook. Cumb —4F 113
Heage. Derbs —5A 86
Healaugh. N Yor —5D 104
(nr. Grinton)
Healaugh. N Yor —5H 99
(nr. York)
Heald Green. G Man —2C 84
Heale. Devn —2G 19
Healey. G Man —3G 91
Healey. Nmbd —4D 114
Healey. N Yor —1D 98
Healeyfield. Dur —5D 114
Healey Hall. Nmbd —4D 114
Healing. NE Lin —3F 95
Heamoor. Corn —3B 4
Heanish. Arg —4B 138
Heanor. Derbs —1B 74
Heanton Punchardon. Devn —3F 19
Heapham. Linc —2F 87
Heartsease. Powy —4D 58
Heasley Mill. Devn —3H 19
Heast. High —2E 147
Heath. Derbs —4B 86
Heath and Reach. Beds —3H 51
Heath Common. W Sus —4C 26
Heathcote. Derbs —4F 85
Heath Cross. Devn —3H 11
Heathencote. Nptn —1F 51
Heath End. Derbs —3A 74
Heath End. Hants —5D 36
Heath End. W Mid —5E 73
Heather. Leics —4A 74
Heatherfield. High —4D 155
Heathfield. Cumb —5C 112
Heathfield. Devn —5B 12
Heathfield. E Sus —3G 27
Heathfield. Ren —3E 126
Heathfield. Som —4E 21
Heath Green. Worc —3E 61
Heathhall. Dum —2A 112
Heath Hayes. Staf —4E 73
Heath Hill. Shrp —4B 72
Heath House. Som —2H 21
Heathon. Shrp —1C 60
Heathrow (London) Airport. G Lon —3B 38
Heathstock. Devn —2F 13
Heath, The. Norf —3E 79
(nr. Buxton)
Heath, The. Norf —3B 78
(nr. Fakenham)
Heath, The. Norf —3D 78
(nr. Heavingham)
Heath, The. Staf —2E 73
Heathton. Suff —2E 55
Heathtop. Derbs —2F 73
Heath Town. W Mid —5D 72
Heatley. G Man —2B 84
Heatley. Staf —3E 73
Heaton. Lanc —3D 96
Heaton. Staf —4D 84
Heaton. Tyne —3F 115
Heaton. W Yor —1B 92
Heaton Moor. G Man —1C 84
Heaton's Bridge. Lanc —3C 90
Heaverham. Kent —5G 39
Heavitree. Devn —3C 12
Hebburn. Tyne —3G 115
Hebden. N Yor —3C 98
Hebden Bridge. W Yor —2H 91
Hebden Green. Ches —4A 84
Hebing End. Herts —3D 52
Hebron. Carm —2F 43
Hebron. Nmbd —1E 115
Heck. Dum —1B 112
Heckdyke. Notts —1E 87
Heckfield. Hants —5F 37
Heckfield Green. Suff —3D 66
Heckfordbridge. Essx —3C 54
Heckington. Linc —1A 76
Heckmondwike. W Yor —2C 92
Heddington. Wilts —5E 35
Heddle. Orkn —6C 172
Heddon. Devn —4G 19
Heddon-on-the-Wall. Nmbd —3E 115
Hedenham. Norf —1F 67
Hedge End. Hants —1C 16
Hedgerley. Buck —2A 38
Hedging. Som —4G 21
Hedley on the Hill. Nmbd —4D 115
Hednesford. Staf —4E 73
Hedon. E Yor —2E 95
Hegdon Hill. Here —5H 59
Heglibister. Shet —6E 173
Heighington. Darl —2F 105
Heighington. Linc —4H 87
Heightington. Worc —3B 60
Heights of Brae. High —2H 157
Heights of Fodderty. High —2H 157
Heights of Kinlochewe. High —2C 156
Heiton. Scot —1B 120
Hele. Devn —5H 11
(nr. Ashburton)
Hele. Devn —2C 12
(nr. Exeter)
Hele. Devn —3D 10
(nr. Holsworthy)
Hele. Devn —2F 19
(nr. Ilfracombe)
Hele. Torb —2F 9
Helensburgh. Arg —1D 126
Helford. Corn —4E 5
Helhoughton. Norf —3A 78
Helions Bumpstead. Essx —1G 53
Helland. Corn —5A 10
Helland. Som —4G 21
Hellandbridge. Corn —5A 10
Hellesdon. Norf —4E 78
Hellesveor. Corn —2C 4
Hellidon. Nptn —5C 62
Hellifield. N Yor —4A 98
Hellingly. E Sus —4G 27
Hellington. Norf —5F 79
Hellister. Shet —7E 173
Helmdon. Nptn —1D 50
Helmingham. Suff —5D 66
Helmington Row. Dur —1E 105
Helmsdale. High —2H 165
Helmshore. Lanc —2F 91
Helmsley. N Yor —1A 100
Helperby. N Yor —3G 99
Helperthorpe. N Yor —2D 100
Helpringham. Linc —1A 76

Helpston—Holborn

Helpston. Pet —5A 76
Helsby. Ches —3G 83
Helsey. Linc —3E 89
Helston. Corn —4D 4
Helstone. Corn —4A 10
Helton. Cumb —2G 103
Helwith. N Yor —4D 105
Helwith Bridge. N Yor —3H 97
Helygain. Flin —3E 82
Hemblington. Norf —4F 79
Hemel Hempstead. Herts —5A 52
Hemerdon. Devn —3B 8
Hemingbrough. N Yor —1G 93
Hemingby. Linc —3B 88
Hemingfield. S Yor —4D 93
Hemingford Abbots. Cambs —3B 64
Hemingford Grey. Cambs —3B 64
Hemingstone. Suff —5D 66
Hemington. Leics —3B 74
Hemington. Nptn —2H 63
Hemington. Som —1C 22
Hemley. Suff —1F 55
Hemlington. Midd —3B 106
Hempholme. E Yor —4E 101
Hempnall. Norf —1E 67
Hempnall Green. Norf —1E 67
Hempriggs. High —4F 169
Hemp's Green. Essx —3C 54
Hempstead. Essx —2G 53
Hempstead. Medw —4B 40
Hempstead. Norf —2D 78
(nr. Holt)
Hempstead. Norf —3G 79
(nr. Stalham)
Hempsted. Glos —4D 48
Hempton. Norf —3B 78
Hempton. Oxon —2C 50
Hemsby. Norf —4G 79
Hemswell. Linc —1G 87
Hemswell Cliff. Linc —2G 87
Hemsworth. Dors —2E 15
Hemsworth. W Yor —3E 93
Hem, The. Shrp —5B 72
Hemyock. Devn —1E 13
Henallt. Carm —3E 45
Henbury. Bris —4A 34
Henbury. Ches —3C 84
Hendomen. Powy —1E 58
Hendon. G Lon —2D 38
Hendon. Tyne —4H 115
Hendra. Corn —3D 6
Hendre. B'End —3C 32
Hendreforgan. Rhon —3C 32
Hendy. Carm —5F 45
Heneglwys. IOA —3D 80
Henfeddau Fawr. Pemb —1G 43
Henfield. S Glo —4B 34
Henfield. W Sus —4D 26
Henford. Devn —3D 10
Hengoed. Cphy —2E 33
Hengoed. Shrp —2E 71
Hengrave. Suff —4H 65
Henham. Essx —3F 53
Heniarth. Powy —5D 70
Henlade. Som —4F 21
Henley. Dors —2B 14
Henley. Shrp —2G 59
(nr. Church Stretton)
Henley. Shrp —3H 59
(nr. Ludlow)
Henley. Som —3H 21
Henley. Suff —5D 66
Henley. W Sus —4G 25
Henley-in-Arden. Warw —4F 61
Henley-on-Thames. Oxon —3F 37
Henley's Down. E Sus —4B 28
Henley Street. Kent —4A 40
Henllan. Cdgn —1D 44
Henllan. Den —4C 82
Henllan. Mon —3F 47
Henllan Amgoed. Carm —2F 43
Henllys. Torf —2F 33
Henlow. Beds —2B 52
Hennock. Devn —4B 12
Henny Street. Essx —2B 54
Henryd. Cnwy —3G 81
Henry's Moat. Pemb —2E 43
Hensall. N Yor —2F 93
Henshaw. Nmbd —3A 114
Hensingham. Cumb —3A 102
Henstead. Suff —2G 67
Hensting. Hants —4C 24
Henstridge. Som —1C 14
Henstridge Ash. Som —4C 22
Henstridge Bowden. Som —4B 22
Henstridge Marsh. Som —4C 22
Henton. Oxon —5F 51
Henton. Som —2H 21
Henwood. Corn —5C 10
Heogan. Shet —7F 173
Heol Senni. Powy —3C 46
Heol-y-Cyw. B'End —3C 32
Hepburn. Nmbd —2E 121
Hepple. Nmbd —4D 121
Hepscott. Nmbd —1F 115
Heptonstall. W Yor —2H 91
Hepworth. Suff —3B 66
Hepworth. W Yor —4B 92
Herbrandston. Pemb —4C 42
Hereford. Here —2A 48
Heribusta. High —1D 154
Heriot. Scot —4H 129
Hermitage. Dors —2B 14
Hermitage. Scot —5H 119
Hermitage. W Ber —4D 36
Hermitage. W Sus —2F 17
Hermon. Carm —3G 45
(nr. Llandeilo)
Hermon. Carm —2D 44
(nr. Newcastle Emlyn)
Hermon. IOA —4C 80
Hermon. Pemb —1G 43
Herne. Kent —4F 41
Herne Bay. Kent —4F 41
Herne Common. Kent —4F 41
Herne Pound. Kent —5A 40
Herner. Devn —4F 19
Hernhill. Kent —4E 41
Herodsfoot. Corn —2G 7
Heronden. Kent —5G 41
Herongate. Essx —1H 39
Heronsford. S Ayr —1G 109
Heronsgate. Herts —1B 38
Heron's Ghyll. E Sus —3F 27
Herra. Shet —2H 173
Herriard. Hants —2E 25
Herringfleet. Suff —1G 67
Herringswell. Suff —4G 65
Herrington. Tyne —4G 115
Hersden. Kent —4G 41
Hersham. Corn —2C 10
Hersham. Surr —4C 38
Herstmonceux. E Sus —4H 27
Herston. Dors —5F 15
Herston. Orkn —8D 172
Hertford. Herts —4D 52
Hertford Heath. Herts —4D 52
Hertingfordbury. Herts —4D 52
Hesketh. Lanc —2C 90
Hesketh Bank. Lanc —2C 90
Hesketh Lane. Lanc —5F 97
Hesket Newmarket. Cumb —1E 103
Heskin Green. Lanc —3D 90
Hesleden. Dur —1B 106
Hesleyside. Nmbd —1B 114
Heslington. York —4A 100
Hessay. York —4H 99
Hessenford. Corn —3H 7
Hessett. Suff —4B 66
Hessilhead. N Ayr —4E 127
Hessle. E Yor —2D 94
Hestaford. Shet —6D 173
Hest Bank. Lanc —3D 96
Hester's Way. Glos —3E 49
Hestinsetter. Shet —7D 173
Heston. G Lon —3C 38
Hestwall. Orkn —6B 172
Heswall. Mers —2E 83
Hethe. Oxon —3D 50
Hethelpit Cross. Glos —3C 48
Hethersett. Norf —5D 78
Hethersgill. Cumb —3F 113
Hetherside. Cumb —3F 113
Hethpool. Nmbd —2C 120
Hett. Dur —1F 105
Hetton. N Yor —4B 98
Hetton-le-Hole. Tyne —5G 115
Hetton Steads. Nmbd —1E 121
Heugh. Nmbd —2D 115
Heugh-head. Aber —2A 152
Heveningham. Suff —3F 67
Hever. Kent —1F 27
Heversham. Cumb —1D 97
Hevingham. Norf —3D 78
Hewas Water. Corn —4D 6
Hewelsfield. Glos —5A 48
Hewish. N Som —5G 33
Hewish. Som —2H 13
Heworth. York —4A 100
Hexham. Nmbd —3C 114
Hextable. Kent —3G 39
Hexton. Herts —2B 52
Hexworthy. Devn —5G 11
Heybridge. Essx —1H 39
(nr. Brentwood)
Heybridge. Essx —5B 54
(nr. Maldon)
Heybridge Basin. Essx —5B 54
Heybrook Bay. Devn —4A 8
Heydon. Cambs —1E 53
Heydon. Norf —3D 78
Heydour. Linc —2H 75
Heylipol. Arg —4A 138
Heyop. Powy —3E 59
Heysham. Lanc —3D 96
Heyshott. W Sus —1G 17
Heytesbury. Wilts —2E 23
Heythrop. Oxon —3B 50
Heywood. G Man —3G 91
Heywood. Wilts —1D 22
Hibaldstow. N Lin —4C 94
Hickleton. S Yor —4E 93
Hickling. Norf —3G 79
Hickling. Notts —3D 74
Hickling Green. Norf —3G 79
Hickling Heath. Norf —3G 79
Hickstead. W Sus —3D 26
Hidcote Bartrim. Glos —1G 49
Hidcote Boyce. Glos —1G 49
Higford. Shrp —5B 72
High Ackworth. W Yor —3E 93
Higham. Derbs —5A 86
Higham. Kent —3B 40
Higham. Lanc —1G 91
Higham. S Yor —4D 92
Higham. Suff —2D 54
(nr. Ipswich)
Higham. Suff —4G 65
(nr. Newmarket)
Higham Dykes. Nmbd —2E 115
Higham Ferrers. Nptn —4G 63
Higham Gobion. Beds —2B 52
Higham on the Hill. Leics —1A 62
Highampton. Devn —2E 11
Higham Wood. Kent —1G 27
High Angerton. Nmbd —1D 115
High Auldgirth. Dum —1G 111
High Bankhill. Cumb —5G 113
High Banton. N Lan —1A 128
High Barnet. G Lon —1D 38
High Beech. Essx —1F 39
High Bentham. N Yor —3F 97
High Bickington. Devn —4G 19
High Biggins. Cumb —2F 97
High Birkwith. N Yor —2G 97
High Blantyre. S Lan —4H 127
High Bonnybridge. Falk —2B 128
High Borrans. Cumb —4F 103
High Bradfield. S Yor —1G 85
High Bray. Devn —3G 19
Highbridge. Cumb —5E 113
Highbridge. High —5D 148
Highbridge. Som —2G 21
Highbrook. W Sus —2E 27
High Brooms. Kent —1G 27
High Bullen. Devn —4F 19
Highburton. W Yor —3B 92
Highbury. Som —2B 22
High Buston. Nmbd —4G 121
High Callerton. Nmbd —2E 115
High Carlingill. Cumb —4H 103
High Catton. E Yor —4B 100
High Church. Nmbd —1E 115
Highclere. Hants —5C 36
Highcliffe. Dors —3H 15
High Cogges. Oxon —5B 50
High Common. Norf —5B 78
High Coniscliffe. Darl —3F 105
High Crosby. Cumb —4F 113
High Cross. Hants —4F 25
High Cross. Herts —4D 52
High Dougarie. N Ayr —2C 122
High Easter. Essx —4G 53
High Eggborough. N Yor —2F 93
High Ellington. N Yor —1D 98
Higher Alham. Som —2B 22
Higher Ansty. Dors —2C 14
Higher Ashton. Devn —4B 12
Higher Ballam. Lanc —1B 90
Higher Bartle. Lanc —1D 90
Higher Bockhampton. Dors —3C 14
High Ercall. Telf —4H 71
Higher Clovelly. Devn —4D 18
Higher Dinting. Derbs —1E 85
Higher End. G Man —4D 90
Higher Gabwell. Devn —2F 9
Higher Heysham. Lanc —3D 96
Higher Hurdsfield. Ches —3D 84
Higher Kingcombe. Dors —3A 14
Higher Kinnerton. Flin —4F 83
Higher Penwortham. Lanc —2D 90
Higher Porthpean. Corn —3E 7
Higher Poynton. Ches —2D 84
Higher Shotton. Flin —4F 83
Higher Shurlach. Ches —3A 84
Higher Tale. Devn —2D 12
Highertown. Corn —4C 6
Higher Town. IOS —1B 4
Higher Town. Som —2C 20
Higher Walton. Lanc —2D 90
Higher Walton. Warr —2A 84
Higher Whatcombe. Dors —2D 14
Higher Wheelton. Lanc —2E 90
Higher Whiteleigh. Corn —3C 10
Higher Whitley. Ches —3A 84
Higher Wincham. Ches —3A 84
Higher Wych. Ches —1G 71
High Etherley. Dur —2E 105
High Ferry. Linc —1C 76
Highfield. E Yor —1H 93
Highfield. N Ayr —4E 126
Highfield. Tyne —4E 115
Highfields. Cambs —5C 64
Highfields. Nmbd —4F 131
High Garrett. Essx —3A 54
Highgate. G Lon —2D 39
Highgate. N Ayr —4E 127
Highgate. Powy —1D 58
High Grange. Dur —1E 105
High Green. Cumb —4F 103
High Green. Norf —5D 78
High Green. Shrp —2B 60
High Green. S Yor —1H 85
High Green. W Yor —3B 92
High Green. Worc —1D 49
Highgreen Manor. Nmbd —5C 120
High Halden. Kent —2C 28
High Halstow. Medw —3B 40
High Ham. Som —3H 21
High Harrington. Cumb —2B 102
High Haswell. Dur —5G 115
High Hatton. Shrp —3A 72
High Hawkser. N Yor —4G 107
High Hesket. Cumb —5F 113
High Hesleden. Dur —1B 106
High Hoyland. S Yor —4C 92
High Hunsley. E Yor —1C 94
High Hurstwood. E Sus —3F 27
High Hutton. N Yor —3B 100
High Ireby. Cumb —1D 102
High Keil. Arg —5A 122
High Kelling. Norf —1D 78
High Kilburn. N Yor —2H 99
High Killerby. N Yor —1E 101
High Knipe. Cumb —3G 103
High Lands. Dur —2E 105
Highlands, The. Shrp —2A 60
Highlane. Ches —4C 84
Highlane. Derbs —2B 86
High Lane. G Man —2D 84
High Lane. Here —4A 60
High Laver. Essx —5F 53
Highlaws. Cumb —5C 112
Highleadon. Glos —3C 48
High Legh. Ches —2A 84
Highleigh. W Sus —3G 17
High Leven. Stoc T —3B 106
Highley. Shrp —2B 60
High Littleton. Bath —1B 22
High Longthwaite. Cumb —5D 112
High Lorton. Cumb —2C 102
High Marishes. N Yor —2C 100
High Marnham. Notts —3F 87
High Melton. S Yor —4F 93
High Mickley. Nmbd —3D 115
Highmoor. Cumb —5D 112
High Moor. Lanc —3D 90
Highmoor. Oxon —3F 37
Highmoor Hill. Mon —3H 33
High Mowthorpe. N Yor —3C 100
Highnam. Glos —4C 48
High Newport. Tyne —4G 115
High Newton. Cumb —1D 96
High Newton-by-the-Sea. Nmbd —2G 121
High Nibthwaite. Cumb —1B 96
High Offley. Staf —3B 72
High Ongar. Essx —5F 53
High Onn. Staf —4C 72
High Orchard. Glos —4D 48
High Park. Mers —3B 90
High Pennyvenie. E Ayr —4E 117
High Roding. Essx —4G 53
High Row. Cumb —1E 103
High Salvington. W Sus —5C 26
High Scales. Cumb —5C 112
High Seaton. Cumb —1B 102
High Shaw. N Yor —5B 104
High Side. Cumb —1D 102
High Spen. Tyne —3E 115
Highsted. Kent —4D 40
High Stoop. Dur —5E 115
High Street. Corn —3D 6
High Street. Suff —5G 67
(nr. Aldeburgh)
High Street. Suff —2F 67
(nr. Bungay)
High Street. Suff —3G 67
(nr. Yoxford)
Highstreet Green. Essx —2A 54
High Street Green. Suff —5C 66
Highstreet Green. Surr —2A 26
Hightae. Dum —2B 112
High Throston. Hart —1B 106
Hightown. Ches —4C 84
Hightown. Mers —4A 90
High Town. Staf —4D 73
Hightown Green. Suff —5B 66
High Toynton. Linc —4B 88
High Trewhitt. Nmbd —4E 121
High Valleyfield. Fife —1D 128
Highway. Here —1H 47
Highweek. Devn —5B 12
High Westwood. Dur —4E 115
Highwood. Staf —2E 73
Highwood. Worc —4A 60
High Worsall. N Yor —4A 106
Highworth. Swin —2H 35
High Wray. Cumb —5E 103
High Wych. Herts —4E 53
High Wycombe. Buck —2G 37
Hilborough. Norf —5H 77
Hilcott. Wilts —1G 23
Hildenborough. Kent —1G 27
Hildersham. Cambs —1F 53
Hilderstone. Staf —2D 72
Hilderthorpe. E Yor —3F 101
Hilfield. Dors —2B 14
Hilgay. Norf —1F 65
Hill. S Glo —2B 34
Hill. Warw —4B 62
Hill. Worc —1E 49
Hillam. N Yor —2F 93
Hillbeck. Cumb —3A 104
Hillberry. IOM —4C 108
Hillborough. Kent —4G 41
Hillbourne. Pool —3F 15
Hillbrae. Aber —4D 160
(nr. Aberchirder)
Hillbrae. Aber —1E 153
(nr. Inverurie)
Hillbrae. Aber —5F 161
(nr. Methlick)
Hill Brow. Hants —4F 25
Hillbutts. Dors —2E 15
Hillcliffane. Derbs —1G 73
Hill Deverill. Wilts —2D 22
Hilldyke. Linc —1C 76
Hill End. Dur —1D 104
Hillend. Fife —1E 129
(nr. Inverkeithing)
Hill End. Fife —4C 136
(nr. Saline)
Hillend. N Lan —3B 128
Hill End. N Yor —4C 98
Hillend. Shrp —1C 60
Hillend. Swan —3D 30
Hillersland. Glos —4A 48
Hillerton. Devn —3H 11
Hillesden. Buck —3E 51
Hillesley. Glos —3C 34
Hillfarrance. Som —4E 21
Hill Furze. Worc —1E 49
Hill Gate. Here —3H 47
Hill Green. Essx —2E 53
Hillgreen. W Ber —4C 36
Hillhead. E Ayr —3D 116
Hill Head. Hants —2D 16
Hillhead. Torb —3F 9
Hilliard's Cross. Staf —4F 73
Hilliclay. High —2D 168
Hillingdon. G Lon —2B 38
Hillington. Norf —3G 77
Hillington. Ren —3G 127
Hillmorton. Warw —3C 62
Hill of Beath. Fife —4D 136
Hill of Fearn. High —1C 158
Hill of Fiddes. Aber —1G 153
Hill of Keillor. Ang —4B 144
Hill of Overbrae. Aber —2F 161
Hill Ridware. Staf —4E 73
Hillsborough. S Yor —1H 85
Hillside. Aber —4G 153
Hillside. Ang —2G 145
Hillside. Devn —2D 8
Hillside. Hants —1F 25
Hillside. Mers —3B 90
Hillside. Orkn —5C 172
Hillside. Shet —5F 173
Hillside. Shrp —2A 60
Hill Side. W Yor —3B 92
Hillside. Worc —4B 60
Hillside of Prieston. Ang —5C 144
Hill Somersal. Derbs —2F 73
Hillstown. Derbs —4B 86
Hillstreet. Hants —1B 16
Hillswick. Shet —4D 173
Hill, The. Cumb —1A 96
Hill Top. Dur —2C 104
(nr. Barnard Castle)
Hill Top. Dur —5F 115
(nr. Durham)
Hill Top. Dur —4E 115
(nr. Stanley)
Hill Top. Hants —2C 16
Hill View. Dors —3E 15
Hillwell. Shet —10E 173
Hill Wootton. Warw —4H 61
Hillyland. Per —1C 136
Hilmarton. Wilts —4F 35
Hilperton. Wilts —1D 22
Hilperton Marsh. Wilts —5D 34
Hilsea. Port —2E 17
Hilston. E Yor —1F 95
Hiltingbury. Hants —4C 24
Hilton. Cambs —4B 64
Hilton. Cumb —2A 104
Hilton. Derbs —2G 73
Hilton. Dors —2C 14
Hilton. Dur —2E 105
Hilton. High —5E 165
Hilton. Shrp —1B 60
Hilton. Staf —5E 73
Hilton. Stoc T —3B 106
Hilton of Cadboll. High —1C 158
Himbleton. Worc —5D 60
Himley. Staf —1C 60
Hincaster. Cumb —1E 97
Hinchcliffe Mill. W Yor —4B 92
Hinchwick. Glos —2G 49
Hinckley. Leics —1B 62
Hinderclay. Suff —3C 66
Hinderwell. N Yor —3E 107
Hindford. Shrp —2F 71
Hindhead. Surr —3G 25
Hindley. G Man —4E 91
Hindley. Nmbd —4D 114
Hindley Green. G Man —4E 91
Hindlip. Worc —5C 60
Hindolveston. Norf —3C 78
Hindon. Wilts —3E 23
Hindringham. Norf —2B 78
Hingham. Norf —5C 78
Hinksford. Staf —2C 60
Hinstock. Shrp —3A 72
Hintlesham. Suff —1D 54
Hinton. Hants —3H 15
Hinton. Here —2G 47
Hinton. Nptn —5C 62
Hinton. Shrp —5G 71
Hinton. S Glo —4C 34
Hinton Ampner. Hants —4D 24
Hinton Blewett. Bath —1A 22
Hinton Charterhouse. Bath —1C 22
Hinton-in-the-Hedges. Nptn —2D 50
Hinton Martell. Dors —2F 15
Hinton on the Green. Worc —1F 49
Hinton Parva. Swin —3H 35
Hinton St George. Som —1H 13
Hinton St Mary. Dors —1C 14
Hinton Waldrist. Oxon —2B 36
Hints. Shrp —3A 60
Hints. Staf —5F 73
Hinwick. Beds —4G 63
Hinxhill. Kent —1E 29
Hinxton. Cambs —1E 53
Hinxworth. Herts —1C 52
Hipley. Hants —1E 16
Hipperholme. W Yor —2B 92
Hipsburn. Nmbd —3G 121
Hipswell. N Yor —5E 105
Hiraeth. Carm —2F 43
Hirn. Aber —3E 153
Hirnant. Powy —3C 70
Hirst. Nmbd —1F 115
Hirst Courtney. N Yor —2G 93
Hirwaen. Den —4D 82
Hirwaun. Rhon —5C 46
Hiscott. Devn —4F 19
Histon. Cambs —4D 64
Hitcham. Suff —5B 66
Hitchin. Herts —3B 52
Hittisleigh. Devn —3H 11
Hittisleigh Barton. Devn —3H 11
Hive. E Yor —1B 94
Hixon. Staf —3E 73
Hoaden. Kent —5G 41
Hoar Cross. Staf —3F 73
Hoarwithy. Here —3A 48
Hoath. Kent —4G 41
Hobarris. Shrp —3F 59
Hobbister. Orkn —7C 172
Hobbles Green. Suff —5G 65
Hobbs Cross. Essx —1F 39
Hobkirk. Scot —3H 119
Hobson. Dur —4E 115
Hoby. Leics —4D 74
Hockering. Norf —4C 78
Hockering Heath. Norf —4C 78
Hockerton. Notts —5E 86
Hockley. Essx —1C 40
Hockley. Staf —5G 73
Hockley. W Mid —2G 61
Hockley Heath. W Mid —3F 61
Hockliffe. Beds —3H 51
Hockwold cum Wilton. Norf —2G 65
Hockworthy. Devn —1D 12
Hoddesdon. Herts —5D 52
Hoddlesden. Bkbn —2F 91
Hoddomcross. Dum —2C 112
Hodgeston. Pemb —5E 43
Hodley. Powy —1D 58
Hodnet. Shrp —3A 72
Hodsoll Street. Kent —4H 39
Hodson. Swin —3G 35
Hodthorpe. Derbs —3C 86
Hoe. Norf —4B 78
Hoe Gate. Hants —1E 17
Hoe, The. Plym —3A 8
Hoff. Cumb —3H 103
Hoffleet Stow. Linc —2B 76
Hogaland. Shet —4E 173
Hogben's Hill. Kent —5E 41
Hoggard's Green. Suff —5A 66
Hoggeston. Buck —3G 51
Hoggrill's End. Warw —1G 61
Hogha Gearraidh. W Isl —1C 170
Hoghton. Lanc —2E 90
Hoghton Bottoms. Lanc —2E 91
Hognaston. Derbs —5G 85
Hogsthorpe. Linc —3E 89
Hogstock. Dors —2E 15
Holbeach. Linc —3C 76
Holbeach Bank. Linc —3C 76
Holbeach Clough. Linc —3C 76
Holbeach Drove. Linc —4C 76
Holbeach Hurn. Linc —3C 76
Holbeach St Johns. Linc —4C 76
Holbeach St Marks. Linc —2C 76
Holbeach St Matthew. Linc —2D 76
Holbeck. Notts —3C 86
Holbeck. W Yor —1C 92
Holberrow Green. Worc —5E 61
Holbeton. Devn —4C 8
Holborn. G Lon —2E 39

Holbrook—Hutton

Holbrook. Derbs —1A 74
Holbrook. S Yor —2B 86
Holbrook. Suff —2E 55
Holburn. Nmbd —1E 121
Holbury. Hants —2C 16
Holcombe. Devn —5C 12
Holcombe. G Man —3F 91
Holcombe. Som —2B 22
Holcombe Brook. G Man —3F 91
Holcombe Rogus. Devn —1D 12
Holcot. Nptn —4E 63
Holden. Lanc —5G 97
Holdenby. Nptn —4D 62
Holder's Green. Essx —3G 53
Holdgate. Shrp —2H 59
Holdingham. Linc —1H 75
Holditch. Dors —2G 13
Holemoor. Devn —2E 11
Hole Street. W Sus —4C 26
Holford. Som —2E 21
Holker. Cumb —2C 96
Holkham. Norf —1A 78
Hollacombe. Devn —2D 11
Holland. Orkn —2D 172 (on Papa Westray)
Holland. Orkn —5F 172 (on Stronsay)
Holland Fen. Linc —1B 76
Holland Lees. Lanc —4D 90
Holland-on-Sea. Essx —4E 55
Holland Park. W Mid —5E 73
Hollandstoun. Orkn —2G 172
Hollesley. Suff —1G 55
Hollinfare. Warr —1A 84
Hollingbourne. Kent —5C 40
Hollingbury. Brig —5E 27
Hollingdon. Buck —3G 51
Hollingrove. E Sus —3A 28
Hollington. Derbs —1G 73
Hollington. E Sus —4B 28
Hollington. Staf —2E 73
Hollington Grove. Derbs —2G 73
Hollingworth. G Man —1E 85
Hollins. Derbs —3H 85
Hollins. G Man —4G 91
Hollinsclough. Staf —4E 85
Hollinswood. Telf —5A 72
Hollinthorpe. W Yor —1D 93
Hollinwood. G Man —4H 91
Hollinwood. Shrp —2H 71
Hollocombe. Devn —1G 11
Holloway. Derbs —5H 85
Hollow Court. Worc —5D 61
Hollowell. Nptn —3D 62
Hollow Meadows. S Yor —2G 85
Hollows. Dum —2E 113
Hollybush. Cphy —5E 47
Hollybush. E Ayr —3C 116
Hollybush. Worc —2C 48
Holly End. Norf —5D 77
Holly Hill. N Yor —4E 105
Hollyhurst. Ches —1H 71
Hollym. E Yor —2G 95
Hollywood. Staf —2D 72
Hollywood. Worc —3E 61
Holmacott. Devn —4F 19
Holmbridge. W Yor —4B 92
Holmbury St Mary. Surr —1C 26
Holmbush. Corn —3E 7
Holmcroft. Staf —3D 72
Holme. Cambs —2A 64
Holme. Cumb —2E 97
Holme. N Lin —4C 94
Holme. N Yor —1F 99
Holme. Notts —5F 87
Holme. W Yor —4B 92
Holmebridge. Dors —4D 15
Holme Chapel. Lanc —2G 91
Holme Hale. Norf —5A 78
Holme Lacy. Here —2A 48
Holme Lane. Notts —2D 74
Holme Marsh. Here —5F 59
Holmend. Dum —4C 118
Holme next the Sea. Norf —1G 77
Holme-on-Spalding-Moor. E Yor —1B 94
Holme on the Wolds. E Yor —5D 100
Holme Pierrepont. Notts —2D 74
Holmer. Here —1A 48
Holmer Green. Buck —2G 37
Holmes. Lanc —3C 90
Holme St Cuthbert. Cumb —5C 112
Holmes Chapel. Ches —4B 84
Holmesfield. Derbs —3H 85
Holmeswood. Lanc —3C 90
Holmewood. Derbs —4B 86
Holmfirth. W Yor —4B 92
Holmhead. E Ayr —2E 117
Holmisdale. High —4A 154
Holm of Drumlanrig. Dum —5H 117
Holmpton. E Yor —2G 95
Holmrook. Cumb —5B 102
Holmsey Green. Suff —3F 65
Holmsgarth. Shet —7F 173
Holmside. Dur —5F 115
Holmwrangle. Cumb —5G 113
Holne. Devn —2D 8
Holsworthy. Devn —2D 10
Holsworthy Beacon. Devn —2D 10
Holt. Dors —2F 15
Holt. Norf —2C 78
Holt. Wilts —5D 34
Holt. Worc —4C 60
Holt. Wrex —5G 83
Holtby. York —4A 100
Holt End. Hants —3E 25
Holt End. Worc —4E 61
Holt Fleet. Worc —4C 60
Holt Green. Lanc —4B 90
Holt Heath. Dors —2F 15
Holt Heath. Worc —4C 60
Holton. Oxon —5E 50
Holton. Som —4B 22
Holton. Suff —3F 67
Holton cum Beckering. Linc —2A 88
Holton Heath. Dors —3E 15
Holton le Clay. Linc —4F 95
Holton le Moor. Linc —1H 87
Holton St Mary. Suff —2D 54
Holt Pound. Hants —2G 25
Holtsmere End. Herts —4A 52
Holtye. E Sus —2F 27
Holwell. Dors —1C 14
Holwell. Herts —2B 52
Holwell. Leics —3E 75
Holwell. Oxon —5H 49
Holwell. Som —2C 22
Holwick. Dur —2C 104
Holworth. Dors —4C 14
Holybourne. Hants —2F 25
Holy Cross. Worc —3D 60
Holyfield. Essx —5D 53
Holyhead. IOA —2B 80
Holy Island. Nmbd —5H 131
Holymoorside. Derbs —4H 85
Holyport. Wind —4G 37
Holystone. Nmbd —4D 120
Holytown. N Lan —3A 128
Holywell. Cambs —3C 64
Holywell. Corn —3B 6
Holywell. Dors —2A 14
Holywell. Flin —3D 82
Holywell. Glos —2C 34
Holywell. Nmbd —2G 115
Holywell. Warw —4F 61
Holywell Green. W Yor —3A 92
Holywell Lake. Som —4E 20
Holywell Row. Suff —3G 65
Holywood. Dum —1G 111
Homer. Shrp —5A 72
Homer Green. Mers —4B 90
Homersfield. Suff —2E 67
Hom Green. Here —3A 48
Homington. Wilts —4G 23
Honeyborough. Pemb —4D 42
Honeybourne. Worc —1G 49
Honeychurch. Devn —2G 11
Honey Hill. Kent —4F 41
Honey Street. Wilts —5G 35
Honey Tye. Suff —2C 54
Honiley. Warw —3G 61
Honing. Norf —3F 79
Honingham. Norf —4D 78
Honington. Linc —1G 75
Honington. Suff —3B 66
Honington. Warw —1A 50
Honiton. Devn —2E 13
Honley. W Yor —3B 92
Honnington. Telf —4B 72
Hoo. Suff —5E 67
Hoobrook. Worc —3C 60
Hood Green. S Yor —4D 92
Hooe. E Sus —5A 28
Hooe. Plym —3A 8
Hooe Common. E Sus —4A 28
Hoohill. Bkpl —1B 90
Hook. Cambs —1D 64
Hook. G Lon —4C 38
Hook. Hants —1F 25 (nr. Basingstoke)
Hook. Hants —2D 16 (nr. Fareham)
Hook. N Lin —2A 94
Hook. Pemb —3D 43
Hook. Wilts —3F 35
Hook-a-Gate. Shrp —5G 71
Hook Bank. Worc —1D 48
Hooke. Dors —2A 14
Hooker Gate. Tyne —4E 115
Hookgate. Staf —2B 72
Hook Green. Kent —2A 28 (nr. Lamberhurst)
Hook Green. Kent —3H 39 (nr. Longfield)
Hook Green. Kent —4H 39 (nr. Meopham)
Hook Norton. Oxon —2B 50
Hook's Cross. Herts —3C 52
Hook Street. Glos —2B 34
Hookway. Devn —3B 12
Hookwood. Surr —1D 26
Hoole. Ches —4G 83
Hooley. Surr —5D 39
Hooley Bridge. G Man —3G 91
Hooley Brow. G Man —3G 91
Hoo St Werburgh. Medw —3B 40
Hooton. Ches —3F 83
Hooton Levitt. S Yor —1C 86
Hooton Pagnell. S Yor —4E 93
Hooton Roberts. S Yor —1B 86
Hoove. Shet —7E 173
Hope. Derbs —2F 85
Hope. Flin —5F 83
Hope. High —3E 167
Hope. Powy —5E 71
Hope. Shrp —5F 71
Hope. Staf —5F 85
Hope Bagot. Shrp —3H 59
Hope Bowdler. Shrp —1G 59
Hopedale. Staf —5F 85
Hope Green. Ches —2D 84
Hopeman. Mor —2F 159
Hope Mansell. Here —4B 48
Hopesay. Shrp —2F 59
Hope's Green. Essx —2B 40
Hopetown. W Yor —2D 93
Hope under Dinmore. Here —5H 59
Hopley's Green. Here —5F 59
Hopperton. N Yor —4G 99
Hop Pole. Linc —4A 76
Hopstone. Shrp —1B 60
Hopton. Derbs —5G 85
Hopton. Powy —1E 59
Hopton. Shrp —3F 71 (nr. Oswestry)
Hopton. Shrp —3H 71 (nr. Wem)
Hopton. Staf —3D 72
Hopton. Suff —3B 66
Hopton Cangeford. Shrp —2H 59
Hopton Castle. Shrp —3F 59
Hoptonheath. Shrp —3F 59
Hopton Heath. Staf —3D 72
Hopton on Sea. Norf —5H 79
Hopton Wafers. Shrp —3A 60
Hopwas. Staf —5F 73
Hopwood. Worc —3E 61
Horam. E Sus —4G 27
Horbling. Linc —2A 76
Horbury. W Yor —3C 92
Horcott. Glos —5G 49
Horden. Dur —5H 115
Horderley. Shrp —2G 59
Hordle. Hants —3A 16
Hordley. Shrp —2F 71
Horeb. Carm —3F 45 (nr. Brechfa)
Horeb. Carm —5E 45 (nr. Llanelli)
Horeb. Cdgn —1D 45
Horfield. Bris —4B 34
Horgabost. W Isl —8C 171
Horham. Suff —3E 66
Horkesley Heath. Essx —3C 54
Horkstow. N Lin —3C 94
Horley. Oxon —1C 50
Horley. Surr —1D 27
Hornblotton Green. Som —3A 22
Hornby. Lanc —3E 97
Hornby. N Yor —4A 106 (nr. Appleton Wiske)
Hornby. N Yor —5F 105 (nr. Catterick Garrison)
Horncastle. Linc —4B 88
Hornchurch. G Lon —2G 39
Horncliffe. Nmbd —5F 131
Horndean. Hants —1E 17
Horndean. Scot —5E 131
Horndon. Devn —4F 11
Horndon on the Hill. Thur —2A 40
Horne. Surr —1E 27
Horner. Som —2C 20
Horning. Norf —4F 79
Horninghold. Leics —1F 63
Horninglow. Staf —3G 73
Horningsea. Cambs —4D 65
Horningsham. Wilts —2D 22
Horningtoft. Norf —3B 78
Hornsby. Cumb —4G 113
Hornsbygate. Cumb —4G 113
Horns Corner. Kent —3B 28
Horns Cross. Devn —4D 19
Hornsea. E Yor —5G 101
Hornsea Burton. E Yor —5G 101
Hornsey. G Lon —2E 39
Hornton. Oxon —1B 50
Horpit. Swin —3H 35
Horrabridge. Devn —2B 8
Horringer. Suff —4H 65
Horringford. IOW —4D 16
Horrocks Fold. G Man —3F 91
Horrocksford. Lanc —5G 97
Horsburgh Ford. Scot —1F 119
Horsebridge. Devn —5E 11
Horsebridge. Hants —3B 24
Horse Bridge. Staf —5D 84
Horsebrook. Staf —4C 72
Horsecastle. N Som —5H 33
Horsehay. Telf —5A 72
Horseheath. Cambs —1G 53
Horsehouse. N Yor —1C 98
Horsell. Surr —5A 38
Horseman's Green. Wrex —1G 71
Horsenden. Buck —5F 51
Horseway. Cambs —2D 64
Horsey. Norf —3G 79
Horsey. Som —3G 21
Horsford. Norf —4D 78
Horsforth. W Yor —1C 92
Horsham. W Sus —2C 26
Horsham. Worc —5B 60
Horsham St Faith. Norf —4E 78
Horsington. Linc —4A 88
Horsington. Som —4C 22
Horsley. Derbs —1A 74
Horsley. Glos —2D 34
Horsley. Nmbd —3D 115 (nr. Prudhoe)
Horsley. Nmbd —5C 120 (nr. Rochester)
Horsley Cross. Essx —3E 54
Horsleycross Street. Essx —3E 54
Horsleyhill. Scot —3H 119
Horsleyhope. Dur —5D 114
Horsley Woodhouse. Derbs —1A 74
Horsmonden. Kent —1A 28
Horspath. Oxon —5D 50
Horstead. Norf —4E 79
Horsted Keynes. W Sus —3E 27
Horton. Buck —4H 51
Horton. Dors —2F 15
Horton. Lanc —4A 98
Horton. Nptn —5F 63
Horton. Shrp —2G 71
Horton. Som —1G 13
Horton. S Glo —3C 34
Horton. Staf —5D 84
Horton. Swan —4D 30
Horton. Wilts —5F 35
Horton. Wind —3B 38
Horton Cross. Som —1G 13
Horton-cum-Studley. Oxon —4D 50
Horton Green. Ches —1G 71
Horton Heath. Hants —1C 16
Horton in Ribblesdale. N Yor —2H 97
Horton Kirby. Kent —4G 39
Hortonwood. Telf —4A 72
Horwich. G Man —3E 91
Horwich End. Derbs —2E 85
Horwood. Devn —4F 19
Hoscar. Lanc —3C 90
Hose. Leics —3E 75
Hosh. Per —1A 136
Hosta. W Isl —1C 170
Hoswick. Shet —9F 173
Hotham. E Yor —1B 94
Hothfield. Kent —1D 28
Hoton. Leics —3C 74
Houbie. Shet —2H 173
Hough. Arg —4A 138
Hough. Ches —5B 84 (nr. Crewe)
Hough. Ches —3C 84 (nr. Wilmslow)
Hougham. Linc —1F 75
Hough Green. Hal —2G 83
Hough-on-the-Hill. Linc —1G 75
Houghton. Cambs —3B 64
Houghton. Cumb —4F 113
Houghton. Hants —3B 24
Houghton. Nmbd —3E 115
Houghton. Pemb —4D 43
Houghton. W Sus —4B 26
Houghton Bank. Darl —2F 105
Houghton Conquest. Beds —1A 52
Houghton Green. E Sus —3D 28
Houghton-le-Side. Darl —2F 105
Houghton-le-Spring. Tyne —5G 115
Houghton on the Hill. Leics —5D 74
Houghton Regis. Beds —3A 52
Houghton St Giles. Norf —2B 78
Houlland. Shet —6E 173 (on Mainland)
Houlland. Shet —4G 173 (on Yell)
Houlsyke. N Yor —4E 107
Hound. Hants —2C 16
Hound Green. Hants —1F 25
Houndslow. Scot —5C 130
Houndsmoor. Som —4E 21
Houndwood. Scot —3E 131
Hounsdown. Hants —1B 16
Hounslow. G Lon —3C 38
Housabister. Shet —6F 173
Housay. Shet —4H 173
Househill. High —3C 158
Housetter. Shet —3E 173
Houss. Shet —8E 173
Houston. Ren —3F 127
Housty. High —5D 168
Houton. Orkn —7C 172
Hove. Brig —5D 27
Hoveringham. Notts —1E 74
Hoveton. Norf —4F 79
Hovingham. N Yor —2A 100
How. Cumb —4G 113
How Caple. Here —2B 48
Howden. E Yor —2H 93
Howden-le-Wear. Dur —1E 105
Howe. Cumb —1D 96
Howe. High —2F 169
Howe. Norf —5E 79
Howe. N Yor —1F 99
Howe Green. Essx —5H 53 (nr. Chelmsford)
Howegreen. Essx —5B 54 (nr. Maldon)
Howell. Linc —1A 76
How End. Beds —1A 52
Howe of Teuchar. Aber —4E 161
Howes. Dum —3C 112
Howe Street. Essx —4G 53 (nr. Chelmsford)
Howe Street. Essx —2G 53 (nr. Finchingfield)
Howe, The. IOM —5A 108
Howey. Powy —5C 58
Howgate. Midl —4F 129
Howgill. Lanc —5H 97
Howgill. N Yor —4C 98
How Green. Kent —1F 27
How Green. Warw —2H 61
How Hill. Norf —4F 79
Howick. Nmbd —3G 121
Howle. Telf —3A 72
Howle Hill. Here —3B 48
Howleigh. Som —1F 13
Howlett End. Essx —2F 53
Howley. Som —2F 13
Howley. Warr —2A 84
Hownam. Scot —3B 120
Howsham. N Lin —4D 94
Howsham. N Yor —3B 100
Howtel. Nmbd —1C 120
Howt Green. Kent —4C 40
Howton. Here —3H 47
Howwood. Ren —3E 127
Hoxne. Suff —3D 66
Hoylake. Mers —2E 82
Hoyland. S Yor —4D 92
Hoylandswaine. S Yor —4C 92
Hoyle. W Sus —4A 26
Hubberholme. N Yor —2B 98
Hubberston. Pemb —4C 42
Hubbert's Bridge. Linc —1B 76
Huby. N Yor —5E 99 (nr. Harrogate)
Huby. N Yor —3H 99 (nr. York)
Huccaby. Devn —5G 11
Hucclecote. Glos —4D 48
Hucking. Kent —5C 40
Hucknall. Notts —1C 74
Huddersfield. W Yor —3B 92
Huddington. Worc —5D 60
Huddlesford. Staf —5F 73
Hudswell. N Yor —4E 105
Huggate. E Yor —4C 100
Hugglescote. Leics —4B 74
Hughenden Valley. Buck —2G 37
Hughley. Shrp —1H 59
Hughton. High —4G 157
Hugh Town. IOS —1B 4
Hugus. Corn —4B 6
Huish. Wilts —5G 35
Huish Champflower. Som —4D 20
Huish Episcopi. Som —4H 21
Huisinis. W Isl —6B 171
Hulcote. Nptn —1F 51
Hulcott. Buck —4G 51
Hulham. Devn —4D 12
Hulland. Derbs —1G 73
Hulland Moss. Derbs —1G 73
Hulland Ward. Derbs —1G 73
Hullavington. Wilts —3D 35
Hullbridge. Essx —1C 40
Hulme. G Man —1C 84
Hulme. Staf —1D 72
Hulme End. Staf —5F 85
Hulme Walfield. Ches —4C 84
Hulverstone. IOW —4B 16
Hulver Street. Suff —2G 67
Humber. Devn —5C 12
Humber Court. Here —5H 59
Humberside Airport. N Lin —3D 94
Humberston. NE Lin —4G 95
Humberstone. Leic C —5D 74
Humbie. E Lot —3A 130
Humbleton. E Yor —1F 95
Humbleton. Nmbd —2D 121
Humby. Linc —2H 75
Hume. Scot —5D 130
Humshaugh. Nmbd —2C 114
Huna. High —1F 169
Huncoat. Lanc —1F 91
Huncote. Leics —1C 62
Hundall. Derbs —3A 86
Hunderthwaite. Dur —2C 104
Hundleby. Linc —4C 88
Hundle Houses. Linc —5B 88
Hundleton. Pemb —4D 42
Hundon. Suff —1H 53
Hundred Acres. Hants —1D 16
Hundred House. Powy —5D 58
Hundred, The. Here —4H 59
Hungarton. Leics —5D 74
Hungerford. Hants —1G 15
Hungerford. Shrp —2H 59
Hungerford. Som —2D 20
Hungerford. W Ber —5B 36
Hungerford Newtown. W Ber —4B 36
Hunger Hill. G Man —4E 91
Hungerton. Linc —2F 75
Hungladder. High —1C 154
Hungryhatton. Shrp —3A 72
Hunmanby. N Yor —2E 101
Hunmanby Sands. N Yor —2F 101
Hunningham. Warw —4A 62
Hunnington. W Mid —2D 60
Hunny Hill. IOW —4C 16
Hunsdon. Herts —4E 53
Hunsingore. N Yor —4G 99
Hunslet. W Yor —1D 92
Hunslet Carr. W Yor —2D 92
Hunsonby. Cumb —1G 103
Hunspow. High —1E 169
Hunstanton. Norf —1F 77
Hunstanworth. Dur —5C 114
Hunston. Suff —4B 66
Hunston. W Sus —2G 17
Hunstrete. Bath —5B 34
Hunt End. Worc —4E 61
Hunterfield. Midl —3G 129
Hunter's Quay. Arg —2C 126
Huntham. Som —4G 21
Hunthill Lodge. Ang —1D 144
Huntingdon. Cambs —3B 64
Huntingfield. Suff —3F 67
Huntingford. Wilts —3D 22
Huntington. Ches —4G 83
Huntington. E Lot —2A 130
Huntington. Here —5E 59
Huntington. Staf —4D 72
Huntington. Telf —5A 72
Huntington. York —4A 100
Huntingtower. Per —1C 136
Huntley. Glos —4C 48
Huntley. Staf —1E 73
Huntly. Aber —4C 160
Huntlywood. Scot —5C 130
Hunton. Hants —3C 24
Hunton. Kent —1B 28
Hunton. N Yor —5E 105
Hunton Bridge. Herts —5A 52
Hunt's Corner. Norf —2C 66
Huntscott. Som —2C 20
Hunt's Cross. Mers —2G 83
Hunts Green. Warw —1F 61
Huntsham. Devn —4D 20
Huntshaw. Devn —4F 19
Huntspill. Som —2G 21
Huntstile. Som —3F 21
Huntstrete. Bath —5B 34
Huntworth. Som —3G 21
Hunwick. Dur —1E 105
Hunworth. Norf —2C 78
Hurcott. Som —1G 13 (nr. Ilminster)
Hurcott. Som —4A 22 (nr. Somerton)
Hurdcott. Wilts —3G 23
Hurdley. Powy —1E 59
Hurdsfield. Ches —3D 84
Hurlet. Glas —3G 127
Hurley. Warw —1G 61
Hurley. Wind —3G 37
Hurlford. E Ayr —1D 116
Hurliston Green. Lanc —3B 90
Hurn. Dors —3G 15
Hursey. Dors —2H 13
Hursley. Hants —4C 24
Hurst. G Man —4H 91
Hurst. N Yor —4D 104
Hurst. Wok —4F 37
Hurstbourne Priors. Hants —2C 24
Hurstbourne Tarrant. Hants —1B 24
Hurst Green. Ches —1H 71
Hurst Green. E Sus —3B 28
Hurst Green. Essx —4D 54
Hurst Green. Lanc —1E 91
Hurst Green. Surr —5E 39
Hurstley. Here —1G 47
Hurstpierpoint. W Sus —4D 27
Hurstway Common. Here —1F 47
Hurst Wickham. W Sus —4D 27
Hurstwood. Lanc —1G 91
Hurtmore. Surr —1A 26
Hurworth-on-Tees. Darl —3A 106
Hurworth Place. Darl —3F 105
Hury. Dur —3C 104
Husbands Bosworth. Leics —2D 62
Husborne Crawley. Beds —2H 51
Husthwaite. N Yor —2H 99
Hutcherleigh. Devn —3D 9
Hut Green. N Yor —2F 93
Huthwaite. Notts —5B 86
Huttoft. Linc —3E 89
Hutton. Cumb —2F 103

Hutton—Keyworth

Hutton. Essx —1H 39
Hutton. Lanc —2C 90
Hutton. N Som —1G 21
Hutton. Scot —4F 131
Hutton Bonville. N Yor —4A 106
Hutton Buscel. N Yor —1D 100
Hutton Conyers. N Yor —2F 99
Hutton Cranswick. E Yor —4E 101
Hutton End. Cumb —1F 103
Hutton Gate. Red C —3C 106
Hutton Henry. Dur —1B 106
Hutton-le-Hole. N Yor —1B 100
Hutton Magna. Dur —3E 105
Hutton Mulgrave. N Yor —3F 107
Hutton Roof. Cumb —2E 97 (nr. Kirkby Lonsdale)
Hutton Roof. Cumb —1E 103 (nr. Penrith)
Hutton Rudby. N Yor —4B 106
Huttons Ambro. N Yor —3B 100
Hutton Sessay. N Yor —2G 99
Hutton Village. Red C —3D 106
Hutton Wandesley. N Yor —4H 99
Huxham. Devn —3C 12
Huxham Green. Som —3A 22
Huxley. Ches —4H 83
Huxter. Shet —6C 173 (on Mainland)
Huxter. Shet —5G 173 (on Whalsay)
Huyton. Mers —1G 83
Hwlffordd. Pemb —3D 42
Hycemoor. Cumb —1A 96
Hyde. Glos —5D 49 (nr. Stroud)
Hyde. Glos —3F 49 (nr. Winchcombe)
Hyde. G Man —1D 84
Hyde Heath. Buck —5H 51
Hyde Lea. Staf —3D 72
Hyde Park. S Yor —4F 93
Hydestile. Surr —1A 26
Hykeham Moor. Linc —4G 87
Hyndford Bridge. S Lan —5C 128
Hynish. Arg —5A 138
Hyssington. Powy —1F 59
Hythe. Hants —2C 16
Hythe. Kent —2F 29
Hythe End. Wind —3B 38
Hythie. Aber —3H 161
Hyton. Cumb —1A 96

Ianstown. Mor —2B 160
Iarsiadar. W Isl —4D 171
Ibberton. Dors —2C 14
Ible. Derbs —5G 85
Ibrox. Glas —3G 127
Ibsley. Hants —2G 15
Ibstock. Leics —4B 74
Ibstone. Buck —2F 37
Ibthorpe. Hants —1B 24
Iburndale. N Yor —4F 107
Ibworth. Hants —1D 24
Icelton. N Som —5G 33
Ichrachan. Arg —5E 141
Ickburgh. Norf —1H 65
Ickenham. G Lon —2B 38
Ickford. Buck —5E 51
Ickham. Kent —5G 41
Ickleford. Herts —2B 52
Icklesham. E Sus —4C 28
Ickleton. Cambs —1E 53
Icklingham. Suff —3G 65
Ickwell. Beds —1B 52
Icomb. Glos —3H 49
Idbury. Oxon —4H 49
Iddesleigh. Devn —2F 11
Ide. Devn —3C 12
Ideford. Devn —5B 12
Ide Hill. Kent —5F 39
Iden. E Sus —3D 28
Iden Green. Kent —2C 28 (nr. Benenden)
Iden Green. Kent —2B 28 (nr. Goudhurst)
Idle. W Yor —1B 92
Idless. Corn —4C 6
Idlicote. Warw —1A 50
Idmiston. Wilts —3G 23
Idole. Carm —4E 45
Idridgehay. Derbs —1G 73
Idrigill. High —2C 154
Idstone. Oxon —3A 36
Iffley. Oxon —5D 50
Ifield. W Sus —2D 26
Ifieldwood. W Sus —2D 26
Ifold. W Sus —2B 26
Iford. E Sus —5F 27
Ifton Heath. Shrp —2F 71
Ightfield. Shrp —2H 71
Ightham. Kent —5G 39
Iken. Suff —5G 67
Ilam. Staf —5F 85
Ilchester. Som —4A 22
Ilderton. Nmbd —2E 121
Ilford. G Lon —2F 39
Ilford. Som —1G 13
Ilfracombe. Devn —2F 19
Ilkeston. Derbs —1B 74
Ilketshall St Andrew. Suff —2F 67
Ilketshall St Lawrence. Suff —2F 67
Ilketshall St Margaret. Suff —2F 67
Ilkley. W Yor —5D 98
Illand. Corn —5C 10
Illey. W Mid —2D 61
Illidge Green. Ches —4B 84
Illington. Norf —2B 66
Illingworth. W Yor —2A 92
Illogan. Corn —4A 6
Illogan Highway. Corn —4A 6
Illston on the Hill. Leics —1E 62
Ilmer. Buck —5F 51
Ilmington. Warw —1H 49
Ilminster. Som —1G 13
Ilsington. Devn —5A 12
Ilsington. Dors —3C 14
Ilston. Swan —3E 31
Ilton. N Yor —2D 98
Ilton. Som —1G 13
Imachar. N Ayr —5G 125
Imber. Wilts —2E 23
Immingham. NE Lin —3E 95
Immingham Dock. NE Lin —3E 95
Impington. Cambs —4D 64
Ince. Ches —3G 83
Ince Blundell. Mers —4B 90
Ince-in-Makerfield. G Man —4D 90
Inchbae Lodge. High —2G 157
Inchbare. Ang —2F 145
Inchberry. Mor —3H 159
Inchbraoch. Ang —3G 145
Inchbrook. Glos —5D 48
Incheril. High —2C 156
Inchinnan. Ren —3F 127
Inchlaggan. High —3D 148
Inchmichael. Per —1E 137
Inchnadamph. High —1G 163
Inchree. High —2E 141
Inchture. Per —1E 137
Inchyra. Per —1D 136
Indian Queens. Corn —3D 6
Ingatestone. Essx —1H 39
Ingbirchworth. S Yor —4C 92
Ingestre. Staf —3D 73
Ingham. Linc —2G 87
Ingham. Norf —3F 79
Ingham. Suff —3A 66
Ingham Corner. Norf —3F 79
Ingleborough. Norf —4D 76
Ingleby. Derbs —3H 73
Ingleby Arncliffe. N Yor —4B 106
Ingleby Barwick. Stoc T —3B 106
Ingleby Greenhow. N Yor —4C 106
Ingleigh Green. Devn —2G 11
Inglemire. Hull —1D 94
Inglesbatch. Bath —5C 34
Ingleton. Dur —2E 105
Ingleton. N Yor —2F 97
Inglewhite. Lanc —5E 97
Ingoe. Nmbd —2D 114
Ingol. Lanc —1D 90
Ingoldisthorpe. Norf —2F 77
Ingoldmells. Linc —4E 89
Ingoldsby. Linc —2H 75
Ingon. Warw —5G 61
Ingram. Nmbd —3E 121
Ingrave. Essx —1H 39
Ingrow. W Yor —1A 92
Ings. Cumb —5F 103
Ingst. S Glo —3A 34
Ingthorpe. Rut —5G 75
Ingworth. Norf —3D 78
Inkberrow. Worc —5E 61
Inkford. Worc —3E 61
Inkpen. W Ber —5B 36
Inkstack. High —1E 169
Innellan. Arg —3C 126
Inner Hope. Devn —5C 8
Innerleith. Fife —2E 137
Innerleithen. Scot —1F 119
Innerleven. Fife —3F 137
Innermessan. Dum —3F 109
Innerwick. E Lot —2D 130
Innerwick. Per —4C 142
Innsworth. Glos —3D 48
Insch. Aber —1D 152
Insh. High —3C 150
Inshegra. High —3C 166
Inshore. High —1D 166
Inskip. Lanc —1C 90
Instow. Devn —3E 19
Intwood. Norf —5D 78
Inver. Aber —4G 151
Inver. High —5F 165
Inver. Per —4H 143
Inverailort. High —5F 147
Inveralligin. High —3H 155
Inverallochy. Aber —2H 161
Inveramsay. Aber —1E 153
Inveran. High —4C 164
Inveraray. Arg —3H 133
Inverarish. High —5E 155
Inverarity. Ang —4D 144
Inverarnan. Arg —2C 134
Inverarnie. High —5A 158
Inverbeg. Arg —4C 134
Inverbervie. Aber —1H 145
Inverboyndie. Aber —2D 160
Invercassley. High —3B 164
Invercharnan. High —4F 141
Inverchoran. High —3E 157
Invercreran. Arg —4E 141
Inverdruie. High —2D 150
Inverebrie. Aber —5G 161
Invereck. Arg —1C 126
Inveresk. E Lot —2G 129
Inveresragan. Arg —5D 141
Inverey. Aber —5E 151
Inverfarigaig. High —1H 149
Invergarry. High —3F 149
Invergeldie. Per —1G 135
Invergordon. High —2B 158
Invergowrie. Per —5C 144
Inverguseran. High —3F 147
Inverharroch. Mor —5A 160
Inverie. High —3F 147
Inverinan. Arg —2G 133
Inverinate. High —1B 148
Inverkeilor. Ang —4F 145
Inverkeithing. Fife —1E 129
Inverkeithny. Aber —4D 160
Inverkip. Inv —2D 126
Inverkirkaig. High —2E 163
Inverlael. High —5F 163
Inverliever Lodge. Arg —3F 133
Inverliver. Arg —5E 141
Inverloch. High —1F 141
Inverlochlarig. Stir —2D 134
Inverlussa. Arg —1E 125
Inver Mallie. High —5D 148
Invermarkie. Aber —5B 160
Invermoriston. High —2G 149
Invermossatt. Aber —2B 152
Invernaver. High —2H 167
Inverneil House. Arg —1G 125
Inverness. High —4A 158
Inverness Airport. High —3B 158
Invernettie. Aber —4H 161
Inverpolly Lodge. High —2E 163
Inverquhomery. Aber —4H 161
Inverroy. High —5E 149
Inversanda. High —3D 140
Invershiel. High —2B 148
Invershin. High —4C 164
Invershore. High —5E 169
Inversnaid. Stir —3C 134
Inverugie. Aber —4H 161
Inveruglas. Arg —3C 134
Inverurie. Aber —1E 153
Invervar. Per —4D 142
Inwardleigh. Devn —3F 11
Inworth. Essx —4B 54
Iochdar. W Isl —4C 170
Iping. W Sus —4G 25
Ipplepen. Devn —2E 9
Ipsden. Oxon —3E 37
Ipstones. Staf —1E 73
Ipswich. Suff —1E 55
Irby. Mers —2E 83
Irby in the Marsh. Linc —4D 88
Irby upon Humber. NE Lin —4E 95
Irchester. Nptn —4G 63
Ireby. Cumb —1D 102
Ireby. Lanc —2F 97
Ireland. Shet —9E 173
Ireleth. Cumb —2B 96
Ireshopeburn. Dur —1B 104
Ireton Wood. Derbs —1G 73
Irlam. G Man —1B 84
Irnham. Linc —3H 75
Iron Acton. S Glo —3B 34
Iron Bridge. Cambs —1D 65
Ironbridge. Telf —5A 72
Iron Cross. Warw —5E 61
Ironville. Derbs —5B 86
Irstead. Norf —3F 79
Irthington. Cumb —3F 113
Irthlingborough. Nptn —3G 63
Irton. N Yor —1E 101
Irvine. N Ayr —1C 116
Irvine Mains. N Ayr —1C 116
Isabella Pit. Nmbd —1G 115
Isauld. High —2B 168
Isbister. Orkn —6D 172
Isbister. Shet —2E 173 (on Mainland)
Isbister. Shet —5G 173 (on Whalsay)
Isfield. E Sus —4F 27
Isham. Nptn —3F 63
Island Carr. N Lin —4C 94
Islay Airport. Arg —4B 124
Isle Abbotts. Som —4G 21
Isle Brewers. Som —4G 21
Isleham. Cambs —3F 65
Isle of Man Airport. IOM —5B 108
Isle of Thanet. Kent —4H 41
Isle of Whithorn. Dum —5B 110
Isleornsay. High —2F 147
Islesburgh. Shet —5E 173
Islesteps. Dum —2A 112
Isleworth. G Lon —3C 38
Isley Walton. Leics —3B 74
Islibhig. W Isl —5B 171
Islington. G Lon —2E 39
Islington. Telf —3B 72
Islip. Nptn —3G 63
Islip. Oxon —4D 50
Islwyn. Cphy —2F 33
Istead Rise. Kent —4H 39
Itchen. Sotn —1C 16
Itchen Abbas. Hants —3D 24
Itchen Stoke. Hants —3D 24
Itchingfield. W Sus —3C 26
Itchington. S Glo —3B 34
Itlaw. Aber —3D 160
Itteringham. Norf —2D 78
Itteringham Common. Norf —3D 78
Itton. Devn —3G 11
Itton Common. Mon —2H 33
Ivegill. Cumb —5F 113
Ivelet. N Yor —5C 104
Iverchaolain. Arg —2B 126
Iver Heath. Buck —2B 38
Iveston. Dur —4E 115
Ivetsey Bank. Staf —4C 72
Ivinghoe. Buck —4H 51
Ivinghoe Aston. Buck —4H 51
Ivington. Here —5G 59
Ivington Green. Here —5G 59
Ivybridge. Devn —3C 8
Ivychurch. Kent —3E 29
Ivy Hatch. Kent —5G 39
Ivy Todd. Norf —5A 78
Iwade. Kent —4D 40
Iwerne Courteney. Dors —1D 14
Iwerne Minster. Dors —1D 14
Ixworth. Suff —3B 66
Ixworth Thorpe. Suff —3B 66

Jackfield. Shrp —5A 72
Jack Hill. N Yor —4E 98
Jacksdale. Notts —5B 86
Jackton. S Lan —4G 127
Jacobstow. Corn —3B 10
Jacobstowe. Devn —2F 11
Jacobswell. Surr —5A 38
Jameston. Pemb —5E 43
Jamestown. Dum —5F 119
Jamestown. Fife —1E 129
Jamestown. High —3G 157
Jamestown. W Dun —1E 127
Janetstown. High —2C 168 (nr. Thurso)
Janetstown. High —3F 169 (nr. Wick)
Jarrow. Tyne —3G 115
Jarvis Brook. E Sus —3G 27
Jasper's Green. Essx —3H 53
Jaywick. Essx —4E 55
Jedburgh. Scot —2A 120
Jeffreyston. Pemb —4E 43
Jellieston. E Ayr —4D 116
Jemimaville. High —2B 158
Jenkins Park. High —3F 149
Jersey Marine. Neat —3G 31
Jesmond. Tyne —3F 115
Jevington. E Sus —5G 27
Jingle Street. Mon —4H 47
Jockey End. Herts —4A 52
Jodrell Bank. Ches —3B 84
Johnby. Cumb —1F 103
John o' Gaunts. W Yor —2D 92
John o' Groats. High —1F 169
John's Cross. E Sus —3B 28
Johnshaven. Aber —2G 145
Johnson's Street. Norf —4F 79
Johnston. Pemb —3D 42
Johnstone. Ren —3F 127
Johnstonebridge. Dum —5D 118
Johnstown. Carm —4D 45
Johnstown. Wrex —1F 71
Joppa. Edin —2G 129
Joppa. S Ayr —3D 116
Jordan Green. Norf —3C 78
Jordans. Buck —1A 38
Jordanston. Pemb —1D 42
Jump. S Yor —4D 93
Jumpers Common. Dors —3G 15
Juniper Green. Edin —3E 129
Jurby East. IOM —2C 108
Jurby West. IOM —2C 108

Kaber. Cumb —3A 104
Kaimend. S Lan —5C 128
Kaimes. Edin —3F 129
Kaimrig End. Scot —5D 129
Kames. Arg —2A 126
Kames. E Ayr —2F 117
Kea. Corn —4C 6
Keadby. N Lin —3B 94
Keal Cotes. Linc —4C 88
Kearsley. G Man —4F 91
Kearsney. Kent —1G 29
Kearstwick. Cumb —1F 97
Kearton. N Yor —5C 104
Kearvaig. High —1C 166
Keasden. N Yor —3G 97
Keason. Corn —2H 7
Keckwick. Hal —2H 83
Keddington. Linc —2C 88
Keddington Corner. Linc —2C 88
Kedington. Suff —1H 53
Kedleston. Derbs —1H 73
Kedlock Feus. Fife —2F 137
Keelby. Linc —4E 95
Keele. Staf —1C 72
Keeley Green. Beds —1A 52
Keeston. Pemb —3D 42
Keevil. Wilts —1E 23
Kegworth. Leics —3B 74
Kehelland. Corn —2D 4
Keig. Aber —2D 152
Keighley. W Yor —5C 98
Keilarsbrae. Clac —4A 136
Keillmore. Arg —1E 125
Keillor. Per —4B 144
Keillour. Per —1B 136
Keiloch. Aber —4F 151
Keils. Arg —3D 124
Keinton Mandeville. Som —3A 22
Keir Mill. Dum —5A 118
Keirsleywell Row. Nmbd —4A 114
Keisby. Linc —3H 75
Keisley. Cumb —2A 104
Keiss. High —2F 169
Keith. Mor —3B 160
Keith Inch. Aber —4H 161
Kelbrook. Lanc —5B 98
Kelby. Linc —1H 75
Keld. Cumb —3G 103
Keld. N Yor —4B 104
Keldholme. N Yor —1B 100
Kelfield. N Lin —4B 94
Kelfield. N Yor —1F 93
Kelham. Notts —5E 87
Kellacott. Devn —4E 11
Kellan. Arg —4G 139
Kellas. Ang —5D 144
Kellas. Mor —3F 159
Kellaton. Devn —5E 9
Kelleth. Cumb —4H 103
Kelling. Norf —1C 78
Kellingley. N Yor —2F 93
Kellington. N Yor —2F 93
Kelloe. Dur —1A 106
Kelloholm. Dum —3G 117
Kells. Cumb —3A 102
Kelly. Devn —4D 11
Kelly Bray. Corn —5D 10
Kelmarsh. Nptn —3E 63
Kelmscott. Oxon —2H 35
Kelsale. Suff —4F 67
Kelsall. Ches —4H 83
Kelshall. Herts —2D 52
Kelsick. Cumb —4C 112
Kelso. Scot —1B 120
Kelstedge. Derbs —4H 85
Kelstern. Linc —1B 88
Kelsterton. Flin —3E 83
Kelston. Bath —5C 34
Keltneyburn. Per —4E 143
Kelton. Dum —2A 112
Kelton Hill. Dum —4E 111
Kelty. Fife —4D 136
Kelvedon. Essx —4B 54
Kelvedon Hatch. Essx —1G 39
Kelvinside. Glas —3G 127
Kelynack. Corn —3A 4
Kemback. Fife —2G 137
Kemberton. Shrp —5B 72
Kemble. Glos —2E 35
Kemerton. Worc —2E 49
Kemeys Commander. Mon —5G 47
Kemnay. Aber —2E 153
Kempley. Glos —3B 48
Kempley Green. Glos —3B 48
Kempsey. Worc —1D 48
Kempsford. Glos —2G 35
Kemps Green. Warw —3F 61
Kempshott. Hants —1E 24
Kempston. Beds —1A 52
Kempston Hardwick. Beds —1A 52
Kempton. Shrp —2F 59
Kemp Town. Brig —5E 27
Kemsing. Kent —5G 39
Kemsley. Kent —4D 40
Kenardington. Kent —2D 28
Kenchester. Here —1H 47
Kencot. Oxon —5A 50
Kendal. Cumb —5G 103
Kendleshire. S Glo —4B 34
Kendray. S Yor —4D 92
Kenfig. B'End —3B 32
Kenfig Hill. B'End —3B 32
Kengharair. Arg —4F 139
Kenidjack. Corn —3A 4
Kenilworth. Warw —3G 61
Kenknock. Stir —5B 142
Kenley. Shrp —5H 71
Kenmore. High —3G 155
Kenmore. Per —4E 143
Kenn. Devn —4C 12
Kenn. N Som —5H 33
Kennacraig. Arg —3G 125
Kenneggy Downs. Corn —4C 4
Kennerleigh. Devn —2B 12
Kennet. Clac —4B 136
Kennethmont. Aber —1C 152
Kennett. Cambs —4F 65
Kennford. Devn —4C 12
Kenninghall. Norf —2C 66
Kennington. Kent —1E 29
Kennington. Oxon —5D 50
Kennoway. Fife —3F 137
Kennyhill. Suff —3F 65
Kennythorpe. N Yor —3B 100
Kenovay. Arg —4A 138
Kensaleyre. High —3D 154
Kensington. G Lon —3D 38
Kenstone. Shrp —3H 71
Kensworth. Beds —4A 52
Kensworth Common. Beds —4A 52
Kentallen. High —3E 141
Kentchurch. Here —3H 47
Kentford. Suff —4G 65
Kentisbeare. Devn —2D 12
Kentisbury. Devn —2G 19
Kentisbury Ford. Devn —2G 19
Kentmere. Cumb —4F 103
Kenton. Devn —4C 12
Kenton. G Lon —2C 38
Kenton. Suff —4D 66
Kenton Bankfoot. Tyne —3F 115
Kentra. High —2A 140
Kentrigg. Cumb —5G 103
Kents Bank. Cumb —2C 96
Kent's Green. Glos —3C 48
Kent's Oak. Hants —4B 24
Kent Street. E Sus —4B 28
Kent Street. Kent —5A 40
Kent Street. W Sus —3D 26
Kenwick. Shrp —2G 71
Kenwyn. Corn —4C 6
Kenyon. Warr —1A 84
Keoldale. High —2D 166
Keppoch. High —1B 148
Kepwick. N Yor —5B 106
Keresley. W Mid —2H 61
Keresley Newlands. W Mid —2H 61
Keristal. IOM —4C 108
Kerne Bridge. Here —4A 48
Kerridge. Ches —3D 84
Kerris. Corn —4B 4
Kerrow. High —5F 157
Kerry. Powy —2D 58
Kerrycroy. Arg —3C 126
Kerry's Gate. Here —2G 47
Kersall. Notts —4E 86
Kersbrook. Devn —4D 12
Kerse. Ren —4E 127
Kersey. Suff —1D 54
Kershopefoot. Cumb —1F 113
Kersoe. Worc —2E 49
Kerswell. Devn —2D 12
Kerswell Green. Worc —1D 48
Kesgrave. Suff —1F 55
Kessingland. Suff —2H 67
Kessingland Beach. Suff —2H 67
Kestle. Corn —4D 6
Kestle Mill. Corn —3C 6
Keston. G Lon —4F 39
Keswick. Cumb —2D 102
Keswick. Norf —2F 79 (nr. North Walsham)
Keswick. Norf —5E 78 (nr. Norwich)
Ketsby. Linc —3C 88
Kettering. Nptn —3F 63
Ketteringham. Norf —5D 78
Kettins. Per —5B 144
Kettlebaston. Suff —5B 66
Kettlebridge. Fife —3F 137
Kettlebrook. Staf —5G 73
Kettleburgh. Suff —4E 67
Kettleholm. Dum —2C 112
Kettleness. N Yor —3F 107
Kettleshulme. Ches —3D 85
Kettlesing. N Yor —4E 99
Kettlesing Bottom. N Yor —4E 99
Kettlestone. Norf —2B 78
Kettlethorpe. Linc —3F 87
Kettletoft. Orkn —4F 172
Kettlewell. N Yor —2B 98
Ketton. Rut —5G 75
Kew. G Lon —3C 38
Kewaigue. IOM —4C 108
Kewstoke. N Som —5G 33
Kexbrough. S Yor —4D 92
Kexby. Linc —2F 87
Kexby. York —4B 100
Keyford. Som —2C 22
Key Green. Ches —4C 84
Key Green. N Yor —4F 107
Keyham. Leics —5D 74
Keyhaven. Hants —3B 16
Keyhead. Aber —3H 161
Keyingham. E Yor —2F 95
Keymer. W Sus —4E 27
Keynsham. Bath —5B 34
Keysoe. Beds —4H 63
Keysoe Row. Beds —4H 63
Key's Toft. Linc —5D 89
Keyston. Cambs —3H 63
Key Street. Kent —4C 40
Keyworth. Notts —2D 74

Knapton—Lenwade

Knapton. York —4H 99
Knapton Green. Here —5G 59
Knapwell. Cambs —4C 64
Knaresborough. N Yor —4F 99
Knarsdale. Nmbd —4H 113
Knatts Valley. Kent —4G 39
Knaven. Aber —4F 161
Knayton. N Yor —1G 99
Knebworth. Herts —3C 52
Knedlington. E Yor —2H 93
Kneesall. Notts —4E 86
Kneesworth. Cambs —1D 52
Kneeton. Notts —1E 74
Knelston. Swan —4D 30
Knenhall. Staf —2D 72
Knightacott. Devn —3G 19
Knightcote. Warw —5B 62
Knightcott. N Som —1G 21
Knightley. Staf —3C 72
Knightley Dale. Staf —3C 72
Knightlow Hill. Warw —3B 62
Knighton. Devn —4B 8
Knighton. Dors —1B 14
Knighton. Leic C —5D 74
Knighton. Powy —3E 59
Knighton. Som —2E 21
Knighton. Staf —3B 72
Knighton. Wilts —4A 36
Knighton. Worc —5E 61
Knighton Common. Worc —3A 60
Knight's End. Cambs —1D 64
Knightswood. Glas —3G 127
Knightwick. Worc —5B 60
Knill. Here —4E 59
Knipton. Leics —2F 75
Knitsley. Dur —5E 115
Kniveton. Derbs —5G 85
Knock. Arg —5G 139
Knock. Cumb —2H 103
Knock. Mor —3C 160
Knockally. High —5D 168
Knockan. Arg —1B 132
Knockan. High —2G 163
Knockandhu. Mor —1G 151
Knockando. Mor —4F 159
Knockarthur. High —3E 165
Knockbain. High —3A 158
Knockbreck. High —2B 154
Knockdee. High —2D 168
Knockdolian. S Ayr —1G 109
Knockdon. S Ayr —3C 116
Knockdown. Wilts —3D 34
Knockenbaird. Aber —1D 152
Knockenkelly. N Ayr —3E 123
Knockentiber. E Ayr —1C 116
Knockfarrel. High —3H 157
Knockglass. High —2C 168
Knockholt. Kent —5F 39
Knockholt Pound. Kent —5F 39
Knockie Lodge. High —2G 149
Knockin. Shrp —3F 71
Knockinlaw. E Ayr —1D 116
Knockinnon. High —5D 169
Knockrome. Arg —2D 124
Knocksharry. IOM —3B 108
Knockvennie. Dum —2E 111
Knodishall. Suff —4G 67
Knole. Som —4H 21
Knollbury. Mon —3H 33
Knolls Green. Ches —3C 84
Knolton. Wrex —2F 71
Knook. Wilts —2E 23
Knossington. Leics —5F 75
Knott. High —3C 154
Knott End-on-Sea. Lanc —5C 96
Knotting. Beds —4H 63
Knotting Green. Beds —4H 63
Knottingley. W Yor —2E 93
Knotts. Cumb —2F 103
Knotty Ash. Mers —1G 83
Knotty Green. Buck —1A 38
Knowbury. Shrp —3H 59
Knowe. Dum —2A 110
Knowefield. Cumb —4F 113
Knowehead. Dum —5F 117
Knowes. E Lot —2C 130
Knowesgate. Nmbd —1C 114
Knoweside. S Ayr —3B 116
Knowle. Bris —4B 34
Knowle. Devn —3E 19
(nr. Braunton)
Knowle. Devn —4D 12
(nr. Budleigh Salterton)
Knowle. Devn —2A 12
(nr. Crediton)
Knowle. Shrp —3H 59
Knowle. W Mid —3F 61
Knowle Green. Lanc —1E 91
Knowle St Giles. Som —1G 13
Knowl Hill. Wind —4G 37
Knowlton. Kent —5G 41
Knowsley. Mers —1G 83
Knowstone. Devn —4B 20
Knucklas. Powy —3E 59
Knuston. Nptn —4G 63
Knutsford. Ches —3B 84
Knypersley. Staf —5C 84
Krumlin. W Yor —3A 92
Kuggar. Corn —5E 5
Kyleakin. High —1F 147
Kyle of Lochalsh. High —1F 147
Kylerhea. High —1F 147
Kylesku. High —5C 166
Kyles Lodge. W Isl —9B 171
Kylesmorar. High —4G 147
Kylestrome. High —5C 166
Kymin. Mon —4A 48
Kynaston. Here —2B 48
Kynaston. Shrp —3F 71
Kynnersley. Telf —4A 72
Kyre Green. Worc —4A 60
Kyre Park. Worc —4A 60
Kyrewood. Worc —4A 60
Kyrle. Som —4D 20

Labost. W Isl —3E 171
Lacasaigh. W Isl —5F 171
Lacasdail. W Isl —4G 171
Laceby. NE Lin —4F 95
Lacey Green. Buck —5G 51
Lach Dennis. Ches —3B 84
Lache. Ches —4F 83
Lackford. Suff —3G 65
Lacock. Wilts —5E 35
Ladbroke. Warw —5B 62
Laddingford. Kent —1A 28
Lade Bank. Linc —5C 88
Ladock. Corn —3C 6
Ladybank. Fife —2F 137
Ladycross. Corn —4D 10
Lady Green. Mers —4B 90
Lady Hall. Cumb —1A 96
Ladykirk. Scot —5E 131
Ladysford. Aber —2G 161
Ladywood. W Mid —2E 61
Ladywood. Worc —4C 60
Laga. High —2A 140
Lagavulin. Arg —5C 124
Lagg. Arg —2D 125
Lagg. N Ayr —3D 122
Laggan. Arg —4A 124
Laggan. High —4E 149
(nr. Fort Augustus)
Laggan. High —4A 150
(nr. Newtonmore)
Laggan. Mor —5H 159
Lagganlia. High —3C 150
Laglingarten. Arg —3A 134
Lagness. W Sus —2G 17
Laid. High —3E 166
Laide. High —4D 162
Laigh Fenwick. E Ayr —5F 127
Laindon. Essx —2A 40
Lairg. High —3C 164
Lairg Muir. High —3C 164
Laithes. Cumb —1F 103
Laithkirk. Dur —2C 104
Lake. Devn —3F 19
Lake. IOW —4D 16
Lake. Wilts —3G 23
Lakenham. Norf —5E 79
Lakenheath. Suff —2G 65
Lakesend. Norf —1E 65
Lakeside. Cumb —1C 96
Laleham. Surr —4B 38
Laleston. B'End —3B 32
Lamancha. Scot —4E 129
Lamarsh. Essx —2B 54
Lamas. Norf —3E 79
Lamb Corner. Essx —2D 54
Lambden. Scot —5D 130
Lamberhead Green. G Man —4D 90
Lamberhurst. Kent —2A 28
Lamberhurst Quarter. Kent —2A 28
Lamberton. Scot —4F 131
Lambeth. G Lon —3E 39
Lambfell Moar. IOM —3B 108
Lambhill. Glas —3G 127
Lambley. Nmbd —4H 113
Lambley. Notts —1D 74
Lambourn. W Ber —4B 36
Lambourne End. Essx —1F 39
Lambourn Woodlands. W Ber —4B 36
Lambrook. Som —4F 21
Lambs Green. Dors —3E 15
Lambs Green. W Sus —2D 26
Lambston. Pemb —3D 42
Lamellion. Corn —2G 7
Lamerton. Devn —5E 11
Lamesley. Tyne —4F 115
Laminess. Orkn —4F 172
Lamington. High —1B 158
Lamington. S Lan —1B 118
Lamlash. N Ayr —2E 123
Lamonby. Cumb —1F 103
Lamorick. Corn —2E 7
Lamorna. Corn —4B 4
Lamorran. Corn —4C 6
Lampeter. Cdgn —1F 45
Lampeter Velfrey. Pemb —3F 43
Lamphey. Pemb —4E 43
Lamplugh. Cumb —2B 102
Lamport. Nptn —3E 63
Lamyatt. Som —3B 22
Lana. Devn —3D 10
(nr. Ashwater)
Lana. Devn —2D 10
(nr. Holsworthy)
Lanark. S Lan —5B 128
Lanarth. Corn —4E 5
Lancaster. Lanc —3D 97
Lanchester. Dur —5E 115
Lancing. W Sus —5C 26
Landbeach. Cambs —4D 64
Landcross. Devn —4E 19
Landerberry. Aber —3E 153
Landewednack. Corn —5E 5
Landford. Wilts —1A 16
Land Gate. G Man —4D 90
Landhallow. High —5D 169
Landimore. Swan —3D 30
Landkey. Devn —3F 19
Landkey Newland. Devn —3F 19
Landore. Swan —3F 31
Landport. Port —2E 17
Landrake. Corn —2H 7
Landscove. Devn —2D 9
Lands End (St Just) Airport. Corn —4A 4
Landshipping. Pemb —3E 43
Landulph. Corn —2A 8
Landywood. Staf —5D 73
Lane. Corn —2C 6
Laneast. Corn —4C 10
Lane Bottom. Lanc —1G 91
Lane End. Buck —2G 37
Lane End. Cumb —5C 102
Lane End. Hants —4D 24
Lane End. IOW —4E 17
Lane End. Wilts —2D 22
Lane Ends. Derbs —2G 73
Lane Ends. Dur —1E 105
Lane Ends. Lanc —4G 97
Laneham. Notts —3F 87
Lanehead. Dur —5B 114
(nr. Cowshill)
Lane Head. Dur —3E 105
(nr. Hutton Magna)
Lane Head. Dur —2D 105
(nr. Woodland)
Lane Head. G Man —1A 84
Lanehead. Nmbd —1A 114
Lane Head. W Yor —4B 92
Lane Heads. Lanc —1C 90
Lanercost. Cumb —3G 113
Laneshaw Bridge. Lanc —5B 98
Laney Green. Staf —5D 72
Langais. W Isl —2D 170
Langal. High —2B 140
Langar. Notts —2E 74
Langbank. Ren —2E 127
Langbar. N Yor —4C 98
Langburnshiels. Scot —4H 119
Langcliffe. N Yor —3H 97
Langdale End. N Yor —5G 107
Langdon. Corn —3C 10
Langdon Beck. Dur —1B 104
Langdon Cross. Corn —4D 10
Langdon Hills. Essx —2A 40
Langdown. Hants —2C 16
Langdyke. Fife —3F 137
Langenhoe. Essx —4D 54
Langford. Beds —1B 52
Langford. Devn —2D 12
Langford. Essx —5B 54
Langford. Notts —5F 87
Langford. Oxon —5H 49
Langford Budville. Som —4E 20
Langham. Dors —4C 22
Langham. Essx —2D 54
Langham. Norf —1C 78
Langham. Rut —4F 75
Langham. Suff —4B 66
Langho. Lanc —1F 91
Langholm. Dum —1E 113
Langland. Swan —4F 31
Langleeford. Nmbd —2D 120
Langley. Ches —3D 84
Langley. Derbs —1B 74
Langley. Essx —2E 53
Langley. Glos —3F 49
Langley. Hants —2C 16
Langley. Herts —3C 52
Langley. Kent —5C 40
Langley. Nmbd —3B 114
Langley. Som —4D 20
Langley. Warw —4F 61
Langley. W Sus —4G 25
Langley. Wind —3B 38
Langley Burrell. Wilts —4E 35
Langleybury. Herts —5A 52
Langley Common. Derbs —2G 73
Langley Green. Derbs —2G 73
Langley Green. Norf —5F 79
Langley Green. Warw —4F 61
Langley Green. W Sus —2D 26
Langley Heath. Kent —5C 40
Langley Marsh. Som —4D 20
Langley Moor. Dur —5F 115
Langley Park. Dur —5F 115
Langley Street. Norf —5F 79
Langney. E Sus —5H 27
Langold. Notts —2C 86
Langore. Corn —4D 10
Langport. Som —4H 21
Langrick. Linc —1B 76
Langridge. Bath —5C 34
Langridgeford. Devn —4F 19
Langrigg. Cumb —5C 112
Langrish. Hants —4F 25
Langsett. S Yor —4C 92
Langshaw. Scot —1H 119
Langstone. Hants —2F 17
Langthorne. N Yor —5F 105
Langthorpe. N Yor —3F 99
Langthwaite. N Yor —4D 104
Langtoft. E Yor —3E 101
Langtoft. Linc —4A 76
Langton. Dur —3E 105
Langton. Linc —4B 88
(nr. Horncastle)
Langton. Linc —3C 88
(nr. Spilsby)
Langton. N Yor —3B 100
Langton by Wragby. Linc —3A 88
Langton Green. Kent —2G 27
Langton Herring. Dors —4B 14
Langton Long Blandford. Dors —2E 15
Langton Matravers. Dors —5F 15
Langtree. Devn —1E 11
Langwathby. Cumb —1G 103
Langwith. Derbs —3C 86
Langworth. Linc —3H 87
Lanivet. Corn —2E 7
Lanjeth. Corn —3D 6
Lank. Corn —5A 10
Lanlivery. Corn —3E 7
Lanner. Corn —5B 6
Lanreath. Corn —3F 7
Lansallos. Corn —3F 7
Lansdown. Glos —3E 49
Lanteglos Highway. Corn —3F 7
Lanton. Nmbd —1D 120
Lanton. Scot —2A 120
Lapford. Devn —2H 11
Laphroaig. Arg —5B 124
Lapley. Staf —4C 72
Lapworth. Warw —3F 61
Larachbeg. High —4A 140
Larbert. Falk —1B 128
Larden Green. Ches —5H 83
Larel. High —3D 169
Largie. Aber —5D 160
Largiemore. Arg —1H 125
Largoward. Fife —3G 137
Largs. N Ayr —4D 126
Largybeg. N Ayr —3E 123
Largymeanoch. N Ayr —3E 123
Largymore. N Ayr —3E 123
Larkfield. Inv —2D 126
Larkfield. Kent —5A 40
Larkhall. Bath —5C 34
Larkhall. S Lan —4A 128
Larkhill. Wilts —2G 23
Larling. Norf —2B 66
Larport. Here —2A 48
Lartington. Dur —3D 104
Lary. Aber —3H 151
Lasham. Hants —2E 25
Lashenden. Kent —1C 28
Lassodie. Fife —4D 136
Lastingham. N Yor —5E 107
Latchford. Herts —3D 53
Latchford. Oxon —5E 51
Latchingdon. Essx —5B 54
Latchley. Corn —5E 11
Latchmere Green. Hants —5E 37
Latham. Lanc —4C 90
Lathbury. Mil —1G 51
Latheron. High —5D 169
Latheronwheel. High —5D 169
Lathom. Lanc —4C 90
Lathones. Fife —3G 137
Latimer. Buck —1B 38
Latteridge. S Glo —3B 34
Lattiford. Som —4B 22
Latton. Wilts —2F 35
Laudale House. High —3B 140
Lauder. Scot —5B 130
Laugharne. Carm —3H 43
Laughterton. Linc —3F 87
Laughton. E Sus —4G 27
Laughton. Leics —2D 62
Laughton. Linc —1F 87
(nr. Gainsborough)
Laughton. Linc —2H 75
(nr. Grantham)
Laughton Common. S Yor —2C 86
Laughton en le Morthen. S Yor —2C 86
Launcells. Corn —2C 10
Launceston. Corn —4D 10
Launcherley. Som —2A 22
Launton. Oxon —3E 50
Laurencekirk. Aber —1G 145
Laurieston. Dum —3D 111
Laurieston. Falk —2C 128
Lavendon. Mil —5G 63
Lavenham. Suff —1C 54
Laverburgh. W Isl —9C 171
Laverhay. Dum —5D 118
Laversdale. Cumb —3F 113
Laverstock. Wilts —3G 23
Laverstoke. Hants —2C 24
Laverton. Glos —2F 49
Laverton. N Yor —2E 99
Laverton. Som —1C 22
Lavister. Wrex —5F 83
Law. S Lan —4B 128
Lawers. Per —5D 142
Lawford. Essx —2D 54
Lawhitton. Corn —4D 10
Lawkland. N Yor —3G 97
Lawnhead. Staf —3C 72
Lawrenny. Pemb —4E 43
Lawshall. Suff —5A 66
Lawton. Here —5G 59
Laxey. IOM —3D 108
Laxfield. Suff —3E 67
Laxfirth. Shet —6F 173
Laxo. Shet —5F 173
Laxton. E Yor —2A 94
Laxton. Nptn —1G 63
Laxton. Notts —4E 86
Laycock. W Yor —5C 98
Layer Breton. Essx —4C 54
Layer-de-la-Haye. Essx —3C 54
Layer Marney. Essx —4C 54
Layland's Green. W Ber —5B 36
Laymore. Dors —2G 13
Laysters Pole. Here —4H 59
Layter's Green. Buck —1A 38
Laytham. E Yor —1H 93
Lazenby. Red C —3C 106
Lazonby. Cumb —1G 103
Lea. Derbs —5H 85
Lea. Here —3B 48
Lea. Linc —2F 87
Lea. Shrp —2F 59
(nr. Bishop's Castle)
Lea. Shrp —5G 71
(nr. Shrewsbury)
Lea. Wilts —3E 35
Leabrooks. Derbs —5B 86
Leac a Li. W Isl —8D 171
Leachd. Arg —4H 133
Leachkin. High —4A 158
Leachpool. Pemb —3D 42
Leadburn. Midl —4F 129
Leadenham. Linc —5G 87
Leaden Roding. Essx —4F 53
Leaderfoot. Scot —1H 119
Leadgate. Cumb —5A 114
Leadgate. Dur —4E 115
Leadgate. Nmbd —4E 115
Leadhills. S Lan —3A 118
Leadingcross Green. Kent —5C 40
Lea End. Worc —3E 61
Leafield. Oxon —4B 50
Leagrave. Lutn —3A 52
Lea Hall. W Mid —2F 61
Lea Heath. Staf —3E 73
Leake. N Yor —5B 106
Leake Common Side. Linc —5C 88
Leake Fold Hill. Linc —5D 88
Leake Hurn's End. Linc —1D 76
Lealholm. N Yor —4E 107
Lealt. Arg —4D 132
Lealt. High —2E 155
Leam. Derbs —3G 85
Lea Marston. Warw —1G 61
Leamington Hastings. Warw —4B 62
Leamington Spa, Royal. Warw —4H 61
Leamonsley. Staf —5F 73
Leamside. Dur —5G 115
Leargybreck. Arg —2D 124
Lease Rigg. N Yor —4F 107
Leasgill. Cumb —1D 97
Leasingham. Linc —1H 75
Leasingthorne. Dur —2F 105
Leasowe. Mers —1E 83
Leatherhead. Surr —5C 38
Leathley. N Yor —5E 99
Leaths. Dum —3E 111
Leaton. Shrp —4G 71
Lea Town. Lanc —1C 90
Leaveland. Kent —5E 40
Leavenheath. Suff —2C 54
Leavening. N Yor —3B 100
Leaves Green. G Lon —4F 39
Lea Yeat. Cumb —1G 97
Leazes. Dur —4E 115
Lebberston. N Yor —1E 101
Lechlade on Thames. Glos —2H 35
Leck. Lanc —2F 97
Leckford. Hants —3B 24
Leckfurin. High —3H 167
Leckgruinart. Arg —3A 124
Leckhampstead. Buck —2F 51
Leckhampstead. W Ber —4C 36
Leckhampstead Street. W Ber —4C 36
Leckhampton. Glos —4E 49
Leckmelm. High —4F 163
Leckwith. V Glam —4E 33
Leconfield. E Yor —5E 101
Ledaig. Arg —5D 140
Ledburn. Buck —3H 51
Ledbury. Here —2C 48
Ledgemoor. Here —5G 59
Ledgowan. High —3D 156
Ledicot. Here —4G 59
Ledmore. High —2G 163
Lednabirichen. High —4E 165
Lednagullin. High —2A 168
Ledsham. Ches —3F 83
Ledsham. W Yor —2E 93
Ledston. W Yor —2E 93
Ledstone. Devn —4D 8
Ledwell. Oxon —3C 50
Lee. Devn —2E 19
(nr. Ilfracombe)
Lee. Devn —4B 20
(nr. South Molton)
Lee. G Lon —3F 39
Lee. Hants —1B 16
Lee. Lanc —4E 97
Lee. Shrp —2G 71
Leeans. Shet —7E 173
Leebotten. Shet —9F 173
Leebotwood. Shrp —1G 59
Lee Brockhurst. Shrp —3H 71
Leece. Cumb —3B 96
Leechpool. Mon —3A 34
Lee Clump. Buck —5H 51
Leeds. Kent —5C 40
Leeds. W Yor —1C 92
Leeds & Bradford Airport. W Yor —5E 98
Leedstown. Corn —3D 4
Leegomery. Telf —4A 72
Lee Head. Derbs —1E 85
Leek. Staf —5D 85
Leekbrook. Staf —5D 85
Leek Wootton. Warw —4G 61
Lee Mill. Devn —3B 8
Leeming. N Yor —1E 99
Leeming Bar. N Yor —5F 105
Lee Moor. Devn —2B 8
Lee Moor. W Yor —2D 92
Lee-on-the-Solent. Hants —2D 16
Lees. Derbs —2G 73
Lees. G Man —4H 91
Lees. W Yor —1A 92
Lees, The. Kent —5E 40
Leeswood. Flin —5E 83
Lee, The. Buck —5H 51
Leetown. Per —1E 136
Leftwich. Ches —3A 84
Legate. E Ayr —3F 117
Legbourne. Linc —2C 88
Legburthwaite. Cumb —3E 102
Legerwood. Scot —5B 130
Legsby. Linc —2A 88
Leicester. Leic C —5C 74
Leicester Forest East. Leics —5C 74
Leigh. Dors —2B 14
Leigh. G Man —4E 91
Leigh. Kent —1G 27
Leigh. Shrp —5F 71
Leigh. Surr —1D 26
Leigh. Wilts —2F 35
Leigh. Worc —5B 60
Leigham. Plym —3B 8
Leigh Beck. Essx —2C 40
Leigh Common. Som —3C 22
Leigh Delamere. Wilts —4D 35
Leigh Green. Kent —2D 28
Leighland Chapel. Som —3D 20
Leigh-on-Sea. S'end —2C 40
Leigh Park. Hants —2F 17
Leigh Sinton. Worc —5B 60
Leighterton. Glos —2D 34
Leigh, The. Glos —3D 48
Leighton. N Yor —2D 98
Leighton. Powy —5E 71
Leighton. Shrp —5A 72
Leighton. Som —2C 22
Leighton Bromswold. Cambs —3A 64
Leighton Buzzard. Beds —3H 51
Leigh-upon-Mendip. Som —2B 22
Leinthall Earls. Here —4G 59
Leinthall Starkes. Here —4G 59
Leintwardine. Here —3G 59
Leire. Leics —1C 62
Leirinmore. High —2E 166
Leishmore. High —4G 157
Leiston. Suff —4G 67
Leitfie. Per —4B 144
Leith. Edin —2F 129
Leitholm. Scot —5D 130
Lelant. Corn —3C 4
Lelant Downs. Corn —3C 4
Lelley. E Yor —1F 95
Lem Hill. Worc —3B 60
Lemington. Tyne —3E 115
Lemmington Hall. Nmbd —3F 121
Lempitlaw. Scot —1B 120
Lemsford. Herts —4C 52
Lenacre. Cumb —1F 97
Lenchie. Aber —5C 160
Lenchwick. Worc —1F 49
Lendalfoot. S Ayr —5A 116
Lendrick. Stir —3E 135
Lenham. Kent —5C 40
Lenham Heath. Kent —1D 28
Lenimore. N Ayr —5G 125
Lennel. Scot —5E 131
Lennoxtown. E Dun —2H 127
Lenton. Linc —2H 75
Lenton. Not C —2C 74
Lentran. High —4H 157
Lenwade. Norf —4C 78

Lenzie—Llanbedr

Lenzie. E Dun —2H 127
Leochel Cushnie. Aber —2C 152
Leogh. Shet —1B 172
Leominster. Here —5G 59
Leonard Stanley. Glos —5D 48
Lepe. Hants —3C 16
Lephenstrath. Arg —5A 122
Lephin. High —4A 154
Lephinchapel. Arg —4G 133
Lephinmore. Arg —4G 133
Leppington. N Yor —3B 100
Lepton. W Yor —3C 92
Lerryn. Corn —3F 7
Lerwick. Shet —7F 173
Lerwick Airport. Shet —7F 173
Lesbury. Nmbd —3G 121
Leslie. Aber —1C 152
Leslie. Fife —3E 137
Lesmahagow. S Lan —1H 117
Lesnewth. Corn —3B 10
Lessingham. Norf —3F 79
Lessonhall. Cumb —4D 112
Leswalt. Dum —3F 109
Letchmore Heath. Herts —1C 38
Letchworth. Herts —2C 52
Letcombe Bassett. Oxon —3B 36
Letcombe Regis. Oxon —3B 36
Letham. Ang —4E 145
Letham. Falk —1B 128
Letham. Fife —2F 137
Lethanhill. E Ayr —3D 116
Lethenty. Aber —4F 161
Letheringham. Suff —5E 67
Letheringsett. Norf —2C 78
Lettaford. Devn —4H 11
Lettan. Orkn —3G 172
Letter. Aber —2E 153
Letterewe. High —1B 156
Letterfearn. High —1A 148
Lettermore. Arg —4F 139
Letters. High —5F 163
Letterston. Pemb —2D 42
Letton. Here —1G 47
(nr. Kington)
Letton. Here —3F 59
(nr. Leintwardine)
Letty Green. Herts —4C 52
Letwell. S Yor —2C 86
Leuchars. Fife —1G 137
Leumrabhagh. W Isl —6F 171
Leusdon. Devn —5H 11
Levaneap. Shet —5F 173
Levedale. Staf —4C 72
Leven. E Yor —5F 101
Leven. Fife —3F 137
Levencorroch. N Ayr —3E 123
Levenhall. E Lot —2G 129
Levens. Cumb —1D 97
Levens Green. Herts —3D 52
Levenshulme. G Man —1C 84
Levenwick. Shet —9F 173
Leverington. Cambs —4D 76
Leverton. Linc —1D 76
Leverton. W Ber —4B 36
Leverton Lucasgate. Linc —1D 76
Leverton Outgate. Linc —1D 76
Levington. Suff —2F 55
Levisham. N Yor —5F 107
Levishie. High —2G 149
Lew. Oxon —5B 50
Lewaigue. IOM —2D 108
Lewannick. Corn —4C 10
Lewdown. Devn —4E 11
Lewes. E Sus —4F 27
Leweston. Pemb —2D 42
Lewisham. G Lon —3E 39
Lewiston. High —1H 149
Lewistown. B'End —3C 32
Lewknor. Oxon —2F 37
Leworthy. Devn —3G 19
(nr. Barnstaple)
Leworthy. Devn —2D 10
(nr. Holsworthy)
Lewson Street. Kent —4D 40
Lewthorn Cross. Devn —5A 12
Lewtrenchard. Devn —4E 11
Ley. Corn —2F 7
Leybourne. Kent —5A 40
Leyburn. N Yor —5E 105
Leycett. Staf —1B 72
Leyfields. Staf —5G 73
Ley Green. Herts —3B 52
Ley Hill. Buck —5H 51
Leyland. Lanc —2D 90
Leylodge. Aber —2E 153
Leymoor. W Yor —3B 92
Leys. Per —5B 144
Leysdown-on-Sea. Kent —3E 41
Leysmill. Ang —4F 145
Leyton. G Lon —2E 39
Leytonstone. G Lon —2F 39
Lezant. Corn —5D 10
Leziate. Norf —4F 77
Lhanbryde. Mor —2G 159
Lhen, The. IOM —1C 108
Liatrie. High —5E 157
Libanus. Powy —3C 46
Libberton. S Lan —5C 128
Libbery. Worc —5D 60
Liberton. Edin —3F 129
Liceasto. W Isl —8D 171
Lichfield. Staf —5F 73
Lickey. Worc —3D 61
Lickey End. Worc —3D 61
Lickfold. W Sus —3A 26
Liddaton. Devn —4E 11
Liddel. Orkn —9D 172
Liddington. Swin —3H 35
Lidgate. Suff —5G 65
Lidgett. Notts —4D 86
Lidham Hill. E Sus —4C 28
Lidlington. Beds —2H 51
Lidsey. W Sus —5A 26
Lidstone. Oxon —3B 50
Lienassie. High —1B 148
Liff. Ang —5C 144
Lifford. W Mid —2E 61
Lifton. Devn —4D 11
Liftondown. Devn —4D 10
Lighthorne. Warw —5H 61
Light Oaks. Staf —1D 72
Lightwater. Surr —4A 38
Lightwood. Staf —1D 72
Lightwood. Stoke —1E 73
Lightwood Green. Ches —1A 72
Lightwood Green. Wrex —1F 71
Lilbourne. Nptn —3C 62
Lilburn Tower. Nmbd —2E 121
Lillesdon. Som —4G 21
Lilleshall. Telf —4B 72
Lilley. Herts —3B 52
Lilliesleaf. Scot —2H 119
Lillingstone Dayrell. Buck —2F 51
Lillingstone Lovell. Buck —1F 51
Lillington. Dors —1B 14
Lilstock. Som —2E 21
Lilybank. Inv —2E 126
Lilyhurst. Shrp —4B 72
Limbrick. Lanc —3E 90
Limbury. Lutn —3A 52
Limekilnburn. S Lan —4A 128
Lime Kiln Nook. Cumb —5E 113
Limekilns. Fife —1D 129
Limerigg. Falk —2B 128
Limestone Brae. Nmbd —5A 114
Lime Street. Worc —2D 48
Limington. Som —4A 22
Limpenhoe. Norf —5F 79
Limpley Stoke. Wilts —5C 34
Limpsfield. Surr —5E 39
Linburn. W Lot —3E 129
Linby. Notts —5C 86
Linchmere. W Sus —3G 25
Lincluden. Dum —2A 112
Lincoln. Linc —3G 87
Lincomb. Worc —4C 60
Lindale. Cumb —1D 96
Lindal in Furness. Cumb —2B 96
Lindean. Scot —1G 119
Linden. Glos —4D 48
Lindfield. W Sus —3E 27
Lindford. Hants —3G 25
Lindores. Fife —2E 137
Lindridge. Worc —4A 60
Lindsell. Essx —3G 53
Lindsey. Suff —1C 54
Lindsey Tye. Suff —1C 54
Linford. Hants —2G 15
Linford. Thur —3A 40
Lingague. IOM —4B 108
Lingdale. Red C —3D 106
Lingen. Here —4F 59
Lingfield. Surr —1E 27
Lingoed. Mon —4G 47
Lingreabhagh. W Isl —9C 171
Ling, The. Norf —1F 67
Lingwood. Norf —5F 79
Lingyclose Head. Cumb —4E 113
Linicro. High —2C 154
Linkend. Worc —2D 48
Linkenholt. Hants —1B 24
Linkinhorne. Corn —5D 10
Linklater. Orkn —9D 172
Linksness. Orkn —7B 172
(on Hoy)
Linksness. Orkn —6E 172
(on Mainland)
Linktown. Fife —4E 137
Linkwood. Mor —2G 159
Linley. Shrp —1F 59
(nr. Bishop's Castle)
Linley. Shrp —1A 60
(nr. Bridgnorth)
Linley Green. Here —5A 60
Linlithgow. W Lot —2C 128
Linlithgow Bridge. Falk —2C 128
Linneraineach. High —3F 163
Linshiels. Nmbd —4C 120
Linsiadar. W Isl —4E 171
Linsidemore. High —4C 164
Linslade. Beds —3H 51
Linstead Parva. Suff —3F 67
Linstock. Cumb —4F 113
Linthwaite. W Yor —3B 92
Lintlaw. Scot —4E 131
Lintmill. Mor —2C 160
Linton. Cambs —1F 53
Linton. Derbs —4G 73
Linton. Here —3B 48
Linton. Kent —5B 40
Linton. N Yor —3B 98
Linton. Scot —2B 120
Linton. W Yor —5F 99
Linton Colliery. Nmbd —5G 121
Linton Hill. Here —3B 48
Linton-on-Ouse. N Yor —3G 99
Lintzford. Tyne —4E 115
Lintzgarth. Dur —5C 114
Linwood. Hants —2G 15
Linwood. Linc —2A 88
Linwood. Ren —3F 127
Lionacleit. W Isl —4C 170
Lionacuidhe. W Isl —4C 170
Lional. W Isl —1H 171
Liphook. Hants —3G 25
Lipley. Shrp —2B 72
Lipyeate. Som —1B 22
Liquo. N Lan —4B 128
Liscard. Mers —1F 83
Liscombe. Som —3B 20
Liskeard. Corn —2G 7
Lisle Court. Hants —3B 16
Liss. Hants —4F 25
Lissett. E Yor —4F 101
Liss Forest. Hants —4F 25
Lissington. Linc —2A 88
Liston. Essx —1B 54
Lisvane. Card —3E 33
Liswerry. Newp —3G 33
Litcham. Norf —4A 78
Litchard. B'End —3C 32
Litchborough. Nptn —5D 62
Litchfield. Hants —1C 24
Litherland. Mers —1F 83
Litlington. Cambs —1D 52
Litlington. E Sus —5G 27
Littemill. Nmbd —3G 121
Litterty. Aber —3E 161
Little Abington. Cambs —1F 53
Little Addington. Nptn —3G 63
Little Airmyn. N Yor —2H 93
Little Alne. Warw —4F 61
Little Ardo. Aber —5F 161
Little Asby. Cumb —4H 103
Little Aston. Staf —5E 73
Little Ayton. N Yor —3C 106
Little Baddow. Essx —5A 54
Little Badminton. S Glo —3D 34
Little Ballinluig. Per —3G 143
Little Bampton. Cumb —4D 112
Little Bardfield. Essx —2G 53
Little Barford. Beds —5A 64
Little Barningham. Norf —2D 78
Little Barrington. Glos —4H 49
Little Barrow. Ches —4G 83
Little Barugh. N Yor —2B 100
Little Bavington. Nmbd —2C 114
Little Bealings. Suff —1F 55
Little Bedwyn. Wilts —5A 36
Little Bentley. Essx —3E 54
Little Billing. Nptn —4F 63
Little Billington. Beds —3H 51
Little Birch. Here —2A 48
Little Bispham. Bkpl —5C 96
Little Blakenham. Suff —1E 54
Little Blencow. Cumb —1F 103
Little Bognor. W Sus —3B 26
Little Bolas. Shrp —3A 72
Little Bollington. Ches —2B 84
Little Bookham. Surr —5C 38
Littleborough. Devn —1B 12
Littleborough. G Man —3H 91
Littleborough. Notts —2F 87
Littlebourne. Kent —5G 41
Little Bourton. Oxon —1C 50
Little Bowden. Leics —2E 63
Little Bradley. Suff —5F 65
Little Brampton. Shrp —2F 59
Little Brechin. Ang —2E 145
Littlebredy. Dors —4A 14
Little Brickhill. Buck —2H 51
Little Bridgeford. Staf —3C 72
Little Brington. Nptn —4D 62
Little Bromley. Essx —3D 54
Little Broughton. Cumb —1B 102
Little Budworth. Ches —4H 83
Little Burstead. Essx —1A 40
Little Burton. E Yor —5F 101
Littlebury. Essx —2F 53
Littlebury Green. Essx —2E 53
Little Bytham. Linc —4H 75
Little Canfield. Essx —3F 53
Little Canford. Dors —3F 15
Little Carlton. Linc —2C 88
Little Carlton. Notts —5E 87
Little Casterton. Rut —5H 75
Little Catwick. E Yor —5F 101
Little Catworth. Cambs —3A 64
Little Cawthorpe. Linc —2C 88
Little Chalfont. Buck —1A 38
Little Chart. Kent —1D 28
Little Chesterford. Essx —1F 53
Little Cheverell. Wilts —1E 23
Little Chishill. Cambs —2E 53
Little Clacton. Essx —4E 55
Little Clanfield. Oxon —5A 50
Little Clifton. Cumb —2B 102
Little Coates. NE Lin —4F 95
Little Comberton. Worc —1E 49
Little Common. E Sus —5B 28
Little Compton. Warw —2A 50
Little Cornard. Suff —2B 54
Littlecote. Buck —3G 51
Littlecott. Wilts —1G 23
Little Cowarne. Here —5A 60
Little Coxwell. Oxon —2A 36
Little Crakehall. N Yor —5F 105
Little Crawley. Mil —1H 51
Little Creich. High —5D 164
Little Cressingham. Norf —5A 78
Little Crosby. Mers —4B 90
Little Crosthwaite. Cumb —2D 102
Little Cubley. Derbs —2F 73
Little Dalby. Leics —4E 75
Little Dawley. Telf —5A 72
Littledean. Glos —4B 48
Little Dens. Aber —4H 161
Little Dewchurch. Here —2A 48
Little Ditton. Cambs —5F 65
Little Down. Hants —1B 24
Little Downham. Cambs —2E 65
Little Drayton. Shrp —2A 72
Little Driffield. E Yor —4E 101
Little Dunham. Norf —4A 78
Little Dunkeld. Per —4H 143
Little Dunmow. Essx —3G 53
Little Easton. Essx —3G 53
Little Eaton. Derbs —1A 74
Little Eccleston. Lanc —5D 96
Little Ellingham. Norf —1C 66
Little Elm. Som —2C 22
Little End. Essx —5F 53
Little Everdon. Nptn —5C 62
Little Eversden. Cambs —5C 64
Little Faringdon. Oxon —5H 49
Little Fencote. N Yor —5F 105
Little Fenton. N Yor —1F 93
Littleferry. High —4F 165
Little Fransham. Norf —4B 78
Little Gaddesden. Herts —4H 51
Little Garway. Here —3H 47
Little Gidding. Cambs —2A 64
Little Glemham. Suff —5F 67
Little Glenshee. Per —5G 143
Little Gransden. Cambs —5B 64
Little Green. Wrex —1G 71
Little Grimsby. Linc —1C 88
Little Habton. N Yor —2B 100
Little Hadham. Herts —3E 53
Little Hale. Linc —1A 76
Little Hallingbury. Essx —4E 53
Littleham. Devn —4E 19
(nr. Bideford)
Littleham. Devn —4D 12
(nr. Exmouth)
Little Hampden. Buck —5G 51
Littlehampton. W Sus —5B 26
Little Haresfield. Glos —5D 48
Little Harrowden. Nptn —3F 63
Little Haseley. Oxon —5E 51
Little Hatfield. E Yor —5F 101
Little Hautbois. Norf —3E 79
Little Haven. Pemb —3C 42
Little Hay. Staf —5F 73
Little Hayfield. Derbs —2E 85
Little Haywood. Staf —3E 73
Little Heath. W Mid —2H 61
Little Heck. N Yor —2F 93
Littlehempston. Devn —2E 9
Little Herbert's. Glos —4E 49
Little Hereford. Here —4H 59
Little Horkesley. Essx —2C 54
Little Hormead. Herts —3E 53
Little Horsted. E Sus —4F 27
Little Horton. W Yor —1B 92
Little Horwood. Buck —2F 51
Little Houghton. Nptn —5F 63
Littlehoughton. Nmbd —3G 121
Little Houghton. S Yor —4E 93
Little Hucklow. Derbs —3F 85
Little Hulton. G Man —4F 91
Little Ingestre. Staf —3D 73
Little Irchester. Nptn —4G 63
Little Kelk. E Yor —3E 101
Little Kimble. Buck —5G 51
Little Kineton. Warw —5H 61
Little Kingshill. Buck —2G 37
Little Langdale. Cumb —4E 102
Little Langford. Wilts —3F 23
Little Laver. Essx —5F 53
Little Lawford. Warw —3B 62
Little Leigh. Ches —3A 84
Little Leighs. Essx —4H 53
Little Leven. E Yor —5E 101
Little Lever. G Man —4F 91
Little Linford. Mil —1G 51
Little London. Buck —4E 51
Little London. E Sus —4G 27
Little London. Hants —2B 24
(nr. Andover)
Little London. Hants —1E 24
(nr. Basingstoke)
Little London. Linc —3D 76
(nr. Long Sutton)
Little London. Linc —3B 76
(nr. Spalding)
Little London. Norf —2E 79
(nr. North Walsham)
Little London. Norf —1G 65
(nr. Northwold)
Little London. Norf —2D 78
(nr. Saxthorpe)
Little London. Norf —1F 65
(nr. Southery)
Little London. Powy —2C 58
Little Longstone. Derbs —3F 85
Little Malvern. Worc —1C 48
Little Maplestead. Essx —2B 54
Little Marcle. Here —2B 48
Little Marlow. Buck —3G 37
Little Massingham. Norf —3G 77
Little Melton. Norf —5D 78
Littlemill. Aber —4H 151
Littlemill. E Ayr —3D 116
Littlemill. High —3D 158
Little Mill. Mon —5G 47
Little Milton. Oxon —5E 50
Little Missenden. Buck —1A 38
Littlemoor. Derbs —4A 86
Littlemoor. Dors —4B 14
Littlemore. Oxon —5D 50
Little Mountain. Flin —4E 83
Little Musgrave. Cumb —3A 104
Little Ness. Shrp —4G 71
Little Neston. Ches —3F 83
Little Newcastle. Pemb —2D 43
Little Newsham. Dur —3E 105
Little Oakley. Essx —3F 55
Little Oakley. Nptn —2F 63
Little Onn. Staf —4C 72
Little Ormside. Cumb —3A 104
Little Orton. Cumb —4E 113
Little Orton. Leics —5H 73
Little Ouse. Norf —2F 65
Little Ouseburn. N Yor —3G 99
Littleover. Dby C —2H 73
Little Packington. Warw —2G 61
Little Paxton. Cambs —4A 64
Little Petherick. Corn —1D 6
Little Plumpton. Lanc —1B 90
Little Plumstead. Norf —4F 79
Little Ponton. Linc —2G 75
Littleport. Cambs —2E 65
Little Posbrook. Hants —2D 16
Little Potheridge. Devn —1F 11
Little Preston. Nptn —5C 62
Little Raveley. Cambs —3B 64
Little Reynoldston. Swan —4D 31
Little Ribston. N Yor —4F 99
Little Rissington. Glos —4G 49
Little Rogart. High —3E 165
Little Rollright. Oxon —2A 50
Little Ryburgh. Norf —3B 78
Little Ryle. Nmbd —3E 121
Little Ryton. Shrp —5G 71
Little Salkeld. Cumb —1G 103
Little Sampford. Essx —2G 53
Little Sandhurst. Brac —5G 37
Little Saredon. Staf —5D 72
Little Saxham. Suff —4G 65
Little Scatwell. High —3F 157
Little Shelford. Cambs —5D 64
Little Shoddesden. Hants —2A 24
Little Singleton. Lanc —1B 90
Little Smeaton. N Yor —3F 93
Little Snoring. Norf —2B 78
Little Sodbury. S Glo —3C 34
Little Somborne. Hants —3B 24
Little Somerford. Wilts —3E 35
Little Soudley. Shrp —3B 72
Little Stainforth. N Yor —3H 97
Little Stainton. Darl —2A 106
Little Stanney. Ches —3G 83
Little Staughton. Beds —4A 64
Little Steeping. Linc —4D 88
Littlester. Shet —3G 173
Little Stoke. Staf —2D 72
Littlestone-on-Sea. Kent —3E 29
Little Stonham. Suff —4D 66
Little Street. Cambs —2E 65
Little Stretton. Leics —5D 74
Little Stretton. Shrp —1G 59
Little Strickland. Cumb —3G 103
Little Stukeley. Cambs —3B 64
Little Sugnall. Staf —2C 72
Little Sutton. Ches —3F 83
Little Sutton. Linc —3D 76
Little Swinburne. Nmbd —2C 114
Little Tew. Oxon —3B 50
Little Tey. Essx —3B 54
Little Thetford. Cambs —3E 65
Little Thirkleby. N Yor —2G 99
Little Thornton. Lanc —5C 96
Littlethorpe. Leics —1C 62
Littlethorpe. N Yor —3F 99
Little Thorpe. W Yor —2B 92
Little Thurlow. Suff —5F 65
Little Thurrock. Thur —3H 39
Littleton. Ches —4G 83
Littleton. G Lon —4B 38
Littleton. Hants —3C 24
Littleton. Som —3H 21
Littleton. Surr —1A 26
Littleton Drew. Wilts —3D 34
Littleton Pannell. Wilts —1E 23
Littleton-upon-Severn. S Glo —2A 34
Little Torboll. High —4E 165
Little Torrington. Devn —1E 11
Little Totham. Essx —4B 54
Little Town. Cumb —3D 102
Littletown. Dur —5G 115
Littletown. High —5E 165
Little Town. Lanc —1E 91
Little Twycross. Leics —5H 73
Little Urswick. Cumb —2B 96
Little Wakering. Essx —2D 40
Little Walden. Essx —1F 53
Little Waldingfield. Suff —1C 54
Little Walsingham. Norf —2B 78
Little Waltham. Essx —4H 53
Little Warley. Essx —1H 39
Little Washbourne. Glos —2E 49
Little Weighton. E Yor —1C 94
Little Welnetham. Suff —5A 66
Little Wenham. Suff —2D 54
Little Wenlock. Telf —5A 72
Little Whittingham Green. Suff —3E 67
Littlewick Green. Wind —4G 37
Little Wilbraham. Cambs —5E 65
Littlewindsor. Dors —2H 13
Little Wisbeach. Linc —2A 76
Little Witcombe. Glos —4E 49
Little Witley. Worc —4B 60
Little Wittenham. Oxon —2D 36
Little Wolford. Warw —2A 50
Littleworth. Beds —1A 52
Littleworth. Glos —2G 49
Littleworth. Oxon —2B 36
Littleworth. Staf —4E 73
(nr. Cannock)
Littleworth. Staf —3B 72
(nr. Eccleshall)
Littleworth. Staf —3D 72
(nr. Stafford)
Littleworth. W Sus —3C 26
Littleworth. Worc —4D 61
(nr. Redditch)
Littleworth. Worc —1D 49
(nr. Worcester)
Little Wratting. Suff —1G 53
Little Wymington. Nptn —4G 63
Little Wymondley. Herts —3C 52
Little Wyrley. Staf —5E 73
Little Yeldham. Essx —2A 54
Littley Green. Essx —4G 53
Litton. Derbs —3F 85
Litton. N Yor —2B 98
Litton. Som —1A 22
Litton Cheney. Dors —3A 14
Liurbost. W Isl —5F 171
Liverpool. Mers —1F 83
Liverpool Airport. Mers —2G 83
Liversedge. W Yor —2B 92
Liverton. Devn —5B 12
Liverton. Red C —3E 107
Liverton Mines. Red C —3E 107
Livingston. W Lot —3D 128
Livingston Village. W Lot —3D 128
Lixwm. Flin —3D 82
Lizard. Corn —5E 5
Llaingoch. IOA —2B 80
Llaithddu. Powy —2C 58
Llampha. V Glam —4C 32
Llan. Powy —5A 70
Llanaber. Gwyn —4F 69
Llanaelhaearn. Gwyn —1C 68
Llanaeron. Cdgn —5D 57
Llanafan. Cdgn —3F 57
Llanafan-fawr. Powy —5B 58
Llanafan-fechan. Powy —5B 58
Llanallgo. IOA —2D 81
Llanandras. Powy —4E 59
Llananno. Powy —3C 58
Llanarmon. Gwyn —2D 68
Llanarmon Dyffryn Ceiriog. Wrex —2D 70
Llanarmon-yn-Ial. Den —5D 82
Llanarth. Cdgn —5D 56
Llanarth. Mon —4G 47
Llanarthney. Carm —3F 45
Llanasa. Flin —2D 82
Llanbabo. IOA —2C 80
Llanbadarn Fawr. Cdgn —2F 57
Llanbadarn Fynydd. Powy —3C 58
Llanbadarn-y-garreg. Powy —1E 46
Llanbadoc. Mon —5G 47
Llanbadrig. IOA —1C 80
Llanbeder. Newp —2G 33
Llanbedr. Gwyn —3E 69
Llanbedr. Powy —3F 47
(nr. Crickhowell)

Llanbedr—Longley Green

Llanbedr. Powy —1E 47 (nr. Hay-on-Wye)
Llanbedr-Dyffryn-Clwyd. Den —5D 82
Llanbedrgoch. IOA —2E 81
Llanbedrog. Gwyn —2C 68
Llanbedr Pont Steffan. Cdgn —1F 45
Llanbedr-y-cennin. Cnwy —4G 81
Llanberis. Gwyn —4E 81
Llanbethery. V Glam —5D 32
Llanbister. Powy —3D 58
Llanblethian. V Glam —4D 32
Llanboidy. Carm —2G 43
Llanbradach. Cphy —2E 33
Llanbrynmair. Powy —5A 70
Llanbydderi. V Glam —5D 32
Llancadle. V Glam —5D 32
Llancarfan. V Glam —4D 32
Llancatal. V Glam —5D 32
Llancayo. Mon —5G 47
Llancloudy. Here —3H 47
Llancoch. Powy —3E 58
Llancynfelyn. Cdgn —1F 57
Llandaff. Card —4E 33
Llandanwg. Gwyn —3E 69
Llandarcy. Neat —3G 31
Llandawke. Carm —3G 43
Llanddaniel-Fab. IOA —3D 81
Llanddarog. Carm —4F 45
Llanddeiniol. Cdgn —3E 57
Llanddeiniolen. Gwyn —4E 81
Llandderfel. Gwyn —2B 70
Llanddeusant. Carm —3A 46
Llanddeusant. IOA —2C 80
Llanddew. Powy —2D 46
Llanddewi. Swan —4D 30
Llanddewi Brefi. Cdgn —5F 57
Llanddewi'r Cwm. Powy —1D 46
Llanddewi Rhydderch. Mon —4G 47
Llanddewi Velfrey. Pemb —3F 43
Llanddewi Ystradenni. Powy —4D 58
Llanddoged. Cnwy —4H 81
Llanddona. IOA —3E 81
Llanddowror. Carm —3G 43
Llanddulas. Cnwy —3B 82
Llanddwywe. Gwyn —3E 69
Llanddyfnan. IOA —3E 81
Llandecwyn. Gwyn —2F 69
Llandefaelog Fach. Powy —2D 46
Llandefaelog-tre'r-graig. Powy —2E 47
Llandefalle. Powy —2E 46
Llandegai. Gwyn —3E 81
Llandegfan. IOA —3E 81
Llandegla. Den —5D 82
Llandegley. Powy —4D 58
Llandegveth. Mon —2G 33
Llandeilo. Carm —3G 45
Llandeilo Graban. Powy —1D 46
Llandeilo'r Fan. Powy —2B 46
Llandeloy. Pemb —2C 42
Llandenny. Mon —5H 47
Llandevaud. Newp —2H 33
Llandevenny. Newp —3H 33
Llandilo. Pemb —2F 43
Llandinabo. Here —3A 48
Llandinam. Powy —2C 58
Llandissilio. Pemb —2F 43
Llandogo. Mon —5A 48
Llandough. V Glam —4C 32 (nr. Cowbridge)
Llandough. V Glam —4E 33 (nr. Penarth)
Llandovery. Carm —2A 46
Llandow. V Glam —4C 32
Llandre. Cdgn —2F 57
Llandrillo. Den —2C 70
Llandrillo-yn-Rhos. Cnwy —2H 81
Llandrindod. Powy —4C 58
Llandrindod Wells. Powy —4C 58
Llandrinio. Powy —4E 71
Llandsadwrn. Carm —2G 45
Llandudno. Cnwy —2G 81
Llandudno Junction. Cnwy —3G 81
Llandudoch. Pemb —1B 44
Llandw. V Glam —4C 32
Llandwrog. Gwyn —5D 80
Llandybie. Carm —4G 45
Llandyfaelog. Carm —4E 45
Llandyfan. Carm —4G 45
Llandyfriog. Cdgn —1D 44
Llandyfrydog. IOA —2D 80
Llandygwydd. Cdgn —1C 44
Llandynan. Den —1D 70
Llandyrnog. Den —4D 82
Llandysilio. Powy —4E 71
Llandyssil. Powy —1D 58
Llandysul. Cdgn —1E 45
Llanedeyrn. Card —3F 33
Llaneglwys. Powy —2D 46
Llanegryn. Gwyn —5F 69
Llanegwad. Carm —3F 45
Llaneilian. IOA —1D 80
Llanelian-yn-Rhos. Cnwy —3A 82
Llanelidan. Den —5D 82
Llanelieu. Powy —2E 47
Llanellen. Mon —4G 47
Llanelli. Carm —3E 31
Llanelltyd. Gwyn —4G 69
Llanelly. Mon —4F 47
Llanelly Hill. Mon —4F 47
Llanelwedd. Powy —5C 58
Llanelwy. Den —3C 82
Llanenddwyn. Gwyn —3E 69
Llanengan. Gwyn —3B 68
Llanerch. Powy —1F 59
Llanerchymedd. IOA —2D 80
Llanerfyl. Powy —5C 70
Llaneuddog. IOA —2D 80
Llanfachraeth. IOA —2C 80
Llanfaelog. IOA —3C 80
Llanfaelrhys. Gwyn —3B 68
Llanfaenor. Mon —4H 47
Llanfaes. IOA —3F 81
Llanfaes. Powy —3D 46
Llanfaethlu. IOA —2C 80
Llanfaglan. Gwyn —4D 80
Llanfair. Gwyn —3E 69
Llanfair. Here —1F 47
Llanfair Caereinion. Powy —5D 70
Llanfair Clydogau. Cdgn —5F 57
Llanfair Dyffryn Clwyd. Den —5D 82
Llanfairfechan. Cnwy —3F 81
Llanfair-Nant-Gwyn. Pemb —1F 43
Llanfair Pwllgwyngyll. IOA —3E 81
Llanfair Talhaiarn. Cnwy —3B 82
Llanfair Waterdine. Shrp —3E 59
Llanfair-ym-Muallt. Powy —5C 58
Llanfairyneubwll. IOA —3C 80
Llanfairynghornwy. IOA —1C 80
Llanfallteg. Carm —3F 43
Llanfallteg West. Carm —3F 43
Llanfaredd. Powy —5C 58
Llanfarian. Cdgn —3E 57
Llanfechain. Powy —3D 70
Llanfechell. IOA —1C 80
Llanfechreth. Gwyn —3G 69
Llanfendigaid. Gwyn —5E 69
Llanferres. Den —4D 82
Llanfflewyn. IOA —2C 80
Llanfihangel Glyn Myfyr. Cnwy —1B 70
Llanfihangel Nant Bran. Powy —2C 46
Llanfihangel-Nant-Melan. Powy —5D 58
Llanfihangel Rhydithon. Powy —4D 58
Llanfihangel Rogiet. Mon —3H 33
Llanfihangel Tal-y-llyn. Powy —3E 46
Llanfihangel-uwch-Gwili. Carm —3E 45
Llanfihangel-yng-ngwynfa. Powy —4C 70
Llanfihangel yn Nhowyn. IOA —3C 80
Llanfihangel-y-pennant. (nr. Golan) Gwyn —1E 69
Llanfihangel-y-pennant. (nr. Tywyn) Gwyn —5F 69
Llanfilo. Powy —2E 46
Llanfinhangel-ar-Arth. Carm —2E 45
Llanfinhangel-y-Creuddyn. Cdgn —3F 57
Llanfihangel-y-traethau. Gwyn —2E 69
Llanfleiddan. V Glam —4C 32
Llanfoist. Mon —4F 47
Llanfor. Gwyn —2B 70
Llanfrechfa. Torf —2G 33
Llanfrothen. Gwyn —1F 69
Llanfrynach. Powy —3D 46
Llanfwrog. Den —5D 82
Llanfwrog. IOA —2C 80
Llanfyllin. Powy —4D 70
Llanfynydd. Carm —3F 45
Llanfynydd. Flin —5E 83
Llanfyrnach. Pemb —1G 43
Llangadfan. Powy —4C 70
Llangadog. Carm —3H 45 (nr. Llandovery)
Llangadog. Carm —5E 45 (nr. Llanelli)
Llangadwaladr. IOA —4C 80
Llangadwaladr. Powy —2D 70
Llangaffo. IOA —4D 80
Llangain. Carm —4D 45
Llangammarch Wells. Powy —1C 46
Llangan. V Glam —4C 32
Llangarron. Here —3A 48
Llangasty-Talyllyn. Powy —3E 47
Llangathen. Carm —3F 45
Llangattock. Powy —4F 47
Llangattock Lingoed. Mon —3G 47
Llangattock-Vibon-Avel. Mon —4H 47
Llangedwyn. Powy —3D 70
Llangefni. IOA —3D 80
Llangeinor. B'End —3C 32
Llangeitho. Cdgn —5F 57
Llangeler. Carm —2D 44
Llangelynin. Gwyn —5E 69
Llangendeirne. Carm —4E 45
Llangennech. Carm —5F 45
Llangennith. Swan —3D 30
Llangenny. Powy —4F 47
Llangernyw. Cnwy —4A 82
Llangian. Gwyn —3B 68
Llangiwg. Neat —5H 45
Llangloffan. Pemb —1D 42
Llanglydwen. Carm —2F 43
Llangoed. IOA —3F 81
Llangoedmor. Cdgn —1C 44
Llangollen. Den —1E 70
Llangolman. Pemb —2F 43
Llangorse. Powy —3E 47
Llangorwen. Cdgn —2F 57
Llangovan. Mon —5H 47
Llangower. Gwyn —2B 70
Llangranog. Cdgn —5C 56
Llangristiolus. IOA —3D 80
Llangrove. Here —4A 48
Llangua. Mon —3G 47
Llangunllo. Powy —3E 58
Llangunnor. Carm —3E 45
Llangurig. Powy —3B 58
Llangwm. Cnwy —1B 70
Llangwm. Mon —5H 47
Llangwm. Pemb —4D 43
Llangwm-isaf. Mon —5H 47
Llangwnnadl. Gwyn —2B 68
Llangwyfan. Den —4D 82
Llangwyfan-isaf. IOA —4C 80
Llangwyllog. IOA —3D 80
Llangwyryfon. Cdgn —3E 57
Llangybi. Cdgn —5F 57
Llangybi. Gwyn —1D 68
Llangybi. Mon —2G 33
Llangyfelach. Swan —3F 31
Llangynhafal. Den —4D 82
Llangynidr. Powy —4E 47
Llangynin. Carm —3G 43
Llangynog. Carm —3H 43
Llangynog. Powy —3C 70
Llangynwyd. B'End —3B 32
Llanhamlach. Powy —3D 46
Llanharan. Rhon —3D 32
Llanharry. Rhon —3D 32
Llanhennock. Mon —2G 33
Llanhilleth. Blae —5F 47
Llanidloes. Powy —2B 58
Llaniestyn. Gwyn —2B 68
Llanigon. Powy —1F 47
Llanilar. Cdgn —3F 57
Llanilid. Rhon —3C 32
Llanilltud Fawr. V Glam —4C 32
Llanishen. Card —3E 33
Llanishen. Mon —5H 47
Llanllawddog. Carm —3E 45
Llanllechid. Gwyn —4F 81
Llanllowell. Mon —2G 33
Llanllugan. Powy —5C 70
Llanllwch. Carm —4D 45
Llanllwchaiarn. Powy —1D 58
Llanllwni. Carm —2E 45
Llanllyfni. Gwyn —5D 80
Llanmadoc. Swan —3D 30
Llanmaes. V Glam —5C 32
Llanmartin. Newp —3G 33
Llanmerwig. Powy —1D 58
Llanmihangel. V Glam —4C 32
Llan-mill. Pemb —3F 43
Llanmiloe. Carm —4G 43
Llanmorlais. Swan —3E 31
Llannefydd. Cnwy —3B 82
Llannon. Carm —5F 45
Llan-non. Cdgn —4E 57
Llannor. Gwyn —2C 68
Llanpumsaint. Carm —3E 45
Llanrhaeadr. Den —4C 82
Llanrhaeadr-ym-Mochnant. Powy —3D 70
Llanrhidian. Swan —3D 31
Llanrhos. Cnwy —2G 81
Llanrhyddlad. IOA —2C 80
Llanrhystud. Cdgn —4E 57
Llanrian. Pemb —1C 42
Llanrothal. Here —4H 47
Llanrug. Gwyn —4E 81
Llanrumney. Card —3F 33
Llanrwst. Cnwy —4G 81
Llansadurnen. Carm —3G 43
Llansadwrn. IOA —3E 81
Llansaint. Carm —5D 45
Llansamlet. Swan —3F 31
Llansanffraid Glan Conwy. Cnwy —3H 81
Llansannan. Cnwy —4B 82
Llansannor. V Glam —4C 32
Llansantffraed. Cdgn —4D 57
Llansantffraed. Powy —3E 46
Llansantffraed Cwmdeuddwr. Powy —4B 58
Llansantffraed in Elwel. Powy —5D 58
Llansantffraid-ym-Mechain. Powy —3E 70
Llansawel. Carm —2G 45
Llansawel. Neat —3G 31
Llansilin. Powy —3E 70
Llansoy. Mon —5H 47
Llanspyddid. Powy —3D 46
Llanstadwell. Pemb —4D 42
Llansteffan. Carm —3H 43
Llanstephan. Powy —1E 46
Llantarnam. Torf —2F 33
Llanteg. Pemb —3F 43
Llanthony. Mon —3F 47
Llantilio Crossenny. Mon —4G 47
Llantilio Pertholey. Mon —4G 47
Llantood. Pemb —1B 44
Llantrisant. Mon —2G 33
Llantrisant. Rhon —3D 32
Llantrithyd. V Glam —4D 32
Llantwit Fardre. Rhon —3D 32
Llantwit Major. V Glam —5C 32
Llanuwchllyn. Gwyn —2A 70
Llanvaches. Newp —2H 33
Llanvair Discoed. Mon —2H 33
Llanvapley. Mon —4G 47
Llanvetherine. Mon —4G 47
Llanveynoe. Here —2G 47
Llanvihangel Crucorney. Mon —3G 47
Llanvihangel Gobion. Mon —5G 47
Llanvihangel Ystern-Llewern. Mon —4H 47
Llanwarne. Here —3A 48
Llanwddyn. Powy —4C 70
Llanwenarth. Mon —4F 47
Llanwenog. Cdgn —1E 45
Llanwern. Newp —3G 33
Llanwinio. Carm —2G 43
Llanwnda. Gwyn —5D 81
Llanwnda. Pemb —1D 42
Llanwnnen. Cdgn —1F 45
Llanwnog. Powy —1C 58
Llanwrda. Carm —2H 45
Llanwrin. Powy —5G 69
Llanwrthwl. Powy —4B 58
Llanwrtyd. Powy —1B 46
Llanwrtyd Wells. Powy —1B 46
Llanwrtud. Powy —1B 46
Llanwyddelan. Powy —5C 70
Llanyblodwel. Shrp —3E 71
Llanybri. Carm —3H 43
Llanybydder. Carm —1F 45
Llanycefn. Pemb —2E 43
Llanychaer. Pemb —1D 43
Llanycil. Gwyn —2B 70
Llanymawddwy. Gwyn —4B 70
Llanymddyfri. Carm —2A 46
Llanymynech. Powy —3E 71
Llanynghenedl. IOA —2C 80
Llanynys. Den —4D 82
Llan-y-pwll. Wrex —5F 83
Llanyrafon. Torf —2G 33
Llanyre. Powy —4C 58
Llanystumdwy. Gwyn —2D 68
Llanywern. Powy —3E 46
Llawhaden. Pemb —3E 43
Llawndy. Flin —2D 82
Llawnt. Shrp —2E 71
Llawr Dref. Gwyn —3B 68
Llawryglyn. Powy —1B 58
Llay. Wrex —5F 83
Llechfaen. Powy —3D 46
Llechryd. Cphy —5E 46
Llechryd. Cdgn —1C 44
Llechrydau. Wrex —2E 71
Lledrod. Cdgn —3F 57
Llethrid. Swan —3E 31
Llidiad-Nenog. Carm —2F 45
Llidiardau. Gwyn —2A 70
Llidiart y Parc. Den —1D 70
Llithfaen. Gwyn —1C 68
Lloc. Flin —3D 82
Llong. Flin —4E 83
Llowes. Powy —1E 47
Lloyney. Powy —3E 59
Llundain-fach. Cdgn —5E 57
Llwydcoed. Rhon —5C 46
Llwyncelyn. Cdgn —5D 56
Llwyncelyn. Swan —5G 45
Llwyndaffydd. Cdgn —5C 56
Llwynderw. Powy —5E 70
Llwyn-du. Mon —4F 47
Llwyngwril. Gwyn —5E 69
Llwynhendy. Carm —3E 31
Llwynmawr. Wrex —2E 71
Llwyn-on Village. Mer T —4D 46
Llwyn-teg. Carm —5F 45
Llwyn-y-brain. Carm —3F 43
Llwynygog. Powy —1A 58
Llwyn-y-groes. Cdgn —5E 57
Llwynypia. Rhon —2C 32
Llynclys. Shrp —3E 71
Llynfaes. IOA —3D 80
Llysfaen. Cnwy —3A 82
Llyswen. Powy —2E 47
Llysworney. V Glam —4C 32
Llys-y-fran. Pemb —2E 43
Llywel. Powy —2B 46
Llywernog. Cdgn —2G 57
Loan. Falk —2C 128
Loanend. Nmbd —4F 131
Loanhead. Midl —3F 129
Loaningfoot. Dum —4A 112
Loanreoch. High —1A 158
Loans. S Ayr —1C 116
Loansdean. Nmbd —1F 115
Lobb. Devn —3E 19
Lobhillcross. Devn —4E 11
Loch a Charnain. W Isl —4D 170
Loch a Ghainmhich. W Isl —5E 171
Lochailort. High —5F 147
Lochaline. High —4A 140
Lochans. Dum —4F 109
Locharbriggs. Dum —1A 112
Lochardil. High —4A 158
Lochassynt Lodge. High —1F 163
Lochavich. Arg —2G 133
Lochawe. Arg —1A 134
Loch Baghasdail. W Isl —7C 170
Lochboisdale. W Isl —7C 170
Lochbuie. Arg —1D 132
Lochcarron. High —5A 156
Loch Choire Lodge. High —5G 167
Lochdochart House. Stir —1D 134
Lochdon. Arg —5B 140
Lochearnhead. Stir —1E 135
Lochee. D'dee —5C 144
Lochend. High —5H 157 (nr. Inverness)
Lochend. High —2E 169 (nr. Thurso)
Locherben. Dum —5B 118
Loch Euphort. W Isl —2D 170
Lochfoot. Dum —2F 111
Lochgair. Arg —4G 133
Lochgarthside. High —2H 149
Lochgelly. Fife —4D 136
Lochgilphead. Arg —1G 125
Lochgoilhead. Arg —3A 134
Loch Head. Dum —5A 110
Lochhill. Mor —2G 159
Lochindorb Lodge. High —5D 158
Lochinver. High —1E 163
Lochlane. Per —1H 135
Loch Loyal Lodge. High —4G 167
Lochluichart. High —2F 157
Lochmaben. Dum —1B 112
Lochmaddy. W Isl —2E 170
Loch nam Madadh. W Isl —2E 170
Lochore. Fife —4D 136
Lochportain. W Isl —1E 170
Lochranza. N Ayr —4H 125
Loch Sgioport. W Isl —5D 170
Lochside. Aber —2G 145
Lochside. High —5A 168 (nr. Auchentoul)
Lochside. High —3C 158 (nr. Nairn)
Lochslin. High —5F 165
Lochstack Lodge. High —4C 166
Lochton. Aber —4E 153
Lochty. Fife —3H 137
Lochuisge. High —3B 140
Lochussie. High —3G 157
Lochwinnoch. Ren —4E 127
Lochyside. High —1F 141
Lockengate. Corn —2E 7
Lockerbie. Dum —1C 112
Lockeridge. Wilts —5G 35
Lockerley. Hants —4A 24
Lockhills. Cumb —5G 113
Locking. N Som —1G 21
Lockington. E Yor —5D 101
Lockington. Leics —3B 74
Lockleywood. Shrp —3A 72
Locksgreen. IOW —3C 16
Locks Heath. Hants —2D 16
Lockton. N Yor —1C 100
Loddington. Leics —5E 75
Loddington. Nptn —3F 63
Loddiswell. Devn —4D 8
Loddon. Norf —1F 67
Lode. Cambs —4E 65
Loders. Dors —3H 13
Lodsworth. W Sus —3A 26
Lofthouse. N Yor —2D 98
Lofthouse. W Yor —2D 92
Lofthouse Gate. W Yor —2D 92
Loftus. Red C —3E 107
Logan. E Ayr —2E 117
Loganlea. W Lot —3C 128
Logaston. Here —5F 59
Loggerheads. Staf —2B 72
Loggie. High —4F 163
Logie. Ang —2F 145
Logie. Fife —1G 137
Logie. Mor —3E 159
Logie Coldstone. Aber —3B 152
Logie Pert. Ang —2F 145
Logierait. Per —3G 143
Login. Carm —2F 43
Lolworth. Cambs —4C 64
Lonbain. High —3F 155
Londesborough. E Yor —5C 100
London. G Lon —2E 39
London Apprentice. Corn —3E 6
London Biggin Hill Airport. Kent —4F 39
London City Airport. G Lon —2F 39
London Colney. Herts —5B 52
Londonderry. N Yor —1F 99
London Gatwick Airport. W Sus —1D 27
London Heathrow Airport. G Lon —3B 38
London Luton Airport. Beds —3B 52
London Southend Airport. Essx —2C 40
London Stansted Airport. Essx —3F 53
Londonthorpe. Linc —2G 75
Londubh. High —5C 162
Lone. High —4D 166
Lonemore. High —5E 165 (nr. Dornoch)
Lonemore. High —1G 155 (nr. Gairloch)
Long Ashton. N Som —4A 34
Long Bank. Worc —3B 60
Longbar. N Ayr —4E 127
Long Bennington. Linc —1F 75
Longbenton. Tyne —3F 115
Longborough. Glos —3G 49
Long Bredy. Dors —3A 14
Longbridge. Warw —4G 61
Longbridge. W Mid —3E 61
Longbridge Deverill. Wilts —2D 22
Long Buckby. Nptn —4D 62
Long Buckby Wharf. Nptn —4D 62
Longburgh. Cumb —4E 112
Longburton. Dors —1B 14
Long Clawson. Leics —3E 74
Longcliffe. Derbs —5G 85
Long Common. Hants —1D 16
Long Compton. Staf —3C 72
Long Compton. Warw —2A 50
Longcot. Oxon —2A 36
Long Crendon. Buck —5E 51
Long Crichel. Dors —1E 15
Longcroft. Cumb —4D 112
Longcroft. Falk —2A 128
Longcross. Surr —4A 38
Longdale. Cumb —4H 103
Longdales. Cumb —5G 113
Longden. Shrp —5G 71
Longden Common. Shrp —5G 71
Long Ditton. Surr —4C 38
Longdon. Staf —4E 73
Longdon. Worc —2D 48
Longdon Green. Staf —4E 73
Longdon on Tern. Telf —4A 72
Longdown. Devn —3B 12
Longdowns. Corn —5B 6
Long Drax. N Yor —2G 93
Long Duckmanton. Derbs —3B 86
Long Eaton. Derbs —2B 74
Longfield. Kent —4H 39
Longfield. Shet —10E 173
Longfield Hill. Kent —4H 39
Longford. Derbs —2G 73
Longford. Glos —3D 48
Longford. G Lon —3B 38
Longford. Shrp —2A 72
Longford. Telf —4B 72
Longford. W Mid —2H 61
Longforgan. Per —1F 137
Longformacus. Scot —4C 130
Longframlington. Nmbd —4F 121
Long Gardens. Essx —2B 54
Long Green. Ches —3G 83
Long Green. Worc —2D 48
Longham. Dors —3F 15
Longham. Norf —4B 78
Long Hanborough. Oxon —4C 50
Longhedge. Wilts —2D 22
Long Hermiston. Edin —2E 129
Longhill. Aber —3H 161
Longhirst. Nmbd —1F 115
Longhope. Glos —4B 48
Longhope. Orkn —8C 172
Longhorsley. Nmbd —5F 121
Longhoughton. Nmbd —3G 121
Long Itchington. Warw —4B 62
Longlands. Cumb —1D 102
Longlane. Derbs —2G 73
Long Lane. Telf —4A 72
Longlane. W Ber —4C 36
Long Lawford. Warw —3B 62
Long Lease. N Yor —4G 107
Longley Green. Worc —5B 60

Long Load—Mains of Auchindachy

Long Load. Som —4H 21
Longmanhill. Aber —2E 161
Long Marston. Herts —4G 51
Long Marston. N Yor —4H 99
Long Marston. Warw —1G 49
Long Marton. Cumb —2H 103
Long Meadow. Cambs —4E 65
Long Meadowend. Shrp —2G 59
Long Melford. Suff —1B 54
Longmoor Camp. Hants —3F 25
Longmorn. Mor —3G 159
Longmoss. Ches —3C 84
Long Newton. Glos —2E 35
Longnewton. Scot —2H 119
Long Newton. Stoc T —3A 106
Longney. Glos —4C 48
Longniddry. E Lot —2H 129
Longnor. Shrp —5G 71
Longnor. Staf —4E 85 (nr. Leek)
Longnor. Staf —4C 72 (nr. Stafford)
Longparish. Hants —2C 24
Longpark. Cumb —3F 113
Long Preston. N Yor —4H 97
Longridge. Lanc —1E 90
Longridge. Staf —4D 72
Longridge. W Lot —3C 128
Longriggend. N Lan —2B 128
Long Riston. E Yor —5F 101
Longrock. Corn —3C 4
Longsdon. Staf —5D 85
Longshaw. G Man —4D 90
Longshaw. Staf —1E 73
Longside. Aber —4H 161
Longslow. Shrp —2A 72
Longstanton. Cambs —4C 64
Longstock. Hants —3B 24
Longstowe. Cambs —5C 64
Long Stratton. Norf —1D 66
Long Street. Mil —1F 51
Longstreet. Wilts —1G 23
Long Sutton. Hants —2F 25
Long Sutton. Linc —3D 76
Long Sutton. Som —4H 21
Longthorpe. Pet —1A 64
Long Thurlow. Suff —4C 66
Longthwaite. Cumb —2F 103
Longton. Lanc —2C 90
Longton. Stoke —1D 72
Longtown. Cumb —3E 113
Longtown. Here —3G 47
Longville in the Dale. Shrp —1H 59
Long Whatton. Leics —3B 74
Longwick. Buck —5F 51
Long Wittenham. Oxon —2D 36
Longwitton. Nmbd —1D 115
Longworth. Oxon —2B 36
Longyester. E Lot —3B 130
Lonmore. High —4B 154
Looe. Corn —3G 7
Loose. Kent —5B 40
Loosegate. Linc —3C 76
Loosley Row. Buck —5G 51
Lootcherbrae. Aber —3D 160
Lopcombe Corner. Wilts —3A 24
Lopen. Som —1H 13
Loppington. Shrp —3G 71
Lorbottle. Nmbd —4E 121
Lorbottle Hall. Nmbd —4E 121
Lordington. W Sus —2F 17
Loscoe. Derbs —1B 74
Loscombe. Dors —3A 14
Losgaintir. W Isl —8C 171
Lossiemouth. Mor —1G 159
Lossit. Arg —4A 124
Lostock Gralam. Ches —3A 84
Lostock Green. Ches —3A 84
Lostock Hall. Lanc —2D 90
Lostock Junction. G Man —4E 91
Lostwithiel. Corn —3F 7
Lothbeg. High —2G 165
Lothersdale. N Yor —5B 98
Lothianbridge. Midl —3G 129
Lothianburn. Edin —3F 129
Lothmore. High —2G 165
Lottisham. Som —3A 22
Loudwater. Buck —1A 38
Loughborough. Leics —4C 74
Loughor. Swan —3E 31
Loughton. Essx —1F 39
Loughton. Mil —2G 51
Loughton. Shrp —2A 60
Lound. Linc —4H 75
Lound. Notts —2D 86
Lound. Suff —1H 67
Lound, The. Cumb —5G 103
Lount. Leics —4A 74
Louth. Linc —2C 88
Love Clough. Lanc —2G 91
Lovedean. Hants —1E 17
Lover. Wilts —4H 23
Loversall. S Yor —1C 86
Loves Green. Essx —5G 53
Loveston. Pemb —4E 43
Lovington. Som —3A 22
Low Ackworth. W Yor —3E 93
Low Angerton. Nmbd —1D 115
Low Ardwell. Dum —5F 109
Low Ballochdoan. S Ayr —2F 109
Lowbands. Glos —2C 48
Low Barlings. Linc —3H 87
Low Bell End. N Yor —5E 107
Low Bentham. N Yor —3F 97
Low Bradfield. S Yor —1G 85
Low Bradley. N Yor —5C 98
Low Braithwaite. Cumb —5F 113
Low Brunton. Nmbd —2C 114
Low Burnham. N Lin —4A 94
Lowca. Cumb —2A 102
Low Catton. E Yor —4B 100
Low Coniscliffe. Dur —3F 105
Low Coylton. S Ayr —3D 116
Low Crosby. Cumb —4F 113
Low Dalby. N Yor —1C 100
Lowdham. Notts —1D 74
Low Dinsdale. Darl —3A 106
Lowe. Shrp —2H 71
Low Ellington. N Yor —1E 98
Lower Amble. Corn —1D 6
Lower Ansty. Dors —2C 14
Lower Arboll. High —5F 165
Lower Arncott. Oxon —4E 50
Lower Ashton. Devn —4B 12
Lower Assendon. Oxon —3F 37
Lower Auchenreath. Mor —2A 160
Lower Badcall. High —4B 166
Lower Ballam. Lanc —1B 90
Lower Basildon. W Ber —4E 36
Lower Beeding. W Sus —3D 26
Lower Benefield. Nptn —2G 63
Lower Bentley. Worc —4D 61
Lower Beobridge. Shrp —1B 60
Lower Boddington. Nptn —5B 62
Lower Bordean. Hants —4E 25
Lower Brailes. Warw —2B 50
Lower Breakish. High —1E 147
Lower Broadheath. Worc —5C 60
Lower Brynamman. Neat —4H 45
Lower Bullingham. Here —2A 48
Lower Bullington. Hants —2C 24
Lower Burgate. Hants —1G 15
Lower Cam. Glos —5C 48
Lower Catesby. Nptn —5C 62
Lower Chapel. Powy —2D 46
Lower Chicksgrove. Wilts —3E 23
Lower Chute. Wilts —1B 24
Lower Clopton. Warw —5F 61
Lower Common. Hants —2E 25
Lower Cumberworth. W Yor —4C 92
Lower Darwen. Bkbn —2E 91
Lower Dean. Beds —4H 63
Lower Dean. Devn —2D 8
Lower Diabaig. High —2G 155
Lower Dicker. E Sus —4G 27
Lower Dounreay. High —2B 168
Lower Down. Shrp —2F 59
Lower Dunsforth. N Yor —3G 99
Lower East Carleton. Norf —5D 78
Lower Egleton. Here —1B 48
Lower Ellastone. Derbs —1F 73
Lower End. Nptn —4F 63
Lower Everleigh. Wilts —1G 23
Lower Failand. N Som —4A 34
Lower Faintree. Shrp —2A 60
Lower Farringdon. Hants —3F 25
Lower Foxdale. IOM —4B 108
Lower Frankton. Shrp —2F 71
Lower Froyle. Hants —2F 25
Lower Gabwell. Devn —2F 9
Lower Gledfield. High —4C 164
Lower Godney. Som —2H 21
Lower Gravenhurst. Beds —2B 52
Lower Green. Essx —2E 53
Lower Green. Norf —2B 78
Lower Green. Staf —5D 72
Lower Green. W Ber —5B 36
Lower Halstow. Kent —4C 40
Lower Hardres. Kent —5F 41
Lower Hardwick. Here —5G 59
Lower Hartshay. Derbs —5A 86
Lower Hawthwaite. Cumb —1B 96
Lower Hayton. Shrp —2H 59
Lower Hergest. Here —5E 59
Lower Heyford. Oxon —3C 50
Lower Heysham. Lanc —3D 96
Lower Higham. Kent —3B 40
Lower Holbrook. Suff —2E 55
Lower Hordley. Shrp —3F 71
Lower Horncroft. W Sus —4B 26
Lower Horsebridge. E Sus —4G 27
Lower Kilcott. Glos —3C 34
Lower Killeyan. Arg —5A 124
Lower Kingcombe. Dors —3A 14
Lower Kingswood. Surr —5D 38
Lower Kinnerton. Ches —4F 83
Lower Langford. N Som —5H 33
Lower Largo. Fife —3G 137
Lower Layham. Suff —1D 54
Lower Ledwyche. Shrp —3H 59
Lower Leigh. Staf —2E 73
Lower Lemington. Glos —2H 49
Lower Lenie. High —1H 149
Lower Ley. Glos —4C 48
Lower Llanfadog. Powy —4B 58
Lower Lode. Glos —2D 49
Lower Loxhore. Devn —3G 19
Lower Loxley. Staf —2E 73
Lower Lydbrook. Glos —4A 48
Lower Lye. Here —4G 59
Lower Machen. Newp —3F 33
Lower Maes-coed. Here —2G 47
Lower Meend. Glos —5A 48
Lower Milovaig. High —3A 154
Lower Moor. Worc —1E 49
Lower Morton. S Glo —2B 34
Lower Mountain. Flin —5F 83
Lower Nazeing. Essx —5D 53
Lower Nyland. Dors —4C 22
Lower Oakfield. Fife —4D 136
Lower Oddington. Glos —3H 49
Lower Ollach. High —5E 155
Lower Penarth. V Glam —5E 33
Lower Penn. Staf —1C 60
Lower Pennington. Hants —3B 16
Lower Peover. Ches —3B 84
Lower Pitkerrie. High —1C 158
Lower Place. G Man —3H 91
Lower Quinton. Warw —1G 49
Lower Rainham. Medw —4C 40
Lower Raydon. Suff —2D 54
Lower Seagry. Wilts —3E 35
Lower Shelton. Beds —1H 51
Lower Shiplake. Oxon —4F 37
Lower Shuckburgh. Warw —4B 62
Lower Sketty. Swan —3F 31
Lower Slaughter. Glos —3G 49
Lower Soudley. Glos —4B 48
Lower Stanton St Quintin. Wilts —3E 35
Lower Stoke. Medw —3C 40
Lower Stonnall. Staf —5E 73
Lower Stow Bedon. Norf —1B 66
Lower Street. Norf —2E 79
Lower Strensham. Worc —1E 49
Lower Sundon. Beds —3A 52
Lower Swanwick. Hants —2C 16
Lower Swell. Glos —3G 49
Lower Tale. Devn —2D 12
Lower Tean. Staf —2E 73
Lower Thurlton. Norf —1G 67
Lower Thurnham. Lanc —4D 96
Lower Thurvaston. Derbs —2G 73
Lowertown. Corn —4D 4
Lower Town. Devn —5H 11
Lower Town. Here —1B 48
Lower Town. IOS —1B 4
Lowertown. Orkn —8D 172
Lower Town. Pemb —1D 42
Lower Tysoe. Warw —1B 50
Lower Upham. Hants —1D 16
Lower Upnor. Medw —3B 40
Lower Vexford. Som —3E 20
Lower Walton. Warr —2A 84
Lower Wear. Devn —4C 12
Lower Weare. Som —1H 21
Lower Welson. Here —5E 59
Lower Whatcombe. Dors —2D 14
Lower Whitley. Ches —3A 84
Lower Wield. Hants —2E 25
Lower Winchendon. Buck —4F 51
Lower Withington. Ches —4C 84
Lower Woodend. Buck —3G 37
Lower Woodford. Wilts —3G 23
Lower Wych. Ches —1G 71
Lower Wyche. Worc —1C 48
Lowesby. Leics —5E 74
Lowestoft. Suff —1H 67
Loweswater. Cumb —2C 102
Low Etherley. Dur —2E 105
Lowfield Heath. W Sus —1D 26
Lowford. Hants —1C 16
Low Fulney. Linc —3B 76
Low Gate. Nmbd —3C 114
Lowgill. Cumb —5H 103
Lowgill. Lanc —3F 97
Low Grantley. N Yor —2E 99
Low Green. N Yor —4E 98
Low Habberley. Worc —3C 60
Low Ham. Som —4H 21
Low Hameringham. Linc —4C 88
Low Hawkser. N Yor —4G 107
Low Hesket. Cumb —5F 113
Low Hesleyhurst. Nmbd —5E 121
Lowick. Cumb —1B 96
Lowick. Nptn —2G 63
Lowick. Nmbd —1E 121
Lowick Bridge. Cumb —1B 96
Lowick Green. Cumb —1B 96
Low Knipe. Cumb —2G 103
Low Leighton. Derbs —2E 85
Low Lorton. Cumb —2C 102
Low Marishes. N Yor —2C 100
Low Marnham. Notts —4F 87
Low Mill. N Yor —5D 106
Low Moor. Lanc —5G 97
Low Moor. W Yor —2B 92
Low Moorsley. Tyne —5G 115
Low Newton-by-the-Sea. Nmbd —2G 121
Lownie Moor. Ang —4D 145
Lowood. Scot —1H 119
Low Row. Cumb —3G 113 (nr. Brampton)
Low Row. Cumb —1E 103 (nr. Caldbeck)
Low Row. Cumb —5C 112 (nr. Wigton)
Low Row. N Yor —5C 104
Lowsonford. Warw —4F 61
Low Street. Norf —5C 78
Low Team. Tyne —3F 115
Lowther. Cumb —2G 103
Lowthorpe. E Yor —3E 101
Lowton. Devn —2G 11
Lowton. G Man —1A 84
Lowton. Som —1E 13
Lowton Common. G Man —1A 84
Low Torry. Fife —1D 128
Low Toynton. Linc —3B 88
Low Valleyfield. Fife —1C 128
Low Walworth. Darl —3F 105
Low Westwood. Dur —4E 115
Low Whinnow. Cumb —4E 112
Low Wood. Cumb —1C 96
Low Worsall. N Yor —4A 106
Low Wray. Cumb —4E 103
Loxbeare. Devn —1C 12
Loxhill. Surr —2B 26
Loxhore. Devn —3G 19
Loxley. S Yor —2H 85
Loxley. Warw —5G 61
Loxley Green. Staf —2E 73
Loxton. N Som —1G 21
Loxwood. W Sus —2B 26
Lubcroy. High —3A 164
Lubenham. Leics —2E 62
Lubinvullin. High —2F 167
Luccombe. Som —2C 20
Luccombe Village. IOW —5D 16
Lucker. Nmbd —1F 121
Luckett. Corn —5D 11
Luckington. Wilts —3D 34
Lucklawhill. Fife —1G 137
Luckwell Bridge. Som —3C 20
Lucton. Here —4G 59
Ludag. W Isl —7C 170
Ludborough. Linc —1B 88
Ludchurch. Pemb —3F 43
Luddenden. W Yor —2A 92
Luddenden Foot. W Yor —2A 92
Luddenham. Kent —4D 40
Ludderburn. Cumb —5F 103
Luddesdown. Kent —4A 40
Luddington. N Lin —3B 94
Luddington. Warw —5F 61
Luddington in the Brook. Nptn —2A 64
Ludford. Linc —2A 88
Ludford. Shrp —3H 59
Ludgershall. Buck —4E 51
Ludgershall. Wilts —1A 24
Ludgvan. Corn —3C 4
Ludham. Norf —4F 79
Ludlow. Shrp —3H 59
Ludstone. Shrp —1C 60
Ludwell. Wilts —4E 23
Ludworth. Dur —5G 115
Luffenhall. Herts —3C 52
Luffincot. Devn —3D 10
Lugar. E Ayr —2E 117
Luggate Burn. E Lot —2C 130
Lugg Green. Here —4G 59
Luggiebank. N Lan —2A 128
Lugton. E Ayr —4F 127
Lugwardine. Here —1A 48
Luib. High —1D 146
Luib. Stir —1D 135
Lulham. Here —1H 47
Lullington. Derbs —4G 73
Lullington. Som —1C 22
Lulsgate Bottom. N Som —5A 34
Lulsley. Worc —5B 60
Lulworth Camp. Dors —4D 14
Lumb. Lanc —2G 91
Lumb. W Yor —2A 92
Lumby. N Yor —1E 93
Lumphanan. Aber —3C 152
Lumphinnans. Fife —4D 136
Lumsdaine. Scot —3E 131
Lumsden. Aber —1B 152
Lunan. Ang —3F 145
Lunanhead. Ang —3D 145
Luncarty. Per —1C 136
Lund. E Yor —5D 100
Lund. N Yor —1G 93
Lundie. Ang —5B 144
Lundin Links. Fife —3G 137
Lundy Green. Norf —1E 67
Lunna. Shet —5F 173
Lunning. Shet —5G 173
Lunnon. Swan —4E 31
Lunsford. Kent —5B 40
Lunsford's Cross. E Sus —4B 28
Lunt. Mers —4B 90
Luppitt. Devn —2E 13
Lupridge. Devn —3D 8
Lupset. W Yor —3D 92
Lupton. Cumb —1E 97
Lurgashall. W Sus —3A 26
Lusby. Linc —4C 88
Luscombe. Devn —3D 9
Luson. Devn —4C 8
Luss. Arg —4C 134
Lussagiven. High —1E 125
Lusta. High —3B 154
Lustleigh. Devn —4A 12
Luston. Here —4G 59
Luthermuir. Aber —2F 145
Luthrie. Fife —2F 137
Lutley. Staf —2C 60
Luton. Devn —2D 12 (nr. Honiton)
Luton. Devn —5C 12 (nr. Teignmouth)
Luton. Lutn —3A 52
Luton. Medw —4B 40
Luton (London) Airport. Beds —3B 52
Lutterworth. Leics —2C 62
Lutton. Devn —3B 8 (nr. Ivybridge)
Lutton. Devn —2C 8 (nr. South Brent)
Lutton. Linc —3D 76
Lutton. Nptn —2A 64
Lutton Gowts. Linc —3D 76
Lutworthy. Devn —1A 12
Luxborough. Som —3C 20
Luxley. Glos —3B 48
Luxulyan. Corn —3E 7
Lybster. High —5E 169
Lydbury North. Shrp —2F 59
Lydcott. Devn —3G 19
Lydd. Kent —3E 29
Lydden. Kent —1G 29
Lyddington. Rut —1F 63
Lydd-on-Sea. Kent —4E 29
Lydeard St Lawrence. Som —3E 21
Lyde Green. Hants —1F 25
Lydford. Devn —4F 11
Lydford Fair Place. Som —3A 22
Lydgate. G Man —4H 91
Lydgate. W Yor —2H 91
Lydham. Shrp —1F 59
Lydiard Millicent. Wilts —3F 35
Lydiate. Mers —4B 90
Lydiate Ash. Worc —3D 61
Lydlinch. Dors —1C 14
Lydney. Glos —5B 48
Lydstep. Pemb —5E 43
Lye. W Mid —2D 60
Lye Green. Buck —5H 51
Lye Green. E Sus —2G 27
Lye Head. Worc —3B 60
Lye, The. Shrp —1A 60
Lyford. Oxon —2B 36
Lyham. Nmbd —1E 121
Lylestone. N Ayr —5E 127
Lymbridge Green. Kent —1F 29
Lyme Regis. Dors —3G 13
Lyminge. Kent —1F 29
Lymington. Hants —3B 16
Lyminster. W Sus —5B 26
Lymm. Warr —2A 84
Lymore. Hants —3A 16
Lympne. Kent —2F 29
Lympsham. Som —1G 21
Lympstone. Devn —4C 12
Lynaberack Lodge. High —4B 150
Lynbridge. Devn —2H 19
Lynch. Som —2C 20
Lynchat. High —3B 150
Lynch Green. Norf —5D 78
Lyndhurst. Hants —2B 16
Lyndon. Rut —5G 75
Lyne. Scot —5F 129
Lyne. Surr —4B 38
Lyneal. Shrp —2G 71
Lyne Down. Here —2B 48
Lyneham. Oxon —3A 50
Lyneham. Wilts —4F 35
Lyneholmeford. Cumb —2G 113
Lynemouth. Nmbd —5G 121
Lyne of Gorthleck. High —1H 149
Lyne of Skene. Aber —2E 153
Lynesack. Dur —2D 105
Lyness. Orkn —8C 172
Lyng. Norf —4C 78
Lyng. Som —4G 21
Lyngate. Norf —2E 79 (nr. North Walsham)
Lyngate. Norf —3F 79 (nr. Worstead)
Lynmouth. Devn —2H 19
Lynn. Staf —5E 73
Lynn. Telf —4B 72
Lynsted. Kent —4D 40
Lynstone. Corn —2C 10
Lynton. Devn —2H 19
Lynwilg. High —2C 150
Lyon's Gate. Dors —2B 14
Lyonshall. Here —5F 59
Lytchett Matravers. Dors —3E 15
Lytchett Minster. Dors —3E 15
Lyth. High —2E 169
Lytham. Lanc —2B 90
Lytham St Anne's. Lanc —2B 90
Lythe. N Yor —3F 107
Lythes. Orkn —9D 172
Lythmore. High —2C 168

Mabe Burnthouse. Corn —5B 6
Mabie. Dum —2G 111
Mablethorpe. Linc —2E 89
Macbiehill. Scot —4E 129
Macclesfield. Ches —3D 84
Macclesfield Forest. Ches —3D 85
Macduff. Aber —2E 160
Machan. S Lan —4A 128
Macharioch. Arg —5B 122
Machen. Cphy —3F 33
Machrie. N Ayr —2C 122
Machrihanish. Arg —3A 122
Machroes. Gwyn —3C 68
Machynlleth. Powy —5G 69
Mackerye End. Herts —4B 52
Mackworth. Dby C —2H 73
Macmerry. E Lot —2H 129
Maddaford. Devn —3F 11
Madderty. Per —1B 136
Maddington. Wilts —2F 23
Maddiston. Falk —2C 128
Madehurst. W Sus —4A 26
Madeley. Staf —1B 72
Madeley. Telf —5A 72
Madeley Heath. Staf —1B 72
Madeley Heath. Worc —3D 60
Madford. Devn —1E 13
Madingley. Cambs —4C 64
Madley. Here —2H 47
Madresfield. Worc —1D 48
Madron. Corn —3B 4
Maenaddwyn. IOA —2D 80
Maenclochog. Pemb —2E 43
Maendy. V Glam —4D 32
Maenporth. Corn —4E 5
Maentwrog. Gwyn —1F 69
Maen-y-groes. Cdgn —1B 44
Maer. Staf —2B 72
Maerdy. Carm —3G 45
Maerdy. Cnwy —1C 70
Maerdy. Rhon —2C 32
Maesbrook. Shrp —3F 71
Maesbury. Shrp —3F 71
Maesbury Marsh. Shrp —3F 71
Maes-glas. Flin —3D 82
Maesgwyn-Isaf. Powy —4D 70
Maeshafn. Den —4E 82
Maes Llyn. Cdgn —1D 44
Maesmynis. Powy —1D 46
Maesteg. B'End —2B 32
Maestir. Cdgn —1F 45
Maesybont. Carm —4F 45
Maesycrugiau. Carm —1E 45
Maesycwmmer. Cphy —2E 33
Maesyrhandir. Powy —1C 58
Magdalen Laver. Essx —5F 53
Maggieknockater. Mor —4H 159
Magham Down. E Sus —4H 27
Maghull. Mers —4B 90
Magna Park. Leics —2C 62
Magor. Mon —3H 33
Magpie Green. Suff —3C 66
Magwyr. Mon —3H 33
Maidenbower. W Sus —2D 27
Maiden Bradley. Wilts —3D 22
Maidencombe. Torb —2F 9
Maidenhayne. Devn —3F 13
Maidenhead. Wind —3G 37
Maiden Law. Dur —5E 115
Maiden Newton. Dors —3A 14
Maidens. S Ayr —4B 116
Maiden's Green. Brac —4G 37
Maidensgrove. Oxon —3F 37
Maidenwell. Corn —5B 10
Maidenwell. Linc —3C 88
Maiden Wells. Pemb —5D 42
Maidford. Nptn —5D 62
Maid's Moreton. Buck —2F 51
Maidstone. Kent —5B 40
Maidwell. Nptn —3E 63
Mail. Shet —9F 173
Maindee. Newp —3G 33
Mainsforth. Dur —1A 106
Mains of Auchindachy. Mor —4B 160

Mains of Drum—Micklethwaite

Mains of Drum. Aber —3F 153
Mains of Edingight. Mor —3C 160
Mainsriddle. Dum —4G 111
Mainstone. Shrp —2E 59
Maisemore. Glos —3D 48
Major's Green. Worc —3F 61
Makeney. Derbs —1A 74
Makerstoun. Scot —1A 120
Malacleit. W Isl —1C 170
Malborough. Devn —5D 8
Malcoff. Derbs —2E 85
Malden Rushett. Surr —4C 38
Maldon. Essx —5B 54
Malham. N Yor —3B 98
Maligar. High —2D 155
Malinslee. Telf —5A 72
Mallaig. High —4E 147
Mallaigvaig. High —4E 147
Malleny Mills. Edin —3E 129
Mallows Green. Essx —3E 53
Malltraeth. IOA —4D 80
Mallwyd. Gwyn —4A 70
Malmesbury. Wilts —3E 35
Malmsmead. Devn —2A 20
Malpas. Ches —1G 71
Malpas. Corn —4C 6
Malpas. Newp —2F 33
Malswick. Glos —3C 48
Maltby. S Yor —1C 86
Maltby. Stoc T —3B 106
Maltby le Marsh. Linc —2D 88
Malt Lane. Arg —3H 133
Maltman's Hill. Kent —1D 28
Malton. N Yor —2B 100
Malvern Link. Worc —1C 48
Malvern Wells. Worc —1C 48
Mamble. Worc —3A 60
Mamhilad. Mon —5G 47
Manaccan. Corn —4E 5
Manafon. Powy —5D 70
Manais. W Isl —9D 171
Manaton. Devn —4A 12
Manby. Linc —2C 88
Mancetter. Warw —1H 61
Manchester. G Man —1C 84
Manchester Airport. G Man —2C 84
Mancot. Flin —4F 83
Manea. Cambs —2D 65
Maney. W Mid —1F 61
Manfield. N Yor —3F 105
Mangotsfield. S Glo —4B 34
Mangurstadh. W Isl —4C 171
Mankinholes. W Yor —2H 91
Manley. Ches —3H 83
Manley. Devn —1C 12
Manmoel. Cphy —5E 47
Mannal. Arg —4A 138
Mannerston. Falk —2D 128
Manningford Bohune. Wilts —1G 23
Manningford Bruce. Wilts —1G 23
Manningham. W Yor —1B 92
Mannings Heath. W Sus —3D 26
Mannington. Dors —2F 15
Manningtree. Essx —2E 54
Mannofield. Aber C —3G 153
Manorbier. Pemb —5E 43
Manorbier Newton. Pemb —5E 43
Manorowen. Pemb —1D 42
Manor Park. G Lon —2F 39
Mansell Gamage. Here —1G 47
Mansell Lacy. Here —1H 47
Mansergh. Cumb —1F 97
Mansewood. Glas —3G 127
Mansfield. E Ayr —3F 117
Mansfield. Notts —4C 86
Mansfield Woodhouse. Notts —4C 86
Mansriggs. Cumb —1B 96
Manston. Dors —1D 14
Manston. Kent —4H 41
Manston. W Yor —1D 92
Manswood. Dors —2E 15
Manthorpe. Linc —4H 75 (nr. Bourne)
Manthorpe. Linc —2G 75 (nr. Grantham)
Manton. N Lin —4C 94
Manton. Notts —3C 86
Manton. Rut —5F 75
Manton. Wilts —5G 35
Manuden. Essx —3E 53
Maperton. Som —4B 22
Maplebeck. Notts —4E 86
Maple Cross. Herts —1B 38
Mapledurham. Oxon —4E 37
Mapledurwell. Hants —1E 25
Maplehurst. W Sus —3C 26
Maplescombe. Kent —4G 39
Mapleton. Derbs —1F 73
Mapperley. Derbs —1B 74
Mapperley. Notts —1C 74
Mapperley Park. Notts —1C 74
Mapperton. Dors —3A 14 (nr. Beaminster)
Mapperton. Dors —3E 15 (nr. Poole)
Mappleborough Green. Warw —4E 61
Mappleton. E Yor —5G 101
Mapplewell. S Yor —4D 92
Mappowder. Dors —2C 14
Maraig. W Isl —7E 171
Marazion. Corn —3C 4
Marbhig. W Isl —6G 171
Marbury. Ches —1H 71
March. Cambs —1D 64
Marcham. Oxon —2C 36
Marchamley. Shrp —3H 71
Marchington. Staf —2F 73
Marchington Woodlands. Staf —3F 73
Marchwiel. Wrex —1F 71
Marchwood. Hants —1B 16
Marcross. V Glam —5C 32
Marden. Here —1A 48
Marden. Kent —1B 28
Marden. Wilts —1F 23
Marden Beech. Kent —1B 28
Marden Thorn. Kent —1B 28
Mardu. Shrp —2E 59
Mardy. Mon —4G 47
Marefield. Leics —5E 75
Mareham le Fen. Linc —4B 88
Mareham on the Hill. Linc —4B 88
Marehay. Derbs —1A 74
Marehill. W Sus —4B 26
Maresfield. E Sus —3F 27
Marfleet. Hull —2E 95
Marford. Wrex —5F 83
Margam. Neat —3A 32
Margaret Marsh. Dors —1D 14
Margaret Roding. Essx —4F 53
Margaretting. Essx —5G 53
Margaretting Tye. Essx —5G 53
Margate. Kent —3H 41
Margery. Surr —5D 38
Margnaheglish. N Ayr —2E 123
Marham. Norf —5G 77
Marhamchurch. Corn —2C 10
Marholm. Pet —5A 76
Marian Cwm. Den —3C 82
Mariandyrys. IOA —2F 81
Marian-glas. IOA —2E 81
Mariansleigh. Devn —4H 19
Marian-y-de. Gwyn —2C 68
Marine Town. Kent —3D 40
Marion-y-mor. Gwyn —2C 68
Marishader. High —2D 155
Marjoriebanks. Dum —1B 112
Mark. Dum —4G 109
Mark. Som —2G 21
Markbeech. Kent —1F 27
Markby. Linc —3D 89
Mark Causeway. Som —2G 21
Mark Cross. E Sus —2G 27
Markeaton. Derbs —2H 73
Market Bosworth. Leics —5B 74
Market Deeping. Linc —4A 76
Market Drayton. Shrp —2A 72
Market End. Warw —2H 61
Market Harborough. Leics —2E 63
Markethill. Per —5B 144
Market Lavington. Wilts —1F 23
Market Overton. Rut —4F 75
Market Rasen. Linc —2A 88
Market Stainton. Linc —3B 88
Market Warsop. Notts —4C 86
Market Weighton. E Yor —5C 100
Market Weston. Suff —3B 66
Markfield. Leics —4B 74
Markham. Cphy —5E 47
Markinch. Fife —3E 137
Markington. N Yor —3E 99
Marksbury. Bath —5B 34
Mark's Corner. IOW —3C 16
Marks Tey. Essx —3C 54
Markwell. Corn —3H 7
Markyate. Herts —4A 52
Marlborough. Wilts —5G 35
Marlcliff. Warw —5E 61
Marldon. Devn —2E 9
Marle Green. E Sus —4G 27
Marlesford. Suff —5F 67
Marley Green. Ches —1H 71
Marley Hill. Tyne —4F 115
Marlingford. Norf —5D 78
Marloes. Pemb —4B 42
Marlow. Buck —3G 37
Marlow. Here —3G 59
Marlow Bottom. Buck —3G 37
Marlpit Hill. Kent —1F 27
Marlpits. E Sus —3F 27
Marlpool. Derbs —1B 74
Marnhull. Dors —1C 14
Marnoch. Aber —3C 160
Marnock. N Lan —3A 128
Marple. G Man —2D 84
Marr. S Yor —4F 93
Marrel. High —2H 165
Marrick. N Yor —5D 105
Marrister. Shet —5G 173
Marros. Carm —4G 43
Marsden. Tyne —3G 115
Marsden. W Yor —3A 92
Marsett. N Yor —1B 98
Marsh. Buck —5G 51
Marsh. Devn —1F 13
Marshall Meadows. Nmbd —4F 131
Marshalsea. Dors —2G 13
Marshalswick. Herts —5B 52
Marsham. Norf —3D 78
Marshaw. Lanc —4E 97
Marsh Baldon. Oxon —2D 36
Marsh Benham. W Ber —5C 36
Marshborough. Kent —5H 41
Marshbrook. Shrp —2G 59
Marshchapel. Linc —1C 88
Marshfield. Newp —3F 33
Marshfield. S Glo —4C 34
Marshgate. Corn —3B 10
Marsh Gibbon. Buck —3E 51
Marsh Green. Devn —3D 12
Marsh Green. Kent —1F 27
Marsh Green. Staf —5C 84
Marsh Green. Telf —4A 72
Marsh Lane. Derbs —3B 86
Marshside. Mers —3B 90
Marsh Side. Norf —1G 77
Marsh Street. Som —2C 20
Marsh, The. Powy —1F 59
Marsh, The. Shrp —3A 72
Marshwood. Dors —3G 13
Marske. N Yor —4E 105
Marske-by-the-Sea. Red C —2D 106
Marston. Ches —3A 84
Marston. Here —5F 59
Marston. Notts —1F 75
Marston. Oxon —5D 50
Marston. Staf —3D 72 (nr. Stafford)
Marston. Staf —4C 72 (nr. Wheaton Aston)
Marston. Warw —1G 61
Marston. Wilts —1E 23
Marston Doles. Warw —5B 62
Marston Green. W Mid —2F 61
Marston Hill. Glos —2G 35
Marston Jabbett. Warw —2A 62
Marston Magna. Som —4A 22
Marston Meysey. Wilts —2G 35
Marston Montgomery. Derbs —2F 73
Marston Moretaine. Beds —1H 51
Marston on Dove. Derbs —3G 73
Marston St Lawrence. Nptn —1D 50
Marston Stannett. Here —5H 59
Marston Trussell. Nptn —2D 62
Marstow. Here —4A 48
Marsworth. Buck —4H 51
Marten. Wilts —5A 36
Marthall. Ches —3C 84
Martham. Norf —4G 79
Marthwaite. Cumb —5H 103
Martin. Hants —1F 15
Martin. Kent —1H 29
Martin. Linc —4B 88 (nr. Horncastle)
Martin. Linc —5A 88 (nr. Metheringham)
Martindale. Cumb —3F 103
Martin Dales. Linc —4A 88
Martin Drove End. Hants —4F 23
Martinhoe. Devn —2G 19
Martinhoe Cross. Devn —2G 19
Martin Hussingtree. Worc —5C 60
Martin Mill. Kent —1H 29
Martinscroft. Warr —2A 84
Martin's Moss. Ches —4C 84
Martinstown. Dors —4B 14
Martlesham. Suff —1F 55
Martlesham Heath. Suff —1F 55
Martletwy. Pemb —3E 43
Martley. Worc —5B 60
Martock. Som —1H 13
Marton. Ches —4C 84
Marton. Cumb —2B 96
Marton. E Yor —3G 101 (nr. Bridlington)
Marton. E Yor —1E 95 (nr. Hull)
Marton. Linc —2F 87
Marton. Midd —3C 106
Marton. N Yor —3G 99 (nr. Boroughbridge)
Marton. N Yor —1B 100 (nr. Pickering)
Marton. Shrp —3G 71 (nr. Myddle)
Marton. Shrp —5E 71 (nr. Worthen)
Marton. Warw —4B 62
Marton Abbey. N Yor —3H 99
Marton-le-Moor. N Yor —2F 99
Martyr's Green. Surr —5B 38
Martyr Worthy. Hants —3D 24
Marwick. Orkn —5B 172
Marwood. Devn —3F 19
Marybank. High —3G 157 (nr. Dingwall)
Marybank. High —1B 158 (nr. Invergordon)
Maryburgh. High —3H 157
Maryfield. Corn —3A 8
Maryhill. Glas —3G 127
Marykirk. Aber —2F 145
Marylebone. G Lon —2D 39
Marylebone. G Man —4D 90
Marypark. Mor —5F 159
Maryport. Cumb —1B 102
Maryport. Dum —5E 109
Marystow. Devn —4E 11
Mary Tavy. Devn —5F 11
Maryton. Ang —3C 144 (nr. Kirriemuir)
Maryton. Ang —3F 145 (nr. Montrose)
Marywell. Aber —4C 152
Marywell. Ang —4F 145
Masham. N Yor —1E 98
Mashbury. Essx —4G 53
Mason. Tyne —2F 115
Masongill. N Yor —2F 97
Masons Lodge. Aber —3F 153
Mastin Moor. Derbs —3B 86
Mastrick. Aber C —3G 153
Matching. Essx —4F 53
Matching Green. Essx —4F 53
Matching Tye. Essx —4F 53
Matfen. Nmbd —2D 114
Matfield. Kent —1A 28
Mathern. Mon —2A 34
Mathon. Here —1C 48
Mathry. Pemb —1C 42
Matlaske. Norf —2D 78
Matlock. Derbs —4G 85
Matlock Bath. Derbs —5G 85
Matterdale End. Cumb —2E 103
Mattersey. Notts —2D 86
Mattersey Thorpe. Notts —1D 86
Mattingley. Hants —1F 25
Mattishall. Norf —4C 78
Mattishall Burgh. Norf —4C 78
Mauchline. E Ayr —2D 117
Maud. Aber —4G 161
Maudlin. Corn —2E 7
Maugersbury. Glos —3G 49
Maughold. IOM —2D 108
Maulden. Beds —2A 52
Maulds Meaburn. Cumb —3H 103
Maunby. N Yor —1F 99
Maund Bryan. Here —5H 59
Mautby. Norf —4G 79
Mavesyn Ridware. Staf —4E 73
Mavis Enderby. Linc —4C 88
Mawbray. Cumb —5B 112
Mawdesley. Lanc —3C 90
Mawdlam. B'End —3B 32
Mawgan. Corn —4E 5
Mawgan Porth. Corn —2C 6
Maw Green. Ches —5B 84
Mawla. Corn —4B 6
Mawnan. Corn —4E 5
Mawnan Smith. Corn —4E 5
Mawthorpe. Linc —3D 88
Maxey. Pet —5A 76
Maxstoke. Warw —2G 61
Maxton. Kent —1H 29
Maxton. Scot —1A 120
Maxwellheugh. Scot —1B 120
Maxwelltown. Dum —2A 112
Maxworthy. Corn —3C 10
Mayals. Swan —4F 31
Maybole. S Ayr —4C 116
Maybush. Sotn —1B 16
Mayes Green. Surr —2C 26
Mayfield. E Sus —3G 27
Mayfield. Midl —3G 129
Mayfield. Per —1C 136
Mayfield. Staf —1F 73
Mayford. Surr —5A 38
Mayhill. Swan —3F 31
Mayland. Essx —5C 54
Maylandsea. Essx —5C 54
Maynard's Green. E Sus —4G 27
Maypole. IOS —1B 4
Maypole. Kent —4G 41
Maypole. Mon —4H 47
Maypole Green. Norf —1G 67
Maypole Green. Suff —5B 66
Mayshill. S Glo —3B 34
Maywick. Shet —9E 173
Mead. Devn —1C 10
Meadgate. Bath —1B 22
Meadle. Buck —5G 51
Meadowbank. Ches —4A 84
Meadowfield. Dur —1F 105
Meadow Green. Here —5B 60
Meadowmill. E Lot —2H 129
Meadows. Not C —2C 74
Meadowtown. Shrp —5F 71
Meadwell. Devn —4E 11
Mealabost. W Isl —2G 171 (nr. Baile Ard)
Mealabost. W Isl —4G 171 (nr. Stornoway)
Mealasta. W Isl —5B 171
Meal Bank. Cumb —5G 103
Mealrigg. Cumb —5C 112
Mealsgate. Cumb —5D 112
Meanwood. W Yor —1C 92
Mearbeck. N Yor —3H 97
Meare. Som —2H 21
Meare Green. Som —4F 21 (nr. Curry Mallet)
Meare Green. Som —4G 21 (nr. Stoke St Gregory)
Mears Ashby. Nptn —4F 63
Measham. Leics —4H 73
Meath Green. Surr —1D 26
Meathop. Cumb —1D 96
Meaux. E Yor —1D 94
Meavy. Devn —2B 8
Medbourne. Leics —1E 63
Medburn. Nmbd —2E 115
Meddon. Devn —1C 10
Meden Vale. Notts —4C 86
Medlam. Linc —5C 88
Medlicott. Shrp —1G 59
Medmenham. Buck —3G 37
Medomsley. Dur —4E 115
Medstead. Hants —3E 25
Medway Towns. Medw —4B 40
Meerbrook. Staf —4D 85
Meer End. W Mid —3G 61
Meers Bridge. Linc —2D 89
Meesden. Herts —2E 53
Meeson. Telf —3A 72
Meeth. Devn —2F 11
Meeting Green. Suff —5G 65
Meidrim. Carm —2G 43
Meifod. Powy —4D 70
Meigle. Per —4B 144
Meikle Earnock. S Lan —4A 128
Meikle Kilchattan Butts. Arg —4B 126
Meikleour. Per —5A 144
Meikle Tarty. Aber —1G 153
Meikle Wartle. Aber —5E 160
Meinciau. Carm —4E 45
Meir. Stoke —1D 72
Meir Heath. Staf —1D 72
Melbourn. Cambs —1D 53
Melbourne. Derbs —3A 74
Melbourne. E Yor —5B 100
Melbury Abbas. Dors —4D 23
Melbury Bubb. Dors —2A 14
Melbury Osmond. Dors —2A 14
Melbury Sampford. Dors —2A 14
Melby. Shet —6C 173
Melchbourne. Beds —4H 63
Melcombe Bingham. Dors —2C 14
Melcombe Regis. Dors —4B 14
Meldon. Devn —3F 11
Meldon. Nmbd —1E 115
Meldreth. Cambs —1D 52
Melfort. Arg —2F 133
Melgarve. High —4G 149
Meliden. Den —2C 82
Melinbyrhedyn. Powy —1H 57
Melincourt. Neat —5B 46
Melin-y-coed. Cnwy —4H 81
Melin-y-ddol. Powy —5C 70
Melin-y-wig. Den —1C 70
Melkington. Nmbd —5E 131
Melkinthorpe. Cumb —2G 103
Melkridge. Nmbd —3A 114
Melksham. Wilts —5E 35
Mellangaun. High —5C 162
Melldalloch. Arg —2H 125
Mellguards. Cumb —5F 113
Melling. Lanc —2E 97
Melling. Mers —4B 90
Melling Mount. Mers —4C 90
Mellis. Suff —3C 66
Mellon Charles. High —4C 162
Mellon Udrigle. High —4C 162
Mellor. G Man —2D 85
Mellor. Lanc —1E 91
Mellor Brook. Lanc —1E 91
Mells. Som —2C 22
Melmerby. Cumb —1H 103
Melmerby. N Yor —1C 98 (nr. Middleham)
Melmerby. N Yor —2F 99 (nr. Ripon)
Melplash. Dors —3H 13
Melrose. Scot —1H 119
Melsetter. Orkn —9B 172
Melsonby. N Yor —4E 105
Meltham. W Yor —3A 92
Meltham Mills. W Yor —3B 92
Melton. E Yor —2C 94
Melton. Suff —5E 67
Meltonby. E Yor —4B 100
Melton Constable. Norf —2C 78
Melton Mowbray. Leics —4E 75
Melton Ross. N Lin —3D 94
Melvaig. High —5B 162
Melverley. Shrp —4F 71
Melverley Green. Shrp —4F 71
Melvich. High —2A 168
Membury. Devn —2F 13
Memsie. Aber —2G 161
Memus. Ang —3D 144
Menabilly. Corn —3E 7
Menai Bridge. IOA —3E 81
Mendham. Suff —2E 67
Mendlesham. Suff —4D 66
Mendlesham Green. Suff —4C 66
Menethorpe. N Yor —3B 100
Menheniot. Corn —2G 7
Menithwood. Worc —4B 60
Menna. Corn —3D 6
Mennock. Dum —4H 117
Menston. W Yor —5D 98
Menstrie. Clac —4H 135
Menthorpe. N Yor —1H 93
Mentmore. Buck —4H 51
Meole Brace. Shrp —4G 71
Meols. Mers —2E 83
Meon. Hants —2D 15
Meonstoke. Hants —1E 16
Meopham. Kent —4H 39
Meopham Green. Kent —4H 39
Meopham Station. Kent —4H 39
Mepal. Cambs —2D 64
Meppershall. Beds —2B 52
Merbach. Here —1G 47
Mercaston. Derbs —1G 73
Merchiston. Edin —2F 129
Mere. Ches —2B 84
Mere. Wilts —3D 22
Mere Brow. Lanc —3C 90
Mereclough. Lanc —1G 91
Mere Green. W Mid —1F 61
Mere Green. Worc —4D 60
Mere Heath. Ches —3A 84
Mereside. Bkpl —1B 90
Meretown. Staf —3B 72
Mereworth. Kent —5A 40
Meriden. W Mid —2G 61
Merkadale. High —5C 154
Merkland. S Ayr —5B 116
Merkland Lodge. High —1A 164
Merley. Pool —3F 15
Merlin's Bridge. Pemb —3D 42
Merridge. Som —3F 21
Merrington. Shrp —3G 71
Merrion. Pemb —5D 42
Merriott. Som —1H 13
Merrivale. Devn —5F 11
Merrow. Surr —5B 38
Merrybent. Darl —3F 105
Merry Lees. Leics —5B 74
Merrymeet. Corn —2G 7
Mersham. Kent —2E 29
Merstham. Surr —5D 39
Merston. W Sus —2G 17
Merstone. IOW —4D 16
Merther. Corn —4C 6
Merthyr. Carm —3D 44
Merthyr Cynog. Powy —2C 46
Merthyr Dyfan. V Glam —5E 32
Merthyr Mawr. B'End —4B 32
Merthyr Tudful. Mer T —5D 46
Merthyr Tydfil. Mer T —5D 46
Merthyr Vale. Mer T —5D 46
Merton. Devn —1F 11
Merton. G Lon —4D 38
Merton. Norf —1B 66
Merton. Oxon —4D 50
Meshaw. Devn —1A 12
Messing. Essx —4B 54
Messingham. N Lin —4B 94
Metcombe. Devn —3D 12
Metfield. Suff —2E 67
Metherell. Corn —2A 8
Metheringham. Linc —4H 87
Methil. Fife —4F 137
Methilhill. Fife —4F 137
Methley. W Yor —2D 93
Methley Junction. W Yor —2D 93
Methlick. Aber —5F 161
Methven. Per —1C 136
Methwold. Norf —1G 65
Methwold Hythe. Norf —1G 65
Mettingham. Suff —1F 67
Metton. Norf —2D 78
Mevagissey. Corn —4E 6
Mexborough. S Yor —4E 93
Mey. High —1E 169
Meysey Hampton. Glos —2G 35
Miabhag. W Isl —7C 171 (nr. Cliasmol)
Miabhag. W Isl —8D 171 (nr. Tarbert)
Miabhig. W Isl —4C 171
Mial. High —1G 155
Michael. IOM —2C 108
Michaelchurch. Here —3A 48
Michaelchurch Escley. Here —2G 47
Michaelchurch-on-Arrow. Powy —5E 59
Michaelcombe. Devn —2C 8
Michaelston-le-Pit. V Glam —4E 33
Michaelston-y-Vedw. Newp —3F 33
Michaelstow. Corn —5A 10
Micheldever. Hants —3D 24
Micheldever Station. Hants —2D 24
Michelmersh. Hants —4B 24
Mickfield. Suff —4D 66
Micklebring. S Yor —1C 86
Mickleby. N Yor —3F 107
Micklefield. W Yor —1E 93
Micklefield Green. Herts —1B 38
Mickleham. Surr —5C 38
Mickleover. Dby C —2H 73
Micklethwaite. Cumb —4D 112

Micklethwaite—Morgan's Vale

Micklethwaite. W Yor —5D 98
Mickleton. Dur —2C 104
Mickleton. Glos —1G 49
Mickletown. W Yor —2D 93
Mickle Trafford. Ches —4G 83
Mickley. N Yor —2E 99
Mickley Green. Suff —5H 65
Mickley Square. Nmbd —3D 115
Mid Ardlaw. Aber —2G 161
Midbea. Orkn —3D 172
Mid Beltie. Aber —3D 152
Mid Calder. W Lot —3D 129
Mid Clyth. High —5E 169
Middle Assendon. Oxon —3F 37
Middle Aston. Oxon —3C 50
Middle Barton. Oxon —3C 50
Middlebie. Dum —2D 112
Middle Chinnock. Som —1H 13
Middle Claydon. Buck —3F 51
Middlecliff. S Yor —4E 93
Middlecott. Devn —4H 11
Middle Drums. Ang —3E 145
Middle Duntisbourne. Glos —5E 49
Middle Essie. Aber —3H 161
Middleforth Green. Lanc —2D 90
Middleham. N Yor —1D 98
Middle Handley. Derbs —3B 86
Middle Harling. Norf —2B 66
Middlehope. Shrp —2G 59
Middle Littleton. Worc —1F 49
Middle Maes-coed. Here —2G 47
Middlemarsh. Dors —2B 14
Middle Marwood. Devn —3F 19
Middle Mayfield. Staf —1F 73
Middlemuir. Aber —4F 161
(nr. New Deer)
Middlemuir. Aber —3G 161
(nr. Strichen)
Middle Rainton. Tyne —5G 115
Middle Rasen. Linc —2H 87
Middlesbrough. Midd —2B 106
Middlesceugh. Cumb —5E 113
Middleshaw. Cumb —1E 97
Middlesmoor. N Yor —2C 98
Middles, The. Dur —4F 115
Middlestone. Dur —1F 105
Middlestone Moor. Dur —1F 105
Middle Stoughton. Som —2H 21
Middlestown. W Yor —3C 92
Middle Street. Glos —5C 48
Middle Taphouse. Corn —2F 7
Middleton. Ang —4E 145
Middleton. Arg —4A 138
Middleton. Cumb —1F 97
Middleton. Derbs —4F 85
(nr. Bakewell)
Middleton. Derbs —5G 85
(nr. Wirksworth)
Middleton. Essx —2B 54
Middleton. G Man —4G 91
Middleton. Hants —2C 24
Middleton. Hart —1C 106
Middleton. Here —4H 59
Middleton. IOW —4B 16
Middleton. Lanc —4D 96
Middleton. Midl —4G 129
Middleton. Norf —4F 77
Middleton. Nptn —1F 63
Middleton. Nmbd —1F 121
(nr. Belford)
Middleton. Nmbd —1D 114
(nr. Morpeth)
Middleton. N Yor —5D 98
(nr. Ilkley)
Middleton. N Yor —1B 100
(nr. Pickering)
Middleton. Per —3D 136
Middleton. Shrp —3H 59
(nr. Ludlow)
Middleton. Shrp —3F 71
(nr. Oswestry)
Middleton. Suff —4G 67
Middleton. Swan —4D 30
Middleton. Warw —1F 61
Middleton. W Yor —2D 92
Middleton Cheney. Nptn —1D 50
Middleton Green. Staf —2D 73
Middleton Hall. Midl —4G 129
Middleton Hall. Nmbd —2D 121
Middleton in Teesdale. Dur —2C 104
Middleton One Row. Darl —3A 106
Middleton-on-Leven. N Yor —4B 106
Middleton-on-Sea. W Sus —5A 26
Middleton on the Hill. Here —4H 59
Middleton-on-the-Wolds. E Yor —5D 100
Middleton Priors. Shrp —1A 60
Middleton Quernhow. N Yor —2F 99
Middleton St George. Darl —3A 106
Middleton Scriven. Shrp —2A 60
Middleton Stoney. Oxon —3D 50
Middleton Tyas. N Yor —4F 105
Middletown. Cumb —4A 102
Middle Town. IOS —1B 4
Middletown. Powy —4F 71
Middle Tysoe. Warw —1B 50
Middle Wallop. Hants —3A 24
Middlewich. Ches —4B 84
Middle Winterslow. Wilts —3H 23
Middlewood. Corn —5C 10
Middlewood. S Yor —1H 85
Middle Woodford. Wilts —3G 23
Middlewood Green. Suff —4C 66
Middleyard. Glos —5D 48
Middlezoy. Som —3G 21
Middridge. Dur —2F 105
Midfield. High —2F 167
Midford. Bath —5C 34
Midge Hall. Lanc —2D 90
Midgeholme. Cumb —4H 113
Midgham. W Ber —5D 36
Midgley. W Yor —2A 92
(nr. Halifax)
Midgley. W Yor —3C 92
(nr. Horbury)
Mid Ho. Shet —2G 173
Midhopestones. S Yor —1G 85
Midhurst. W Sus —4G 25
Mid Kirkton. N Ayr —4C 126
Mid Lambrook. Som —1H 13
Midland. Orkn —7C 172
Mid Lavant. W Sus —2G 17
Midlem. Scot —2H 119
Midney. Som —4A 22
Midsomer Norton. Bath —1B 22
Midton. Inv —2D 126
Midtown. High —5C 162
(nr. Poolewe)
Midtown. High —2F 167
(nr. Tongue)
Midville. Linc —5C 88
Mid Walls. Shet —6C 173
Midway. Derbs —3H 73
Mid Yell. Shet —2G 173
Migdale. High —4D 164
Migvie. Aber —3B 152
Milborne Port. Som —1B 14
Milborne St Andrew. Dors —3D 14
Milborne Wick. Som —4B 22
Milbourne. Nmbd —2E 115
Milbourne. Wilts —3E 35
Milburn. Cumb —2H 103
Milbury Heath. S Glo —2B 34
Milby. N Yor —3G 99
Milcombe. Oxon —2C 50
Milden. Suff —1C 54
Mildenhall. Suff —3G 65
Mildenhall. Wilts —5H 35
Milebrook. Powy —3F 59
Milebush. Kent —1B 28
Mile End. Cambs —2F 65
Mile End. Essx —3C 54
Mileham. Norf —4B 78
Mile Oak. Brig —5D 26
Miles Green. Staf —5C 84
Miles Hope. Here —4H 59
Milesmark. Fife —1D 128
Mile Town. Kent —3D 40
Milfield. Nmbd —1D 120
Milford. Derbs —1A 74
Milford. Devn —4C 18
Milford. Powy —1C 58
Milford. Staf —3D 73
Milford. Surr —1A 26
Milford Haven. Pemb —4D 42
Milford on Sea. Hants —3A 16
Milkwall. Glos —5A 48
Milkwell. Wilts —4E 23
Milland. W Sus —4G 25
Millbank. High —2D 168
Mill Bank. W Yor —2A 92
Millbeck. Cumb —2D 102
Millbounds. Orkn —4E 172
Millbreck. Aber —4H 161
Millbridge. Surr —2G 25
Millbrook. Beds —2A 52
Millbrook. Corn —3A 8
Millbrook. G Man —1D 85
Millbrook. Sotn —1B 16
Mill Common. Suff —2G 67
Mill Corner. E Sus —3C 28
Milldale. Staf —5F 85
Millden Lodge. Ang —1E 145
Milldens. Ang —3E 145
Millearn. Per —2B 136
Mill End. Buck —3F 37
Mill End. Cambs —5F 65
Millend. Glos —2C 34
(nr. Dursley)
Mill End. Glos —4G 49
(nr. Northleach)
Mill End. Herts —2D 52
Millerhill. Midl —3G 129
Miller's Dale. Derbs —3F 85
Millers Green. Derbs —5G 85
Millerston. Glas —3H 127
Millfield. Aber —4B 152
Millfield. Pet —1A 64
Millgate. Lanc —3G 91
Mill Green. Norf —2D 66
Mill Green. Shrp —3A 72
Mill Green. Staf —3E 73
Mill Green. Suff —1C 54
Mill Greep. Essx —5G 53
Millhalf. Here —1F 47
Millhall. E Ren —4G 127
Millhayes. Devn —2F 13
(nr. Honiton)
Millhayes. Devn —1E 13
(nr. Wellington)
Millhead. Lanc —2D 97
Millheugh. S Lan —4A 128
Mill Hill. Bkbn —2E 91
Mill Hill. G Lon —1D 38
Millholme. Cumb —5G 103
Millhouse. Arg —2A 126
Millhousebridge. Dum —1C 112
Millhouses. S Yor —2H 85
Millikenpark. Ren —3F 127
Millington. E Yor —4C 100
Millington Green. Derbs —1G 73
Mill Knowe. Arg —3B 122
Mill Lane. Hants —1F 25
Millmeece. Staf —2C 72
Mill of Craigievar. Aber —2C 152
Mill of Fintray. Aber —2F 153
Mill of Haldane. W Dun —1E 127
Millom. Cumb —1A 96
Millow. Beds —1C 52
Mill Place. N Lin —4C 94
Millpool. Corn —5B 10
Millport. N Ayr —4C 126
Mill Side. Cumb —1D 96
Mill Street. Norf —4C 78
(nr. Lyng)
Mill Street. Norf —4C 78
(nr. Swanton Morley)
Mill Street. Suff —3C 66
Millthorpe. Derbs —3H 85
Millthorpe. Linc —2A 76
Millthrop. Cumb —5H 103
Milltimber. Aber C —3F 153
Milltown. Aber —3G 151
(nr. Corgarff)
Milltown. Aber —2B 152
(nr. Lumsden)
Milltown. Corn —3F 7
Milltown. Derbs —4A 86
Milltown. Devn —3F 19
Milltown. Dum —2E 113
Milltown. High —3E 157
Milltown. Mor —4C 160
Milltown of Aberdalgie. Per —1C 136
Milltown of Auchindoun. Mor —4A 160
Milltown of Campfield. Aber —3D 152
Milltown of Edinville. Mor —5G 159
Milltown of Towie. Aber —2B 152
Milnacraig. Ang —3B 144
Milnathort. Per —3D 136
Milngavie. E Dun —2G 127
Milnholm. Stir —1A 128
Milnrow. G Man —3H 91
Milnthorpe. Cumb —1D 97
Milnthorpe. W Yor —3D 92
Milovaig. High —4A 154
Milson. Shrp —3A 60
Milstead. Kent —5D 40
Milston. Wilts —2G 23
Milthorpe. Nptn —1D 50
Milton. Ang —4C 144
Milton. Cambs —4D 65
Milton. Cumb —3G 113
Milton. Derbs —3H 73
Milton. Dum —2F 111
(nr. Crocketford)
Milton. Dum —1F 111
(nr. Dunscore)
Milton. Dum —4H 109
(nr. Glenluce)
Milton. E Ayr —2D 116
Milton. Glas —2H 127
Milton. High —3F 157
(nr. Achnasheen)
Milton. High —4G 155
(nr. Applecross)
Milton. High —5G 157
(nr. Drumnadrochit)
Milton. High —1B 158
(nr. Invergordon)
Milton. High —4H 157
(nr. Inverness)
Milton. High —3F 169
(nr. Wick)
Milton. Mor —2C 160
(nr. Cullen)
Milton. Mor —2F 151
(nr. Tomintoul)
Milton. N Som —5G 33
Milton. Notts —3E 86
Milton. Oxon —2C 50
(nr. Banbury)
Milton. Oxon —2C 36
(nr. Didcot)
Milton. Pemb —4E 43
Milton. Per —3A 144
Milton. Port —3E 17
Milton. Som —4H 21
Milton. Stir —3E 135
(nr. Aberfoyle)
Milton. Stir —4D 134
(nr. Drymen)
Milton. Stoke —5D 84
Milton. W Dun —2F 127
Milton Abbas. Dors —2D 14
Milton Abbot. Devn —5E 11
Milton Auchlossan. Aber —3C 152
Milton Bridge. Midl —3F 129
Milton Bryan. Beds —2H 51
Milton Clevedon. Som —3B 22
Milton Coldwells. Aber —5G 161
Milton Combe. Devn —2A 8
Milton Damerel. Devn —1D 11
Miltonduff. Mor —2F 159
Milton End. Glos —5G 49
Milton Ernest. Beds —5H 63
Milton Green. Ches —5G 83
Milton Hill. Devn —5C 12
Milton Hill. Oxon —2C 36
Milton Keynes. Mil —2G 51
Milton Keynes Village. Mil —2G 51
Milton Lilbourne. Wilts —5G 35
Milton Malsor. Nptn —5E 63
Milton Morenish. Per —5D 142
Milton of Auchinhove. Aber —3C 152
Milton of Balgonie. Fife —3F 137
Milton of Barras. Aber —1H 145
Milton of Campsie. E Dun —2H 127
Milton of Cultoquhey. Per —1A 136
Milton of Cushnie. Aber —2C 152
Milton of Finavon. Ang —3D 145
Milton of Gollanfield. High —3B 158
Milton of Lesmore. Aber —1B 152
Milton of Tullich. Aber —4A 152
Milton on Stour. Dors —4C 22
Milton Regis. Kent —4C 40
Milton Street. E Sus —5G 27
Milton-under-Wychwood. Oxon —4A 50
Milverton. Som —4E 20
Milverton. Warw —4H 61
Milwich. Staf —2D 72
Mimbridge. Surr —4A 38
Minard. Arg —4G 133
Minchington. Dors —1E 15
Minchinhampton. Glos —5D 49
Mindrum. Nmbd —1C 120
Minehead. Som —2C 20
Minera. Wrex —5E 83
Minety. Wilts —2F 35
Minffordd. Gwyn —2E 69
Mingarrypark. High —2A 140
Mingary. High —2G 139
Miningsby. Linc —4C 88
Minions. Corn —5C 10
Minishant. S Ayr —3C 116
Minllyn. Gwyn —4A 70
Minngearraidh. W Isl —6C 170
Minnigaff. Dum —3B 110
Minorca. IOM —3D 108
Minskip. N Yor —3F 99
Minstead. Hants —1A 16
Minsted. W Sus —4G 25
Minster. Kent —4H 41
(nr. Ramsgate)
Minster. Kent —3D 40
(nr. Sheerness)
Minsteracres. Nmbd —4D 114
Minsterley. Shrp —5F 71
Minster Lovell. Oxon —4B 50
Minsterworth. Glos —4C 48
Minterne Magna. Dors —2B 14
Minterne Parva. Dors —2B 14
Minting. Linc —3A 88
Mintlaw. Aber —4H 161
Minto. Scot —2H 119
Minton. Shrp —1G 59
Minwear. Pemb —3E 43
Minworth. W Mid —1F 61
Miodar. Arg —4B 138
Mirbister. Orkn —6C 172
Mirehouse. Cumb —3A 102
Mireland. High —2F 169
Mirfield. W Yor —3C 92
Miserden. Glos —5E 49
Miskin. Rhon —3D 32
Misson. Notts —1D 86
Misterton. Leics —2C 62
Misterton. Notts —1E 87
Misterton. Som —2H 13
Mistley. Essx —2E 54
Mistley Heath. Essx —2E 55
Mitcham. G Lon —4D 39
Mitcheldean. Glos —4B 48
Mitchell. Corn —3C 6
Mitchel Troy. Mon —4H 47
Mitcheltroy Common. Mon —5H 47
Mitford. Nmbd —1E 115
Mithian. Corn —3B 6
Mitton. Staf —4C 72
Mixbury. Oxon —2E 50
Mixenden. W Yor —2A 92
Mixon. Staf —5E 85
Moarfield. Shet —1G 173
Moat. Cumb —2F 113
Moats Tye. Suff —5C 66
Mobberley. Ches —3B 84
Mobberley. Staf —1E 73
Moccas. Here —1G 47
Mochdre. Cnwy —3H 81
Mochdre. Powy —2C 58
Mochrum. Dum —5A 110
Mockbeggar. Hants —2G 15
Mockerkin. Cumb —2B 102
Modbury. Devn —3C 8
Moddershall. Staf —2D 72
Modsarie. High —2G 167
Moelfre. Cnwy —3B 82
Moelfre. IOA —2E 81
Moelfre. Powy —3D 70
Moffat. Dum —4C 118
Mogerhanger. Beds —1B 52
Mogworthy. Devn —1B 12
Moira. Leics —4H 73
Molash. Kent —5E 41
Mol-chlach. High —2C 146
Mold. Flin —4E 83
Molehill Green. Essx —3F 53
Molescroft. E Yor —5E 101
Molesden. Nmbd —1E 115
Molesworth. Cambs —3H 63
Moll. High —5E 155
Molland. Devn —4B 20
Mollington. Ches —3F 83
Mollington. Oxon —1C 50
Mollinsburn. N Lan —2A 128
Monachty. Cdgn —4E 57
Monachylemore. Stir —1D 134
Monar Lodge. High —4E 156
Monaughty. Powy —4E 59
Monewden. Suff —5E 67
Moneydie. Per —1C 136
Moneyrow Green. Wind —4G 37
Moniaive. Dum —5G 117
Monifieth. Ang —5E 145
Monikie. Ang —5E 145
Monimail. Fife —2E 137
Monington. Pemb —1B 44
Monk Bretton. S Yor —4D 92
Monken Hadley. G Lon —1D 38
Monk Fryston. N Yor —2F 93
Monk Hesleden. Dur —1B 106
Monkhide. Here —1B 48
Monkhill. Cumb —4E 113
Monkhopton. Shrp —1A 60
Monkland. Here —5G 59
Monkleigh. Devn —4E 19
Monknash. V Glam —4C 32
Monkokehampton. Devn —2F 11
Monkseaton. Tyne —2G 115
Monks Eleigh. Suff —1C 54
Monk's Gate. W Sus —3D 26
Monk's Heath. Ches —3C 84
Monk Sherborne. Hants —1E 24
Monkshill. Aber —4E 161
Monksilver. Som —3D 20
Monks Kirby. Warw —2B 62
Monk Soham. Suff —4E 66
Monk Soham Green. Suff —4E 66
Monkspath. W Mid —3F 61
Monks Risborough. Buck —5G 51
Monksthorpe. Linc —4D 88
Monk Street. Essx —3G 53
Monkswood. Mon —5G 47
Monkton. Devn —2E 13
Monkton. Kent —4G 41
Monkton. Pemb —4D 42
Monkton. S Ayr —2C 116
Monkton Combe. Bath —5C 34
Monkton Deverill. Wilts —3D 22
Monkton Farleigh. Wilts —5D 34
Monkton Heathfield. Som —4F 21
Monktonhill. S Ayr —2C 116
Monkton Up Wimborne. Dors —1F 15
Monkton Wyld. Dors —3G 13
Monkwearmouth. Tyne —4H 115
Monkwood. Hants —3E 25
Monmarsh. Here —1A 48
Monmouth. Mon —4A 48
Monnington on Wye. Here —1G 47
Monreith. Dum —5A 110
Montacute. Som —1H 13
Montford. Arg —3C 126
Montford. Shrp —4G 71
Montford Bridge. Shrp —4G 71
Montgarrie. Aber —2C 152
Montgarswood. E Ayr —2E 117
Montgomery. Powy —1E 58
Montgreenan. N Ayr —5E 127
Montrave. Fife —3F 137
Montrose. Ang —3G 145
Monxton. Hants —2B 24
Monyash. Derbs —4F 85
Monymusk. Aber —2D 152
Monzie. Per —1A 136
Moodiesburn. N Lan —2H 127
Moon's Green. Kent —3C 28
Moonzie. Fife —2F 137
Moor Allerton. W Yor —1C 92
Moorbath. Dors —3H 13
Moorbrae. Shet —3F 173
Moorby. Linc —4B 88
Moorcot. Here —5F 59
Moor Crichel. Dors —2E 15
Moor Cross. Devn —3C 8
Moordown. Bour —3F 15
Moore. Hal —2H 83
Moorend. Dum —2D 112
Moor End. E Yor —1B 94
Moorend. Glos —5C 48
(nr. Dursley)
Moorend. Glos —4D 48
(nr. Gloucester)
Moorends. S Yor —3G 93
Moorgate. S Yor —1B 86
Moorgreen. Hants —1C 16
Moorgreen. Notts —1B 74
Moor Green. Wilts —5D 34
Moorhaigh. Notts —4C 86
Moorhall. Derbs —3H 85
Moorhampton. Here —1G 47
Moorhouse. Cumb —4E 113
(nr. Carlisle)
Moorhouse. Cumb —4D 112
(nr. Wigton)
Moorhouse. Notts —4E 87
Moorhouse. Surr —5F 39
Moorhouses. Linc —5B 88
Moorland. Som —3G 21
Moorlinch. Som —3G 21
Moor Monkton. N Yor —4H 99
Moor of Granary. Mor —3E 159
Moor Row. Cumb —3B 102
(nr. Whitehaven)
Moor Row. Cumb —5D 112
(nr. Wigton)
Moorsholm. Red C —3D 107
Moorside. Dors —1C 14
Moorside. G Man —4H 91
Moor, The. Kent —3B 28
Moortown. Devn —3D 10
Moortown. Hants —2G 15
Moortown. IOW —4C 16
Moortown. Linc —1H 87
Moortown. Telf —4A 72
Moortown. W Yor —1D 92
Moortown. W Yor —1D 92
Morangie. High —5E 165
Morar. High —4E 147
Morborne. Cambs —1A 64
Morchard Bishop. Devn —2A 12
Morcombelake. Dors —3H 13
Morcott. Rut —5G 75
Morda. Shrp —3E 71
Morden. Dors —3E 15
Morden. G Lon —4D 38
Mordiford. Here —2A 48
Mordon. Dur —2A 106
More. Shrp —1F 59
Morebath. Devn —4C 20
Morebattle. Scot —2B 120
Morecambe. Lanc —3D 96
Morefield. High —4F 163
Morehouse, The. Shrp —1H 59
Moreleigh. Devn —3D 8
Morely St Botolph. Norf —1C 66
Morenish. Per —5C 142
Moresby. Cumb —2A 102
Moresby Parks. Cumb —3A 102
Morestead. Hants —4D 24
Moreton. Dors —4D 14
Moreton. Essx —5F 53
Moreton. Here —4H 59
Moreton. Mers —1E 83
Moreton. Oxon —5E 51
Moreton. Staf —4B 72
Moreton Corbet. Shrp —3H 71
Moretonhampstead. Devn —4A 12
Moreton-in-Marsh. Glos —2H 49
Moreton Jeffries. Here —1B 48
Moreton Morrell. Warw —5H 61
Moreton on Lugg. Here —1A 48
Moreton Pinkney. Nptn —1D 50
Moreton Say. Shrp —2A 72
Moreton Valence. Glos —5C 48
Morfa. Cdgn —5C 56
Morfa Bach. Carm —4D 44
Morfa Bychan. Gwyn —2E 69
Morfa Glas. Neat —5B 46
Morfa Nefyn. Gwyn —1B 68
Morganstown. Card —3E 33
Morgan's Vale. Wilts —4G 23

Newcastle Airport—North Hayling

Newcastle Airport. Tyne —2E 115
Newcastle Emlyn. Carm —1D 44
Newcastleton. Scot —1F 113
Newcastle-under-Lyme. Staf —1C 72
Newcastle upon Tyne. Tyne —3F 115
Newchapel. Pemb —1G 43
Newchapel. Powy —2B 58
Newchapel. Staf —5C 84
Newchapel. Surr —1E 27
New Cheriton. Hants —4D 24
Newchurch. Carm —3D 45
Newchurch. Here —5F 59
Newchurch. IOW —4D 16
Newchurch. Kent —2E 29
Newchurch. Lanc —1G 91
(nr. Nelson)
Newchurch. Lanc —2G 91
(nr. Rawtenstall)
Newchurch. Mon —2H 33
Newchurch. Powy —5E 58
Newchurch. Staf —3F 73
New Costessey. Norf —4D 78
Newcott. Devn —2F 13
New Cowper. Cumb —5C 112
Newcraighall. Edin —2G 129
New Crofton. W Yor —3D 93
New Cross. Cdgn —3F 57
New Cumnock. E Ayr —3F 117
New Deer. Aber —4F 161
New Denham. Buck —2B 38
Newdigate. Surr —1C 26
New Duston. Nptn —4E 62
New Earswick. York —4A 100
New Edlington. S Yor —1C 86
New Elgin. Mor —2G 159
New Ellerby. E Yor —1E 95
Newell Green. Brac —4G 37
New Eltham. G Lon —3F 39
New End. Warw —4F 61
New End. Worc —5E 61
Newenden. Kent —3C 28
New England. Essx —1H 53
New England. Pet —5A 76
Newent. Glos —3C 48
New Ferry. Mers —2F 83
Newfield. Dur —4F 115
(nr. Chester-le-Street)
Newfield. Dur —1F 105
(nr. Willington)
Newfound. Hants —1D 24
New Fryston. W Yor —2E 93
New Galloway. Dum —2D 110
Newgate. Norf —1C 78
Newgate. Pemb —2C 42
Newgate Street. Herts —5D 52
New Greens. Herts —5B 52
New Grimsby. IOS —1A 4
New Hainford. Norf —4E 78
Newhall. Ches —1A 72
Newhall. Staf —3G 73
Newham. Nmbd —2F 121
New Hartley. Nmbd —2G 115
Newhaven. Derbs —4F 85
Newhaven. E Sus —5F 27
Newhaven. Edin —2F 129
New Haw. Surr —4B 38
New Hedges. Pemb —4F 43
New Herrington. Tyne —4G 115
Newhey. G Man —3H 91
New Holkham. Norf —2A 78
New Holland. N Lin —2D 94
Newholm. N Yor —3F 107
New Horton Grange. Nmbd —2F 115
New Houghton. Derbs —4C 86
New Houghton. Norf —3G 77
Newhouse. N Lan —3A 128
New Houses. N Yor —2H 97
New Hutton. Cumb —5G 103
New Hythe. Kent —5B 40
Newick. E Sus —3F 27
Newington. Edin —2F 129
Newington. Kent —2F 29
(nr. Folkestone)
Newington. Kent —4C 40
(nr. Sittingbourne)
Newington. Notts —1D 86
Newington. Oxon —2E 36
Newington Bagpath. Glos —2D 34
New Inn. Carm —2E 45
New Inn. Mon —5H 47
New Inn. N Yor —2H 97
New Inn. Torf —2G 33
New Invention. Shrp —3E 59
New Kelso. High —4B 156
New Lanark. S Lan —5B 128
Newland. Glos —5A 48
Newland. Hull —1D 94
Newland. N Yor —2G 93
Newland. Som —3B 20
Newland. Worc —1C 48
Newlandrig. Midl —3G 129
Newlands. Cumb —1E 103
Newlands. Essx —2C 40
Newlands. High —4B 158
Newlands. Nmbd —4D 115
Newlands. Notts —4C 86
Newlands. Staf —3E 73
Newlands of Geise. High —2C 168
Newlands of Tynet. Mor —2A 160
New Lane. Lanc —3C 90
New Lane End. Warr —1A 84
New Langholm. Dum —1E 113
New Leake. Linc —5D 88
New Leeds. Aber —3G 161
New Longton. Lanc —2D 90
Newlot. Orkn —6E 172
New Luce. Dum —3G 109
Newlyn. Corn —4B 4
Newmachar. Aber —2F 153
Newmains. N Lan —4B 128
New Mains of Ury. Aber —5F 153
New Malden. G Lon —4D 38
Newman's Green. Suff —1B 54
Newmarket. Suff —4F 65
Newmarket. W Isl —4G 171
New Marske. Red C —2D 106
New Marton. Shrp —2F 71
New Mill. Aber —4E 160
New Mill. Corn —3B 4
New Mill. Herts —4H 51
Newmill. Mor —3B 160
Newmill. Scot —3G 119
New Mill. W Yor —4B 92
New Mill. Wilts —5G 35
Newmillerdam. W Yor —3D 92
New Mills. Corn —3D 6
New Mills. Derbs —2E 85
Newmills. Fife —1D 128
Newmills. High —2A 158
New Mills. Mon —5A 48
New Mills. Powy —5C 70
Newmiln. Per —5A 144
Newmilns. E Ayr —1E 117
New Milton. Hants —3H 15
New Mistley. Essx —2E 54
New Moat. Pemb —2E 43
Newmore. High —3H 157
(nr. Dingwall)
Newmore. High —1A 158
(nr. Invergordon)
Newnham. Cambs —5D 64
Newnham. Glos —4B 48
Newnham. Hants —1F 25
Newnham. Herts —2C 52
Newnham. Kent —5D 40
Newnham. Nptn —5C 62
Newnham. Warw —4F 61
Newnham Bridge. Worc —4A 60
New Ollerton. Notts —4D 86
New Oscott. W Mid —1F 61
Newpark. Fife —2G 137
New Park. N Yor —4E 99
New Pitsligo. Aber —3F 161
New Polzeath. Corn —1D 6
Newport. Corn —4D 10
Newport. Devn —3F 19
Newport. E Yor —1B 94
Newport. Essx —2F 53
Newport. Glos —2B 34
Newport. High —1H 165
Newport. IOW —4D 16
Newport. Newp —3G 33
Newport. Norf —4H 79
Newport. Pemb —1E 43
Newport. Som —4G 21
Newport. Telf —4B 72
Newport-on-Tay. Fife —1G 137
Newport Pagnell. Mil —1G 51
Newpound Common. W Sus —3B 26
New Prestwick. S Ayr —2C 116
New Quay. Cdgn —5C 56
Newquay. Corn —2C 6
Newquay Cornwall (St Mawgan) Airport. Corn —2C 6
New Rackheath. Norf —4E 79
New Radnor. Powy —4E 58
New Rent. Cumb —1F 103
New Ridley. Nmbd —4D 114
New Romney. Kent —3E 29
New Rossington. S Yor —1D 86
New Row. Cdgn —3G 57
New Row. Lanc —1E 91
New Row. N Yor —3D 106
New Sauchie. Clac —4A 136
Newsbank. Ches —4C 84
New Scone. Per —1D 136
Newseat. Aber —5E 160
Newsham. Lanc —1D 90
Newsham. Nmbd —2G 115
Newsham. N Yor —3E 105
(nr. Richmond)
Newsham. N Yor —1F 99
(nr. Thirsk)
New Sharlston. W Yor —3D 93
Newsholme. E Yor —2H 93
Newsholme. Lanc —4H 97
New Shoreston. Nmbd —1F 121
New Springs. G Man —4E 90
Newstead. Notts —5C 86
Newstead. Scot —1H 119
New Stevenston. N Lan —3A 128
New Street. Here —5F 59
Newstreet Lane. Shrp —2A 72
New Swanage. Dors —4F 15
New Swannington. Leics —4B 74
Newthorpe. N Yor —1E 93
Newthorpe. Notts —1B 74
Newton. Arg —4H 133
Newton. B'End —4B 32
Newton. Cambs —1E 53
(nr. Cambridge)
Newton. Cambs —4D 76
(nr. Wisbech)
Newton. Ches —4G 83
(nr. Chester)
Newton. Ches —5H 83
(nr. Tattenhall)
Newton. Cumb —2B 96
Newton. Derbs —5B 86
Newton. Dum —2D 112
(nr. Annan)
Newton. Dum —5D 118
(nr. Moffat)
Newton. G Man —1D 84
Newton. Here —2G 47
(nr. Ewyas Harold)
Newton. Here —5H 59
(nr. Leominster)
Newton. High —2B 158
(nr. Cromarty)
Newton. High —4B 158
(nr. Inverness)
Newton. High —5C 166
(nr. Kylestrome)
Newton. High —4F 169
(nr. Wick)
Newton. Lanc —2E 97
(nr. Carnforth)
Newton. Lanc —4G 97
(nr. Clitheroe)
Newton. Lanc —1C 90
(nr. Kirkham)
Newton. Linc —2H 75
Newton. Mers —2E 83
Newton. Mor —2F 159
Newton. Norf —4H 77
Newton. Nptn —2F 63
Newton. Nmbd —3D 114
Newton. Notts —1D 74
Newton. Scot —2A 120
Newton. Shet —8E 173
Newton. Shrp —1B 60
(nr. Bridgnorth)
Newton. Shrp —2G 71
(nr. Wem)
Newton. Som —3E 20
Newton. S Lan —3H 127
(nr. Glasgow)
Newton. S Lan —1B 118
(nr. Lanark)
Newton. Staf —3E 73
Newton. Suff —1C 54
Newton. Swan —4F 31
Newton. Warw —3C 62
Newton. W Lot —2D 129
Newton. Wilts —4H 23
Newton Abbot. Devn —5B 12
Newtonairds. Dum —1F 111
Newton Arlosh. Cumb —4D 112
Newton Aycliffe. Dur —2F 105
Newton Bewley. Hart —2B 106
Newton Blossomville. Mil —5G 63
Newton Bromswold. Nptn —4G 63
Newton Burgoland. Leics —5A 74
Newton by Toft. Linc —2H 87
Newton Ferrers. Devn —4B 8
Newton Flotman. Norf —1E 66
Newtongarry Croft. Aber —5C 160
Newtongrange. Midl —3G 129
Newton Green. Mon —2A 34
Newton Hall. Dur —5F 115
Newton Hall. Nmbd —3D 114
Newton Harcourt. Leics —1D 62
Newton Heath. G Man —4G 91
Newtonhill. Aber —4G 153
Newtonhill. High —4H 157
Newton Hill. W Yor —2D 92
Newton Ketton. Darl —2A 106
Newton Kyme. N Yor —5G 99
Newton-le-Willows. Mers —1H 83
Newton-le-Willows. N Yor —1E 98
Newton Longville. Buck —2G 51
Newton Mearns. E Ren —4G 127
Newtonmore. High —4B 150
Newton Morrell. N Yor —4F 105
Newton Mulgrave. N Yor —3E 107
Newton of Ardtoe. High —1A 140
Newton of Balcanquhal. Per —2D 136
Newton of Beltrees. Ren —4E 127
Newton of Falkland. Fife —3E 137
Newton of Mountblairy. Aber —3D 160
Newton of Pitcairns. Per —2C 136
Newton-on-Ouse. N Yor —3H 99
Newton-on-Rawcliffe. N Yor —5F 107
Newton on the Hill. Shrp —3G 71
Newton-on-the-Moor. Nmbd —4F 121
Newton on Trent. Linc —3F 87
Newton Poppleford. Devn —4D 12
Newton Purcell. Oxon —2E 51
Newton Regis. Warw —5G 73
Newton Reigny. Cumb —1F 103
Newton Rigg. Cumb —1F 103
Newton St Cyres. Devn —3B 12
Newton St Faith. Norf —4E 78
Newton St Loe. Bath —5C 34
Newton St Petrock. Devn —1E 11
Newton Solney. Derbs —3G 73
Newton Stacey. Hants —2C 24
Newton Stewart. Dum —3B 110
Newton Toney. Wilts —2H 23
Newton Tracey. Devn —4F 19
Newton under Roseberry. Red C —3C 106
Newton Unthank. Leics —5B 74
Newton upon Ayr. S Ayr —2C 116
Newton upon Derwent. E Yor —5B 100
Newton Valence. Hants —3F 25
Newton with Scales. Lanc —1B 90
Newtown. Aber —2E 160
Newtown. Cambs —4H 63
Newtown. Ches —1A 72
Newtown. Corn —5C 10
Newtown. Cumb —5B 112
(nr. Aspatria)
Newtown. Cumb —3G 113
(nr. Brampton)
Newtown. Cumb —2G 103
(nr. Penrith)
Newtown. Derbs —2D 85
Newtown. Devn —4A 20
Newtown. Dors —2H 13
(nr. Beaminster)
New Town. Dors —1E 15
(nr. Sixpenny Handley)
Newtown. Dum —4G 117
New Town. E Lot —2H 129
Newtown. Falk —1D 128
Newtown. Glos —5B 48
(nr. Lydney)
Newtown. Glos —2E 49
(nr. Tewkesbury)
Newtown. Hants —1D 16
(nr. Bishop's Waltham)
Newtown. Hants —1A 16
(nr. Lyndhurst)
Newtown. Hants —5C 36
(nr. Newbury)
Newtown. Hants —4B 24
(nr. Romsey)
Newtown. Hants —2C 16
(nr. Warsash)
Newtown. Hants —1E 16
(nr. Wickham)
Newtown. Here —2B 48
(nr. Ledbury)
Newtown. Here —2A 48
(nr. Little Dewchurch)
Newtown. Here —1B 48
(nr. Stretton Grandison)
Newtown. High —3F 149
Newtown. IOM —4C 108
Newtown. IOW —3C 16
Newtown. Lanc —3D 90
New Town. Lutn —3A 52
Newtown. Nmbd —4E 121
(nr. Rothbury)
Newtown. Nmbd —2E 121
(nr. Wooler)
Newtown. Pool —3F 15
Newtown. Powy —1D 58
Newtown. Rhon —2D 32
Newtown. Shet —3F 173
Newtown. Shrp —2G 71
Newtown. Som —1F 13
Newtown. Staf —4D 84
(nr. Biddulph)
Newtown. Staf —5D 73
(nr. Cannock)
Newtown. Staf —4E 85
(nr. Longnor)
New Town. W Yor —2E 93
Newtown. Wilts —4E 23
Newtown-in-St Martin. Corn —4E 5
Newtown Linford. Leics —4C 74
Newtown St Boswells. Scot —1H 119
New Tredegar. Cphy —5E 47
Newtyle. Ang —4B 144
New Village. E Yor —1D 94
New Village. S Yor —4F 93
New Walsoken. Cambs —5D 76
New Waltham. NE Lin —4F 95
New Wimpole. Cambs —1D 52
New Winton. E Lot —2H 129
New World. Cambs —1C 64
New Yatt. Oxon —4B 50
Newyears Green. G Lon —2B 38
New York. Linc —5B 88
New York. Tyne —2G 115
Nextend. Here —5F 59
Neyland. Pemb —4D 42
Nib Heath. Shrp —4G 71
Nicholashayne. Devn —1E 12
Nicholaston. Swan —4E 31
Nidd. N Yor —3F 99
Niddrie. Edin —2F 129
Niddry. W Lot —2D 129
Nigg. Aber C —3G 153
Nigg. High —1C 158
Nigg Ferry. High —2B 158
Nightcott. Som —4B 20
Nine Ashes. Essx —5F 53
Ninebanks. Nmbd —4A 114
Nine Elms. Swin —3G 35
Ninemile Bar. Dum —2F 111
Nine Mile Burn. Midl —4E 129
Ninfield. E Sus —4B 28
Ningwood. IOW —4C 16
Nisbet. Scot —2A 120
Nisbet Hill. Scot —4E 130
Niton. IOW —5D 16
Nitshill. E Ren —4G 127
Niwbwrch. IOA —4D 80
Noak Hill. G Lon —1G 39
Nobold. Shrp —4G 71
Nobottle. Nptn —4D 62
Nocton. Linc —4H 87
Nogdam End. Norf —5F 79
Noke. Oxon —4D 50
Nolton. Pemb —3C 42
Nolton Haven. Pemb —3C 42
No Man's Heath. Ches —1H 71
No Man's Heath. Warw —5G 73
Nomansland. Devn —1B 12
Nomansland. Wilts —1A 16
Noneley. Shrp —3G 71
Noness. Shet —9F 173
Nonikiln. High —1A 158
Nonington. Kent —5G 41
Nook. Cumb —2F 113
(nr. Longtown)
Nook. Cumb —1E 97
(nr. Milnthorpe)
Noranside. Ang —2D 144
Norbreck. Bkpl —5C 96
Norbridge. Here —1C 48
Norbury. Ches —1H 71
Norbury. Derbs —1F 73
Norbury. Shrp —1F 59
Norbury. Staf —3B 72
Norby. N Yor —1G 99
Norby. Shet —6C 173
Norcross. Lanc —5C 96
Nordelph. Norf —5E 77
Norden. G Man —3G 91
Nordley. Shrp —1A 60
Norham. Nmbd —5F 131
Norland Town. W Yor —2A 92
Norley. Ches —3H 83
Norleywood. Hants —3B 16
Normanby. N Lin —3B 94
Normanby. N Yor —1B 100
Normanby. Red C —3C 106
Normanby-by-Spital. Linc —2H 87
Normanby le Wold. Linc —1A 88
Norman Cross. Cambs —1A 64
Normandy. Surr —5A 38
Norman's Bay. E Sus —5A 28
Norman's Green. Devn —2D 12
Normanton. Dby C —2H 73
Normanton. Leics —1F 75
Normanton. Linc —1G 75
Normanton. Notts —5E 86
Normanton. W Yor —2D 93
Normanton le Heath. Leics —4A 74
Normanton on Soar. Notts —3C 74
Normanton-on-the-Wolds. Notts —2D 74
Normanton on Trent. Notts —4E 87
Normoss. Lanc —1B 90
Norrington Common. Wilts —5D 35
Norris Green. Mers —1F 83
Norris Hill. Leics —4H 73
Norristhorpe. W Yor —2C 92
North Acre. Norf —1B 66
Northall. Buck —3H 51
Northallerton. N Yor —5A 106
Northam. Devn —4E 19
Northam. Sotn —1C 16
Northampton. Nptn —4E 63
North Anston. S Yor —2C 86
North Ascot. Brac —4A 38
North Aston. Oxon —3C 50
Northaw. Herts —5C 52
Northay. Som —1F 13
North Baddesley. Hants —4B 24
North Balfern. Dum —4B 110
North Ballachulish. High —2E 141
North Barrow. Som —4B 22
North Barsham. Norf —2B 78
Northbeck. Linc —1H 75
North Benfleet. Essx —2B 40
North Bersted. W Sus —5A 26
North Berwick. E Lot —1B 130
North Bitchburn. Dur —1E 105
North Blyth. Nmbd —1G 115
North Boarhunt. Hants —1E 16
North Bockhampton. Dors —3G 15
Northborough. Pet —5A 76
Northbourne. Kent —5H 41
Northbourne. Oxon —3D 36
North Bovey. Devn —4H 11
North Bradley. Wilts —1D 22
North Brentor. Devn —4E 11
North Brewham. Som —3C 22
Northbrook. Oxon —3C 50
North Brook End. Cambs —1C 52
North Buckland. Devn —2E 19
North Burlingham. Norf —4F 79
North Cadbury. Som —4B 22
North Carlton. Linc —3G 87
North Cave. E Yor —1B 94
North Cerney. Glos —5F 49
North Chailey. E Sus —3E 27
Northchapel. W Sus —3A 26
North Charford. Hants —1G 15
North Charlton. Nmbd —2F 121
North Cheriton. Som —4B 22
North Chideock. Dors —3H 13
Northchurch. Herts —5H 51
North Cliffe. E Yor —1B 94
North Clifton. Notts —3F 87
North Close. Dur —1F 105
North Cockerington. Linc —1C 88
North Coker. Som —1A 14
North Collafirth. Shet —3E 173
North Common. E Sus —3E 27
North Commonty. Aber —4F 161
North Coombe. Devn —1B 12
North Corbelly. Dum —3A 112
North Cornelly. B'End —3B 32
North Cotes. Linc —4G 95
Northcott. Devn —3D 10
Northcourt. Oxon —2D 36
North Cove. Suff —2G 67
North Cowton. N Yor —4F 105
North Craigo. Ang —2F 145
North Crawley. Mil —1H 51
North Cray. G Lon —3F 39
North Creake. Norf —2A 78
North Curry. Som —4G 21
North Dalton. E Yor —4D 100
North Deighton. N Yor —4F 99
North Dronley. Ang —5C 144
North Duffield. N Yor —1G 93
Northdyke. Orkn —5B 172
Northedge. Derbs —4A 86
North Elkington. Linc —1B 88
North Elmham. Norf —3B 78
North Elmsall. W Yor —3E 93
North End. E Yor —1F 95
North End. Essx —4G 53
(nr. Great Dunmow)
North End. Essx —2A 54
(nr. Great Yeldham)
North End. Hants —5C 36
North End. Leics —4C 74
North End. Linc —1B 76
North End. Norf —1B 66
North End. N Som —5H 33
Northend. Oxon —2F 37
North End. Port —2E 17
Northend. Warw —5A 62
North End. W Sus —5C 26
North End. Wilts —2F 35
North Erradale. High —5B 162
North Evington. Leic C —5D 74
North Fambridge. Essx —1C 40
North Fearns. High —5E 155
North Featherstone. W Yor —2E 93
North Feorline. N Ayr —3D 122
North Ferriby. E Yor —2C 94
Northfield. Aber C —3F 153
Northfield. E Yor —2D 94
Northfield. Som —3F 21
Northfield. W Mid —3E 61
Northfleet. Kent —3H 39
North Frodingham. E Yor —4F 101
Northgate. Linc —3A 76
North Gluss. Shet —4E 173
North Gorley. Hants —1G 15
North Green. Norf —2E 66
North Green. Suff —4F 67
(nr. Framlingham)
North Green. Suff —3F 67
(nr. Halesworth)
North Green. Suff —4F 67
(nr. Saxmundham)
North Greetwell. Linc —3H 87
North Grimston. N Yor —3C 100
North Halling. Medw —4B 40
North Hayling. Hants —2F 17

North Hazelrigg—Osmaston

North Hazelrigg. Nmbd —1E 121
North Heasley. Devn —3H 19
North Heath. W Sus —3B 26
North Hill. Corn —5C 10
North Hinksey Village. Oxon —5C 50
North Holmwood. Surr —1C 26
North Huish. Devn —3D 8
North Hykeham. Linc —4G 87
Northiam. E Sus —3C 28
Northill. Beds —1B 52
Northington. Hants —3D 24
North Kelsey. Linc —4D 94
North Kelsey Moor. Linc —4D 94
North Kessock. High —4A 158
North Killingholme. N Lin —3E 95
North Kilvington. N Yor —1G 99
North Kilworth. Leics —2D 62
North Kyme. Linc —5A 88
North Lancing. W Sus —5C 26
Northlands. Linc —5C 88
Northleach. Glos —4G 49
North Lee. Buck —5G 51
North Lees. N Yor —2F 99
Northleigh. Devn —3G 19
(nr. Barnstaple)
Northleigh. Devn —3E 13
(nr. Honiton)
North Leigh. Kent —1F 29
North Leigh. Oxon —4B 50
North Leverton with Habblesthorpe. Notts —2E 87
Northlew. Devn —3F 11
North Littleton. Worc —1F 49
North Lopham. Norf —2C 66
North Luffenham. Rut —5G 75
North Marden. W Sus —1G 17
North Marston. Buck —3F 51
North Middleton. Midl —4G 129
North Middleton. Nmbd —2E 121
North Molton. Devn —4H 19
North Moor. N Yor —1D 100
Northmoor. Oxon —5C 50
Northmoor Green. Som —3G 21
North Moreton. Oxon —3D 36
Northmuir. Ang —3C 144
North Mundham. W Sus —2G 17
North Murie. Per —1E 137
North Muskham. Notts —5E 87
North Ness. Orkn —8C 172
North Newbald. E Yor —1C 94
North Newington. Oxon —2C 50
North Newnton. Wilts —1G 23
North Newton. Som —3F 21
Northney. Hants —2F 17
North Nibley. Glos —2C 34
North Oakley. Hants —1D 24
North Ockendon. G Lon —2G 39
Northolt. G Lon —2C 38
Northop. Flin —4E 83
Northop Hall. Flin —4E 83
North Ormesby. Midd —2C 106
North Ormsby. Linc —1B 88
Northorpe. Linc —4H 75
(nr. Bourne)
Northorpe. Linc —2B 76
(nr. Donington)
Northorpe. Linc —1F 87
(nr. Gainsborough)
North Otterington. N Yor —1F 99
Northover. Som —3H 21
(nr. Glastonbury)
Northover. Som —4A 22
(nr. Yeovil)
North Owersby. Linc —1H 87
Northowram. W Yor —2B 92
North Perrott. Som —2H 13
North Petherton. Som —3F 21
North Petherwin. Corn —4C 10
North Pickenham. Norf —5A 78
North Piddle. Worc —5D 60
North Poorton. Dors —3A 14
North Port. Arg —1H 133
Northport. Dors —4E 15
North Queensferry. Fife —1E 129
North Radworthy. Devn —3A 20
North Rauceby. Linc —1H 75
Northrepps. Norf —2E 79
North Rigton. N Yor —5E 99
North Rode. Ches —4C 84
North Roe. Shet —3E 173
North Ronaldsay Airport. Orkn —2G 172
North Row. Cumb —1D 102
North Runcton. Norf —4F 77
North Sannox. N Ayr —5B 126
North Scale. Cumb —3A 96
North Scarle. Linc —4F 87
North Seaton. Nmbd —1F 115
North Seaton Colliery. Nmbd —1F 115
North Sheen. G Lon —3C 38
North Shian. Arg —4D 140
North Shields. Tyne —3G 115
North Shoebury. Essx —2D 40
North Shore. Bkpl —1B 90
North Side. Cumb —2B 102
North Skelton. Red C —3D 106
North Somercotes. Linc —1D 88
North Stainley. N Yor —2E 99
North Stainmore. Cumb —3B 104
North Stifford. Thur —2H 39
North Stoke. Bath —5C 34
North Stoke. Medw —3C 40
North Stoke. Oxon —3E 36
North Stoke. W Sus —4B 26
North Street. Hants —3E 25
North Street. Kent —5E 40
North Street. Medw —3C 40
North Street. W Ber —4E 37
North Sunderland. Nmbd —1G 121
North Tamerton. Corn —3D 10
North Tawton. Devn —2G 11
North Thoresby. Linc —1B 88
North Tidworth. Wilts —2H 23
North Town. Devn —2F 11
Northtown. Orkn —8D 172
North Town. Shet —10E 173
North Tuddenham. Norf —4C 78
North Walbottle. Tyne —3E 115
Northwall. Orkn —3G 172
North Walsham. Norf —2E 79
North Waltham. Hants —2D 24
North Warnborough. Hants —1F 25
North Water Bridge. Ang —2F 145
North Watten. High —3E 169
Northway. Glos —2E 49
Northway. Swan —4E 31
North Weald Bassett. Essx —5F 53
North Weston. N Som —4H 33
North Wheatley. Notts —2E 87
North Whilborough. Devn —2E 9
Northwich. Ches —3A 84
North Wick. Bath —5A 34
Northwick. Som —2G 21
Northwick. S Glo —3A 34
North Widcombe. Bath —1A 22
North Willingham. Linc —2A 88
North Wingfield. Derbs —4B 86
North Witham. Linc —3G 75
Northwold. Norf —1G 65
Northwood. Derbs —4G 85
Northwood. G Lon —1B 38
Northwood. IOW —3C 16
Northwood. Kent —4H 41
Northwood. Shrp —2G 71
Northwood. Stoke —1C 72
Northwood Green. Glos —4C 48
North Wootton. Dors —1B 14
North Wootton. Norf —3F 77
North Wootton. Som —2A 22
North Wraxall. Wilts —4D 34
North Wroughton. Swin —3G 35
North Yardhope. Nmbd —4D 120
Norton. Devn —3E 9
Norton. Glos —3D 48
Norton. Hal —2H 83
Norton. Herts —2C 52
Norton. IOW —4B 16
Norton. Mon —3H 47
Norton. Nptn —4D 62
Norton. N Yor —2B 100
Norton. Notts —3C 86
Norton. Powy —4F 59
Norton. Shrp —2G 59
(nr. Ludlow)
Norton. Shrp —5B 72
(nr. Madeley)
Norton. Shrp —5H 71
(nr. Shrewsbury)
Norton. S Yor —3F 93
(nr. Askern)
Norton. S Yor —2A 86
(nr. Sheffield)
Norton. Stoc T —2B 106
Norton. Suff —4B 66
Norton. Swan —4F 31
Norton. W Sus —5A 26
(nr. Arundel)
Norton. W Sus —3G 17
(nr. Selsey)
Norton. Wilts —3D 35
Norton. Worc —1F 49
(nr. Evesham)
Norton. Worc —5C 60
(nr. Worcester)
Norton Bavant. Wilts —2E 23
Norton Bridge. Staf —2C 72
Norton Canes. Staf —5E 73
Norton Canon. Here —1G 47
Norton Corner. Norf —3C 78
Norton Disney. Linc —5F 87
Norton East. Staf —5E 73
Norton Ferris. Wilts —3C 22
Norton Fitzwarren. Som —4F 21
Norton Green. IOW —4B 16
Norton Green. Stoke —5D 84
Norton Hawkfield. Bath —5A 34
Norton Heath. Essx —5G 53
Norton in Hales. Shrp —2B 72
Norton in the Moors. Stoke —5C 84
Norton-Juxta-Twycross. Leics —5H 73
Norton-le-Clay. N Yor —2G 99
Norton Lindsey. Warw —4G 61
Norton Little Green. Suff —4B 66
Norton Malreward. Bath —5B 34
Norton Mandeville. Essx —5F 53
Norton St Philip. Som —1C 22
Norton Subcourse. Norf —1G 67
Norton sub Hamdon. Som —1H 13
Norton Woodseats. S Yor —2A 86
Norwell. Nptn —4E 87
Norwell Woodhouse. Notts —4E 87
Norwich. Norf —5E 79
Norwich Airport. Norf —4E 78
Norwick. Shet —1H 173
Norwood. Derbs —2B 86
Norwood Green. W Yor —2B 92
Norwood Hill. Surr —1D 26
Norwood Park. Som —3A 22
Norwoodside. Cambs —1D 64
Noseley. Leics —1E 63
Noss Mayo. Devn —4B 8
Nosterfield. N Yor —1E 99
Nostie. High —1A 148
Notgrove. Glos —3G 49
Nottage. B'End —4B 32
Nottingham. Not C —1C 74
Nottington. Dors —4B 14
Notton. W Yor —3D 92
Notton. Wilts —5E 35
Nounsley. Essx —4A 54
Noutard's Green. Worc —4B 60
Nox. Shrp —4G 71
Noyadd Trefawr. Cdgn —1C 44
Nuffield. Oxon —3E 37
Nunburnholme. E Yor —5C 100
Nuncargate. Notts —5C 86
Nunclose. Cumb —5F 113
Nuneaton. Warw —1A 62
Nuneham Courtenay. Oxon —2D 36
Nun Monkton. N Yor —4H 99
Nunnerie. S Lan —3B 118
Nunney. Som —2C 22
Nunnington. N Yor —2A 100
Nunnykirk. Nmbd —5E 121
Nunsthorpe. NE Lin —4F 95
Nunthorpe. Midd —3C 106
Nunthorpe. York —5H 99
Nunton. Wilts —4G 23
Nunwick. Nmbd —2B 114
Nunwick. N Yor —2F 99
Nupend. Glos —5C 48
Nursling. Hants —1B 16
Nursted. Hants —4F 25
Nursteed. Wilts —5F 35
Nurston. V Glam —5D 32
Nutbourne. W Sus —2F 17
(nr. Chichester)
Nutbourne. W Sus —4B 26
(nr. Pulborough)
Nutfield. Surr —5E 39
Nuthall. Notts —1B 74
Nuthampstead. Herts —2E 53
Nuthurst. Warw —3F 61
Nuthurst. W Sus —3C 26
Nutley. E Sus —3F 27
Nuttall. G Man —3F 91
Nutwell. S Yor —4G 93
Nybster. High —2F 169
Nyetimber. W Sus —3G 17
Nyewood. W Sus —4G 25
Nymet Rowland. Devn —2H 11
Nymet Tracey. Devn —2H 11
Nympsfield. Glos —5D 48
Nynehead. Som —4E 21
Nyton. W Sus —5A 26

Oadby. Leics —5D 74
Oad Street. Kent —4C 40
Oakamoor. Staf —1E 73
Oakbank. Arg —5B 140
Oakbank. W Lot —3D 129
Oakdale. Cphy —2E 33
Oakdale. Pool —3F 15
Oake. Som —4E 21
Oaken. Staf —5C 72
Oakenclough. Lanc —5E 97
Oakengates. Telf —4B 72
Oakenholt. Flin —3E 83
Oakenshaw. Dur —1F 105
Oakenshaw. W Yor —2B 92
Oakerthorpe. Derbs —5A 86
Oakford. Cdgn —5D 56
Oakford. Devn —4C 20
Oakfordbridge. Devn —4C 20
Oakgrove. Ches —4D 84
Oakham. Rut —5F 75
Oakhanger. Ches —5B 84
Oakhanger. Hants —3F 25
Oakhill. Som —2B 22
Oakington. Cambs —4D 64
Oaklands. Powy —5C 58
Oakle Street. Glos —4C 48
Oakley. Beds —5H 63
Oakley. Buck —4E 51
Oakley. Fife —1D 128
Oakley. Hants —1D 24
Oakley. Suff —3D 66
Oakley Green. Wind —3A 38
Oakley Park. Powy —2B 58
Oakmere. Ches —4H 83
Oakridge. Glos —5E 49
Oaks. Shrp —5G 71
Oaksey. Wilts —2E 35
Oaks Green. Derbs —2F 73
Oakshaw Ford. Cumb —2G 113
Oakshott. Hants —4F 25
Oakthorpe. Leics —4H 73
Oak Tree. Darl —3A 106
Oakwood. Dby C —2A 74
Oakwood. W Yor —1D 92
Oakwoodhill. Surr —2C 26
Oakworth. W Yor —1A 92
Oape. High —3B 164
Oare. Kent —4E 40
Oare. Som —2B 20
Oare. W Ber —4D 36
Oare. Wilts —5G 35
Oareford. Som —2B 20
Oasby. Linc —2H 75
Oath. Som —4G 21
Oathlaw. Ang —3D 145
Oatlands. N Yor —4F 99
Oban. Arg —1F 133
Oban. W Isl —7D 171
Oborne. Dors —1B 14
Obsdale. High —2A 158
Obthorpe. Linc —4H 75
Occlestone Green. Ches —4A 84
Occold. Suff —3D 66
Ochiltree. E Ayr —2E 117
Ochtermuthill. Per —2H 135
Ochtertyre. Per —1H 135
Ockbrook. Derbs —2B 74
Ockeridge. Worc —4B 60
Ockham. Surr —5B 38
Ockle. High —1G 139
Ockley. Surr —1C 26
Ocle Pychard. Here —1A 48
Octofad. Arg —4A 124
Octomore. Arg —4A 124
Octon. E Yor —3E 101
Odcombe. Som —1A 14
Odd Down. Bath —5C 34
Oddingley. Worc —5D 60
Oddington. Oxon —4D 50
Oddsta. Shet —2G 173
Odell. Beds —5G 63
Odie. Orkn —5F 172
Odiham. Hants —1F 25
Odsey. Cambs —2C 52
Odstock. Wilts —4G 23
Odstone. Leics —5A 74
Offchurch. Warw —4A 62
Offenham. Worc —1F 49
Offenham Cross. Worc —1F 49
Offerton. G Man —2D 84
Offerton. Tyne —4G 115
Offham. E Sus —4F 27
Offham. Kent —5A 40
Offham. W Sus —5B 26
Offleyhay. Staf —3C 72
Offley Hoo. Herts —3B 52
Offleymarsh. Staf —3B 72
Offord Cluny. Cambs —4B 64
Offord D'Arcy. Cambs —4B 64
Offton. Suff —1D 54
Offwell. Devn —3E 13
Ogbourne Maizey. Wilts —4G 35
Ogbourne St Andrew. Wilts —4G 35
Ogbourne St George. Wilts —4H 35
Ogden. G Man —3H 91
Ogle. Nmbd —2E 115
Ogmore. V Glam —4B 32
Ogmore-by-Sea. V Glam —4B 32
Ogmore Vale. B'End —3C 32
Okeford Fitzpaine. Dors —1D 14
Okehampton. Devn —3F 11
Okehampton Camp. Devn —3F 11
Okraquoy. Shet —8F 173
Okus. Swin —3G 35
Old. Nptn —3E 63
Old Aberdeen. Aber C —3G 153
Old Alresford. Hants —3D 24
Oldany. High —5B 166
Old Arley. Warw —1G 61
Old Barns. Nmbd —4G 121
Old Basford. Not C —1C 74
Old Basing. Hants —1E 25
Oldberrow. Warw —4F 61
Old Bewick. Nmbd —2E 121
Old Bexley. G Lon —3F 39
Old Blair. Per —2F 143
Old Bolingbroke. Linc —4C 88
Oldborough. Devn —2A 12
Old Brampton. Derbs —3H 85
Old Bridge of Tilt. Per —2F 143
Old Bridge of Urr. Dum —3E 111
Old Buckenham. Norf —1C 66
Old Burghclere. Hants —1C 24
Oldbury. Shrp —1B 60
Oldbury. Warw —1H 61
Oldbury. W Mid —2D 61
Oldbury-on-Severn. S Glo —2B 34
Oldbury on the Hill. Glos —3D 34
Old Byland. N Yor —1H 99
Old Cassop. Dur —1A 106
Oldcastle. Mon —3G 47
Oldcastle Heath. Ches —1G 71
Old Clee. NE Lin —4F 95
Old Cleeve. Som —2D 20
Old Clipstone. Notts —4D 86
Old Colwyn. Cnwy —3A 82
Oldcotes. Notts —2C 86
Old Coulsdon. G Lon —5E 39
Old Dailly. S Ayr —5B 116
Old Dalby. Leics —3D 74
Old Dam. Derbs —3F 85
Old Deer. Aber —4G 161
Old Dilton. Wilts —2D 22
Old Down. S Glo —3B 34
Oldeamere. Cambs —1C 64
Old Edlington. S Yor —1C 86
Old Eldon. Dur —2F 105
Old Ellerby. E Yor —1E 95
Old Fallings. W Mid —5D 72
Oldfallow. Staf —4D 72
Old Felixstowe. Suff —2G 55
Oldfield. Shrp —2A 60
Oldfield. Worc —4C 60
Old Fletton. Pet —1A 64
Oldford. Som —1C 22
Old Forge. Here —4A 48
Old Glossop. Derbs —1E 85
Old Goole. E Yor —2H 93
Old Gore. Here —3B 48
Old Graitney. Dum —3E 112
Old Grimsbury. Oxon —1C 50
Old Grimsby. IOS —1A 4
Old Hall. E Yor —3F 95
Oldhall. High —3E 169
Old Hall Street. Norf —2F 79
Oldham. G Man —4H 91
Oldhamstocks. E Lot —2D 130
Old Heathfield. E Sus —3G 27
Old Hill. W Mid —2D 60
Old Hunstanton. Norf —1F 77
Old Hurst. Cambs —3B 64
Old Hutton. Cumb —1E 97
Old Kea. Corn —4C 6
Old Kilpatrick. W Dun —2F 127
Old Kinnernie. Aber —3E 152
Old Knebworth. Herts —3C 52
Oldland. S Glo —4B 34
Old Laxey. IOM —3D 108
Old Leake. Linc —5D 88
Old Llanberis. Gwyn —5F 81
Old Malton. N Yor —2B 100
Oldmeldrum. Aber —1F 153
Oldmill. Corn —5D 10
Oldmixon. N Som —1G 21
Old Monkland. N Lan —3A 128
Old Newton. Suff —4C 66
Old Park. Telf —5A 72
Old Pentland. Midl —3F 129
Old Philpstoun. W Lot —2D 128
Old Quarrington. Dur —1A 106
Old Radnor. Powy —5E 59
Old Rayne. Aber —1D 152
Oldridge. Devn —3B 12
Old Romney. Kent —3E 29
Old Scone. Per —1D 136
Oldshore Beg. High —3B 166
Oldshoremore. High —3C 166
Old Snydale. W Yor —2E 93
Old Sodbury. S Glo —3C 34
Old Somerby. Linc —2G 75
Old Spital. Dur —3C 104
Oldstead. N Yor —1H 99
Old Stratford. Nptn —1F 51
Old Swan. Mers —1F 83
Old Tebay. Cumb —4H 103
Old Town. Cumb —5F 113
Old Town. E Sus —5G 27
Oldtown. High —5C 164
Old Town. IOS —1B 4
Old Town. Nmbd —5C 120
Oldtown of Ord. Aber —3D 160
Old Trafford. G Man —1C 84
Old Tupton. Derbs —4A 86
Oldwall. Cumb —3F 113
Oldwalls. Swan —3D 31
Old Warden. Beds —1B 52
Oldways End. Som —4B 20
Old Westhall. Aber —1D 152
Old Weston. Cambs —3H 63
Oldwhat. Aber —3F 161
Old Windsor. Wind —3A 38
Old Wives Lees. Kent —5E 41
Old Woking. Surr —5B 38
Oldwood Common. Worc —4H 59
Old Woodstock. Oxon —4C 50
Olgrinmore. High —3C 168
Oliver's Battery. Hants —4C 24
Ollaberry. Shet —3E 173
Ollerton. Ches —3B 84
Ollerton. Notts —4D 86
Ollerton. Shrp —3A 72
Olmarch. Cdgn —5F 57
Olmstead Green. Cambs —1G 53
Olney. Mil —5F 63
Olrig. High —2D 169
Olton. W Mid —2F 61
Olveston. S Glo —3B 34
Ombersley. Worc —4C 60
Ompton. Notts —4D 86
Omunsgarth. Shet —7E 173
Onchan. IOM —4D 108
Onecote. Staf —5E 85
Onehouse. Suff —5C 66
Onen. Mon —4H 47
Ongar Hill. Norf —3E 77
Ongar Street. Here —4F 59
Onibury. Shrp —3G 59
Onich. High —2E 141
Onllwyn. Neat —4B 46
Onneley. Shrp —1B 72
Onslow Green. Essx —4G 53
Onslow Village. Surr —1A 26
Onthank. E Ayr —1D 116
Openwoodgate. Derbs —1A 74
Opinan. High —1G 155
(nr. Gairloch)
Opinan. High —4C 162
(nr. Poolewe)
Orasaigh. W Isl —6F 171
Orbost. High —4B 154
Orby. Linc —4D 89
Orchard Hill. Devn —4E 19
Orchard Portman. Som —4F 21
Orcheston. Wilts —2F 23
Orcop. Here —3H 47
Orcop Hill. Here —3H 47
Ord. High —2E 147
Ordale. Shet —1H 173
Ordhead. Aber —2D 152
Ordie. Aber —3B 152
Ordiquish. Mor —3H 159
Ordley. Nmbd —4C 114
Ordsall. Notts —3E 86
Ore. E Sus —4C 28
Oreham Common. W Sus —4D 26
Oreton. Shrp —2A 60
Orford. Linc —1B 88
Orford. Suff —1H 55
Orford. Warr —1A 84
Organford. Dors —3E 15
Orgil. Orkn —7B 172
Orgreave. Staf —4F 73
Oridge Street. Glos —3C 48
Orlestone. Kent —2D 28
Orleton. Here —4G 59
Orleton. Worc —4A 60
Orleton Common. Here —4G 59
Orlingbury. Nptn —3F 63
Ormacleit. W Isl —5C 170
Ormathwaite. Cumb —2D 102
Ormesby. Midd —3C 106
Ormesby St Margaret. Norf —4G 79
Ormesby St Michael. Norf —4G 79
Ormiscaig. High —4C 162
Ormiston. E Lot —3H 129
Ormsaigbeg. High —2F 139
Ormsaigmore. High —2F 139
Ormsary. Arg —2F 125
Ormsgill. Cumb —2A 96
Ormskirk. Lanc —4C 90
Orphir. Orkn —7C 172
Orpington. G Lon —4F 39
Orrell. G Man —4D 90
Orrell. Mers —1F 83
Orrisdale. IOM —2C 108
Orsett. Thur —2H 39
Orslow. Staf —4C 72
Orston. Notts —1E 75
Orthwaite. Cumb —1D 102
Orton. Cumb —4H 103
Orton. Nptn —3F 63
Orton. Staf —1C 60
Orton Longueville. Pet —1A 64
Orton-on-the-Hill. Leics —5H 73
Orton Waterville. Pet —1A 64
Orton Wistow. Pet —1A 64
Orwell. Cambs —5C 64
Osbaldeston. Lanc —1E 91
Osbaldwick. York —4A 100
Osbaston. Leics —5B 74
Osbaston. Shrp —3F 71
Osbournby. Linc —2H 75
Osclay. High —5E 169
Oscroft. Ches —4H 83
Ose. High —4C 154
Osgathorpe. Leics —4B 74
Osgodby. Linc —1H 87
Osgodby. N Yor —1E 101
(nr. Scarborough)
Osgodby. N Yor —1G 93
(nr. Selby)
Oskaig. High —5E 155
Oskamull. Arg —4F 139
Osleston. Derbs —2G 73
Osmaston. Dby C —2A 74

Osmaston—Pentre

Osmaston. Derbs —1G 73
Osmington. Dors —4C 14
Osmington Mills. Dors —4C 14
Osmondthorpe. W Yor —1D 92
Osmondwall. Orkn —9C 172
Osmotherley. N Yor —5B 106
Osnaburgh. Fife —2G 137
Ospisdale. High —5E 164
Ospringe. Kent —4E 40
Ossett. W Yor —2C 92
Ossington. Notts —4E 87
Ostend. Essx —1D 40
Ostend. Norf —2F 79
Osterley. G Lon —3C 38
Oswaldkirk. N Yor —2A 100
Oswaldtwistle. Lanc —2F 91
Oswestry. Shrp —3E 71
Otby. Linc —1A 88
Otford. Kent —5G 39
Otham. Kent —5B 40
Otherton. Staf —4D 72
Othery. Som —3G 21
Otley. Suff —5E 66
Otley. W Yor —5E 98
Otterbourne. Hants —4C 24
Otterburn. Nmbd —5C 120
Otterburn. N Yor —4A 98
Otterburn Camp. Nmbd —5C 120
Otterburn Hall. Nmbd —5C 120
Otter Ferry. Arg —1H 125
Otterford. Som —1F 13
Otterham. Corn —3B 10
Otterhampton. Som —2F 21
Otterham Quay. Kent —4C 40
Ottershaw. Surr —4B 38
Otterspool. Mers —2F 83
Otterswick. Shet —3G 173
Otterton. Devn —4D 12
Otterwood. Hants —2C 16
Ottery St Mary. Devn —3E 12
Ottinge. Kent —1F 29
Ottringham. E Yor —2F 95
Oughterby. Cumb —4D 112
Oughtershaw. N Yor —1A 98
Oughterside. Cumb —5C 112
Oughtibridge. S Yor —1H 85
Oughtrington. Warr —2A 84
Oulston. N Yor —2H 99
Oulton. Cumb —4D 112
Oulton. Norf —3D 78
Oulton. Staf —3B 72
(nr. Gnosall Heath)
Oulton. Staf —2D 72
(nr. Stone)
Oulton. Suff —1H 67
Oulton. W Yor —2D 92
Oulton Broad. Suff —1H 67
Oulton Street. Norf —3D 78
Oundle. Nptn —2H 63
Ousby. Cumb —1H 103
Ousdale. High —1H 165
Ousden. Suff —5G 65
Ousefleet. E Yor —2B 94
Ouston. Dur —4F 115
Ouston. Nmbd —4A 114
(nr. Bearsbridge)
Ouston. Nmbd —2D 114
(nr. Stamfordham)
Outer Hope. Devn —4C 8
Outertown. Orkn —6B 172
Outgate. Cumb —5E 103
Outhgill. Cumb —4A 104
Outlands. Staf —2B 72
Outlane. W Yor —3A 92
Out Newton. E Yor —2G 95
Out Rawcliffe. Lanc —5D 96
Outwell. Norf —5E 77
Outwick. Hants —1G 15
Outwood. Surr —1E 27
Outwood. W Yor —2D 92
Outwood. Worc —3D 60
Outwoods. Leics —4B 74
Outwoods. Staf —4B 72
Ouzlewell Green. W Yor —2D 92
Ovenden. W Yor —2A 92
Over. Cambs —3C 64
Over. Ches —4A 84
Over. Glos —4D 48
Over. S Glo —3A 34
Overbister. Orkn —3F 172
Over Burrows. Derbs —2G 73
Overbury. Worc —2E 49
Overcombe. Dors —4B 14
Over Compton. Dors —1A 14
Over End. Cambs —1H 63
Over Finlarg. Ang —4D 144
Overgreen. Derbs —3H 85
Over Green. W Mid —1F 61
Over Haddon. Derbs —4G 85
Over Hulton. G Man —4E 91
Over Kellet. Lanc —2E 97
Over Kiddington. Oxon —3C 50
Overleigh. Som —3H 21
Overley. Staf —4F 73
Over Monnow. Mon —4A 48
Over Norton. Oxon —3B 50
Over Peover. Ches —3B 84
Overpool. Ches —3F 83
Overscaig. High —1B 164
Overseal. Derbs —4G 73
Over Silton. N Yor —5B 106
Oversland. Kent —5E 41
Overstone. Nptn —4F 63
Over Stowey. Som —3E 21
Overstrand. Norf —1E 79
Over Stratton. Som —1H 13
Over Street. Wilts —3F 23
Overthorpe. Nptn —1C 50
Overton. Aber C —2F 153
Overton. Ches —3H 83
Overton. Hants —2D 24
Overton. High —5E 169
Overton. Lanc —4D 96
Overton. N Yor —4H 99
Overton. Shrp —2A 60
(nr. Bridgnorth)
Overton. Shrp —3H 59
(nr. Ludlow)
Overton. Swan —4D 30
Overton. W Yor —3C 92
Overton. Wrex —1F 71
Overtown. N Lan —4B 128
Overtown. Swin —4G 35
Over Wallop. Hants —3A 24
Over Whitacre. Warw —1G 61
Over Worton. Oxon —3C 50
Oving. Buck —3F 51
Oving. W Sus —5A 26
Ovingdean. Brig —5E 27
Ovingham. Nmbd —3D 115
Ovington. Dur —3E 105
Ovington. Essx —1A 54
Ovington. Hants —3D 24
Ovington. Norf —5B 78
Ovington. Nmbd —3D 114
Owen's Bank. Staf —3G 73
Ower. Hants —2C 16
(nr. Holbury)
Ower. Hants —1B 16
(nr. Totton)
Owermoigne. Dors —4C 14
Owlbury. Shrp —1F 59
Owler Bar. Derbs —3G 85
Owlerton. S Yor —2H 85
Owlswick. Buck —5F 51
Owmby. Linc —4D 94
Owmby-by-Spital. Linc —2H 87
Ownham. W Ber —4C 36
Owrytn. Wrex —1F 71
Owslebury. Hants —4D 24
Owston. Leics —5E 75
Owston. S Yor —3F 93
Owston Ferry. N Lin —4B 94
Owstwick. E Yor —1F 95
Owthorne. E Yor —2G 95
Owthorpe. Notts —2D 74
Owton Manor. Hart —2B 106
Oxborough. Norf —5G 77
Oxcombe. Linc —3C 88
Oxen End. Essx —3G 53
Oxenhall. Glos —3C 48
Oxenholme. Cumb —5G 103
Oxenhope. W Yor —1A 92
Oxen Park. Cumb —1C 96
Oxenpill. Som —2H 21
Oxenton. Glos —2E 49
Oxenwood. Wilts —1B 24
Oxford. Oxon —5D 50
Oxgangs. Edin —3F 129
Oxhey. Herts —1C 38
Oxhill. Warw —1B 50
Oxley. W Mid —5C 72
Oxley Green. Essx —4C 54
Oxley's Green. E Sus —3A 28
Oxlode. Cambs —2D 65
Oxnam. Scot —3B 120
Oxshott. Surr —4C 38
Oxspring. S Yor —4C 92
Oxted. Surr —5E 39
Oxton. Mers —2E 83
Oxton. N Yor —5H 99
Oxton. Notts —5D 86
Oxton. Scot —4A 130
Oxwich. Swan —4D 31
Oxwich Green. Swan —4D 31
Oxwick. Norf —3B 78
Oykel Bridge. High —3A 164
Oyne. Aber —1D 152
Oystermouth. Swan —4F 31

Pabail Iarach. W Isl —4H 171
Pabail Uarach. W Isl —4H 171
Pachesham. Surr —5C 38
Packers Hill. Dors —1C 14
Packington. Leics —4A 74
Packmoor. Stoke —5C 84
Packmores. Warw —4G 61
Packwood. W Mid —3F 61
Packwood Gullett. W Mid —3F 61
Padanaram. Ang —3D 144
Padbury. Buck —2F 51
Paddington. G Lon —2D 38
Paddington. Warr —2A 84
Paddlesworth. Kent —2F 29
Paddock. Kent —5D 40
Paddockhole. Dum —1D 112
Paddock Wood. Kent —1A 28
Paddolgreen. Shrp —2H 71
Padeswood. Flin —4E 83
Padiham. Lanc —1F 91
Padside. N Yor —4D 98
Padson. Devn —3F 11
Padstow. Corn —1D 6
Padworth. W Ber —5E 36
Page Bank. Dur —1F 105
Pagham. W Sus —3G 17
Paglesham Churchend. Essx —1D 40
Paglesham Eastend. Essx —1D 40
Paibeil. W Isl —2C 170
Paibeil. W Isl —8C 171
Paignton. Torb —2E 9
Pailton. Warw —2B 62
Paine's Corner. E Sus —3H 27
Painleyhill. Staf —2E 73
Painscastle. Powy —1E 47
Painshawfield. Nmbd —3D 114
Painsthorpe. E Yor —4C 100
Painswick. Glos —5D 48
Painter's Forstal. Kent —5D 40
Painthorpe. W Yor —3D 92
Pairc Shiaboist. W Isl —3E 171
Paisley. Ren —3F 127
Pakefield. Suff —1H 67
Pakenham. Suff —4B 66
Pale. Gwyn —2B 70
Palehouse Common. E Sus —4F 27
Palestine. Hants —2A 24
Paley Street. Wind —4G 37
Palgowan. Dum —1A 110
Palgrave. Suff —3D 66
Pallington. Dors —3C 14
Palmarsh. Kent —2F 29
Palmer Moor. Derbs —2F 73
Palmers Cross. W Mid —5C 72
Palmerstown. V Glam —5E 33
Palnackie. Dum —4F 111
Palnure. Dum —3B 110
Palterton. Derbs —4B 86
Pamber End. Hants —1E 24
Pamber Green. Hants —1E 24
Pamber Heath. Hants —5E 36
Pamington. Glos —2E 49
Pamphill. Dors —2E 15
Pampisford. Cambs —1E 53
Panborough. Som —2H 21
Panbride. Ang —5E 145
Pancakehill. Glos —4F 49
Pancrasweek. Devn —2C 10
Pandy. Gwyn —3A 70
(nr. Bala)
Pandy. Gwyn —5F 69
(nr. Tywyn)
Pandy. Mon —3G 47
Pandy. Powy —5B 70
Pandy. Wrex —2D 70
Pandy Tudur. Cnwy —4A 82
Panfield. Essx —3H 53
Pangbourne. W Ber —4E 37
Pannal. N Yor —4F 99
Pannal Ash. N Yor —4E 99
Pannanich. Aber —4A 152
Pant. Shrp —3E 71
Pant. Wrex —1F 71
Pantasaph. Flin —3D 82
Pant Glas. Gwyn —1D 68
Pant-glas. Shrp —2E 71
Pantgwyn. Carm —3F 45
Pantgwyn. Cdgn —1C 44
Pant-lasau. Swan —3F 31
Panton. Linc —3A 88
Pant-pastynog. Den —4C 82
Pantperthog. Gwyn —5G 69
Pant-teg. Carm —3E 45
Pant-y-Caws. Carm —2F 43
Pant-y-dwr. Powy —3B 58
Pant-y-ffridd. Powy —5D 70
Pantyffynnon. Carm —4G 45
Pantygasseg. Torf —5F 47
Pant-y-llyn. Carm —4G 45
Pant-yr-awel. B'End —3C 32
Pant y Wacco. Flin —3D 82
Panxworth. Norf —4F 79
Papa Westray Airport. Orkn —2D 172
Papcastle. Cumb —1C 102
Papigoe. High —3F 169
Papil. Shet —8E 173
Papple. E Lot —2B 130
Papplewick. Notts —5C 86
Papworth Everard. Cambs —4B 64
Papworth St Agnes. Cambs —4B 64
Par. Corn —3E 7
Paramour Street. Kent —4G 41
Parbold. Lanc —3C 90
Parbrook. Som —3A 22
Parbrook. W Sus —3B 26
Parc. Gwyn —2A 70
Parcllyn. Cdgn —5B 56
Parc-Seymour. Newp —2H 33
Pardown. Hants —2D 24
Pardshaw. Cumb —2B 102
Parham. Suff —4F 67
Park. Aber —4E 153
Park. Arg —4D 140
Park. Dum —5B 118
Park Bottom. Corn —4A 6
Parkburn. Aber —5E 161
Park Corner. E Sus —2G 27
Park Corner. Oxon —3E 37
Parkend. Glos —5B 48
Park End. Nmbd —2B 114
Parkeston. Essx —2F 55
Parkfield. Corn —2H 7
Parkgate. Ches —3E 83
Parkgate. Cumb —5D 112
Parkgate. Dum —1B 112
Park Gate. Hants —2D 16
Parkgate. Surr —1D 26
Park Gate. Worc —3D 60
Parkhall. W Dun —2F 127
Parkham. Devn —4D 19
Parkham Ash. Devn —4D 18
Parkhead. Cumb —5E 113
Parkhead. Glas —3H 127
Park Hill. Mers —4C 90
Parkhouse. Mon —5H 47
Parkhurst. IOW —3C 16
Park Lane. G Man —4F 91
Park Lane. Staf —5C 72
Parkmill. Swan —4E 31
Park Mill. W Yor —3C 92
Parkneuk. Aber —1G 145
Parkside. N Lan —4B 128
Parkstone. Pool —3F 15
Park Street. Herts —5B 52
Park Street. W Sus —2C 26
Park Town. Oxon —5D 50
Park Village. Nmbd —3H 113
Parkway. Here —2C 48
Parley Cross. Dors —3F 15
Parmoor. Buck —3F 37
Parr. Mers —1H 83
Parracombe. Devn —2G 19
Parrog. Pemb —1E 43
Parsonage Green. Essx —4H 53
Parsonby. Cumb —1C 102
Parson Cross. S Yor —1A 86
Parson Drove. Cambs —5C 76
Partick. Glas —3G 127
Partington. G Man —1B 84
Partney. Linc —4D 88
Parton. Cumb —2A 102
(nr. Whitehaven)
Parton. Cumb —4D 112
(nr. Wigton)
Parton. Dum —2D 111
Partridge Green. W Sus —4C 26
Parwich. Derbs —5F 85
Passenham. Nptn —2F 51
Passfield. Hants —3G 25
Passingford Bridge. Essx —1G 39
Paston. Norf —2F 79
Pasturefields. Staf —3D 73
Patchacott. Devn —3E 11
Patcham. Brig —5E 27
Patchetts Green. Herts —1C 38
Patching. W Sus —5B 26
Patchole. Devn —2G 19
Patchway. S Glo —3B 34
Pateley Bridge. N Yor —3D 98
Pathe. Som —3G 21
Pathhead. Aber —2G 145
Pathhead. E Ayr —3F 117
Pathhead. Fife —4E 137
Pathhead. Midl —3G 129
Pathlow. Warw —5F 61
Path of Condie. Per —2C 136
Pathstruie. Per —2C 136
Patmore Heath. Herts —3E 53
Patna. E Ayr —3D 116
Patney. Wilts —1F 23
Patrick. IOM —3B 108
Patrick Brompton. N Yor —5F 105
Patrington. E Yor —2G 95
Patrington Haven. E Yor —2G 95
Patrixbourne. Kent —5F 41
Patterdale. Cumb —3E 103
Pattiesmuir. Fife —1D 129
Pattingham. Staf —1C 60
Pattishall. Nptn —5D 62
Pattiswick. Essx —3B 54
Patton Bridge. Cumb —5G 103
Paul. Corn —4B 4
Paulerspury. Nptn —1F 51
Paull. E Yor —2E 95
Paulton. Bath —1B 22
Pauperhaugh. Nmbd —5F 121
Pave Lane. Telf —4B 72
Pavenham. Beds —5G 63
Pawlett. Som —2G 21
Pawston. Nmbd —1C 120
Paxford. Glos —2G 49
Paxton. Scot —4F 131
Payhembury. Devn —2D 12
Paythorne. Lanc —4H 97
Peacehaven. E Sus —5F 27
Peak Dale. Derbs —3E 85
Peak Forest. Derbs —3F 85
Peak Hill. Linc —4B 76
Peakirk. Pet —5A 76
Peanmeanach. High —5F 147
Pearsie. Ang —3C 144
Peasedown St John. Bath —1C 22
Peaseland Green. Norf —4C 78
Peasemore. W Ber —4C 36
Peasenhall. Suff —4F 67
Pease Pottage. W Sus —2D 26
Peaslake. Surr —1B 26
Peasley Cross. Mers —1H 83
Peasmarsh. E Sus —3C 28
Peasmarsh. Surr —1A 26
Peaston. E Lot —3H 129
Peastonbank. E Lot —3H 129
Peathill. Aber —2G 161
Peat Inn. Fife —3G 137
Peatling Magna. Leics —1C 62
Peatling Parva. Leics —1C 62
Peaton. Arg —1D 126
Peaton. Shrp —2H 59
Peats Corner. Suff —4D 66
Pebmarsh. Essx —2B 54
Pebworth. Worc —1G 49
Pecket Well. W Yor —2H 91
Peckforton. Ches —5H 83
Peckham Bush. Kent —5A 40
Peckleton. Leics —5B 74
Pedair-ffordd. Powy —3D 70
Pedlinge. Kent —2F 29
Pedmore. W Mid —2D 60
Pedwell. Som —3H 21
Peebles. Scot —5F 129
Peel. IOM —3B 108
Peel. Scot —1G 119
Peel Common. Hants —2D 16
Peening Quarter. Kent —3C 28
Pegg's Green. Leics —4B 74
Pegsdon. Beds —2B 52
Pegswood. Nmbd —1F 115
Peinchorran. High —5E 155
Peinlich. High —3D 154
Pelaw. Tyne —3G 115
Pelcomb Bridge. Pemb —3D 42
Pelcomb Cross. Pemb —3D 42
Peldon. Essx —4C 54
Pelsall. W Mid —5E 73
Pelton. Dur —4F 115
Pelutho. Cumb —5C 112
Pelynt. Corn —3G 7
Pemberton. Carm —5F 45
Pembrey. Carm —5E 45
Pembridge. Here —5F 59
Pembroke. Pemb —4D 43
Pembroke Dock. Pemb —4D 42
Pembroke Ferry. Pemb —4D 42
Pembury. Kent —1H 27
Penallt. Mon —5A 48
Penally. Pemb —5F 43
Penalt. Here —3A 48
Penalum. Pemb —5F 43
Penarth. V Glam —4E 33
Penbeagle. Corn —3C 4
Penberth. Corn —4B 4
Pen-bont Rhydybeddau. Cdgn —2F 57
Penbryn. Cdgn —5B 56
Pencader. Carm —2E 45
Pen-cae. Cdgn —5D 56
Pencaenewydd. Gwyn —1D 68
Pencaerau. Neat —3G 31
Pencaitland. E Lot —3H 129
Pencarnisiog. IOA —3C 80
Pencarreg. Carm —1F 45
Pencarrow. Corn —4B 10
Pencelli. Powy —3D 46
Pen-clawdd. Swan —3E 31
Pencoed. B'End —3C 32
Pencombe. Here —5H 59
Pencraig. Here —3A 48
Pencraig. Powy —3C 70
Pendeen. Corn —3A 4
Pendeford. Staf —5D 72
Penderyn. Rhon —5C 46
Pendine. Carm —4G 43
Pendlebury. G Man —4F 91
Pendleton. G Man —1C 84
Pendleton. Lanc —1F 91
Pendock. Worc —2C 48
Pendoggett. Corn —5A 10
Pendomer. Som —1A 14
Pendoylan. V Glam —4D 32
Pendre. B'End —3C 32
Penegoes. Powy —5G 69
Penelewey. Corn —4C 6
Penffordd. Pemb —2E 43
Penffordd-Las. Powy —1A 58
Penfro. Pemb —4D 43
Pengam. Cphy —2E 33
Pengam. Card —4F 33
Penge. G Lon —3E 39
Pengelly. Corn —4A 10
Pengenffordd. Powy —2E 47
Pengorffwysfa. IOA —1D 80
Pengover Green. Corn —2G 7
Pengwern. Den —3C 82
Penhale. Corn —5D 5
(nr. Mullion)
Penhale. Corn —3D 6
(nr. St Austell)
Penhale Camp. Corn —3B 6
Penhallow. Corn —3B 6
Penhalvean. Corn —5B 6
Penhelig. Gwyn —1F 57
Penhill. Swin —3G 35
Penhow. Newp —2H 33
Penhurst. E Sus —4A 28
Peniarth. Gwyn —5F 69
Penicuik. Midl —3F 129
Peniel. Carm —3E 45
Penifiler. High —4D 155
Peninver. Arg —3B 122
Penisa'r Waun. Gwyn —4E 81
Penistone. S Yor —4C 92
Penketh. Warr —2H 83
Penkill. S Ayr —5B 116
Penkridge. Staf —4D 72
Penley. Wrex —2G 71
Penllech. Gwyn —2B 68
Penllergaer. Swan —3F 31
Pen-llyn. IOA —2C 80
Penmachno. Cnwy —5G 81
Penmaen. Swan —4E 31
Penmaenmawr. Cnwy —3G 81
Penmaenpool. Gwyn —4F 69
Penmaen Rhos. Cnwy —3A 82
Penmark. V Glam —5D 32
Penmarth. Corn —5B 6
Penmon. IOA —2F 81
Penmorfa. Gwyn —1E 69
Penmyndd. IOA —3E 81
Penn. Buck —1A 38
Penn. Dors —3G 13
Penn. W Mid —1C 60
Pennal. Gwyn —5G 69
Pennan. Aber —2F 161
Pennant. Cdgn —4E 57
Pennant. Den —2C 70
Pennant. Gwyn —3B 70
Pennant. Powy —1A 58
Pennant Melangell. Powy —3C 70
Pennar. Pemb —4D 42
Pennard. Swan —4E 31
Pennerley. Shrp —1F 59
Pennington. Cumb —2B 96
Pennington. G Man —1A 84
Pennington. Hants —3B 16
Pennorth. Powy —3E 46
Penn Street. Buck —1A 38
Pennsylvania. Devn —3C 12
Pennsylvania. S Glo —4C 34
Penny Bridge. Cumb —1C 96
Pennycross. Plym —3A 8
Pennygate. Norf —3F 79
Pennyghael. Arg —1C 132
Penny Hill. Linc —3C 76
Pennylands. Lanc —4C 90
Pennymoor. Devn —1B 12
Pennyvenie. E Ayr —4D 117
Pennywell. Tyne —4G 115
Penparc. Cdgn —1C 44
Penparcau. Cdgn —2E 57
Penpedairheol. Cphy —2E 33
Penperlleni. Mon —5G 47
Penpillick. Corn —3E 7
Penpol. Corn —5C 6
Penpoll. Corn —3F 7
Penponds. Corn —3D 4
Penpont. Corn —5A 10
Penpont. Dum —5H 117
Penpont. Powy —3C 46
Penprysg. B'End —3C 32
Penquit. Devn —3C 8
Penrherber. Carm —1G 43
Penrhiw. Pemb —1C 44
Penrhiwceiber. Rhon —2D 32
Pen Rhiwfawr. Neat —4H 45
Penrhiw-llan. Cdgn —1D 44
Penrhiw-pal. Cdgn —1D 44
Penrhos. Gwyn —2C 68
Penrhos. Here —5F 59
Penrhos. IOA —2B 80
Penrhos. Mon —4H 47
Penrhos. Powy —4B 46
Penrhos garnedd. Gwyn —3E 81
Penrhyn. IOA —1C 80
Penrhyn Bay. Cnwy —2H 81
Penrhyn-coch. Cdgn —2F 57
Penrhyndeudraeth. Gwyn —2F 69
Penrhyn Side. Cnwy —2H 81
Penrice. Swan —4D 31
Penrith. Cumb —2G 103
Penrose. Corn —1C 6
Penruddock. Cumb —2F 103
Penryn. Corn —5B 6
Pensarn. Carm —4E 45
Pen-sarn. Gwyn —3E 69
Pensax. Worc —4B 60
Pensby. Mers —2E 83
Penselwood. Som —3C 22
Pensford. Bath —5B 34
Pensham. Worc —1E 49
Penshaw. Tyne —4G 115
Penshurst. Kent —1G 27
Pensilva. Corn —2G 7
Pensnett. W Mid —2D 60
Penston. E Lot —2H 129
Penstone. Devn —2A 12
Pente-tafarn-y-fedw. Cnwy —4H 81
Pentewan. Corn —4E 6
Pentir. Gwyn —4E 81
Pentire. Corn —2B 6
Pentlepoir. Pemb —4F 43
Pentlow. Essx —1B 54
Pentney. Norf —4G 77
Penton Mewsey. Hants —2B 24
Pentraeth. IOA —3E 81
Pentre. Powy —1E 59
(nr. Church Stoke)
Pentre. Powy —2D 58
(nr. Kerry)
Pentre. Powy —2C 58
(nr. Mochdre)

Pentre—Portreath

Pentre. Rhon —2C 32
Pentre. Shrp —4F 71
Pentre. Wrex —2D 70
(nr. Llanfyllin)
Pentre. Wrex —1E 71
(nr. Rhosllanerchrugog)
Pentrebach. Carm —2B 46
Pentre-bach. Cdgn —1F 45
Pentrebach. Mer T —5D 46
Pentre-bach. Powy —2C 46
Pentrebach. Swan —5G 45
Pentre Berw. IOA —3D 80
Pentre-bont. Cnwy —5G 81
Pentrecagal. Carm —1D 44
Pentre-celyn. Den —5D 82
Pentre-clawdd. Shrp —2E 71
Pentreclwydau. Neat —5B 46
Pentre-cwrt. Carm —2D 45
Pentre Dolau Honddu. Powy —1C 46
Pentre-du. Cnwy —5G 81
Pentre-dwr. Neat —3F 31
Pentrefelin. Carm —3F 45
Pentrefelin. Cdgn —1G 45
Pentrefelin. Cnwy —3H 81
Pentrefelin. Gwyn —2E 69
Pentrefoelas. Cnwy —5A 82
Pentre Galar. Pemb —1F 43
Pentregat. Cdgn —5C 56
Pentre Gwenlais. Carm —4G 45
Pentre Gwynfryn. Gwyn —3E 69
Pentre Halkyn. Flin —3E 82
Pentre Hodre. Shrp —3F 59
Pentre-Llanrhaeadr. Den —4C 82
Pentre Llifior. Powy —1D 58
Pentrellwyn. IOA —2E 81
Pentre-llwyn-llwyd. Powy —5B 58
Pentre-llyn-cymmer. Cnwy —5B 82
Pentre Meyrick. V Glam —4C 32
Pentre-piod. Gwyn —2A 70
Pentre-poeth. Newp —3F 33
Pentre'r Beirdd. Powy —4D 70
Pentre'r-felin. Powy —2C 46
Pentre-ty-gwyn. Carm —2B 46
Pentre-uchaf. Gwyn —2C 68
Pentrich. Derbs —5A 86
Pentridge. Dors —1F 15
Pen-twyn. Cphy —5F 47
(nr. Oakdale)
Pentwyn. Cphy —5E 46
(nr. Rhymney)
Pentwyn. Card —3F 33
Pentyrch. Card —3E 32
Pentywyn. Carm —4G 43
Penuwch. Cdgn —4E 57
Penwithick. Corn —3E 7
Penwyllt. Powy —4B 46
Penybanc. Carm —4G 45
(nr. Ammanford)
Pen-y-banc. Carm —3G 45
(nr. Llandeilo)
Pen-y-bont. Carm —2H 43
Penybont. Powy —4D 58
(nr. Llandrindod Wells)
Pen-y-bont. Powy —3E 70
(nr. Llanfyllin)
Pen-y-Bont Ar Ogwr. B'End —3C 32
Penybontfawr. Powy —3C 70
Penybryn. Cphy —2E 33
Pen-y-bryn. Pemb —1B 44
Pen-y-bryn. Wrex —1E 71
Pen-y-cae. Powy —4B 46
Penycae. Wrex —1E 71
Pen-y-cae-mawr. Mon —2H 33
Penycaerau. Gwyn —3A 68
Pen-y-cefn. Flin —3D 82
Pen-y-clawdd. Mon —5H 47
Pen-y-coedcae. Rhon —3D 32
Penycwm. Pemb —2C 42
Pen-y-darren. Mer T —5D 46
Pen-y-fai. B'End —3B 32
Penyffordd. Flin —4F 83
(nr. Mold)
Pen-y-ffordd. Flin —2D 82
(nr. Prestatyn)
Penyffridd. Gwyn —5E 81
Pen-y-garn. Cdgn —2F 57
Pen-y-garnedd. IOA —3E 81
Penygarnedd. Powy —3D 70
Pen-y-graig. Gwyn —2A 68
Penygraig. Rhon —2C 32
Pen-y-groes. Carm —4F 45
Penygroes. Gwyn —5D 80
Penygroes. Pemb —1F 43
Penymynydd. Flin —4F 83
Penyrheol. Cphy —3E 33
Pen-yr-heol. Mon —4H 47
Penyrheol. Swan —3E 31
Pen-yr-Heolgerrig. Mer T —5D 46
Penysarn. IOA —1D 80
Pen-y-stryt. Den —5E 82
Penywaun. Rhon —5C 46
Penzance. Corn —4B 4
Penzance Heliport. Corn —3B 4
Peopleton. Worc —5D 60
Peover Heath. Ches —3B 84
Peper Harow. Surr —1A 26
Peplow. Shrp —3A 72
Pepper Arden. N Yor —4F 105
Perceton. N Ayr —5E 127
Percyhorner. Aber —2G 161
Perham Down. Wilts —2A 24
Periton. Som —2C 20
Perkinsville. Dur —4F 115
Perlethorpe. Notts —3D 86
Perranarworthal. Corn —5B 6
Perranporth. Corn —3B 6
Perranuthnoe. Corn —4C 4
Perranwell. Corn —5B 6
Perranzabuloe. Corn —3B 6
Perrott's Brook. Glos —5F 49
Perry. W Mid —1E 61
Perry Barr. W Mid —1E 61
Perry Crofts. Staf —5G 73
Perry Green. Essx —3B 54
Perry Green. Herts —4E 53
Perry Green. Wilts —3E 35
Perry Street. Kent —3H 39
Perry Street. Som —2G 13
Perrywood. Kent —5E 41
Pershall. Staf —2C 72
Pershore. Worc —1E 49
Pertenhall. Beds —4H 63
Perth. Per —1D 136
Perthy. Shrp —2F 71
Perton. Staf —1C 60
Pertwood. Wilts —3D 23
Peterborough. Pet —1A 64
Peterburn. High —5B 162
Peterchurch. Here —2G 47
Peterculter. Aber C —3F 153
Peterhead. Aber —4H 161
Peterlee. Dur —5H 115
Petersfield. Hants —4F 25
Petersfinger. Wilts —4G 23
Peter's Green. Herts —4B 52
Peters Marland. Devn —1E 11
Peterstone Wentlooge. Newp —3F 33
Peterston-super-Ely. V Glam —4D 32
Peterstow. Here —3A 48
Peter Tavy. Devn —5F 11
Petertown. Orkn —7C 172
Petham. Kent —5F 41
Petherwin Gate. Corn —4C 10
Petrockstowe. Devn —2F 11
Petsoe End. Mil —1G 51
Pett. E Sus —4C 28
Pettaugh. Suff —5D 66
Petteridge. Kent —1A 28
Petteril Green. Cumb —5F 113
Pettinain. S Lan —5C 128
Pettistree. Suff —5E 67
Petton. Devn —4D 20
Petton. Shrp —3G 71
Petts Wood. G Lon —4F 39
Pettycur. Fife —1F 129
Pettywell. Norf —3C 78
Petworth. W Sus —3A 26
Pevensey. E Sus —5H 27
Pevensey Bay. E Sus —5A 28
Pewsey. Wilts —5G 35
Pheasant's Hill. Buck —3F 37
Philadelphia. Tyne —4G 115
Philham. Devn —4C 18
Philiphaugh. Scot —2G 119
Phillack. Corn —3C 4
Philleigh. Corn —5C 6
Philpstoun. W Lot —2D 128
Phocle Green. Here —3B 48
Phoenix Green. Hants —1F 25
Pibsbury. Som —4H 21
Pibwrlwyd. Carm —4E 45
Pica. Cumb —2B 102
Piccadilly. Warw —1G 61
Piccadilly Corner. Norf —2E 67
Piccotts End. Herts —5A 52
Pickering. N Yor —1B 100
Picket Piece. Hants —2B 24
Picket Post. Hants —2G 15
Pickford. W Mid —2G 61
Pickhill. N Yor —1F 99
Picklenash. Glos —3C 48
Picklescott. Shrp —1G 59
Pickletillem. Fife —1G 137
Pickmere. Ches —3A 84
Pickstock. Telf —3B 72
Pickwell. Devn —2E 19
Pickwell. Leics —4E 75
Pickworth. Linc —2H 75
Pickworth. Rut —4G 75
Picton. Ches —3G 83
Picton. Flin —2D 82
Picton. N Yor —4B 106
Piddinghoe. E Sus —5F 27
Piddington. Buck —2G 37
Piddington. Nptn —5F 63
Piddington. Oxon —4E 51
Piddlehinton. Dors —3C 14
Piddletrenthide. Dors —2C 14
Pidley. Cambs —3C 64
Pidney. Dors —2C 14
Pie Corner. Here —4A 60
Piercebridge. Darl —3F 105
Pierowall. Orkn —3D 172
Pigdon. Nmbd —1E 115
Pightley. Som —3F 21
Pikehall. Derbs —5F 85
Pikeshill. Hants —2A 16
Pilford. Dors —2F 15
Pilgrims Hatch. Essx —1G 39
Pilham. Linc —1F 87
Pill. N Som —4A 34
Pillaton. Corn —2H 7
Pillerton Hersey. Warw —1A 50
Pillerton Priors. Warw —1A 50
Pilleth. Powy —4E 59
Pilley. Hants —3B 16
Pilley. S Yor —4D 92
Pillgwenlly. Newp —3G 33
Pilling. Lanc —5D 96
Pilling Lane. Lanc —5C 96
Pillowell. Glos —5B 48
Pill, The. Mon —3H 33
Pillwell. Dors —1C 14
Pilning. S Glo —3A 34
Pilsbury. Derbs —4F 85
Pilsdon. Dors —3H 13
Pilsgate. Pet —5H 75
Pilsley. Derbs —3G 85
(nr. Bakewell)
Pilsley. Derbs —4B 86
(nr. Clay Cross)
Pilson Green. Norf —4F 79
Piltdown. E Sus —3F 27
Pilton. Edin —2F 129
Pilton. Nptn —2H 63
Pilton. Rut —5G 75
Pilton. Som —2A 22
Pilton Green. Swan —4D 30
Pimperne. Dors —2E 15
Pinchbeck. Linc —3B 76
Pinchbeck Bars. Linc —3A 76
Pinchbeck West. Linc —3B 76
Pinfold. Lanc —3B 90
Pinford End. Suff —5H 65
Pinged. Carm —5E 45
Pinhoe. Devn —3C 12
Pinkerton. E Lot —2D 130
Pinkneys Green. Wind —3G 37
Pinley. W Mid —3A 62
Pinley Green. Warw —4G 61
Pin Mill. Suff —2F 55
Pinmore. S Ayr —5B 116
Pinner. G Lon —2C 38
Pins Green. Worc —1C 48
Pinsley Green. Ches —1H 71
Pinvin. Worc —1E 49
Pinwherry. S Ayr —1G 109
Pinxton. Derbs —5B 86
Pipe and Lyde. Here —1A 48
Pipe Aston. Here —3G 59
Pipe Gate. Shrp —1B 72
Pipehill. Staf —5E 73
Piperhill. High —3C 158
Pipe Ridware. Staf —4E 73
Pipers Pool. Corn —4C 10
Pipewell. Nptn —2F 63
Pippacott. Devn —3F 19
Pipton. Powy —2E 47
Pirbright. Surr —5A 38
Pirnmill. N Ayr —5G 125
Pirton. Herts —2B 52
Pirton. Worc —1D 49
Pisgah. Stir —3G 135
Pishill. Oxon —3F 37
Pistyll. Gwyn —1C 68
Pitagowan. Per —2F 143
Pitcairn. Per —3F 143
Pitcairngreen. Per —1C 136
Pitcalnie. High —1C 158
Pitcaple. Aber —1E 152
Pitchcombe. Glos —5D 48
Pitchcott. Buck —3F 51
Pitchford. Shrp —5H 71
Pitch Green. Buck —5F 51
Pitch Place. Surr —5A 38
Pitcombe. Som —3B 22
Pitcox. E Lot —2C 130
Pitcur. Per —5B 144
Pitfichie. Aber —2D 152
Pitgrudy. High —4E 165
Pitkennedy. Ang —3E 145
Pitlessie. Fife —3F 137
Pitlochry. Per —3G 143
Pitmachie. Aber —1D 152
Pitmaduthy. High —1B 158
Pitmedden. Aber —1F 153
Pitminster. Som —1F 13
Pitnacree. Per —3G 143
Pitney. Som —4H 21
Pitroddie. Per —1E 136
Pitscottie. Fife —2G 137
Pitsea. Essx —2B 40
Pitsford. Nptn —4E 63
Pitsford Hill. Som —3E 20
Pitsmoor. S Yor —2A 86
Pitstone. Buck —4H 51
Pitstone Green. Buck —4H 51
Pitt. Hants —4C 24
Pittaton. Staf —4D 72
Pitt Court. Glos —2C 34
Pittentrail. High —3E 164
Pittenweem. Fife —3H 137
Pittington. Dur —5G 115
Pitton. Swan —4D 30
Pitton. Wilts —3H 23
Pittswood. Kent —1H 27
Pittulie. Aber —2G 161
Pittville. Glos —3E 49
Pitversie. Per —2D 136
Pityme. Corn —1D 6
Pity Me. Dur —5F 115
Pixey Green. Suff —3E 67
Pixley. Here —2B 48
Place Newton. N Yor —2C 100
Plaidy. Aber —3E 161
Plaidy. Corn —3G 7
Plain Dealings. Pemb —3E 43
Plains. N Lan —3A 128
Plainsfield. Som —3E 21
Plaish. Shrp —1H 59
Plaistow. Here —1B 48
Plaistow. W Sus —2B 26
Plaitford. Hants —1A 16
Plas Llwyd. Cnwy —3B 82
Plastow Green. Hants —5D 36
Plas yn Cefn. Den —3C 82
Platt. Kent —5H 39
Platt Bridge. G Man —4E 90
Platt Lane. Shrp —2H 71
Platts Common. S Yor —4D 92
Platt's Heath. Kent —5C 40
Platt, The. E Sus —2G 27
Plawsworth. Dur —5F 115
Plaxtol. Kent —5H 39
Playden. E Sus —3D 28
Playford. Suff —1F 55
Play Hatch. Oxon —4F 37
Playing Place. Corn —4C 6
Playley Green. Glos —2C 48
Plealey. Shrp —5G 71
Plean. Stir —1B 128
Pleasington. Bkbn —2E 91
Pleasley. Derbs —4C 86
Pledgdon Green. Essx —3F 53
Plenmeller. Nmbd —3A 114
Pleshey. Essx —4G 53
Plockton. High —5H 155
Plocrapol. W Isl —8D 171
Ploughfield. Here —1G 47
Plowden. Shrp —2F 59
Ploxgreen. Shrp —5F 71
Pluckley. Kent —1D 28
Plumbland. Cumb —1C 102
Plumgarths. Cumb —5F 103
Plumley. Ches —3B 84
Plummers Plain. W Sus —3D 26
Plumpton. Cumb —1F 103
Plumpton. E Sus —4E 27
Plumpton. Nptn —1D 50
Plumptonfoot. Cumb —1F 103
Plumpton Green. E Sus —4E 27
Plumpton Head. Cumb —1G 103
Plumstead. G Lon —3F 39
Plumstead. Norf —2D 78
Plumtree. Notts —2D 74
Plumtree Park. Notts —2D 74
Plungar. Leics —2E 75
Plush. Dors —2C 14
Plushabridge. Corn —5D 10
Plwmp. Cdgn —5C 56
Plymouth. Plym —3A 8
Plymouth Airport. Plym —2B 8
Plympton. Plym —3B 8
Plymstock. Plym —3B 8
Plymtree. Devn —2D 12
Pockley. N Yor —1A 100
Pocklington. E Yor —5C 100
Pode Hole. Linc —3B 76
Podimore. Som —4A 22
Podington. Beds —4G 63
Podmore. Staf —2B 72
Poffley End. Oxon —4B 50
Point Clear. Essx —4D 54
Pointon. Linc —2A 76
Pokesdown. Bour —3G 15
Polbae. Dum —2H 109
Polbain. High —3E 163
Polbathic. Corn —3H 7
Polbeth. W Lot —3D 128
Polbrock. Corn —2E 6
Polchar. High —3C 150
Polebrook. Nptn —2H 63
Pole Elm. Worc —1D 48
Polegate. E Sus —5G 27
Pole Moor. W Yor —3A 92
Poles. High —4E 165
Polesworth. Warw —5G 73
Polglass. High —3E 163
Polgooth. Corn —3D 6
Poling. W Sus —5B 26
Poling Corner. W Sus —5B 26
Polio. High —1B 158
Polkerris. Corn —3E 7
Polla. High —3D 166
Pollard Street. Norf —2F 79
Pollicott. Buck —4F 51
Pollington. E Yor —3G 93
Polloch. High —2B 140
Pollok. Glas —3G 127
Pollokshaws. Glas —3G 127
Pollokshields. Glas —3G 127
Polmaily. High —5G 157
Polmassick. Corn —4D 6
Polmont. Falk —2C 128
Polnessan. E Ayr —3D 116
Polnish. High —5F 147
Polperro. Corn —3G 7
Polruan. Corn —3F 7
Polscoe. Corn —2F 7
Polsham. Som —2A 22
Polskeoch. Dum —4F 117
Polstead. Suff —2C 54
Polstead Heath. Suff —1C 54
Poltescoe. Corn —5E 5
Poltimore. Devn —3C 12
Polton. Midl —3G 129
Polwarth. Scot —4D 130
Polyphant. Corn —4C 10
Polzeath. Corn —1D 6
Ponde. Powy —2E 46
Pondersbridge. Cambs —1B 64
Ponders End. G Lon —1E 39
Pond Street. Essx —2E 53
Pondtail. Hants —1G 25
Ponsanooth. Corn —5B 6
Ponsongath. Corn —5E 5
Ponsworthy. Devn —5H 11
Pontamman. Carm —4G 45
Pontantwn. Carm —4E 45
Pontardawe. Neat —5H 45
Pontardulais. Swan —5F 45
Pontarfynach. Cdgn —3G 57
Pont-ar-gothi. Carm —3F 45
Pont ar Hydfer. Powy —3B 46
Pontarllechau. Carm —3H 45
Pontarsais. Carm —3E 45
Pontblyddyn. Flin —4E 83
Pontbren Llwyd. Rhon —5C 46
Pont Cyfyng. Cnwy —5G 81
Pontdolgoch. Powy —1C 58
Pontefract. W Yor —2E 93
Ponteland. Nmbd —2E 115
Ponterwyd. Cdgn —2G 57
Pontesbury. Shrp —5G 71
Pontesford. Shrp —5G 71
Pontfadog. Wrex —2E 71
Pontfaen. Pemb —1E 43
Pont-faen. Powy —2C 46
Pont-Faen. Shrp —2E 71
Pontgarreg. Cdgn —5C 56
Pont-Henri. Carm —5E 45
Ponthir. Torf —2G 33
Ponthirwaun. Cdgn —1C 44
Pontllanfraith. Cphy —2E 33
Pontlliw. Swan —5G 45
Pont Llogel. Powy —4C 70
Pontllyfni. Gwyn —5D 80
Pontlottyn. Cphy —5E 46
Pontneddfechan. Rhon —5C 46
Pont-newydd. Carm —5E 45
Pont-newydd. Flin —4D 82
Pontnewydd. Torf —2G 33
Ponton. Shet —6E 173
Pont Pen-y-benglog. Gwyn —4F 81
Pontrhydfendigaid. Cdgn —4G 57
Pont Rhyd-y-cyff. B'End —3B 32
Pontrhydyfen. Neat —2A 32
Pont-rhyd-y-groes. Cdgn —3G 57
Pontrhydyrun. Torf —2F 33
Pont Rhythallt. Gwyn —4E 81
Pontrilas. Here —3G 47
Pontrilas Road. Here —3G 47
Pontrobert. Powy —4D 70
Pont-rug. Gwyn —4E 81
Ponts Green. E Sus —4A 28
Pontshill. Here —3B 48
Pont-Sian. Cdgn —1E 45
Pontsticill. Mer T —4D 46
Pont-Walby. Neat —5B 46
Pontwelly. Carm —2E 45
Pontwgan. Cnwy —3G 81
Pontyates. Carm —5E 45
Pontyberem. Carm —4F 45
Pontybodkin. Flin —5E 83
Pontyclun. Rhon —3D 32
Pontycymer. B'End —2C 32
Pontyglazier. Pemb —1F 43
Pontygwaith. Rhon —2D 32
Pont-y-pant. Cnwy —5G 81
Pontypool. Torf —2F 33
Pontypridd. Rhon —2D 32
Pontypwl. Torf —2F 33
Pontywaun. Cphy —2F 33
Pooksgreen. Hants —1B 16
Pool. Corn —4A 6
Pool. IOS —1A 4
Pool. W Yor —5E 99
Poole. N Yor —2E 93
Poole. Pool —3F 15
Poole Green. Ches —5A 84
Poole Keynes. Glos —2E 35
Poolend. Staf —5D 84
Poolewe. High —5C 162
Pooley Bridge. Cumb —2F 103
Poolfold. Staf —5C 84
Pool Head. Here —5H 59
Pool Hey. Lanc —3B 90
Poolhill. Glos —3C 48
Poolmill. Here —3A 48
Pool o' Muckhart. Clac —3B 136
Pool Quay. Powy —4E 71
Poolsbrook. Derbs —3B 86
Pool Street. Essx —2A 54
Pootings. Kent —1F 27
Pope Hill. Pemb —3D 42
Pope's Hill. Glos —4B 48
Popeswood. Brac —5G 37
Popham. Hants —2D 24
Poplar. G Lon —2E 39
Popley. Hants —1E 25
Porchfield. IOW —3C 16
Porin. High —3F 157
Poringland. Norf —5E 79
Porkellis. Corn —5A 6
Porlock. Som —2B 20
Porlock Wier. Som —2B 20
Portachoillan. Arg —4F 125
Port Ann. Arg —1H 125
Port Appin. Arg —4D 140
Port Askaig. Arg —3C 124
Portavadie. Arg —3H 125
Port Bannatyne. Arg —3B 126
Portbury. N Som —4A 34
Port Carlisle. Cumb —3D 112
Port Charlotte. Arg —4A 124
Portchester. Hants —2E 16
Port Clarence. Stoc T —2B 106
Port Dinorwig. Gwyn —4E 81
Port Driseach. Arg —2A 126
Port Dundas. Glas —3H 127
Port Ellen. Arg —5B 124
Port Elphinstone. Aber —2E 153
Portencross. N Ayr —5C 126
Port Erin. IOM —5A 108
Port Erroll. Aber —5H 161
Porter's Fen Corner. Norf —5E 77
Portesham. Dors —4B 14
Portessie. Mor —2B 160
Port e Vullen. IOM —2D 108
Port-Eynon. Swan —4D 30
Portfield Gate. Pemb —3D 42
Portgate. Devn —4E 11
Port Gaverne. Corn —4A 10
Port Glasgow. Inv —2E 127
Portgordon. Mor —2A 160
Portgower. High —2H 165
Porth. Corn —2C 6
Porth. Rhon —2D 32
Porthaethwy. Per —3E 81
Porthallow. Corn —3G 7
(nr. Looe)
Porthallow. Corn —4E 5
(nr. St Keverne)
Porthalong. High —5C 154
Porthcawl. B'End —4B 32
Porthcothan. Corn —1C 6
Porthcurno. Corn —4A 4
Port Henderson. High —1G 155
Porthgain. Pemb —1C 42
Porthgwarra. Corn —4A 4
Porthill. Shrp —4G 71
Porthkerry. V Glam —5D 32
Porthleven. Corn —4D 4
Porthllechog. IOA —1D 80
Porthmadog. Gwyn —2E 69
Porthmeirion. Gwyn —2E 69
Porthmeor. Corn —3B 4
Porth Navas. Corn —4E 5
Portholland. Corn —4D 6
Porthoustock. Corn —4F 5
Porthtowan. Corn —4A 6
Porth Tywyn. Carm —5E 45
Porth-y-felin. IOA —2B 80
Porthyrhyd. Carm —4F 45
(nr. Carmarthen)
Porthyrhyd. Carm —2H 45
(nr. Llandovery)
Porth-y-waen. Shrp —3E 71
Portincaple. Arg —4B 134
Portington. E Yor —1A 94
Portinnisherrich. Arg —2G 133
Portinscale. Cumb —2D 102
Port Isaac. Corn —1D 6
Portishead. N Som —4H 33
Portknockie. Mor —2B 160
Port Lamont. Arg —2B 126
Portlethen. Aber —4G 153
Portlethen Village. Aber —4G 153
Portling. Dum —4F 111
Port Lion. Pemb —4D 43
Portloe. Corn —5D 6
Port Logan. Dum —5F 109
Portmahomack. High —5G 165
Port Mary. Arg —2E 133
Port Mead. Swan —3F 31
Portmellon. Corn —4E 6
Port Mholair. W Isl —4H 171
Port Mor. High —1F 139
Portmore. Hants —3B 16
Port Mulgrave. N Yor —3E 107
Portnacroish. Arg —4D 140
Portnahaven. Arg —4A 124
Portnalong. High —5C 154
Portnaluchaig. High —5E 147
Portnancon. High —2E 167
Port Nan Giuran. W Isl —4H 171
Port nan Long. W Isl —1D 170
Port Nis. W Isl —1H 171
Portobello. Edin —2G 129
Portobello. W Yor —3D 92
Port of Menteith. Stir —3E 135
Porton. Wilts —3G 23
Portormin. High —5D 168
Portpatrick. Dum —4F 109
Port Quin. Corn —1D 6
Port Ramsay. Arg —4C 140
Portreath. Corn —4A 6

Renishaw—Ruishton

Renishaw. Derbs —3B 86
Rennington. Nmbd —3G 121
Renton. W Dun —2E 127
Renwick. Cumb —5H 113
Repps. Norf —4G 79
Repton. Derbs —3H 73
Resaurie. High —4B 158
Rescassa. Corn —4D 6
Rescobie. Ang —3E 145
Rescorla. Corn —3E 7
(nr. Rosevean)
Rescorla. Corn —4D 6
(nr. St Ewe)
Resipole. High —2B 140
Resolfen. Neat —5B 46
Resolis. High —2A 158
Resolven. Neat —5B 46
Rest and be Thankful. Arg —3B 134
Reston. Scot —3E 131
Restrop. Wilts —3F 35
Retford. Notts —2E 86
Retire. Corn —2E 6
Rettendon. Essx —1B 40
Retyn. Corn —3C 6
Revesby. Linc —4C 88
Rew. Devn —5D 8
Rewe. Devn —3C 12
Rew Street. IOW —3C 16
Rexon. Devn —4E 11
Reybridge. Wilts —5E 35
Reydon. Suff —3H 67
Reymerston. Norf —5C 78
Reynalton. Pemb —4E 43
Reynoldston. Swan —4D 31
Rezare. Corn —5D 10
Rhadyr. Mon —5G 47
Rhaeadr Gwy. Powy —4B 58
Rhandirmwyn. Carm —1A 46
Rhayader. Powy —4B 58
Rheindown. High —4H 157
Rhemore. High —3G 139
Rhenetra. High —3D 154
Rhewl. Den —1D 70
(nr. Llangollen)
Rhewl. Den —4D 82
(nr. Ruthin)
Rhewl. Shrp —2F 71
Rhewl-Mostyn. Flin —2D 82
Rhian. High —2C 164
Rhian Breck. High —3C 164
Rhicarn. High —1E 163
Rhiconich. High —3C 166
Rhicullen. High —1A 158
Rhidorroch. High —4F 163
Rhifail. High —4H 167
Rhigos. Rhon —5C 46
Rhilochan. High —3E 165
Rhiroy. High —5F 163
Rhitongue. High —3G 167
Rhiw. Gwyn —3B 68
Rhiwabon. Wrex —1F 71
Rhiwbina. Card —3E 33
Rhiwbryfdir. Gwyn —1F 69
Rhiwderin. Newp —3F 33
Rhiwlas. Gwyn —2B 70
(nr. Bala)
Rhiwlas. Gwyn —4E 81
(nr. Bangor)
Rhiwlas. Powy —2D 70
Rhodes. G Man —4G 91
Rhodesia. Notts —3C 86
Rhodes Minnis. Kent —1F 29
Rhodiad-y-Brenin. Pemb —2B 42
Rhonehouse. Dum —4E 111
Rhoose. V Glam —5D 32
Rhos. Carm —2D 45
Rhos. Neat —5H 45
Rhosaman. Carm —4H 45
Rhoscefnhir. IOA —3E 81
Rhoscolyn. IOA —3B 80
Rhos Common. Powy —4E 71
Rhoscrowther. Pemb —4D 42
Rhos-ddu. Gwyn —2B 68
Rhosdylluan. Gwyn —3A 70
Rhosesmor. Flin —4E 82
Rhos-fawr. Gwyn —2C 68
Rhosgadfan. Gwyn —5E 81
Rhosgoch. IOA —2D 80
Rhosgoch. Powy —1E 47
Rhos Haminiog. Cdgn —4E 57
Rhos-hill. Pemb —1B 44
Rhoshirwaun. Gwyn —3A 68
Rhoslan. Gwyn —1D 69
Rhoslefain. Gwyn —5E 69
Rhosllanerchrugog. Wrex —1E 71
Rhos Lligwy. IOA —2D 81
Rhosmaen. Carm —3G 45
Rhosmeirch. IOA —3D 80
Rhosneigr. IOA —3C 80
Rhos-on-Sea. Cnwy —2H 81
Rhossili. Swan —4D 30
Rhosson. Pemb —2B 42
Rhos, The. Pemb —3E 43
Rhostrenwfa. IOA —3D 80
Rhostryfan. Gwyn —5D 81
Rhostyllen. Wrex —1F 71
Rhoswiel. Shrp —2E 71
Rhosybol. IOA —2D 80
Rhos-y-brithdir. Powy —3D 70
Rhos-y-garth. Cdgn —3F 57
Rhos-y-gwaliau. Gwyn —2B 70
Rhos-y-llan. Gwyn —2B 68
Rhos-y-meirch. Powy —4E 59
Rhu. Arg —1D 126
Rhuallt. Den —3C 82
Rhubadach. Arg —2B 126
Rhubha Stoer. High —1E 163
Rhuddall Heath. Ches —4H 83
Rhuddlan. Cdgn —1E 45
Rhuddlan. Den —3C 82
Rhue. High —4E 163
Rhulen. Powy —5D 58
Rhunahaorine. Arg —5F 125
Rhuthun. Den —5D 82
Rhuvoult. High —3C 166
Rhyd. Gwyn —1F 69
Rhydaman. Carm —4G 45
Rhydargaeau. Carm —3E 45
Rhydcymerau. Carm —2F 45
Rhydd. Worc —1D 48
Rhyd-Ddu. Gwyn —5E 81
Rhydding. Neat —3G 31
Rhydfudr. Cdgn —4E 57
Rhydlanfair. Cnwy —5H 81
Rhydlewis. Cdgn —1D 44
Rhydlios. Gwyn —2A 68
Rhydlydan. Cnwy —5A 82
Rhyd-meirionydd. Cdgn —2F 57
Rhydowen. Cdgn —1E 45
Rhyd-Rosser. Cdgn —4E 57
Rhydspence. Powy —1F 47
Rhydtalog. Flin —5E 83
Rhyd-uchaf. Gwyn —2B 70
Rhydwyn. IOA —2C 80
Rhyd-y-clafdy. Gwyn —2C 68
Rhydycroesau. Shrp —2E 71
Rhydyfelin. Cdgn —3E 57
Rhydyfelin. Rhon —3E 32
Rhyd-y-foel. Cnwy —3B 82
Rhyd-y-fro. Neat —5H 45
Rhydymain. Gwyn —3H 69
Rhyd-y-meirch. Mon —5G 47
Rhyd-y-meudwy. Den —5D 82
Rhydymwyn. Flin —4E 82
Rhyd-yr-onen. Gwyn —5F 69
Rhyd-y-sarn. Gwyn —1F 69
Rhyl. Den —2C 82
Rhymney. Cphy —5E 46
Rhymni. Cphy —5E 46
Rhynd. Per —1D 136
Rhynie. Aber —1B 152
Ribbesford. Worc —3B 60
Ribbleton. Lanc —1D 90
Ribby. Lanc —1C 90
Ribchester. Lanc —1E 91
Riber. Derbs —5H 85
Ribigill. High —3F 167
Riby. Linc —4E 95
Riccall. N Yor —1G 93
Riccarton. E Ayr —1D 116
Richards Castle. Here —4G 59
Richborough Port. Kent —4H 41
Richings Park. Buck —3B 38
Richmond. G Lon —3C 38
Richmond. N Yor —4E 105
Rickarton. Aber —5F 153
Rickerby. Cumb —4F 113
Rickerscote. Staf —3D 72
Rickford. N Som —1H 21
Rickham. Devn —5D 8
Rickinghall Superior. Suff —3C 66
Rickleton. Tyne —4F 115
Rickling. Essx —2E 53
Rickling Green. Essx —3F 53
Rickmansworth. Herts —1B 38
Riddings. Derbs —5B 86
Riddlecombe. Devn —1G 11
Riddlesden. W Yor —5C 98
Ridge. Dors —4E 15
Ridge. Herts —5C 52
Ridge. Wilts —3E 23
Ridgebourne. Powy —4C 58
Ridge Lane. Warw —1G 61
Ridgeway. Derbs —5A 86
(nr. Alfreton)
Ridgeway. Derbs —2B 86
(nr. Sheffield)
Ridgeway. Staf —5C 84
Ridgeway Cross. Here —1C 48
Ridgeway Moor. Derbs —2B 86
Ridgewell. Essx —1H 53
Ridgewood. E Sus —3F 27
Ridgmont. Beds —2H 51
Ridgwardine. Shrp —2A 72
Riding Mill. Nmbd —3D 114
Ridley. Kent —4H 39
Ridley. Nmbd —3A 114
Ridlington. Norf —2F 79
Ridlington. Rut —5F 75
Ridsdale. Nmbd —1C 114
Rieff. High —2D 162
Riemore Lodge. Per —4H 143
Rievaulx. N Yor —1H 99
Rift House. Hart —1B 106
Rigg. Dum —3D 112
Riggend. N Lan —2A 128
Rigmaden Park. Cumb —1F 97
Rigsby. Linc —3D 88
Rigside. S Lan —1A 118
Riley Green. Lanc —2E 90
Rileyhill. Staf —4F 73
Rilla Mill. Corn —5C 10
Rillington. N Yor —2C 100
Rimington. Lanc —5H 97
Rimpton. Som —4B 22
Rimsdale. High —4H 167
Rimswell. E Yor —2G 95
Ringasta. Shet —10E 173
Ringford. Dum —4D 111
Ringing Hill. Leics —4B 74
Ringinglow. S Yor —2G 85
Ringland. Norf —4D 78
Ringlestone. Kent —5C 40
Ringmer. E Sus —4F 27
Ringmore. Devn —4C 8
(nr. Kingsbridge)
Ringmore. Devn —5C 12
(nr. Teignmouth)
Ring o' Bells. Lanc —3C 90
Ring's End. Cambs —5C 76
Ringsfield. Suff —2G 67
Ringsfield Corner. Suff —2G 67
Ringshall. Buck —4H 51
Ringshall. Suff —5C 66
Ringshall Stocks. Suff —5C 66
Ringstead. Norf —1G 77
Ringstead. Nptn —3G 63
Ringwood. Hants —2G 15
Ringwould. Kent —1H 29
Rinmore. Aber —2B 152
Rinnigill. Orkn —8C 172
Rinsey. Corn —4C 4
Riof. W Isl —4D 171
Ripe. E Sus —4G 27
Ripley. Derbs —1B 74
Ripley. Hants —3G 15
Ripley. N Yor —3E 99
Ripley. Surr —5B 38
Riplingham. E Yor —1C 94
Riplington. Hants —4E 25
Ripon. N Yor —2F 99
Rippingale. Linc —3H 75
Ripple. Kent —1H 29
Ripple. Worc —2D 48
Ripponden. W Yor —3A 92
Rireavach. High —4E 163
Risabus. Arg —5B 124
Risbury. Here —5H 59
Risby. E Yor —1D 94
Risby. N Lin —3C 94
Risby. Suff —4G 65
Risca. Cphy —2F 33
Rise. E Yor —5F 101
Riseden. E Sus —2H 27
Riseden. Kent —2B 28
Rise End. Derbs —5G 85
Risegate. Linc —3B 76
Riseholme. Linc —3G 87
Riseley. Beds —4H 63
Riseley. Wok —5F 37
Rishangles. Suff —4D 66
Rishton. Lanc —1F 91
Rishworth. W Yor —3A 92
Risley. Derbs —2B 74
Risley. Warr —1A 84
Risplith. N Yor —3E 99
Rispond. High —2E 167
Rivar. Wilts —5B 36
Rivenhall. Essx —4B 54
Rivenhall End. Essx —4B 54
River. Kent —1G 29
River. W Sus —3A 26
River Bank. Cambs —4E 65
Riverhead. Kent —5G 39
Rivington. Lanc —3E 91
Roach Bridge. Lanc —2D 90
Roachill. Devn —4B 20
Roade. Nptn —5E 63
Road Green. Norf —1E 67
Roadhead. Cumb —2G 113
Roadmeetings. S Lan —5B 128
Roadside. High —2D 168
Roadside of Catterline. Aber —1H 145
Roadside of Kinneff. Aber —1H 145
Roadwater. Som —3D 20
Road Weedon. Nptn —5D 62
Roag. High —4B 154
Roa Island. Cumb —3B 96
Roath. Card —4E 33
Roberton. Scot —3G 119
Roberton. S Lan —2B 118
Robertsbridge. E Sus —3B 28
Robertstown. Mor —4G 159
Robertstown. Rhon —5C 46
Roberttown. W Yor —2B 92
Robeston Back. Pemb —3E 43
Robeston Wathen. Pemb —3E 43
Robeston West. Pemb —4C 42
Robin Hood. Lanc —3D 90
Robin Hood. W Yor —2D 92
Robinhood End. Essx —2H 53
Robin Hood's Bay. N Yor —4G 107
Roborough. Devn —1F 11
(nr. Great Torrington)
Roborough. Devn —2B 8
(nr. Plymouth)
Rob Roy's House. Arg —2A 134
Roby Mill. Lanc —4D 90
Rocester. Staf —2F 73
Roch. Pemb —2C 42
Rochdale. G Man —3G 91
Roche. Corn —2D 6
Rochester. Medw —4B 40
Rochester. Nmbd —5C 120
Rochford. Essx —1C 40
Rock. Corn —1D 6
Rock. Nmbd —2G 121
Rock. W Sus —4C 26
Rock. Worc —3B 60
Rockbeare. Devn —3D 12
Rockbourne. Hants —1G 15
Rockcliffe. Cumb —3E 113
Rockcliffe. Dum —4F 111
Rockcliffe Cross. Cumb —3E 113
Rock Ferry. Mers —2F 83
Rockfield. High —5G 165
Rockfield. Mon —4H 47
Rockford. Hants —2G 15
Rockgreen. Shrp —3H 59
Rockhampton. S Glo —2B 34
Rockhead. Corn —4A 10
Rockingham. Nptn —1F 63
Rockland All Saints. Norf —1B 66
Rockland St Mary. Norf —5F 79
Rockland St Peter. Norf —1B 66
Rockley. Wilts —4G 35
Rockwell End. Buck —3F 37
Rockwell Green. Som —1E 13
Rodborough. Glos —5D 48
Rodbourne. Wilts —3E 35
Rodd. Here —4F 59
Roddam. Nmbd —2E 121
Rodden. Dors —4B 14
Roddymoor. Dur —1E 105
Rode. Som —1D 22
Rodeheath. Ches —4C 84
Rode Heath. Ches —5C 84
Roden. Telf —4H 71
Rodenloft. E Ayr —2D 117
Rodhuish. Som —3D 20
Rodington. Telf —4H 71
Rodington Heath. Telf —4H 71
Rodley. Glos —4C 48
Rodmarton. Glos —2E 35
Rodmell. E Sus —5F 27
Rodmersham. Kent —4D 40
Rodmersham Green. Kent —4D 40
Rodney Stoke. Som —2H 21
Rodsley. Derbs —1G 73
Rodway. Som —2F 21
Rodway. Telf —4A 72
Rodwell. Dors —5B 14
Roecliffe. N Yor —3F 99
Roe Green. Herts —2D 52
Roehampton. G Lon —3D 38
Roesound. Shet —5E 173
Roffey. W Sus —2C 26
Rogart. High —3E 165
Rogate. W Sus —4G 25
Roger Ground. Cumb —5E 103
Rogerstone. Newp —3F 33
Roghadal. W Isl —9C 171
Rogiet. Mon —3H 33
Rogue's Alley. Cambs —5C 76
Roke. Oxon —2E 37
Rokemarsh. Oxon —2E 36
Roker. Tyne —4H 115
Rollesby. Norf —4G 79
Rolleston. Leics —5E 75
Rolleston. Notts —5E 87
Rolleston on Dove. Staf —3G 73
Rolston. E Yor —5G 101
Rolvenden. Kent —2C 28
Rolvenden Layne. Kent —2C 28
Romaldkirk. Dur —2C 104
Roman Bank. Shrp —1H 59
Romanby. N Yor —5A 106
Roman Camp. W Lot —2D 129
Romannobridge. Scot —5E 129
Romansleigh. Devn —4H 19
Romers Common. Worc —4H 59
Romesdal. High —3D 154
Romford. Dors —2F 15
Romford. G Lon —2G 39
Romiley. G Man —1D 84
Romsey. Hants —4B 24
Romsley. Shrp —2B 60
Romsley. Worc —3D 60
Ronague. IOM —4B 108
Ronaldsvoe. Orkn —8D 172
Rookby. Cumb —3B 104
Rookhope. Dur —5C 114
Rooking. Cumb —3F 103
Rookley. IOW —4D 16
Rooks Bridge. Som —1G 21
Rooksey Green. Suff —5B 66
Rooks Nest. Som —3D 20
Rookwood. W Sus —3F 17
Roos. E Yor —1F 95
Roosebeck. Cumb —3B 96
Roosecote. Cumb —3B 96
Rootfield. High —3H 157
Rootham's Green. Beds —5A 64
Rootpark. S Lan —4C 128
Ropley. Hants —3E 25
Ropley Dean. Hants —3E 25
Ropsley. Linc —2G 75
Rora. Aber —3H 161
Rorandle. Aber —2D 152
Rorrington. Shrp —5F 71
Rose. Corn —3B 6
Roseacre. Lanc —1C 90
Rose Ash. Devn —4A 20
Rosebank. S Lan —5B 128
Rosebush. Pemb —2E 43
Rosedale Abbey. N Yor —5E 107
Roseden. Nmbd —2E 121
Rose Green. Essx —3B 54
Rose Green. Suff —1C 54
Rosehall. High —3B 164
Rosehearty. Aber —2G 161
Rose Hill. E Sus —4F 27
Rose Hill. Lanc —1G 91
Rosehill. Shrp —2A 72
(nr. Market Drayton)
Rosehill. Shrp —4G 71
(nr. Shrewsbury)
Roseisle. Mor —2F 159
Rosemarket. Pemb —4D 42
Rosemarkie. High —3B 158
Rosemary Lane. Devn —1E 13
Rosemount. Per —4A 144
Rosenannon. Corn —2D 6
Roser's Cross. E Sus —3G 27
Rosevean. Corn —3E 7
Rosewell. Midl —3F 129
Roseworth. Stoc T —2B 106
Roseworthy. Corn —3D 4
Rosgill. Cumb —3G 103
Roshven. High —1B 140
Roskhill. High —4B 154
Roskorwell. Corn —4E 5
Rosley. Cumb —5E 112
Roslin. Midl —3F 129
Rosliston. Derbs —4G 73
Rosneath. Arg —1D 126
Ross. Dum —5D 110
Ross. Nmbd —1F 121
Ross. Per —1G 135
Ross. Scot —3F 131
Rossendale. Lanc —2G 91
Rossett. Wrex —5F 83
Rossington. S Yor —1D 86
Rosskeen. High —2A 158
Rossland. Ren —2F 127
Ross-on-Wye. Here —3B 48
Roster. High —4E 169
Rostherne. Ches —2B 84
Rostholme. S Yor —4F 93
Rosthwaite. Cumb —3D 102
Roston. Derbs —1F 73
Rosudgeon. Corn —4C 4
Rosyth. Fife —1E 129
Rothbury. Nmbd —4E 121
Rotherby. Leics —4D 74
Rotherfield. E Sus —3G 27
Rotherfield Greys. Oxon —3F 37
Rotherfield Peppard. Oxon —3F 37
Rotherham. S Yor —1B 86
Rothersthorpe. Nptn —5E 62
Rotherwick. Hants —1F 25
Rothes. Mor —4G 159
Rothesay. Arg —3B 126
Rothienorman. Aber —5E 160
Rothiesholm. Orkn —5F 172
Rothley. Leics —4C 74
Rothley. Nmbd —1D 114
Rothwell. Linc —1A 88
Rothwell. Nptn —2F 63
Rothwell. W Yor —2D 92
Rothwell Haigh. W Yor —2D 92
Rotsea. E Yor —4E 101
Rottal. Ang —2C 144
Rotten End. Suff —4F 67
Rottenhill. Aber —3H 161
Rotten Row. Norf —4C 78
Rotten Row. W Ber —4D 36
Rotten Row. W Mid —3F 61
Rottingdean. Brig —5E 27
Rottington. Cumb —3A 102
Roud. IOW —4D 16
Rougham. Norf —3H 77
Rougham. Suff —4B 66
Rough Close. Staf —2D 72
Rough Common. Kent —5F 41
Roughcote. Staf —1D 72
Rough Haugh. High —4H 167
Rough Hay. Staf —3G 73
Roughlee. Lanc —5H 97
Roughley. W Mid —1F 61
Roughsike. Cumb —2G 113
Roughton. Linc —4B 88
Roughton. Norf —2E 78
Roughton. Shrp —1B 60
Roundbush Green. Essx —4F 53
Roundham. Som —2H 13
Roundhay. W Yor —1D 92
Round Hill. Torb —2F 9
Roundhurst Common. W Sus —2A 26
Round Oak. Shrp —2F 59
Roundstreet Common. W Sus —3B 26
Roundthwaite. Cumb —4H 103
Roundway. Wilts —5F 35
Roundyhill. Ang —3C 144
Rousdon. Devn —3F 13
Rousham. Oxon —3C 50
Rous Lench. Worc —5E 61
Routh. E Yor —5E 101
Rout's Green. Buck —2F 37
Row. Corn —5A 10
Row. Cumb —1D 96
(nr. Kendal)
Row. Cumb —1H 103
(nr. Penrith)
Rowanburn. Dum —2F 113
Rowardennan. Stir —4C 134
Rowarth. Derbs —2E 85
Row Ash. Hants —1D 16
Rowberrow. Som —1H 21
Rowde. Wilts —5E 35
Rowden. Devn —3G 11
Rowden Hill. Wilts —4E 35
Rowen. Cnwy —3G 81
Rowfoot. Nmbd —3H 113
Row Green. Essx —3H 53
Row Heath. Essx —4E 55
Rowhedge. Essx —3D 54
Rowhook. W Sus —2C 26
Rowington. Warw —4G 61
Rowland. Derbs —3G 85
Rowland's Castle. Hants —1F 17
Rowlands Gill. Tyne —4E 115
Rowledge. Surr —2G 25
Rowley. Dur —5D 115
Rowley. E Yor —1C 94
Rowley. Shrp —5F 71
Rowley. Staf —3F 73
Rowley Hill. W Yor —3B 92
Rowley Regis. W Mid —2D 60
Rowlstone. Here —3G 47
Rowly. Surr —1B 26
Rowner. Hants —2D 16
Rowney Green. Worc —3E 61
Rownhams. Hants —1B 16
Rowrah. Cumb —3B 102
Rowsham. Buck —4G 51
Rowsley. Derbs —4G 85
Rowstock. Oxon —3C 36
Rowston. Linc —5H 87
Row, The. Lanc —2D 96
Rowthorne. Derbs —4B 86
Rowton. Ches —4G 83
Rowton. Shrp —2G 59
(nr. Ludlow)
Rowton. Shrp —4F 71
(nr. Shrewsbury)
Rowton. Telf —4A 72
Row Town. Surr —4B 38
Roxburgh. Scot —1B 120
Roxby. N Lin —3C 94
Roxby. N Yor —3E 107
Roxton. Beds —5A 64
Roxwell. Essx —5G 53
Royal Leamington Spa. Warw —4H 61
Royal Oak. Darl —2F 105
Royal Oak. Lanc —4C 90
Royal Oak. N Yor —2F 101
Royal's Green. Ches —1A 72
Royal Tunbridge Wells. Kent —2G 27
Roybridge. High —5E 149
Roydon. Essx —4E 53
Roydon. Norf —2C 66
(nr. Diss)
Roydon. Norf —3G 77
(nr. King's Lynn)
Roydon Hamlet. Essx —5E 53
Royston. Herts —1D 52
Royston. S Yor —3D 92
Royston Water. Som —1F 13
Royton. G Man —4H 91
Ruabon. Wrex —1F 71
Ruaig. Arg —4B 138
Ruan High Lanes. Corn —5D 6
Ruan Lanihorne. Corn —4C 6
Ruan Minor. Corn —5E 5
Ruarach. High —1B 148
Ruardean. Glos —4B 48
Ruardean Hill. Glos —4B 48
Ruardean Woodside. Glos —4B 48
Rubery. W Mid —3D 61
Ruchazie. Glas —3H 127
Ruckcroft. Cumb —5G 113
Ruckinge. Kent —2E 29
Ruckland. Linc —3C 88
Rucklers Lane. Herts —5A 52
Ruckley. Shrp —5H 71
Rudbaxton. Pemb —2D 42
Rudby. N Yor —4B 106
Ruddington. Notts —2C 74
Rudford. Glos —3C 48
Rudge. Shrp —1C 60
Rudge. Wilts —1D 22
Rudge Heath. Shrp —1B 60
Rudgeway. S Glo —3B 34
Rudgwick. W Sus —2B 26
Rudhall. Here —3B 48
Rudheath. Ches —3A 84
Rudheath Woods. Ches —3B 84
Rudley Green. Essx —5B 54
Rudloe. Wilts —4D 34
Rudry. Cphy —3E 33
Rudston. E Yor —3E 101
Rudyard. Staf —5D 84
Rufford. Lanc —3C 90
Rufforth. York —4H 99
Rugby. Warw —3C 62
Rugeley. Staf —4E 73
Ruilick. High —4H 157
Ruisaurie. High —4G 157
Ruishton. Som —4F 21

Ruisigearraidh—Scalpaigh

Ruisigearraidh. W Isl —1E 170
Ruislip. G Lon —2B 38
Ruislip Common. G Lon —2B 38
Rumbling Bridge. Per —4C 136
Rumburgh. Suff —2F 67
Rumford. Corn —1C 6
Rumford. Falk —2C 128
Rumney. Card —4F 33
Rumwell. Som —4E 21
Runcorn. Hal —2H 83
Runcton. W Sus —2G 17
Runcton Holme. Norf —5F 77
Rundlestone. Devn —5F 11
Runfold. Surr —2G 25
Runhall. Norf —5C 78
Runham. Norf —4G 79
Runnington. Som —4E 20
Runshaw Moor. Lanc —3D 90
Runswick. N Yor —3F 107
Runtaleave. Ang —2B 144
Runwell. Essx —1B 40
Ruscombe. Wok —4F 37
Rushall. Here —2B 48
Rushall. Norf —2D 66
Rushall. W Mid —5E 73
Rushall. Wilts —1G 23
Rushbrooke. Suff —4A 66
Rushbury. Shrp —1H 59
Rushden. Herts —2D 52
Rushden. Nptn —4G 63
Rushenden. Kent —3D 40
Rushford. Devn —5E 11
Rushford. Suff —2B 66
Rush Green. Herts —3C 52
Rushlake Green. E Sus —4H 27
Rushmere. Suff —2G 67
Rushmere St Andrew. Suff —1E 55
Rushmoor. Surr —2G 25
Rushock. Worc —3C 60
Rusholme. G Man —1C 84
Rushton. Ches —4H 83
Rushton. Nptn —2F 63
Rushton. Shrp —5A 72
Rushton Spencer. Staf —4D 84
Rushwick. Worc —5C 60
Rushyford. Dur —2F 105
Ruskie. Stir —3F 135
Ruskington. Linc —5H 87
Rusland. Cumb —1C 96
Rusper. W Sus —2D 26
Ruspidge. Glos —4B 48
Russell's Water. Oxon —3F 37
Russel's Green. Suff —3E 67
Russ Hill. Surr —1D 26
Russland. Orkn —6C 172
Rusthall. Kent —2G 27
Rustington. W Sus —5B 26
Ruston. N Yor —1D 100
Ruston Parva. E Yor —3E 101
Ruswarp. N Yor —4F 107
Rutherglen. S Lan —3H 127
Ruthernbridge. Corn —2E 6
Ruthin. Den —5D 82
Ruthin. V Glam —4C 32
Ruthrieston. Aber C —3G 153
Ruthven. Aber —4C 160
Ruthven. Ang —4B 144
Ruthven. High —5C 158 (nr. Inverness)
Ruthven. High —4B 150 (nr. Kingussie)
Ruthvoes. Corn —2D 6
Ruthwaite. Cumb —1D 102
Ruthwell. Dum —3C 112
Ruxton Green. Here —4A 48
Ruyton-XI-Towns. Shrp —3F 71
Ryal. Nmbd —2D 114
Ryall. Dors —3H 13
Ryall. Worc —1D 48
Ryarsh. Kent —5A 40
Rychraggan. High —5G 157
Rydal. Cumb —4E 103
Ryde. IOW —3D 16
Rye. E Sus —3D 28
Ryecroft Gate. Staf —4D 84
Ryeford. Here —3B 48
Rye Foreign. E Sus —3D 28
Rye Harbour. E Sus —4D 28
Ryehill. E Yor —2F 95
Rye Street. Worc —2C 48
Ryhall. Rut —4H 75
Ryhill. W Yor —3D 93
Ryhnie. Aber —1B 152
Ryhope. Tyne —4H 115
Ryhope Colliery. Tyne —4H 115
Rylands. Notts —2C 74
Rylstone. N Yor —4B 98
Ryme Intrinseca. Dors —1A 14
Ryther. N Yor —1F 93
Ryton. Glos —2C 48
Ryton. N Yor —2B 100
Ryton. Shrp —5B 72
Ryton. Tyne —3E 115
Ryton. Warw —2A 62
Ryton-on-Dunsmore. Warw —3A 62
Ryton Woodside. Tyne —3E 115

S

Saasaig. High —3E 147
Sabden. Lanc —1F 91
Sacombe. Herts —4D 52
Sacriston. Dur —5F 115
Sadberge. Darl —3A 106
Saddell. Arg —2B 122
Saddington. Leics —1D 62
Saddle Bow. Norf —4F 77
Saddlescombe. W Sus —4D 26
Saddleworth. G Man —4H 91
Sadgill. Cumb —4F 103
Saffron Walden. Essx —2F 53
Sageston. Pemb —4E 43
Saham Hills. Norf —5B 78
Saham Toney. Norf —5A 78
Saighdinis. W Isl —2D 170
Saighton. Ches —4G 83
Sain Dunwyd. V Glam —5C 32
Sain Hilari. V Glam —4D 32
St Abbs. Scot —3F 131
St Agnes. Corn —3B 6
St Albans. Herts —5B 52
St Allen. Corn —3C 6
St Andrews. Fife —2H 137
St Andrews Major. V Glam —4E 33
St Anne's. Lanc —2B 90
St Ann's. Dum —5C 118
St Ann's Chapel. Corn —5E 11
St Ann's Chapel. Devn —4C 8
St Anthony. Corn —4E 5 (nr. Helford)
St Anthony. Corn —5C 6 (nr. St Mawes)
St Arvans. Mon —2A 34
St Asaph. Den —3C 82
St Athan. V Glam —5D 32
Sain Tathan. V Glam —5D 32
St Austell. Corn —3E 6
St Bartholomew's Hill. Wilts —4E 23
St Bees. Cumb —3A 102
St Blazey. Corn —3E 7
St Blazey Gate. Corn —3E 7
St Boswells. Scot —1A 120
St Breock. Corn —1D 6
St Breward. Corn —5A 10
St Briavels. Glos —5A 48
St Brides. Pemb —3B 42
St Bride's Major. V Glam —4B 32
St Bride's Netherwent. Mon —3H 33
St Bride's-super-Ely. V Glam —4D 32
St Brides Wentlooge. Newp —3F 33
St Budeaux. Plym —3A 8
Saintbury. Glos —2G 49
St Buryan. Corn —4B 4
St Catherine. Bath —4C 34
St Catherines. Arg —3A 134
St Clears. Carm —3G 43
St Cleer. Corn —2G 7
St Clement. Corn —4C 6
St Clether. Corn —4C 10
St Colmac. Arg —3B 126
St Columb Major. Corn —2D 6
St Columb Minor. Corn —2C 6
St Columb Road. Corn —3D 6
St Combs. Aber —2H 161
St Cross. Hants —4C 24
St Cross South Elmham. Suff —2E 67
St Cyrus. Aber —2G 145
St David's. Pemb —2B 42
St David's. Per —1B 136
St Day. Corn —4B 6
St Dennis. Corn —3D 6
St Dogmaels. Pemb —1B 44
St Dominick. Corn —2H 7
St Donat's. V Glam —5C 32
St Edith's Marsh. Wilts —5E 35
St Endellion. Corn —1D 6
St Enoder. Corn —3C 6
St Erme. Corn —4C 6
St Erney. Corn —3H 7
St Erth. Corn —3C 4
St Erth Praze. Corn —3C 4
St Ervan. Corn —1C 6
St Eval. Corn —2C 6
St Ewe. Corn —4D 6
St Fagans. Card —4E 32
St Fergus. Aber —3H 161
St Fillans. Per —1F 135
St Florence. Pemb —4E 43
St Gennys. Corn —3B 10
St George. Cnwy —3B 82
St George's. N Som —5G 33
St Georges. V Glam —4D 32
St Germans. Corn —3H 7
St Gile's Hill. Hants —4C 24
St Giles in the Wood. Devn —1F 11
St Giles on the Heath. Devn —4D 10
St Gluvias. Corn —5B 6
St Harmon. Powy —3B 58
St Helena. Warw —5G 73
St Helen Auckland. Dur —2E 105
St Helens. Cumb —1B 102
St Helens. E Sus —4C 28
St Helens. IOW —4E 17
St Helens. Mers —1G 83
St Hilary. Corn —3C 4
St Hilary. V Glam —4D 32
Saint Hill. Devn —2D 12
Saint Hill. W Sus —2E 27
St Illtyd. Blae —5F 47
St Ippollitts. Herts —3B 52
St Ishmael. Carm —5D 44
St Ishmael's. Pemb —4C 42
St Issey. Corn —1D 6
St Ive. Corn —2H 7
St Ives. Cambs —3C 64
St Ives. Corn —2C 4
St Ives. Dors —2G 15
St James End. Nptn —4E 63
St James South Elmham. Suff —2F 67
St Jidgey. Corn —2D 6
St John. Corn —3A 8
St John's. IOM —3B 108
St Johns. Worc —5C 60
St John's Chapel. Devn —4F 19
St John's Chapel. Dur —1B 104
St John's Fen End. Norf —4E 77
St John's Hall. Dur —1D 104
St John's Town of Dalry. Dum —1D 110
St Judes. IOM —2D 108
St Just. Corn —5C 6 (nr. Falmouth)
St Just. Corn —3A 4 (nr. Penzance)
St Just in Roseland. Corn —5C 6
St Katherines. Aber —5E 161
St Keverne. Corn —4E 5
St Kew. Corn —5A 10
St Kew Highway. Corn —5A 10
St Keyne. Corn —2G 7
St Lawrence. Corn —2E 7
St Lawrence. Essx —5C 54
St Lawrence. IOW —5D 16
St Leonards. Buck —5H 51
St Leonards. Dors —2G 15
St Leonards. E Sus —5B 28
St Levan. Corn —4A 4
St Lythans. V Glam —4E 32
St Mabyn. Corn —5A 10
St Madoes. Per —1D 136
St Margarets. Here —2G 47
St Margaret's. Herts —4A 52 (nr. Hemel Hempstead)
St Margarets. Herts —4D 53 (nr. Hoddesdon)
St Margaret's. Wilts —5G 35
St Margaret's at Cliffe. Kent —1H 29
St Margaret's Hope. Orkn —8D 172
St Margaret South Elmham. Suff —2F 67
St Mark's. IOM —4C 108
St Martin. Corn —4E 5 (nr. Helston)
St Martin. Corn —3G 7 (nr. Looe)
St Martins. Per —5A 144
St Martin's. Shrp —2F 71
St Mary Bourne. Hants —1C 24
St Marychurch. Torb —2F 9
St Mary Church. V Glam —4D 32
St Mary Cray. G Lon —4F 39
St Mary Hill. V Glam —4C 32
St Mary Hoo. Medw —3C 40
St Mary in the Marsh. Kent —3E 29
St Mary's. Orkn —7D 172
St Mary's Airport. IOS —1B 4
St Mary's Bay. Kent —3E 29
St Mary's Grove. N Som —5H 33
St Maughan's Green. Mon —4H 47
St Mawes. Corn —5C 6
St Mawgan. Corn —2C 6
St Mellion. Corn —2H 7
St Mellons. Card —3F 33
St Merryn. Corn —1C 6
St Mewan. Corn —3D 6
St Michael Caerhays. Corn —4D 6
St Michael Penkevil. Corn —4C 6
St Michaels. Kent —2C 28
St Michaels. Torb —3E 9
St Michaels. Worc —4H 59
St Michael's on Wyre. Lanc —5D 96
St Michael South Elmham. Suff —2F 67
St Minver. Corn —1D 6
St Monans. Fife —3H 137
St Neot. Corn —2F 7
St Neots. Cambs —4A 64
St Newlyn East. Corn —3C 6
St Nicholas. Pemb —1D 42
St Nicholas. V Glam —4D 32
St Nicholas at Wade. Kent —4G 41
St Nicholas South Elmham. Suff —2F 67
St Ninians. Stir —4H 135
St Olaves. Norf —1G 67
St Osyth. Essx —4E 54
St Osyth Heath. Essx —4E 55
St Owen's Cross. Here —3A 48
St Paul's Cray. G Lon —4F 39
St Paul's Walden. Herts —3B 52
St Peter's. Kent —4H 41
St Peter the Great. Worc —5C 60
St Petrox. Pemb —5D 42
St Pinnock. Corn —2G 7
St Quivox. S Ayr —2C 116
St Ruan. Corn —5E 5
St Stephen. Corn —3D 6
St Stephens. Corn —4D 10 (nr. Launceston)
St Stephens. Corn —3A 8 (nr. Saltash)
St Teath. Corn —4A 10
St Thomas. Devn —3C 12
St Thomas. Swan —3F 31
St Tudy. Corn —5A 10
St Twynnells. Pemb —5D 42
St Veep. Corn —3F 7
St Vigeans. Ang —4F 145
St Wenn. Corn —2D 6
St Weonards. Here —3H 47
St Winnolls. Corn —3H 7
St Winnow. Corn —3F 7
Salcombe. Devn —5D 8
Salcombe Regis. Devn —4E 13
Salcott. Essx —4C 54
Sale. G Man —1B 84
Saleby. Linc —3D 88
Sale Green. Worc —5D 60
Salehurst. E Sus —3B 28
Salem. Carm —3G 45
Salem. Cdgn —2F 57
Salem. Gwyn —5E 81
Salen. Arg —4G 139
Salen. High —2A 140
Salesbury. Lanc —1E 91
Saleway. Worc —5D 60
Salford. Beds —2H 51
Salford. G Man —1C 84
Salford. Oxon —3A 50
Salford Priors. Warw —5E 61
Salfords. Surr —1D 27
Salhouse. Norf —4F 79
Saligo. Arg —3A 124
Saline. Fife —4C 136
Salisbury. Wilts —3G 23
Salkeld Dykes. Cumb —1G 103
Sallachan. High —2D 141
Sallachy. High —5B 156 (nr. Darnie)
Sallachy. High —3C 164 (nr. Lairg)
Salle. Norf —3D 78
Salmonby. Linc —3C 88
Salmond's Muir. Ang —5E 145
Salperton. Glos —3F 49
Salph End. Beds —5H 63
Salsburgh. N Lan —3B 128
Salt. Staf —3D 72
Salta. Cumb —5B 112
Saltaire. W Yor —1B 92
Saltash. Corn —3A 8
Saltburn. High —2B 158
Saltburn-by-the-Sea. Red C —2D 106
Saltby. Leics —3F 75
Saltcoats. Cumb —5B 102
Saltcoats. N Ayr —5D 126
Saltdean. Brig —5E 27
Salt End. E Yor —2E 95
Salter. Lanc —3F 97
Salterforth. Lanc —5A 98
Salters Lode. Norf —5E 77
Salterswall. Ches —4A 84
Salterton. Wilts —3G 23
Saltfleet. Linc —1D 88
Saltfleetby All Saints. Linc —1D 88
Saltfleetby St Clements. Linc —1D 88
Saltfleetby St Peter. Linc —2D 88
Saltford. Bath —5B 34
Salthouse. Norf —1C 78
Saltmarshe. E Yor —2A 94
Saltmead. Card —4E 33
Saltness. Orkn —8B 172
Saltness. Shet —7D 173
Saltney. Flin —4F 83
Salton. N Yor —1B 100
Saltrens. Devn —4E 19
Saltwick. Nmbd —2E 115
Saltwood. Kent —2F 29
Salum. Arg —4B 138
Salwarpe. Worc —4C 60
Salwayash. Dors —3H 13
Samalaman. High —1A 140
Sambourne. Warw —4E 61
Sambourne. Wilts —2D 22
Sambrook. Telf —3B 72
Samhia. W Isl —2C 170
Samlesbury. Lanc —1D 90
Samlesbury Bottoms. Lanc —2E 90
Sampford Arundel. Som —1E 12
Sampford Brett. Som —2D 20
Sampford Courtenay. Devn —2G 11
Sampford Peverell. Devn —1D 12
Sampford Spiney. Devn —5F 11
Samsonlane. Orkn —5F 172
Samuelston. E Lot —2A 130
Sanaigmore. Arg —2A 124
Sancreed. Corn —4B 4
Sancton. E Yor —1C 94
Sand. High —4D 162
Sand. Shet —7E 173
Sand. Som —2H 21
Sandaig. High —3F 147
Sandale. Cumb —5D 112
Sandal Magna. W Yor —3D 92
Sandavore. High —5C 146
Sanday Airport. Orkn —3F 172
Sandbach. Ches —4B 84
Sandbank. Arg —1C 126
Sandbanks. Pool —4F 15
Sandend. Aber —2C 160
Sanderstead. G Lon —4E 39
Sandfields. Neat —3G 31
Sandford. Cumb —3A 104
Sandford. Devn —2B 12
Sandford. Dors —4E 15
Sandford. Hants —2G 15
Sandford. IOW —4D 16
Sandford. N Som —1H 21
Sandford. Shrp —3F 71 (nr. Oswestry)
Sandford. Shrp —2H 71 (nr. Whitchurch)
Sandford. S Lan —5A 128
Sandfordhill. Aber —4H 161
Sandford-on-Thames. Oxon —5D 50
Sandford Orcas. Dors —4B 22
Sandford St Martin. Oxon —3C 50
Sandgate. Kent —2F 29
Sandgreen. Dum —4C 110
Sandhaven. Aber —2G 161
Sandhead. Dum —4F 109
Sandhill. Cambs —2E 65
Sandhills. Dors —1B 14
Sandhills. Surr —2A 26
Sandhoe. Nmbd —3C 114
Sand Hole. E Yor —1B 94
Sandholme. E Yor —1B 94
Sandholme. Linc —2C 76
Sandhurst. Brac —5G 37
Sandhurst. Glos —3D 48
Sandhurst. Kent —3B 28
Sandhurst Cross. Kent —3B 28
Sandhutton. N Yor —1F 99 (nr. Thirsk)
Sand Hutton. N Yor —4A 100 (nr. York)
Sandiacre. Derbs —2B 74
Sandilands. Linc —2E 89
Sandiway. Ches —3A 84
Sandleheath. Hants —1G 15
Sandling. Kent —5B 40
Sandlow Green. Ches —4B 84
Sandness. Shet —6C 173
Sandon. Essx —5H 53
Sandon. Herts —2D 52
Sandon. Staf —3D 72
Sandonbank. Staf —3D 72
Sandown. IOW —4D 16
Sandplace. Corn —3G 7
Sandridge. Herts —4B 52
Sandridge. Wilts —5E 35
Sandringham. Norf —3F 77
Sandsend. N Yor —3F 107
Sandside. Cumb —2C 96
Sandsound. Shet —7E 173
Sands, The. Surr —2G 25
Sandtoft. N Lin —4H 93
Sandvoe. Shet —2E 173
Sandway. Kent —5C 40
Sandwich. Kent —5H 41
Sandwick. Cumb —3F 103
Sandwick. Orkn —6B 172 (on Mainland)
Sandwick. Orkn —9D 172 (on South Ronaldsay)
Sandwick. Shet —9F 173 (on Mainland)
Sandwick. Shet —5G 173 (on Whalsay)
Sandwith. Cumb —3A 102
Sandy. Beds —1B 52
Sandy. Carm —5E 45
Sandy Bank. Linc —5B 88
Sandycroft. Flin —4F 83
Sandy Cross. Here —5A 60
Sandygate. Devn —5B 12
Sandygate. IOM —2C 108
Sandy Haven. Pemb —4C 42
Sandyhills. Dum —4F 111
Sandylands. Lanc —3D 96
Sandylane. Swan —4E 31
Sandy Lane. Wilts —5E 35
Sandypark. Devn —4H 11
Sandystones. Scot —2H 119
Sandyway. Here —3H 47
Sangobeg. High —2E 167
Sangomore. High —2E 166
Sankyn's Green. Worc —4B 60
Sanna. High —2F 139
Sanndabhaig. W Isl —4G 171 (on Lewis)
Sanndabhaig. W Isl —4D 170 (on South Uist)
Sannox. N Ayr —5B 126
Sanquhar. Dum —3G 117
Santon. Cumb —4C 102
Santon Bridge. Cumb —4C 102
Santon Downham. Suff —2H 65
Sapcote. Leics —1B 62
Sapey Common. Here —4B 60
Sapiston. Suff —3B 66
Sapley. Cambs —3B 64
Sapperton. Derbs —2F 73
Sapperton. Glos —5E 49
Sapperton. Linc —2H 75
Saracen's Head. Linc —3C 76
Sarclet. High —4F 169
Sardis. Carm —5F 45
Sardis. Pemb —4D 42 (nr. Milford Haven)
Sardis. Pemb —4F 43 (nr. Tenby)
Sarisbury. Hants —2D 16
Sarn. B'End —3C 32
Sarn. Powy —1E 58
Sarnau. Carm —3E 45
Sarnau. Cdgn —5C 56
Sarnau. Gwyn —2B 70
Sarnau. Powy —2D 46 (nr. Brecon)
Sarnau. Powy —4E 71 (nr. Welshpool)
Sarn Bach. Gwyn —3C 68
Sarnesfield. Here —5F 59
Sarn Meyllteyrn. Gwyn —2B 68
Saron. Carm —4G 45 (nr. Ammanford)
Saron. Carm —2D 45 (nr. Newcastle Emlyn)
Saron. Gwyn —4E 81 (nr. Bethel)
Saron. Gwyn —5D 80 (nr. Bontnewydd)
Sarratt. Herts —1B 38
Sarre. Kent —4G 41
Sarsden. Oxon —3A 50
Satley. Dur —5E 115
Satron. N Yor —5C 104
Satterleigh. Devn —4G 19
Satterthwaite. Cumb —5E 103
Satwell. Oxon —3F 37
Sauchen. Aber —2D 152
Saucher. Per —5A 144
Saughall. Ches —3F 83
Saughtree. Scot —5H 119
Saul. Glos —5C 48
Saundby. Notts —2E 87
Saundersfoot. Pemb —4F 43
Saunderton. Buck —5F 51
Saunderton Lee. Buck —2G 37
Saunton. Devn —3E 19
Sausthorpe. Linc —4C 88
Saval. High —3C 164
Saverley Green. Staf —2D 72
Sawbridge. Warw —4C 62
Sawbridgeworth. Herts —4E 53
Sawdon. N Yor —1D 100
Sawley. Derbs —2B 74
Sawley. Lanc —5G 97
Sawley. N Yor —3E 99
Sawston. Cambs —1E 53
Sawtry. Cambs —2A 64
Saxby. Leics —3F 75
Saxby. Linc —2H 87
Saxby All Saints. N Lin —3C 94
Saxelby. Leics —3D 74
Saxham Street. Suff —4C 66
Saxilby. Linc —3F 87
Saxlingham. Norf —2C 78
Saxlingham Green. Norf —1E 67
Saxlingham Nethergate. Norf —1E 67
Saxlingham Thorpe. Norf —1E 66
Saxmundham. Suff —4F 67
Saxondale. Notts —1D 74
Saxon Street. Cambs —5F 65
Saxtead. Suff —4E 67
Saxtead Green. Suff —4E 67
Saxthorpe. Norf —2D 78
Saxton. N Yor —1E 93
Sayers Common. W Sus —4D 26
Scackleton. N Yor —2A 100
Scadabhagh. W Isl —8D 171
Scaftworth. Notts —1D 86
Scagglethorpe. N Yor —2C 100
Scaitcliffe. Lanc —2F 91
Scalasaig. Arg —4A 132
Scalby. E Yor —2B 94
Scalby. N Yor —5H 107
Scalby Mills. N Yor —5H 107
Scaldwell. Nptn —3E 63
Scaleby. Cumb —3F 113
Scaleby Hill. Cumb —3F 113
Scale Houses. Cumb —5G 113
Scales. Cumb —2B 96 (nr. Barrow-in-Furness)
Scales. Cumb —2E 103 (nr. Keswick)
Scalford. Leics —3E 75
Scaling. Red C —3E 107
Scaling Dam. Red C —3E 107
Scalloway. Shet —8E 173
Scalpaigh. W Isl —8E 171

Scalpay House—Shuttleworth

Scalpay House. High —1E 147
Scamblesby. Linc —3B 88
Scamodale. High —1C 140
Scampston. N Yor —2C 100
Scampton. Linc —3G 87
Scaniport. High —5A 158
Scapa. Orkn —7D 172
Scapegoat Hill. W Yor —3A 92
Scar. Orkn —3F 172
Scarasta. W Isl —8C 171
Scarborough. N Yor —1E 101
Scarcliffe. Derbs —4B 86
Scarcroft. W Yor —5F 99
Scardroy. High —3E 156
Scarfskerry. High —1E 169
Scargill. Dur —3D 104
Scarinish. Arg —4B 138
Scarisbrick. Lanc —3B 90
Scarning. Norf —4B 78
Scarrington. Notts —1E 75
Scarth Hill. Lanc —4C 90
Scartho. NE Lin —4F 95
Scarvister. Shet —7E 173
Scat Ness. Shet —10E 173
Scatwell. High —3F 157
Scaur. Dum —4F 111
Scawby. N Lin —4C 94
Scawsby. S Yor —4F 93
Scawton. N Yor —1H 99
Scayne's Hill. W Sus —3E 27
Scethrog. Powy —3E 46
Scholar Green. Ches —5C 84
Scholes. G Man —4E 90
Scholes. W Yor —2B 92
(nr. Bradford)
Scholes. W Yor —4B 92
(nr. Holmfirth)
Scholes. W Yor —1D 93
(nr. Leeds)
Scholey Hill. W Yor —2D 93
School Aycliffe. Darl —2F 105
School Green. Ches —4A 84
School Green. Essx —2H 53
Scissett. W Yor —3C 92
Scleddau. Pemb —1D 42
Scofton. Notts —2D 86
Scole. Norf —3D 66
Scolpaig. W Isl —1C 170
Scolton. Pemb —2D 43
Sconser. High —5E 155
Scoonie. Fife —3F 137
Scopwick. Linc —5H 87
Scoraig. High —4E 163
Scorborough. E Yor —5E 101
Scorrier. Corn —4B 6
Scorriton. Devn —2D 8
Scorton. Lanc —5E 97
Scorton. N Yor —4F 105
Sco Ruston. Norf —3E 79
Scotby. Cumb —4F 113
Scotch Corner. N Yor —4F 105
Scotforth. Lanc —3D 97
Scot Hay. Staf —1C 72
Scothern. Linc —3H 87
Scotland End. Oxon —2B 50
Scotlandwell. Per —3D 136
Scot Lane End. G Man —4E 91
Scotsburn. High —1B 158
Scotsdike. Cumb —2E 113
Scots Gap. Nmbd —1D 114
Scotstoun. Glas —3G 127
Scotstown. High —2C 140
Scotswood. Tyne —3F 115
Scottas. High —3F 147
Scotter. Linc —4B 94
Scotterthorpe. Linc —4B 94
Scottlethorpe. Linc —3H 75
Scotton. Linc —1F 87
Scotton. N Yor —5E 105
(nr. Catterick Garrison)
Scotton. N Yor —4F 99
(nr. Harrogate)
Scottow. Norf —3E 79
Scoulton. Norf —5B 78
Scounslow Green. Staf —3E 73
Scourie. High —4B 166
Scourie More. High —4B 166
Scousburgh. Shet —10E 173
Scout Green. Cumb —4G 103
Scouthead. G Man —4H 91
Scrabster. High —1C 168
Scrafield. Linc —4C 88
Scrainwood. Nmbd —4D 121
Scrane End. Linc —1C 76
Scraptoft. Leics —5D 74
Scratby. Norf —4H 79
Scrayingham. N Yor —3B 100
Scredington. Linc —1H 75
Scremby. Linc —4D 88
Scremerston. Nmbd —5G 131
Screveton. Notts —1E 75
Scrivelsby. Linc —4B 88
Scriven. N Yor —4F 99
Scronkey. Lanc —5D 96
Scrooby. Notts —1D 86
Scropton. Derbs —2F 73
Scrub Hill. Linc —5B 88
Scruton. N Yor —5A 106
Scuggate. Cumb —2F 113
Sculcoates. Hull —1D 94
Sculthorpe. Norf —2A 78
Scunthorpe. N Lin —3B 94
Scurlage. Swan —4D 30
Sea. Som —1G 13
Seaborough. Dors —2H 13
Seabridge. Staf —1C 72
Seabrook. Kent —2F 29
Seaburn. Tyne —4H 115
Seacombe. Mers —1F 83
Seacroft. Linc —4E 89
Seacroft. W Yor —1D 92
Seadyke. Linc —2C 76
Seafield. High —5G 165
Seafield. Midl —3F 129
Seafield. S Ayr —2C 116
Seafield. W Lot —3D 128
Seaford. E Sus —5F 27
Seaforth. Mers —1F 83
Seagrave. Leics —4D 74
Seaham. Dur —5H 115
Seahouses. Nmbd —1G 121
Seal. Kent —5G 39
Sealand. Flin —4F 83
Seale. Surr —2G 25
Seamer. N Yor —1E 101
(nr. Scarborough)
Seamer. N Yor —3B 106
(nr. Stokesley)
Seamill. N Ayr —5C 126
Sea Mills. Bris —4A 34
Sea Palling. Norf —3G 79
Searby. Linc —4D 94
Seasalter. Kent —4E 41
Seascale. Cumb —4B 102
Seaside. Per —1E 137
Seater. High —1F 169
Seathorne. Linc —4E 89
Seathwaite. Cumb —3D 102
(nr. Borrowdale)
Seathwaite. Cumb —5D 102
(nr. Ulpha)
Seatle. Cumb —1C 96
Seatoller. Cumb —3D 102
Seaton. Corn —3H 7
Seaton. Cumb —1B 102
Seaton. Devn —3F 13
Seaton. Dur —5G 115
Seaton. E Yor —5F 101
Seaton. Nmbd —2G 115
Seaton. Rut —1G 63
Seaton Burn. Tyne —2F 115
Seaton Carew. Hart —2C 106
Seaton Delaval. Nmbd —2G 115
Seaton Junction. Devn —3F 13
Seaton Ross. E Yor —5B 100
Seaton Sluice. Nmbd —2G 115
Seatown. Dors —3H 13
Seatown. Mor —2C 160
(nr. Cullen)
Seatown. Mor —1G 159
(nr. Lossiemouth)
Seatown. Mor —2C 160
(nr. Portsoy)
Seave Green. N Yor —4C 106
Seaview. IOW —3E 17
Seaville. Cumb —4C 112
Seavington St Mary. Som —1H 13
Seavington St Michael. Som —1H 13
Seawick. Essx —4E 55
Sebastopol. Cphy —5E 47
Sebastopol. Torf —2F 33
Sebergham. Cumb —5E 113
Seckington. Warw —5G 73
Second Coast. High —4D 162
Sedbergh. Cumb —5H 103
Sedbury. Glos —2A 34
Sedbusk. N Yor —5B 104
Sedgeberrow. Worc —2F 49
Sedgebrook. Linc —2F 75
Sedgefield. Dur —2A 106
Sedgeford. Norf —2G 77
Sedgehill. Som —4D 22
Sedgley. W Mid —1D 60
Sedgwick. Cumb —1E 97
Sedlescombe. E Sus —4B 28
Seend. Wilts —5E 35
Seend Cleeve. Wilts —5E 35
Seer Green. Buck —1A 38
Seething. Norf —1F 67
Sefton. Mers —4B 90
Sefton Park. Mers —2F 83
Seggat. Aber —4E 161
Seghill. Nmbd —2F 115
Seifton. Shrp —2G 59
Seighford. Staf —3C 72
Seilebost. W Isl —8C 171
Seisdon. Staf —1C 60
Seisiadar. W Isl —4H 171
Selattyn. Shrp —2E 71
Selborne. Hants —3F 25
Selby. N Yor —1G 93
Selham. W Sus —3A 26
Selkirk. Scot —2G 119
Sellack. Here —3A 48
Sellafirth. Shet —2G 173
Sellindge. Kent —2E 29
Selling. Kent —5E 41
Sells Green. Wilts —5E 35
Selly Oak. W Mid —2E 61
Selmeston. E Sus —5G 27
Selsdon. G Lon —4E 39
Selsey. W Sus —3G 17
Selsfield Common. W Sus —2E 27
Selside. Cumb —5G 103
Selside. N Yor —2G 97
Selsley. Glos —5D 48
Selsted. Kent —1G 29
Selston. Notts —5B 86
Selworthy. Som —2C 20
Semblister. Shet —6E 173
Semer. Suff —1D 54
Semington. Wilts —5D 35
Semley. Wilts —4D 23
Send. Surr —5B 38
Send Marsh. Surr —5B 38
Senghenydd. Cphy —2E 32
Sennen. Corn —4A 4
Sennen Cove. Corn —4A 4
Sennicotts. W Sus —2G 17
Sennybridge. Powy —3C 46
Serlby. Notts —2D 86
Sessay. N Yor —2G 99
Setchey. Norf —4F 77
Setley. Hants —2B 16
Setter. Shet —3F 173
Settiscarth. Orkn —6C 172
Settle. N Yor —3H 97
Settrington. N Yor —2C 100
Seven Ash. Som —3E 21
Sevenhampton. Glos —3F 49
Sevenhampton. Swin —2H 35
Sevenoaks. Kent —5G 39
Sevenoaks Weald. Kent —5G 39
Seven Sisters. Neat —5B 46
Seven Springs. Glos —4E 49
Severn Beach. S Glo —3A 34
Severn Stoke. Worc —1D 48
Sevington. Kent —1E 29
Sewards End. Essx —2F 53
Sewardstone. Essx —1E 39
Sewell. Beds —3H 51
Sewerby. E Yor —3F 101
Seworgan. Corn —5B 6
Sewstern. Leics —3F 75
Sgallairidh. W Isl —9B 170
Sgarasta Mhor. W Isl —8C 171
Sgiogarstaigh. W Isl —1H 171
Sgreadan. Arg —4A 132
Shabbington. Buck —5E 51
Shackerley. Shrp —5C 72
Shackerstone. Leics —5A 74
Shackleford. Surr —1A 26
Shadforth. Dur —5G 115
Shadingfield. Suff —2G 67
Shadoxhurst. Kent —2D 28
Shadsworth. Bkbn —2E 91
Shadwell. Norf —2B 66
Shadwell. W Yor —1D 92
Shaftesbury. Dors —4D 22
Shafton. S Yor —3D 93
Shafton Two Gates. S Yor —3D 93
Shaggs. Dors —4D 14
Shakesfield. Glos —2B 48
Shalbourne. Wilts —5B 36
Shalcombe. IOW —4B 16
Shalden. Hants —2E 25
Shaldon. Devn —5C 12
Shalfleet. IOW —4C 16
Shalford. Essx —3H 53
Shalford. Surr —1B 26
Shalford Green. Essx —3H 53
Shallochpark. S Ayr —5A 116
Shallowford. Devn —2H 19
Shallowford. Staf —3C 72
Shalmsford Street. Kent —5E 41
Shalstone. Buck —2E 51
Shamley Green. Surr —1B 26
Shandon. Arg —1D 126
Shandwick. High —1C 158
Shangton. Leics —1E 62
Shankhouse. Nmbd —2F 115
Shanklin. IOW —4D 16
Shannochie. N Ayr —3D 122
Shap. Cumb —3G 103
Shapwick. Dors —2E 15
Shapwick. Som —3H 21
Sharcott. Wilts —1G 23
Shardlow. Derbs —2B 74
Shareshill. Staf —5D 72
Sharlston. W Yor —3D 93
Sharlston Common. W Yor —3D 93
Sharnal Street. Medw —3B 40
Sharnbrook. Beds —5G 63
Sharneyford. Lanc —2G 91
Sharnford. Leics —1B 62
Sharnhill Green. Dors —2C 14
Sharow. N Yor —2F 99
Sharpe Green. Lanc —1D 90
Sharpenhoe. Beds —2A 52
Sharperton. Nmbd —4D 120
Sharpness. Glos —5B 48
Sharp Street. Norf —3F 79
Sharpthorne. W Sus —2E 27
Sharrington. Norf —2C 78
Shatterford. Worc —2B 60
Shatton. Derbs —2F 85
Shaugh Prior. Devn —2B 8
Shavington. Ches —5B 84
Shaw. G Man —4H 91
Shaw. W Ber —5C 36
Shaw. Wilts —5D 35
Shawbirch. Telf —4A 72
Shawbury. Shrp —3H 71
Shawdon Hall. Nmbd —3E 121
Shawell. Leics —2C 62
Shawford. Hants —4C 24
Shawforth. Lanc —2G 91
Shaw Green. Lanc —3D 90
Shawhead. Dum —2F 111
Shaw Mills. N Yor —3E 99
Shawwood. E Ayr —2E 117
Shearington. Dum —3B 112
Shearsby. Leics —1D 62
Shearston. Som —3F 21
Shebbear. Devn —2E 11
Shebdon. Staf —3B 72
Shebster. High —2C 168
Shedfield. Hants —1D 16
Shedog. N Ayr —2D 122
Sheen. Staf —4F 85
Sheepbridge. Derbs —3A 86
Sheep Hill. Dur —4E 115
Sheepscar. W Yor —1D 92
Sheepscombe. Glos —4D 49
Sheepstor. Devn —2B 8
Sheepwash. Devn —2E 11
Sheepwash. Nmbd —1F 115
Sheepway. N Som —4H 33
Sheepy Magna. Leics —5H 73
Sheepy Parva. Leics —5H 73
Sheering. Essx —4F 53
Sheerness. Kent —3D 40
Sheerwater. Surr —4B 38
Sheet. Hants —4F 25
Sheffield. S Yor —2H 85
Sheffield Bottom. W Ber —5E 37
Sheffield City Airport. S Yor —2B 86
Sheffield Green. E Sus —3F 27
Shefford. Beds —2B 52
Shefford Woodlands. W Ber —4B 36
Sheigra. High —2B 166
Sheinton. Shrp —5A 72
Shelderton. Shrp —3G 59
Sheldon. Derbs —4F 85
Sheldon. Devn —2E 12
Sheldon. W Mid —2F 61
Sheldwich. Kent —5E 40
Sheldwich Lees. Kent —5E 40
Shelf. W Yor —2B 92
Shelfanger. Norf —2D 66
Shelfield. Warw —4F 61
Shelfield. W Mid —5E 73
Shelford. Notts —1D 74
Shelford. Warw —2B 62
Shell. Worc —5D 60
Shelley. Suff —2D 54
Shelley. W Yor —3C 92
Shell Green. Hal —2H 83
Shellingford. Oxon —2B 36
Shellow Bowells. Essx —5G 53
Shelsley Beauchamp. Worc —4B 60
Shelsley Walsh. Worc —4B 60
Shelthorpe. Leics —4C 74
Shelton. Beds —4H 63
Shelton. Norf —1E 67
Shelton. Notts —1E 75
Shelton. Shrp —4G 71
Shelton Green. Norf —1E 67
Shelton Lock. Dby C —2A 74
Shelve. Shrp —1F 59
Shelwick. Here —1A 48
Shelwick Green. Here —1A 48
Shenfield. Essx —1H 39
Shenington. Oxon —1B 50
Shenley. Herts —5B 52
Shenley Brook End. Mil —2G 51
Shenleybury. Herts —5B 52
Shenley Church End. Mil —2G 51
Shenmore. Here —2G 47
Shennanton. Dum —3A 110
Shenstone. Staf —5F 73
Shenstone. Worc —3C 60
Shenstone Woodend. Staf —5F 73
Shenton. Leics —5A 74
Shenval. Mor —1G 151
Shepeau Stow. Linc —4C 76
Shephall. Herts —3C 52
Shepherd's Bush. G Lon —2D 38
Shepherds Gate. Norf —4E 77
Shepherd's Green. Oxon —3F 37
Shepherd's Port. Norf —2F 77
Shepherdswell. Kent —1G 29
Shepley. W Yor —4B 92
Sheppardstown. High —4D 169
Shepperdine. S Glo —2B 34
Shepperton. Surr —4B 38
Shepreth. Cambs —1D 53
Shepshed. Leics —4B 74
Shepton Beauchamp. Som —1H 13
Shepton Mallet. Som —2B 22
Shepton Montague. Som —3B 22
Shepway. Kent —5B 40
Sheraton. Dur —1B 106
Sherborne. Bath —1A 22
Sherborne. Dors —1B 14
Sherborne. Glos —4G 49
Sherborne Causeway. Dors —4D 22
Sherborne St John. Hants —1E 24
Sherbourne. Warw —4G 61
Sherburn. Dur —5G 115
Sherburn. N Yor —2D 100
Sherburn Hill. Dur —5G 115
Sherburn in Elmet. N Yor —1E 93
Shere. Surr —1B 26
Shereford. Norf —3A 78
Sherfield English. Hants —4A 24
Sherfield on Loddon. Hants —1E 25
Sherford. Devn —4D 9
Sherford. Dors —3E 15
Sheriffhales. Shrp —4B 72
Sheriff Hutton. N Yor —3A 100
Sheriffston. Mor —2G 159
Sheringham. Norf —1D 78
Sherington. Mil —1G 51
Shermanbury. W Sus —4D 26
Shernal Green. Worc —4D 60
Shernborne. Norf —2G 77
Sherrington. Wilts —3E 23
Sherston. Wilts —3D 34
Sherwood. Not C —1C 74
Sherwood Green. Devn —4F 19
Shettleston. Glas —3H 127
Shevington. G Man —4D 90
Shevington Moor. G Man —3D 90
Shevington Vale. G Man —4D 90
Sheviock. Corn —3H 7
Shiel Bridge. High —2B 148
Shieldaig. High —1H 155
(nr. Charlestown)
Shieldaig. High —3H 155
(nr. Loch Shieldaig)
Shieldhill. Dum —1B 112
Shieldhill. Falk —2B 128
Shieldhill. S Lan —5D 128
Shieldmuir. N Lan —4A 128
Shielfoot. High —2A 140
Shielhill. Aber —3H 161
Shielhill. Ang —3D 144
Shifnal. Shrp —5B 72
Shilbottle. Nmbd —4F 121
Shilbottle Grange. Nmbd —4G 121
Shildon. Dur —2F 105
Shillford. E Ren —4F 127
Shillingford. Devn —4C 20
Shillingford. Oxon —2D 36
Shillingford St George. Devn —4C 12
Shillingstone. Dors —1D 14
Shillington. Beds —2B 52
Shillmoor. Nmbd —4C 120
Shilton. Oxon —5A 50
Shilton. Warw —2B 62
Shilvinghampton. Dors —4B 14
Shilvington. Nmbd —1E 115
Shimpling. Norf —2D 66
Shimpling. Suff —5A 66
Shimpling Street. Suff —5A 66
Shincliffe. Dur —5F 115
Shiney Row. Tyne —4G 115
Shinfield. Wok —5F 37
Shingay. Cambs —1D 52
Shingham. Norf —5G 77
Shingle Street. Suff —1G 55
Shinner's Bridge. Devn —2D 9
Shinness. High —2C 164
Shipbourne. Kent —5G 39
Shipdham. Norf —5B 78
Shipham. Som —1H 21
Shiphay. Torb —2E 9
Shiplake. Oxon —4F 37
Shipley. Derbs —1B 74
Shipley. Nmbd —3F 121
Shipley. Shrp —1C 60
Shipley. W Sus —3C 26
Shipley. W Yor —1B 92
Shipley Bridge. Surr —1E 27
Shipmeadow. Suff —1F 67
Shippon. Oxon —2C 36
Shipston on Stour. Warw —1A 50
Shipton. Buck —3F 51
Shipton. Glos —4F 49
Shipton. N Yor —4H 99
Shipton. Shrp —1H 59
Shipton Bellinger. Hants —2H 23
Shipton Gorge. Dors —3H 13
Shipton Green. W Sus —3G 17
Shipton Moyne. Glos —3D 35
Shipton-on-Cherwell. Oxon —4C 50
Shiptonthorpe. E Yor —5C 100
Shipton-under-Wychwood. Oxon —4A 50
Shirburn. Oxon —2E 37
Shirdley Hill. Lanc —3B 90
Shire. Cumb —1H 103
Shirebrook. Derbs —4C 86
Shiregreen. S Yor —1A 86
Shirehampton. Bris —4A 34
Shiremoor. Tyne —2G 115
Shirenewton. Mon —2H 33
Shireoaks. Notts —2C 86
Shires Mill. Fife —1D 128
Shirkoak. Kent —2D 28
Shirland. Derbs —5A 86
Shirley. Derbs —1G 73
Shirley. Sotn —1C 16
Shirley. W Mid —3F 61
Shirleywich. Staf —3D 73
Shirl Heath. Here —5G 59
Shirrell Heath. Hants —1D 16
Shirwell. Devn —3F 19
Shiskine. N Ayr —3D 122
Shobdon. Here —4F 59
Shobnall. Staf —3G 73
Shobrooke. Devn —2B 12
Shoby. Leics —3D 74
Shocklach. Ches —1G 71
Shoeburyness. S'end —2D 40
Sholden. Kent —5H 41
Sholing. Sotn —1C 16
Sholver. G Man —4H 91
Shoot Hill. Shrp —4G 71
Shop. Corn —1C 10
(nr. Bude)
Shop. Corn —1C 6
(nr. Padstow)
Shop. Devn —1D 11
Shopford. Cumb —2G 113
Shop Street. Suff —4E 66
Shoreditch. G Lon —2E 39
Shoreditch. Som —4F 21
Shoreham. Kent —4G 39
Shoreham-by-Sea. W Sus —5D 26
Shoresdean. Nmbd —5F 131
Shoreswood. Nmbd —5F 131
Shore, The. Fife —2E 137
Shorncote. Glos —2F 35
Shorne. Kent —3A 40
Shorne Ridgeway. Kent —3A 40
Shortacombe. Devn —4F 11
Shortbridge. E Sus —3F 27
Shortgate. E Sus —4F 27
Short Green. Norf —2C 66
Shorthampton. Oxon —3B 50
Short Heath. Leics —4H 73
Short Heath. W Mid —1E 61
(nr. Erdington)
Short Heath. W Mid —5D 73
(nr. Wednesfield)
Shortlanesend. Corn —4C 6
Shorton. Torb —2E 9
Shortstown. Beds —1A 52
Shortwood. S Glo —4B 34
Shorwell. IOW —4C 16
Shoscombe. Bath —1C 22
Shotesham. Norf —1E 67
Shotgate. Essx —1B 40
Shotley. Suff —2F 55
Shotley Bridge. Dur —4D 115
Shotleyfield. Nmbd —4D 114
Shotley Gate. Suff —2F 55
Shottenden. Kent —5E 41
Shottermill. Surr —3G 25
Shottery. Warw —5F 61
Shotteswell. Warw —1C 50
Shottisham. Suff —1G 55
Shottle. Derbs —1H 73
Shotton. Dur —1B 106
(nr. Peterlee)
Shotton. Dur —2A 106
(nr. Sedgefield)
Shotton. Flin —4E 83
Shotton. Nmbd —2F 115
(nr. Morpeth)
Shotton. Nmbd —1C 120
(nr. Town Yetholm)
Shotton Colliery. Dur —5G 115
Shotts. N Lan —3B 128
Shotwick. Ches —3F 83
Shouldham. Norf —5F 77
Shouldham Thorpe. Norf —5F 77
Shoulton. Worc —5C 60
Shrawardine. Shrp —4F 71
Shrawley. Worc —4C 60
Shreding Green. Buck —2B 38
Shrewley. Warw —4G 61
Shrewsbury. Shrp —4G 71
Shrewton. Wilts —2F 23
Shripney. W Sus —5A 26
Shrivenham. Oxon —3H 35
Shropham. Norf —1B 66
Shroton. Dors —1D 14
Shrub End. Essx —3C 54
Shucknall. Here —1A 48
Shudy Camps. Cambs —1G 53
Shulista. High —1D 154
Shurdington. Glos —4E 49
Shurlock Row. Wind —4G 37
Shurrery. High —3C 168
Shurton. Som —2F 21
Shustoke. Warw —1G 61
Shute. Devn —3F 13
(nr. Axminster)
Shute. Devn —2B 12
(nr. Crediton)
Shutford. Oxon —1B 50
Shut Heath. Staf —3C 72
Shuthonger. Glos —2D 49
Shutlanehead. Staf —1C 72
Shutlanger. Nptn —1F 51
Shutt Green. Staf —5C 72
Shuttington. Warw —5G 73
Shuttlewood. Derbs —3B 86
Shuttleworth. G Man —3G 91

Siabost—Southwater Street

Siabost. W Isl —3E 171
Siabost bho Dheas. W Isl —3E 171
Siabost bho Thuath. W Isl —3E 171
Siadar. W Isl —2F 171
Siadar Uarach. W Isl —2F 171
Sibbaldbie. Dum —1C 112
Sibbertoft. Nptn —2D 62
Sibdon Carwood. Shrp —2G 59
Sibertswold. Kent —1G 29
Sibford Ferris. Oxon —2B 50
Sibford Gower. Oxon —2B 50
Sible Hedingham. Essx —2A 54
Sibsey. Linc —5C 88
Sibsey Fen Side. Linc —5C 88
Sibson. Cambs —1H 63
Sibson. Leics —5A 74
Sibster. High —3F 169
Sibthorpe. Notts —1E 75
Sibton. Suff —4F 67
Sicklesmere. Suff —4A 66
Sicklinghall. N Yor —5F 99
Sid. Devn —4E 13
Sidbury. Devn —3E 13
Sidbury. Shrp —2A 60
Sidcot. N Som —1H 21
Sidcup. G Lon —3F 39
Siddick. Cumb —1B 102
Siddington. Ches —3C 84
Siddington. Glos —2F 35
Side of the Moor. G Man —3F 91
Sidestrand. Norf —2E 79
Sidford. Devn —3E 13
Sidlesham. W Sus —3G 17
Sidley. E Sus —5B 28
Sidlowbridge. Surr —1D 26
Sidmouth. Devn —4E 13
Sigford. Devn —5A 12
Sigglesthorne. E Yor —5F 101
Sighthill. Edin —2E 129
Sigingstone. V Glam —4C 32
Signet. Oxon —4H 49
Silchester. Hants —5E 37
Sildinis. W Isl —6E 171
Sileby. Leics —4D 74
Silecroft. Cumb —1A 96
Silfield. Norf —1D 66
Silian. Cdgn —5E 57
Silkstone. S Yor —4C 92
Silkstone Common. S Yor —4C 92
Silksworth. Tyne —4G 115
Silk Willoughby. Linc —1H 75
Silloth. Cumb —4C 112
Sills. Nmbd —4C 120
Sillyearn. Mor —3C 160
Silpho. N Yor —5G 107
Silsden. W Yor —5C 98
Silsoe. Beds —2A 52
Silverbank. Aber —4E 152
Silverburn. Midl —3F 129
Silverdale. Lanc —2D 96
Silverdale. Staf —1C 72
Silverdale Green. Lanc —2D 96
Silver End. Essx —4B 54
Silver End. W Mid —2D 60
Silvergate. Norf —3D 78
Silverhillocks. Aber —2E 161
Silverley's Green. Suff —3E 67
Silverstone. Nptn —1E 51
Silverton. Devn —2C 12
Silverton. W Dun —2F 127
Silvington. Shrp —3A 60
Simm's Cross. Hal —2H 83
Simm's Lane End. Mers —1H 83
Simonburn. Nmbd —2B 114
Simonsbath. Som —3A 20
Simonstone. Lanc —1F 91
Simprim. Scot —5E 131
Simpson. Pemb —3C 42
Simpson Cross. Pemb —3C 42
Sinclairston. E Ayr —3D 116
Sinclairtown. Fife —4E 137
Sinderby. N Yor —1F 99
Sinderhope. Nmbd —4B 114
Sindlesham. Wok —5F 37
Sinfin. Dby C —2A 74
Singleborough. Buck —2F 51
Singleton. Kent —1D 28
Singleton. Lanc —1B 90
Singleton. W Sus —1G 17
Singlewell. Kent —3A 40
Sinkhurst Green. Kent —1C 28
Sinnahard. Aber —2B 152
Sinnington. N Yor —1B 100
Sinton Green. Worc —4C 60
Sipson. G Lon —3B 38
Sirhowy. Blae —4E 47
Sissinghurst. Kent —2B 28
Siston. S Glo —4B 34
Sithney. Corn —4D 4
Sittingbourne. Kent —4D 40
Six Ashes. Staf —2B 60
Six Bells. Blae —5F 47
Six Hills. Leics —3D 74
Sixhills. Linc —2A 88
Six Mile Bottom. Cambs —5E 65
Sixpenny Handley. Dors —1E 15
Sizewell. Suff —4G 67
Skail. High —4H 167
Skaill. Orkn —6B 172
Skaills. Orkn —7E 172
Skares. E Ayr —3E 117
Skateraw. E Lot —2D 130
Skaw. Shet —5G 173
Skeabost. High —4D 154
Skeabrae. Orkn —5B 172
Skeeby. N Yor —4E 105
Skeffington. Leics —5E 75
Skeffling. E Yor —3G 95
Skegby. Notts —4B 86
(nr. Mansfield)
Skegby. Notts —4E 87
(nr. Tuxford)
Skegness. Linc —4E 89
Skelberry. Shet —10E 173
(nr. Boddam)
Skelberry. Shet —3E 173
(nr. Housetter)
Skelbo. High —4E 165
Skelbo Street. High —4E 165
Skelbrooke. S Yor —3F 93
Skeldyke. Linc —2C 76
Skelfhill. Scot —4G 119
Skellingthorpe. Linc —3G 87
Skellister. Shet —6F 173
Skellorn Green. Ches —2D 84
Skellow. S Yor —3F 93
Skelmanthorpe. W Yor —3C 92
Skelmersdale. Lanc —4C 90
Skelmorlie. N Ayr —3C 126
Skelpick. High —3H 167
Skelton. Cumb —1F 103
Skelton. E Yor —2A 94
Skelton. N Yor —4D 105
(nr. Richmond)
Skelton. N Yor —3F 99
(nr. Ripon)
Skelton. Red C —3D 106
Skelton. York —4H 99
Skelton Green. Red C —3D 106
Skelwick. Orkn —3D 172
Skelwith Bridge. Cumb —4E 103
Skendleby. Linc —4D 88
Skendleby Psalter. Linc —3D 88
Skenfrith. Mon —3H 47
Skerne. E Yor —4E 101
Skeroblingarry. Arg —3B 122
Skerray. High —2G 167
Skerray. High —2G 167
Skerricha. High —3C 166
Skerton. Lanc —3D 96
Sketchley. Leics —1B 62
Sketty. Swan —3F 31
Skewen. Neat —3G 31
Skewsby. N Yor —2A 100
Skeyton. Norf —3E 79
Skeyton Corner. Norf —3E 79
Skiall. High —2C 168
Skidbrooke. Linc —1D 88
Skidbrooke North End. Linc —1D 88
Skidby. E Yor —1D 94
Skilgate. Som —4C 20
Skillington. Linc —3F 75
Skinburness. Cumb —4C 112
Skinflats. Falk —1C 128
Skinidin. High —4B 154
Skinnet. High —2F 167
Skinningrove. Red C —2E 107
Skipness. Arg —4G 125
Skippool. Lanc —5C 96
Skiprigg. Cumb —5E 113
Skipsea. E Yor —4F 101
Skipsea Brough. E Yor —4F 101
Skipton. N Yor —4B 98
Skipton-on-Swale. N Yor —2F 99
Skipwith. N Yor —1G 93
Skirbeck. Linc —1C 76
Skirbeck Quarter. Linc —1C 76
Skirlaugh. E Yor —1E 95
Skirling. Scot —1C 118
Skirmett. Buck —2F 37
Skirpenbeck. E Yor —4B 100
Skirwith. Cumb —1H 103
Skirwith. N Yor —2G 97
Skirza. High —2F 169
Skitby. Cumb —3F 113
Skitham. Lanc —5D 96
Skittle Green. Buck —5F 51
Skroo. Shet —1B 172
Skulamus. High —1E 147
Skullomie. High —2G 167
Skyborry Green. Shrp —3E 59
Skye Green. Essx —3B 54
Skye of Curr. High —1D 151
Slack. W Yor —2H 91
Slackhall. Derbs —2E 85
Slack Head. Cumb —2D 97
Slackhead. Mor —2B 160
Slackholme End. Linc —3E 89
Slacks of Cairnbanno. Aber —4F 161
Slack, The. Dur —2E 105
Slad. Glos —5D 48
Slade. Devn —2F 19
Slade. Swan —4D 31
Slade End. Oxon —2D 36
Slade Field. Cambs —2C 64
Slade Green. G Lon —3G 39
Slade Heath. Staf —5D 72
Slade Hooton. S Yor —2C 86
Sladesbridge. Corn —5A 10
Slade, The. W Ber —5D 36
Slaggyford. Nmbd —4H 113
Slaidburn. Lanc —4G 97
Slaid Hill. W Yor —5F 99
Slaithwaite. W Yor —3A 92
Slaley. Derbs —5G 85
Slaley. Nmbd —4C 114
Slamannan. Falk —2B 128
Slapton. Buck —3H 51
Slapton. Devn —4E 9
Slapton. Nptn —1E 51
Slattock. G Man —4G 91
Slaugham. W Sus —3D 26
Slaughterford. Wilts —4D 34
Slawston. Leics —1E 63
Sleaford. Hants —3G 25
Sleaford. Linc —1H 75
Sleagill. Cumb —3G 103
Sleap. Shrp —3G 71
Sledmere. E Yor —3D 100
Sleightholme. Dur —3C 104
Sleights. N Yor —4F 107
Slepe. Dors —3E 15
Slickly. High —2E 169
Sliddery. N Ayr —3D 122
Sligachan. High —1C 146
Slimbridge. Glos —5C 48
Slindon. Staf —2C 72
Slindon. W Sus —5A 26
Slinfold. W Sus —2C 26
Slingsby. N Yor —2A 100
Slip End. Herts —4A 52
Slipton. Nptn —3G 63
Slitting Mill. Staf —4E 73
Slochd. High —1C 150
Slockavullin. Arg —4F 133
Sloley. Norf —3E 79
Sloncombe. Devn —4H 11
Sloothby. Linc —3D 89
Slough. Slo —3A 38
Slough Green. Som —4F 21
Slough Green. W Sus —3D 27
Sluggan. High —1C 150
Slyne. Lanc —3D 97
Smailholm. Scot —1A 120
Smallbridge. G Man —3H 91
Smallbrook. Devn —3B 12
Smallburgh. Norf —3F 79
Smallburn. E Ayr —2F 117
Smalldale. Derbs —3E 85
Small Dole. W Sus —4D 26
Smalley. Derbs —1B 74
Smallfield. Surr —1E 27
Small Heath. W Mid —2F 61
Smallholm. Dum —2C 112
Small Hythe. Kent —2C 28
Smallrice. Staf —2D 72
Smallridge. Devn —2G 13
Smallwood Hey. Lanc —5C 96
Smallworth. Norf —2C 66
Smannell. Hants —2B 24
Smardale. Cumb —4A 104
Smarden. Kent —1C 28
Smarden Bell. Kent —1C 28
Smart's Hill. Kent —1G 27
Smeatharpe. Devn —1F 13
Smeeth. Kent —2E 29
Smeeth, The. Norf —4E 77
Smeeton Westerby. Leics —1D 62
Smeircleit. W Isl —7C 170
Smerral. High —5D 169
Smestow. Staf —1C 60
Smethwick. W Mid —2E 61
Smirisary. High —1A 140
Smisby. Derbs —4H 73
Smitham Hill. Bath —1A 22
Smith End Green. Worc —5B 60
Smithfield. Cumb —3F 113
Smith Green. Lanc —4D 97
Smithies, The. Shrp —1A 60
Smithincott. Devn —1D 12
Smith's Green. Essx —3F 53
Smithstown. High —1G 155
Smithton. High —4B 158
Smithwood Green. Suff —5B 66
Smithy Bridge. G Man —3H 91
Smithy Green. Ches —3B 84
Smithy Lane Ends. Lanc —3C 90
Smockington. Warw —2B 62
Smoogro. Orkn —7C 172
Smyth's Green. Essx —4C 54
Snaigow House. Per —4H 143
Snailbeach. Shrp —5F 71
Snailwell. Cambs —4F 65
Snainton. N Yor —1D 100
Snaith. E Yor —2G 93
Snape. N Yor —1E 99
Snape. Suff —5F 67
Snape Green. Lanc —3B 90
Snarestone. Leics —5H 73
Snarford. Linc —2H 87
Snargate. Kent —3D 28
Snave. Kent —3E 28
Sneachill. Worc —5D 60
Snead. Powy —1F 59
Snead Common. Worc —4B 60
Sneaton. N Yor —4F 107
Sneatonthorpe. N Yor —4G 107
Snelland. Linc —2H 87
Snelston. Derbs —1F 73
Snetterton. Norf —1B 66
Snettisham. Norf —2F 77
Snibston. Leics —4B 74
Snig's End. Glos —3C 48
Sniseabhal. W Isl —6C 170
Snitter. Nmbd —4E 121
Snitterby. Linc —1G 87
Snitterfield. Warw —5G 61
Snitton. Shrp —3H 59
Snodhill. Here —1G 47
Snodland. Kent —4A 40
Snods Edge. Nmbd —4D 114
Snowshill. Glos —2F 49
Snow Street. Norf —2C 66
Snydale. W Yor —3E 93
Soake. Hants —1E 17
Soar. Carm —3G 45
Soar. Gwyn —2F 69
Soar. Powy —2C 46
Soberton. Hants —1E 16
Soberton Heath. Hants —1E 16
Sockbridge. Cumb —2F 103
Sockburn. Darl —4A 106
Sodom. Den —3C 82
Sodom. Shet —5G 173
Soham. Cambs —3E 65
Soham Cotes. Cambs —3E 65
Solas. W Isl —1D 170
Soldon Cross. Devn —1D 10
Soldridge. Hants —3E 25
Solent Breezes. Hants —2D 16
Sole Street. Kent —4A 40
(nr. Meopham)
Sole Street. Kent —1E 29
(nr. Waltham)
Solihull. W Mid —3F 61
Sollers Dilwyn. Here —5G 59
Sollers Hope. Here —2B 48
Sollom. Lanc —3C 90
Solva. Pemb —2B 42
Somerby. Leics —4E 75
Somerby. Linc —4D 94
Somercotes. Derbs —5B 86
Somerford. Dors —3G 15
Somerford. Staf —5C 72
Somerford Keynes. Glos —2F 35
Somerley. W Sus —3G 17
Somerleyton. Suff —1G 67
Somersal Herbert. Derbs —2F 73
Somersby. Linc —3C 88
Somersham. Cambs —3C 64
Somersham. Suff —1D 54
Somerton. Oxon —3C 50
Somerton. Som —4H 21
Somerton. Suff —5H 65
Sompting. W Sus —5C 26
Sonning. Wok —4F 37
Sonning Common. Oxon —3F 37
Sookholme. Notts —4C 86
Sopley. Hants —3G 15
Sopworth. Wilts —3D 34
Sorbie. Dum —5B 110
Sordale. High —2D 168
Sorisdale. Arg —2D 138
Sorn. E Ayr —2E 117
Sornhill. E Ayr —1E 117
Sortat. High —2E 169
Sotby. Linc —3B 88
Sots Hole. Linc —4A 88
Sotterley. Suff —2G 67
Soudley. Shrp —1G 59
(nr. Church Stretton)
Soudley. Shrp —3B 72
(nr. Market Drayton)
Soughton. Flin —4E 83
Soulbury. Buck —3G 51
Soulby. Cumb —3A 104
(nr. Appleby)
Soulby. Cumb —2F 103
(nr. Penrith)
Souldern. Oxon —2D 50
Souldrop. Beds —4G 63
Sound. Shet —7F 173
(nr. Lerwick)
Sound. Shet —6E 173
(nr. Tresta)
Soundwell. S Glo —4B 34
Sourhope. Scot —2C 120
Sourin. Orkn —4D 172
Sourton. Devn —3F 11
Soutergate. Cumb —1B 96
South Acre. Norf —4H 77
Southall. G Lon —3C 38
South Allington. Devn —5D 9
South Alloa. Falk —4A 136
Southam. Glos —3E 49
Southam. Warw —4B 62
South Ambersham. W Sus —3A 26
Southampton. Sotn —1C 16
Southampton Airport. Hants —1C 16
Southannan. N Ayr —4D 126
South Anston. S Yor —2C 86
South Ascot. Wind —4A 38
South Baddesley. Hants —3B 16
South Balfern. Dum —4B 110
South Ballachulish. High —3E 141
South Bank. Red C —2C 106
South Barrow. Som —4B 22
South Beach. Nmbd —2G 115
South Benfleet. Essx —2B 40
South Bents. Tyne —3H 115
South Bersted. W Sus —5A 26
Southborough. Kent —1G 27
Southbourne. Bour —3G 15
Southbourne. W Sus —2F 17
South Brent. Devn —2D 8
South Brewham. Som —3C 22
South Broomage. Falk —1B 128
South Broomhill. Nmbd —5G 121
Southburgh. Norf —5B 78
South Burlingham. Norf —5F 79
Southburn. E Yor —4D 101
South Cadbury. Som —4B 22
South Carlton. Linc —3G 87
South Cave. E Yor —1C 94
South Cerney. Glos —2F 35
South Chard. Som —2G 13
South Charlton. Nmbd —2F 121
South Cheriton. Som —4B 22
South Church. Dur —2F 105
Southchurch. S'end —2D 40
South Cleatlam. Dur —3E 105
South Cliffe. E Yor —1B 94
South Clifton. Notts —3F 87
South Clunes. High —4H 157
South Cockerington. Linc —2C 88
South Common. E Sus —4E 27
South Cornelly. B'End —3B 32
Southcott. Devn —1E 11
(nr. Great Torrington)
Southcott. Devn —3F 11
(nr. Okehampton)
Southcott. Wilts —1G 23
Southcourt. Buck —4G 51
South Cove. Suff —2G 67
South Creagan. Arg —4D 141
South Creake. Norf —2A 78
South Crosland. W Yor —3B 92
South Croxton. Leics —4D 74
South Dalton. E Yor —5D 100
South Darenth. Kent —4G 39
Southdean. Scot —4A 120
Southdown. Bath —5C 34
South Duffield. N Yor —1G 93
Southease. E Sus —5F 27
South Elkington. Linc —2B 88
South Elmsall. W Yor —3E 93
Southend. Arg —5A 122
South End. Cumb —3B 96
Southend. Glos —2C 34
South End. N Lin —2E 94
South End. W Ber —4D 36
Southend (London) Airport. Essx —2C 40
Southend-on-Sea. S'end —2C 40
Southerfield. Cumb —5C 112
Southerhouse. Shet —8E 173
Southerly. Devn —4F 11
Southernden. Kent —1C 28
Southerndown. V Glam —4B 32
Southerness. Dum —4A 112
South Erradale. High —1G 155
Southerton. Devn —3D 12
Southery. Norf —1F 65
Southey Green. Essx —2A 54
South Fambridge. Essx —1C 40
South Fawley. W Ber —3B 36
South Feorline. N Ayr —3D 122
South Ferriby. N Lin —2C 94
South Field. E Yor —2D 94
Southfleet. Kent —3H 39
South Garvan. High —1D 141
Southgate. Cdgn —2E 57
Southgate. G Lon —1E 39
Southgate. Norf —3D 78
(nr. Aylsham)
Southgate. Norf —2F 77
(nr. Dersingham)
Southgate. Norf —2A 78
(nr. Fakenham)
Southgate. Swan —4E 31
South Gluss. Shet —4E 173
South Godstone. Surr —1E 27
South Gorley. Hants —1G 15
South Green. Essx —1A 40
(nr. Billericay)
South Green. Essx —4D 54
(nr. Colchester)
South Green. Kent —4C 40
South Hanningfield. Essx —1B 40
South Harting. W Sus —1F 17
South Hayling. Hants —3F 17
South Hazelrigg. Nmbd —1E 121
South Heath. Buck —5H 51
South Heath. Essx —4E 54
South Heighton. E Sus —5F 27
South Hetton. Dur —5G 115
South Hiendley. W Yor —3D 93
South Hill. Corn —5D 10
South Hill. Som —4H 21
South Hinksey. Oxon —5D 50
South Hole. Devn —4C 18
South Holme. N Yor —2B 100
South Holmwood. Surr —1C 26
South Hornchurch. G Lon —2G 39
South Huish. Devn —4C 8
South Hykeham. Linc —4G 87
South Hylton. Tyne —4G 115
Southill. Beds —1B 52
Southington. Hants —2D 24
South Kelsey. Linc —1H 87
South Kessock. High —4A 158
South Killingholme. N Lin —3E 95
South Kilvington. N Yor —1G 99
South Kilworth. Leics —2D 62
South Kirkby. W Yor —3E 93
South Kirton. Aber —3E 153
South Kyme. Linc —1A 76
South Lancing. W Sus —5C 26
South Ledaig. Arg —5D 140
Southleigh. Devn —3F 13
South Leigh. Oxon —5B 50
South Leverton. Notts —2E 87
South Limmerhaugh. E Ayr —2F 117
South Littleton. Worc —1F 49
South Lopham. Norf —2C 66
South Luffenham. Rut —5G 75
South Malling. E Sus —4F 27
South Marston. Swin —3G 35
South Middleton. Nmbd —2E 121
South Milford. N Yor —1E 93
South Milton. Devn —4D 8
South Mimms. Herts —5C 52
Southminster. Essx —1D 40
South Molton. Devn —4H 19
South Moor. Dur —4E 115
Southmoor. Oxon —2B 36
South Moreton. Oxon —3D 36
South Mundham. W Sus —2G 17
South Muskham. Notts —5E 87
South Newbald. E Yor —1C 94
South Newington. Oxon —2C 50
South Newsham. Nmbd —2G 115
South Newton. N Ayr —4H 125
South Newton. Wilts —3F 23
South Normanton. Derbs —5B 86
South Norwood. G Lon —4E 39
South Nutfield. Surr —1E 27
South Ockendon. Thur —2G 39
Southoe. Cambs —4A 64
Southolt. Suff —4D 66
South Ormsby. Linc —3C 88
Southorpe. Pet —5H 75
South Otterington. N Yor —1F 99
South Owersby. Linc —1H 87
Southowram. W Yor —2B 92
South Oxhey. Herts —1C 38
South Perrott. Dors —2H 13
South Petherton. Som —1H 13
South Petherwin. Corn —4D 10
South Pickenham. Norf —5A 78
South Pool. Devn —4D 9
South Port. Arg —1H 133
Southport. Mers —3B 90
Southpunds. Shet —10F 173
South Queensferry. Edin —2E 129
South Radworthy. Devn —3A 20
South Rauceby. Linc —1H 75
South Raynham. Norf —3A 78
Southrepps. Norf —2E 79
South Reston. Linc —2D 88
Southrey. Linc —4A 88
Southrop. Glos —5G 49
Southrope. Hants —2E 25
South Runcton. Norf —5F 77
South Scarle. Notts —4F 87
Southsea. Port —3E 17
South Shields. Tyne —3G 115
South Shore. Bkpl —1B 90
Southside. Orkn —5E 172
South Somercotes. Linc —1D 88
South Stainley. N Yor —3F 99
South Stainmore. Cumb —3B 104
South Stifford. Thur —3G 39
Southstoke. Bath —5C 34
South Stoke. Oxon —3D 36
South Stoke. W Sus —4B 26
South Street. E Sus —4E 27
South Street. Kent —5E 41
(nr. Faversham)
South Street. Kent —4F 41
(nr. Whitstable)
South Tawton. Devn —3G 11
South Thoresby. Linc —3D 88
South Tidworth. Wilts —2H 23
South Town. Devn —4C 12
South Town. Hants —3E 25
Southtown. Norf —5H 79
Southtown. Orkn —8D 172
South View. Shet —7E 173
Southwaite. Cumb —5F 113
South Walsham. Norf —4F 79
South Warnborough. Hants —2F 25
Southwater. W Sus —3C 26
Southwater Street. W Sus —3C 26

Southway—Stonegate

Southway. Som —2A 22
South Weald. Essx —1G 39
South Weirs. Hants —2A 16
Southwell. Dors —5B 14
Southwell. Notts —5D 86
South Weston. Oxon —2F 37
South Wheatley. Corn —3C 10
South Wheatley. Notts —2E 87
Southwick. Hants —2E 17
Southwick. Nptn —1H 63
Southwick. Tyne —4G 115
Southwick. W Sus —5D 26
Southwick. Wilts —1D 22
South Widcombe. Bath —1A 22
South Wigston. Leics —1C 62
South Willingham. Linc —2A 88
South Wingfield. Derbs —5A 86
South Witham. Linc —4G 75
Southwold. Suff —3H 67
South Wonston. Hants —3C 24
Southwood. Norf —5F 79
Southwood. Som —3A 22
South Woodham Ferrers. Essx —1C 40
South Wootton. Norf —3F 77
South Wraxall. Wilts —5D 34
South Zeal. Devn —3G 11
Soval Lodge. W Isl —5F 171
Sowerby. N Yor —1G 99
Sowerby. W Yor —2A 92
Sowerby Bridge. W Yor —2A 92
Sowerby Row. Cumb —5E 113
Sower Carr. Lanc —5C 96
Sowley Green. Suff —5G 65
Sowood. W Yor —3A 92
Sowton. Devn —3C 12
Soyal. High —4C 164
Soyland Town. W Yor —2A 92
Spacey Houses. N Yor —4F 99
Spa Common. Norf —2E 79
Spalding. Linc —3B 76
Spaldington. E Yor —1A 94
Spaldwick. Cambs —3A 64
Spalford. Notts —4F 87
Spanby. Linc —2H 75
Sparham. Norf —4C 78
Sparhamhill. Norf —4C 78
Spark Bridge. Cumb —1C 96
Sparket. Cumb —2F 103
Sparkford. Som —4B 22
Sparkwell. Devn —3B 8
Sparrow Green. Norf —4B 78
Sparrowpit. Derbs —2E 85
Sparrow's Green. E Sus —2H 27
Sparsholt. Hants —3C 24
Sparsholt. Oxon —3B 36
Spartylea. Nmbd —5B 114
Spath. Staf —2E 73
Spaunton. N Yor —1B 100
Spaxton. Som —3F 21
Spean Bridge. High —5E 149
Spear Hill. W Sus —4C 26
Speen. Buck —2G 37
Speen. W Ber —5C 36
Speeton. N Yor —2F 101
Speke. Mers —2G 83
Speldhurst. Kent —1G 27
Spellbrook. Herts —4E 53
Spelsbury. Oxon —3B 50
Spencers Wood. Wok —5F 37
Spennithorne. N Yor —1D 98
Spennymoor. Dur —1F 105
Spernall. Warw —4E 61
Spetchley. Worc —5C 60
Spetisbury. Dors —2E 15
Spexhall. Suff —2F 67
Speybank. High —3C 150
Spey Bay. Mor —2A 160
Speybridge. High —1E 151
Speyview. Mor —4G 159
Spilsby. Linc —4C 88
Spindlestone. Nmbd —1F 121
Spinkhill. Derbs —3B 86
Spinney Hills. Leic C —5D 74
Spinningdale. High —5D 164
Spital. Mers —2F 83
Spitalhill. Derbs —1F 73
Spital in the Street. Linc —2G 87
Spithurst. E Sus —4F 27
Spittal. Dum —4A 110
Spittal. E Lot —2A 130
Spittal. High —3D 168
Spittal. Nmbd —4G 131
Spittal. Pemb —2D 43
Spittalfield. Per —4A 144
Spittal of Glenmuick. Aber —5H 151
Spittal of Glenshee. Per —1A 144
Spittal-on-Rule. Scot —3H 119
Spixworth. Norf —4E 79
Splatt. Corn —4C 10
Spofforth. N Yor —4F 99
Spondon. Dby C —2B 74
Spon End. W Mid —3H 61
Spooner Row. Norf —1C 66
Sporle. Norf —4H 77
Spott. E Lot —2C 130
Spratton. Nptn —3E 62
Spreakley. Surr —2G 25
Spreyton. Devn —3H 11
Spridlington. Linc —2H 87
Springburn. Glas —3H 127
Springfield. Dum —3E 113
Springfield. Fife —2F 137
Springfield. High —2A 158
Springfield. W Mid —2E 61
Springhill. Staf —5D 73
Springholm. Dum —3F 111
Springside. N Ayr —1C 116
Springthorpe. Linc —2F 87
Spring Vale. IOW —3E 16
Spring Valley. IOM —4C 108
Springwell. Tyne —4F 115
Sproatley. E Yor —1E 95
Sproston Green. Ches —4B 84
Sprotbrough. S Yor —4F 93
Sproughton. Suff —1E 54
Sprouston. Scot —1B 120
Sprowston. Norf —4E 79
Sproxton. Leics —3F 75
Sproxton. N Yor —1A 100
Sprunston. Cumb —5F 113
Spurstow. Ches —5H 83
Squires Gate. Lanc —1B 90
Sraid Ruadh. Arg —4A 138
Srannda. W Isl —9C 171
Sronphadruig Lodge. Per —1E 142
Sruth Mor. W Isl —2E 170
Stableford. Shrp —1B 60
Stackhouse. N Yor —3H 97
Stackpole. Pemb —5D 43
Stackpole Elidor. Pemb —5D 43
Stacksford. Norf —1C 66
Stacksteads. Lanc —2G 91
Staddiscombe. Plym —3B 8
Staddlethorpe. E Yor —2B 94
Staddon. Devn —2D 10
Staden. Derbs —3E 85
Stadhampton. Oxon —2E 36
Stadhlaigearraidh. W Isl —5C 170
Staffield. Cumb —5G 113
Staffin. High —2D 155
Stafford. Staf —3D 72
Stafford Park. Telf —5B 72
Stagden Cross. Essx —4G 53
Stagsden. Beds —1H 51
Stag's Head. Devn —4G 19
Stainburn. Cumb —2B 102
Stainburn. N Yor —5E 99
Stainby. Linc —3G 75
Staincliffe. W Yor —2C 92
Staincross. S Yor —3D 92
Staindrop. Dur —2E 105
Staines. Surr —3B 38
Stainfield. Linc —3H 75 (nr. Bourne)
Stainfield. Linc —3A 88 (nr. Lincoln)
Stainforth. N Yor —3H 97
Stainforth. S Yor —3G 93
Staining. Lanc —1B 90
Stainland. W Yor —3A 92
Stainsacre. N Yor —4G 107
Stainton. Cumb —4E 113 (nr. Carlisle)
Stainton. Cumb —1E 97 (nr. Kendal)
Stainton. Cumb —2F 103 (nr. Penrith)
Stainton. Dur —3D 104
Stainton. Midd —3B 106
Stainton. N Yor —5E 105
Stainton. S Yor —1C 86
Stainton by Langworth. Linc —3H 87
Staintondale. N Yor —5G 107
Stainton le Vale. Linc —1A 88
Stainton with Adgarley. Cumb —2B 96
Stair. Cumb —2D 102
Stair. E Ayr —2D 116
Staithes. N Yor —3E 107
Stakeford. Nmbd —1F 115
Stake Pool. Lanc —5D 96
Stakes. Hants —2E 17
Stalbridge. Dors —1C 14
Stalbridge Weston. Dors —1C 14
Stalham. Norf —3F 79
Stalham Green. Norf —3F 79
Stalisfield Green. Kent —5D 40
Stallen. Dors —1B 14
Stallingborough. NE Lin —3F 95
Stalling Busk. N Yor —1B 98
Stallington. Staf —1D 72
Stalmine. Lanc —5C 96
Stalybridge. G Man —1D 84
Stambourne. Essx —2H 53
Stamford. Linc —5H 75
Stamford. Nmbd —3G 121
Stamford Bridge. Ches —4G 83
Stamford Bridge. E Yor —4B 100
Stamfordham. Nmbd —2D 115
Stamperland. E Ren —4G 127
Stanah. Lanc —5C 96
Stanborough. Herts —4C 52
Stanbridge. Beds —3H 51
Stanbridge. Dors —2F 15
Stanbury. W Yor —1A 92
Stand. N Lan —3A 128
Standburn. Falk —2C 128
Standeford. Staf —5D 72
Standen. Kent —1C 28
Standen Street. Kent —2C 28
Standerwick. Som —1D 22
Standford. Hants —3G 25
Standford Bridge. Telf —3B 72
Standingstone. Cumb —1B 102 (nr. Maryport)
Standingstone. Cumb —5D 112 (nr. Wigton)
Standish. Glos —5D 48
Standish. G Man —3D 90
Standish Lower Ground. G Man —4D 90
Standlake. Oxon —5C 50
Standon. Hants —4C 24
Standon. Herts —3D 53
Standon. Staf —2C 72
Standon Green End. Herts —4D 52
Standwell Green. Suff —3D 66
Stane. N Lan —3B 128
Stanecastle. N Ayr —1C 116
Stanfield. Norf —3B 78
Stanford. Beds —1B 52
Stanford. Kent —2F 29
Stanford Bishop. Here —5A 60
Stanford Bridge. Worc —4B 60
Stanford Dingley. W Ber —4D 36
Stanford in the Vale. Oxon —2B 36
Stanford-le-Hope. Thur —2A 40
Stanford on Avon. Nptn —3C 62
Stanford on Soar. Notts —3C 74
Stanford on Teme. Worc —4B 60
Stanford Rivers. Essx —5F 53
Stanfree. Derbs —3B 86
Stanghow. Red C —3D 107
Stanground. Pet —1B 64
Stanhoe. Norf —2H 77
Stanhope. Dur —1C 104
Stanhope. Scot —1D 118
Stanion. Nptn —2G 63
Stanley. Derbs —1B 74
Stanley. Dur —4E 115
Stanley. Per —5A 144
Stanley. Shrp —2B 60
Stanley. Staf —5D 84
Stanley. W Yor —2D 93
Stanley Common. Derbs —1B 74
Stanley Crook. Dur —1E 105
Stanley Hill. Here —1B 48
Stanlow. Ches —3G 83
Stanmer. Brig —5E 27
Stanmore. G Lon —1C 38
Stanmore. Hants —4C 24
Stanmore. W Ber —4C 36
Stannersburn. Nmbd —1A 114
Stanningfield. Suff —5A 66
Stannington. Nmbd —2F 115
Stannington. S Yor —2H 85
Stansbatch. Here —4F 59
Stansfield. Suff —5G 65
Stanshope. Staf —5F 85
Stanstead. Suff —1B 54
Stanstead Abbotts. Herts —4D 53
Stansted. Kent —4H 39
Stansted (London) Airport. Essx —3F 53
Stansted Mountfitchet. Essx —3F 53
Stanthorne. Ches —4A 84
Stanton. Derbs —4G 73
Stanton. Glos —2F 49
Stanton. Nmbd —5F 121
Stanton. Staf —1F 73
Stanton. Suff —3B 66
Stanton by Bridge. Derbs —3A 74
Stanton by Dale. Derbs —2B 74
Stanton Chare. Suff —3B 66
Stanton Drew. Bath —5A 34
Stanton Fitzwarren. Swin —2G 35
Stanton Harcourt. Oxon —5C 50
Stanton Hill. Notts —4B 86
Stanton in Peak. Derbs —4G 85
Stanton Lacy. Shrp —3G 59
Stanton Long. Shrp —1H 59
Stanton-on-the-Wolds. Notts —2D 74
Stanton Prior. Bath —5B 34
Stanton St Bernard. Wilts —5F 35
Stanton St John. Oxon —5D 50
Stanton St Quintin. Wilts —4E 35
Stanton Street. Suff —4B 66
Stanton under Bardon. Leics —4B 74
Stanton upon Hine Heath. Shrp —3H 71
Stanton Wick. Bath —5B 34
Stanwardine in the Fields. Shrp —3G 71
Stanwardine in the Wood. Shrp —3G 71
Stanway. Essx —3C 54
Stanway. Glos —2F 49
Stanwell. Surr —3B 38
Stanwell Moor. Surr —3B 38
Stanwick. Nptn —3G 63
Stanydale. Shet —6D 173
Staoinebrig. W Isl —5C 170
Stape. N Yor —5E 107
Stapehill. Dors —2F 15
Stapeley. Ches —1A 72
Stapenhill. Staf —3G 73
Staple. Kent —5G 41
Staple Cross. Devn —4D 20
Staplecross. E Sus —3B 28
Staplefield. W Sus —3D 27
Staple Fitzpaine. Som —1F 13
Stapleford. Cambs —5D 64
Stapleford. Herts —4D 52
Stapleford. Leics —4F 75
Stapleford. Linc —5F 87
Stapleford. Notts —2B 74
Stapleford. Wilts —3F 23
Stapleford Abbotts. Essx —1G 39
Stapleford Tawney. Essx —1G 39
Staplegrove. Som —4F 21
Staplehay. Som —4F 21
Staple Hill.. S Glo —4B 34
Staplehurst. Kent —1B 28
Staplers. IOW —4D 16
Stapleton. Bris —4B 34
Stapleton. Cumb —2G 113
Stapleton. Here —4F 59
Stapleton. Leics —1B 62
Stapleton. N Yor —3F 105
Stapleton. Shrp —5G 71
Stapleton. Som —4H 21
Stapley. Som —1E 13
Staploe. Beds —4A 64
Staplow. Here —1B 48
Star. Fife —3F 137
Star. Pemb —1G 43
Starbeck. N Yor —4F 99
Starbotton. N Yor —2B 98
Starcross. Devn —4C 12
Stareton. Warw —3H 61
Starkholmes. Derbs —5H 85
Starkigarth. Shet —9F 173
Starling. G Man —3F 91
Starling's Green. Essx —2E 53
Starston. Norf —2E 67
Start. Devn —4E 9
Startforth. Dur —3D 104
Start Hill. Essx —3F 53
Startley. Wilts —3E 35
Stathe. Som —4G 21
Stathern. Leics —2E 75
Station Town. Dur —1B 106
Staughton Green. Cambs —4A 64
Staughton Highway. Cambs —4A 64
Staunton. Glos —3C 48 (nr. Cheltenham)
Staunton. Glos —4A 48 (nr. Monmouth)
Staunton in the Vale. Notts —1F 75
Staunton on Arrow. Here —4F 59
Staunton on Wye. Here —1G 47
Staveley. Cumb —5F 103
Staveley. Derbs —3B 86
Staveley. N Yor —3F 99
Staveley-in-Cartmel. Cumb —1C 96
Staverton. Devn —2D 9
Staverton. Glos —3D 49
Staverton. Nptn —4C 62
Staverton. Wilts —5D 34
Stawell. Som —3G 21
Stawley. Som —4D 20
Staxigoe. High —3F 169
Staxton. N Yor —2E 101
Staylittle. Powy —1A 58
Staynall. Lanc —5C 96
Staythorpe. Notts —5E 87
Stean. N Yor —2C 98
Stearsby. N Yor —2A 100
Steart. Som —2F 21
Stebbing. Essx —3G 53
Stebbing Green. Essx —3G 53
Stedham. W Sus —4G 25
Steel. Nmbd —4C 114
Steel Cross. E Sus —2G 27
Steelend. Fife —4C 136
Steele Road. Scot —5H 119
Steel Heath. Shrp —2H 71
Steen's Bridge. Here —5H 59
Steep. Hants —4F 25
Steep Lane. W Yor —2A 92
Steeple. Dors —4E 15
Steeple. Essx —5C 54
Steeple Ashton. Wilts —1E 23
Steeple Aston. Oxon —3C 50
Steeple Barton. Oxon —3C 50
Steeple Bumpstead. Essx —1G 53
Steeple Claydon. Buck —3E 51
Steeple Gidding. Cambs —2A 64
Steeple Langford. Wilts —3F 23
Steeple Morden. Cambs —1C 52
Steeton. W Yor —5C 98
Stein. High —3B 154
Steinmanhill. Aber —4E 161
Stelling Minnis. Kent —1F 29
Stembridge. Som —4H 21
Stemster. High —2D 169 (nr. Halkirk)
Stemster. High —2C 168 (nr. Westfield)
Stenalees. Corn —3E 6
Stenhill. Devn —1D 12
Stenhouse. Edin —2F 129
Stenhousemuir. Falk —1B 128
Stenigot. Linc —2B 88
Stenscholl. High —2D 155
Stenso. Orkn —5C 172
Stenson. Derbs —3H 73
Stenton. E Lot —2C 130
Stenwith. Linc —2F 75
Steornabhagh. W Isl —4G 171
Stepaside. Pemb —4F 43
Stepford. Dum —1F 111
Stepney. G Lon —2E 39
Steppingley. Beds —2A 52
Stepps. Glas —3H 127
Sterndale Moor. Derbs —4F 85
Sternfield. Suff —4F 67
Stert. Wilts —1F 23
Stetchworth. Cambs —5F 65
Stevenage. Herts —3C 52
Stevenston. N Ayr —5D 126
Steventon. Hants —2D 24
Steventon. Oxon —2C 36
Stevington. Beds —5G 63
Stevington End. Cambs —1F 53
Stewartby. Beds —1A 52
Stewarton. Arg —4A 122
Stewarton. E Ayr —5F 127
Stewkley. Buck —3G 51
Stewkley Dean. Buck —3G 51
Stewley. Som —1G 13
Stewton. Linc —2C 88
Steyning. W Sus —4C 26
Steynton. Pemb —4D 42
Stibb. Corn —1C 10
Stibbard. Norf —3B 78
Stibb Cross. Devn —1E 11
Stibb Green. Wilts —5H 35
Stibbington. Pet —1H 63
Stichill. Scot —1B 120
Sticker. Corn —3D 6
Stickford. Linc —4C 88
Sticklepath. Devn —3G 11
Sticklinch. Som —3A 22
Stickling Green. Essx —2E 53
Stickney. Linc —5C 88
Stiffkey. Norf —1B 78
Stifford's Bridge. Here —1C 48
Stileway. Som —2H 21
Stillingfleet. N Yor —5H 99
Stillington. N Yor —3H 99
Stillington. Stoc T —2A 106
Stilton. Cambs —2A 64
Stinchcombe. Glos —2C 34
Stinsford. Dors —3C 14
Stiperstones. Shrp —5F 71
Stirchley. Telf —5B 72
Stirchley. W Mid —2E 61
Stirling. Aber —4H 161
Stirling. Stir —4G 135
Stirton. N Yor —4B 98
Stisted. Essx —3A 54
Stitchcombe. Wilts —5H 35
Stithians. Corn —5B 6
Stittenham. High —1A 158
Stivichall. W Mid —3H 61
Stixwould. Linc —4A 88
Stoak. Ches —3G 83
Stobo. Scot —1D 118
Stobo Castle. Scot —1D 118
Stoborough. Dors —4E 15
Stobs Castle. Scot —4H 119
Stobswood. Nmbd —5G 121
Stock. Essx —1A 40
Stockbridge. Hants —3B 24
Stockbridge. W Yor —5C 98
Stockbury. Kent —4C 40
Stockcross. W Ber —5C 36
Stockdalewath. Cumb —5E 113
Stocker's Head. Kent —5D 40
Stockerston. Leics —1F 63
Stock Green. Worc —5D 61
Stocking. Here —2B 48
Stockingford. Warw —1H 61
Stocking Green. Essx —2F 53
Stocking Pelham. Herts —3E 53
Stockland. Devn —2F 13
Stockland Bristol. Som —2F 21
Stockleigh English. Devn —2B 12
Stockleigh Pomeroy. Devn —2B 12
Stockley. Wilts —5F 35
Stocklinch. Som —1G 13
Stockport. G Man —2D 84
Stocksbridge. S Yor —1G 85
Stocksfield. Nmbd —3D 114
Stocks, The. Kent —3D 28
Stockstreet. Essx —3B 54
Stockton. Here —4H 59
Stockton. Norf —1F 67
Stockton. Shrp —1B 60 (nr. Bridgnorth)
Stockton. Shrp —5E 71 (nr. Chirbury)
Stockton. Telf —4B 72
Stockton. Warw —4B 62
Stockton. Wilts —3E 23
Stockton Brook. Staf —5D 84
Stockton Cross. Here —4H 59
Stockton Heath. Warr —2A 84
Stockton-on-Tees. Stoc T —3B 106
Stockton on Teme. Worc —4B 60
Stockton-on-the-Forest. York —4A 100
Stockwell Heath. Staf —3E 73
Stockwood. Bris —5B 34
Stock Wood. Worc —5E 61
Stodmarsh. Kent —4G 41
Stody. Norf —2C 78
Stoer. High —1E 163
Stoford. Som —1A 14
Stoford. Wilts —3F 23
Stogumber. Som —3D 20
Stogursey. Som —2F 21
Stoke. Devn —4C 18
Stoke. Hants —1C 24 (nr. Andover)
Stoke. Hants —2F 17 (nr. South Hayling)
Stoke. Medw —3C 40
Stoke. W Mid —3A 62
Stoke Abbott. Dors —2H 13
Stoke Albany. Nptn —2F 63
Stoke Ash. Suff —3D 66
Stoke Bardolph. Notts —1D 74
Stoke Bliss. Worc —4A 60
Stoke Bruerne. Nptn —1F 51
Stoke by Clare. Suff —1H 53
Stoke-by-Nayland. Suff —2C 54
Stoke Canon. Devn —3C 12
Stoke Charity. Hants —3C 24
Stoke Climsland. Corn —5D 10
Stoke Cross. Here —5A 60
Stoke D'Abernon. Surr —5C 38
Stoke Doyle. Nptn —2H 63
Stoke Dry. Rut —1F 63
Stoke Edith. Here —1B 48
Stoke Farthing. Wilts —4F 23
Stoke Ferry. Norf —1G 65
Stoke Fleming. Devn —4E 9
Stokeford. Dors —4D 14
Stoke Gabriel. Devn —3E 9
Stoke Gifford. S Glo —4B 34
Stoke Golding. Leics —1A 62
Stoke Goldington. Mil —1G 51
Stokeham. Notts —3E 87
Stoke Hammond. Buck —3G 51
Stoke Heath. Shrp —3A 72
Stoke Holy Cross. Norf —5E 79
Stokeinteignhead. Devn —5C 12
Stoke Lacy. Here —1B 48
Stoke Lyne. Oxon —3D 50
Stoke Mandeville. Buck —4G 51
Stokenchurch. Buck —2F 37
Stoke Newington. G Lon —2E 39
Stokenham. Devn —4E 9
Stoke on Tern. Shrp —3A 72
Stoke-on-Trent. Stoke —1C 72
Stoke Orchard. Glos —3E 49
Stoke Pero. Som —2B 20
Stoke Poges. Buck —2A 38
Stoke Prior. Here —5H 59
Stoke Prior. Worc —4D 60
Stoke Rivers. Devn —3G 19
Stoke Rochford. Linc —3G 75
Stoke Row. Oxon —3E 37
Stoke St Gregory. Som —4G 21
Stoke St Mary. Som —4F 21
Stoke St Michael. Som —2B 22
Stoke St Milborough. Shrp —2H 59
Stokesay. Shrp —2G 59
Stokesby. Norf —4G 79
Stokesley. N Yor —4C 106
Stoke sub Hamdon. Som —1H 13
Stoke Talmage. Oxon —2E 37
Stoke Trister. Som —4C 22
Stolford. Som —2F 21
Stondon Massey. Essx —5F 53
Stone. Buck —4F 51
Stone. Glos —2B 34
Stone. Kent —3G 39
Stone. Som —3A 22
Stone. Staf —2D 72
Stone. Worc —3C 60
Stonea. Cambs —1D 64
Stoneacton. Shrp —1H 59
Stone Allerton. Som —1H 21
Ston Easton. Som —1B 22
Stonebridge. N Som —5G 33
Stonebridge. Som —2C 22
Stonebridge. Surr —1C 26
Stone Bridge Corner. Pet —5B 76
Stonebroom. Derbs —5B 86
Stonebyres. S Lan —5B 128
Stone Chair. W Yor —2B 92
Stone Cross. E Sus —5H 27
Stone Cross. Kent —2G 27
Stone-edge-Batch. N Som —4H 33
Stoneferry. Hull —1D 94
Stonefield. Arg —5D 140
Stonefield. S Lan —4H 127
Stonegate. E Sus —3A 28
Stonegate. N Yor —4E 107

Tunstall—Waddingham

Tunstall. E Yor —1G 95
Tunstall. Kent —4C 40
Tunstall. Lanc —2F 97
Tunstall. Norf —5G 79
Tunstall. N Yor —5F 105
Tunstall. Staf —3B 72
Tunstall. Stoke —5C 84
Tunstall. Suff —5F 67
Tunstall. Tyne —4G 115
Tunstead. Derbs —3F 85
Tunstead. Norf —3E 79
Tunstead Milton. Derbs —2E 85
Tunworth. Hants —2E 25
Tupsley. Here —1A 48
Tupton. Derbs —4A 86
Turfholm. S Lan —1H 117
Turfmoor. Devn —2F 13
Turgis Green. Hants —1E 25
Turkdean. Glos —4G 49
Turkey Island. Hants —1D 16
Tur Langton. Leics —1E 62
Turleigh. Wilts —5D 34
Turlin Moor. Dors —3E 15
Turnant. Here —3G 47
Turnastone. Here —2G 47
Turnberry. S Ayr —4B 116
Turnchapel. Plym —3A 8
Turnditch. Derbs —1G 73
Turners Hill. W Sus —2E 27
Turners Puddle. Dors —3D 14
Turnford. Herts —5D 52
Turnhouse. Edin —2E 129
Turnworth. Dors —2D 14
Turriff. Aber —4E 161
Tursdale. Dur —1A 106
Turton Bottoms. Bkbn —3F 91
Turtory. Mor —4C 160
Turves Green. W Mid —3E 61
Turvey. Beds —5G 63
Turville. Buck —2F 37
Turville Heath. Buck —2F 37
Turweston. Buck —2E 50
Tushielaw. Scot —3F 119
Tutbury. Staf —3G 73
Tutnall. Worc —3D 61
Tutsbill. Glos —2A 34
Tuttington. Norf —3E 79
Tutts Clump. W Ber —4D 36
Tutwell. Corn —5D 11
Tuxford. Notts —3E 87
Twatt. Orkn —5B 172
Twatt. Shet —6E 173
Twechar. E Dun —2A 128
Tweedale. Telf —5A 72
Tweedmouth. Nmbd —4F 131
Tweedsmuir. Scot —2C 118
Twelveheads. Corn —4B 6
Twemlow Green. Ches —4B 84
Twenty. Linc —3A 76
Twerton. Bath —5C 34
Twickenham. G Lon —3C 38
Twigworth. Glos —3D 48
Twineham. W Sus —3D 26
Twinhoe. Bath —1C 22
Twinstead. Essx —2B 54
Twinstead Green. Essx —2B 54
Twiss Green. Warr —1A 84
Twiston. Lanc —5H 97
Twitchen. Devn —3A 20
Twitchen. Shrp —3F 59
Two Bridges. Devn —5G 11
Two Bridges. Glos —5B 48
Two Dales. Derbs —4G 85
Two Gates. Staf —5G 73
Two Mile Oak Cross. Devn —2E 9
Twycross. Leics —5H 73
Twyford. Buck —3E 51
Twyford. Derbs —3H 73
Twyford. Dors —1D 14
Twyford. Hants —4C 24
Twyford. Leics —4E 75
Twyford. Norf —3C 78
Twyford. Wok —4F 37
Twyford Common. Here —2A 48
Twyncarno. Cphy —5E 46
Twynholm. Dum —4D 110
Twyning. Glos —2D 49
Twyning Green. Glos —2E 49
Twynllanan. Carm —3A 46
Twynmynydd. Carm —4G 45
Twyn-y-Sheriff. Mon —5H 47
Twywell. Nptn —3G 63
Tyberton. Here —2G 47
Tyburn. W Mid —1F 61
Tyby. Norf —3C 78
Tycroes. Carm —4G 45
Tycrwyn. Powy —4D 70
Tyddewi. Pemb —2B 42
Tydd Gote. Linc —4D 76
Tydd St Giles. Cambs —4D 76
Tydd St Mary. Linc —4D 76
Tye. Hants —2F 17
Tye Green. Essx —3F 53
(nr. Bishop's Stortford)
Tye Green. Essx —3A 54
(nr. Braintree)
Tye Green. Essx —2F 53
(nr. Saffron Walden)
Tyersal. W Yor —1B 92
Ty Issa. Powy —3D 70
Tyldesley. G Man —4E 91
Tyle. Carm —3G 45
Tyler Hill. Kent —4F 41
Tylers Green. Buck —2G 37
Tyler's Green. Essx —5F 53
Tylorstown. Rhon —2D 32
Tylwch. Powy —2B 58
Ty-nant. Cnwy —1B 70
Tyndrum. Stir —5H 141
Tyneham. Dors —4D 15
Tynehead. Midl —4G 129
Tynemouth. Tyne —3G 115
Tyneside. Tyne —3F 115
Tyne Tunnel. Tyne —3G 115
Tynewydd. Rhon —2C 32
Tyninghame. E Lot —2C 130
Tynron. Dum —5H 117
Ty'n-y-bryn. Rhon —3D 32
Tyn-y-celyn. Wrex —2D 70
Tyn-y-cwm. Swan —5G 45
Tyn-y-ffridd. Powy —2D 70
Tynygongl. IOA —2E 81
Tynygraig. Cdgn —4F 57
Tyn-y-groes. Cnwy —3G 81
Ty'n-yr-eithin. Cdgn —4F 57
Tyn-y-rhyd. Powy —4C 70
Tyn-y-wern. Powy —3C 70
Tyringham. Mil —1G 51
Tythecott. Devn —1E 11
Tythegston. B'End —4B 32
Tytherington. Ches —3D 84
Tytherington. Som —2C 22
Tytherington. S Glo —3B 34
Tytherington. Wilts —2E 23
Tytherleigh. Devn —2G 13
Tywardreath. Corn —3E 7
Tywardreath Highway. Corn —3E 7
Tywyn. Cnwy —3G 81
Tywyn. Gwyn —5E 69

Uachdar. W Isl —3D 170
Uags. High —5G 155
Ubbeston Green. Suff —3F 67
Ubley. Bath —1A 22
Uckerby. N Yor —4F 105
Uckfield. E Sus —3F 27
Uckinghall. Worc —2D 48
Uckington. Glos —3E 49
Uckington. Shrp —5H 71
Uddingston. S Lan —3H 127
Uddington. S Lan —1A 118
Udimore. E Sus —4C 28
Udny Green. Aber —1F 153
Udny Station. Aber —1G 153
Udston. S Lan —4A 128
Udstonhead. S Lan —5A 128
Uffcott. Swin —4G 35
Uffculme. Devn —1D 12
Uffington. Linc —5H 75
Uffington. Oxon —3B 36
Uffington. Shrp —4H 71
Ufford. Pet —5H 75
Ufford. Suff —5E 67
Ufton. Warw —4A 62
Ufton Nervet. W Ber —5E 37
Ugadale. Arg —3B 122
Ugborough. Devn —3C 8
Ugford. Wilts —3F 23
Uggeshall. Suff —3G 67
Ugglebarnby. N Yor —4F 107
Ugley. Essx —3F 53
Ugley Green. Essx —3F 53
Ugthorpe. N Yor —3E 107
Uidh. W Isl —9B 170
Uig. Arg —3C 138
Uig. High —3A 154
(nr. Dunvegan)
Uig. High —2C 154
(nr. Glen Uig)
Uigshader. High —4D 154
Uisken. Arg —1A 132
Ulbster. High —4F 169
Ulcat Row. Cumb —2F 103
Ulceby. Linc —3D 88
Ulceby. N Lin —3E 94
Ulceby Skitter. N Lin —3E 94
Ulcombe. Kent —1C 28
Uldale. Cumb —1D 102
Uley. Glos —2C 34
Ulgham. Nmbd —5G 121
Ullapool. High —4F 163
Ullenhall. Warw —4F 61
Ulleskelf. N Yor —1F 93
Ullesthorpe. Leics —2C 62
Ulley. S Yor —2B 86
Ullingswick. Here —1A 48
Ullinish. High —5C 154
Ullock. Cumb —2B 102
Ulpha. Cumb —5D 102
Ulrome. E Yor —4F 101
Ulsta. Shet —3F 173
Ulting. Essx —5B 54
Ulva House. Arg —5F 139
Ulverston. Cumb —2B 96
Ulwell. Dors —4F 15
Umberleigh. Devn —4G 19
Unapool. High —5C 166
Underbarrow. Cumb —5F 103
Undercliffe. W Yor —1B 92
Underdale. Shrp —4H 71
Underhoull. Shet —1G 173
Underriver. Kent —5G 39
Under Tofts. S Yor —2H 85
Underton. Shrp —1A 60
Underwood. Notts —5B 86
Underwood. Plym —3B 8
Undley. Suff —2F 65
Undy. Mon —3H 33
Union Mills. IOM —4C 108
Union Street. E Sus —2B 28
Unst Airport. Shet —1H 173
Unstone. Derbs —3A 86
Unstone Green. Derbs —3A 86
Unthank. Cumb —5E 113
(nr. Carlisle)
Unthank. Cumb —5H 113
(nr. Gamblesby)
Unthank. Cumb —1F 103
(nr. Penrith)
Unthank End. Cumb —1F 103
Upavon. Wilts —1G 23
Up Cerne. Dors —2B 14
Upchurch. Kent —4C 40
Upcott. Devn —2F 11
Upcott. Here —5F 59
Upend. Cambs —5G 65
Up Exe. Devn —2C 12
Upgate. Norf —4D 78
Upgate Street. Norf —1C 66
Uphall. W Lot —2D 128
Uphall Station. W Lot —2D 128
Upham. Devn —2B 12
Upham. Hants —4D 24
Uphampton. Here —4F 59
Uphampton. Worc —4C 60
Up Hatherley. Glos —3E 49
Uphill. N Som —1G 21
Up Holland. Lanc —4D 90
Uplawmoor. E Ren —4F 127
Upleadon. Glos —3C 48
Upleatham. Red C —3D 106
Uplees. Kent —4D 40
Uploders. Dors —3A 14
Uplowman. Devn —1D 12
Uplyme. Devn —3G 13
Up Marden. W Sus —1F 17
Upminster. G Lon —2G 39
Up Nately. Hants —1E 25
Upottery. Devn —2F 13
Uppat. High —3F 165
Upper Affcot. Shrp —2G 59
Upper Arley. Worc —2B 60
Upper Armley. W Yor —1C 92
Upper Arncott. Oxon —4E 50
Upper Astrop. Nptn —2D 50
Upper Badcall. High —4B 166
Upper Bangor. Gwyn —3E 81
Upper Basildon. W Ber —4D 36
Upper Batley. W Yor —2C 92
Upper Beeding. W Sus —4C 26
Upper Benefield. Nptn —2G 63
Upper Bentley. Worc —4D 61
Upper Bighouse. High —3A 168
Upper Boddam. Aber —5D 160
Upper Boddington. Nptn —5B 62
Upper Booth. Derbs —2F 85
Upper Borth. Cdgn —2F 57
Upper Boyndlie. Aber —2G 161
Upper Brailes. Warw —2B 50
Upper Breakish. High —1E 147
Upper Breinton. Here —1H 47
Upper Broadheath. Worc —5C 60
Upper Broughton. Notts —3D 74
Upper Brynamman. Carm —4H 45
Upper Bucklebury. W Ber —5D 36
Upper Bullington. Hants —2C 24
Upper Burgate. Hants —1G 15
Upper Caldecote. Beds —1B 52
Upper Canterton. Hants —1A 16
Upper Catesby. Nptn —5C 62
Upper Chapel. Powy —1D 46
Upper Cheddon. Som —4F 21
Upper Chicksgrove. Wilts —4E 23
Upper Church Village. Rhon —3D 32
Upper Chute. Wilts —1A 24
Upper Clatford. Hants —2B 24
Upper Coberley. Glos —4E 49
Upper Coedcae. Torf —5F 47
Upper Cokeham. W Sus —5C 26
Upper Common. Hants —2E 25
Upper Cound. Shrp —5H 71
Upper Cudworth. S Yor —4D 93
Upper Cumberworth. W Yor —4C 92
Upper Cuttlehill. Aber —4B 160
Upper Cwmbran. Torf —2F 33
Upper Dallachy. Mor —2A 160
Upper Dean. Beds —4H 63
Upper Dean. Devn —2D 8
Upper Denby. W Yor —4C 92
Upper Derraid. High —5E 159
Upper Diabaig. High —2H 155
Upper Dicker. E Sus —5G 27
Upper Dinchope. Shrp —2G 59
Upper Dochcarty. High —2H 157
Upper Dounreay. High —2B 168
Upper Dovercourt. Essx —2F 55
Upper Dunsforth. N Yor —3G 99
Upper Dunsley. Herts —4H 51
Upper Eastern Green. W Mid —3G 61
Upper Elkstone. Staf —5E 85
Upper Ellastone. Staf —1F 73
Upper End. Derbs —3E 85
Upper Enham. Hants —2B 24
Upper Farringdon. Hants —3F 25
Upper Framilode. Glos —4C 48
Upper Froyle. Hants —2F 25
Upper Gills. High —1F 169
Upper Glenfintaig. High —5E 149
Upper Godney. Som —2H 21
Upper Gravenhurst. Beds —2B 52
Upper Green. Essx —2E 53
Upper Green. W Ber —5B 36
Upper Green. W Yor —2C 92
Upper Grove Common. Here —3A 48
Upper Hackney. Derbs —4G 85
Upper Hale. Surr —2G 25
Upper Halliford. Surr —4B 38
Upper Halling. Medw —4A 40
Upper Hambleton. Rut —5G 75
Upper Hardwick. Here —5G 59
Upper Hartfield. E Sus —2F 27
Upper Haugh. S Yor —1B 86
Upper Hayton. Shrp —2H 59
Upper Heath. Shrp —2H 59
Upper Hellesdon. Norf —4E 79
Upper Helmsley. N Yor —4A 100
Upper Hengoed. Shrp —2E 71
Upper Hergest. Here —5E 59
Upper Heyford. Nptn —5D 62
Upper Heyford. Oxon —3C 50
Upper Hill. Here —5G 59
Upper Hindhope. Scot —4B 120
Upper Hopton. W Yor —3B 92
Upper Horsebridge. E Sus —4C 28
Upper Howsell. Worc —1C 48
Upper Hulme. Staf —4E 85
Upper Inglesham. Swin —2H 35
Upper Kilcott. S Glo —3C 34
Upper Killay. Swan —3E 31
Upper Kirkton. Aber —5E 161
Upper Kirkton. N Ayr —4C 126
Upper Knockando. Mor —4F 159
Upper Knockchoilum. High —2G 149
Upper Lambourn. W Ber —3B 36
Upper Langford. N Som —1H 21
Upper Langwith. Derbs —4C 86
Upper Largo. Fife —3G 137
Upper Latheron. High —5D 169
Upper Layham. Suff —1D 54
Upper Leigh. Staf —2E 73
Upper Lenie. High —1H 149
Upper Lochton. Aber —4D 152
Upper Longdon. Staf —4E 73
Upper Longwood. Shrp —5A 72
Upper Lybster. High —5E 169
Upper Lydbrook. Glos —4B 48
Upper Lye. Here —4F 59
Upper Maes-coed. Here —2G 47
Uppermill. G Man —4H 91
Upper Millichope. Shrp —2H 59
Upper Milovaig. High —4A 154
Upper Minety. Wilts —2F 35
Upper Mitton. Worc —3C 60
Upper Nash. Pemb —4E 43
Upper Neepaback. Shet —3G 173
Upper Netchwood. Shrp —1A 60
Upper Nobut. Staf —2E 73
Upper North Dean. Buck —2G 37
Upper Norwood. W Sus —4A 26
Upper Nyland. Dors —4C 22
Upper Oddington. Glos —3H 49
Upper Ollach. High —5E 155
Upper Outwoods. Staf —3G 73
Upper Padley. Derbs —3G 85
Upper Pennington. Hants —3B 16
Upper Poppleton. York —4H 99
Upper Quinton. Warw —1G 49
Upper Rochford. Worc —4A 60
Upper Rusko. Dum —3C 110
Upper Sandaig. High —2F 147
Upper Sanday. Orkn —7E 172
Upper Sapey. Here —4A 60
Upper Seagry. Wilts —3E 35
Upper Shelton. Beds —1H 51
Upper Sheringham. Norf —1D 78
Upper Skelmorlie. N Ayr —3C 126
Upper Slaughter. Glos —3G 49
Upper Sonachan. Arg —1H 133
Upper Soudley. Glos —4B 48
Upper Staploe. Beds —5A 64
Upper Stoke. Norf —5E 79
Upper Stondon. Beds —2B 52
Upper Stowe. Nptn —5D 62
Upper Street. Hants —1G 15
Upper Street. Norf —4F 79
(nr. Horning)
Upper Street. Norf —4F 79
(nr. Hoveton)
Upper Street. Suff —2E 55
Upper Strensham. Worc —2E 49
Upper Studley. Wilts —1D 22
Upper Sundon. Beds —3A 52
Upper Swell. Glos —3G 49
Upper Tankersley. S Yor —1H 85
Upper Tean. Staf —2E 73
Upperthong. W Yor —4B 92
Upperthorpe. N Lin —4A 94
Upper Thurnham. Lanc —4D 96
Upper Tillyrie. Per —3D 136
Upperton. W Sus —3A 26
Upper Tooting. G Lon —3D 38
Uppertown. Derbs —4H 85
(nr. Ashover)
Upper Town. Derbs —5G 85
(nr. Bonsall)
Upper Town. Derbs —5G 85
(nr. Hognaston)
Upper Town. Here —1A 48
Uppertown. High —1F 169
Upper Town. N Som —5A 34
Uppertown. Nmbd —2B 114
Uppertown. Orkn —8D 172
Upper Tysoe. Warw —1B 50
Upper Upham. Wilts —4H 35
Upper Upnor. Medw —3B 40
Upper Urquhart. Fife —3D 136
Upper Wardington. Oxon —1C 50
Upper Weald. Mil —2F 51
Upper Weedon. Nptn —5D 62
Upper Wellingham. E Sus —4F 27
Upper Whiston. S Yor —2B 86
Upper Wield. Hants —3E 25
Upper Winchendon. Buck —4F 51
Upperwood. Derbs —5G 85
Upper Woodford. Wilts —3G 23
Upper Wootton. Hants —1D 24
Upper Wraxall. Wilts —4D 34
Upper Wyche. Here —1C 48
Uppincott. Devn —2B 12
Uppingham. Rut —1F 63
Uppington. Shrp —5H 71
Upsall. N Yor —1G 99
Upsettlington. Scot —5E 131
Upshire. Essx —5E 53
Up Somborne. Hants —3B 24
Upstreet. Kent —4G 41
Up Sydling. Dors —2B 14
Upthorpe. Suff —3B 66
Upton. Buck —4F 51
Upton. Cambs —3A 64
Upton. Ches —4G 83
Upton. Corn —2C 10
(nr. Bude)
Upton. Corn —5C 10
(nr. Liskeard)
Upton. Cumb —1E 102
Upton. Devn —2D 12
(nr. Honiton)
Upton. Devn —4D 8
(nr. Kingsbridge)
Upton. Dors —3E 15
(nr. Poole)
Upton. Dors —4C 14
(nr. Weymouth)
Upton. E Yor —4F 101
Upton. Hants —1B 24
(nr. Andover)
Upton. Hants —1B 16
(nr. Southampton)
Upton. IOW —3D 16
Upton. Leics —1A 62
Upton. Linc —2F 87
Upton. Mers —2E 83
Upton. Norf —4F 79
Upton. Nptn —4E 62
Upton. Notts —3E 87
(nr. East Retford)
Upton. Notts —5E 87
(nr. Southwell)
Upton. Oxon —3D 36
Upton. Pemb —4E 43
Upton. Pet —5A 76
Upton. Slo —3A 38
Upton. Som —4H 21
(nr. Somerton)
Upton. Som —4C 20
(nr. Wiveliscombe)
Upton. Warw —5F 61
Upton. W Yor —3E 93
Upton. Wilts —3D 22
Upton Bishop. Here —3B 48
Upton Cheyney. S Glo —5B 34
Upton Cressett. Shrp —1A 60
Upton Crews. Here —3B 48
Upton Cross. Corn —5C 10
Upton End. Beds —2B 52
Upton Grey. Hants —2E 25
Upton Heath. Ches —4G 83
Upton Hellions. Devn —2B 12
Upton Lovell. Wilts —2E 23
Upton Magna. Shrp —4H 71
Upton Noble. Som —3C 22
Upton Pyne. Devn —3C 12
Upton St Leonards. Glos —4D 48
Upton Scudamore. Wilts —2D 22
Upton Snodsbury. Worc —5D 60
Upton upon Severn. Worc —1D 48
Upton Warren. Worc —4D 60
Upwaltham. W Sus —4A 26
Upware. Cambs —3E 65
Upwell. Cambs —5D 77
Upwey. Dors —4B 14
Upwick Green. Herts —3E 53
Upwood. Cambs —2B 64
Urafirth. Shet —4E 173
Uragaig. Arg —3A 132
Urchany. High —4C 158
Urchfont. Wilts —1F 23
Urdimarsh. Here —1A 48
Ure. Shet —4D 173
Ure Bank. N Yor —2F 99
Urgha. W Isl —8D 171
Urlay Nook. Stoc T —3B 106
Urmston. G Man —1B 84
Urquhart. Mor —2G 159
Urra. N Yor —4C 106
Urray. High —3H 157
Usan. Ang —3G 145
Ushaw Moor. Dur —5F 115
Usk. Mon —5G 47
Usselby. Linc —1H 87
Usworth. Tyne —4G 115
Uton. Devn —3B 12
Utterby. Linc —1C 88
Uttoxeter. Staf —2E 73
Uwchmynydd. Gwyn —3A 68
Uxbridge. G Lon —2B 38
Uyeasound. Shet —1G 173
Uzmaston. Pemb —3D 42

Valley. IOA —3B 80
Valley End. Surr —4A 38
Valley Truckle. Corn —4B 10
Valsgarth. Shet —1H 173
Valtos. High —2E 155
Van. Powy —2B 58
Vange. Essx —2B 40
Varteg. Torf —5F 47
Vatsetter. Shet —3G 173
Vatten. High —4B 154
Vaul. Arg —4B 138
Vauld,The. Here —1A 48
Vaynol. Gwyn —3E 81
Vaynor. Mer T —4D 46
Veensgarth. Shet —7F 173
Velindre. Powy —2E 47
Vellow. Som —3D 20
Velly. Devn —4C 18
Veness. Orkn —5E 172
Venhay. Devn —1A 12
Venn. Devn —4D 8
Venngreen. Devn —1D 11
Vennington. Shrp —5F 71
Venn Ottery. Devn —3D 12
Venny's Green. Here —1A 48
Venny Tedburn. Devn —3B 12
Venterdon. Corn —5D 10
Ventnor. IOW —5D 16
Vernham Dean. Hants —1B 24
Vernham Street. Hants —1B 24
Vernolds Common. Shrp —2G 59
Verwood. Dors —2F 15
Veryan. Corn —5D 6
Veryan Green. Corn —4D 6
Vicarage. Devn —4F 13
Vickerstown. Cumb —3A 96
Victoria. Corn —2D 6
Vidlin. Shet —5F 173
Viewpark. N Lan —3A 128
Vigo. W Mid —5E 73
Vigo Village. Kent —4H 39
Vinehall Street. E Sus —3B 28
Vine's Cross. E Sus —4G 27
Viney Hill. Glos —5B 48
Virginia Water. Surr —4A 38
Virginstow. Devn —3D 11
Vobster. Som —2C 22
Voe. Shet —5F 173
(nr. Hillside)
Voe. Shet —3E 173
(nr. Swinister)
Vole. Som —2G 21
Vowchurch. Here —2G 47
Voxter. Shet —4E 173
Voy. Orkn —6B 172
Vulcan Village. Warr —1H 83

Wackerfield. Dur —2E 105
Wacton. Norf —1D 66
Wadbister. Shet —7F 173
Wadborough. Worc —1E 49
Waddesdon. Buck —4F 51
Waddeton. Devn —3E 9
Waddicar. Mers —1F 83
Waddingham. Linc —1G 87

West Buckland—Whiteinch

West Buckland. Devn —3G 19
West Buckland. Som —4E 21
West Burnside. Aber —1G 145
West Burrafirth. Shet —6D 173
West Burton. N Yor —1C 98
West Burton. W Sus —4A 26
Westbury. Buck —2E 50
Westbury. Shrp —5F 71
Westbury. Wilts —1D 22
Westbury Leigh. Wilts —2D 22
Westbury-on-Severn. Glos —4C 48
Westbury on Trym. Bris —4A 34
Westbury-sub-Mendip. Som —2A 22
West Butsfield. Dur —5E 115
West Butterwick. N Lin —4B 94
Westby. Linc —3G 75
West Byfleet. Surr —4B 38
West Caister. Norf —4H 79
West Calder. W Lot —3D 128
West Camel. Som —4A 22
West Carr. N Lin —4H 93
West Chaldon. Dors —4C 14
West Challow. Oxon —3B 36
West Charleton. Devn —4D 8
West Chelborough. Dors —2A 14
West Chevington. Nmbd —5G 121
West Chiltington. W Sus —4B 26
West Chiltington Common. W Sus —4B 26
West Chinnock. Som —1H 13
West Chisenbury. Wilts —1G 23
West Clandon. Surr —5B 38
Westcliff. IOW —5D 16
West Cliffe. Kent —1H 29
Westcliffe-on-Sea. S'end —2C 40
West Clyne. High —3F 165
West Coker. Dors —1A 14
Westcombe. Som —3B 22 (nr. Evercreech)
Westcombe. Som —4H 21 (nr. Somerton)
West Common. Linc —3G 87
West Compton. Dors —3A 14
West Compton. Som —2A 22
West Cornforth. Dur —1A 106
Westcot. Oxon —3B 36
Westcote. Glos —3H 49
Westcott. Buck —4F 51
Westcott. Devn —2D 12
Westcott. Surr —1C 26
Westcott Barton. Oxon —3C 50
West Cowick. E Yor —2G 93
West Cranmore. Som —2B 22
West Croftmore. High —2D 150
West Cross. Swan —4F 31
West Cullerley. Aber —3E 153
West Culvennan. Dum —3H 109
West Curry. Corn —3C 10
West Curthwaite. Cumb —5E 113
Westdean. E Sus —5G 27
West Dean. W Sus —1G 17
West Dean. Wilts —4A 24
West Deeping. Linc —5A 76
West Derby. Mers —1F 83
West Dereham. Norf —5F 77
West Down. Devn —2F 19
Westdowns. Corn —4A 10
West Drayton. G Lon —3B 38
West Drayton. Notts —3E 86
West Dunnet. High —1E 169
West Ella. E Yor —2D 94
West End. Beds —5G 63
West End. Cambs —1D 64
West End. Dors —2E 15
West End. E Yor —3E 101 (nr. Kilham)
West End. E Yor —1E 95 (nr. Preston)
West End. E Yor —1C 94 (nr. South Cove)
West End. E Yor —4F 101 (nr. Ulrome)
West End. G Lon —2D 39
West End. Hants —1C 16
West End. Herts —5C 52
West End. Kent —4F 41
West End. Linc —1C 76
West End. Norf —4G 79
West End. N Som —5H 33
West End. N Yor —4D 98
West End. S Glo —3C 34
West End. S Lan —5C 128
West End. Surr —4A 38
West End. Wilts —4E 23
West End. Wind —4G 37
West End. Worc —2F 49
West End Green. Hants —5E 37
Westenhanger. Kent —2F 29
Wester Aberchalder. High —2H 149
Wester Balgedie. Per —3D 136
Wester Brae. High —2A 158
Wester Culbeuchly. Aber —2D 160
Westerdale. High —3D 168
Westerdale. N Yor —4D 106
Wester Dechmont. W Lot —2D 128
Wester Fearn. High —5D 164
Westerfield. Suff —1E 55
Wester Galcantray. High —4C 158
Westergate. W Sus —5A 26
Wester Gruinards. High —4C 164
Westerham. Kent —5F 39
Westerleigh. S Glo —4B 34
Westerloch. High —3F 169
Wester Mandally. High —3E 149
Wester Parkgate. Dum —1B 112
Wester Quarff. Shet —8F 173
Wester Rarichie. High —1C 158
Wester Skeld. Shet —7D 173
Westerton. Ang —3F 145
Westerton. Dur —1F 105
Westerton. W Sus —2G 17
Westerwick. Shet —7D 173
West Farleigh. Kent —5B 40
West Farndon. Nptn —5C 62
West Felton. Shrp —3F 71
Westfield. Cumb —2A 102
Westfield. E Sus —4C 28
Westfield. High —2C 168
Westfield. Norf —5B 78
Westfield. N Lan —2A 128
Westfield. W Lot —2C 128
Westfields. Dors —2C 14
Westfields of Rattray. Per —4A 144
West Firle. E Sus —5F 27
West Fleetham. Nmbd —2F 121
West Garforth. W Yor —1D 93
Westgate. Dur —1C 104
Westgate. Norf —1B 78
Westgate. N Lin —4A 94
Westgate on Sea. Kent —3H 41
West Ginge. Oxon —3C 36
West Grafton. Wilts —5H 35
West Green. Hants —1F 25
West Grimstead. Wilts —4H 23
West Grinstead. W Sus —3C 26
West Haddlesey. N Yor —2F 93
West Haddon. Nptn —3D 62
West Hagbourne. Oxon —3D 36
West Hagley. Worc —2C 60
West Hall. Cumb —3G 113
Westhall. Suff —2G 67
West Hallam. Derbs —1B 74
Westhall Terrace. Ang —5D 144
West Halton. N Lin —2C 94
Westham. Dors —5B 14
Westham. E Sus —5H 27
West Ham. G Lon —2E 39
Westham. Som —2H 21
Westhampnett. W Sus —2G 17
West Handley. Derbs —3A 86
West Hanney. Oxon —2C 36
West Hanningfield. Essx —1B 40
West Hardwick. W Yor —3E 93
West Harnham. Wilts —4G 23
West Harptree. Bath —1A 22
West Harting. W Sus —4F 25
West Harton. Tyne —3G 115
West Hatch. Som —4F 21
Westhay. Som —2H 21
Westhead. Lanc —4C 90
West Head. Norf —5E 77
West Heath. Hants —1D 24 (nr. Basingstoke)
West Heath. Hants —1G 25 (nr. Farnborough)
West Helmsdale. High —2H 165
West Hendred. Oxon —3C 36
West Heogaland. Shet —4D 173
West Heslerton. N Yor —2D 100
West Hewish. N Som —5G 33
Westhide. Here —1A 48
Westhill. Aber —3F 153
West Hill. Devn —3D 12
West Hill. E Yor —3F 101
Westhill. High —4B 158
West Hill. N Som —4H 33
West Hill. W Sus —2E 27
West Hoathly. W Sus —2E 27
West Holme. Dors —4D 15
Westhope. Here —5G 59
Westhope. Shrp —2G 59
West Horndon. Essx —2H 39
Westhorp. Nptn —5C 62
Westhorpe. Linc —2B 76
Westhorpe. Suff —4C 66
West Horrington. Som —2A 22
West Horsley. Surr —5B 38
West Horton. Nmbd —1E 121
West Hougham. Kent —1G 29
Westhoughton. G Man —4E 91
West Houlland. Shet —6D 173
Westhouse. N Yor —2F 97
West Howe. Bour —3F 15
Westhumble. Surr —5C 38
West Huntspill. Som —2G 21
West Hyde. Herts —1B 38
West Hynish. Arg —4A 138
West Hythe. Kent —2F 29
West Ilsley. W Ber —3C 36
Westing. Shet —1G 173
West Itchenor. W Sus —2F 17
West Keal. Linc —4C 88
West Kennett. Wilts —5G 35
West Kilbride. N Ayr —5D 126
West Kingsdown. Kent —4G 39
West Kington. Wilts —4D 34
West Kirby. Mers —2E 82
West Knapton. N Yor —2C 100
West Knighton. Dors —4C 14
West Knoyle. Wilts —3D 22
Westlake. Devn —3C 8
West Lambrook. Som —1H 13
West Langdon. Kent —1H 29
West Langwell. High —3D 164
West Lavington. W Sus —4G 25
West Lavington. Wilts —1F 23
West Layton. N Yor —3E 105
West Leake. Notts —3C 74
West Learmouth. Nmbd —1C 120
Westleigh. Devn —4E 19 (nr. Bideford)
Westleigh. Devn —1D 12 (nr. Tiverton)
West Leigh. Devn —2G 11 (nr. Winkleigh)
Westleigh. G Man —4E 91
West Leith. Herts —4H 51
Westleton. Suff —4G 67
West Lexham. Norf —4H 77
Westley. Shrp —5F 71
Westley. Suff —4H 65
Westley Waterless. Cambs —5F 65
West Lilling. N Yor —3A 100
Westlington. Buck —4F 51
Westlinton. Cumb —3E 113
West Linton. Scot —4E 129
West Littleton. S Glo —4C 34
West Looe. Corn —3G 7
West Lulworth. Dors —4D 14
West Lutton. N Yor —3D 100
West Lydford. Som —3A 22
West Lynn. Norf —4F 77
West Mains. Per —2B 136
West Malling. Kent —5A 40
West Malvern. Worc —1C 48
Westmancote. Worc —2E 49
West Marden. W Sus —1F 17
West Markham. Notts —3E 86
Westmarsh. Kent —4G 41
West Marsh. NE Lin —4F 95
West Marton. N Yor —4A 98
West Meon. Hants —4E 25
West Mersea. Essx —4D 54
Westmeston. E Sus —4E 27
Westmill. Herts —3D 52 (nr. Buntingford)
Westmill. Herts —2B 52 (nr. Hitchin)
West Milton. Dors —3A 14
Westminster. G Lon —3D 39
West Molesey. Surr —4C 38
West Monkton. Som —4F 21
Westmoor End. Cumb —1B 102
West Moors. Dors —2F 15
West Morden. Dors —3E 15
West Muir. Ang —2E 145 (nr. Brechin)
Westmuir. Ang —3C 144 (nr. Forfar)
West Murkle. High —2D 168
West Ness. N Yor —2A 100
Westness. Orkn —5C 172
Westnewton. Cumb —5C 112
West Newton. E Yor —1E 95
West Newton. Norf —3F 77
Westnewton. Nmbd —1D 120
West Norwood. G Lon —3E 39
Westoe. Tyne —3G 115
West Ogwell. Devn —2E 9
Weston. Bath —5C 34
Weston. Ches —5B 84 (nr. Crewe)
Weston. Ches —3D 84 (nr. Macclesfield)
Weston. Devn —4E 13
Weston. Dors —5B 14
Weston. Hal —2H 83
Weston. Hants —4F 25
Weston. Here —5F 59
Weston. Herts —2C 52
Weston. Linc —3B 76
Weston. Nptn —1D 50
Weston. Notts —4E 87
Weston. Shrp —1H 59 (nr. Bridgnorth)
Weston. Shrp —3F 59 (nr. Knighton)
Weston. Shrp —3H 71 (nr. Wem)
Weston. S Lan —5D 128
Weston. Staf —3D 73
Weston. Suff —2G 67
Weston. W Ber —4B 36
Weston Bampfylde. Som —4B 22
Weston Beggard. Here —1A 48
Westonbirt. Glos —3D 34
Weston by Welland. Nptn —1E 63
Weston Colville. Cambs —5F 65
Westoncommon. Shrp —3G 71
Weston Coyney. Stoke —1D 72
Weston Ditch. Suff —3F 65
Weston Favell. Nptn —4E 63
Weston Green. Cambs —5F 65
Weston Green. Norf —4D 78
Weston Heath. Shrp —4B 72
Weston Hills. Linc —4B 76
Weston in Arden. Warw —2A 62
Westoning. Beds —2A 52
Weston-in-Gordano. N Som —4H 33
Weston Jones. Staf —3B 72
Weston Longville. Norf —4D 78
Weston Lullingfields. Shrp —3G 71
Weston-on-Avon. Warw —5F 61
Weston-on-the-Green. Oxon —4D 50
Weston-on-Trent. Derbs —3B 74
Weston Patrick. Hants —2E 25
Weston Rhyn. Shrp —2E 71
Weston Subedge. Glos —1G 49
Weston-super-Mare. N Som —5G 33
Weston Town. Som —2C 22
Weston Turville. Buck —4G 51
Weston under Lizard. Staf —4C 72
Weston under Penyard. Here —3B 48
Weston under Wetherley. Warw —4A 62
Weston Underwood. Derbs —1G 73
Weston Underwood. Mil —5F 63
Westonzoyland. Som —3G 21
West Orchard. Dors —1D 14
West Overton. Wilts —5G 35
Westow. N Yor —3B 100
West Panson. Devn —3D 10
West Park. Hart —1B 106
West Parley. Dors —3F 15
West Peckham. Kent —5H 39
West Pelton. Dur —4F 115
West Pennard. Som —3A 22
West Pentire. Corn —2B 6
West Perry. Cambs —4A 64
West Pitcorthie. Fife —3H 137
West Plean. Stir —1B 128
West Poringland. Norf —5E 79
West Porlock. Som —2B 20
Westport. Som —4G 21
West Putford. Devn —1D 10
West Quantoxhead. Som —2E 20
Westra. V Glam —4E 33
West Rainton. Dur —5G 115
West Rasen. Linc —2H 87
West Ravendale. NE Lin —1B 88
Westray Airport. Orkn —2D 172
West Raynham. Norf —3A 78
Westrigg. W Lot —3C 128
West Rounton. N Yor —4B 106
West Row. Suff —3F 65
West Rudham. Norf —3H 77
West Runton. Norf —1D 78
Westruther. Scot —5C 130
Westry. Cambs —1C 64
West Saltoun. E Lot —3A 130
West Sandford. Devn —2B 12
West Sandwick. Shet —3F 173
West Scrafton. N Yor —1C 98
Westside. Orkn —5C 172
West Sleekburn. Nmbd —1F 115
West Somerton. Norf —4G 79
West Stafford. Dors —4C 14
West Stockwith. Notts —1E 87
West Stoke. W Sus —2G 17
West Stonesdale. N Yor —4B 104
West Stoughton. Som —2H 21
West Stour. Dors —4C 22
West Stourmouth. Kent —4G 41
West Stow. Suff —3H 65
West Stowell. Wilts —5G 35
West Strathan. High —2F 167
West Stratton. Hants —2D 24
West Street. Kent —5D 40
West Tanfield. N Yor —2E 99
West Taphouse. Corn —2F 7
West Tarbert. Arg —3G 125
West Thirston. Nmbd —4F 121
West Thorney. W Sus —2F 17
West Thurrock. Thur —3G 39
West Tilbury. Thur —3A 40
West Tisted. Hants —4E 25
West Tofts. Norf —1H 65
West Torrington. Linc —2A 88
West Town. Bath —5A 34
West Town. Hants —3F 17
West Town. N Som —5H 33
West Tytherley. Hants —4A 24
West Tytherton. Wilts —4E 35
West View. Hart —1C 106
Westville. Notts —1C 74
West Walton. Norf —4D 76
Westward. Cumb —5D 112
Westward Ho!. Devn —4E 19
Westwell. Kent —1D 28
Westwell. Oxon —5H 49
Westwell Leacon. Kent —1D 28
West Wellow. Hants —1A 16
West Wemyss. Fife —4F 137
Westwick. Cambs —4D 64
Westwick. Dur —3D 104
Westwick. Norf —3E 79
West Wick. N Som —5G 33
West Wickham. Cambs —1G 53
West Wickham. G Lon —4E 39
West Williamston. Pemb —4E 43
West Willoughby. Linc —1G 75
West Winch. Norf —4F 77
West Winterslow. Wilts —3H 23
West Wittering. W Sus —3F 17
West Witton. N Yor —1C 98
Westwood. Devn —3D 12
Westwood. Kent —4H 41
Westwood. Pet —1A 64
Westwood. S Lan —4H 127
Westwood. Wilts —1D 22
West Woodburn. Nmbd —1B 114
West Woodhay. W Ber —5B 36
West Woodlands. Som —2C 22
West Woodside. Cumb —5E 112
Westwoodside. N Lin —1E 87
West Worldham. Hants —3F 25
West Worlington. Devn —1A 12
West Worthing. W Sus —5C 26
West Wratting. Cambs —5F 65
West Wycombe. Buck —2G 37
West Wylam. Nmbd —3E 115
West Yatton. Wilts —4D 34
West Yell. Shet —3F 173
West Youlstone. Corn —1C 10
Wetheral. Cumb —4F 113
Wetherby. W Yor —5G 99
Wetherden. Suff —4C 66
Wetheringsett. Suff —4D 66
Wethersfield. Essx —2H 53
Wethersta. Shet —5E 173
Wetherup Street. Suff —4D 66
Wetley Rocks. Staf —1D 72
Wettenhall. Ches —4A 84
Wetton. Staf —5F 85
Wetwang. E Yor —4D 100
Wetwood. Staf —2B 72
Wexcombe. Wilts —1A 24
Wexham Street. Buck —2A 38
Weybourne. Norf —1D 78
Weybourne. Surr —2G 25
Weybread. Suff —2E 67
Weybridge. Surr —4B 38
Weycroft. Devn —3G 13
Weydale. High —2D 168
Weyhill. Hants —2B 24
Weymouth. Dors —5B 14
Weythel. Powy —5E 59
Whaddon. Buck —2G 51
Whaddon. Cambs —1D 52
Whaddon. Glos —4D 48
Whaddon. Wilts —4G 23
Whale. Cumb —2G 103
Whaley. Derbs —3C 86
Whaley Bridge. Derbs —2E 85
Whaley Thorns. Derbs —3C 86
Whalley. Lanc —1F 91
Whalton. Nmbd —1E 115
Wham. N Yor —3G 97
Whaplode. Linc —3C 76
Whaplode Drove. Linc —4C 76
Whaplode St Catherine. Linc —3C 76
Wharfe. N Yor —3G 97
Wharles. Lanc —1C 90
Wharley End. Beds —1H 51
Wharncliffe Side. S Yor —1G 85
Wharram-le-Street. N Yor —3C 100
Wharton. Ches —4A 84
Wharton. Here —5H 59
Whashton. N Yor —4E 105
Whasset. Cumb —1E 97
Whatcote. Warw —1A 50
Whateley. Warw —1G 61
Whatfield. Suff —1D 54
Whatley. Som —2G 13 (nr. Chard)
Whatley. Som —2C 22 (nr. Frome)
Whatlington. E Sus —4B 28
Whatmore. Shrp —3A 60
Whatstandwell. Derbs —5H 85
Whatton. Notts —2E 75
Whauphill. Dum —5B 110
Whaw. N Yor —4C 104
Wheatacre. Norf —1G 67
Wheatcroft. Derbs —5A 86
Wheathampstead. Herts —4B 52
Wheathill. Shrp —2A 60
Wheatley. Devn —3B 12
Wheatley. Hants —2F 25
Wheatley. Oxon —5D 50
Wheatley. W Yor —2A 92
Wheatley Hill. Dur —1A 106
Wheatley Lane. Lanc —1G 91
Wheatley Park. S Yor —4F 93
Wheaton Aston. Staf —4C 72
Wheatstone Park. Staf —5C 72
Wheddon Cross. Som —3C 20
Wheelerstreet. Surr —1A 26
Wheelock. Ches —5B 84
Wheelock Heath. Ches —5B 84
Wheelton. Lanc —2E 90
Wheldrake. York —5A 100
Whelford. Glos —2G 35
Whelpley Hill. Buck —5H 51
Whelpo. Cumb —1E 102
Whelston. Flin —3E 82
Whenby. N Yor —3A 100
Whepstead. Suff —5H 65
Wherstead. Suff —1E 55
Wherwell. Hants —2B 24
Wheston. Derbs —3F 85
Whetsted. Kent —1A 28
Whetstone. G Lon —1D 38
Whetstone. Leics —1C 62
Whicham. Cumb —1A 96
Whichford. Warw —2B 50
Whickham. Tyne —3F 115
Whiddon. Devn —2E 11
Whiddon Down. Devn —3G 11
Whigstreet. Ang —4D 145
Whilton. Nptn —4D 62
Whimble. Devn —2D 10
Whimple. Devn —3D 12
Whimpwell Green. Norf —3F 79
Whinburgh. Norf —5C 78
Whin Lane End. Lanc —5C 96
Whinnyfold. Aber —5H 161
Whinny Hill. Stoc T —3A 106
Whippingham. IOW —3D 16
Whipsnade. Beds —4A 52
Whipton. Devn —3C 12
Whirlow. S Yor —2H 85
Whisby. Linc —4G 87
Whissendine. Rut —4F 75
Whissonsett. Norf —3B 78
Whisterfield. Ches —3C 84
Whistley Green. Wok —4F 37
Whiston. Mers —1G 83
Whiston. Nptn —4F 63
Whiston. S Yor —1B 86
Whiston. Staf —1E 73 (nr. Cheadle)
Whiston. Staf —4C 72 (nr. Penkridge)
Whiston Cross. Shrp —5B 72
Whiston Eaves. Staf —1E 73
Whitacre Heath. Warw —1G 61
Whitbeck. Cumb —1A 96
Whitbourne. Here —5B 60
Whitburn. Tyne —3H 115
Whitburn. W Lot —3C 128
Whitburn Colliery. Tyne —3H 115
Whitby. Ches —3F 83
Whitby. N Yor —3F 107
Whitbyheath. Ches —3F 83
Whitchester. Scot —4D 130
Whitchurch. Bath —5B 34
Whitchurch. Buck —3G 51
Whitchurch. Card —4E 33
Whitchurch. Devn —5E 11
Whitchurch. Hants —2C 24
Whitchurch. Here —4A 48
Whitchurch. Pemb —2B 42
Whitchurch. Shrp —1H 71
Whitchurch Canonicorum. Dors —3G 13
Whitchurch Hill. Oxon —4E 37
Whitchurch-on-Thames. Oxon —4E 37
Whitcombe. Dors —4C 14
Whitcot. Shrp —1F 59
Whitcott Keysett. Shrp —2E 59
Whiteash Green. Essx —2A 54
Whitebog. High —2B 158
Whitebridge. High —2G 149
Whitebrook. Mon —5A 48
Whitecairns. Aber —2G 153
White Chapel. Lanc —5E 97
Whitechurch. Pemb —1F 43
White Colne. Essx —3B 54
White Coppice. Lanc —3E 90
White Corries. High —3G 141
Whitecraig. E Lot —2G 129
Whitecroft. Glos —5B 48
Whitecross. Corn —1D 6
White Cross. Corn —4D 5
Whitecross. Falk —2C 128
White End. Worc —2C 48
Whiteface. High —5E 164
Whitefaulds. S Ayr —4B 116
Whitefield. Dors —3E 15
Whitefield. G Man —4G 91
Whitefield. Som —4D 20
Whiteford. Aber —1E 152
Whitegate. Ches —4A 84
Whitehall. Devn —1E 13
Whitehall. Hants —1F 25
Whitehall. Orkn —5F 172
Whitehall. W Sus —3C 26
Whitehaven. Cumb —3A 102
Whitehaven. Shrp —3E 71
Whitehill. Hants —3F 25
Whitehill. N Ayr —4D 126
Whitehills. Aber —2D 160
Whitehills. Ang —3D 144
White Horse Common. Norf —3F 79
Whitehough. Derbs —2E 85
Whitehouse. Aber —2D 152
Whitehouse. Arg —3G 125
Whiteinch. Glas —3G 127

Woodfalls—Zouch

Woodfalls. Wilts —4G 23
Woodfield. Oxon —3D 50
Woodfields. Lanc —1E 91
Woodford. Corn —1C 10
Woodford. Devn —3D 9
Woodford. Glos —2B 34
Woodford. G Lon —1E 39
Woodford. G Man —2C 84
Woodford. Nptn —3G 63
Woodford. Plym —3B 8
Woodford Green. G Lon —1F 39
Woodford Halse. Nptn —5C 62
Woodgate. Norf —4C 78
Woodgate. W Mid —2D 61
Woodgate. W Sus —5A 26
Woodgate. Worc —4D 60
Wood Green. G Lon —1D 39
Woodgreen. Hants —1G 15
Wood Hall. E Yor —1E 95
Woodhall. Inv —2E 127
Woodhall. Linc —4B 88
Woodhall. N Yor —5C 104
Woodhall Spa. Linc —4A 88
Woodham. Surr —4B 38
Woodham Ferrers. Essx —1B 40
Woodham Mortimer. Essx —5B 54
Woodham Walter. Essx —5B 54
Woodhaven. Fife —1G 137
Wood Hayes. W Mid —5D 72
Woodhead. Aber —2G 161
(nr. Fraserburgh)
Woodhead. Aber —5E 161
(nr. Fyvie)
Woodhill. N Som —4H 33
Woodhill. Shrp —2B 60
Woodhorn. Nmbd —1G 115
Woodhouse. Leics —4C 74
Woodhouse. S Yor —2B 86
Woodhouse. W Yor —1C 92
(nr. Leeds)
Woodhouse. W Yor —2D 93
(nr. Normanton)
Woodhouse Eaves. Leics —4C 74
Woodhouses. Ches —3H 83
Woodhouses. G Man —4H 91
(nr. Failsworth)
Woodhouses. G Man —1B 84
(nr. Sale)
Woodhouses. Staf —4F 73
Woodhuish. Devn —3F 9
Woodhurst. Cambs —3C 64
Woodingdean. Brig —5E 27
Woodland. Devn —2D 9
Woodland. Dur —2D 104
Woodland Head. Devn —3A 12
Woodlands. Aber —4E 153
Woodlands. Dors —2F 15
Woodlands. Hants —1B 16
Woodlands. Kent —4G 39
Woodlands. N Yor —4F 99
Woodlands. S Yor —4F 93
Woodlands Park. Wind —4G 37
Woodlands St Mary. W Ber —4B 36
Woodlane. Shrp —3A 72
Woodlane. Staf —3F 73
Woodleigh. Devn —4D 8
Woodlesford. W Yor —2D 92
Woodley. G Man —1D 84
Woodley. Wok —4F 37
Woodmancote. Glos —3E 49
(nr. Cheltenham)
Woodmancote. Glos —5F 49
(nr. Cirencester)
Woodmancote. W Sus —2F 17
(nr. Chichester)
Woodmancote. W Sus —4D 26
(nr. Henfield)
Woodmancote. Worc —1E 49
Woodmancott. Hants —2D 24
Woodmansey. E Yor —1D 94
Woodmansgreen. W Sus —4G 25
Woodmansterne. G Lon —5D 39
Woodmanton. Devn —4D 12
Woodmill. Staf —3F 73
Woodminton. Wilts —4F 23
Woodnesborough. Kent —5H 41
Woodnewton. Nptn —1H 63
Woodnook. Linc —2G 75
Wood Norton. Norf —3C 78
Woodplumpton. Lanc —1D 90
Woodrising. Norf —5B 78
Woodrow. Cumb —5D 112
Woodrow. Dors —2C 14
Wood Row. W Yor —2D 93
Woods Eaves. Here —1F 47
Woodseaves. Shrp —2A 72
Woodseaves. Staf —3B 72
Woodsend. Wilts —4H 35
Woodsetts. S Yor —2C 86
Woodsford. Dors —3C 14
Wood's Green. E Sus —2H 27
Woodshaw. Wilts —3F 35
Woodside. Aber C —3G 153
Woodside. Brac —3A 38
Woodside. Cumb —1B 102
Woodside. Derbs —1A 74
Woodside. Dum —2B 112
Woodside. Dur —2E 105
Woodside. Fife —3G 137
Woodside. Herts —5C 52
Woodside. Per —5B 144
Wood Stanway. Glos —2F 49
Woodstock. Oxon —4C 50
Woodstock Slop. Pemb —2E 43
Woodston. Pet —1A 64
Wood Street. Village. Surr —5A 38
Woodthorpe. Derbs —3B 86
Woodthorpe. Leics —4C 74
Woodthorpe. Linc —2D 88
Woodthorpe. York —5H 99
Woodton. Norf —1E 67
Woodtown. Devn —4E 19
(nr. Bideford)
Woodtown. Devn —4E 19
(nr. Littleham)
Woodvale. Mers —3B 90
Woodville. Derbs —4H 73
Woodwalton. Cambs —2B 64
Woodwick. Orkn —5C 172
Woodyates. Dors —1F 15
Woody Bay. Devn —2G 19
Woofferton. Shrp —4H 59
Wookey. Som —2A 22
Wookey Hole. Som —2A 22
Wool. Dors —4D 14
Woolacombe. Devn —2E 19
Woolage Green. Kent —1G 29
Woolaston. Glos —2A 34
Woolavington. Som —2G 21
Woolbeding. W Sus —4G 25
Woolcotts. Som —3C 20
Wooldale. W Yor —4B 92
Wooler. Nmbd —2D 121
Woolfardisworthy. Devn —4D 18
(nr. Bideford)
Woolfardisworthy. Devn —2B 12
(nr. Crediton)
Woolfords. S Lan —4D 128
Woolgarston. Dors —4E 15
Woolhampton. W Ber —5D 36
Woolhope. Here —2B 48
Woolland. Dors —2C 14
Woollard. Bath —5B 34
Woolley. Bath —5C 34
Woolley. Cambs —3A 64
Woolley. Corn —1C 10
Woolley. Derbs —4A 86
Woolley. W Yor —3D 92
Woolley Green. Wilts —5D 34
Woolmere Green. Worc —4D 60
Woolmer Green. Herts —4C 52
Woolminstone. Som —2H 13
Woolpit. Suff —4B 66
Woolridge. Glos —3D 48
Woolscott. Warw —4B 62
Woolsery. Devn —4D 18
Woolsington. Tyne —3E 115
Woolstaston. Shrp —1G 59
Woolsthorpe. Linc —3G 75
(nr. Colsterworth)
Woolsthorpe. Linc —2F 75
(nr. Grantham)
Woolston. Devn —4D 8
Woolston. Shrp —2G 59
(nr. Church Stretton)
Woolston. Shrp —3F 71
(nr. Oswestry)
Woolston. Som —4B 22
Woolston. Sotn —1C 16
Woolston. Warr —1A 84
Woolstone. Glos —2E 49
Woolstone. Oxon —3A 36
Woolston Green. Devn —2D 9
Woolton. Mers —2G 83
Woolton Hill. Hants —5C 36
Woolverstone. Suff —2E 55
Woolverton. Som —1C 22
Woolwell. Devn —2B 8
Woolwich. G Lon —3F 39
Woonton. Here —5F 59
(nr. Kington)
Woonton. Here —4H 59
(nr. Leominster)
Wooperton. Nmbd —2E 121
Woore. Shrp —1B 72
Wooton. Shrp —2B 60
Wootton. Beds —1A 52
Wootton. Hants —3H 15
Wootton. IOW —3D 16
Wootton. Kent —1G 29
Wootton. Nptn —5E 63
Wootton. N Lin —3D 94
Wootton. Oxon —5C 50
(nr. Abingdon)
Wootton. Oxon —4C 50
(nr. Woodstock)
Wootton. Shrp —3G 59
(nr. Ludlow)
Wootton. Shrp —3F 71
(nr. Oswestry)
Wootton. Staf —3C 72
(nr. Eccleshall)
Wootton. Staf —1F 73
(nr. Ellastone)
Wootton Bassett. Wilts —3F 35
Wootton Bridge. IOW —3D 16
Wootton Common. IOW —3D 16
Wootton Courtenay. Som —2C 20
Wootton Fitzpaine. Dors —3G 13
Wootton Rivers. Wilts —5G 35
Woottons. Staf —2E 73
Wootton St Lawrence. Hants —1D 24
Wootton Wawen. Warw —4F 61
Worcester. Worc —5C 60
Worcester Park. G Lon —4D 38
Wordsley. W Mid —2C 60
Worfield. Shrp —1B 60
Work. Orkn —6D 172
Workhouse Green. Suff —2C 54
Workington. Cumb —2A 102
Worksop. Notts —3C 86
Worlaby. N Lin —3D 94
Worlds End. Hants —1E 17
Worldsend. Shrp —1G 59
World's End. W Ber —4C 36
Worlds End. W Mid —2F 61
World's End. W Sus —4E 27
Worle. N Som —5G 33
Worleston. Ches —5A 84
Worley. Glos —2D 34
Worlingham. Suff —1G 67
Worlington. Suff —3F 65
Worlingworth. Suff —4E 67
Wormbridge. Here —2H 47
Wormegay. Norf —4F 77
Wormelow Tump. Here —2H 47
Wormhill. Derbs —3F 85
Wormiehills. Ang —5F 145
Wormingford. Essx —2C 54
Worminghall. Buck —5E 51
Wormington. Glos —2F 49
Worminster. Som —2A 22
Wormit. Fife —1F 137
Wormleighton. Warw —5B 62
Wormley. Herts —5D 52
Wormley. Surr —2A 26
Wormshill. Kent —5C 40
Wormsley. Here —1H 47
Worplesdon. Surr —5A 38
Worrall. S Yor —1H 85
Worsbrough. S Yor —4D 92
Worsley. G Man —4F 91
Worstead. Norf —3F 79
Worsthorne. Lanc —1G 91
Worston. Lanc —5G 97
Worth. Kent —5H 41
Worth. W Sus —2E 27
Wortham. Suff —3C 66
Worthen. Shrp —5F 71
Worthenbury. Wrex —1G 71
Worthing. Norf —4B 78
Worthing. W Sus —5C 26
Worthington. Leics —3B 74
Worth Matravers. Dors —5E 15
Worting. Hants —1E 24
Wortley. Glos —2C 34
Wortley. S Yor —1H 85
Wortley. W Yor —1C 92
Worton. N Yor —5C 104
Worton. Wilts —1E 23
Wortwell. Norf —2E 67
Wotherton. Shrp —5E 71
Wothorpe. Nptn —5H 75
Wotter. Devn —2B 8
Wotton. Glos —4D 48
Wotton. Surr —1C 26
Wotton-under-Edge. Glos —2C 34
Wotton Underwood. Buck —4E 51
Wouldham. Kent —4B 40
Wrabness. Essx —2E 55
Wrafton. Devn —3E 19
Wragby. Linc —3A 88
Wragby. W Yor —3E 93
Wramplingham. Norf —5D 78
Wrangbrook. W Yor —3E 93
Wrangle. Linc —5D 88
Wrangle Lowgate. Linc —5D 88
Wrangway. Som —1E 13
Wrantage. Som —4G 21
Wrawby. N Lin —4D 94
Wraxall. Dors —2A 14
Wraxall. N Som —4H 33
Wraxall. Som —3B 22
Wray. Lanc —3F 97
Wrayland. Devn —4A 12
Wraysbury. Wind —3B 38
Wrayton. Lanc —2F 97
Wrea Green. Lanc —1B 90
Wreay. Cumb —5F 113
(nr. Carlisle)
Wreay. Cumb —2F 103
(nr. Penrith)
Wrecclesham. Surr —2G 25
Wrecsam. Wrex —5F 83
Wrekenton. Tyne —4F 115
Wrelton. N Yor —1B 100
Wrenbury. Ches —1H 71
Wreningham. Norf —1D 66
Wrentham. Suff —2G 67
Wrenthorpe. W Yor —2D 92
Wrentnall. Shrp —5G 71
Wressle. E Yor —1H 93
Wressle. N Lin —4C 94
Wrestlingworth. Beds —1C 52
Wretham. Norf —1B 66
Wretton. Norf —5F 77
Wrexham. Wrex —5F 83
Wrexham Industrial Estate. Wrex —1F 71
Wrickton. Shrp —2A 60
Wrightlington Bar. Lanc —3D 90
Wright's Green. Essx —4F 53
Wrinehill. Staf —1B 72
Wrington. N Som —5H 33
Writtle. Essx —5G 53
Wrockwardine. Telf —4A 72
Wroot. N Lin —4H 93
Wrotham. Kent —5H 39
Wrotham Heath. Kent —5H 39
Wroughton. Swin —3G 35
Wroxall. IOW —5D 16
Wroxall. Warw —3G 61
Wroxeter. Shrp —5H 71
Wroxham. Norf —4F 79
Wroxton. Oxon —1C 50
Wyaston. Derbs —1F 73
Wyatt's Green. Essx —1G 39
Wybers Wood. NE Lin —4F 95
Wyberton. Linc —1C 76
Wyboston. Beds —5A 64
Wybunbury. Ches —1A 72
Wychbold. Worc —4D 60
Wych Cross. E Sus —2F 27
Wychnor. Staf —4F 73
Wychnor Bridges. Staf —4F 73
Wyck. Hants —3F 25
Wyck Hill. Glos —3G 49
Wyck Rissington. Glos —3G 49
Wycliffe. Dur —3E 105
Wycombe Marsh. Buck —2G 37
Wyddial. Herts —2D 52
Wye. Kent —1E 29
Wyesham. Mon —4A 48
Wyfold Grange. Oxon —3E 37
Wyfordby. Leics —4E 75
Wyke. Devn —2B 12
Wyke. Dors —4C 22
Wyke. Shrp —5A 72
Wyke. Surr —5A 38
Wyke. W Yor —2B 92
Wyke Champflower. Som —3B 22
Wykeham. Linc —3B 76
Wykeham. N Yor —2C 100
(nr. Malton)
Wykeham. N Yor —1D 100
(nr. Scarborough)
Wyken. Shrp —1B 60
Wyken. W Mid —2A 62
Wyke Regis. Dors —5B 14
Wyke, The. Shrp —5B 72
Wykey. Shrp —3F 71
Wykin. Leics —1B 62
Wylam. Nmbd —3E 115
Wylde Green. W Mid —1F 61
Wylye. Wilts —3F 23
Wymering. Port —2E 17
Wymeswold. Leics —3D 74
Wymington. Beds —4G 63
Wymondham. Leics —4F 75
Wymondham. Norf —5D 78
Wyndham. B'End —2C 32
Wynford Eagle. Dors —3A 14
Wyng. Orkn —8C 172
Wyre Piddle. Worc —1E 49
Wysall. Notts —3D 74
Wyson. Here —4H 59
Wythall. Worc —3E 61
Wytham. Oxon —5C 50
Wythburn. Cumb —3E 103
Wythenshawe. G Man —2C 84
Wythop Mill. Cumb —2C 102
Wyton. Cambs —3B 64
Wyton. E Yor —1E 95
Wyverstone. Suff —4C 66
Wyverstone Street. Suff —4C 66
Wyville. Linc —3F 75
Wyvis Lodge. High —1G 157

Yaddlethorpe. N Lin —4B 94
Yafford. IOW —4C 16
Yafforth. N Yor —5A 106
Yalberton. Torb —3E 9
Yalding. Kent —5A 40
Yanley. N Som —5A 34
Yanwath. Cumb —2G 103
Yanworth. Glos —4F 49
Yapham. E Yor —4B 100
Yapton. W Sus —5A 26
Yarburgh. Linc —1C 88
Yarcombe. Devn —2F 13
Yarde. Som —3D 20
Yardley. W Mid —2F 61
Yardley Gobion. Nptn —1F 51
Yardley Hastings. Nptn —5F 63
Yardley Wood. W Mid —2F 61
Yardro. Powy —5E 58
Yarhampton. Worc —4B 60
Yarkhill. Here —1B 48
Yarlet. Staf —3D 72
Yarley. Som —2A 22
Yarlington. Som —4B 22
Yarm. Stoc T —3B 106
Yarmouth. IOW —4B 16
Yarnbrook. Wilts —1D 22
Yarnfield. Staf —2C 72
Yarnscombe. Devn —4F 19
Yarnton. Oxon —4C 50
Yarpole. Here —4G 59
Yarrow. Nmbd —1A 114
Yarrow. Scot —2F 119
Yarrow. Som —2G 21
Yarrow Feus. Scot —2F 119
Yarrow Ford. Scot —1G 119
Yarsop. Here —1H 47
Yarwell. Nptn —1H 63
Yate. S Glo —3C 34
Yateley. Hants —5G 37
Yatesbury. Wilts —4F 35
Yattendon. W Ber —4D 36
Yatton. Here —4G 59
(nr. Leominster)
Yatton. Here —2B 48
(nr. Ross-on-Wye)
Yatton. N Som —5H 33
Yatton Keynell. Wilts —4D 34
Yaverland. IOW —4E 16
Yawl. Devn —3G 13
Yaxham. Norf —4C 78
Yaxley. Cambs —1A 64
Yaxley. Suff —3D 66
Yazor. Here —1H 47
Y Bala. Gwyn —2B 70
Y Bont-Faen. V Glam —4C 32
Y Dref. Gwyn —2D 69
Y Drenewydd. Powy —1D 58
Yeading. G Lon —2C 38
Yeadon. W Yor —5E 98
Yealand Conyers. Lanc —2E 97
Yealand Redmayne. Lanc —2E 97
Yealmpton. Devn —3B 8
Yearby. Red C —2D 106
Yearngill. Cumb —5C 112
Yearsett. Here —5B 60
Yearsley. N Yor —2H 99
Yeaton. Shrp —4G 71
Yeaveley. Derbs —1F 73
Yeavering. Nmbd —1D 120
Yedingham. N Yor —2C 100
Yelden. Beds —4H 63
Yeldersley Hollies. Derbs —1G 73
Yelford. Oxon —5B 50
Yelland. Devn —3E 19
Yelling. Cambs —4B 64
Yelsted. Kent —4C 40
Yelvertoft. Nptn —3C 62
Yelverton. Devn —2B 8
Yelverton. Norf —5E 79
Yenston. Som —4C 22
Yeoford. Devn —3A 12
Yeolmbridge. Corn —4D 10
Yeo Mill. Devn —4B 20
Yeovil. Som —1A 14
Yeovil Marsh. Som —1A 14
Yeovilton. Som —4A 22
Yerbeston. Pemb —4E 43
Yesnaby. Orkn —6B 172
Yetlington. Nmbd —4E 121
Yetminster. Dors —1A 14
Yett. N Lan —4A 128
Yett. S Ayr —2D 116
Yettington. Devn —4D 12
Yetts o' Muckhart. Clac —3C 136
Y Felinheli. Gwyn —4E 81
Y Fenni. Mon —4G 47
Y Ferwig. Cdgn —1B 44
Y Fflint. Flin —3E 83
Y Ffor. Gwyn —2C 68
Y Gelli Gandryll. Powy —1F 47
Yieldshields. S Lan —4B 128
Yiewsley. G Lon —2B 38
Yinstay. Orkn —6E 172
Ynysboeth. Rhon —2D 32
Ynysddu. Cphy —2E 33
Ynysforgan. Swan —3F 31
Ynyshir. Rhon —2D 32
Ynyslas. Cdgn —1F 57
Ynysmaerdy. Neat —3G 31
Ynysmaerdy. Rhon —3D 32
Ynysmeudwy. Neat —5H 45
Ynystawe. Swan —5G 45
Ynyswen. Powy —4B 46
Ynys-wen. Rhon —2C 32
Ynys y Barri. V Glam —5E 32
Ynysybwl. Rhon —2D 32
Yockenthwaite. N Yor —2B 98
Yockleton. Shrp —4G 71
Yokefleet. E Yor —2B 94
Yoker. Glas —3G 127
Yonder Bognie. Aber —4D 160
York. York —4A 100
Yorkletts. Kent —4E 41
Yorkley. Glos —5B 48
Yorton. Shrp —3H 71
Yorton Heath. Shrp —3H 71
Youlgreave. Derbs —4G 85
Youlthorpe. E Yor —4B 100
Youlton. N Yor —3G 99
Young's End. Essx —4H 53
Young Wood. Linc —3A 88
Yoxall. Staf —4F 73
Yoxford. Suff —4F 67
Yr Hob. Flin —5F 83
Y Rhws. V Glam —5D 32
Yr Wyddgrug. Flin —4E 83
Ysbyty Cynfyn. Cdgn —3G 57
Ysbyty Ifan. Cnwy —1H 69
Ysbyty Ystwyth. Cdgn —3G 57
Ysceifiog. Flin —3D 82
Yspitty. Carm —3E 31
Ystalyfera. Neat —5A 46
Ystrad. Rhon —2C 32
Ystrad Aeron. Cdgn —5E 57
Ystradfellte. Powy —4C 46
Ystradffin. Carm —1A 46
Ystradgynlais. Powy —4A 46
Ystradmeurig. Cdgn —4G 57
Ystrad Mynach. Cphy —2E 33
Ystradowen. Neat —4A 46
Ystradowen. V Glam —4D 32
Ystumtuen. Cdgn —3G 57
Ythanbank. Aber —5G 161
Ythanwells. Aber —5D 160
Y Trallwng. Powy —5E 70
Y Waun. Wrex —2E 71

Zeal Monachorum. Devn —2H 11
Zeals. Wilts —3C 22
Zelah. Corn —3C 6
Zennor. Corn —3B 4
Zouch. Notts —3C 74

Limited Interchange Motorway Junctions, are shown on the maps by RED junction indicators

M1

Junction 2
Northbound: No exit, access from A1 only
Southbound: No access, exit to A1 only

Junction 4
Northbound: No exit, access from A41 only
Southbound: No access, exit to A41 only

Junction 6a
Northbound: No exit, access from M25 only
Southbound: No access, exit to M25 only

Junction 7
Northbound: No exit, access from M10 only
Southbound: No access, exit to M10 only

Junction 17
Northbound: No access, exit to M45 only
Southbound: No exit, access from M45 only

Junction 19
Northbound: Exit to M6 only,
            access from A14 only
Southbound: Access from M6 only,
            exit to A14 only

Junction 21a
Northbound: No access, exit to A46 only
Southbound: No exit, access from A46 only

Junction 24a
Northbound: Access from A50 only
Southbound: Exit to A50 only

Junction 35a
Northbound: No access, exit to A616 only
Southbound: No exit, access from A616 only

Junction 43
Northbound: Exit to M621 only
Southbound: Access from M621 only

Junction 45
Not open until completion of A63

Junction 48
Eastbound: Exit to A1(M)
Northbound only
Westbound: Access from A1(M) Southbound
only

M2

Junction 1
Eastbound: Access from A2 Eastbound only
Westbound: Exit to A2 Westbound only

M3

Junction 8
Westbound: No access, exit to A303 only
Eastbound: No exit, access from A303 only

Junction 10
Northbound: No access from A31
Southbound: No exit to A31

Junction 13
Southbound: No access from A335 onto
M3 leading to M27 Eastbound

M4

Junction 1
Westbound: Access from A4 Westbound only
Eastbound: Exit to A4 Eastbound only

Junction 21
Westbound: No access from M48
Eastbound: No exit onto M48

Junction 23
Westbound: No exit onto M48
Eastbound: No access from M48

Junction 25
Westbound: No access
Eastbound: No exit

Junction 25a
Westbound: No access
Eastbound: No exit

Junction 29
Westbound: No access, exit to A48(M) only
Eastbound: No exit, access from A48(M) only

Junction 38
Westbound: No access, exit to A48 only

Junction 39
Westbound: No exit, access from A48 only
Eastbound: No exit or access

Junction 42
Westbound: No exit to A48
Eastbound: No access from A48

Junction 46
Westbound: No access, exit to A48 only
Eastbound: No exit, access from A48 only

M5

Junction 10
Southbound: No access, exit to A4019 only
Northbound: No exit, access from A4019 only

Junction 11a
Southbound: No exit to A417 Westbound

Junction 12
Southbound: No access, exit to A38 only
Northbound: No access, exit to A38 only

M6

Junction 4
Northbound: No exit to M42 Northbound
            No access from M42 Southbound
Southbound: No exit to M42
            No access from M42 Southbound

Junction 4a
Northbound: No exit, access from M42
Southbound only
Southbound: No access, exit to M42 only

Junction 5
Northbound: No access, exit to A452 only
Southbound: No exit, access from A452 only

Junction 10a
Northbound: No access, exit to M54 only
Southbound: No exit, access from M54 only

Junction 20
Northbound: No exit to M56 Eastbound
Southbound: No access from M56 Westbound

Junction 24
Northbound: No exit, access from A58 only
Southbound: No access, exit to A58 only

Junction 25
Northbound: No access, exit to A49 only
Southbound: No exit, access from A49 only

Junction 30
Northbound: No exit, access from M61
Northbound only
Southbound: No access, exit to M61
Southbound only

Junction 31a
Northbound: No access, exit to B road only
Southbound: No exit, access from B road only

M8

Junction 8
Westbound: No access from M73 Southbound
Eastbound: No exit to M73 Northbound

Junction 9
Westbound: No exit, access only
Eastbound: No access, exit only

Junction 13
Westbound: No exit to M80 Northbound
Eastbound: No access from M80 Southbound

Junction 14
Westbound: No exit, access only
Eastbound: No access, exit only

Junction 16
Westbound: No access, exit only
Eastbound: No exit, access only

Junction 17
Westbound: No access, exit to A82 only
Eastbound: No exit, access from A82 only

Junction 18
Westbound: No exit, access only

Junction 19
Westbound: No access from A814 Westbound
Eastbound: No exit to A814 Eastbound

Junction 20
Westbound: No exit, access only
Eastbound: No exit, access only

Junction 21
Westbound: No exit, access only
Eastbound: No access, exit only

Junction 22
Westbound: No access, exit to M77 only
Eastbound: No exit, access from M77 only

Junction 23
Westbound: No access, exit to B768 only
Eastbound: No exit, access from B768 only

Junction 25
Westbound and Eastbound:
   Exit to A739 Northbound only
   Access from A739 Southbound only

Junction 25a
Eastbound: Access only
Westbound: Exit only

Junction 28
Westbound: no access, exit to airport only
Eastbound: no exit, access from airport only

M9

Junction 1a
Northbound: No access, exit to A8000 only
Southbound: No exit, access from A8000 only

Junction 2
Northbound: No exit, access from B8046 only
Southbound: No access, exit to B8046 only

Junction 3
Northbound: No access, exit to A803 only
Southbound: No exit, access from A803 only

Junction 6
Northbound: No access only
Southbound: No access, exit to A905 only

Junction 8
Northbound: No access, exit to M876 only
Southbound: No exit, access from M876 only

M10

Junction with M1 (M1 Junc. 7)
Northbound: No exit to M1 Southbound
Southbound: No access from M1 Northbound

M11

Junction 4
Northbound: No exit, access from A406
Eastbound only
Southbound: No access, exit to A406
Westbound only

Junction 5
Northbound: No access, exit to A1168 only
Southbound: No exit, access from A1168 only

Junction 9
Northbound: No access, exit only
Southbound: No exit, access only

Junction 13
Northbound: No access, exit only
Southbound: No exit, access only

Junction 14
Northbound: No access from A428 Eastbound
            No exit to A428 Westbound
Southbound: No exit, access from A428
            Eastbound only

M20

Junction 2
Eastbound: No access, exit to A20 only
   (access via M26 Junction 2a)
Westbound: No exit, access only
   (exit via M26 Junction 2a)

Junction 3
Eastbound: No access, access from M26
Eastbound only
Westbound: No access, exit to M26
Westbound only

Junction 11a
Westbound: No exit to Channel Tunnel
Eastbound: No access from Channel Tunnel

M23

Junction 7
Southbound: No access from A23 Northbound
Northbound: No exit to A23 Southbound

Junction 10a
Northbound: No access, exit only
Southbound: No access, exit only

M25

Junction 5
Clockwise: No exit to M26 Eastbound
Anti-clockwise: No access from M26
            Westbound

Spur to A21
Southbound: No access from M26 Westbound
Northbound: No exit to M26 Eastbound

Junction 19
Clockwise: No access exit only
Anti-clockwise: No exit access only

Junction 21
Clockwise and Anti-clockwise:
   No exit to M1 Southbound
   No access from M1 Northbound

Junction 31
Southbound: No exit access only
   (exit via Junction 30)
Northbound: No access exit only
   (access via Junction 30)

M26

Junction with M25
Westbound: No exit to M25 anti-clockwise
   or spur to A21 Southbound
Eastbound: No access from M25 clockwise
   or spur to A21 Northbound

Junction with M20
(M20 Junction 3)
Eastbound: No exit to M20 Westbound
Westbound: No access from M20 Eastbound

M27

Junction 4
Eastbound and Westbound: No exit to A33
   Southbound (Southampton)
   No access from A33 Northbound

Junction 10
Eastbound: No exit, access from A32 only
Westbound: No access, exit to A32 only

M40

Junction 3
North-Westbound: No access,
            exit to A40 only
South-Eastbound: No exit,
            access from A40 only

Junction 7
South-Eastbound: No exit, access only
North-Westbound: No access, exit only

Junction 13
South-Eastbound: No access, exit only
North-Westbound: No access, exit only

Junction 14
South-Eastbound: No exit, access only
North-Westbound: No access, exit only

Junction 16
South-Eastbound: No access, exit only
North-Westbound: No exit, access only

M42

Junction 1
Eastbound: No exit
Westbound: No access

Junction 7
Northbound: No access, exit to M6 only
Southbound: No exit, access from M6
Northbound only

Junction 8
Northbound: No exit, access from M6
Southbound only
Southbound: Exit to M6 Northbound only
            Access from M6 Southbound only

M45

Junction with M1
Eastbound: No exit to M1 Northbound
Westbound: No access from M1 Southbound

Junction with A45 east
of Dunchurch
Eastbound: No access, exit to A45 only
Westbound: No exit, access from A45
Northbound only

M48
Junction with M4 near Magor
Westbound: No exit onto M4 Eastbound
Eastbound: No access from M4 Westbound

M53
Junction 11
Southbound and Northbound: No access from M56 Eastbound, no exit to M56 Westbound

M56
Junction 1
Westbound: No access from M60 South-Eastbound
No access from A34 Northbound
Eastbound: No exit to M60 North-Westbound
No exit to A34 Southbound
Junction 2
Westbound: No access, exit to A560 only
Eastbound: No exit, access from A560 only
Junction 3
Westbound: No exit, access only
Eastbound: No access, exit only
Junction 4
Westbound: No exit, access only
Eastbound: No access, exit only
Junction 7
Westbound: No exit, access only
Junction 8
Westbound: No exit, access from A556 only
Eastbound: No access, no exit
Junction 9
Westbound: No exit to M6 Southbound
Eastbound: No access from M6 Northbound
Junction 15
Westbound: No access from M53
Eastbound: No exit to M53

M57
Junction 3
Northbound: No exit, access only
Southbound: No access, exit only
Junction 5
Northbound: No exit, access from A580
Westbound only
Southbound: No access, exit to A580
Eastbound only

M58
Junction 1
Eastbound: No exit, access from A506 only
Westbound: No access, exit to A506 only

M60
Junction 2
Nth.-Eastbound: No access, exit to A560 only
Sth.-Westbound: No exit, access from A560 only
Junction 3
Westbound: No exit to A34 Northbound
Eastbound: No access from A34 Southbound
Junction 4
Westbound: No access from A34 Southbound
No access from M56 Eastbound
Eastbound: No exit to M56 South-Westbound
No exit to A34 Northbound
Junction 5
South-Eastbound: No access from or exit to A5103 Northbound
North-Westbound: No access from or exit to A5103 Southbound
Junction 14
Eastbound: No exit to A580
No access from A580 Westbound
Westbound: No exit to A580 Eastbound
No access from A580
Junction 16
Eastbound: No exit, access from A666 only
Westbound: No access, exit to A666 only
Junction 20
Eastbound: No access from A664
Westbound: No exit to A664
Junction 22
Westbound: No access from A62
Junction 25
South-Westbound: No access from A560/A6017
Junction 26
North-Eastbound: No access or exit

Junction 27
North-Eastbound: No access, exit only
South-Westbound: No exit, access only

M61
Junctions 2 and 3
North-Westbound:
No access from A580 Eastbound
Sth.-Eastbound: No exit to A580 Westbound
Junction with M6
(M6 Junction 30)
North-Westbound:
No exit to M6 Southbound
South-Eastbound:
No access from M6 Northbound

M62
Junction 23
Eastbound: No access, exit to A640 only
Westbound: No exit, access from A640 only

M65
Junction 9
Nth.-Eastbound: No access, exit to A679 only
Sth.-Westbound:
No exit, access from A679 only
Junction 11
North-Eastbound: No exit, access only
South-Westbound: No access, exit only

M66
Junction 1
Southbound: No exit, access from A56 only
Northbound: No access, exit to A56 only

M67
Junction 1
Eastbound: No access, exit to A6017 only
Westbound: No exit, access from A6017 only
Junction 2
Eastbound: No access, exit to A57 only
Westbound: No access, exit to A57 only

M69
Junction 2
North-Eastbound:
No exit, access from B4669 only
South-Westbound:
No exit, access to B4669 only

M73
Junction 1
Northbound: No access from A74 Eastbound
Southbound: No exit to A74 Eastbound
Junction 2
Northbound: No access from M8 Eastbound
No exit to A89 Eastbound
Southbound: No exit to M8 Westbound
No access from A89 Westbound
Junction 3
Northbound: No exit to A80 South-Westbound
Southbound:
No access from A80 North-Eastbound

M74
Junction 2
Eastbound: No exit
Westbound: No access
Junction 3
Eastbound: No access
Westbound: No exit
Junction 7
Southbound: No access, exit to A72 only
Northbound: No exit, access from A72 only
Junction 9
Southbound: No access, exit to B7078 only
Northbound: No access, no exit
Junction 10
Southbound: No exit, access from B7078 only
Junction 11
Southbound: No access, exit to B7078 only
Northbound: No exit, access from B7078 only
Junction 12
Southbound: No exit, access from A70 only
Northbound: No access, exit to A70 only

M77
Junction with M8 (M8 Junc. 22)
Northbound: No exit to M8 Westbound
Southbound: No access from M8 Eastbound
Junction 4
Southbound: No access
Northbound: No exit
Junction with A77
Southbound: No exit onto A77 Northbound

M80
Junction 1
Northbound: No access from M8 Westbound
Southbound: No exit to M8 Eastbound
Junction 5
Northbound: No access from M876
Southbound: No exit to M876

M90
Junction 2a
Northbound: No access, exit to A92 only
Southbound: No exit, access from A92 only
Junction 7
Northbound: No exit, access from A91 only
Southbound: No access, exit to A91 only
Junction 8
Northbound: No access, exit to A91 only
Southbound: No exit, access from A91 only
Junction 10
Northbound: No access from A912
Exit to A912 Northbound only
Southbound: No exit to A912
Access from A912 Southbound only

M180
Junction 1
Eastbound: No access, exit only
Westbound: No exit, access from A18 only

M606
Junction with Merrydale Road, Bradford
Northbound: No access, exit only

M621
Junction 2a
Eastbound: Access only, no exit
Westbound: No access, exit only
Junction 4
Southbound: No access from A61
Junction 5
Northbound: No access, exit to A61 only
Southbound: No exit, access from A61 only
Junction 6
Northbound: No exit, access only
Southbound: No access, exit only

M876
Junction with M80 (M80 Junc. 5)
North-Eastbound:
No access from M80 Southbound
South-Westbound: No exit to M80 Northbound
Junction 2
North-Eastbound: No access, exit only
South-Westbound: No exit, access only
Junction with M9 (M9 Junc. 8)
North-Eastbound: No exit to M9 Northbound
South-Westbound:
No access from M9 Southbound

A1(M) (Hertfordshire Section)
Junction 2
Southbound: No exit, access from A1001 only
Northbound: No access, exit only
Junction 3
Southbound: No access, exit only
Junction 5
Northbound: No access, exit only
Southbound: No exit or access

A1(M) (Cambridgeshire Section)
Junction 13a
Northbound: No exit to B1043
Southbound: No access from B1043

Junction 14
Northbound: No exit, access only
Southbound: No access, exit only

A1(M) (Leeds Section)
Junction 44
Northbound: Access from M1 Eastbound only
Southbound: Exit to M1 Westbound only

A1(M) (Durham Section)
Junction 57
Northbound: No access, exit to A66(M) only
Southbound: No exit, access from A66(M)
Junction 65
Northbound: Exit to A1 North-Westbound, and to A194(M)
Southbound: Access from A1 South-Eastbound, and from A194(M)

A3(M)
Junction 4
Northbound: No access, exit only
Southbound: No exit, access only

A38(M) Aston Expressway
Junction with Victoria Road, Aston
Northbound: No exit, access only
Southbound: No access, exit only

A48(M)
Junction with M4 (M4 Junction 29)
South-Westbound: access from M4 Westbound
North-Eastbound: exit to M4 Eastbound only
Junction 29a
South-Westbound: Exit to A48 Westbound only
North-Eastbound:
Access from A48 Eastbound only

A57(M) Mancunian Way
Junction with A34 Brook Street, Manchester
Eastbound: No access, exit to A34 Brook Street Southbound only
Westbound: No exit, access only

A58(M) Leeds Inner Ring Road
Junction with Park Lane/Westgate
Southbound: No access, exit only

A64(M) Leeds Inner Ring Road
(Continuation of A58(M))
Junction with A58 Clay Pit Lane
Eastbound: No Access
Westbound: No exit

A66(M)
Junction with A1(M) SW of Darlington
South-Westbound:
Exit to A1(M) Southbound only
North-Eastbound:
Access from A1(M) Northbound only

A74(M)
Junction 14
Southbound: No exit
Junction 18
Northbound: No access
Southbound: No exit

A167(M) Newcastle Central Motorway
Junction with Camden Street
Northbound: No exit, access only
Southbound: No exit or access

A194(M)
Junction with A1(M) and A1 Gateshead Western By-Pass
Southbound: Exit to A1(M) only
Northbound: Access from A1(M) only

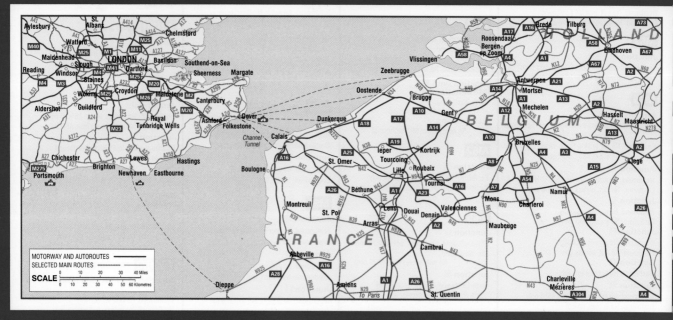

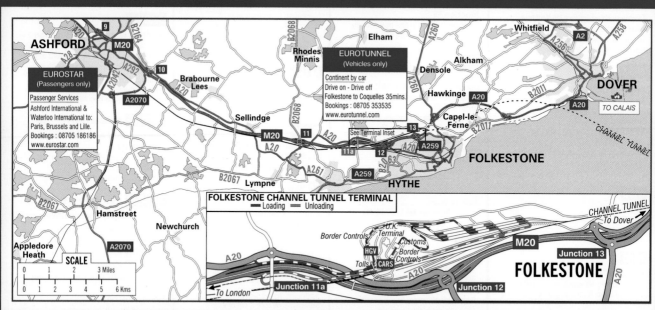

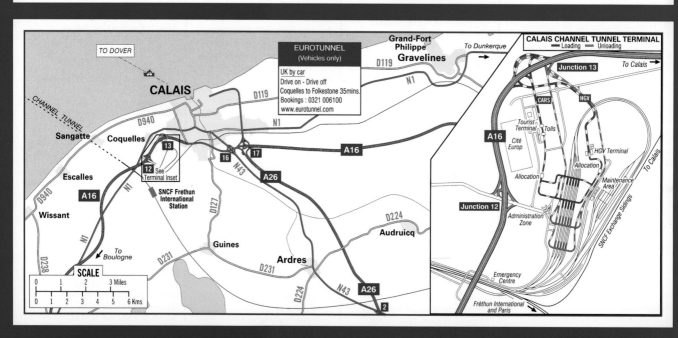